t = time

PI = profitability index

r = Internal rate of Return

NI = net income

D = depreciation

t = marginal tax rate

Δ = incremental or change

k_{proj} = required rate of return on a project

β = beta

k_d = cost of debt

k_a = weighted average cost of capital

k_p = cost of preferred stock

k_e = cost of shareholders' equity

D_1 = expected dividend on common stock

g = constant growth rate of dividends per share

p = price per unit

v = variable cost per unit

DOL_x = degree of operating leverage (units)

DOL_s = degree of operating leverage (dollars)

DFL_x = degree of financial leverage (units)

DFL_s = degree of financial leverage (dollars)

F_O = fixed operating costs

F_f = fixed financial costs

DCL_x = degree of combined leverage (units)

DCL_s = degree of combined leverage (dollars)

EBIT = earnings before interest and taxes

EPS = earnings per share

EBIT* = EBIT at which EPS is the same for different financing options

I = total interest in dollars

N = number of common stock shares

n = number of periods

k_l = cost of levered equity

k_u = cost of unlevered equity

D/E = ratio of debt to equity

V_{tl} = total value of levered firm

V_{tu} = total value of unlevered firm

D = total market value of debt

t_i = personal tax rate on interest income

t_c = corporate tax rate

t_e = personal tax rate on equity income

r = return on equity

I = inflation

GEORGE A. ARAGON
Boston College

FINANCIAL MANAGEMENT

ALLYN AND BACON
BOSTON • LONDON • SYDNEY • TORONTO

This book is dedicated to Margaret and George Oscar.

Series Editor ● *Cary Tengler*
Developmental Editor ● *Allen Workman*
Cover Administrator ● *Linda Dickinson*
Manufacturing Buyer ● *Bill Alberti*
Editorial-Production Service ● *York Production Services*
Cover Designer ● *Lynda Fishbourne*

Copyright © 1989 by Allyn and Bacon
A Division of Simon & Schuster
160 Gould Street
Needham Heights, Massachusetts 02194

Aragon, George A.
    Financial management/George A. Aragon.
       p. cm.
    Includes index.
    ISBN 0-205-11240-4
    International Edition ISBN 0-205-11596-9
    1. Business enterprises—Finance.   I. Title.
    HG4026.A743 1988
    658.1'5—dc19

87-32533
CIP

Printed in the United States of America.
10 9 8 7 6 5 4 3 2   93 92 91 90 89

C O N T E N T S

11

ACCOUNTS RECEIVABLE MANAGEMENT 380

12

INVENTORY MANAGEMENT 418

13

SHORT TERM FINANCING 452

P A R T
V

INVESTMENT DECISIONS

14

INTRODUCTION TO CAPITAL BUDGETING
488

15

ESTIMATING CASH FLOWS
534

16
CAPITAL BUDGETING UNDER RISK 580

COST OF CAPITAL AND VALUATION

P A R T
VI

17
THE COST OF CAPITAL 618

18
FINANCIAL STRUCTURE DECISIONS 648

22
LONG TERM DEBT

23
LEASING, "HYBRID" SECURITIES, AND WARRANTS

 ## SPECIAL FINANCING SITUATIONS

P A R T

VII

24
MERGERS, ACQUISITIONS, AND BANKRUPTCY

PREFACE

Writing a textbook is a long and difficult enterprise that requires some motivating purpose. Mine was to make a book that would be readable without being superficial, and, conversely, a book that would be technically complete without being sterile. I also wanted very much to stress that the teaching of financial management must preserve the rich managerial context in which modern financial ideas are applied. My own appreciation for the managerial perspective is influenced by my work experience with industrial firms, as well as my exposure to the managerial point of view at Harvard Business School.

I feel that this managerial viewpoint is especially needed in today's teaching of finance, to help correct what has been an accelerating emphasis toward an excessively market-centered view of the firm. Books teaching from this extreme market-centered view have very nearly relegated the firm to a sort of black box that simply generates expected cash flow streams for pricing out in efficient markets. From the context of managing the firm, such a perspective is necessarily incomplete, since the firm's financial manager must work in both imperfect markets and in efficient markets. Some implications of this managerial viewpoint in today's markets are highlighted in the Postscript, "Black Monday," which appears at the end of the text. Management decisions have significant impacts on the amounts, timing, and variability of cash flows. Students need to know what goes on inside the black box, and what financial managers can do to create value for shareholders. In short, there are two sides to the corporate finance process and they should both be part of a student's education in financial management.

INTENDED AUDIENCE

This book is intended for use in the first course in business finance at either undergraduate or graduate level. Typically such courses will have a mixture of finance majors and non-finance majors. When writing this text, I had such a mixed audience constantly in mind. For the finance major, my intent has been to provide more than an introduction to the major concepts and techniques of business finance. Throughout this text I have stressed that to be effective, financial managers must have an appreciation for the managerial context in which principles are applied. This means that the financial manager must understand the interelatedness of management functions. Indeed, it is from the marketing, administrative, and production managers of the firm that the financial managers get most of the raw material for "financial" decisions. The significant contribution of the financial manager is to draw upon the efficient market paradigm in order to provide an integrated, value-oriented framework for making marketing, administrative, and production, as well as financing, decisions.

For their part, the non-finance majors must have an understanding of the financial repercussions of business decisions. The approach in this book is to illustrate that important financial principles are consistent with common sense. Without such a connection, abstract principles cannot be persuasive. Toward this end I have made the book readable and uncomplicated. This does not mean that important issues have been swept under the rug or that concepts have been watered down. All major concepts and techniques typically covered in the first course are included in this book. In addition, the book contains material that interested students can use to further their independent study of financial management.

FEATURES OF THE BOOK

Solved Problems. The solved problems at the end of each chapter go beyond what is normally included in two respects:

First, the solutions in key chapters are quite detailed. For example, the illustrated solutions for Chapter 15, "Estimating Cash Flows," cover sixteen pages in the book. Solutions to the problems in Chapter 8, "Financial Planning and Forecasting," cover eight pages in the book.

Second, in most chapters the first group of non-solved problems are virtually identical in format with the corresponding solved problems, though with different numbers. Thus the student may work through the solved problems, then follow the same procedure with a non-solved problem to gain further confidence in setting up problems. In addition to the tutorial problems, a variety of other problems are included.

Case Exercises. Most key chapters contain a short case example to allow the instructor to bring out issues or problems of application which students might not otherwise appreciate. For example, the case exercise in Chapter 1 raises the agency problem in the context of a shareholder's meeting and provides opportunities to examine the diversity of situations in which management and ownership interests might conflict. The case exercise in Chapter 4 demonstrates how the time value of money is relevant to product pricing decisions.

Unique multiple-choice questions as well as discussion questions appear at the end of each chapter to reinforce important concepts and serve as a self-teaching check on learning. Answers for the multiple choice questions appear at the end of the book.

Flexible Organization. The book has been organized and written with the objective of allowing instructors considerable flexibility in sequencing coverage. In particular, the early materials dealing with financial analysis and forecasting (chapters 7 and 8) and working capital management (chapters 9 through 13) may be postponed, if the instructor wishes to present capital budgeting, the cost of capital and capital structure decisions early. The coverage in these chapters allows for this early treatment.

ORGANIZATION OF THE BOOK

This book is organized into seven major parts. Part I, Background, provides an overview of the environmental context, both economic and governmental, for financial decisions. The tax environment and the Tax Reform Act of 1986 are specifically incorporated into pertinent parts of these discussions.

Part II presents the basic concepts of modern business finance: the importance of the time value of money, its application to the valuation of stocks and bonds, and the relationship between risk and the rate of return. The capital asset pricing model is presented and applied.

Part III, Evaluation and Forecasting, reviews financial analysis and planning, the purpose of financial ratio analysis, and the use of ratios in financial models.

Part IV, Working Capital Management, first provides an overview chapter, and then discusses the firm's operating cycle, dealing with methods for cash management, and illustrating the development of a marketable securities portfolio. The final three chapters describe choices in credit policies and practices, inventory investments, and short-term financing. Each chapter carefully illustrates the managerial implications for the topic covered.

Part V, Investment Decisions, deals with capital budgeting decisions, including evaluation techniques, estimation of cash flows, and the methods used in adjusting for risk differences among the investment proposals. The provisions of the 1986 Tax Reform Act are explicitly incorporated.

Part VI contains seven chapters dealing with the flow and cost of long-term capital to the corporation. In th first four chapters there is a full discussion of the cost of capital concept, followed by coverage of financial and capital structure as well as dividend decisions, both from a theoretical and practical perspective. The remaining chapters describe how firms raise funds through sale of equity and debt, and how they manage leasing and hybrid financing.

Part VII, Special Financing Situations, covers mergers and acquisitions, bankruptcies, and the international financial environment.

ANCILLARY MATERIALS

The following ancillary materials are available.

Instructor's Manual contains solutions to all questions, problems, and case exercises.

Study Guide, prepared by Professors John Bowdidge and George Swales of Southwest Missouri State University, contains chapter overviews, outlines, short-answer questions, and multiple-choice and true-false questions and problems.

Test Bank Booklet contains approximately 1250 test items for testing concepts and problem-solving quizzes and exams.

Micro Test Computerized Test Bank presents the above test items in flexible computerized format available for IBM-PC, Apple II, and Macintosh computers.

Transparency Masters display key examples and examples for classroom discussion.

The Allyn and Bacon Financial Toolkit contains computer software for structured problem solving by students working independently or in a laboratory environment.

Lotus 1-2-3 Templates allow students to run "what-if" scanarios with many of the end-chapter cases and problems.

Allyn and Bacon Finance Video Library allows qualified adopters one or more of the following videos: *Fast Buck—Or Faith in the Future*, Edward L. Hennessey, Jr.'s address to Bentley College's Seventh Annual College Conference on Business Ethics dealing with the ethics of corporate raiders and greenmailers; *Trader*, a compelling and fascinating look at Paul Tudor Jones II, the dynamic, young president of Tudor Investment Corporation; *The Ethics of Bankruptcy*, featuring Dr. Kenneth Goodpaster, Harvard Business School, and Thomas Stephens, CEO of Manville Corporation, discussing the ethical implications of bankruptcy filings of both Manville and Braniff International; and several of the highly acclaimed *Enterprise* videotapes.

ACKNOWLEDGEMENTS

My appreciation for the power of modern financial theory is due in large part to the patient and generous efforts of my teacher and thesis chairman, John Lintner at the Harvard Business School. In the process of writing this book I also owe a great debt of gratitude to Professors Robert W. Johnson of Purdue University and Ronald W. Melicher of the University of Colorado at Boulder. Their many substantial contributions are evident throughout this text. In addition, I am grateful to Professor William Folks for his contribution to the chapter on International Finance.

My colleague, Elizabeth Strock, provided me with valuable reviews of the valuation, risk, and capital budgeting materials. Many other outstanding academic reviewers, listed below, provided insightful and constructive reviews of portions of the manuscript at various stages: John S. Bowdidge, Southwest Missouri State; Sinan Cebenovan, Hofstra University; David M. Cordell, Louisiana State University; Andrea DeMaskey, University of Nevada-Reno; John Dunkelberg, Wake Forest University; John W. Ellis, Colorado State University; Peter Erwald, Long Island University-C.W. Post; Keith Fairchild, University of Texas; Joseph E. Finnerty, University of Illinois, Urbana; William F. Hardin, University of Arkansas; James O. Horrigan, University of New Hampshire; Duncan Kretovich, Northeastern University; Martin Laurence, William Paterson College; James T. Lindsley, University of Alabama; Dean R. Longmore, Idaho State University; James A. Millar, University of Arkansas; James Miles, Pennsylvania State University; John Mussachia, Loyola Marymount, Los Angeles; Zane A. Dennick-Ream, Miami University; Debra K. Reed, Texas A&M University; Alan Stephens, Utah State University; Michael C. Walker, University of Cincinnati; J. Daniel Williams, University of Akron.

I am grateful for the reviews and suggestions from the following business professionals: Rubin C. Trevino, Colonial Management; William J. Brett, Barclay Chemical; Dana Seero, Santin Engineering, Inc.; Richard Stockton, Alexander Hamilton Institute; Richard Arscott, CIGNA Securities, Inc.

I also wish to thank my editors at Allyn and Bacon, Cary Tengler and Rich Carle, for their help and support. Senior Developmental Editor Allen Workman provided truly exceptional assistance in keeping me on schedule. At York Production Services, Susan Bogle demonstrated skill and patience in preparing the final copy. Of course, I assume responsibility for any deficiencies which may remain.

I am grateful to Dean John Neuhauser of Boston College and Dean John Wholihan, Loyola Marymount, for their support in this project, and to my colleagues in the Finance Departments at Boston College and Loyola Marymount for their congeniality and encouragement. I want to thank my research assistants, Juan Jurado and Albin C. Halquist, III, for their enthusiastic and timely help.

Last, but definitely not least, my appreciation to H.S. for all the H.S.

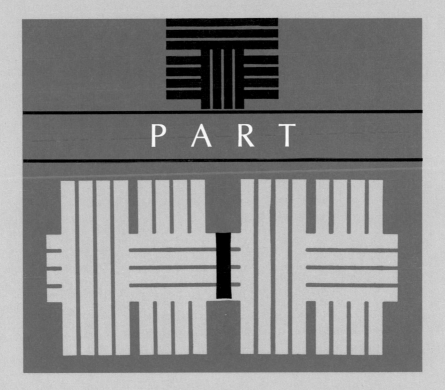

PART

I

BACKGROUND

CHAPTER 1

INTRODUCTION TO FINANCIAL MANAGEMENT

his book is written from the viewpoint of financial managers—the people whose role is planning a business organization's needs and uses for funds, raising the necessary funds, and evaluating the effectiveness with which those funds are used.

In order to explain the scope and functions of financial management clearly, we will describe financial management as it is applied in large corporations with publicly traded stocks. However, the basic precepts and techniques presented here apply to businesses of all types and sizes. Indeed, with minor modifications most of them are applicable to the effective management of not-for-profit organizations as well.

Objectives and Organization of this Chapter

This introductory chapter provides an overview of financial management. After demonstrating that the financial perspective is crucial to all organizations regardless of their individual goals or characteristics, the chapter examines the financial perspective in detail in the context of a business firm.

The first section of the chapter demonstrates the generality and comprehensiveness of the financial perspective. It shows that all types of organizations share common financial problems and that without the financial perspective, organizations usually fail to realize their goals. The second section examines the goals of the business firm and concludes that the preeminent goal should be to maximize the value of the firm to its owners. Practical problems in realizing this goal are addressed.

The third section of the chapter examines the determinants of a firm's stock price and how they influence the firm's operating, investment, and financing activities. The fourth section defines the firm's financial policies and how they are necessary to guide management decisions toward maximizing share price. The fifth section describes the managerial organization of a typical business firm. The sixth describes the organization of the finance function within the firm and the roles of the controller and treasurer. The final section describes the organization of the book.

Every active organization, whether it is a business, political party, social club, government, or theater group, shares three common activities:

- Operating activities
- Investing activities
- Financing activities

Consider a not-for-profit organization such as a large city hospital. The hospital's operating activities include the provision of a wide range of health care services. To support its services, the hospital must undertake investment activities such as the construction of buildings and the purchase of beds and instruments. Finally, to support its operating and investment activities, the hospital must undertake financing activities such as securing funding from government agencies, loans from banks, and contributions from individuals and foundations.

A profit-making business organization performs the same types of activities. For example, the operating activities of a manufacturer are directed to producing and distributing goods. To support them, the manufacturer must undertake investments in materials, supplies, and equipment. Finally, to pay for these activities, the firm must arrange financing from lenders and owners.

Try to think of other examples of these activities and it is easy to see how general they are. For example, can you identify the operating, investing, and financing activities involved in your life as a student? Certainly, the investing aspect should be clear. You are investing considerable time and money in pursuing your education. Likewise, you must arrange for financing by seeking scholarships, loans, and part-time work. Finally, your operating activity involves not only completing a prescribed course of study but also providing for meals, housing, clothing, and entertainment. While the specific characteristics of your operating, investing, and financing activities differ from those of a corporation, the activities themselves are analytically the same.

The Financial Perspective

Each of the three basic activities involves the flow of cash, regardless of the form or goals of the organization. Hospitals must pay for employees, supplies and medicines, buildings, beds, and equipment. Cash is also involved in financing, for example, when the hospital borrows or repays loans.

All three activities must be coordinated if an organization is to pursue its goals effectively. If the flow of cash into and out of each activity is not directed, there is no assurance the organization will move toward its goals, let alone achieve them. For example, if a hospital technician is allowed to order expensive equipment without consulting the finance administrator, there may not be enough money to pay employees. Similarly, if a manu-facturing corporation produces more products than it can sell, money will be tied up in inventory and there may not be enough left to support advertising to generate sales. Exhibit 1-1 presents a diagram of the various cash inflows and outflows through an organization.

Notice that the focal point of Exhibit 1-1 is the cash balance. Think of the cash balance as a reservoir. Cash inflows from operating, investing, and financing activities increase the reservoir. For example, cash received from sales of goods and services is an operating inflow; cash received from selling a piece of equipment represents the reversal of an investing (i.e., "divesting") activity; and cash from a bank loan represents inflow from a financing activity.

Conversely, cash outflows from operating, investing, and financing activities decrease the cash-balance reservoir. For example, payment of cash for employee wages represents an operating cash outflow; purchase of

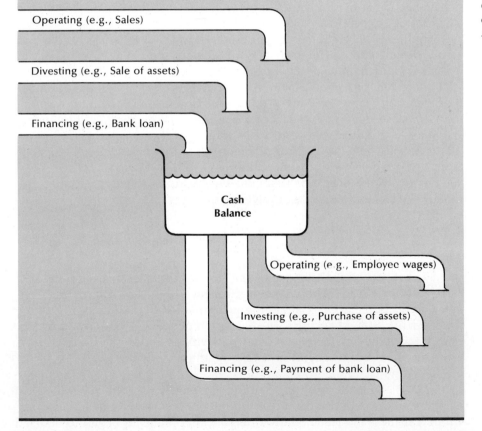

EXHIBIT 1-1
Cash Flows In and Out of Organizational Activities

equipment represents an investing outflow; and repayment of a bank loan represents a financing outflow.

Someone in an organization has to monitor, direct, and evaluate the flow of cash into and out of each basic organizational activity to make sure organizational goals are served effectively. This is the essence of financial management.

Three things should be evident about the financial perspective. First, it is quite general and applies to organizations of all types. Second, it is comprehensive; it encompasses all the fundamental activities of organizations. Third, it is integrative, providing a central focus for the diverse activities of the organization.

Subfields of Finance

While organizations are analytically similar, their characteristics, including goals and cultures, can be quite different.

corporate finance

public finance

not-for-profit finance

personal finance

financial institutions and markets

international finance

investments

Over time, finance specialties have emerged to deal with the unique characteristics of different types of organizations. For example, the study of *corporate finance* deals primarily with the operating, investment, and financing activities of nonfinancial corporations. *Public finance* deals with the activities of governments; the study of *not-for-profit organizations* addresses the activities of educational institutions, hospitals, charitable groups, and similar organizations. The study of *personal finance* deals with the operating, investing, and financing activities of individuals. The study of *financial institutions and markets* deals with the activities of banks, insurance companies, pension funds, and other financial institutions. The study of *international finance* deals with the foreign operating, investment, and financing activities of multinational firms. In addition to these aspects of finance, which are based on organizational distinctions, there is the study of *investments*, which deals with the valuation of securities by investors.

Finance is a large field. It should be, because, above all, it concerns money. Whenever money is involved, finance is involved.

Evolution of Financial Management

The practice of financial management and the financial environment in which firms operate have changed dramatically in recent decades. Consider, for example, that as late as the 1920s the dominant finance text of the time, Arthur Stone Dewing's *The Financial Policy of Corporations,* was primarily concerned with the financing activity of business. Little, if any, attention was paid to operating and investment activities.

The origins of modern financial teaching and practice began to emerge in the 1940s with the rise of "scientific" management. The Second World War fostered the development of quantitative methods and models useful for business management. Mathematical approaches began to be used in making financial choices. By the 1950s, firms were applying financial models to investment decisions.

Contemporaneously, financial markets had become much more developed. The passage of wide-ranging legislation requiring full financial disclosures by publicly traded firms (produced in part by the collapse of the stock market in 1929) exposed management performance more readily to the scrutiny of the investing public. Financial institutions—such as pension funds, mutual funds, and insurance companies—with billions of dollars became important investors in the stocks and bonds of corporations. These developments increased management's accountability to stockholders and creditors and thereby elevated the importance of financial analysis in decision making.

The stage was set for the development of useful financial theory, and in the late 1950s the foundations of modern finance were established. The most seminal of the financial theories were proposed by Harry Markowitz in the field of management science, who laid the groundwork for quantifying the risk-return tradeoff; and Franco Modigliani and Merton Miller (popularly referred to as "M & M"), both in the field of economics, who established a framework for valuing corporate financial decision making in the context of efficient markets.

We will examine their theories and others in more detail in later chapters of this text. For now it is enough simply to note that the development of modern finance can be dated with reasonable precision to the 1950s. The speed with which theory has developed and transformed the teaching and practice of finance should not be underestimated. The integration of research, theory, and practice in the field of financial management continues to accelerate at a pace unequalled in other management disciplines.

GOALS OF THE BUSINESS FIRM

Organizational goals provide direction for operating, investing, and financing activities. In addition, organizational goals can serve as guides to evaluate the effectiveness with which each activity is managed. Goals can differ dramatically from one type of organization to another. Since the primary concern here is with business organizations, we will discuss business goals and how firms are organized to pursue them.

In this book, we assume the primary goal of a business firm should be to maximize the value of its owners' investment by maximizing the price of their common stock.[1] In large firms, professionals are hired to manage in the interests of shareholders. In this capacity, they act as *agents*, or representatives, of the owners. Their relationship to owners, then, is one of "agency."

agency relationship

1. This is consistent with the prevailing belief that our capital markets are efficient. In an efficient stock market, stock prices fully reflect all information about the associated firms and instantaneously adjust to new information.

The Agency Relationship

A difficulty with the *agency relationship* is that stockholders in large corporations have little information about the day-to-day choices and decisions faced by management. Hence, they cannot know whether management strives in their best interests. This situation can give rise to "agency problems" of many types. For example, the owners may want management to borrow funds. Borrowing is usually advantageous for a company, but it also increases financial risks and the danger of bankruptcy. If the company should go bankrupt, the stockholders lose their investments, but top managers may lose their entire professional careers. Thus it is not surprising that management's interests might be at odds with those of shareholders.

Other principal areas of potential conflict are management's decisions with respect to dividends and investments. Generally shareholders prefer more dividends. However, since this reduces the amount of cash the company has, management may prefer to keep dividends low. Shareholders also prefer the company to take reasonable risks in investment choices in hopes of greater profits. Management's preference tends toward taking fewer investment risks because the consequences of failure can be catastrophic for managers.

Owners may choose to provide incentives that encourage management to keep their concerns active. The most direct way to do this is to give key employees stock options that allow them to buy stock in the firm at bargain prices. The idea is that, if managers are also stockholders, they will have a strong interest in maximizing the company's stock price. In addition, many firms tie the compensation of their managers to corporate performance.[2] The costs associated in persuading or forcing managers to work in the interests of owners are known as *agency costs*.

agency costs

Agency costs also arise in borrowing arrangements. When a bank or other financial institution lends money to a business, it does so with the expectation that management will comply with the terms of the loan. For example, if management requests a loan for the purchase of a piece of equipment, lenders expect management to use the money for that purpose and not to use it to increase management salaries. Creditors attempt to solve this problem by setting forth very specific requirements with which the borrower must comply. Of course, the more stringent these requirements are, the less flexibility management has in day-to-day decision making. To some extent, management can "buy" more flexibility and less stringent requirements by offering to pay higher interest rates. But the higher borrowing cost reduces shareholders' profits and must be viewed as another cost of the agency relationship.

---

2. For example, the chief executive officer of one large corporation has a 12-year contract providing yearly pay equal to .36 percent of the company's annual revenue, with the only constraint being that the pay is limited to 2.5 percent of total operating profit. Many CEOs receive a combination of fixed salary plus various performance incentives. Such compensation packages are reported annually by both *Forbes* and *Fortune* magazines.

Societal Interests

Social goals embodied in law and culture must also be addressed by the corporation. Increasingly, society expects more from corporations than mere compliance with the laws. Many investors demand that their companies avoid profitable activities if they are not morally justifiable, even though they might still be legal. For example, recently many universities, religious organizations, charitable foundations, and government retirement funds refused to own stock in companies doing business with South Africa. When one considers that such organizations invest enormous amounts of money in corporate stocks and bonds, it is understandable that corporations listen to what they have to say.

FRAMEWORK FOR FINANCIAL MANAGEMENT

Having identified a central business goal—maximization of the value of shareholders' investment, we need a framework that links the firm's activities to share price maximization.

Risk and Return Tradeoff

In general, the greater the level of risk a firm has in its operating, investment, and financing activities, the lower its stock price will be. Conversely, the more profitable a firm is (i.e., the higher its rate of return), the higher its stock price will be.

One would think that maximizing a firm's stock price is simple: maximize return and minimize risk. Unfortunately, risk and return are also related: Generally, the greater the rate of return pursued by the company, the more risk to which it exposes itself.

The *risk-return tradeoff* is so pervasive that it is fundamental to every important business activity. In each of the operating, investment, and financing activities, the objective of financial management is to orient these activities toward the optimal balance between risk and return in order to maximize the firm's stock price. In order to achieve this objective, a financial manager must understand these activities intimately in the context of his or her own firm. In part, this means the financial manager must think like a *manager.* In addition, the financial manager must organize the finance function so that each important aspect of the firm's activities is addressed and directed toward the financial objective.

risk-return tradeoff

FINANCIAL POLICIES

Financial policies are general rules to guide management in making decisions that are consistent with the firm's goals. Financial policies are set by the board of directors. However, the chief financial officer usually plays an important role in designing and managing them. Financial policies address operating, investment, and financing activities.

Operating Policies

Operating policies address a broad range of decisions that come up daily in the normal business routine. For example, decisions with respect to granting credit to customers or maintaining inventory for production and marketing purposes affect operating performance. Such decisions affect not only the firm's cash balances but also its risk and return profile. For example, a liberal credit policy may increase profits and simultaneously increase the firm's risk level. The financial operating policies we will examine in later chapters are designed to balance this tradeoff in order to maximize the firm's stock price.

Investment Policies

Investment policies refer to the evaluation and selection of investments that will last more than one year. Investment decisions are difficult to reverse and typically involve relatively large amounts of cash. Thus, investment policies provide rules for deciding which investments should be made and which should be rejected. In this area, the tradeoff between risk and return is particularly crucial. The investment decision rules examined in subsequent chapters are designed to enable the risk-return tradeoff to be made with reference to stock price.

Financing Policies

These policies are directed toward questions such as how much money the firm should borrow and how much, if any, of the profits should be paid out as dividends. Financing policies clearly affect the cash position and the firm's risk profile in important ways. For example, borrowing increases the firm's cash balance but also increases risk level. Payment of large dividends to stockholders depletes cash and increases risk level. Policies are of great importance in helping make such decisions in ways that maximize the firm's stock price.

 ## ORGANIZATION OF THE FIRM AND THE FINANCE FUNCTION

While the shareholders of a corporation are its legal owners, in large corporations they delegate their control to a board of directors, which they elect. The members of the board, in effect, act as agents or representatives of the owners.

The board of directors is responsible for setting the general goals and policies of the corporation, but day-to-day management is delegated to a chief executive officer (CEO) who may have a variety of titles depending on the company. The CEO, in turn, hires key top management. Through the process of delegation, the firm's managers likewise become agents of the shareholders. The relationships of the various groups are depicted in Exhibit 1-2.

The scale and complexity of large businesses necessitate a further specialization of managerial functions. Decision-making responsibilities are often allocated according to the functional nature of the decision, e.g., manufacturing or production, personnel, marketing and sales, or finance. Vice-presidents for sales, personnel, manufacturing, and finance are identified in Exhibit 1-2.

The Finance Function

Many business firms and other organizations give the title, "Vice President–Finance," to their chief financial officers. The financial vice president is responsible for managing the finance function and reports directly to the president or chief executive officer, as is depicted in Exhibit 1-2.

EXHIBIT 1-2
Typical Corporate Organizational Structure

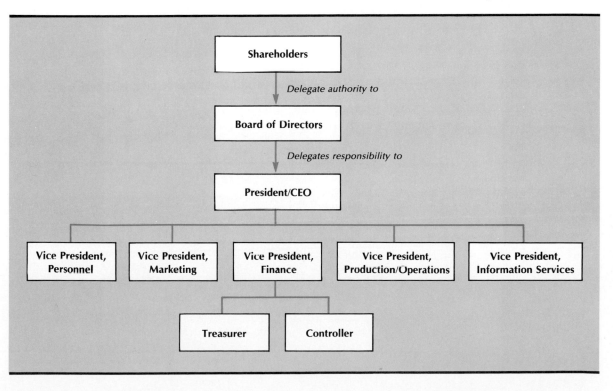

It is extremely important to keep in mind that the financial vice president is first and foremost a *manager*. That means he or she must participate in establishing overall business strategies and policies and become familiar with the full range of business operations, including activities on the "shop floor," the company's personnel policies, the marketing and distribution of products, and other matters. All these activities affect profitability and risk level and, hence, the company's stock value.

Reporting to the financial vice president are the treasurer and controller (sometimes called the comptroller). In general, the controller is concerned with the firm's operating and investing activities while the treasurer is concerned primarily with financing activities. The specific tasks and responsibilities addressed in these activities are listed in Exhibit 1-3.

controller

The Controller. In general, the controller is the chief accounting officer and is responsible for carrying out the overall accounting or record-keeping activities, which include the preparation of tax, accounting, and financial statements. The controller is also responsible for budgeting and analyzing the company's actual performance relative to budgeted performance.

treasurer

The Treasurer. The treasurer is responsible for managing the firm's cash and marketable securities and for acquiring the funds necessary to meet its financing needs. This entails planning the financial structure, obtaining short- and intermediate-term funds, and selling stocks and bonds. To carry out these responsibilities effectively, the treasurer must stay abreast of developments in the financial markets, including the outlooks for interest rates, inflation, and other credit market conditions.

Financial Management in Small Businesses

In small firms, the chief financial manager must often perform both the controller's and the treasurer's functions because the business cannot

EXHIBIT 1-3
Typical Responsibilities Of Corporate Treasurers And Controllers

Controller	Treasurer
1. Budgeting	1. Cash management
2. Financial analysis	2. Banking relationships
3. Financial reporting	3. Financial planning
4. Management reports	4. Credit management
5. Tax planning	5. Pension & profit sharing administration
6. Internal auditing	6. Investor relations
7. Management information systems	7. Government relations
8. Management performance appraisal	8. Credit market analysis

support the salaries of specialists in both areas. Yet, if anything, the small scale of operations makes the financial manager's duties more complex. For example, access to funds from the financial markets is much more difficult and the terms on which funds are acquired are more onerous and difficult to negotiate.

In addition, in small firms, all managers including the financial manager are looked upon for advice in planning business strategies and making a variety of operating decisions. Conversely, other managers, such as the marketing and production managers, have more direct input into credit and purchasing decisions that affect the financial performance and condition of the company.

For small businesses, time shortens considerably with regard to financial analysis of operating choices. Finally, the small capitalizations of such businesses make the risks of incorrect decisions much more severe.

ORGANIZATION OF THE BOOK

This book provides a comprehensive review of the techniques, concepts, and theories important to effective financial decision making. Part I provides background on the organization and taxation of business firms and addresses important features of the financial environment. Part II provides background on the basic tools of financial analysis, including the very important concept of the time value of money and its application to investment valuation. This part also examines the concept and measurement of risk and the relationship between risk and the rate of return from investments. Part III introduces the techniques of financial statement analysis and the use of ratios and financial models for financial planning. Part IV addresses the manager's concern to operate efficiently. It examines the importance of proper working capital management to the value of the firm and offers principles to guide working capital decisions. Part V addresses the manager's concern for profitable investment. It focuses on long-term investment decisions, referred to as capital budgeting decisions. The objective of this part is to provide decision rules that may be used to evaluate alternative investments under uncertainty.

Part VI addresses the manager's concern to raise capital at minimum cost. It presents techniques and theories that can be applied to estimating the firm's cost of capital. In addition, a comparison of the characteristics of alternative sources of long-term funds is provided. Finally, this part presents an examination of the key considerations in determining dividend policy. Part VII, the last part of the text, provides a detailed look at special topics, including the analysis of mergers and acquisitions, bankruptcy, and the financial management of international firms.

SUMMARY

Every active organization exhibits three common types of activities: operating activities, investment activities, and financing activities. All these activities absorb and release cash flows and hence possess a financial dimension. Unless they are coordinated and directed, organizational goals will not be achieved. In this text, the goal of business firms is presumed to be the maximization of common stock price. This involves a continual trade-off between risk and return.

In large corporations, the owners need to provide incentives to management to make sure managers act in the owners' interests. Creditors attempt to control management behavior by imposing stringent requirements on the use of funds lent to the corporation. The financial manager should develop policies to guide decision making in operating, investment, and financing activities toward maximizing the firm's stock price.

MULTIPLE CHOICE QUESTIONS

1. In the early part of the century, the teaching of finance could be described as:
   a) Theoretical
   b) Descriptive
   c) "Scientific"
   d) Analytical

2. The financial manager should seek to maximize the company's:
   a) Sales
   b) Assets
   c) Profits
   d) Stock price

3. In larger companies, the development and control of the company's budgets is typically the direct responsibility of the:
   a) Chief executive officer
   b) Board of directors

c) Treasurer

d) Controller

4. In large companies, banking relationships are typically the direct responsibility of the:

a) Chairman of the board

b) Treasurer

c) Controller

d) Firm's shareholders

5. The basic tradeoff a financial manager must face is:

a) Short-term vs. long-term

b) Debt vs. equity

c) Shareholders vs. bondholders

d) Risk vs. return

6. The market price of the firm's common stock is determined by the company's:

a) Sales

b) Assets

c) Profits

d) Return and risk

7. The subfield of finance that deals primarily with the study of financial securities is known as:

a) Personal finance

b) Public finance

c) Capital markets and institutions

d) Investments

8. The "agency problem" refers to:

a) The possibility that creditors will take over the company

b) The conflict between shareholders' interests and management's interests

c) The need to supervise owners

d) The conflict between management and unions

DISCUSSION QUESTIONS

1. Identify and explain the three common activities of all active organizations.

2. Discuss what is meant by the terms, "agency relationship," "agency problem," and "agency costs."

3. What is the goal of the business firm, according to this text?

4. Identify and briefly explain the major functions of financial management.

5. Identify and describe the principal financial policies of a firm.

6. Suggest ways in which the interests of management of a corporation may conflict with those of common stockholders.

7. Identify and compare the major subfields of finance.
8. Define and explain what is meant by the "risk-return" tradeoff.
9. Compare the typical responsibilities of the treasurer and controller in a large corporation.
10. Identify some similarities in the financial management of a not-for-profit organization with that of a large corporation.

REFERENCES

Barnea, Amir, Robert A. Haugen, and Lemma W. Senbet. "Market Imperfections, Agency Problems, and Capital Structure: A Review." *Financial Management,* Summer 1981, pp. 7-22.

Donaldson, Gordon. "Financial Goals: Management vs. Stockholders." *Harvard Business Review,* May–June 1963, pp. 116-129.

Donaldson, Gordon. "Financial Goals and Strategic Consequences." *Harvard Business Review,* May–June 1985, pp. 57-66.

Meckling, William H., and Michael C. Jensen. "Reflections on the Corporation as a Social Invention." *Midland Corporate Finance Journal,* Vol. 1, Fall 1983, pp. 6-15.

Seitz, Neil. "Shareholder Goals, Firm Goals and Firm Financing Decisions." *Financial Management,* Autumn 1982, pp. 20-26.

CASE EXERCISE

Management vs. Shareholders

The annual shareholders' meeting at the Bieder Company brought some shock to management and the board of directors when a group of shareholders complained vigorously about the company's financial policies. While expressions of dissatisfaction by one or two shareholders had not been uncommon in the past, the company's senior executives were surprised by the degree of support for the protest group voiced by other stockholders.

Shareholder Complaints

The initial target of the complaints was the company's policy of not paying dividends in almost two years. The chairman of the board, Mr. Michael Bieder, responded that the company had been experiencing poor profitability and had needed all available funds to maintain its investments. Other shareholders rose to complain that the company's policy of not using borrowed money limited its ability to make investments and pay dividends. Again the chairman responded, this time citing the need for caution in the way the company was financed. He gave several examples of large companies that had been heavy borrowers and had recently gone bankrupt. To this another shareholder complained that, if the company were more aggressive in its investment policies there would be enough money for everything. "Until you start taking some chances on new ideas and new products, our stock prices will continue to go down instead of up. I could have earned more by putting my money in government bonds," complained the shareholder.

"Admit it," another shareholder shouted, "you fat cats with your fancy salaries and fancy offices couldn't care less about us little guys. But then why would you? Most of you don't even own stock in the Company." Losing his temper, the Chairman replied angrily that his own ancestors had founded the business and still owned almost 10 percent of the shares outstanding. He added that the company's management group was doing an outstanding job of running the company, adding, "And I'm not saying that just because my son, Jimmy, is president. After all, nobody forced you to buy your stock and nobody's forcing you to keep it. In fact, I would personally be more than happy to buy your stock from you with my own money. Now I ask the rest of you shareholders," concluded the Chairman broadly, "would you rather have your company be safe and secure or bankrupt?"

Case Questions

1. Identify the principal financial policies being debated.
2. Considering the perspective of management only, what tendencies do you see in each of these financial policies?

3. Considering the perspective of shareholders only, what preferences do you see in each of these financial policies?

4. The Bieder Company's creditors are not directly mentioned in the case, but what do you think their preferences would be with regard to each of the financial policies?

5. Use some ideas from the chapter and some ideas of your own to indicate how Bieder Company's shareholders might persuade management to move in the direction of shareholders' preferences.

CHAPTER

2

BUSINESS ORGANIZATION AND TAXES

business may take the form of a sole proprietorship, partnership, or corporation. The legal form of organization selected affects the flexibility of management, the risk position of the owners, and the amount of taxes paid on business income.

Each of the three business forms has important advantages and disadvantages. However, the larger the scope and size of the business, the more likely it is to require the corporate form of organization.

Business decisions almost always have tax consequences. While it is illegal to evade taxes, business managers should strive to minimize the amount of taxes that have to be paid. This requires understanding the tax consequences of business decisions *before* they are made.

● Objectives and Organization of this Chapter

This chapter introduces several important ideas that reappear throughout the remainder of the text. First it considers the characteristics of the principal forms of business organization and explains why the corporate form is prevalent for large businesses. Second, it presents basic features of the federal tax laws which most commonly affect business decisions.

The first section of the chapter describes the principal forms of business organization. The second compares the relative advantages and disadvantages of proprietorships, partnerships, and corporations. The third section of the chapter briefly introduces the main financial statements used by businesses. The final section presents tax aspects of business decisions.

THE BASIC FORMS OF BUSINESS ORGANIZATION

There are three main forms of business organization: sole proprietorships, partnerships, and corporations. Table 2-1 presents a comparison of these various types, including numbers of units and relative sizes.

While the majority of businesses are sole proprietorships, corporations are by far the dominant form of organization in terms of sales. And, just as

TABLE 2-1   Major Forms of Business Organization as of 1982

	Number (Thousands)	Sales ($Billions)	Average Sales ($Thousands)
Proprietorships	10,106	$ 434	$ 42.9
Partnerships	1,514	297	196.2
Corporations	2,926	7,024	2,400.5

Source: U.S. Internal Revenue Service, *Statistics of Income*

corporations are more financially significant than proprietorships and partnerships, so big corporations are more significant than small ones — but again, small corporations outnumber the giants. For example, in 1982, corporations with sales of $1 million and over accounted for about 15 percent of all corporations and over 92 percent of all corporate sales. Consequently, the great majority of corporations are fairly small and many have the same financial problems as proprietorships and partnerships.

Sole Proprietorships

sole proprietorship

A sole proprietorship is a firm owned by a single person who owns all the assets and is responsible for the liabilities (debts). The owner receives the profits or suffers the losses incurred in operations. A sole proprietorship can be established easily. Aside from any local licensing requirements for certain types of businesses (such as barbershops), the owner need only start up operations.

Partnerships

general partnership

Partnerships are almost as easy to form as sole proprietorships. A partnership differs from a proprietorship chiefly in that there is more than one owner. The most common form of partnership is the *general partnership*, under which all partners are liable for the debts of the business. The partnership agreement should specify the capital contributions to be made by the partners, their salaries or other compensations, and how profits and losses are to be divided. If there is no agreement, partners share profits and losses equally, regardless of their capital contributions.

limited partnerships

Limited partnerships[1] may be formed under the statutes of some states. In such organizations there must always be at least one general partner who

---

[1]This is the customary form of organization used for Broadway plays and musicals. The "angels" (people who put up the money) are made limited partners, while the playwright, producer, and possibly others are general partners. The agreements usually specify that the angels must be repaid their investment before subsequent earnings are shared with the general partners. This form is also commonly used for oil drilling ventures.

has all the rights and responsibilities of the general partners described above. However, there are also one or more people designated as limited partners, who may not exercise any managerial rights but may share in the profits to an extent specified in the partnership agreement. Most important, the liability of a limited partner for losses and debts is restricted to the amount of his or her original contribution. Thus, creditors of the partnership may not proceed against the limited partner's personal assets.

Corporations

A *corporation* is a creation of the law. It is a legal entity that is empowered to own property, to contract debts, and to engage in certain activities. The classic definition of a corporation is that of Chief Justice Marshall.

> *A corporation is an artificial being, invisible, intangible, and existing only in contemplation of law. Being a mere creature of law, it possesses only those properties which the charter of its creation confers upon it, either expressly, or as incidental to its very existence {Dartmouth College* v. *Woodward, 4 Wheaton (U.S.) 518 (1819).}*

This definition should not obscure the fact that there are real people who have joined for a common purpose through the means of the corporation. The corporation is simply a remarkable device that permits this group of people to act and be treated as a single person.

The first step in forming a corporation is to select the *state of incorporation.* The choice depends primarily on the state in which the owners plan to do business and the liberality of the state's laws pertaining to the corporations it charters. Delaware is a favorite state of incorporation due to a combination of liberal laws and a large body of case law that establishes precedents for almost every corporate legal matter. In 1987, Wells Fargo & Co., a California corporation, announced its decision to reincorporate in Delaware in order to protect its directors from shareholder suits and allow the company to resist hostile takeovers by other companies more effectively. In California, unlike Delaware, a company's board of directors can be sued for negligent or grossly negligent business decisions. The threat of suits has made it difficult for some companies to attract directors to their boards unless director liability insurance, which is expensive, is provided.

Once the state of incorporation is chosen, the owners must file a *certificate of incorporation* with the proper state official, usually the secretary of state. This specifies such matters as the name of the corporation, the location of the principal office, the operating objectives of the firm, the amount of stock authorized, names and addresses of the incorporators and those subscribing to the stock, and the length of time for which the corporation is being formed.

When this document and the accompanying fees are accepted by the state official, a *charter* is issued. This document sets forth the relationship between the state and the corporation as expressed in the general corporation laws of the state and the specifics of the certificate of incorporation.

corporation

state of incorporation

certificate of incorporation

charter

The nature of charters granted by Delaware is illustrated by the following excerpt taken from a "Delaware corporation."

ARTICLE III. *The nature of the business or purpose to be conducted or promoted is:*

To engage in any lawful act or activity for which corporations may be organized under the General Corporation Law of Delaware.

Without in any way limiting the generality of the foregoing, to engage in any and every kind of business enterprise, venture or activity, whether manufacturing, sales, service or otherwise; to design, invent or develop; and to buy or otherwise acquire, sell or otherwise dispose of, and otherwise deal in and with real and personal property of every kind and character, tangible and intangible.

Before a corporation begins business, one other step is necessary. There must be a preliminary meeting of the incorporators or stockholders at which they adopt *bylaws*. These are a set of regulations for the internal management of the corporation. They specify such matters as the issuance and transfer of stock, the time and place of stockholders' and directors' meetings, and the selection and qualifications of directors, officers, and various committees.

bylaws

COMPARING THE MAJOR BUSINESS FORMS

Many factors determine the selection of organizational form. Some of these have to do with finance, but others relate to the owners' attitudes toward risk and control. The form of organization should be suitable to the amount and type of funds needed to finance the company. Thus, a corner grocery store may not find the corporate form of organization suitable to its financial needs, while a company that plans to manufacture steel might find the corporate form essential to obtain the necessary funds. Let us examine the aspects of proprietorships, partnerships, and corporations that should be considered in selecting the form of organization.

Liability of Owners

liability

Both sole proprietors and general partners are fully and personally liable for business debts or other obligations of their businesses. In contrast, because a corporation has a legal existence separate from its owners, the owners have limited liability. In this respect they are like limited partners. Consequently, when substantial personal assets exist, a prospective owner may elect to incorporate a business. Otherwise an incompetent partner could incur excessive debts on behalf of the business for which the other general partners would be personally liable. For this reason, many people find it more attractive to be stockholders in corporations than proprietors or partners. However, the owner-manager of a small corporation is likely to find that liability extends further than expected. Creditors may ask the owner-manager personally to endorse the corporation's promises to pay, so that personal assets are added as backing to the assets pledged by the corporation.

Transferability of Ownership

Another reason why it can be less difficult to raise funds for a corporation is the relative ease of transferring ownership. A sole proprietor who wishes to sell his or her interests might have to search long and hard to find a buyer. A partner cannot transfer his or her interest in a partnership to another by sale, by gift, or through a will without the consent of all other partners. There is value in marketability, and the poor marketability of ownership interests in proprietorships and partnerships hinders the ability to raise funds for these types of organization.

transferability

In contrast, the stockholder of a corporation does not need the approval of other owners to sell his or her shares. One may sell all or a portion of one's holdings without disturbing the continued existence of the corporation. If one's shares are held in a large corporation, one can estimate the market price of the shares and sell them within a few minutes. While shareholders of small, family-owned corporations—*closed corporations*, as they are called—have the legal right to dispose of their shares as they choose, they may have almost as much difficulty finding buyers as do proprietors and partners. Only a small fraction of corporations have securities that are readily marketable, although these few corporations hold the great majority of corporate assets.

closed corporations

Continuity

Prospective investors are also interested in the continuity of a business. A proprietorship ceases with the death, withdrawal, or retirement of the proprietor. A partnership is legally terminated upon the withdrawal, death, bankruptcy, or insanity of any one of the partners. In many of these cases, it is necessary to liquidate the business to raise the cash to pay the share of assets due the partner or his or her heirs. Such a forced liquidation can substantially reduce the values of all the partners' holdings. Thus the uncertain life of proprietorships and partnerships also hampers the raising of funds from owners and creditors.

continuity

In contrast, the legal existence of a corporation is not jeopardized by the withdrawal or death of any of its owners. When stockholders die, the shares go to their heirs.

Control

A sole proprietor or partner can be sure that he or she will retain control or at least partial control of a business. A partner can even force an end to the partnership rather than share control with someone he or she does not like or trust. In contrast, those in control of a corporation today can find themselves in a different position tomorrow. When the officers own less than half the voting stock, control of the corporation can be gained by outsiders. For example, in November 1986 the management of the Gillette Company learned that Ronald Perelman, chairman of the Revlon Company, was purchasing Gillette's common stock with the longer-term intention of taking over Gillette. Gillette's management was reportedly so disturbed at the prospect that Gillette paid Perelman a premium of $39 million to repurchase his shares. Under similar circumstances, the Goodyear Tire and Rubber Company reportedly paid Sir James Goldsmith a premium of $90 million if he would leave the company alone.[2]

Corporations are also more subject to external control from government agencies than are proprietorships and partnerships. In large part, this results from the greater size and economic power of many corporations plus the fact that the corporate mechanism was used in early trust movements and in other attempts to gain monopoly power. Moreover, the separation of management and ownership characteristic of large corporations has raised concern that managers may not be fulfilling their responsibilities to the owners or their full range of obligations to society. Consequently, a body of rules and regulations that were designed to curb abuses of power by large corporations also affects the operations of small corporations.

maneuverability

Maneuverability

How quickly can the business organization respond to change in its environment or internal needs? Sole proprietors need to consult no one. If they have an opportunity to buy property or to change the line of business, they can seize the chance immediately. Partners, on the other hand, may need to consult other partners, while corporate officers may need to obtain approval from their directors, possibly even their stockholders. It may be necessary to amend the bylaws before action can be taken. Of course, the speed of decision depends partly on the size of the organization, but the form of organization also establishes certain rules and regulations that affect management's maneuverability.

---

[2]When Irwin Jacobs and another group bought a large block of shares in the Enron Corporation, the chairman reportedly claimed it had such a destabilizing effect that Enron ended up repurchasing the shares at a $20 million premium. Enron then sold the shares to an employee stock ownership plan (ESOP) to take the stock out of circulation.

FINANCIAL STATEMENTS

All forms of business organization need some method of accounting to monitor, evaluate, and direct activities toward organizational goals. This need increases dramatically when a business is large and decentralized, because top management cannot possibly supervise every activity directly. In addition, the corporation's owners and creditors typically rely on the financial statements as their primary source of information about the firm.

To insure objectivity, such statements are often *audited* by independent accounting firms. Audited financial statements have more credibility than financial statements prepared by a firm's management.[3]

audited

The principal financial statements of a business are organized around the operating, investing, and financing activities of the business. For example, the *income statement* reports the financial results of operations over a period of time. The *balance sheet* represents the results of investing and financing activities as of a point in time. The *statement of cash flows* presents the flows of cash into and out of the various operating, investing, and financing activities of the business over a period of time.[4] The *statement of retained earnings* reports any transactions affecting the retained earnings account during the accounting period. In addition to these formal financial statements, companies prepare tax statements to determine the amount of taxes owed during a period of time. To the list of important financial statements must be added three principal statements prepared for internal management and planning. These are the cash budget, the proforma (i.e., forecast) income statement, and the proforma balance sheet. These internal statements will be discussed in Chapter 8.

income statement
balance sheet
statement of cash flows

statement of retained earnings

Income Statement (Operating Activities)

The income statement is a report of the profits made during the reporting period (e.g., for the last 12 months of operations). The "bottom line" of the statement indicates the net profits earned for the owners. The income statement also indicates the total sales produced during the period, the total expenses incurred in producing those sales, and the tax liability generated. Equation 2-1 shows the relationship algebraically.

$$\text{Net income} = \text{Sales revenues} - \text{expenses} - \text{taxes} \qquad (2\text{-}1)$$

Exhibit 2-1 presents a very general picture of what an income statement looks like.

---

[3]The expense of independent audits can, in some sense, be considered part of the costs of the agency relationship discussed in Chapter 1.
[4]These and other financial statements are discussed in more detail in Chapter 7.

EXHIBIT 2-1
Income Statement for the
year ending 12/31/87

Sales	$1,000,000
Expenses	600,000
Profit before taxes	400,000
Taxes (34%)	136,000
Net income	$ 264,000

Balance Sheet (Investing and Financing Activities)

The balance sheet reflects the results of investing and financing activities as of a single point in time. It is something like a "snapshot" of these activities. The balance sheet has three main parts. The first part (the left-hand side) indicates all the items (assets) owned by the corporation. This represents the investing activities of the company. The right-hand side indicates all the money owed to creditors (liabilities) and all the money invested by the owners (shareholders' equity). This reflects the financing activities of the company. The firm's total assets must equal the total of its liabilities and shareholders' equity. This relationship is expressed algebraically in Equation 2-2.

$$\text{Assets} = \text{Liabilities} + \text{shareholders' equity} \qquad (2\text{-}2)$$

Exhibit 2-2 shows a summary balance sheet. Note that the balance sheet is dated "as of 12/31/87," indicating that it represents results at a single point in time.

Statement of Cash Flows (Operating, Investing, and Financing Activities)

The statement of cash flows integrates information from the income statement and balance sheet. The statement summarizes the cash inflows and outflows from the firm's operating, investing, and financing activities. At the time of this writing this statement is expected to replace the previously used "Statement of Changes in Financial Position" and provides a more uniform and understandable format. The statement of cash flows has three main sections:

- Operating activities, which summarizes cash inflows and outflows relating to the production and marketing of goods and services.
- Investing activities, which summarizes cash inflows and outflows relating to the purchases or sales of assets.

EXHIBIT 2-2
Summary Balance Sheet
as of 12/31/88

Assets	$500,000	Liabilities	$200,000
		Shareholders' equity	$300,000
		Total	$500,000

- Financing activities, which summarizes cash inflows and outflows relating to borrowing and repaying loans, selling and repurchasing common stock, and paying dividends.

An example of what the statement of cash flows looks like is shown in Exhibit 2-3.

Cash flows from operating activities	$160,000
Cash flows from investing activities	($300,000)
Cash flows from financing activities	$100,000
Net increase (decrease) in cash	$ (40,000)

EXHIBIT 2-3
Statement of Cash Flows
for the year ending
12/31/87

TAXATION

Taxes enter virtually every important business transaction. In addition to domestic federal taxes, businesses must deal with state taxes, municipal taxes, and possibly foreign taxes. The scope and complexity of tax provisions necessitates that we consider only the principal tax factors facing businesses. In addition, since many state and municipal tax principles are based on the federal tax codes, we will focus on federal tax factors.

Federal Income Taxes

Since a sole proprietorship is owned by one person—the proprietor of the business—any taxable income is treated as personal income and taxed at the personal income tax rate of the proprietor. According to the Tax Reform Act of 1986, there are two basic personal tax rates: 15 percent and 28 percent (plus a surtax within certain income ranges). The taxable income brackets for which these rates apply are shown in Table 2-2. More precisely, Table 2-2 shows the *marginal income tax rates* for taxpayers in different income tax brackets.

Tax Reform Act of 1986

marginal income tax rate

TABLE 2-2 Tax Rates Versus Personal Income Levels

Single		Married (Joint Filing)	
Taxable Income	*Marginal Rate*	*Taxable Income*	*Marginal Rate*
0-17,850	15%	0-29,750	15%
17,850-43,150	28%	29,750-71,900	28%
43,150-89,560	33%	71,900-149,250	33%
>89,560	28%	>149,250	28%

Notice that, for example, the single taxpayer has a 5-percent surcharge for income in the $43,150 to $89,560 range. This surcharge is intended to balance off the lower 15-percent bracket income. In essence, the effective tax rate is a straight 28 percent for taxable income above $89,560.

Marginal Vs. Effective (Average) Tax Rates

It is important to distinguish between marginal and effective tax rates. The federal income tax is known as a progressive tax system, meaning that people who earn more pay more taxes on the additional income.[5] A married couple filing jointly with taxable income of $29,750 pays a tax rate of 15 percent. But, if their taxable income goes above $29,750 (but less than $71,900), they pay taxes at a 28 percent rate on the increase, or *marginal* income. Thus, the marginal tax rate is the rate paid on the next dollar of income.

marginal

effective tax rate

The effective tax rate is the ratio of total taxes paid to total taxable income. This is expressed algebraically in Equation 2-3.

$$\text{Effective tax rate} = \text{Total taxes paid/taxable income} \qquad (2\text{-}3)$$

Example

Personal Taxes

Mary Lou has income of $89,560. Her tax liability would be:

Taxable Income	Marginal Tax Rate	Tax Liability
$17,850	.15	= 2,677.50
$43,150–17,850	.28	= 7,084.00
$89,560–43,150	.33	= 15,315.30
Total		25,076.80

Mary Lou's total tax liability is $25,076.80. Her effective tax rate is:

$$\$25,076.80/\$89,560 = .28$$

Notice that the surtax has just balanced the 15-percent lower bracket rate so that the effective tax is just equal to 28 percent.

$$.28(\$89,560) = 25,076.80$$

---

[5]Under the Tax Reform Act of 1986, the progressivity effectively ceases at the 28-percent rate.

For personal incomes above $89,560, the marginal tax rate will be constant and will be the same as the effective tax rate.

The personal tax rates that apply to Mary Lou as an individual also apply to businesses organized as sole proprietorships and partnerships.

Example

Taxation of Partnership Income

Joe Smith is a partner in The Leather Shop which has taxable income of $400,000. Joe is in a 28-percent tax bracket (i.e., his marginal tax rate is 28 percent). If Joe gets half the partnership income, his tax liability generated by the leather business is:

$$\text{Income from partnership} \times \text{personal tax rate} = \text{Tax liability}$$
$$\$200,000 \times .28 = \$56,000$$

Corporation Tax Rates

Under existing tax laws, the corporation has the legal status of a person and has its own applicable tax schedule on income, as shown in Table 2-3.

TABLE 2-3   Corporate Tax Schedule

Taxable Income	Marginal Tax Rate
0–$50,000	15%
$50,001–$75,000	25%
$75,001–$100,000	34%
100,001–335,000	39% (5% surtax)
over $335,000	34%

Example

Taxable Liability on Income of $400,000

Tax Bracket	Marginal Tax Rate	Tax Liability
First $50,000	×.15	$ 7,500
Income between $50,000 and $75,000	×.25	6,250
Income between $75,000 and $100,000	×.34	8,500
Income between $100,000 and $335,000	×.39	91,650
Income over $335,000	×.34	22,100
Total		$136,000

The 5-percent surcharge on income between $100,000 and $335,000 is applied to offset the lower 15-percent tax rate applied to the first $50,000 of income. The effective tax rate is:

$$\$136,000/\$400,000 = .34$$

Thus, as a shortcut, the company's tax liability can be determined by simply multiplying taxable income (if the total exceeds $335,000) by 34 percent.

Double Taxation

One of the important disadvantages with the corporate form of organization is the double taxation of dividends. When a corporation pays out dividends to shareholders, the shareholders must pay taxes on the dividend income (at the personal tax rates). However the dividends paid by the corporation are not tax deductible. Thus, business income is taxed once at the corporate level and again at the personal level if dividends are paid.[6]

In contrast to the double taxation of corporate dividends, the owners of sole proprietorships and partnerships pay taxes on business income only once, even if they withdraw the profits for personal use (similar to dividends).

Example

Taxation of Partnerships Versus Corporations

Three investors have decided to start a business. They estimate that taxable income will be $1 million. Each of the investors is in a 28-percent personal tax bracket, and each will share equally in the business profits. Assume all profits will be distributed to the investors.

From the standpoint of tax liability only, the investors will be better off organizing as a partnership than a corporation. The calculations are shown in Table 2-4. The higher rate of the corporation and the double taxation of dividend income both make the tax liability much greater for the corporate form ($524,800) than for the partnership form ($280,000) of organization. The effective overall tax rate as a corporation would be 52.48 percent (i.e., $524,800/$1,000,000) compared to 28 percent as a partnership.

---

[6] The double taxation of dividends has the effect of encouraging firms to reinvest profits in the business rather than pay them out as dividends. If the corporation tries to avoid this double taxation by not paying dividends, the IRS might prove that the company is unnecessarily accumulating profits to avoid the tax. If so, the IRS might levy an "Excess Profits Accumulation Tax."

TABLE 2-4   Tax Comparison: Partnership Vs. Corporation

As partnership

Partnership income	$1,000,000	
Tax rate of partners	.28	
Partners' total tax liability		$280,000
Net partners' after-tax income		$720,000

As corporation

Corporation taxable income	$1,000,000	
Corporate tax liability (34% rate)		$340,000
Net corporate income		$660,000
Dividends to owners	$660,000	
Tax on dividend income at personal tax rates of 28%		$184,800
Net after-tax owners' income		$475,200
Total tax liability (corporate + personal taxes):		$524,800

Sub-Chapter S Corporation

The Internal Revenue Service allows small corporations to be taxed as partnerships. These are known as *Sub-Chapter S*, or simply as *S* corporations. To qualify, the corporation must have no more than 35 owners and meet certain other requirements.[7] The owners can take advantage of the many benefits of corporate organization but, by organizing as an S corporation, avoid the larger tax liability.

S corporation

Master Limited Partnership (MLP)

Master limited partnerships have increased in popularity as a result of the personal tax rate reductions of the Tax Reform Act of 1986. These forms of organization offer many of the benefits of a corporate form (e.g., limited liability, transferability of ownership, and continuity of existence) and a partnership form (e.g., avoidance of double taxation and lower effective tax rates). In these respects MLPs are similar to S Corporations, but they are much more flexible. For example, MLPs are not limited to a maximum of 35 shareholders, and ownership interests can be sold easily. Partnership interests, called "units," are like common stock shares in that they may be bought and sold on stock exchanges. For example, in 1986 the owners of the Boston Celtics basketball team sold 2.6 million partnership units at a price

Master limited partnership

[7]Other requirements are: a) Shareholders must be U.S. citizens or U.S. residents; b) only one class of stock can be issued; c) and the company may not own 80 percent or more of the stock of a subsidiary.

of $18.50 per unit. The partnership units are traded on the New York Stock Exchange just as if they were shares of common stock in a corporation.

As a partnership, any income earned by the master limited partnership is exempt from federal income taxes and flows through directly to holders of the partnership units. Since, under the Tax Reform Act of 1986, personal tax rates are generally much lower than corporate rates, incentives to convert corporate organizations into MLPs have increased. However, at the time of this writing, Congress is considering changes in legislation to tax MLPs as corporations.

Business Losses and Taxes

When businesses are profitable, they pay taxes on profits. However, if businesses experience losses, they may be eligible to receive tax refunds from past taxes paid or to reduce future tax liabilities. Under existing tax laws, companies may "carry back" a current operating loss three years or "carry forward" a current operating loss 15 years in order to offset taxable income.[8] If carried back, the company may request a refund of taxes previously paid. If carried forward, future tax liabilities are reduced.

carry back
carry forward

To illustrate the manner in which operating losses in the current year can be used to reduce taxes, consider the following example.

Example

Taxes and Operating Losses

The Frankel Company has been in business two years. In its first year, the company had a taxable income of $500,000 on which it paid taxes of $170,000, producing a net income of $330,000. In its second year, the company experienced severe reverses and had a pre-tax loss of $600,000.

The company will carry back $500,000 of its pre-tax loss to year one by filing an amended return for year one. The amended return will indicate a pre-tax profit of zero for year one and, thus, a zero tax liability. The actual taxes paid in year one of $170,000 will be refunded to the company. The calculations are shown in Table 2-5.

TABLE 2-5 Tax Loss Carry Back			
Year	1	2	Combined
Taxable Income	$500,000	($600,000)	($100,000)
Tax Liability	$170,000	($204,000)	($34,000)
Net Income	$330,000	($396,000)	($66,000)

[8]Losses must first be applied to the past three years.

The remaining $100,000 operating loss of year 2 is available to carry-forward against taxable income over the next 15 years. At current tax rates, it will provide potential tax savings of $34,000.

Dividend Income

Corporations often invest in the stocks of other companies to take advantage of preferential tax treatment of intercompany dividends. Eighty percent of the dividends which one company receives from another are exempt from federal taxes. Thus, if Company A receives dividends of $1 million from Company B, only $200 thousand is taxable income. The $200,000 is taxed at the company's marginal tax rate on ordinary income (34 percent).

intercompany dividends

Interest Income and Expense

The interest that a business pays on borrowed money is tax deductible, which has the effect of reducing the amount of taxes paid. The interest that is received by a taxpayer, however, is taxed as ordinary income. Contrast this with dividends. Dividends paid by a business are not tax deductible, but dividends received are taxed.

interest and taxes

Capital Gains

When an asset is sold for more than its original cost, a capital gain is realized. Prior to the Tax Reform Act of 1986, long-term capital gains received favorable tax treatment in that 60 percent of the gains were tax exempt. The remaining 40 percent of the gains were taxed at ordinary income rates. This favorable treatment was eliminated by the Act, and all capital gains are now taxed at regular income tax rates.

capital gains

Investment Tax Credit

From time to time, Congress amends the Tax Code to allow an investment tax credit. This gives business a tax credit on long-term equipment purchased. The credit can be used to reduce the company's current tax liability. For example, prior to the Tax Reform Act of 1986, Congress granted a 10-percent tax credit. This meant that, for eligible equipment, a company that purchased $1 million worth of equipment would be able to reduce its tax liability by $100 thousand. When allowed, the investment tax credit

investment tax credit

provides incentives for business investment in hopes of increasing productivity and employment. The Tax Reform Act of 1986 abolished the investment tax credit, but it may come back someday.[9]

DEPRECIATION AND TAXES

depreciation

Accelerated Cost Recovery System (ACRS) straight-line depreciation

When a company buys a piece of equipment or other asset which will last for more than one year, some portion of the cost of the asset can be written off as an expense, called *depreciation*, each year. The treatment of depreciation as an expense has the effect of reducing corporate taxes. The more rapid the depreciation applied, the sooner the tax savings are realized. The Tax Reform Act of 1986 provides for two principal forms of depreciation: the Accelerated Cost Recovery System (ACRS) and the straight-line depreciation method. Because different types of assets have different economic lives, the IRS has spelled out various categories (class lives) to indicate how rapid the depreciation can be.

double-declining balance depreciation

For most business equipment (except real estate) purchased after 1986, companies must use either the straight-line or 200 percent declining balance (commonly referred to as double-declining balance) methods of depreciation.[10]

Additional Modifications

While the depreciation methods themselves are not complicated, some modifications must be incorporated in applying them.

half-year convention

Half-Year Convention.   The depreciation allowed in the first year of an asset's life must conform to the half-year convention, meaning that only half of the depreciation for the year is allowed. No matter when during a year the asset is actually acquired, it is assumed to be acquired on July 1 of the year. In effect, this means that "three-year" depreciation is spread over parts of four years.

switch in depreciation method

Switch in Depreciation Method.   Although the double declining balance method of depreciation results in larger depreciation in the early years of an asset's class life, in later years the straight-line method may actually

---

[9]More precisely, the Tax Reform Act repeals the investment tax credit only on property placed in service on or after January 1, 1986. Tax credits on property placed in service before January 1, 1986 were not abolished.

[10]The 200 percent declining balance method is also known as the declining balance method. Prior to the ACRS depreciation regulations, other methods of depreciation, such as the sum-of-the-years-digits method, could be used for tax purposes. Such methods are still acceptable for equipment purchased prior to ACRS.

produce larger depreciation write-offs. A company is allowed to switch from the accelerated method to the straight-line method when straight-line produces higher depreciation.

Salvage Value. At the end of an asset's class life, the asset may still have resale value (salvage value). The proceeds from the salvage value (assuming the asset is fully depreciated) are taxable at the company's ordinary income tax rate. Salvage value is not considered in calculating the annual depreciation allowances for tax purposes.

salvage value

Straight-Line Depreciation

To use the straight-line method of depreciation, one first determines the cost to be depreciated (the *depreciable basis*) and the number of years over which it can be depreciated (*class life*). To determine the annual straight-line depreciation (S-L), divide the cost (C) of the asset by the number of years of its class life (*n*). The straight-line method results in the same amount of depreciation each year. Note that salvage value is ignored for tax depreciation purposes.[11]

$$S - L = C/n \qquad (2\text{-}4)$$

Example

Straight-Line Depreciation

Assume an asset costs $100,000 and has a class life of three years. The annual straight-line depreciation is $33,333. However, due to the "half-year" convention, in the first year only one-half (16,667) is allowed. The shortfall is made up in the fourth year. Thus, the actual depreciation schedule would be as shown in Table 2-6.

TABLE 2-6   Straight-Line Depreciation Schedule

Year	1	2	3	4
Beginning Book Value	$100,000	83,333	50,000	16,667
−Depreciation	16,667	33,333	33,333	16,667
Ending Book Value	83,333	50,000	16,667	0

Notice that the total depreciation ($100,000) is equal to the original cost of the asset.

---

[11]In Chapter 15 we will distinguish tax depreciation from financial accounting depreciation methods.

ACRS Method

The ACRS method employs the double declining balance (DDB) method of depreciation for most business equipment. To calculate double declining balance depreciation, (DDB), one divides the asset's net book value (B) by the number of years in the asset's class life (n) and multiplies by two. The asset's net book value is equal to its original cost less all previous depreciation taken on it.

$$DDB = 2(B/n) \qquad (2\text{-}5)$$

Example

ACRS Three-Year Property

American Corporation has acquired a new machine tool for $100,000. The machine tool qualifies as three-year property. The DDB depreciation for each year is shown in Table 2-7:

TABLE 2-7 ACRS Depreciation: 3-Year Property

Year	1	2	3	4
Beginning Book Value	$100,000	66,667	22,222	7,407
−Depreciation	33,333	44,444	14,815	7,407
Ending Book Value	66,667	22,222	7,407	0

Notice that the first year's depreciation is only half of what it should be (i.e., $2 \times \$100,000/3 = \$66,667$) due to the half-year convention. Also note that some depreciation is taken in the fourth year.

The ACRS method results in higher depreciation in the early years than the straight-line method. This advantage reduces the tax liability of the corporation in the early years and gives the company more cash to invest in the short term.

TAX REPORTS AND FINANCIAL STATEMENTS

Accelerated depreciation methods and other accounting rules reduce taxable income and result in lower taxes. This could lead to a dilemma for the financial manager: should I report higher profits and pay more taxes or report lower profits and pay less taxes? Fortunately, the financial manager does not have to choose. The IRS allows companies to keep two sets of books: one set for preparing tax reports and the other for financial reports. For example, the company might use ACRS depreciation methods in its tax reports and straight line for its financial reports. The straight line method is used by more than 90% of U.S. Corporations for financial reporting. The ACRS method would produce higher depreciation in the early years and reduce profits before taxes, hence tax liability. However, for financial statement purposes, straight-line would show lower depreciation, higher net income, and higher taxes. Of course, the actual tax liability would be the one shown in tax reports. Table 2-8 shows how tax liability and profits can differ between the two statements.

TABLE 2-8 Tax Reporting Vs. Financial Reporting

	Tax Report	Financial Report
Profits before depreciation and taxes	$600,000	$600,000
less depreciation expense	$200,000	$100,000
Profit before taxes	$400,000	$500,000
Taxes (34%)	$136,000	$170,000
Net income	$264,000	$330,000

Tax Payment Dates

Businesses are required to estimate the amount of their tax liability for the year and to pay installments on the overall liability. Tax payment due dates are the fifteenth of April, June, September, and December. Since there is a temptation to understate the annual tax liability, the IRS assesses a penalty on firms which substantially understate the tax liability.

SUMMARY

Many legal, business, and personal factors enter the selection of the form of business organization. Taxes are very important to a business, regardless of its organizational form, because every dollar of taxes reduces the amount of earnings received by owners. Nonetheless, taxes are only one of several factors which determine the organizational form of a business. Other important considerations are liability exposure of owners, permanence of the business organization, transferability of all or part ownership in the business, and access to financial markets. Generally, the larger the business, the more likely it is to be organized as a corporation.

MULTIPLE CHOICE QUESTIONS

1. A partnership is taxed:
   a) Twice—once as a corporation, then again as personal income
   b) At the personal tax rates of the partners
   c) As a proprietorship
   d) Only if dividends are paid

2. Ignoring the 5-percent tax surcharge, the maximum corporate tax rate on business income is:
   a) 28 percent
   b) Dependent on other income levels of owners
   c) 34 percent
   d) Dependent on the total sales of the corporation

3. Ignoring the 5-percent tax surcharge, the maximum corporate tax rate on long-term capital gains is:
   a) 28 percent
   b) Dependent on the book value of the asset
   c) 34 percent
   d) Twice the straight-line rate

4. An operating loss may be:

   a) Carried back seven years and forward three years
   b) Carried back three years and forward 15 years
   c) Carried back and forward a maximum of three years
   d) Carried back and forward a maximum of 15 years

5. In terms of transferability of ownership, the most flexible form of organization is:

   a) Proprietorship
   b) Partnership
   c) Corporation
   d) S corporation

6. Personal liability would be greatest in a.

   a) Proprietorship
   b) Limited partnership
   c) Corporation
   d) S corporation

7. For tax purposes straight-line depreciation is calculated by:

   a) Dividing the original cost minus salvage value by the economic life of the asset
   b) Dividing the book value of the asset by twice the economic life of the asset
   c) Dividing the original cost of the asset by the economic life of the asset
   d) Dividing the original cost of the asset by one-half the economic life of the asset.

8. According to the half-year convention:

   a) Half of the asset's cost can be deducted in the first year
   b) Half of the annual depreciation is deducted in the first year
   c) Half of the economic life of the asset is used to compute depreciation in the first year
   d) Half of the net book value is deducted in the first year

9. Under the Tax Reform Act of 1986, the investment tax credit is:

   a) 10 percent
   b) 6 percent
   c) Variable
   d) Zero

10. The total depreciation produced by the double-declining-balance method is:

    a) Equal to that of the straight-line method
    b) Twice that of the straight-line method
    d) One-half that of the straight-line method
    d) Twice the original cost of the asset

11. Dividend income received by one corporation from another is:
    a) 50-percent tax exempt
    b) 34-percent tax exempt
    c) 80-percent tax exempt
    d) 85-percent tax exempt

DISCUSSION QUESTIONS

1. Briefly describe the major differences among the three main forms of business organization.
2. What is the main difference between general and limited partnerships?
3. Why is Delaware the most popular state of incorporation for businesses?
4. Explain the advantages of a master limited partnership.
5. What are the main advantages of an S corporation?
6. What is the difference between marginal and effective tax rates?
7. In calculating corporate taxes, why is a surcharge assessed on income between $100,000 and $335,000?
8. What is meant by the double taxation of corporate income?
9. Explain the tax treatments of operating loss carrybacks and carryforwards.
10. What is the purpose of the investment tax credit? How was it affected by the Tax Reform Act of 1986?
11. What are the two principal depreciation methods provided under the Tax Reform Act of 1986? Compare the financial and tax consequences of the two methods.
12. What is meant by the half-year convention in calculating depreciation?
13. Briefly describe the primary financial statements used by businesses.

SOLVED PROBLEMS

personal vs. corporate taxes

SP-1. The Blivens Sanitation Corporation earned taxable income of $150,000 in 1987.
    a) Calculate the company's tax liability.
    b) What is the company's marginal tax rate?
    c) What is the company's effective tax rate?
    d) Assume that the company is solely owned by Mr. Blivens and his wife, that all profits after corporate taxes are paid out as dividends, and that the Blivens' marginal tax rate is 28 percent. What taxes will have to be paid on the dividends?

e) Combining corporate and personal tax liabilities on the original taxable income of $150,000, calculate the effective tax rate paid by the Blivens.

SP-2. The Williams Company purchased a machine for $200,000. The machine qualifies as three-year property for purposes of depreciation. Develop depreciation schedules for each year using the straight-line and double-declining balance methods.   *depreciation methods*

SP-3. The PRT Corporation had losses its first two years of operations and became profitable in year three, as shown below: *operating losses*

	Year		
	1	*2*	*3*
Operating profit (loss) before taxes	−$100,000	$−50,000	$100,000

a) Calculate PRT's taxes in each of the three years, assuming that the tax rates of the Tax Reform Act of 1986 apply.
b) What is PRT's tax status at the end of year three?
c) Assume that taxable income in year four is $75,000. What will PRT's tax situation be?

PROBLEMS

1. The Jacobs Janitorial Service Corporation earned taxable income of $400,000 in 1987.   *personal vs. corporate taxes*

a) Calculate the company's tax liability.
b) What is the company's marginal tax rate?
c) What is the company's effective tax rate?
d) Assume that the company is solely owned by Mr. Jacobs and his wife, that all profits after corporate taxes are paid out as dividends, and that the Jacobs' marginal tax rate is 28 percent. What taxes will have to be paid on the dividends?
e) Combining corporate and personal tax liabilities on the original taxable income of $400,000, calculate the effective tax rate paid by the Jacobs.

2. The Binetti Company purchased a machine for $400,000. The machine qualifies as three-year property for purposes of depreciation. Develop depreciation schedules for each year using the straight-line and double declining balance methods.   *depreciation methods*

3. Wholey Mackeral Corporation had losses its first two years of operations and became profitable in year three, as shown below: *operating losses*

	Year		
	1	*2*	*3*
Operating profit (loss) before taxes	−$300,000	−$100,000	$800,000

  a) Calculate Wholey's taxes in each of the three years, assuming that the tax rates of the Tax Reform Act of 1986 apply.
  b) What is the company's tax status at the end of year three?
  c) Assume that in year four the company has a loss of $100,000, what will its tax situation be?

personal taxes

4. Dr. and Mrs. Jones have total combined taxable income of $130,000.
  a) What is the Jones' tax liability if they file jointly?
  b) What is the Jones' marginal tax rate?
  c) What is the Jones' effective tax rate?

corporate vs. sole proprietorship taxes

5. The Smith Company earned taxable income of $300,000 in 1987.
  a) Calculate the company's tax liability.
  b) What is the company's marginal tax rate?
  c) What is the company's effective tax rate?
  d) Assume that the company is solely owned by Mr. Smith, that all profits after corporate taxes are paid out as dividends, and that his marginal tax rate is 28 percent. What taxes will have to be paid on the dividends?
  e) Combining corporate and personal tax liabilities on the original taxable income of $300,000, calculate the effective tax rate paid by Mr. Smith.

depreciation methods

6. The Trache Company purchased a machine for $800,000. The machine qualifies as five-year property for purposes of depreciation. Develop depreciation schedules for each year using the straight-line and double declining balance methods.

operating losses

7. Southern Company had profits its first two years of operations and had an operating loss in year three, as shown below:

	Year		
	1	*2*	*3*
Operating profit (loss) before taxes	$600,000	$800,000	−$400,000

  a) Calculate Southern's taxes in each of the three years, assuming that the tax rates of the Tax Reform Act of 1986 apply.
  b) What is Southern's tax status at the end of year three?

    c) Assume that taxable income in year four is $1 million. What will Southern's tax situation be?

8. The Fisher Corporation is expected to earn $80,000 in taxable income this year.
    a) What is the dollar amount of income taxes that will have to be paid? *corporate taxes*
    b) What are Fisher's marginal and effective income tax rates?

9. Mr. and Mrs. Sand have a taxable income of $25,000 while their neighbors, the Joneses, have a taxable income of $50,000. *personal taxes*
    a) Calculate the income tax liabilities for the Sands and the Joneses.
    b) Compare the marginal and effective tax rates for the two couples.

10. Compare the marginal and effective tax rates for a corporation with taxable income of $50,000 with the tax rates applicable for a corporation with taxable income earnings of $500,000. *marginal vs. effective tax rates*

11. The Carter Maintenance Corporation had sales of $500,000 during the year. Business expenses were $400,000. *corporate taxes*
    a) What is the after-tax income for Carter?
    b) What are Carter's marginal and effective income tax rates?
    c) If Carter had also received $100,000 in dividend income from the Ajax Corporation, what would its after-tax net income have been?

12. The Webster Products Corporation was formed in 1983. While it has generally been profitable, a $200,000 loss was incurred in 1987. Webster's annual taxable income was as follows: *operating losses*

Year	Taxable Income
1983	$20,000
1984	50,000
1985	80,000
1986	40,000
1987	−200,000

    Revise Webster's income tax liability for each year of operation.

13. Willy has taxable income of $90,500. Calculate his tax liability and effective tax rate. *personal taxes*

14. John Mathis is a partner in The Toy Shop, which has taxable income of 600,000. John is in a 28-percent tax bracket. If John gets half the partnership income, calculate his tax liability. *partnership taxes*

15. Four investors have decided to start a business. They estimate that business taxable income will be $2 million. Each of the investors is in a 28-percent personal tax bracket, and each will share equally in the *partnership vs. corporate taxes*

business profits. Assume that all profits will be paid in dividends to the four investors.

a) Calculate total taxes paid under a partnership and corporate form of organization.
b) Compute the effective tax rate under each form of organization.
c) What form of organization would you recommend on the basis of tax liability?

SOLUTIONS TO SOLVED PROBLEMS

SP-1. a) Using the information in the chapter, construct the following table:

Taxable Income	Marginal Tax Rate	Tax Liability
up to $50,000	.15	$7,500
between 50,000 and 75,000	.25	6,250
between 75,000 and 100,000	.34	8,500
between 100,000 and 150,000	.39	19,500
Total		41,750

b) The marginal tax rate is the rate on the next dollar of taxable income. For taxable income between $100,000 and $335,000, the 5-percent tax surcharge applies. The Blivens Corporation is still within this bracket, and thus its marginal tax rate is 39 percent.
c) The effective corporate tax rate is simply the ratio of total corporate taxes to total taxable income. For the Blivens Corporation the effective tax rate on taxable income of $150,000 is 27.8 percent.

$$\text{Effective tax rate} = \text{tax liability/taxable income}$$
$$= \$41,750/\$150,000 = 27.8\%$$

d) The company's taxes of $41,750 on taxable income of $150,000 mean that $108,250 is income after taxes. All of this is presumed paid out as dividends to the Blivens. Since they are in the 28-percent marginal tax bracket, the tax liability on the dividends is $30,310 (i.e., $108,250 × .28). This problem demonstrates the double taxation of corporate dividends: they are taxed once at the corporate level and again at the personal level.
e) Total taxes will be $72,060 (i.e., corporate taxes of $41,750 plus personal taxes of $30,310). Overall, the effective tax rate is 48 percent! The Blivens definitely should consider organizing as an S corporation.

Straight-Line Method

Year	1	2	3	4
Beginning Book Value	$200,000	166,667	100,000	33,333
−Depreciation	33,333	66,667	66,667	33,333
Ending Book Value	166,667	100,000	33,333	0

Double-Declining-Balance Method

Year	1	2	3	4
Beginning Book Value	$200,000	133,333	44,444	14,815
−Depreciation	66,667	88,889	29,629	14,815
Ending Book Value	133,333	44,444	14,815	0

Summary

Year	1	2	3	4	Total
S-L depreciation	$33,333	$66,667	$66,667	$33,333	$200,000
DDB depreciation	$66,667	$88,889	$29,629	$14,815	$200,000

Both methods produce the same total depreciation, but the pattern is different. The DDB method produces more depreciation early and less later.

SP-3. a) In years one and two, losses were experienced and no taxes were due. In year three, although profits before taxes of $100,000 are earned, no taxes are due since losses in prior years can be carried forward to more than offset the profits in year three.

  b) Year three's taxable income of $100,000 is offset with year one's operating loss of $100,000. However, year two's operating loss of $50,000 is still available to offset against taxable income in year four and subsequently.

  c) In year four, $50,000 of the $75,000 taxable income can be offset by the operating loss in year two. Thus, only $25,000 of year four's taxable income is subject to tax. The tax rate for this level of income is 15 percent, which produces a tax liability in year four of $3,750.

REFERENCES

Commerce Clearing House, *Tax Reform Act* of 1986.

Coopers and Lybrand, Tax Reform Act of 1986, Washington, D.C., 1986.

Mack, T. "Disincorporating America." *Forbes*, August 1, 1983, pp. 76-78.

C H A P T E R

3

THE ECONOMIC ENVIRONMENT

hapter 2 presented important features of the legal and tax environment as they relate to financial decisions. This chapter takes up important features of the economic environment and their relation to a firm's financial decisions. The most important of these economic factors are the effects of business cycles, economic policies of the federal government, the behavior of interest rates, and the organization and operation of financial markets. Chapter 4 considers more systematically the importance of interest rates to financial management.

● Objectives and Organization of this Chapter

This chapter has a limited but very important objective: to enable one to read and interpret financial news of immediate relevance to a firm. For example, a financial manager must know what the prospect of a recession means, what references to monetary policy imply for interest rates, or why commercial banks and insurance companies are important to a firm. Included here are the basic framework, concepts, and terminology to provide an understanding of these and many other factors in the economic environment.

The first section of the chapter describes the importance of business cycles to financial management. The second section contains a discussion of the primary economic policies of the federal government and how they affect a firm. The third section considers the determinants of interest rates and the behavior of interest rates over time. The fourth section discusses the important concept of the term structure of interest rates and the insights which may be drawn about expected future interest rates and inflation. In the final section of the chapter, the organization and operation of financial markets are described.

BUSINESS CYCLES AND FINANCIAL MANAGEMENT

A company's profits depend heavily on the level of sales it achieves. For the typical firm, high and rising sales levels result in greater profits. The rise in profits is viewed favorably by the stock market, and the firm's stock price increases. Conversely, declines in sales result in lower profits and lower stock prices. The level of sales a firm achieves is clearly important to the maximization of its stock price.

business cycle

Many factors determine sales level. For example, the degree of competition, the attractiveness of the firm's products, and the prices it charges all play important roles in sales success. Another factor that strongly affects the sales levels of most firms is the business cycle. The financial manager must understand the behavior of business cycles and try to recognize changes quickly enough to take proper action.

What Are Business Cycles?

A business cycle refers to the rise and fall of overall economic activity as measured by the Gross National Product (GNP). The GNP is the total value of all goods and services produced by the economy.

expansion
recession

Business cycles are a recurring feature of the economic environment and typically contain two principal phases: expansion and recession. The highest point of an expansion is called the *peak,* and the lowest part of a recession is known as the *trough.* A business cycle expansion starts with the recession trough and ends with the subsequent expansionary peak. A recession begins with the peak and ends with the subsequent recessionary trough. Exhibit 3-1 shows what such a pattern might look like.

EXHIBIT 3-1
Business Cycles Stages

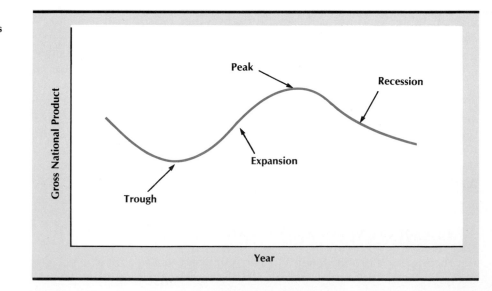

The Expansion

During a period of expansion, overall spending in the economy increases. This means that a company will see a rise in sales and increases in profits. The longer and more intense the expansion, the greater the rise in sales and profits. As expansions reach their peak, most companies are operating at close to maximum capacity. If sales demand increases even further, prices begin to rise and price inflation begins to develop.

Expansionary periods are good for business because companies realize large profits and generate more money to build new and more efficient facilities. Since they represent unusual opportunities, business expansions must be fully exploited by companies. This means that the financial manager must plan for the financing needed to hire more employees, purchase and produce more inventories, build larger facilities, and extend more credit to customers.

The Recession

The recessionary phase of the business cycle is of most concern to business managers. In this phase, companies have trouble finding customers. The inventories of goods being produced begin to increase faster than sales. Instead of hiring more workers, companies begin to lay workers off. Instead of building more production facilities, companies have idled machines. Unemployment throughout the economy grows, and consumers have less money to spend. Sales, profits, and stock prices decline. This pattern was evident, for example, during the recession that lasted from July 1981 (the peak) to November 1982 (the trough). In that period, corporate profits after taxes dropped almost 27 percent and stock prices overall dropped about 7 percent. The historical relation between corporate profits and recessions can be seen in Exhibit 3-2.

Recessions typically last less than two years, and some are of very short duration. The 1980 recession lasted only seven months, from January (peak) to July (trough). It is important to note, in addition, that particular industries may experience recessions even though the overall economy is not affected.

During the recession, the company must be careful to conserve cash. However, many expenses, such as payment of loan obligations, dividends to shareholders, top management salaries, rents, and leases of facilities are, to some extent, fixed and cannot be reduced immediately. These represent significant cash drains on a company when cash inflows from sales are dwindling. If the financial manager fails to recognize a recession soon enough and does not institute contingency plans, the company can easily go bankrupt.

Sensitivity to Business Cycles

Some firms are much more sensitive to business cycle changes than others. Firms in the food industry, for example, are less affected than firms

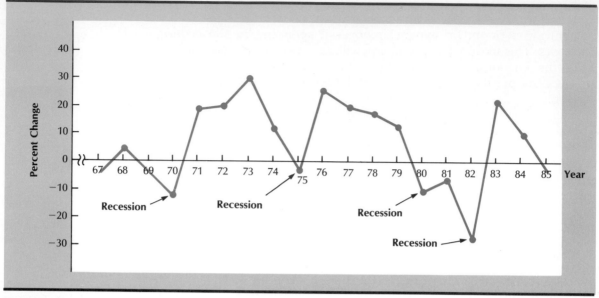

EXHIBIT 3-2
Percentage Changes in
Corporate Profits
1967–1985

in the automotive industry. Consumers may not drastically cut back on grocery purchases during a recession, but they may very well postpone buying a new car. Thus, it is important for the firm's financial manager to estimate how sensitive his or her firm is to changes in the business cycle.

Example

Sensitivity to Business Cycles

By studying the Arec Company's sales behavior during past business cycles, the firm's financial manager determined that, on average, Arec's sales were twice as volatile as the overall economy. If GNP increased by 5 percent, Arec's sales increased by about 10 percent; and if GNP declined by 5 percent, Arec's sales decreased by about 10 percent.

The company's financial manager believes that a recession is likely and that GNP may decline by as much as 6 percent. Thus, plans have been prepared to adjust production schedules, raw materials purchases, and proposed capital expenditures consistent with a sales level 12 percent lower. The plans will be instituted when the company is certain that the recession has begun.

Forecasting Business Cycles

Much effort is put into trying to forecast the business cycle. The U.S. Department of Commerce publishes an index of *leading indicators*. A leading

leading indicators

52

indicator usually provides clues about changes ("turning points") in the business cycle.

For example, the Arec Company's financial manager carefully follows an index of the average number of hours worked per week in all manufacturing businesses. This is because other firms, like Arec, adjust their production schedules to conform with their sales orders. When sales increase, companies ask their crews to work longer hours. This increases the average number of hours worked per week and signals an increase in overall economic activity (i.e., an expansion). Conversely, companies are reluctant to lay off workers. Thus when sales start to decrease, companies reduce the number of hours worked by employees. Average hours worked per week begin to decline, and this signals the onset of a recession.

For many years, the stock market has been considered a leading indicator. The rationale is that, if the economy is expected to expand, profits of corporations will be higher, making their stocks more attractive. Presumably, when stock prices overall begin to rise, there is general expectation that the economy is going to expand. If overall stock prices fall, this reflects an expectation that corporate profits will fall.

Other popular indicators of business conditions are durable goods orders, inventory purchases, and "help wanted" ads. The idea is that these will tend to increase with expansions and decrease with recessions.

Weaknesses in Leading Indicators

Leading indicators have two principal weaknesses. First, they may indicate the onset of an expansion or recession, but they do not indicate how soon either will occur or their magnitudes and duration. For example, a recession may be indicated but might not actually be evident for six months or more. Second, often the indicated change in the business cycle may not materialize. This fact has led to the saying that "leading indicators have predicted 10 out of the last seven recessions."

Unreliable leading indicators may have the same financial consequences as no indicators at all. If a firm's financial manager reacts too quickly to an indicated recession, for example, the company might start cutting back on production too quickly and miss sales in the event the recession is late in developing or, perhaps, never develops. However, if the financial manager stays abreast of economic news and develops contingency plans, the company may have plenty of time to react even after the recession (or expansion) has begun.

NATIONAL ECONOMIC POLICIES AND THE FIRM

In 1946 the U.S. Government formally committed itself to the economic goals of full employment, economic growth, and reasonable price stability. In pursuing these goals, the government employs two major economic policy instruments. They are known as fiscal and monetary policies.

Fiscal Policy

fiscal policy

Generally, fiscal policy refers to taxation policies and spending decisions of the federal government. The federal government is an enormous force in the economy. For example, in 1986 total GNP was just above $4 trillion and federal spending on goods and services was almost $400 billion (about 10 percent).[1] At the same time, the federal government takes enormous quantities of income out of the hands of consumers through taxes. If the government takes in more tax revenues than it spends, it has a budget surplus and overall spending in the economy is reduced. Conversely, if the government spends more than it takes in, it has a budget deficit and overall spending in the economy is increased. By altering the amount of surplus or deficit it produces, the federal government tries to moderate the business cycle. Thus, if the economy is heading toward a recession, the government may spend more than it takes in from tax revenues and, by producing a budget deficit, increase spending in the economy. Conversely, if an expansion is becoming inflationary, the government may produce a budget surplus (i.e., more tax revenues than spending), thereby reducing total spending in the economy.

Budget surpluses have become a rarity, as indicated by Exhibit 3-3. In fact, recent budget deficits have increased at alarming rates. The budget deficit in 1979 was $56.3 billion, but by 1986 the deficit had increased to $245.2 billion. One of the many severe problems such deficits create is that fiscal policy becomes less flexible and less effective. This in turn increases the reliance on monetary policy.

Monetary Policy

monetary policy

Monetary policy refers primarily to controls over the supply of money. One objective of monetary policy is, like fiscal policy, to moderate business cycles.

Federal Reserve System

Monetary policy is administered by the Board of Governors of the Federal Reserve System (popularly known as the "Fed") through the banking system (most large banks are members of the Federal Reserve System). The idea behind monetary policy is that, by controlling the amount of money in the financial system, the supply and cost of money can be altered to encourage or discourage economic activity.[2]

In order to anticipate the availability and cost of funds, many financial managers monitor changes in the money supply. For example, if the Fed

---

[1] When one considers multiplier effects, the impact of changes in federal taxation and spending is much larger. For a further discussion of the multiplier, see any introductory economics textbook.
[2] The focus of monetary policy has typically been on maintaining price stability (i.e., to fight inflation) while that of fiscal policy has been on employment and economic growth. The Fed also attempts to influence interest rates by raising or lowering the interest rate it charges member banks (the discount rate), but this tool has been seriously impaired in recent years.

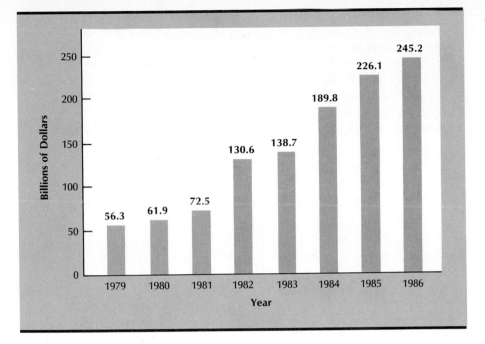

EXHIBIT 3-3
Federal Budget Deficit
1979–1986

appears to be increasing the money supply at a rapid rate ("monetary ease"), financial managers expect to find money more readily available and less expensive (i.e., lower interest rates). Conversely, a period of "tight" money reflects the Fed's intention of slowing down the growth in the money supply in order to slow down the pace of business activity. In such a case, the financial manager can expect higher interest rates and more difficulty in raising funds.

The Effects of Monetary and Fiscal Policies

In the 1960s there was widespread belief that the proper mix of fiscal and monetary policies could moderate the swings in business cycles and guide the economy to full employment without inflation. That view is not widely held now. Failures to control inflation, prevent severe recessions, and balance the budget in the 1970s and 1980s undermined the credibility of economic policies.[3] Indeed, some skeptics believe that fiscal and monetary policies have actually been *pro-cyclical* and thus made expansions more inflationary and recessions more severe.

---

[3]The most stunning statement of disillusionment was the imposition of mandatory wage and price controls by President Nixon in 1971.

In addition, in the 1980s there have been increasing budget deficits of such alarming magnitudes that the financial requirements of the Treasury Department threaten to "crowd out" the financial needs of businesses.[4]

The enormous and active involvements by the federal government in the economy have made it more important than ever for financial managers to stay alert to the economic environment. This point was made clearly by the chief financial officer of the Exxon Corporation, John Bennett, one of the most respected financial officers in the United States, when he said:

> People worry a lot about business cycles, and they're important. But most of the disruption that hits the market is clearly government created. . . . I spend half my time chasing around the world, looking for a way to exploit some obstacle or another that a government has put in my way.[5]

In addition to business cycles and government policies, the financial manager must try to understand the behavior of interest rates. In the following section, we will examine why this is important to effective financial management.

INTEREST RATES AND FINANCIAL MANAGEMENT

Like any other raw material, money has a cost. The cost of money is generally calculated as a percentage of the amount of money received. This percentage is referred to as the interest rate, or *yield,* of the funds raised. Often, interest rates are referred to in terms of basis points. There are 100 basis points in 1 percent. Saving even one basis point on borrowings of large amounts can be significant in terms of dollars. In the business literature, the terms interest rates and yields on securities are used interchangeably. In this chapter we will follow that convention, and we will defer discussing the distinction between the two to chapter 4.

interest rate
basis point

yield

Example

Interest Rates

Assume that the financial manager for the Jones Company borrows $1 million for one year from a bank. The banker specifies that, at the end of a year, the Jones Company must repay the principal amount borrowed ($1 million) plus interest of $120 thousand. The interest rate would be 12 percent (i.e., $120,000/$1,000,000). If the Jones Company can borrow the $1 million from another bank at a rate of 11.9 percent, the savings (10 basis points) will amount to $1,000.

---

[4]The crowding-out effect occurs when the Treasury borrows so heavily in the financial markets that insufficient capital is left for any but the largest, best-known business firms.
[5]Boston Globe, page A7, February 1, 1987.

Interest rates vary considerably over time and among firms. Everything else equal, the higher the firm's interest rate, the lower its profits will be and the lower its stock price will be. For many companies, a period of high interest rates can result in payments of interest that are greater than the profits received by stockholders. Clearly, finding ways to save on interest expense is an important responsibility of the financial manager.

Interest Rate Determinants

Interest rates are determined by several factors. Analytically, these factors can be distinguished as shown in Equation 3-1:

$$I = I^* + P + R \qquad (3\text{-}1)$$

Where I is the nominal or stated rate of interest; I^* is the real rate of interest in the economy; P is a premium to compensate for expected price inflation; R is a premium to compensate for risk.

nominal interest rate

The Real Rate of Interest (I^*)

The simplest way to define the real interest rate is that it is the interest rate that would prevail if there were no inflation, and no risk. It represents compensation to a saver for passing up other uses of the money (such as spending the money for personal consumption). The real rate of interest is generally assumed to be relatively stable over time.

real rate of interest

Example

The Real Rate of Interest

Let us assume that Joe Marx is in the mood for a pizza and decides to order one. Just as he is about to place the order, his friend Fred shows up and asks Joe for a $5 loan. If Joe lends Fred the $5, he will not have enough cash to buy his pizza. So Joe turns Fred down. But Fred is insistent. "Look, Joe," pleads Fred, "lend me the five bucks and I'll give you $10 bucks next Friday." Joe figures that if he lends Fred the money now, next Friday he will be able to buy pizzas for himself and his girl friend, Sue. Thus, Joe accepts Fred's offer, knowing that Fred never reneges on a promise.

Joe's real rate of interest is very high. So high, in fact, that if he were lending commercially at these rates he would be breaking laws against usury (the charging of excessive interest rates). Joe's case was also somewhat extreme in that the $5 was all he had and Fred was desperate. However if Joe's wealthy roommate, Bill, had been present, he might have lent Fred the $5 at a zero interest rate. For the economy as a whole, the real rate depends on the supply and demand for loanable funds.

inflation premium

Inflation Premium (*P*)

When an investor foregoes current consumption for more consumption in the future, the investor also wants to be protected against higher future prices. This is accomplished by demanding an inflation premium. The inflation premium is added to the real interest rate. Thus, if Joe Marx expects the cost of pizza to double by next Friday (as it can easily do in some economies), Fred's $10 payment will only buy one pizza rather than the two Joe wants. Inflation would result in a zero real interest rate for Joe. If Joe really expects the cost of pizza to rise by Friday, he would insist on more than $10 from Fred. In fact, if Joe wants the equivalent of two pizzas on Friday, he will insist on $20 Friday in exchange for $5 now. Inflation rates have been very volatile in the recent past as shown in Exhibit 3-4.

Example

Inflation and Interest Rates

Assume that the real rate of interest is expected to be 3 percent over the next year. In addition, inflation is expected to be 5 percent over the next

**EXHIBIT 3-4
Annual Rate of Inflation
1967–1984**

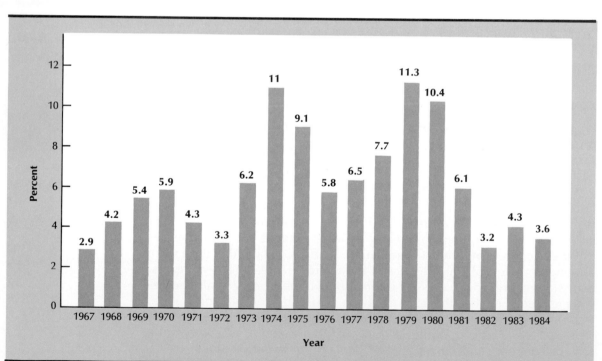

year. The nominal rate of interest on a one-year risk-free investment is, therefore, 8 percent.[6]

59
CHAPTER 3
THE ECONOMIC
ENVIRONMENT

Risk Premium (R)

Interest rates also reflect the relative risk of the borrower. This risk is the possibility that interest and principal will not be paid when due and that the borrower will default on the loan. For Treasury securities, the probability of default is zero and the risk premium is zero. The relationship between risk and the interest rate is so important that we will devote an entire chapter to it (Chapter 6, "Risk and the Rate of Return"). The relationship is also examined less formally in Chapter 5, "Valuation."

The risk premium varies widely among companies on the basis of the borrower's size and financial strength. For example, when large, financially strong companies borrow from banks, they are likely to receive the bank's lowest interest rate (usually referred to as the prime rate). Weaker companies may have to pay interest rates one or more percentage points above prime.

prime rate

Example

Interest Rates and the Risk Premium

The Arec Company's five-year securities are considered much riskier than Treasury's. Five-year Treasury securities have a yield of 8 percent. Investors require a risk premium of 4 percent for lending Arec funds. Thus, the Arec Company must provide a total yield of 12 percent (i.e., 8 percent plus 4 percent risk premium).

Risk premiums change over time. This difference is associated with investor optimism or pessimism concerning the outlook for economic activity. When the economy is expected to be heading into a recession, investors become more pessimistic and require larger risk premiums if they are to invest in riskier securities. During more optimistic times, risk premiums shrink.

For example in the 1980 recession, the risk premium between Treasury bonds and lower-quality corporate bonds increased from 1.42 percent (i.e., 142 basis points) to 2.38 percent.

---

[6]This is normally a close approximation. The nominal rate is actually equal to:
$(I^* + P + I^*P)$. At low inflation rates, the cross-product term, I^*P is usually low and can be ignored. In Joe's case, both the real and inflation rates are so high that the cross-product term should not be ignored.

In addition to risk, interest rates reflect the marketability of an investment. Marketability refers to the ability to liquidate or terminate an investment by selling it to someone else. For instance, an investor who buys Treasury bills can get his or her money back by selling the Treasury bills to another investor. The number of investors buying and selling Treasury bills is so great that the bills are considered perfectly marketable. Thus, the marketability premium on Treasury bills is zero. At the other extreme, a personal loan to a small company might be very unmarketable since it might be difficult to liquidate the investment on short notice. The less marketable securities are, the higher the interest rate they must offer investors.

INTEREST RATES AND TERM TO MATURITY

term to maturity

Interest rates or yields also vary on the basis of term to maturity. For example, the annual yield on a 10-year Treasury Bond is different from that of a 20-year Treasury Bond. Since both bonds have zero risk and perfect marketability, the differences are mainly due to the term to maturity.[7]

term structure
yield curve

The relationship between term to maturity and yield is known as the *term structure.* The term structure is often presented graphically in the form of a "yield curve" such as the one in Exhibit 3-5, which is constructed by plotting the yields on U.S. government securities of varying maturities as of a particular date.

Notice that the pattern of the yield curve changes from one period to another. Sometimes long-term bonds have lower yields than short-term bonds (the March 14, 1980 curve), and at other times long-term bonds have higher yields than short-term bonds (the October 31, 1986 curve).

Financial managers analyze the shape of the yield curve to gain insights about expected future interest rates and inflation. To see how this is done, we will examine three popular explanations for the shape of the yield curve: the *expectations* theory, the *liquidity premium* theory, and the *market segmentation* theory.

expectations theory
liquidity premium theory
market segmentation theory

Expectations Theory

According to the expectations theory, long-term interest rates are an average of short-term rates. For example, the interest rate (yield) on a two-year security is an *average* of the two one-year rates it encompasses. Think of a two-year security as made up of two one-year segments, a three-year security as made up of three one-year segments, and so on. Thus, when one refers to the yield of, say, a two-year security being

---

[7]We are ignoring certain differences in various provisions associated with different issues. For example, Treasury "Flower" bonds have lower yields than one would expect. The reason is that the bonds have tax advantages in settling estate taxes (hence the term "flower" bonds).

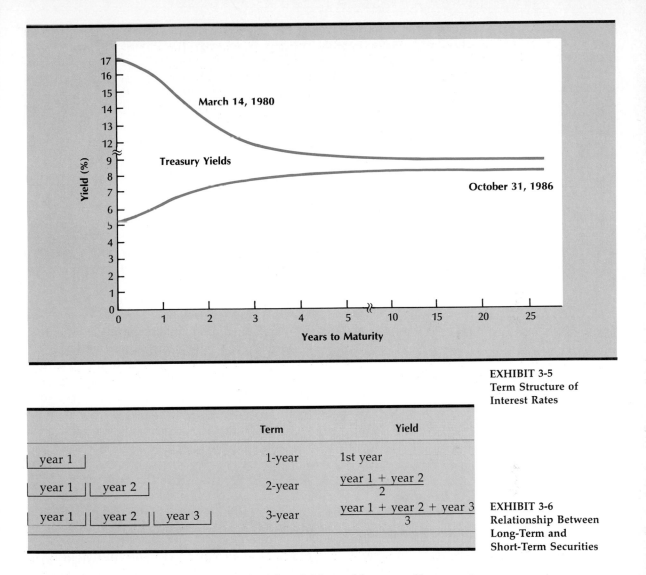

EXHIBIT 3-5
Term Structure of Interest Rates

		Term	Yield
year 1		1-year	1st year
year 1 | year 2		2-year	$\dfrac{\text{year 1 + year 2}}{2}$
year 1 | year 2 | year 3		3-year	$\dfrac{\text{year 1 + year 2 + year 3}}{3}$

EXHIBIT 3-6
Relationship Between Long-Term and Short-Term Securities

11 percent, it is understood to mean that the yield would *average* 11 percent per year if the security were owned for two years. Exhibit 3-6 provides an illustration.

Example

Expectations Theory

Assume that the yield on a one-year Treasury Bill as of January 1, 1988 is 10 percent. Further assume that investors expect the yield on a one-year Treasury Bill as of January 1, 1989 to be 12 percent. According to the expectations theory, the rate on a two-year Treasury as of January 1, 1988 should be approximately 11 percent per year. [i.e., (10% + 12%)/2].[8]

	Term	Yield
└─ 10% ─┘	1-year	10%
└─ 10% ─┴─ 12% ─────┘	2-year	(10% + 12%)/2 = 11%

If the yield curve is rising, it means that short-term interest rates are expected to rise. If the yield curve is sloping downward, short-term rates are expected to decline. If the yield curve is flat, short-term interest rates are expected to remain constant. In "normal" economic times, the shape of the yield curve is upward sloping.

An examination of the term structure of Treasury security yields may be used to develop insights about expected inflation. For example, Treasury bills, notes, and bonds all have different maturities. Yet, the risk premiums for all these securities are zero. Thus, any difference in yields between, say, a one-year Treasury bill and a two-year Treasury note would be due to differences in the real rate of interest and inflation, according to Equation 3-1. If one further assumes that the real rate of interest is roughly constant, then the difference in yields must be due entirely to expectations about inflation rates.

Example

Inflation Expectations

The yield on a one-year Treasury bill is 5 percent while the yield on a two-year Treasury note is 7 percent. According to the expectations theory, and assuming a constant real rate of interest, the rate of inflation is expected to be 4 percent higher over the next year. To determine this, first one has to determine the one-year rate in the second year needed to produce an average of 7 percent per year for two years. If the one-year rate in the first year is 5 percent, the one-year rate in the second year is

---

[8]This is an approximation, since it is an arithmetic average of the two rates. More precisely, the two-year yield should be a geometric, or compound, average. The difference is not material. The compound method is described in Chapter 4.

expected to be 9 percent, producing an average of 7 percent per year over the two years (i.e., (5% + 9%)/2). Graphically, this can be shown as:

	Term	Yield
└─ 5% ─┘	1-year	5%
└─ 5% ──┘ └─ 9% ─────────┘	2-year	(5% + 9%)/2 = 7%

Liquidity Premium Theory

According to the liquidity premium theory, long-term rates tend to be higher than short-term rates because investors are reluctant to tie up their funds for long periods of time. In order to attract investors to longer-term securities, a bonus *premium* interest rate must be paid. The existence of a liquidity premium will affect the implied future short-term rates and inflation indicated by the expectations theory alone.

Market Segmentation Theory

According to the market segmentation theory, short-term, intermediate-term, and long-term rates are affected by unique supply and demand relationships in each segment of the term structure. An important aspect of this theory is that investors and borrowers do not exploit interest differentials in other maturity groups. For example, short-term lenders may receive lower yields than longer-term lenders. But the short-term lenders do not switch to long-term lending in order to get the higher yields.

FINANCIAL MARKETS

Financial markets are vast and constantly changing. Although most financial managers have access to specialized advice from investment bankers, financial managers need to have a working understanding of financial markets in order to meet their firms' financing requirements in a timely fashion and on favorable terms. We will review the principal characteristics of financial markets in this chapter and defer more detailed discussions for subsequent chapters.

Money Markets and Capital Markets

By convention, money markets refer to the supply of and demand for short-term funds. *Short-term* means funds that must be repaid in a year or less. Governments as well as corporations are major participants in this *money markets* market. For example, if the Treasury Department needs to borrow for three months, it may issue a three-month Treasury Bill. If a corporation needs to borrow for 60 days, it may issue 60-day commercial paper. If a bank wants to borrow for a year, it may sell one-year certificates of deposit. Table 3-1 contains a brief description of major money market securities.

Table 3-2 shows recent yields on various money market securities, all with a three-month yield to maturity.

The interest, or yield, on money market securities is strongly affected by business cycles and economic policies. That is, short-term rates typically

---

TABLE 3-1   Major Money Market Securities

Treasury Bills

Treasury bills are sold by the United States Treasury Department to generate cash for the federal government. They have maturities of one year or less. They do not pay interest but are sold at a discount. "T bills," as they are commonly called, are readily marketable, even in very large amounts.

Commercial Paper

Commercial paper is sold by large, financially very strong industrial corporations and finance companies. Since these securities are available for any maturity up to 270 days, the issuer can schedule maturities to match cash needs precisely.

Negotiable Certificates of Deposit

These are promissory notes sold by commercial banks and can be re-sold to other investors in the open market. They are very similar to commercial paper.

Bankers' Acceptances

Bankers' acceptances are checks ("drafts") that a bank has promised to pay at some future date. An importer of goods is usually not required to pay for them immediately. The seller may send the buyer an order to pay with a draft with, say, a three-month maturity. If the seller wishes to be particularly certain of being paid, he or she may ask that the buyer have the draft *accepted* by a commercial bank. By this process the bank guarantees the payment of the draft at maturity, and the buyer gains ready access to credit (after payment of an appropriate fee to the banker for the service). Once accepted by the bank, the draft becomes a *banker's acceptance*. If the seller does not wish to wait for the funds for three months, he or she can readily sell it in the money market.

Repurchase Agreements

Generally referred to as "repos," repurchase agreements are arrangements whereby a corporation buys a large amount of Treasury securities from a bond dealer for a few days (frequently over a weekend), with the understanding that the dealer will then repurchase the securities at an agreed price. Thus the corporation aids the dealer in carrying the inventory of securities and obtains a yield that is slightly above the available yield on a Treasury obligation of similar maturity.

TABLE 3-2	Comparative Yields on Three-Month Money Market Securities	
	U.S. Treasury Bills	5.21%
	Commercial paper	5.57%
	Bankers' acceptances	5.60%
	Certificates of Deposit	5.71%

rise with an expanding economy and fall as business activity declines. The money market is important to the financial manager both for meeting short-term financing needs and for investing temporary excess cash. Often, large, financially strong companies can raise funds less expensively by selling commercial paper than by borrowing from their banks at the prime rate. For example, at the end of October 1986, prime commercial paper cost 5.62 percent compared to a prime bank borrowing rate of 7.50 percent, a difference of 188 basis points. When large amounts of borrowing are involved, even slightly lower rates can result in significant savings at the lower rates.

In contrast to money markets, capital markets include the supply of and demand for long-term funds. There are two principal types of long-term funds: debt funds and equity (ownership) funds. Among the instruments traded are Treasury, agency, municipal, and corporate securities. Table 3-3 contains a brief description of major capital market securities.

capital markets

Capital Market Yields

By keeping the term to maturity constant and focusing only on the relationship of risk differentials to interest rates (or yields), one can observe that the higher the risk in a given security, the greater the interest rate or yield it must provide. This general pattern is described in Exhibit 3-7.

PRIMARY MARKETS AND SECONDARY MARKETS

The distinction between primary and secondary markets is simple but very significant to a firm. A primary-market transaction refers to the first (primary) sale of a security. A secondary-market transaction refers to the resale of a security.

primary market
secondary market

Example

Primary Vs. Secondary Market

The Arec Company sold a 20-year bond to investor A. At the time of sale, Arec received $1,000 and the investor received a bond certificate. This first

TABLE 3-3 Major Capital Market Securities

Treasury Notes and Bonds

These securities are issued by the Treasury Department to finance the federal government. Treasury notes have maturities of 10 years or less. Treasury bonds have maturities in excess of 10 years. Like Treasury bills, bonds and notes have zero default risk.

U.S. Agency Securities

Various agencies owned or sponsored by the federal government raise funds to finance their operations by selling notes and bonds. These agency securities are considered almost as safe as Treasury securities. But, because they do not have the same marketability, they offer slightly higher yields. The largest agencies are involved in supplying funds to the mortgage market to facilitate home and farm ownership. Some of the better known issuers of agency securities are listed below:

Government National Mortgage Association, popularly known as "Ginnie May" due to its acronym (GNMA).

Federal National Mortgage Association (FNMA or "Fannie May")

Federal Home Loan Banks (FHLB)

Federal Housing Administration (FHA)

Municipal Securities

general obligations

revenue bonds

States, counties and municipalities issue securities to finance their operations. There are two principal types of municipal securities: General obligations (G.O.s) are backed by the taxing power of the issuer. For example, a general obligation bond issued by the state of California is guaranteed by the full taxing power of the state. If for any reason the State were unable to pay the interest or principal required, the State would raise taxes to generate the needed funds. *Revenue bonds* are repaid from specific revenue sources. For example, if a governmental authority issues revenue bonds to raise money to build a bridge, interest and principal on the bonds would be paid from toll revenues.

Corporate Securities

corporate securities

There are two basic types of corporate securities: debt securities and common stock. Debt securities reflect borrowing by the corporation while common stock represents ownership in the corporation. Some securities represent a mixture of debt and common stock and are known as "hybrid" or "derivative" securities. These are discussed in much more detail later in this text.

debentures

Debentures are unsecured bonds and are backed by the overall financial strength of the corporation.

mortgages

Mortgages are secured loans backed by real estate or other assets.

convertible debentures

Convertible debentures are debt securities that can be exchanged for common stock in the company at the option of the investor.

preferred stock

Preferred stock is a form of nonvoting, nonownership equity. Investors receive a stipulated dividend at specified payment periods.

common stock

Common stock represents ownership in the corporation. All the profits earned by the corporation (less preferred stock dividends) go to the common stockholders. These profits may be paid out to the common stockholders as dividends or reinvested by the corporation to produce future profits.

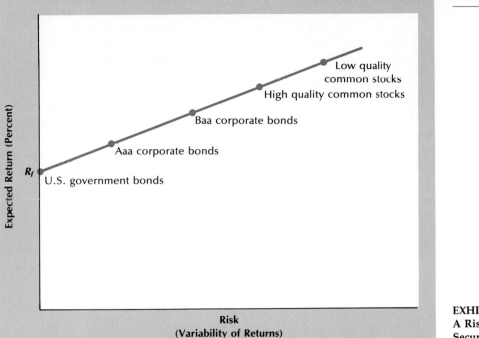

EXHIBIT 3-7
A Risk-Return Line for
Securities Traded in the
Capital Markets

sale represents a primary-market transaction. Later, if investor A sells the bond to investor B, A gets cash and B gets the security. This second sale is a secondary-market transaction. Note, however, that Arec receives money only on the primary sale and is not affected by any subsequent secondary transactions.

Secondary markets are important because they make primary-market transactions safer by providing marketability to investors. For example, if there is no secondary market for Arec bonds, investor A may be locked into the bond purchase until the bonds are repaid, in 20 years. In the absence of good secondary markets, the risk premium demanded by investors is higher and thus raises the costs of financing to the firm.

While the distinction between a primary and secondary transaction is all-important to the corporation selling the security, it is much less important to the investor. For example, when IBM sells a new issue of common stock, the proceeds will go to IBM only from the primary sale. However, from the standpoint of investors, the new IBM shares will be identical to all those already outstanding. Thus, buying the "new" shares is no different from buying the "old" shares.[9]

---

[9]We are ignoring special discounts which may be offered to existing shareholders through a rights offering. These are discussed in Chapter 21.

Stock Markets

New York Stock Exchange
NYSE
organized exchanges
American Stock Exchange
(ASE)
regional stock exchanges

Primary and secondary-market transactions are carried out on stock exchanges. The largest of the exchanges by far is the New York Stock Exchange (NYSE). It is an *organized* exchange because it has a distinct central location. Other organized exchanges are the American Stock Exchange (ASE) and regional stock exchanges such as the Midwest Stock Exchange (in Chicago) and the Pacific Stock Exchange. The NYSE accounts for between 80 and 90 percent of all stock transactions in terms of dollars compared to 3 to 5 percent for the AMEX. The remainder is accounted for by the regional exchanges. In addition to the organized stock exchanges, stock and bond trading is carried out on the Over-The-Counter (OTC)

Over-The-Counter (OTC)

market, a computerized network of individual securities dealers who buy and sell in limited numbers of securities. Stocks of smaller, local, or less-well-known companies are traded on the OTC market. In addition, most corporate bond transactions take place in the OTC market, although some bond trading takes place on the organized exchanges. The OTC market is now linked into a national computer network known as the

NASDAQ

NASDAQ (National Association of Securities Dealers Automated Quotation) system. More than 3,000 companies have their stocks traded on the NASDAQ system.

Public and Private Securities Markets

When a company sells bonds or other securities to the general public, the transaction is known as a public issue. Public issues involve many costs and require much public disclosure of the borrower's financial situation. Many companies prefer to sell securities directly to a private group of

private placement

investors. A private placement allows the issuer to avoid many legal and selling costs associated with a public issue and restricts disclosure to a few investors. Typically, private placements are made to financial institutions such as insurance companies because of the large amounts of money involved.

FLOW OF FUNDS THROUGH THE FINANCIAL SYSTEM

Funds supplied to firms through the money and capital markets originate largely from savings of individuals. In addition, actions of the Federal Reserve to expand or contract the money supply affect the flow of investible funds from the banking system. To a lesser extent, foreign investors also supply funds to the money and capital markets.

financial intermediation

Most personal savings flows are accumulated in financial institutions, or intermediaries, through the process of financial intermediation. The financial institutions, in turn, perform the function of channeling funds to government and business, the principal users of savings flows.

The flow of funds from individuals to business is illustrated in Exhibit 3-8.

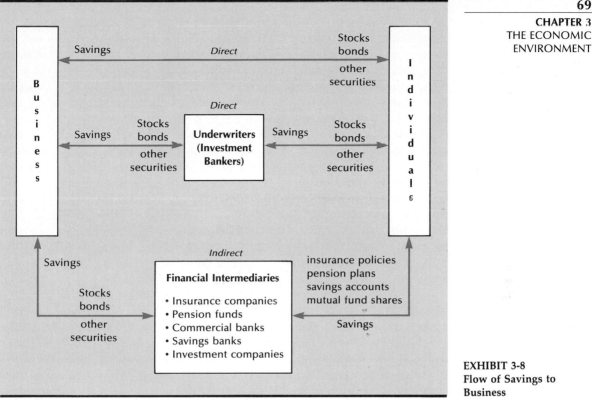

EXHIBIT 3-8
Flow of Savings to Business

The savings of individuals are channeled to business and government units directly or indirectly. Individuals transfer savings directly by purchasing security issues from the issuer or by purchasing them through an investment banker. For example, if IBM issues bonds, an individual investor may buy them directly from the company (through his or her agent banker) or may buy them from an underwriter who has previously purchased them. In both cases, the investor holds a bond issued by IBM and which will be paid off by IBM.

In contrast, an indirect transfer of savings from individuals to businesses or government units occurs when the individual places savings in a financial institution such as a bank, insurance company, pension fund, mutual fund, or savings and loan association. The financial institution then uses the money to purchase the bonds, for example, IBM's. However, the individual now holds a security created by the institution rather than IBM. In essence, the institution has substituted a security of its creation (such as a pension-plan policy) for those of the ultimate user. This process of *security substitution* is what distinguishes financial intermediaries. All financial institutions that create new securities are intermediaries.

security substitution

Individuals make their personal savings available to these institutions by making deposits (commercial banks and mutual savings banks), by purchasing shares (savings and loan associations and credit unions), by paying insurance premiums, a portion of which is invested (insurance companies), and by making contributions to retirement funds (insurance companies and corporate and government retirement funds). Occasionally individuals also purchase securities newly issued by sales finance and consumer credit companies.

Individuals place their savings in these financial institutions for two main reasons. First, the small saver finds it impossible or prohibitively expensive to make direct financial investments. Instead savings are channeled into financial institutions, which accept savings in small amounts and then reinvest them in large amounts. Second, even if one could afford to purchase several hundred dollars worth of some stock, the individual saver *diversification* would not be able to obtain much diversification. All his or her "eggs would be in one basket," which would not be a sound investment practice. By putting the savings in financial institutions, risk is spread out by obtaining a share in at least several hundred different investments.

Although it is not shown on the exhibit, nonfinancial corporations also furnish funds to each other and to financial institutions. The most common form is the extension of credit by one business firm to another at the time *trade credit* goods are sold. Some large corporations also temporarily invest idle funds in the short-term obligations of other corporations, including those of the financial institutions that provide funds to consumers. By adding to their deposits at commercial banks, savings banks, and savings and loan associations, business firms provide funds that these institutions may then make available to other borrowers. In addition some government agencies lend to business concerns funds that the government has borrowed or acquired from taxes. Thus the money and capital markets are tied together with a complex system of channels through which funds flow in all directions.

Relative Importance of Institutions and Channels

depository institutions Commercial banks usually provide the most funds in each year. This is due to their role as *depository institutions* and because the banking system has the ability to expand credit.

contractual savings institutions Insurance companies and pension funds, known as *contractual savings institutions* because of fixed commitments by savers, rank second as a group as suppliers of funds to the financial markets.

thrift institutions Thrift institutions, which like commercial banks are deposit organizations, represent the third largest source of funds for the money and capital markets. This group is dominated by savings and loan associations, which rank only behind commercial banks in terms of individual institutional suppliers. It should be recognized, however, that, since commercial banks and thrift institutions depend heavily on the non contractual savings of individuals, funds supplied by these institutions may vary greatly from year to year.

Intermediation Vs. Disintermediation

The process of accumulating savings in financial institutions is referred to as intermediation. When savers take their money out of financial institutions and invest directly, the process is known as disintermediation. Disintermediation takes place when alternative investments such as U.S. government securities offer higher yields than do financial intermediaries.

disintermediation

Example

Disintermediation

Assume that the Super Mutuals Savings Bank offers depositors an interest rate of 5 percent per year and that the Treasury Department is selling Treasury bills with an equivalent interest yield of 7 percent. Many depositors take their money out of the Savings Bank and buy Treasury bills. This results in disintermediation. If it continues, Super will have difficulty coming up with enough cash to meet depositors' withdrawals.

SUMMARY

This chapter discussed several important factors in a firm's economic environment. They include business cycles, economic policies of the federal government, the behavior of interest rates, and the organization and operation of financial markets.

Business cycles have dramatic impacts on sales, profits, and stock prices of companies. Thus, the finance manager must understand the behavior of business cycles and try to recognize changes quickly enough to allow the company to take corrective actions.

The federal government is another enormous influence on all economic activity. In pursuing national economic objectives of full employment, growth, and price stability, the government employs fiscal and monetary policies. The diverse involvements of the federal government in the economy have made it more important than ever for finance managers to stay alert to changes in economic policies.

In addition to business cycles and government policies, the finance manager must try to understand the behavior of interest rates. For many companies, a period of high interest rates can result in payments of interest that are greater than the profits received by stockholders.

Funds are supplied to the financial markets by individuals directly and indirectly through financial institutions such as commercial banks, thrift institutions, and insurance companies. Finance managers need to have a working understanding of the flow of funds through the financial markets in order to meet their firms' financing requirements in a timely fashion and on favorable terms.

MULTIPLE CHOICE QUESTIONS

1. The principal source of savings funds supplied to the money and capital markets is:
   a) Borrowings by large corporations
   b) Loans by large corporations
   c) Insurance companies
   d) Individuals

2. The process of accumulating savings in financial institutions is referred to as:

    a) Speculation
    b) Intermediation
    c) Disintermediation
    d) Hoarding

3. Disintermediation occurs when:

    a) A cadaver is dug up
    b) A dispute cannot be resolved
    c) Investors remove funds from institutions and invest directly
    d) Investors remove funds from direct investment and place them in financial institutions

4. Long-term interest rates or yields are said to be an average of short-term rates according to:

    a) Federal law
    b) Liquidity theory
    c) Expectations theory
    d) Fair play

5. In "normal" times, the liquidity preference theory would suggest:

    a) A humped yield curve
    b) A horizontal yield curve
    c) An upward-sloping yield curve
    d) A downward-sloping yield curve

6. If one holds time-to-maturity constant, differences in yields among securities can be attributed principally to:

    a) Maturity differentials
    b) The expectations theory
    c) Risk differentials
    d) Coupon rate differentials

7. A drop in sales is most likely when the business cycle is:

    a) Recessionary
    b) Expansionary
    c) In deficit
    d) In surplus

8. The main instruments of economic policy are monetary policy and:

    a) Credit policy
    b) Interest rate policy
    c) Fiscal policy
    d) Insurance policy

9. Leading indicators are primarily used to forecast changes in:

    a) The stock market
    b) Interest rates
    c) The business cycle
    d) Top management

10. A private placement refers to:

a) Reserved seating
b) A direct sale of securities to the public
c) A direct sale of securities to a small group of investors
d) A direct sale of securities to the Treasury

DISCUSSION QUESTIONS

1. Explain the concept of the business cycle. Define and explain what the expansionary and recessionary phases mean to the firm's financial performance.
2. Identify and discuss the major economic policies employed by the federal government. What types of budgetary and monetary policies are considered appropriate during expansions? Recessions?
3. Define each of the principal determinants of interest rates for securities with the same term to maturity.
4. Define what is meant by the interest-rate risk premium. Why does this premium change over time?
5. Briefly describe how the money market differs from the capital market.
6. What is meant by financial disintermediation?
7. Explain how monetary policy can affect interest rates.
8. Describe what is meant by the term structure of interest rates. Define the expectations, liquidity preference, and market segmentation theories.
9. Define and contrast private placements and public issues of securities.
10. Explain the process of financial intermediation.

SOLVED PROBLEMS

term structure

SP-1. Below is a series of interest rates and maturities for debt instruments of equal risk.

Security	Term to Maturity	Yield
1	3 months	14%
2	6 months	13%
3	1 year	12%
4	5 years	11%
5	10 years	10%

a) Plot the series on graph paper, with term to maturity on the horizontal axis and yield on the vertical axis.
b) Interpret the term structure from the standpoint of the expectations theory

SP-2. Below are average yields for three classes of long-term bonds for the years 19X1, 19X2, and 19X3. The year 19X1 was one of high economic expansion, 19X2 was a recession year, and 19X3 was a year of moderate (e.g., "normal") economic activity.

risk premium

	Average Yields		
	19X1	*19X2*	*19X3*
Long-Term Treasury Bonds	11.46%	7.99%	6.84%
High-Quality Corporate Bonds	11.94%	8.83%	7.44%

a) Calculate the risk premiums of the corporate bonds relative to the Treasury bonds for each year.
b) What pattern, if any, can you draw about the relationship between economic activity and risk premiums?

PROBLEMS

1. Below is a series of interest rates and maturities for debt instruments of equal risk.

term structure

Security	Term to Maturity	Yield
1	3 months	10%
2	6 months	11%
3	1 year	12%
4	5 years	13%
5	10 years	14%

a) Plot the series on graph paper with term to maturity on the horizontal axis and yield on the vertical axis.
b) Interpret the term structure from the standpoint of the expectations theory.

2. Assume the following Treasury securities and their yields were reported:

term structure

Term	Yield (annual rate)
1 year	8.00
2 years	7.67
3 years	7.16
4 years	7.12

a) Graph and label the term structure implied by these rates.
b) Considering only the one-, two-, and three-year Treasuries, what are the expected one-year rates for each of the next three years according to the expectations theory?

risk premium

3. Assume that the "normal" yield spread between high-risk corporate bonds and Treasury bonds is about 200 basis points. Also assume that the economy is expected to expand vigorously over the next 12 months. The corporate bonds are currently yielding 15.67 percent and the Treasuries are currently yielding 12.38 percent.

a) Calculate the current risk premium on the corporate bonds.
b) Compare the current risk premium with the normal premium.
c) In light of the economic environment, what would you expect to happen to the premium over the next 12 months?

4. Assume the following Treasury securities and their yields were reported:

expectations theory

Term	Yield (annual rate)
1 year	7.30%
2 years	8.72%
3 years	9.00%

a) What are the expected one-year rates according to the expectations theory?
b) As the financial manager of a company, assume that you must borrow $1 million for two years. If you forecast the one-year rate in year two to be 9.00%, would you be better off with a two-year loan or two one-year loans? (Calculate the cost of each alternative.)

5. (Library Assignment) Obtain interest-rate or yield data from the Federal Reserve Bulletin, or from the Federal Reserve banks (e.g., the St. Louis Bank) on U.S. Government securities covering a variety of maturity dates.

term structure

a) Prepare a schedule indicating the term structure of interest rates.
b) Plot the data from Part (a) on a graph to show the term structure or yield curve for U.S. Government securities. This should be done by

plotting the yield percentage on the vertical axis and the years to maturity on the horizontal axis.

c) How does the expectations theory explain the shape of your yield curve?

SOLUTIONS TO SOLVED PROBLEMS

SP-1. a) See Exhibit SP-1.
b) The yield curve is downward sloping which suggests that short-term interest rates are expected to decline in the future.

SP-2. a)

	Risk Premiums		
	19X1	19X2	19X3
Corporate-Treasury Yields	.48%	.84%	.60%

b) Given that 19X1 was an expansion year, 19X2 was a recession year, and 19X3 was an average year, one might guess that risk

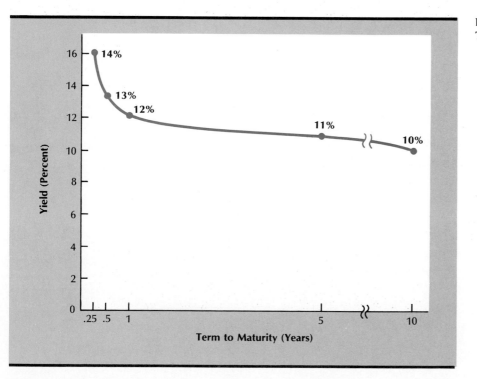

EXHIBIT SP-1
Term Structure

premiums are lower than average during expansions and higher than average during recessions.

REFERENCES

Dougall, Herbert E., and Jack E. Gaumnitz. Capital Markets and Institutions. 4th ed. Englewood Cliffs, N.J.: Prentice-Hall, 1980.

The Federal Reserve System — Its Purposes and Functions. Washington: Board of Governors of the Federal Reserve System, 1974.

Van Horne, James C. Financial Market Rates and Flows. Englewood Cliffs, N.J.: Prentice-Hall, 1984.

Welshans, Merle T., and Ronald W. Melicher. Finance, An Introduction to Financial Markets and Institutions, 6th ed. Cincinnati: South-Western Publishing Co., 1985.

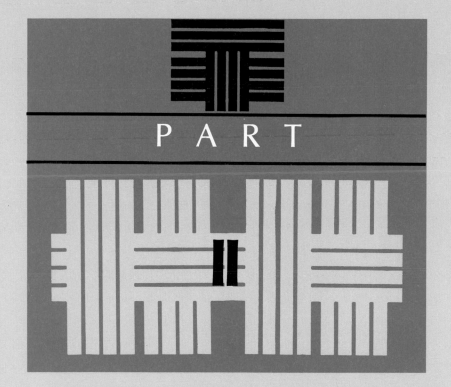

PART

II

BASIC CONCEPTS

CHAPTER

4

TIME VALUE
OF MONEY

I

n Chapter 1, we noted that the objective of financial management is the maximization of a company's common stock price. To achieve this objective, the financial manager must help direct the firm's operating, investing, and financing cash flows toward that end. This task becomes especially complex and vital when cash flow decisions span several years. For example, an investment decision may easily absorb the majority of a company's available cash, and yet the cash benefits from the investment might only be realized gradually. If such decisions are not made carefully, the firm can easily go bankrupt or have such low profitability that its stock price is depressed.

Fortunately, financial managers have a reliable tool for directing cash flows over time toward the objective of maximizing share price. This tool is known as the time value of money.

The time value of money must be considered whenever the element of time enters a financial transaction. For this reason, the time value of money is the most pervasive concept in finance. It enters virtually every significant financial transaction in one form or another. It is used not only in directing investment decisions that may last several years, but also in the valuation of stocks and bonds and in setting terms in every type of credit transaction from corporate borrowing to personal installment-payment plans. The time value of money idea plays a central role in the daily transactions of every financial institution in making loans to individuals and businesses, managing pension plans, and designing insurance policies. In short, the time value of money is such a key concept that little of finance can be understood without it. Because the time value idea is broad in scope, this chapter provides a survey of it. However, financial management is primarily concerned with one aspect of the time value idea known as present value. The present value aspect will provide the financial manager with a reliable technique for making optimal investment and financing decisions.

Objectives and Organization of this Chapter

The primary objective of this chapter is to explain the time value of money concept and to show how it works. In addition, since time value considerations arise in many different forms, we will show how time value relationships can be arranged to answer a variety of questions that arise in common financial transactions.

The first section of the chapter introduces the time value of money idea and illustrates its usefulness and importance. Section two examines the concept of compound interest and illustrates the power of compounding. Section three presents the basic time value equation and shows how it can be applied. Section four introduces the very important concept of present value and its relationship to the basic time value equation.

THE TIME VALUE OF MONEY

The *time value of money* is a standard term expressing the idea that the value of money is affected by the passage of time. This change in value results from the interest-earning potential of money. According to the time value of money concept, a dollar today is equivalent in value to more than one dollar in the future.

As an example, assume that one deposits $100 in a bank savings account that pays interest of 10 percent per year. At the end of one year, the account will have $110 in it. This is made up of the original deposit plus $10 of interest which the bank has paid for using the money for one year.

Notice that, because of the interest-earning ability of money (10 percent in this case), $100 at the beginning of the year is equal in value to $110 at the end of the year. And, conversely, $110 one year from now is equivalent to $100 today, given an interest-earning potential of 10 percent per year.

THE POWER OF COMPOUND INTEREST

The effect of time on the value of money is magnified through the power of compound interest. Compound interest means that interest earned in one period will itself earn interest in subsequent periods. Here is how it works. Assume someone deposits $100 in the bank today at 10 percent compounded annually and does not withdraw any of the balance for three years. In the first year, the depositor earns $10 on the original deposit, producing a total of $110 in the account. In the second year, the interest earned is $11 (i.e., 10% × $110). Now there is $121 in the account. In the third year, the interest earned is $12.10 (i.e., 10% × $121), giving a total of $133.10 in the account. Since the original deposit was only $100, the depositor has earned total interest of $33.10 in three years, given an interest rate of 10 percent per year. The account is growing; compounding means growing.

Graphing the money values with respect to time produces a graph like the one shown in Exhibit 4-1.

The upper curve, the 10-percent curve, traces out what would happen to a $1.00 deposit if left in a bank account at 10 percent compounded

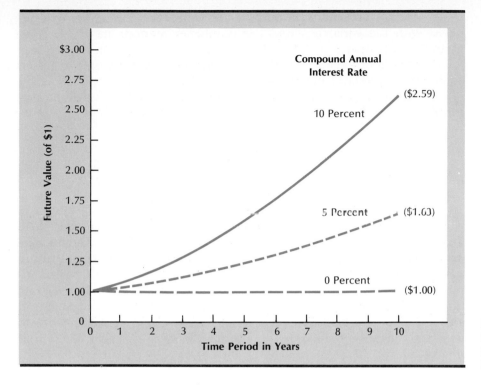

EXHIBIT 4-1
Future Value, Interest Rate, and Time Period Relationships

annually. For example at the end of 10 years, the $1.00 would have grown to $2.59. By similar reasoning, a $100 deposit would have grown to $259 in 10 years. At lower interest rates, growth would be slower. In Exhibit 4-1, the graph also shows the growth produced by interest rates of 5 percent and 0 percent. Note that, at a 5-percent interest rate, a $1.00 deposit would only have increased to $1.63; and at a 0% interest rate, no interest would be earned during the 10 years and the $1.00 original deposit would not have increased at all. The power of compound interest is what makes high interest rates on savings accounts and other investments so desirable.

Exhibit 4-1 also illustrates the important point that the time value of money depends on the compound interest rate and the number of periods the interest is earned.

THE BASIC TIME VALUE FORMULA

Considering the simple examples above in an analytical way, one can see that they each involve four elements, or variables. The present amount (such as the $100 deposit), which can be designated by the variable PV_0, meaning the present value at time zero; the future amount, which can be designated FV_n at some point in time, n; the interest rate, which is designated with the variable i; and the number of periods in which compounding takes place, which is designated by the variable n. Finally, it is the interaction of the interest rate and number of periods variables which equate some present value to its future value.

These four variables are mathematically related in the basic time value formula shown in equation 4-1.

$$FV_n = PV_0(1 + i)^n \tag{4-1}$$

In the bank deposit example, the future value of $100 at a 10 percent annual compound rate for two years would be:

$$FV_2 = \$100(1.10)^2 = \$121$$

The basic time value formula is powerful because it makes it possible to analyze a broad variety of time value questions. For example, the formula can be rearranged to determine the present-value equivalent of some future value, given some compound interest rate and the number of compounding periods. It is also possible to solve for the compound interest rate implied by a given present value, future value, and number of compound periods. Finally, it is possible to solve for the number of periods needed to equate some present amount with a future amount, given the compound interest rate.

Example

Mike deposits $100 in a savings account. How much will he have in his account in 10 years, assuming the bank pays him interest of 10 percent per year, compounded annually?

$$FV_n = PV_0(1 + i)^n$$

$$FV_{10} = \$100(1.10)^{10}$$

$$FV_{10} = \$100(2.594)$$

$$FV_{10} = \$259.40$$

The Future Value Table

The above example is not complex, but without a calculator, it is difficult to find for instance what $(1.10)^{10}$ is. The tables in Appendix A to this text contain calculations for a number of common combinations for n periods and i interest rates. The $(1 + i)^n$ factor is known as the *future value interest factor* or, FVIF, for short. An excerpt from the more extensive table in Appendix A is shown in Table 4-1. Notice that the FVIF value where n

future value interest factor
FVIF

TABLE 4-1 Future Value of $1 (FVIF)

Year n	3%	4%	5%	6%	7%	8%	9%	10%
1	1.030	1.040	1.050	1.060	1.070	1.080	1.090	1.100
2	1.061	1.082	1.102	1.124	1.145	1.166	1.188	1.210
3	1.093	1.125	1.158	1.191	1.225	1.260	1.295	1.331
4	1.126	1.170	1.216	1.262	1.311	1.360	1.412	1.464
5	1.159	1.217	1.276	1.338	1.403	1.469	1.539	1.611
6	1.194	1.265	1.340	1.419	1.501	1.587	1.677	1.772
7	1.230	1.316	1.407	1.504	1.606	1.714	1.828	1.949
8	1.267	1.369	1.477	1.594	1.718	1.851	1.993	2.144
9	1.305	1.423	1.551	1.689	1.838	1.999	2.172	2.358
10	1.344	1.480	1.629	1.791	1.967	2.159	2.367	2.594

equals 10 and i equals 10 percent is 2.594, which is the same number calculated above.

Example

Using the FVIF Table

Let us try an example using the FVIF table. Joe is going to deposit $1,000 in a bank account earning 9 percent per year compounded annually. How much will he have at the end of five years? How much of that represents interest earned over the five years?

First, set the problem up, then define the variables which are known and the variable which is to be determined.

$$FV_n = PV_0(1 + i)^n$$

$$FV_n = PV_0(FVIF_{i,n})$$

$$FV_5 = PV_0(FVIF_{9\%,5})$$

$$FV_5 = \$1,000\ (1.539)$$

$$FV_5 = \$1,539$$

Notice that the term, $(1 + i)^n$ was replaced with $(FVIF_{9\%,5})$. Then the FVIF table yielded the value that corresponds to n equals 5 and i equals 9 percent. The FVIF value is 1.539, which, multiplied by the deposit of $1,000, gives the future compounded amount of $1,539. Since Joe will only deposit $1,000 and will have $1,539 in his account, the amount of interest he will earn over the 5 years is $539.

Compound Annuities

The preceding examples were simplistic in that only one amount was assumed to be deposited and left for a period of time. However, many meaningful time value problems involve a series of deposits. For example, if a company expects to pay employees retirement benefits in the future, funds must be set aside each year to make sure the payments can be made. *sinking-fund* Also, many long-term loan arrangements, known as sinking-fund arrangements, require the borrower to make periodic deposits to a bank account to make sure the debt can be repaid at a later date. If the deposits are all equal in amount and if they are deposited in a continuous series, they are called *compound annuities* compound annuities.

Annuity Due Vs. Regular Annuity

annuities due

regular annuities

Annuities involving cash flows at the *beginning* of each period are known as annuities due. Examples include annuity savings plans and lease arrangements whereby the lessee makes the initial lease payment at the start of the lease. Annuities involving cash flows at the *end* of each period are known as deferred or regular annuities. Examples of this type include the repayment of loans involving equal annual installments over the life of the loan, as well as the repayment of debt through sinking-fund arrangements. Unless otherwise specified, in the remainder of this text, when we refer to annuities, we will mean regular annuities. The annuity tables in the Appendix apply to regular annuities.

Example

The Tech Corporation sets aside $50,000 at the end of each year to fund its employee pension plan. The money is put into a bank trust account where it earns 10-percent interest per year, compounded annually. How much money will be in the account at the end of four years? How much of this represents interest earned?

The first $50,000 deposit will occur at the end of year one and will earn interest during years two, three, and four. The second $50,000 deposit will occur at the end of year two and will earn interest during years three and four. The third deposit will occur at the end of year three and will earn interest in year four only. The deposit at the end of year four will not have had a chance to earn any interest. We can express this future value of an annuity (FVA) as follows:

$$\text{FVA}_4 = \$50,000(1.10)^3 + \$50,000(1.10)^2 + \$50,000(1.10)^1 + \$50,000(1.10)^0$$

$$\text{FVA}_4 = \$50,000(1.331) + \$50,000(1.210) + \$50,000(1.100) \\ + \$50,000(1.000)$$

By factoring out the $50,000, we get,

$$FVA_4 = \$50{,}000[1.331 + 1.210 + 1.100 + 1.000]$$

$$FVA_4 = \$50{,}000(4.641)$$

$$FVA_4 = \$232{,}050$$

We can also illustrate this future value of an annuity in the following fashion:

	End of Year			
	1	2	3	4
Annual deposit	$50,000	$50,000	$50,000	$50,000
				$55,000
				$60,500
				$66,550
		Total future value		$232,050

89

CHAPTER 4
TIME VALUE
OF MONEY

It is useful to note that the future value of an annuity, involving, as it does, a series of cash flows, is still developed from the basic time value formula. However, when annuities are involved, a shortcut can be employed in calculating the future value. When one factors out the amount of the annuity ($50,000) in the last example, one simply adds up the individual FVIF values and multiplies by the annuity amount. The FVIFA table automatically adds these up. When using the FVIFA table, the future value of an annuity is found by using Equation 4-2.

future value

interest factor of an annuity
FVIFA

$$FVA_n = A(FVIFA_{i,n}) \tag{4-2}$$

Where FVA_n is the future value of an annuity as of period n; A is the amount of the annuity each period; and $FVIFA_{i,n}$ is the future value interest factor of an annuity given an interest rate of i percent compounded for n periods. The FVIFA value is taken from Table 3 in Appendix A, an excerpt from which is shown in Table 4-2. In the above example, i is equal to 10 percent and n is equal to four years. The FVIFA value is 4.641. Multiply the annuity, $50,000, by 4.641 to get the value of the annuity at the end of year 4.

$$FVA_4 = A(FVIFA_{10\%,4})$$

$$FVA_4 = \$50{,}000(4.641)$$

$$FVA_4 = \$232{,}050$$

At the end of four years, the company will have $232,050 set aside. Since the company deposited a total of $200,000, interest earned is $32,050 over the four years.

TABLE 4-2 Future Sum or Value of a $1 Annuity (FVIFA)

Year n	3%	4%	5%	6%	7%	8%	9%	10%
1	1.000	1.000	1.000	1.000	1.000	1.000	1.000	1.000
2	2.030	2.040	2.050	2.060	2.070	2.080	2.090	2.100
3	3.091	3.122	3.152	3.184	3.215	3.246	3.278	3.310
4	4.184	4.246	4.310	4.375	4.440	4.506	4.573	4.641
5	5.309	5.416	5.526	5.637	5.751	5.867	5.985	6.105
6	6.468	6.633	6.802	6.975	7.153	7.336	7.523	7.716
7	7.662	7.898	8.142	8.394	8.654	8.923	9.200	9.487
8	8.892	9.214	9.549	9.897	10.260	10.637	11.028	11.436
9	10.159	10.583	11.027	11.491	11.978	12.488	13.021	13.579
10	11.464	12.006	12.578	13.181	13.816	14.487	15.193	15.937

PRESENT VALUE

present value

Investment choices involve an outflow of cash in the present, generally, in exchange for a series of future cash inflows. In order to make proper investment decisions, the financial manager must determine the present value of the future cash flows. If the present value exceeds the cost of the investment, the investment should be made. This simple decision rule will guide the financial manager's investment decisions in the direction of maximizing the firm's stock price.

Because of its importance to valuation of investments, the present-value analysis will be employed often in the remainder of the text. Let us first examine how present value formulas are derived from the basic time value formula in Equation 4-1, then illustrate its use through selected examples.

Present Value Formula

The present value formula is simply a rearrangement of the basic time value formula, replacing the FV_n variable on the left-hand side of the equation with the PV_0 variable. In other words, rearrange Equation 4-1 to solve for PV_0. This is shown in Equation 4-3.

$$FV_n = PV_0(1 + i)^n \tag{4-1}$$

$$PV_0 = \frac{FV_n}{(1 + i)^n} \tag{4-3}$$

Equation 4-3 can be further rearranged, as shown in Equation 4-3a.

$$PV_0 = FV_n \left[\frac{1}{(1 + i)^n} \right] \tag{4-3a}$$

The term $[1/(1 + i)^n]$ is known as the *present value interest factor,* or, PVIF, for short. Substituting, the present value equation appears in a form that can be used with present value tables, as shown in Equation 4-3b.

present value interest factor
PVIF

$$PV_0 = FV_n(PVIF_{i,n}) \qquad (4\text{-}3b)$$

Where PV_0 is the present value of a future cash amount, or cash flow, FV_n to be received in period n assuming a compound interest rate of i percent per period. As a matter of convention, in dealing with present value analysis, the interest rate is called the *discount rate*. This is because present value involves discounting future cash flows. However, the discount rate and the rate of interest are the same thing. We will follow conventional use and refer to the *discount* rate when calculating present values and the *interest* rate when computing future values.

discount rate

Relationship of Present Value to Future Value

As indicated in Equation 4-3a, present value and future value are fundamentally linked. The present value interest factor, $[1/(1 + i)^n]$ is just the inverse of the future value interest factor, $(1 + i)^n$. Thus, it is easy enough to calculate the PVIF values for combinations of i and n once the FVIF values are known. The PVIF values for each i and n combination are the reciprocals of the corresponding FVIF values. In other words, PVIF = 1/FVIF. The PVIF values are more extensively contained in Appendix A, Table 2. Table 4-3 contains an excerpt from the larger table. To show that the PVIF table's values are reciprocals of the FVIF values, we have shown the FVIF value for i equal to 6 percent and n equal to 10, along with the PVIF value for the same discount (interest) rate and n periods.

TABLE 4-3   Present Value of $1 (PVIF)

Year n	3%	4%	5%	6%	7%	8%	9%	10%
1	.971	.962	.952	.943	.935	.926	.917	.909
2	.943	.925	.907	.890	.873	.857	.842	.826
3	.915	.889	.864	.840	.816	.794	.772	.751
4	.889	.855	.823	.792	.763	.735	.708	.683
5	.863	.822	.784	.747	.713	.681	.650	.621
6	.838	.790	.746	.705	.666	.630	.596	.564
7	.813	.760	.711	.665	.623	.583	.547	.513
8	.789	.731	.677	.627	.582	.540	.502	.467
9	.766	.703	.645	.592	.544	.500	.460	.424
10	.744	.676	.614	.558	.508	.463	.422	.386

91

$$FVIF_{6\%,10} = 1.791$$

$$PVIF_{6\%,10} = .558$$

$$PVIF_{6\%,10} = \frac{1}{FVIF_{6\%,10}} = \frac{1}{1.791} = .558$$

The present value equivalent of a future dollar decreases with time due to the discounting effect. This is evident in Table 4-3. Note that the present value equivalent of $1.00 to be received in one year at a 10% discount rate is only 90.9 cents. The present value equivalent of one dollar to be received in two years is only 82.6 cents, and the present value equivalent of a dollar to be received in three years is only 75.1 cents. The present value equivalents for years 1 through 10, assuming a 10-percent discount rate are shown in Exhibit 4-2. The present value depends not only on the number of periods into the future a dollar is to be received, but also on the discount rate. At lower discount rates, the present value equivalents do not decrease as quickly with respect to time. This is evident in the 5-percent curve in Exhibit 4-2. The present value equivalent of $1.00 to be received in 10 years is only about 39 cents, assuming a discount rate of 10 percent; but, at a 5-percent discount rate, the present value equivalent is about 61 cents.

EXHIBIT 4-2
Present Value, Discount Rate, and Time Period Relationships

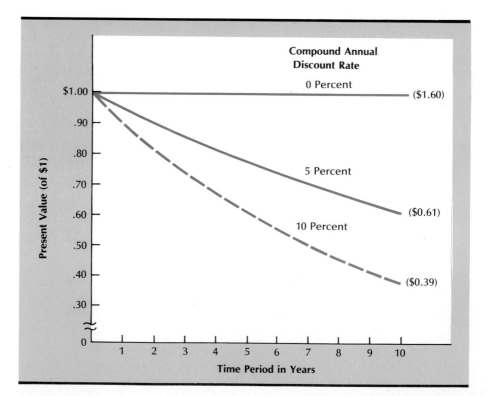

about 39 cents, assuming a discount rate of 10 percent; but, at a 5-percent discount rate, the present value equivalent is about 61 cents.

Example

May sees an advertisement for a bank certificate of deposit. If she buys the certificate, she will get $1,000 at the end of two years. What is the present value of the certificate at a discount rate of 10 percent per year?

Using the PVIF table, one can find the value that corresponds to a discount rate of 10 percent and two years. The value is .826. Thus, the present value of the certificate is $826. If May pays this much for the certificate, she will earn a compound annual rate of return of 10 percent per year for two years on her $826 investment.

$$PV_0 = FV_n(PVIF_{i,n})$$

$$PV_0 = FV_2(PVIF_{10\%,2})$$

$$PV_0 = \$1,000(.826)$$

$$PV_0 = \$826$$

Present Value of Multiple Cash Flows

Investments typically involve the receipt of more than one future amount, or cash flow. In order to determine the total present value of multiple cash flows, the present value of each future cash flow must be calculated and summed.

Example

Let us assume that the Arc Corporation is considering an investment that will produce the stream of future cash flows shown in Table 4-4. Note that $1,500 will be received at the end of the first year, $500 at the end of each of the second and third years, and $1,500 at the end of the fourth year. If the discount rate is 10 percent per year, each cash inflow must be multiplied by the 10 percent PVIF value for the corresponding year. (The PVIF values are taken from Table 4-3). Then, the individual present values of the yearly cash flows must be summed in order to find the present value of the total stream of cash flows, as is illustrated in Table 4-4. Note that the present worth of the $4,000 stream of cash inflows is only $3,176.50.

It should be apparent from the example that the present value of a stream of future cash flows will depend on the pattern of cash flows (the

TABLE 4-4 Calculating the Present Value of an Uneven Stream of Cash Inflows

End of Year	Cash Inflows	×	10% PVIF	=	Present Value of Cash Inflows
1	$1,500		.909		$1,363.50
2	500		.826		413.00
3	500		.751		375.50
4	1,500		.683		1,024.50
Total	$4,000				$3,176.50

sooner a cash flow is received the higher will be its present value) and the rate at which the cash flows are discounted.

Present Value of Annuity

Earlier in this chapter, we discussed compound annuities (i.e., a constant series of deposits growing to some future amount). The present value of an annuity is the present value of a series of constant cash flows. While most investment and financing arrangements will not involve constant cash flows, many important ones will. For example, a company's lease arrangement may require a constant lease payment to be made for many years into the future. Likewise, employee retirement benefit plans may require a company to make regular pension payments to employees for many years. In addition, if a company sells goods on an installment plan basis, the terms to be offered can be determined by use of the present value of an annuity method.

The present value of an annuity can be calculated easily with the use of annuity tables by using Equation 4-5.

$$PVA = A(PVIFA_{i,n}) \qquad (4\text{-}5)$$

present value interest factor of an annuity PVIFA

Where PVA is the present value of the annuity, A, and PVIFA represents the present value interest factor of an annuity, given a discount rate of i percent and n periods over which the annuity will be received.

Table 4-5 contains an excerpt from the more extensive PVIFA table in Appendix A.

Example

Bill has inherited an insurance annuity of $1,000 per year for 10 years. Instead of receiving the annuity, Bill has the option of cashing it for a lump sum now. Assuming the insurance company uses a discount rate of 8 percent per year, what will Bill get if he chooses a lump sum?

The annual amount of cash is $1,000, the PVIFA value for a discount rate of 8 percent and 10 years is 6.710 (from Table 4-5). Thus, the lump sum Bill would receive is $6,710.

$$PVA = A(PVIFA_{i,n})$$

$$PVA = A(PVIFA_{8\%,10})$$

$$PVA = \$1,000(6.710)$$

$$PVA = \$6,710$$

INTRA-YEAR COMPOUNDING AND DISCOUNTING

The future value and present value discussions have assumed that interest (or the discount rate) was compounded or discounted once each year. However, compounding or discounting is often computed more than once per year. Perhaps the most common example is the compounding performed on savings accounts at banks and thrift institutions. For example, a bank might offer an interest rate on savings accounts of 8 percent per year, compounded daily. This simply means that the bank calculates the interest earned on your savings everyday. In comparison, with annual compounding, interest is computed once at the end of the year. This means the customer has to wait a year before interest can begin earning more interest.

intra-year compounding and discounting

In a similar fashion, discounting more than once a year results in a lower present value than annual discounting.

Table 4-6 illustrates the effects on future values and present values when compounding and discounting are performed more than once a year. For example, the future value column assumes that $1,000 is deposited for one year. The present value column assumes that $1,000 will be received at

TABLE 4-5   Present Amount or Value of a $1 Annuity (PVIFA)

Year *n*	3%	4%	5%	6%	7%	8%	9%	10%
1	0.971	0.962	0.952	0.943	0.935	0.926	0.917	0.909
2	1.913	1.886	1.859	1.833	1.808	1.783	1.759	1.736
3	2.829	2.775	2.723	2.673	2.624	2.577	2.531	2.487
4	3.717	3.630	3.546	3.465	3.387	3.312	3.240	3.170
5	4.580	4.452	4.329	4.212	4.100	3.993	3.890	3.791
6	5.417	5.242	5.076	4.917	4.767	4.623	4.486	4.355
7	6.230	6.002	5.786	5.582	5.389	5.206	5.033	4.868
8	7.020	6.733	6.463	6.210	5.971	5.747	5.535	5.335
9	7.786	7.435	7.108	6.802	6.515	6.247	5.995	5.759
10	8.530	8.111	7.722	7.360	7.024	6.710	6.418	6.145

TABLE 4-6 Effect of Compounding and Discounting More Than Once Per Year (Interest at 12% per year)		
Frequency	Future Value	Present Value
Annual	$1,120	$893
Semi-annual	$1,124	$890
Quarterly	$1,126	$888
Monthly	$1,127	$887

the end of one year. The general pattern is evident. The more frequent the compounding is done, the higher the future value for a specified interest rate; and the more frequently discounting is done, the lower the present value for a specified discount rate.

Banks and thrift institutions got heavily into the practice of compounding interest more than once a year as a way of getting around interest-rate ceilings established by the Federal Reserve Board. The interest-rate ceilings have been phased out but, before they were phased out commercial banks were limited to paying a maximum interest rate on savings deposits of 5 percent per year. To attract deposits, the banks needed to provide more competitive savings rates. Since the interest rate ceiling said nothing about how often interest could be compounded, commercial banks found a way around the ceilings: they simply compounded more and more frequently, producing annual earnings rates that were effectively above the ceilings.

When compounding or discounting takes place more than once per year, Equation 4-1 must be modified. Generally, the number of periods must be increased and the interest rate should be decreased. For example, if m is the number of compounding or discounting periods per year, Equation 4-1 should be modified as shown in Equation 4-6.

$$FV_n = PV_0\left(1 + \frac{i}{m}\right)^{mn} \tag{4-6}$$

For example, if compounding is done quarterly, the annual interest rate, i, is divided by 4 and the number of periods is multiplied by 4.

$$FV_n = PV_0\left(1 + \frac{i}{4}\right)^{4n}$$

CONTINUOUS COMPOUNDING AND DISCOUNTING

continuous compounding and discounting

As the frequency of compounding or discounting becomes infinitely large, the term $(1+i/m)^{mn}$ approaches the value e^{in} where e is approximately 2.71828, the base of natural logarithms.

and equation 4-6 becomes

$$FV_n = PV_0 e^{in} \qquad (4\text{-}7)$$

The present value formula, assuming continuous discounting is thus,

$$PV_0 = FV_n \left[\frac{1}{e^{in}} \right] \qquad (4\text{-}8)$$

GROWTH RATES

Interest rates measure the rate of growth of a sum of money. For example, $100 deposited at 10% will *grow* to $110 in one year, $121 in two years and so on. Often in finance, we want to know growth rates of such things as sales, earnings per share, dividends and other financial variables. Growth rates resemble compound interest and, thus, we can solve for the growth rate between some beginning (i.e. present value) and ending (i.e., future value) amount in the same way we solve for the effective interest rate: It is the rate that makes the beginning and ending values equivalent for a given number of periods.

To find the compound growth rate, we take the ending number (FV) and divide by the beginning number (PV). This gives the FVIF value. We look in the FVIF table along the number of periods until we find the FVIF value closest to the calculated value. The corresponding interest rate represents the growth rate.

Example

The Mead Company has had the following sales figures for the last 8 years:

Year	Sales ($000)
1980	$2,000
1981	2,125
1982	2,750
1983	2,500
1984	2,750
1985	3,125
1986	3,500
1987	3,898

Calculate the compound rate of growth in sales in the 7 years between 1980 and 1987.

$$FV_{1987} = PV_{1980}(FVIF_{i\%,7})$$

$$\$3,898 = \$2,000(FVIF_{i\%,7})$$

$$FVIF_{i\%,7} = \$3,898/\$2,000$$

$$FVIF_{i\%,7} = 1.949$$

We divide the ending value ($3,898) by the beginning value ($2,000). The calculated value is 1.949. Since the number of periods between 1980 and 1987 is 7, we look in the FVIF table, along the row for 7 periods until we find the value closest to 1.949. When we find the value closest to 1.949, we look to see what interest rate column it is under. In this case, reading along the 7 year row we find the exact value, 1.949, corresponding to an interest rate of 10%. Thus, the compound growth rate in sales over the 7 year period is 10% per year.

The growth rate we calculated represents the increase in sales in 1987 relative to 1980. In that sense, it represents a rough estimate of the average growth per year. Individual year to year changes may be more or less than 10%.

In this example, the calculated value, 1.949 was exactly equal to the one in the table. This will not usually be the case, simply because the tables cannot contain every combination of i and n. If we can't find the exact number in the table to match the calculated number, we have two alternatives: use the closest number or interpolate. Interpolation gives a better estimate of the true growth rate but requires additional computation.

 INTERPOLATION

When using the present value or future value tables to solve for effective interest rates or growth rates, we may not find the exact value in the table to match the one we have calculated. This is simply because the tables cannot contain every possible combination of i and n. If the value in the table is reasonably close to the one we are looking for, we might safely use that as an approximation of the interest rate or growth rate we are looking for. If the number in the table is not close enough, we may find it desirable to interpolate. The purpose of this section is to demonstrate the use of interpolation in terms of an example.

Example

The Arick Corporation has negotiated a loan of $1,000,000 with the Eternal Life Insurance Company. The loan is to be repaid in 5 annual installments of $310,000 each. What effective interest rate is being charged on the borrowing?

The loan repayment involves an annuity. Since the present value is given, $1,000,000, we use the PVIFA table.

$$PV = \$1,000,000 \text{(amount of loan)}$$

$$A = \$310,000 \text{(annual payment)}$$

$$n = 5 \text{ years(number of annual installments)}$$

$$i = ? \text{(effective annual interest rate)}$$

$$PVA = A(PVIFA_{i\%,n})$$

$$\$1,000,000 = \$310,000(PVIFA_{i\%,5})$$

$$PVIFA_{i\%,5} = \frac{\$1,000,000}{\$310,000}$$

$$PVIFA_{i\%,5} = 3.226$$

We need to find what interest rate for 5 years results in a value of 3.226 in the PVIFA table. Searching along the 5 year row, we find that 3.226 lies between the 16% and 17% columns. We will need to interpolate to get a better estimate of the true interest rate.

For $n = 5$	
i	PVIFA
16%	3.274
?	3.226
17%	3.199

In interpolating, we first find the total difference between the 16% and 17% PVIFA values:

16%	3.274
17%	3.199
difference	0.075

We then find the difference between the calculated PVIFA value (3.226) and the 16% PVIFA value.

$$
\begin{array}{ll}
16\% & 3.274 \\
? & \underline{3.226} \\
\text{Partial difference} & 0.048
\end{array}
$$

We then take the ratio of the partial difference (0.048) to the total difference (0.075).

$$
\frac{.048}{.075} = .64
$$

The ratio, .64 is then added to the 16% rate to get the estimated effective interest rate of 16.64%.

KNOWING WHICH TABLE TO USE

Beginning finance students often ask, "How do I know which formula or table to use for a particular time value problem?" This is a reasonable question, since time value problems arise in so many different forms. The best answer is to determine exactly what you want to know. This takes some practice, but the task is simplified when you realize that every time value problem obeys certain rules that usually make the proper approach clear. The following guide is meant to help you become more adept in solving most time value problems.

Annuity Vs. Nonannuity

The first thing to determine is whether the problem involves a simple annuity cash flow. In other words, annuity problems should be solved with the annuity tables, FVIFA or PVIFA. This is not essential, of course, but it is easier. Learn to recognize the many synonyms for an annuity cash flow. For example, words such as *constant*, *level*, *regular*, *periodic*, *even*, and *equal* often signal that an annuity is involved.

If the problem does not involve an annuity, use the FVIF or PVIF tables.

Four Variables

Every time value formula has four variables. To be solved, three of these variables must be given a numerical value in the problem itself. Through the process of elimination, the variable without a numerical value is the one for which to solve.

To see this more clearly, consider the basic time value formula:

$$
FV_n = PV_0(1 + i)^n
$$

The four variables are FV, PV, i, and n. Three of these must be specified in the problem in order to solve for the fourth. In problems involving an annuity, the annuity replaces either the FV or PV variable — so there are still four variables. If the annuity problem contains the FV variable, use the FVIFA table. If the annuity problem contains the PV variable, use the PVIFA table.

Table 4-7 shows how the variables relate for nonannuity time value problems. Tables 4-8 and 4-9 show how the variables relate to annuity problems.

TABLE 4-7   Solving Nonannuity Problems

	FV	PV	i	n	Use Table
1.	?	✓	✓	✓	FVIF
2.	✓	?	✓	✓	PVIF
3.	✓	✓	?	✓	FVIF or PVIF
4.	✓	✓	✓	?	FVIF or PVIF

To interpret the table, consider line 1. The PV, i and n variables are known, hence the FV variable is not known. In such a case use the FVIF table.

TABLE 4-8   Solving Annuity Problems Which Include PV

A	PV	i	n	Use Table
?	✓	✓	✓	PVIFA
✓	?	✓	✓	PVIFA
✓	✓	?	✓	PVIFA
✓	✓	✓	?	PVIFA

TABLE 4-9   Solving Annuity Problems Which Include FV

A	FV	i	n	Use Table
?	✓	✓	✓	FVIFA
✓	?	✓	✓	FVIFA
✓	✓	?	✓	FVIFA
✓	✓	✓	?	FVIFA

S U M M A R Y

This chapter has examined the time value concept and presented the principal variations of the basic time value formula that appear in financial decision making. By manipulating these variations, any time value problem can be evaluated. The principal time value structures, in forms that can be solved with the tables in Appendix A are:

$$FV_n = PV_0(FVIF_{i\%,n}),$$

which gives the future value of some single present amount.

$$FVA = PV_0(FVIFA_{i\%,n}),$$

which gives the cumulated future sum of an annuity.

$$PV_0 = FV_n(PVIF_{i\%,n})$$

which gives the present value of a single future amount.

$$PV_0 = \sum_{n=1}^{n} FV_n(PVIF_{i\%,n})$$

which gives the present value of an uneven stream of future cash flows.

$$PVA = A(PVIFA_{i\%,n})$$

which gives the present value of an even stream of future cash flows (i.e., an annuity).

Each time value structure involves four variables. If any three are known, the fourth can be solved for.

MULTIPLE CHOICE QUESTIONS

1. Compound interest means:
   a) Double-counting interest expenses
   b) Earning interest on interest

   c) Finding the present value
   d) More than one interest rate is used

2. Adjusting for the time value of money is accomplished by:

   a) Ignoring it
   b) Taking the reciprocal of each year's cash flow
   c) Dividing each year's cash flow by 2.0
   d) Discounting

3. An annuity is:

   a) A celebration marking the passage of another year
   b) Any irregular series of cash flows
   c) An obligation that must be repaid
   d) A stream of equal cash flows

4. Annuities involving cash flows at the beginning of each period are known as:

   a) Little known annuities
   b) Annuities due
   c) Reverse annuities
   d) Discount annuities

5. The basic time value formula can be shown as:

   a) $FV_n = FV_0(1 + i)^n$
   b) $FV_0 = PV_n(1 + n)^{(1+i)}$
   c) $PV_n = FV_0(1 + i)^{(1+n)}$
   d) $FV_n = PV_0(1 + i)^n$

6. In present value analysis, the interest rate is often referred to as:

   a) The time value of money
   b) The discount rate
   c) The PVIF
   d) The compounded rate

7. The present value interest factor is just the inverse of:

   a) The annuity present value factor
   b) The discount rate
   c) The future value interest factor
   d) The factor interest value present

8. When discounting on a quarterly basis, one should:

   a) Multiply the annual interest rate by four
   b) Divide the number of annual periods by four
   c) Divide the annual interest rate by three
   d) Divide the annual interest rate by four

9. To solve a problem involving a sinking fund, one would probably use:

   a) The FVIF table
   b) The PVIF table
   c) The FVIFA table
   d) The PVIFA table

10. In time value problems, interpolating refers to:

    a) Finding the future value of a sum of money

    b) Adjusting interest rates to reflect intra-year compounding

    c) Finding discounting or compounding interest rates that are not in tables

    d) Trying to guess which variable is missing

DISCUSSION QUESTIONS

1. What is meant by the time value of money?

2. Briefly describe what is meant by compound interest. Express the compound interest concept in the form of a general equation.

3. What is an annuity? Give an example of an annuity. What is the difference between a regular annuity and an annuity due? Which type of annuity is represented in the Appendix tables?

4. What is meant by intra-year compounding periods? How does the frequency of compounding affect future values?

5. Identify the four variables present in all time value problems. In your answer, distinguish between the variables in annuity and nonannuity time value problems.

6. Explain what is meant by the phrase, "PVIF factors are simply the inverse of FVIF factors."

7. Explain the connection between the PVIF table and the PVIFA table. In particular, comment on the relationship between the factors (numbers) in each table.

8. Explain the connection between the FVIF table and the FVIFA table. In particular, comment on the relationship between the factors (numbers) in each table.

9. Explain why discounting is used more than compounding in investment analyses.

10. How must the interest rate and number of periods be adjusted when discounting more than once per year?

SOLVED PROBLEMS

compounding

SP-1. Barbara deposits $1,000 in the bank. The bank pays interest of 8 percent compounded annually. How much will Barbara have in 10 years?

sinking fund

SP-2. John wants to have a fund of $50,000 in 10 years. He thinks he can earn interest of 8 percent compounded annually. How much should he deposit each year to have the fund he wants?

annuity

SP-3. Margo plans to buy a car on an installment plan. The car costs $20,000. Margo wants to pay in 24 equal monthly installments. The interest rate on the financing is 12 percent per year, compounded monthly.

a) What will her monthly payment be?

b) How much total interest will Margo pay over the 24 months?

SP-4. The Scotch Corporation has a pension fund of $20,000 per employee. The corporation will earn interest of 8 percent per year on money in the fund until it is all paid out. *annuity*

a) What will the annual pension be for an employee who retires, assuming payments start one year from now and are designed to exhaust the $20,000 at the end of 20 years?

b) How much money will each employee receive over the entire 20 years?

SP-5. The Argus Corporation has a loan agreement with an insurance company. According to the agreement, Argus will pay the insurance company $100,000 at the end of 10 years. In the interim, Argus is required to make quarterly deposits in a special bank account to make sure it has the needed $100,000 when due. (This arrangement is known as a *sinking fund*.) Argus can earn 8 percent per year, compounded quarterly, on the savings account. *sinking fund*

a) How much should Argus deposit each quarter, assuming the payments are all the same amount?

b) How much of the $100,000 payment in 10 years will represent deposits made by Argus? How much will come from interest earned on the sinking fund?

SP-6. The Wilcox Company needs as much debt as it can get. The finance manager believes that the company will have $40,000 per quarter in cash available for the next five years which can be used to make payments on any debt the company secures. An insurance company is willing to lend the company the needed funds at an interest rate of 20 percent per year. *annuity*

a) What is the maximum loan Wilcox could handle with its quarterly cash flow? Assume the loan will be repaid in even quarterly installments over a five-year period and will have an interest cost of 20 percent per year.

b) How much interest (in dollars) will Wilcox pay on the loan?

SP-7. The Plyneer Company sells furniture. The Company recently began advertising a "convenient purchase plan" on a line of living room sets. The sets cost $1,500 if purchased for cash. Customers may also pay in installments. For example, a $1,500 living room set can be purchased for a "low, low" $100 per month for 18 months. *annuity*

a) What interest rate is Plyneer charging its credit customers?

b) How much interest (in dollars) will customers pay over the 18 months?

compound growth **SP-8.** The Mead Company's sales have grown from $2,000,000 in 1980 to $3,898,000 in 1987. Compute the compounded annual growth rate over the period.

present value **SP-9.** The Minik Corporation is considering an investment proposal which will produce the following future cash flows each year:

	1	2	3	4	5
Cash flow ($000)	$100	$150	$200	$140	$80

The discount rate applicable to the investment is 15 percent per year. Calculate the present value of the investment.

interpolation **SP-10.** The Arick Corporation has negotiated a loan of $1,000,000 with the Eternal Life Insurance Company. The loan is to be repaid in five annual installments of $310,000 each. What effective interest rate is being charged on the borrowing. Use interpolation of the figures in the table.

PROBLEMS

compounding **1.** Betty deposits $15,000 in the bank. The bank pays interest of 6 percent compounded annually. How much will Betty have in 20 years?

sinking fund **2.** Margaret wants to have a fund of $100,000 in 20 years. She thinks she can earn interest of 7 percent compounded annually over the 20 years. How much should she deposit each year to have the fund she wants in 20 years?

annuity **3.** Oscar plans to buy a car on an installment plan. The car costs $30,000. Oscar wants to pay in 12 equal monthly installments. The interest rate on the financing is 12 percent per year, compounded monthly.

    a) What will his monthly payment be?
    b) How much total interest will Oscar pay over the 12 months?

annuity **4.** The Tuner Company has a pension fund of $80,000 per employee. The company can earn interest of 7 percent per year on money in the fund until it is all paid out.

    a) What will the annual pension be for an employee who retires, assuming payments start one year from now and are designed to exhaust the $80,000 at the end of 15 years?
    b) How much money will each employee receive over the entire 15 years?

5. The Stub Corporation has a loan agreement with an insurance company. According to the agreement, Stub will pay the insurance company $200,000 at the end of 20 years. In the interim, Stub is required to make semiannual deposits in a special bank account to make sure it has the needed $200,000 when due. (This arrangement is known as a sinking fund.) Stub can earn 10 percent per year, compounded semiannually, on the savings account.

   a) How much should Stub deposit each six months, assuming the payments are all the same amount?

   b) How much of the $200,000 payment in 20 years will represent deposits made by Stub? How much will come from interest earned on the sinking fund?

6. The Dray Company needs as much debt as it can get. The finance manager believes that the company will have $100,000 per year in cash available for the next 15 years which can be used to make payments on any debt the company secures. An insurance company is willing to lend the company the needed funds at an interest rate of 12 percent per year. *annuity*

   a) What is the maximum loan Dray could handle with its annual cash flow? Assume the loan will be repaid in equal annual installments over a 15-year period and will have an interest cost of 12 percent per year.

   b) How much interest (in dollars) will Dray pay on the loan?

7. The Trial Company sells furniture. The Company recently began advertising a "convenient purchase plan" on a line of living room sets. The sets cost $1,450 if purchased for cash. Customers may also pay in installments. For example, a $1,450 living room set can be purchased for a "low, low" $200 per month for 18 months. *annuity*

   a) What annual interest rate is the Trial Company charging its credit customers?

   b) How much interest (in dollars) will customers pay over the 18 months?

8. The Bead Company's sales have grown from $4,000,000 in 1980 to $8,844,000 in 1987. Compute the compounded annual growth rate over the period. *compound growth*

9. The Milk Company is considering an investment proposal which will produce the following future cash flows each year. *present value*

	1	2	3	4	5
Cash flow ($000)	$200	$450	$700	$500	$300

The discount rate applicable to the investment is 12 percent per year. Calculate the present value of the investment.

10. The Fish Corporation has negotiated a loan of $2,000,000 with the Eternal Life Insurance Company. The loan is to be repaid in 10 annual *interpolation*

intra-year compounding

installments of $380,000 each. What effective interest rate is being charged on the borrowing? Use interpolation of the figures in the table.

11. Calculate the future value of a $500 investment made now under each of the following interest rate and investment period alternatives.

   a) Assume annual compounding.
   b) Assume semiannual compounding.
   c) Assume quarterly compounding.

Investment Alternative	Interest Rate (%)	Investment Time Period
A	8	6 years
B	12	3
C	16	5
D	4	10
E	20	5

intra-year discounting

12. You will receive $2,500 at the end of some future time period. Calculate the present value or worth to you of the $2,500 under each of the following reinvestment or discount rate and receipt period alternatives.

   a) Assume annual discounting.
   b) Assume semiannual discounting.
   c) Assume quarterly discounting.

Receipt Alternative	Discount Rate (per year)	Receipt Time Period (year end)
A	16%	4 years
B	8	1
C	12	5
D	20	10
E	4	6

compounding

13. You have $5,000 to invest now in a savings account. When your "nest egg" reaches $10,000, you plan to vacation in the Caribbean.

   a) If you plan to take your vacation at the end of five years from now, what annual rate of interest will you have to earn on your savings account?
   b) If you are willing to wait eight years before taking your vacation, what annual rate of interest would be necessary on your savings account?

c) If you can earn 8 percent per year compounded annually on your savings account, how long will it take before you have adequate funds to take the vacation?

d) How soon could you take the vacation if your savings account pays a 16-percent interest rate annually but compounds your interest quarterly?

compounding

14. You need $15,000 seven years from now in order to take advantage of a "once-in-a-lifetime" investment opportunity.

a) If you have $6,000 to invest now, what interest rate would you have to earn on your investment assuming annual compounding?

b) If you have the opportunity of earning 12 percent compounded annually on your investment, what dollar amount would you have to invest now in order to make your "once-in-a-lifetime" investment?

c) How would your answer in Part (b) be altered if semiannual compounding occurred on your initial investment?

future value and present value

15. Following are several cash flow streams available to the DeAngelo Company. The prevailing interest and discount rates are 9 percent with annual compounding.

Cash Flow Stream	End of Year Cash Flows				
	1	2	3	4	5
A	$700	$700	$700	$700	$700
B	500	600	700	800	900
C	900	900	−100	900	900

a) Calculate the future values of the three cash flow streams at the end of the fifth year. Why do they differ?

b) Calculate the present values of the three cash flow streams. Why do they differ?

sinking fund

16. The Birch Corporation will need $100,000 to renovate its sales offices six years from now. The firm will invest an equal amount each year.

a) If the firm can earn 10 percent per year compounded annually, how much will it have to invest each year beginning one year from now?

b) If the firm invests $10,000 per year beginning one year from now, what annual rate of interest would it have to earn on its investment?

c) If the firm does not make its first investment until one year from now and can earn 12 percent per year, how much will it have to invest each year?

annuity

17. The Shale Corporation will loan $200,000 to another corporation and will receive equal annual dollar payments in return.

a) If Shale requires an annual $25,000 payment beginning one year after the loan is initiated and covering 12 years, what will be the annual rate of return?

b) If the loan is for eight years with the first payment being required one year from now and Shale wants a 10-percent annual return, what must be the dollar amount of each payment?

annuity

18. The Rank Company is planning to save $12,000 per year for five years. Assume deposits are made at the end of the year and earn interest at 8 percent per year.

a) Calculate the future value for this annuity if interest is compounded semiannually.

b) Calculate the future value for this annuity if interest is compounded quarterly.

annuity

19. The Dairy Corporation will be receiving rental payments made by a client in the amount of $17,000 per year for two years, with the first payment to be received one year from now. Present discount rates are 12 percent per year.

a) What is the present value of the annuity?

b) What is the present value of the annuity if discounting occurs semiannually?

compounding

20. Mark deposits $100 in the bank. Assuming he can earn 8 percent per year and that he makes no withdrawals from the account, how much will he have:

a) At the end of one year

b) At the end of three years

c) At the end of 10 years

d) At the end of 20 years

intra-year compounding

21. Jill deposits $1,000 in the bank. If Jill earns 12 percent per year on the account and makes no withdrawals, how much will she have in her account at the end of the two years, assuming:

a) Annual compounding

b) Semiannual compounding

c) Quarterly compounding

d) Monthly compounding

compounding

22. Karen borrows $1,000 from the bank at an interest rate of 24 percent per year. If she has to repay the loan plus accumulated interest, how much will she have to repay if she borrows for:

a) Six months

b) One year

c) 18 months

d) Two years

23. Marcia borrows $1,000 for 10 years. She will be required to repay $2,159 in one lump sum at the end of 10 years. The $2,159 will represent payment of principal and accumulated interest. What is the effective interest rate on Marcia's loan?   *unknown interest rate*

24. George can earn an interest rate of 7 percent per year on his savings. How long will it take for a $1,000 deposit to grow to $2,759?   *compounding*

25. The Xcess Corporation has had the following sales and earnings per share for the last seven years.   *growth rate*

Year	Sales ($000)	Earnings Per Share
1980	$1,000	$1.00
1981	1,050	1.09
1982	1,102	1.19
1983	1,158	1.30
1984	1,216	1.41
1985	1,276	1.54
1986	1,340	1.68

   a) Calculate the compound annual growth rate in sales from 1980 to 1986.
   b) Calculate the compound annual growth rate in earnings per share from 1980 to 1986.

26. Margo deposits $1,000 in a bank account. At the end of 10 years, she expects to have a total of $1,879 in the account. Assuming no withdrawals or other deposits within the 10 years, calculate the interest rate Margo expects to earn on her bank account.   *unknown interest rate*

27. Jack deposits $3,250 in his bank account. How much will be in that account at the end of 10 years assuming: *compounding*

   a) An interest rate of 6 percent per year
   b) An interest rate of 12 percent per year
   c) How much more interest will be earned at the 12 percent rate compared to the 6 percent rate, in dollars?

28. Maple has been offered an interesting investment opportunity. If she invests $1,000 at the end of every four months, she is "guaranteed" a rate of return of 20% per year, compounded quarterly for as long as her deposits continue. If Maple accepts the offer, how much will she have accumulated: *compounding*

   a) At the end of one year
   b) At the end of five years
   c) At the end of 10 years

29. Dave wants to have $50,000 in 10 years, when he plans to retire. He can earn a rate of 12 percent per year compounded quarterly. How much will he have to deposit at the end of each quarter?

30. Inflation represents the growth in prices. Calculate the inflation rate for each of the following:

Item	Price in	
	1977	*1987*
toothpaste	$1.85	$4.38
marbles	.95	5.88
paper	.15	.32

31. Agil Corp. has not raised any of its prices for the last three years. In that time, inflation has increased at the rate of 7 percent per year. How much should Agil Corp. raise its prices to reflect inflation?

Product	Price
X	$ 15.60
Y	$100.41
Z	$ 57.85

32. Ambrose Corp. has a loan for $100,000 which will have to be paid off in 10 years. The Corporation pays interest each year, but the principal ($100,000) will be paid in one lump sum at the end of 10 years. According to its loan agreement, Ambrose is obligated to make deposits at the end of each quarter into a special sinking-fund savings account to make sure it has the $100,000 in 10 years. If Ambrose earns 8 percent per year, compounded quarterly, on the sinking fund account, how much should the corporation deposit at the end of each quarter?

33. Calculate the present value of $1,000 to be received at the end of five years, assuming a discount rate of:
   a) 10 percent per year
   b) 20 percent per year
   c) 5 percent per year

34. Calculate the present value of $1,000 to be received in 10 years, assuming a discount rate of 12 percent per year, discounted:
   a) Annually
   b) Semiannually
   c) Quarterly

35. Calculate the present value of $100 to be received at the end of one year, assuming a discount rate of 10 percent per year, discounted semi-annually. *intra-year discounting*

36. Calculate the present value of 40 dollars to be received at the end of every six months for five years *plus* $1,000 at the end of the fifth year, assuming semiannual discounting, discounted at: *intra-year discounting*

a) 10 percent per year
b) 8 percent per year
c) 4 percent per year

37. Milt has inherited $100,000. He plans to deposit the money in a bank where he can earn 12 percent per year. At the end of each year, Milt will withdraw a constant amount of money. What is the most he can withdraw at the end of each year if he wants the money to last: *annuity*

a) 10 years
b) 20 years
c) five years

38. The Armor Company has made an investment that will produce the following cash flows at the end of each year. What is the present value of the investment opportunity at a discount rate of 14 percent per year: *present value*

	1	2	3	4	5
Cash flow ($000)	$10,000	$20,000	$15,000	$8,000	$5,000

39. The Mafoll Company is trying to develop a credit plan for its refrigerator sales. The refrigerator is sold for $1,500. Mafoll will let customers pay for the refrigerators in 18 equal monthly installments. What will the installments be if Mafoll charges the following interest rate on the plan: *annuity*

a) 12 percent per year
b) 24 percent per year

SOLUTIONS TO SOLVED PROBLEMS

SP-1. *Step 1:* List the variables known in order to identify which one to solve for:

$$PV = \$1,000 \text{(her deposit now)}$$

$$i = 8 \text{ percent}$$

$$n = 10 \text{ years}$$

$$FV = ?$$

113

Step 2: Since the FV variable is not known and the problem does not involve an annuity, use the FVIF table.

$$FV = PV(FVIF_{i\%,n})$$

$$FV_{10} = \$1,000(2.159)$$

$$FV_{10} = \$2,159$$

SP-2. This problem involves an annuity: the amount to save each year. Since the future value, $50,000 is specified, use the FVIFA table.

$$FV = A(FVIFA_{i\%,n})$$

$$\$50,000 = A(14.487)$$

$$A = \$50,000/14.487$$

$$A = \$3,451.37$$

SP-3. a) *Step 1:* List the variables known in order to identify which one to solve for:

$$PV = \$20,000 \text{(the price of the car now)}$$

$$i = 12 \text{ percent per year}$$

$$n = 24 \text{ months}$$

$$A = ? \text{(the amount of the monthly payment)}$$

Step 2: Convert the annual interest rate to a monthly rate, since the payments will be monthly. The number of periods n does not have to be converted because it is already on a monthly basis.

Monthly interest rate = Annual rate/12 months

$$= 12\%/12 = 1\% \text{ per month}$$

Step 3: Since an annuity is involved and the PV variable is known, use the PVIFA table.

$$PV = A(PVIFA_{i\%,n})$$

$$\$20,000 = A(21.244)$$

$$A = \$941.44$$

b) Margo's monthly payments will be $941.44. In 24 months she will have paid $22,594.56 (i.e., 24 months times $941.44 per month). Since the car costs $20,000, Margo will pay total interest of $2,594.56 over the 24 months.

SP-4. a) *Step 1:* List the variables known to identify which one to solve for:

$$PV = \$20{,}000 \text{(the amount in the fund now)}$$

$$i = 8 \text{ percent per year}$$

$$n = 20 \text{ years}$$

$$A = ? \text{(the amount of the pension per year)}$$

Step 2: Since an annuity is involved (the annual pension payment) and the PV variable is known, use the PVIFA table.

$$PV = A(\text{PVIFA}_{i\%,n})$$

$$\$20{,}000 = A(9.818)$$

$$A = \$2{,}037.07$$

b) The annual pension will be $2,037.07. The total cash received by each employee will be $40,741.40 (i.e., $2,037.07 per year times 20 years).

SP-5. a) *Step 1:* List the variables known in order to identify which one to solve for:

$$FV = \$100{,}000 \text{(the loan to be paid at the end of 10 years)}$$

$$i = 8 \text{ percent per year}$$

$$n = 10 \text{ years}$$

$$A = ? \text{(the amount of the quarterly payment)}$$

Step 2: Convert the annual interest rate to a quarterly rate, since the deposits will be quarterly. The number of periods *n* also has to be changed to reflect the quarterly deposits.

$$\text{Quarterly interest rate} = \text{annual rate/four months}$$

$$= 8\%/4 = 2\% \text{ per quarter}$$

$$\text{Number of quarterly periods} = \text{number of years times four}$$

$$= 10 \times 4 = 40 \text{ quarterly periods}$$

Step 3: Since an annuity is involved and the FV variable is known, use the FVIFA table.

$$FV = A(\text{FVIFA}_{i\%,n})$$

$$\$100{,}000 = A(60.401)$$

$$A - \$1{,}655.60$$

b) Argus needs to deposit $1,655.60 per quarter in the sinking fund. Over the 40 quarters, Argus will deposit a total of $66,224.00 (i.e., $1,655.60 × 40) in the fund. Interest earnings during the 40 quarters will provide the additional $33,776.00 needed to pay the total $100,000 due in 10 years.

SP-6. a) *Step 1:* List the variables known in order to identify which one to solve for:

$$PV = ?(\text{Amount to be borrowed now})$$

$$i = 20 \text{ percent per year}$$

$$n = \text{five years}$$

$$A = \$40,000 \text{ will be paid each quarter}$$

Step 2: Convert the annual interest rate to a quarterly rate, since the payments will be quarterly. The number of periods n also has to be changed to reflect the quarterly payments.

Quarterly interest rate = annual rate/four

$$= 20 \text{ percent}/4 = 5 \text{ percent per quarter}$$

Number of quarterly periods = number of years times four

$$= 5 \times 4 = 20 \text{ quarterly periods}$$

Step 3: Since an annuity is involved and the PV variable is not known, use the PVIFA table.

$$PV = A(\text{PVIFA}_{i\%,n})$$

$$PV = \$40,000(12.462)$$

$$PV = \$498,480$$

With its cash flow projections, Wilcox can borrow approximately $498,480.
   b) Wilcox will pay a total of $800,000 ($40,000 per quarter times 20 quarters). Since the amount borrowed will be $498,480, the difference of $301,520 represents the interest on the loan. This will be an expensive loan!

SP-7. a) *Step 1:* List the variables known in order to identify which one to solve for:

$$PV = \$1,500 \text{ (the price of the living room set now)}$$

$$i = ?$$

$$n = 18 \text{ months}$$

$$A = \$100 \text{ (the amount of the monthly payment)}$$

Step 2: Since an annuity is involved and both the PV and A variables are known, use the PVIFA table.

$$PV = A(\text{PVIFA}_{i\%,n})$$

$$\$1,500 = \$100(\text{PVIFA}_{i\%,18})$$

$$(\text{PVIFA}_{i\%,18}) = \$1,500/\$100 = 15.000$$

The interest rate required is one which, together with $n = 18$, results in a PVIFA value of approximately 15. Since the tables cannot contain every combination of interest rates and periods, look for the closest value or use interpolation as described in the chapter. The PVIFA value closest to 15.000 for $n = 18$, is 14.992, at an interest rate of 2 percent per month, or 24 percent per year. Since the PVIFA value is so close to 15.000, interpolation is not necessary in this case.

b) Total payments over the 18 months will be $1,800 for a $1,500 purchase. The difference, $300, represents interest payments.

SP-8. Growth problems are a variation of the time value problem. In finding growth rates, you are looking for a compound factor (the interest rate equivalent in a time value problem) which relates a beginning amount (i.e., the PV in a time value problem) with the ending amount (i.e., the FV in a time value problem) over a specified number of periods (i.e., the n in a time value problem). Growth problems can be solved with either the PVIF or FVIF tables.

Step 1: Identify the beginning amount, ending amount, and number of growth periods.

$$\text{Beginning sales} = \$2,000,000$$

$$\text{Ending Sales} = \$3,898,000$$

$$\text{Number of growth periods} = \text{seven}$$

$$\text{Growth rate} = ?$$

Step 2: Set up the time value relationship between a present amount and a future amount. Solve for the interest rate which, for seven periods, makes the beginning and ending amounts equal. This is the annual compound growth rate in sales.

$$PV = FV(PVIF_{i\%,n})$$

$$\$2,000,000 = \$3,898,000(PVIF_{i\%,7})$$

$$(PVIF_{i\%,7}) = \$2,000,000/\$3,898,000$$

$$= .513$$

The PVIF factor of .513 is produced by an interest rate of 10 percent and 7 periods. Thus, the annual compound growth rate in sales is 10 percent.

SP-9. The problem clearly involves present value. Since no annuity is involved (i.e., the cash flows are uneven), the PVIF table should be used. However, since more than one cash flow is involved, each must be discounted separately and summed. The simplest way to approach this would be to set up a table such as the one shown below.

	1	2	3	4	5
Cash flow ($000)	$100	$150	$200	$140	$80
$PVIF_{15\%,n}$	.870	.756	.658	.572	.497
PV	$ 87	$113.40	$131.60	$ 80.08	$39.76

$\Sigma = \$87 + \$113.40 + \$131.60 + \$80.08 + \$39.76 = \$451.84$

SP-10. *Step 1:* List the variables known in order to identify which one to solve for:

$$PV = \$1,000,000 \text{ (amount of loan)}$$

$$i = ? \text{ (effective interest rate to be determined)}$$

$$n = \text{five years}$$

$$A = \$310,000 \text{ to be paid each year}$$

Step 2: Since both the annuity amount and the PV variable are known, use the PVIFA table.

$$PV = A(PVIFA_{i\%,n})$$

$$\$1,000,000 = \$310,000(PVIFA_{i\%,5})$$

$$(PVIFA_{i\%,5}) = \$1,000,000/\$310,000 = 3.226$$

Step 3: You need to find what interest rate for five years results in a value of 3.226 in the PVIFA table. Searching along the five-year row, it can be seen that 3.226 lies between the 16-percent (i.e., PVIFA = 3.274) and 17-percent (i.e., PVIFA = 3.199) columns. It is necessary to interpolate to get a better estimate of the true interest rate.

For n = 5

i	PVIFA
16%	3.274
?	3.226
17%	3.199

Step 4: In interpolating, find the total difference between the 16 percent and 17 percent PVIFA values:

16%	3.274
—	—
17%	3.199
difference:	0.075

Step 5: Then find the difference between the calculated PVIFA value (3.226) and the 16 percent PVIFA value.

16%		3.274
?		3.226
	partial difference:	0.048

Step 6: Take the ratio of the partial difference (0.046) to the total difference (0.075).

$$.048/.075 = .64$$

Step 7: The ratio (0.64) is then added to the 16-percent rate to get the estimated effective interest rate of 16.64 percent.

REFERENCES

Cissell, Robert, Helen Cissell, and David C. Flaspohler. *Mathematics of Finance,* 5th Ed. Boston: Houghton Mifflin, 1978.

Clayton, Gary E., and Christopher B. Spivery. *The Time Value of Money.* Philadelphia: W. B. Saunders Co., 1978.

CASE EXERCISE

Chip-Tek, Inc.

Chip-Tek's top management was seriously concerned over the dismal sales performance of the "The Lapper" portable computer, which the Company had introduced with high hopes a few months earlier.

At one meeting, the marketing manager voiced the opinion that a more aggressive sales effort was needed to keep sales of the "The Lapper" from vanishing altogether by the end of the year. Perplexed, the president responded, "I want you to study the sales program for the 'The Lapper' and report back to us what you think is missing."

At the following meeting, the marketing manager reported that the major weakness in the sales program was that the computer was not competitively financed. Potential customers were having difficulty financing the $2,500 cost of the basic unit plus another $500 for peripherals and software. These customers were turning to Chip-Tek's competitors because they could get immediate financing which let them pay for equipment and software in installments. Some competitors had banking arrangements whereby the bank provided the financing to customers, while others provided financing to customers directly.

Hearing the marketing report, the president turned to the finance manager and said, "See what we can do to provide more competitive financing for the 'The Lapper' and report back next week."

The finance manager reported that Chip-Tek's main competitor, Cheapo, was offering customers installment-plan financing at very low interest rates. Since Chip-Tek did not have the financial resources to provide such financing, the company would have to develop an arrangement through a bank to provide installment financing.

A problem with this alternative was that Chip-Tek's customers would not be able to secure credit terms as favorable as Cheapo was offering its customers. "Of course, one way around that would be for us to provide an interest 'rebate' to make up the difference," noted the finance manager. When asked to explain, he said "The rebate would really just be a price reduction on the 'The Lapper' to keep the installment payments equal to what they would be at a lower interest rate. Since our customers would be paying a higher interest rate, the amount needed to finance would have to be lower to keep the installment payments competitive. The difference between the lower financing amount and our current price would be the rebate."

"I'm sorry, but I still don't completely follow," remarked the president. "Run that by me again."

"Well," noted the finance manager, "assume that one of our customers wants to buy $3,000 worth of equipment. If he buys it on credit from Cheapo with interest at, say, 12 percent per year and four quarterly payments, that would come to . . . ," he paused, punching some numbers into his calculator, "four installment payments of $807.08 each. But if he buys the same equipment from us and our bank charges 16 percent per year, his payments will be $826.45 each quarter." "I'll be...," the president exclaimed, "...in other words, our computer is actually higher priced than theirs if you buy it on time, and simply because our bankers are charging higher interest rates." "Right," responded the financial manager. "And to make ours competitive, we would have to cut the computer price down to about $2,930 so that the quarterly payments would come out to $807.10." At this, the marketing manager, who had attentively followed the explanation, exclaimed, "Isn't that something? Things really are topsy turvy when our *credit* customers are charged less than our cash customers. That just doesn't seem right."

Case Questions

1. Determine the quarterly installment payment which Cheapo's customers will pay if the average amount financed is $3,000, carries an interest rate of 20 percent per year, and is to be paid in four quarterly installments.

2. a) Assuming Chip-Tek's customers purchase an average of $3,000, what would their four quarterly installment payments be if bank financing is at 24 percent.
   b) Examine the "rebate" idea. How much of a price discount from the $3,000 average sale would be required to produce the same quarterly payments as Cheapo (question 1)?

3. Assume that $3,000 of equipment/software is purchased; that Chip-Tek supplies the financing itself at 16 percent per year; and that customers pay in four equal quarterly installments. If Cheapo's customers have to pay an annual interest rate of 20 percent (see question 1) how much of a price discount from the $3,000 is Chip-Tek providing its customers?

4. Assume that a consumer finance company makes the following proposal: Chip-Tek will provide customers installment purchase plans at an interest rate of 16 percent. Chip-Tek will then sell the installment contracts to the finance company. The finance company will pay Chip-Tek the present value of each installment contract discounted at an interest rate of 24 percent. How much will Chip-Tek receive from the finance company on each contract?

CHAPTER

5

VALUATION

n Chapter 4, we introduced the ideas and mechanics of present value analysis. In this chapter, we will apply those methods to the process of valuation.

Valuation means finding the financial worth of an investment. This is important because investing is one of the three central activities of business. For example, introducing a new product, purchasing a more efficient machine, or extending easier credit terms to customers are all investment decisions. Without a clear idea of what an investment is worth, the financial manager can easily make mistakes. When investments involve large amounts of money, even one mistake can bankrupt a company.

To illustrate the valuation process, we will examine financial investments such as stocks and bonds. Working with these types of investments makes it possible to develop the principles of valuation in a straightforward manner. Later, when we discuss business investments in detail, we will apply these principles to more complex investments.

Another reason for examining the valuation of a company's stocks and bonds is that the financial manager must know how the values of these securities are determined in order to maximize their values. By knowing the determinants of stock price, he or she can guide operating, investing, and financing activities toward maximizing stock price. Finally, as we shall see later, the valuation of bonds and stocks is important in helping management determine the costs of money it raises in financial markets.

● Objectives and Organization of this Chapter

The primary objective of this chapter is to illustrate how the present value concept can be applied to the important task of investment valuation. While Chapter 4 contained some brief illustrations in this regard, investment cash flows and discount rates were both assumed. This chapter examines how investment cash flows can be estimated from financial securities. In Chapter 6, we will consider ways of estimating the discount rates to be applied to investments of different types.

The first section of the chapter discusses the connection between present value and valuation. The second section describes the process of investment valuation. Section three examines the valuation of bonds. Section four explains valuation of preferred stock. Section five covers the valuation of common stock. The final section provides an analytic summary of investment types.

KNOW YOUR INVESTMENT!

The first rule of investment valuation is to know the unique characteristics of the investment itself. Whether one is interested in valuing securities or business investments, it is critical to know both how the investment will produce the necessary rewards for investors and what sources and magnitudes of risk the investment possesses. In the following discussion of financial securities, we review the particular characteristics of different types of securities to illustrate how these features determine an investment's risks and rewards.

Price Vs. Value

In this chapter, methods are illustrated for estimating the value of an investment. But, keep in mind that the actual price of an investment can be higher or lower than its value. By comparing an investment's value with its price, decisions as to whether the investment should be accepted or rejected are made.

For example, assume that financial analysis indicates the value of a share of stock of the Jones Corporation is worth $50 but the stock can be purchased on the New York Stock Exchange for $45. In this case, the stock is worth buying because its price is less than its value.

When securities markets are efficient, the prices of financial instruments reflect their values, and so price and value are the same. Chapter 6 discusses the price and value relationship in more detail. For present purposes, however, we will assume that securities are correctly priced and that their prices and values are equal.

THE VALUATION CONCEPT

Investment value can be defined as the present value of expected future cash flows to be produced by the investment.[1] The general present value equation can be expressed as follows:

$$P_0 = \sum_{t=1}^{n} CF_t/(1 + k)^t \qquad (5\text{-}1)$$

[1] Recall from Chapter 4 that present value refers to the value today of a set of future cash flows from an investment and that the determinants of present value are the timing, amounts, and level of uncertainty of the cash flows.

where P_0 is the value of the investment at time 0; CF_t represents the dollar amount of cash flow received in period t discounted at the required rate of return, k; and Σ represents the summation of all discounted cash flows for periods one through n.[2] Thus, valuation involves finding the present value of an investment's cash flows given some specified rate of return. Table 5-1 contains a checklist of the steps in the valuation process. In the succeeding sections we will follow these steps in valuing bonds, preferred stock, and common stock.

TABLE 5-1   Steps in the Valuation Process

Step 1:	Determine *how much* each cash flow is.
Step 2:	Determine *when* each cash flow will occur.
Step 3:	Determine the *required rate of return*.
Step 4:	Determine the *present value of* each cash flow.
Step 5:	*Sum* each of the present values.

Basic Bond Features

Bonds are debt securities. A person who buys a bond becomes a lender (creditor) to the borrower (issuer). In other words, the buyer is owed money. For example, if someone purchases a bond issued by AT&T, he or she becomes a creditor of AT&T. By purchasing a United States Treasury Bond, one becomes a creditor of the United States Government.   *bonds*

Most bonds share certain basic features: maturity date, par value, and coupon interest rate.

Maturity Date.   A bond's maturity date specifies when it will be paid off. The *term to maturity* indicates the time remaining until the bond is paid off.[3] A *"seasoned" issue* is a bond which has been outstanding for a while. Of course, the longer a bond has been outstanding, the shorter its term to maturity. The *original maturity* of a bond refers to term to maturity at the time of issue. For example, when a 20-year bond is issued, its original maturity is 20 years. Five years later the bond's term to maturity is 15 years, but its original maturity is still 20 years.   *term to maturity*
seasoned issue

original maturity

Par Value.   The par value of a bond is also known as its *face value* or *principal*. These terms are used interchangeably, but face value is probably   *face value*
principal

---

[2]When applied to investments, the term *present value* is often used interchangeably with synonyms such as *economic value, intrinsic value, fair value,* and *investment worth*. The underlying idea is the same: the value of an investment is determined by its expected cash flows and the investor's required rate of return.
[3]Recall that Chapter 3 discussed the term to maturity in reference to interest rate behavior.

coupon rate

more common. It is the amount the issuer promises to pay at maturity. The face value of most corporate bonds is $1,000, although some bonds have denominations of $5,000 and $10,000.

Coupon Interest Rate.   A bond's coupon interest rate indicates the rate of interest per year the borrower will pay to the holder of the bond. To determine the interest in dollars that will be paid each year, multiply the coupon interest rate times the face value of the bond. For example, if the AT&T bond has a coupon interest rate of $8\frac{3}{4}$ percent and a face value of $1,000, AT&T will pay the bondholder $87.50 per year. This calculation is shown in Equation 5-2.

$$\text{Interest payment } (I) = \text{Coupon rate } (C) \times \text{Face value } (F) \qquad (5\text{-}2)$$

$$\$87.50 = .0875 \times \$1,000$$

Interest payments are usually made semiannually. Thus, the holder of the AT&T bond would receive $43.75 ($87.50/2) every six months.

Bond Ratings

The level of risk of a bond varies from company to company, depending on the issuer's financial strength, operating profitability, and outlook for its products and services. All these factors are combined in developing an estimate of risk.

As an aid to investors, Moody's Investors Service and Standard & Poor's Corporation rate widely traded bonds. Moody's, for example, rates bonds on a scale ranging from Aaa, which is the highest-grade bond issued by corporations, down to a level of C, which is the lowest ranking. Ratings of Ba or lower are considered speculative.

Standard & Poor's assigns AAA ratings to the highest-quality bonds. Its lowest rating, D, indicates that the bond has defaulted, meaning that the issuer has failed to pay interest or meet some other provision of the bond agreement. Table 5-2 shows the various ratings of bonds established by Moody's and Standard & Poor's and what these ratings indicate.

Bond Quotations

The basic bond features can readily be identified in bond quotations (*quotes*), which are published in most daily newspapers. Bond quotes indicate the issuer, coupon rate, maturity date, price and other characteristics of traded bonds. A typical bond quote is shown in Table 5-3.

The first few columns describe the bonds by issuer (Tandy Corporation), coupon rate (10s, for 10 percent, ignore the *s*), maturity date (94, meaning 1994). A bond trader would read the quote as "the Tandy tens of 94." The current yield of 9.7 means that, if you bought the bond at its closing price, you would receive a rate of return of 9.7 percent over the next

TABLE 5-2 Moody's and S & P corporate quality ratings

Moody's	S & P	
Aaa	AAA	Highest-grade obligations. They possess the maximum degree of protection for principal and interest.
Aa	AA	High-quality obligations, differing from AAA or Aaa only to a small degree. These issues, along with the "triple A" issues, are generally known as high-grade bonds.
A	A	These are regarded as upper-medium bonds. They are of fairly good quality, but factors are present that may lead to impairment.
Baa	BBB	These are considered medium-grade obligations. They provide sufficient safety, but elements are present that make them susceptible to changing business and economic conditions. They have investment characteristics, but certain speculative characteristics also exist.
Ba	BB	Lower-medium grade obligations. They have speculative elements that jeopardize their investment quality.
B	B	Speculative. Interest payments are not assured under difficult economic conditions.
	CCC-CC	Outright speculations, but interest is being paid. In difficult economic conditions, continuation is unlikely.
Caa		Poor standing. May be in default.
	C	Income bonds with no interest being paid.
Ca		Highly speculative. Often in default.
	DDD-D	In default, with DDD, DD, D indicating relative salvage value.
C		Lowest ranking. Bonds with this ranking have very poor prospects.

TABLE 5-3

Bonds	Cur. Yld.	Vol.	High	Low	Close	Net Chg.
Tandy 10s94	9.7	7	103½	103⅛	103½	½

year from the interest alone. (We will discuss the current yield in more detail later, including how this calculation can be misleading.) The volume column indicates the number of Tandy bonds traded on this day, seven.

Information on trading prices is also reported, including the highest price paid for one of the bonds (high) during the day, the lowest price paid (low), the last transaction price (close) and the net change in bond price since the previous close (net change). Bond prices are quoted as a percentage of face value. To translate a bond price quote into a dollar equivalent, multiply the quoted percentage times the face value. For example, the

Tandy bond quoted at $103\frac{1}{2}$ would mean $103\frac{1}{2}$ percent of face value or, $1,035, as shown in Equation 5-3.

$$\text{Bond price } (P) = \text{Quoted percentage } (\%) \times \text{face value } (F) \qquad (5\text{-}3)$$

$$\$1,035 = 103.5\% \times \$1,000$$

If there is any accrued interest on the bond at the time of purchase, the amount will be added to the price of the bond. For example, assume that the Tandy bonds pay $100 interest December 31st of each year. If you buy bonds on, say, December 30th, you would get the annual interest payment the next day. However almost all that interest is really owed to the seller of the bond.

Estimating Bond Cash Flows

Knowing the features of a bond is important because they determine the cash flows to be received by the bondholder and the risk level of the bond. To illustrate this, let us examine the cash flows of the Tandy bonds described above.

Example

Estimating The Tandy Bond Cash Flows

Bond cash flows are made up of two parts: interest received each year (or six months if paid semiannually) and face value paid at maturity. Assume that you are considering the Tandy bonds as of January 1, 1988 and the bonds will mature December 31, 1994. Also assume that the bonds pay interest once a year on December 31st. The cash flows to be produced by the Tandy bonds can be represented by a time line such as that shown in Exhibit 5-1.

Bond Valuation

The value of the Tandy bonds can be determined by discounting each of the cash flows to be received and summing. Of course, this is equivalent to finding the present value of a stream of cash flows, as discussed in Chapter 4. Recall that, in order to find the present value, a discount rate is needed—i.e., the rate of return which the investment should provide given its relative risk level. Algebraically, the bond's value is determined by Equation 5-4.

$$P_0 = \sum_{t=1}^{n} I_t/(1 + k)^t + F_n/(1 + k)^n \qquad (5\text{-}4)$$

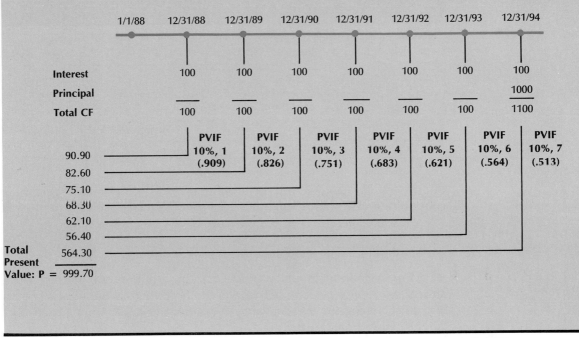

EXHIBIT 5-1
Tandy Bond Cash Flows:
Time Line and Present
Value

Where I_t is the interest payment received in year t; F_n is the face value received in year n; and k is the rate of return, or yield, required from the bond given its level of risk.

Using Present Value Tables. Exhibit 5-1 shows the present value of each cash flow discounted at a required yield to maturity of 10 percent.[4] The total present value of the Tandy bonds is $1,000 ignoring rounding differences. The present value interest factors (PVIF) come from Table 2 in the Appendix.

Table 5-4 shows an easier way to calculate the bond's present value. Note that since the interest payments are the same amount each year, they represent a seven-year annuity of $100 per year. The face value of $1,000 represents a lump-sum cash flow to be received at the end of year seven.[5]

Note that the value of the bond, $1,000, is equal to the face value of the bond. This is an important result and occurs only because the coupon rate (C) on the bond is equal to the required rate (i.e., k). As a general proposi-

---

[4]In this chapter, we will assume that the required yield to maturity has already been determined. In Chapter 6, we will discuss the method for estimating the required yield to maturity.
[5]In you are unsure of the procedure followed, review the present value discussion in Chapter 4.

TABLE 5-4   Calculation of Tandy Bond Value

Bond: 10% coupon; seven-year maturity; interest paid annually; yield-to-maturity 10%

Cash Flow	Amount	Received	PVIFA$_{10\%,7}$	PVIF$_{10\%,7}$	Present Value
Interest	$ 100	1-7	4.868		$486.80
Principal	$1000	7		.513	513.00
				Bond value:	$ 999.80
				or approximately:	$1,000.00*

*Ignore 20-cent rounding difference.

tion, it can be stated that, whenever the yield on a bond is equal to its coupon rate, the bond's value will be equal to its face value.

Semiannual Interest Payments

Most corporate bonds provide for the payment of interest semi-annually, or twice a year. Such bonds can be valued in the same way, but one must convert the present value calculations to a semiannual basis. This is reflected in Equation 5-5.

$$P_0 = \sum_{t=1}^{2n} (I_t/2)/[1 + (k/2)]^t + F_{2n}/(1 + k/2)^{2n} \tag{5-5}$$

If the Tandy bond pays interest semiannually, a bondholder would receive $50 every six months for 14 semiannual periods and a $1,000 payment at the end of the 14th period.

Since the cash flows are on a semiannual basis, the required yield to maturity should also be on a semiannual basis. As an approximation of the semiannual yield, simply divide the annual rate by two to get 5 percent semiannually.[6] When adjusting the yield to a semiannual basis, one must also adjust the number of periods. There are two semiannual periods per year, and thus the number of periods is multiplied by two. The calculations, assuming semiannual interest payments, will produce the values shown in Table 5-5. Note that the value of the bond is still $1,000. The reason is that the semiannual yield (5 percent) is equal to the semiannual coupon rate (5 percent). As long as the yield equals the coupon rate, bonds sell at par ($1,000).

---

[6]More precisely, if the annual yield is 10 percent compounded semiannually, the semiannual yield would be 4.88 percent rather than 5 percent, as shown below. This involves using an approximation, as is common practice, for convenience in using the tables.

Let x be the semiannual compounded rate and y be the annual rate. Then:

$$(1 + x)^2 = 1 + y$$

$$1 + x = \sqrt{1.10} = 1.0488$$

$$x = .0488 = 4.88\%$$

TABLE 5-5 Calculation of Bond Value: Semiannual Compounding

Bond: 10% coupon; seven-year maturity; interest paid semiannually; yield-to-maturity 10% per year or 5% semiannually.

Cash Flow	Amount	Received	PVIFA$_{5\%,14}$	PVIF$_{5\%,\ 14}$	Present Value
Interest	$ 50	1-14	9.899		$ 494.95
Principal	$1000	14		.505	505.00
				Bond value:	$ 999.95
				or approximately:	$1,000.00*

*Ignore 5-cent rounding difference.

Relationship of Bond Price to Yield

As shown in Chapter 4, the present value of future cash flows decreases as the discount rate increases. The same principle applies to bond values. In other words, there is an inverse relationship between bond price and yield: if yields go up, bond prices will go down; if yields go down, bond prices go up. Since the bond's cash flows are set by the coupon rate and face value of the bond, an increase in the yield to maturity reduces the (present) value of the bond. Conversely, a decrease in the yield to maturity produces an increase in the value of the bond. This principle is illustrated in Table 5-6. Note that, at a yield of 12 percent compounded annually, the value of the bond is $908.40 and that at a yield of 8 percent, the value of the bond is $1,103.60. The bond values in the table are calculated using Equation 5-4. In order to emphasize the relationship between bond value and the yield-to-maturity, the full present value calculations have not been shown.

The results in Table 5-6 indicate the following bond relationships:

1. When the bond's yield to maturity is less than the bond's coupon rate, (i.e., $k<C$) the bond will sell at a *premium*, meaning that the bond's price will be greater than its face value. For example, a yield to maturity of 8 percent is less than the bond's coupon rate (10 percent) and the price of the bond ($1,103.60) is greater than the face value ($1,000).

bond premium

2. When the bond's yield to maturity is equal to the bond's coupon rate ($k=C$) the bond will sell at *par*, meaning the bond's price will be equal

par value bond

yield to maturity

TABLE 5-6 Relationship of Bond Value and Yield-to-Maturity

Bond: 10% coupon; seven-year maturity; interest paid once per year.

Yield-to-Maturity	Bond Value
8%	$1103.60
10%	$1000.00
12%	$ 908.40

discount bond

to its face value. Thus, a yield to maturity of 10 percent is equal to the bond's coupon rate and the price of the bond is equal to the face value.

3. When the yield to maturity on a bond is greater than the bond's coupon rate, $(k>C)$ the bond will sell at a *discount,* meaning the bond's price will be less than its face value. For example, a yield to maturity of 12 percent is greater than the bond's coupon rate (10 percent) and the price of the bond ($908.40) is less than the face value ($1,000).

Bond Prices and Maturity Date

Assuming no default, at maturity the holder of the bond will receive $1,000 from the borrower. Thus, regardless of the yield-to-maturity, as a bond approaches its maturity date, the price of the bond will approach $1,000. Investors who purchased the bond at a discount will find the value of the bond appreciating. Bonds such as the "Tandy tens" that are selling at a premium will drop in price as they approach maturity, since at maturity the holder will only get $1,000 in payment for the bond. Exhibit 5-2 shows the behavior of bond values for discount, par, and premium-priced bonds as each approaches maturity. Note that the par-value bond does not change in price regardless of the term to maturity. The reason is that the yield is exactly equal to the coupon rate, and the yield reflects neither capital gain nor loss at any point.

EXHIBIT 5-2
Relationship of Bond Price to Maturity Date

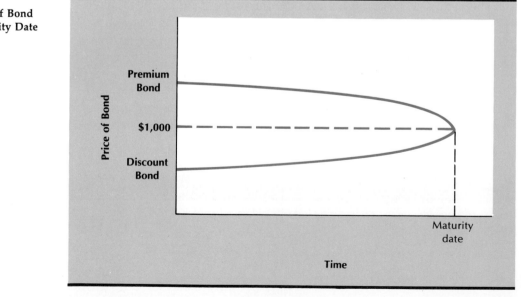

We have discussed the Tandy bonds in terms of yield-to-maturity, i.e., assuming one would hold the bonds until 1994. But suppose an investor only wants to invest in the bonds for one year. How would the 12 percent yield be produced? To answer this, consider the following example.

Example

Assume that the Tandy bonds are priced at a yield-to-maturity of 12 percent. Interest of $100 is paid once per year, and there are seven years remaining to maturity. Table 5-7 shows that, at a yield of 12 percent, the bonds would be selling for $908.40 with seven years to maturity. By using the same methodology in Table 5-8, the price of the bonds can be determined to be $918.10 when there are only six years remaining to maturity (i.e., one year later).[7]

TABLE 5-7 Calculation of Bond Value — Annual Compounding, Seven-Year Maturity

Bond: 10% coupon; seven-year maturity; interest paid annually; yield-to-maturity 12% per year.

Cash Flow	Amount	Received	$PVIFA_{12\%,7}$	$PVIF_{12\%,\ 7}$	Present Value
Interest	$ 100	1-7	4.564		$ 456.40
Principal	$1000	7		.452	452.00
				Bond value:	$ 908.40

TABLE 5-8 Calculation of Bond Value — Annual Compounding, Six-Year Maturity

Bond: 10% coupon; six-year maturity; interest paid annually; yield-to-maturity 12% per year.

Cash Flow	Amount	Received	$PVIFA_{12\%,6}$	$PVIF_{12\%,\ 6}$	Present Value
Interest	$ 100	1-6	4.111		$ 411.10
Principal	$1000	6		.507	507.00
				Bond value:	$ 918.10

---

[7]We are assuming, for illustrative purposes, that the yield on a seven-year bond is the same as the yield on a six-year bond of equivalent risk. This implies a term structure of interest rates that is flat, meaning the yield on securities is not affected by the term to maturity. In actuality, this would be unusual.

At a price of $908.40, the bond in the above example is providing a current yield of 11.01% (i.e., $100/908.40). If the bond is sold at the end of one year for $918.10, the capital gain will be $9.70 or, in percentage terms, 1.07% (i.e., $9.70/908.40). The current yield plus capital gain will produce an overall yield of approximately 12 percent (i.e., 11.01 percent + 1.07 percent).

$$\text{Annual yield} = \text{Current yield} + \text{capital gain(loss)} \qquad (5\text{-}6)$$

$$= \$100/908.40 + (918.10 - 908.40)/908.40$$

$$= 11.01\% + 1.07\%$$

$$= 12\%, \text{approximately}$$

Each year, part of the investment yield or rate of return is produced by a change in the price of the bond (appreciation or reduction) and part is produced by the coupon interest received. For "high" coupon bonds, most of the return is produced by interest income and relatively little (perhaps even a negative return) is produced by price appreciation. "Low" coupon bonds are just the reverse. Little return is produced by interest income and most of the return is accounted for by price appreciation in the bond. An extreme example of this latter case is the *zero-coupon* bond, which pays no interest at all.

Zero Coupon Bonds

In 1984, the Exxon Corporation sold 20-year bonds in Japan with a total face value of $1.8 billion. The cash Exxon received in exchange for the bonds was only $199 million. Without knowing anything else about the bonds or the issuer, one might speculate that the Exxon bonds were providing enormous yields-to-maturity. On the contrary, the actual cost of the funds raised, $199 million, was only about 11.64 percent. At the time of issue, the Exxon bonds had a lower yield than 20-year U.S. Treasury bonds!

The Exxon bonds are zero-coupon bonds, meaning that Exxon will not have to pay any interest on them. Instead, bondholders will receive their entire return from capital appreciation of the bonds from one year to the next. At maturity, in the year 2004, Exxon will pay bondholders a total of $1.8 billion. It should be clear from this example that zero-coupon bonds will sell at very deep discounts from face value.

When "zeros" were first introduced in the United States, they were very popular because of favorable tax treatment; namely, the return from price appreciation was taxed at lower rates than the return from interest income. This is no longer the case (although, in Japan, holders of the Exxon bonds did receive important tax advantages). A main attraction of zero coupon bonds now is that they can eliminate an important type of risk known as reinvestment-rate risk.

In order to demonstrate the valuation of zero-coupon bonds with the use of the present value tables in the Appendix, let us assume that the zero-coupon Exxon bonds have a yield of 12 percent. The value of the total bond issue is simply the present value of $1.9 billion to be received in 20 years at a yield of 12 percent per year.

$$\text{Value of zero-coupon bonds} = \text{Face value} \times (\text{PVIF}_{12\%,20}) \qquad (5\text{-}7)$$

$$= \$1.9 \text{ billion} \times (.104)$$

$$= \$197.6 \text{ million}$$

Since Exxon actually received $199 million, the yield must be slightly less than 12 percent.

Zero Coupon Bonds and Reinvestment Rate Risk

"Regular" bonds pay the holder interest on a periodic basis until the bond matures. Interest payments can produce an important type of risk for the bondholder: the risk that interest rates will drop and any cash flows from coupon interest will have to be reinvested at a lower rate. Zero-coupon bonds eliminate reinvestment rate risk because they do not pay the bearer interest. Instead, the bonds are sold at a large discount so that the yield to maturity is derived entirely from capital appreciation of the bond.

Example

Assume that you have a choice between a five-year zero-coupon bond providing a yield of 15 percent and a five-year, 15 percent coupon bond also providing a yield of 15 percent. Using Table 2 in the Appendix, it can be determined that the zero-coupon bond will cost $497 while the coupon bond will cost $1,000. Thus, for an investment of $1,000 you can buy slightly more than two zero bonds (i.e., $1,000/$497) or one coupon bond. For simplicity, assume that you will hold either bond until it matures, and that as soon as you purchase the bond, interest rates in the market drop to zero. Which investment will produce more cash over the five years?

At the end of the five years, the zeros mature and yield slightly more than $2,000 (remember, you bought two of them for $1,000). However, the coupon bond has produced five coupon payments of $150 each; or $750 in interest. Since market interest rates have fallen to zero, none of the coupons can earn any further interest. In addition, the coupon bond gives you $1,000 at maturity. But the total cash from the coupon bond is only $1,750 compared to the $2,000 you receive from the zeros.

The reason for this example's result is entirely due to the assumption made about the drop in the market interest rate, and thus the coupon bond's reinvestment rate. The chance that this may drop is what is meant by reinvestment rate risk. Zeros avoid this risk because they do not produce any cash until maturity.

Zeros and Interest Rate Risk

Unfortunately, while zeros eliminate reinvestment rate risk, they increase exposure to interest rate risk. Interest rate risk refers to the effect of changes in bond yields on bond prices. As is apparent from earlier discussions, higher yields produce lower bond values. All bonds have some exposure to interest rate risk, but zeros are affected to a much larger extent, especially zeros with long-term maturities. Table 5-9 illustrates the greater volatility of zero-coupon bonds for a given increase in interest rates. The bond prices are calculated at various yields, using the formulas described earlier.

Note that, as yields move from 10 percent to 12 percent, the percentage drop in the price of the zero is more than twice that of the coupon bond. Of course, zeros will increase in price at a faster rate if interest rates drop. Interest rate risk is a problem if the investor has to sell the bond before it matures. However, if the investor plans to hold the bonds until maturity (and zeros are often recommended for retirement-plan investments) interest rate risk can also be avoided. At maturity and assuming the issuer does not default, the bonds will be worth $1,000, regardless of prevailing interest rates.

STRIPS

While the variety of bond instruments is increasing every day, the Separate Trading of Registered Interest and Principle Securities, known by the acronym, STRIPS, should be mentioned. STRIPS are zeros issued by the U.S. Treasury Department. Since these securities have no default risk, an investor who buys and holds them to maturity can avoid reinvestment rate risk, interest rate risk, and default risk.

TABLE 5-9   Interest Rate Risk: Zeros Vs. Coupon Bonds

	Yield-To-Maturity		
	10%	*12%*	*Change*
Price of Zero	$ 149.00	$104.00	−30.20%
Price of Coupon	$1,000.00	$850.90	−14.91%

Consols

Consols are the opposite of zero-coupon bonds. Zeros pay no interest but have a relatively large maturity value. Consols pay only interest and have no maturity value. The cash flows of a consol thus represent a *perpetuity.* For this type of bond, the bond value equation reduces to:

$$P_0 = I/k \qquad (5\text{-}8)$$

Where I is the annual interest payment, and k is the yield to maturity of the bond.

Junk Bonds and Default Risk

In recent years junk bonds have become increasingly popular. Junk bonds are considered high risk and offer very high yields to investors willing to take risks. For example, in August 1986, the Wedtech corporation, a defense contractor, sold $75 million worth of bonds. These bonds were considered *speculative grade,* meaning high-risk, and had to offer a high yield, 14 percent, to attract investors. The bonds were sold at par value, $1,000. Four months later, the company was in bankruptcy and the bonds were selling for $200. Investors who buy high-yield bonds hope to have enough good bonds to offset the large losses which may be realized with the bad ones.

BOND YIELDS

In many cases investors want to know what rate of return they will earn if they buy a bond at its given price and estimated future cash flows. Most typically, this is known as the yield to maturity on a bond, but yields for different holding periods can also be calculated. Following is a description of the most common yield calculations.

Current Yield

A bond's current yield is calculated by simply dividing its interest payment by the current price of the bond. Using the information for the Tandy Corporation "tens" above, the current yield is calculated to be 9.7 percent. Note that this is the same as the current yield indicated in the bond quote.

$$\text{Current yield} = I/P_0 \qquad (5\text{-}9)$$

$$= \$100/1035.00$$

$$= .0966 = 9.7\%$$

As we have seen, the current yield is an incomplete measure of the bond's true yield because it ignores any capital appreciation or capital loss during the year which may occur as the bond moves toward its maturity date. This is particularly important when a bond is selling at a deep discount from par value or at a large premium over par value.

Yield to Maturity

The yield to maturity is the compound rate of return a buyer will receive from a bond, including interest income and capital gains, assuming the bond is held until its maturity date. More formally, the yield to maturity can be defined as the discount rate of return which makes the present value of the bond's cash flows equal to its selling price. Thus, Equation 5-4 can be used to solve for k, given the price of the bond and the estimated cash flows. Without the aid of a calculator, finding the exact yield to maturity can be a tedious, trial-and-error process. Let us demonstrate the procedure using the tables in the Appendixes.

Example

The Track Company has a 12-percent coupon, 10-year maturity bond outstanding. Interest is paid annually, and the bond is selling for $896. To find the yield to maturity on the bond, one must begin by realizing that the bond is selling at a discount from face value. Thus, the yield on the bond must be more than the coupon rate (12 percent). As shown in Table 5-10, at a 15-percent discount rate, the value of the bond is $849.28; since this is too low, one must try a lower discount rate. It is found that, at a 14-percent rate, the value of the bond is $895.92. Since this is very close to the selling price, it can be concluded that the yield to maturity is 14 percent.[8]

---

approximate yield to maturity

[8]Many bond investors calculate the bond's *approximate yield to maturity.* The equation for calculating approximate yield to maturity (YTM) is shown below:

$$\text{YTM} = \frac{(F_n - P_0)/n + I}{(F_n + P_0)/2} \qquad (5\text{-}10)$$

where YTM = approximate yield to maturity; F_n=face value of bond; P_0 = current price of bond; n = number of years remaining until maturity; I = dollar amount of annual interest income.

Given the information for the Track Company, we can estimate the approximate yield to maturity. Using Equation 5-10:

$$\text{YTM} = \frac{(1000 - 896)/10 + 120}{(1000 + 896)/2}$$

$$= 13.76\%$$

By comparison with the true yield to maturity of 14 percent, the approximate yield to maturity is close.

TABLE 5-10   Calculation of Bond Yield-To-Maturity: Track Company Bond

Bond: 12% coupon; 10-year maturity; interest paid annually; price: $896.

Try discount rate of 15%

Cash Flow	Amount	Received	$PVIFA_{15\%,10}$	$PVIF_{15\%,10}$	Present Value
Interest	$ 120	1-10	5.019		$ 602.28
Principal	$1000	10		.247	247.00
				Bond value:	$ 849.28

Since computed value is less than price of $896, try a lower yield.

Try discount rate of 14%

Cash Flow	Amount	Received	$PVIFA_{14\%,10}$	$PVIF_{14\%,10}$	Present Value
Interest	$ 120	1-10	5.216		$ 625.92
Principal	$1000	10		.270	270.00
				Bond value:	$ 895.92

Since computed value is approximately equal to bond price, bond yield to maturity is approximately 14 percent.

Yield to Call

Most corporate bonds are issued with a call provision, which means they can be *called in* and repaid before maturity. The corporation typically has to pay bondholders a penalty if the bonds are called before maturity. This penalty, known as the *call premium*, is usually set at one-year's interest; it declines with the length of time the bonds are outstanding.

call premium

Bonds are most likely to be called when interest rates drop significantly. The old bonds (plus any penalty) are repaid, or refunded, by selling new bonds with lower coupon rates. By refunding at lower coupon rates, the corporation can save substantial interest costs. However, note that the corporation's gain is the bondholders' loss. The bondholders will have to cash in the bond and reinvest the proceeds at lower interest rates which will then prevail. When there is a substantial risk of the corporation's calling in the bond, investors will want higher yields on the bonds, and the bond value will be lower because of it.

The yield to call is an estimate of the return on a bond investment if the bond is called in at its earliest call date. For example, if a bond was originally scheduled to mature in the year 2010, but was callable in 1995 or thereafter, the yield to call would be calculated on the assumption that the bond would be called in 1995.

yield to call

Bonds are usually vulnerable to call when their market prices are at a large premium[9] over face value, because this signifies that the bonds are paying relatively high interest and the corporation has an incentive to re-fund the old debt with new borrowings at lower rates. The yield to call

---

[9]Bonds are not so likely to be called when selling at big discounts.

should be considered especially when the market price of the bond is greater than par plus one year's interest.

Example

Yield-to-Call

Assume that the Banner Corporation has a 15 percent, 20-year bond outstanding. Interest rates have fallen, and the bond is selling for $1,152. According to the bond's terms, it can be called in five years. If called, the corporation must pay a call premium of one year's interest. The Banner bond's yield to call is 13 percent as shown in Table 5-11.[10]

 PREFERRED STOCK

Instead of bonds or common stock, corporations may sell shares of preferred stock. Although preferred stock is not a major source of financing for companies, it is considered at this point because it has features of both debt and equity.

The term *preferred* refers to the fact that the stockholders holding this kind of stock have priority over common stockholders in the payment of dividends. Although the preferred dividend is not a legal obligation as in the case of interest on bonds, companies would not ordinarily issue preferred stock unless they planned to make the dividend payments. One reason for this is that most preferred stock dividends are *cumulative*. This means that, if a scheduled dividend is not paid, it must be made up later before any common stock dividends can be paid.

cumulative

The amount of preferred dividends is usually fixed according to the specific terms of the issue. This fixed-income feature is similar to that of a bond. On the other hand, since, like common stock, preferred stock does not have a maturity date, dividends are the only cash received by owners

---

[10]The yield to call can be estimated with an alternative version of Equation 5-10 used to estimate the yield to maturity.

$$\text{YTC} = \frac{(F_n - P_0)/n + I}{(F_n + P_0)/2} \tag{5-11}$$

The equation is virtually identical with Equation 5-10 except that the number of years until maturity, n, is replaced by the number of years until call; and the maturity value, F_n, is replaced by the face value plus call premium. The bond's yield to call using Equation 5-11 is 13.00 percent.

$$\text{YTC} = \frac{(\$1,150 - 1,152)/5 + \$150}{(\$1,150 + 1,152)/2}$$

$$= 13.00\%$$

TABLE 5-11   Calculation of Bond Yield-To-Call: Banner Corporation

Bond: 15% coupon; five-year call; call premium $150; price: $1,152.
Try discount rate of 12%:

Cash Flow	Amount	Received	PVIFA$_{12\%, 5}$	PVIF$_{12\%, 5}$	Present Value
Interest	$ 150	1-5	3.605		$ 540.75
Principal	$1150	5		.567	652.05
				Bond value:	$1192.80

Since computed value of $1,192.80 is greater than price, try a higher yield.

Try discount rate of 13%:

Cash Flow	Amount	Received	PVIFA$_{13\%, 5}$	PVIF$_{13\%, 5}$	Present Value
Interest	$ 150	1-5	3.517		$ 527.55
Principal	$1150	5		.543	624.45
				Bond value:	$1152.00

Since computed value is equal to bond price, the bond's yield to call is 13 percent.

of preferred stock. Sometimes the dividend payment is specified by dollar amount, such as $2.60 per share; and sometimes it is specified as some percentage of par, or face value, such as "10 percent, $60 par," meaning that the annual dividend is 10 percent of the $60 face value, or $6.00.

Since preferred dividends are typically fixed in amount and are expected to continue indefinitely, their cash flow pattern represents a perpetuity. As shown in Chapter 4, the present value of a perpetuity may be easily calculated by dividing the annual cash flow by the required rate of return:[11]

$$P_0 = D/k \qquad (5\text{-}12)$$

where D represents the annual preferred dividend and k is the required return on this risk class of preferred stock.

---

[11]According to the valuation equation, the value of a share of preferred stock can be calculated as the present value of all future dividends into infinity since the preferred stock being discussed does not mature.

$$\text{Value} = \sum_{t=1}^{\infty} D_t/(1 + k)^t$$

However, since D_t is a constant, this is equivalent to:

$$\text{Value} = D \sum_{t=1}^{\infty} 1/(1 + k)^t$$

The term $\sum_{t=1}^{\infty} 1/(1 + k)^t$ is the sum of a geometric progression and is equivalent to $1/k$. Substituting we have:

$$\text{Value} = D(1/k) = D/k$$

Example

The Exec Company preferred stock pays a dividend of $6.00 per share annually. At a required rate of return of 14 percent Exec's preferred stock (using Equation 5-12) has a value of, approximately, $42.86 per share.

$$P_0 = D/k = \$6.00/.14 = \$42.86$$

Yield Changes and Preferred Stock Prices

Preferred stocks are more sensitive to interest rates than are bonds. The reason is that preferred stocks typically do not mature and hence are more vulnerable to the interest rate risk described earlier. For example, if yields on the Exec preferred stock should drop to 10 percent, the stock price would rise to $60 per share. An increase in yields from 14 percent to 18 percent would drop the stock's price to $33.33 per share.

Preferred Stock Yield

The rate of return on preferred stock is known as the *yield*. The yield is the discount rate of return which will make the present value of expected dividends equal to the current price of the stock. By a simple rearrangement of Equation 5-12, the preferred stock yield can be calculated as shown in Equation 5-13:

$$k = D/P_0 \qquad\qquad (5\text{-}13)$$

Example

The Laric Company preferred stock is selling for $50 per share and pays an annual dividend of $8. The yield on the preferred stock is 16 percent (i.e., $8/50 = .16$).

COMMON STOCK

Common stock shares represent ownership in a corporation. The stocks of large, publicly held companies are traded on the major stock exchanges, such as the New York Stock Exchange (NYSE) and the American Stock Exchange (ASE).

eighths of a point

Stock prices are quoted in multiples of eighths of a dollar (i.e., 12.5 cents). A *point* is a full dollar. Thus, if stock is "up a point," that means the stock price has risen by $1.00. Conversely, a share that is "down three-eighths" has dropped in price by 37.5 cents.

Stock Quotes

Stock quotes are reported for all NYSE and ASE companies in most daily newspapers. Let us examine Table 5-12, which presents a typical stock quote for the Tandy Corporation as it might be reported in the *Wall Street Journal*.

The first two columns indicate the highest and lowest closing prices in the last 52 weeks. The highest previous close was $49\frac{7}{8}$, and the lowest was $30\frac{1}{2}$. The next column indicates the name of the company that issued the stock, Tandy Corporation. The *Div.* column indicates the annualized dividend rate based on the most recent dividend paid. Thus, the dividend paid for Tandy is at a rate of 25 cents per share per year. The *Yld %* column refers to the *dividend yield* of the stock and is calculated by dividing the annual dividend (25 cents) by the closing stock price ($48.75). Tandy's dividend yield is .5 percent. Note the similarity in the calculation between the dividend yield on common stock and the current yield on bonds. The dividend yield represents part of the total return which an investor would realize during the next 12 months if the stock were purchased at its closing price. Like the current yield calculation on bonds, the dividend yield does not include any capital gains expected during the year.

dividend yield

The *price-to-earnings*, or *P/E, ratio* is calculated by dividing the closing stock price by the company's last four quarters earnings per share. The P/E ratio is a measure of how attractively the company's stock is viewed by investors. Tandy's P/E of 20 is relatively high, suggesting that the company's prospects are favorably viewed by investors. The next column, *Sales 100s* indicates how many Tandy shares changed hands during the day. The number "5393" is multiplied by 100. Thus, 539,300 shares of Tandy stock were traded.

P/E ratio

The last four columns relate to price activity during the day. The *high* and *low* columns indicate the highest and lowest prices at which Tandy stock traded. The *close* is the price at which the last trade took place. The *net change* indicates how the closing stock price compares with the previous day's closing price. For example, Tandy stock was up $\frac{5}{8}$ (62.5 cents).

Common Stock Valuation

As with any other investment, common stock values are equal to the present values of future cash flows discounted at the required rate of return. We are deferring the problem of estimating the required rate of

TABLE 5-12

52 Weeks		Stock	Div.	Yld %	P/E Ratio	Sales 100s	High	Low	Close	Net Chg
High	Low									
$49\frac{7}{8}$	$30\frac{1}{2}$	Tandy	.25	.5	20	5393	$48\frac{7}{8}$	48	$48\frac{3}{4}$	$+\frac{5}{8}$

return on common stock investment until Chapter 6. This chapter concentrates on estimating the future cash flows from common stock.

Estimating Common Stock Cash Flows

The benefit of ownership in a company is, primarily, a *pro-rata* share of the profits earned by the company. However, profits are not the same as cash flows. Some of the profits earned by the company must be reinvested to maintain the current level of sales and profits or to exploit new, profitable investment opportunities. Shareholders expect such reinvestment of profits to be reflected by a rise in stock price as the firm becomes more valuable.

An Important Distinction

It is important to distinguish the set of transactions *between* the corporation and its shareholders as a group from transactions *among* shareholders. Shareholders may buy and sell a company's stock among each other many times, but the company receives none of the proceeds from any except the first sale of the stock (in Chapter 3, this was called a primary transaction). The only cash ever received by investors from the corporation is in the form of dividends including, possibly, a liquidating dividend. Therefore, the only thing shareholders trade is the claim on future dividends to be paid by the corporation.

Of all the topics in valuation, this gives students the most difficulty. What is most important from a theoretical standpoint — dividends — seems least important from a student standpoint. In contrast, what is irrelevant from a theoretical standpoint, capital gains, seem the most important from a student standpoint. And there is always the problem of stocks that currently pay no dividends. Students wonder how such stocks can have any value from a theoretical (i.e., dividend) standpoint.

The problem arises from confusing the two sets of transactions: transactions *between* the corporation and shareholders as a group and transactions *among* shareholders. When this confusion afflicts many investors, serious investment errors can occur, such as the wild overvaluation of securities prior to the stock market collapse in 1929. Such errors occur when investors think only in terms of each other and not in terms of the corporation. To see this distinction more clearly, consider the following somewhat extreme example.

Example

The Banning of Dividends in Euphoria

Assume that a national law is passed in the land of Euphoria prohibiting the payment of dividends of any type (including *liquidating* dividends,

i.e., dividends paid from the proceeds of a liquidation of the company)
forever. Companies are allowed to operate, product profits, expand, and do everything they normally do except pay dividends. Proceeds from companies that are liquidated due to bankruptcy or other reasons are put in perpetual trusts for stockholders. Stockholders are still entitled to *pro-rata* ownership of the company and all its reinvested profits. But, they will never get them because dividends are forbidden.

The value of stock in Euphoria (aside from the psychic feeling of wealth) would have to be zero. The capital gains potential, regardless of how large and profitable the firm becomes, would also have to be zero because no other investor would pay for the stock. Nor would investors be able to borrow against such ownership, because the shares would have zero collateral value.

Now let us consider an amendment to the law, an amendment that stipulates corporations will be allowed to pay dividends once and only once 20 years later. All corporations announce that on that date they will liquidate and pay out to shareholders all earnings that have been accumulated during those 20 years. Now the shares would be worth something. But what? Investors would try to estimate how much cash dividends would be on that special day 20 years later. During the 20 years before "liquidation day," shareholders would actively buy and sell stock, realizing capital gains sometimes and capital losses other times. But all they would be exchanging would be the right to receive that one dividend 20 years later.

Stock prices would fluctuate whenever the estimates of that 20-year dividend changed. Indeed, there could be wild swings in the prices of certain stocks if exceptionally good or bad news were announced affecting estimates of the future dividend. The stock, with its 20-year liquidating dividend, would now resemble a 20-year zero-coupon bond. The only real difference would be the greater uncertainty about the face value or liquidating dividend 20 years later.

Thus, stocks that pay no dividends are like zero-coupon bonds. If someone were asked to buy a zero-coupon bond that never matured and, hence, never gave any cash, he or she would have to conclude it was worthless. When investors as a group forget that they are trading claims on future dividends, they lose sight of the true value of the stock certificates. Then prices can get far out of line with their underlying value.

An Algebraic Explanation of Stock Valuation

The relevance of dividends can be demonstrated more directly with a few algebraic relationships, but the point is the same as that made above. A stock's value is the present value of the dividends it will produce.

Suppose an investor wants to buy a share of stock and sell it one year later. The value of the stock would be the present value of dividends, if any, received plus the present value of selling price at the end of the year. This is shown algebraically in Equation 5-14.

$$P_0 = D_1/(1 + k) + P_1/(1 + k) \qquad (5\text{-}14)$$

Where, P_0 is the value of the stock; D_1 is the dividend to be received at the end of the year[12]; P_1 is the selling price at the end of the year; and, k is the required rate of return on the stock.

Before solving for the value of the stock, it is necessary to estimate the dividend and the selling price one year later. Companies follow different dividend policies, and we will discuss them in detail later. For present purposes, let us assume that the dividend, whatever it is, can be estimated one year in advance. The question is what the selling price, P_1, will be one year later. Assuming other investors also have one-year holding periods, the price at P_1 will be equal to the present value of expected dividend plus selling price at P_2.

$$P_1 = D_2/(1 + k) + P_2/(1 + k) \qquad (5\text{-}15)$$

Substituting P_1 in Equation 5-14, we have:

$$P_0 = D_1/(1 + k) + D_2/(1 + k)(1 + k) + P_2/(1 + k)(1 + k) \qquad (5\text{-}16)$$

And, simplifying, we have:

$$P_0 = D_1/(1 + k) + D_2/(1 + k)^2 + P_2/(1 + k)^2 \qquad (5\text{-}17)$$

If one continued expanding the prices in Equation 5-17 forever, the result would be

$$P_0 = \sum_{t=1}^{\infty} D_t/(1 + k)^t + P_\infty/(1 + k)^\infty \qquad (5\text{-}18)$$

The term, $P_\infty/(1 + k)^\infty$ will approach zero since the discount factor $1/(1 + k)^\infty$ approaches zero. This reduces Equation 5-18 to:

$$P_0 = \sum_{t=1}^{\infty} D_t/(1 + k)^t \qquad (5\text{-}19)$$

Where P_0 represents the value of the common stock; D_t is the cash dividend expected at time t; k represents the required rate of return on the stock, and Σ represents the summation of all the discounted future dividends to infinity.

A Brief Digression on *Infinity*

Referring to the present value of cash flows throughout infinity is done for theoretical precision. In practice, most of the present value for an

---

[12]Common stock dividends are typically paid quarterly. If so, Equation 5-19 should be on a quarterly basis. For convenience, however, assume that dividends are paid annually.

"infinite" investment is received within 50 years, more or less. To see this clearly, consider a perpetuity of $100 per year. Since it is a perpetuity, the $100 is received each year forever. At a discount rate of, say, 20 percent per year, the present value of this perpetuity is $500.

Now consider the present value of an annuity of $100 to be received for only 50 years. At a discount rate of 20 percent per year, it can be determined from Table 4 in the Appendix that the present value of the annuity would be $499.90 (i.e., $100 × 4.999). Thus, the present value of $100 per year forever is only 10 cents more than the present value of $100 per year for 50 years! At lower discount rates, the difference will be larger. For example, at a 10-percent discount rate, the value of the $100 perpetuity is $1,000 while the value of the 50-year annuity is $991.50. Thus, 99.15 percent of the perpetuity's value (i.e., $991.50/1,000) is accounted for in the first 50 years.

The Gordon Constant Growth Model

Professor Myron Gordon demonstrated that if dividends are assumed to grow at a constant rate into the foreseeable future, Equation 5-19 may be simplified to the form shown in Equation 5-20. This model is often referred to as the Gordon model.[13]

---

[13]The model is derived as follows:

a) $P_0 = \dfrac{D_1}{(1 + k)} + \dfrac{D_2}{(1 + k)^2} + \dfrac{D_3}{(1 + k)^3} + \ldots + \dfrac{D_n}{(1 + k)^n}$

Substitute $D_1 = D_0(1 + g)$; $D_2 = D_0(1 + g)^2$; $D_3 = D_0(1 + g)^3$

b) $P_0 = \dfrac{D_0(1 + g)}{(1 + k)} + \dfrac{D_0(1 + g)^2}{(1 + k)^2} + \dfrac{D_0(1 + g)^3}{(1 + k)^3} + \ldots + \dfrac{D_0(1 + g)^n}{(1 + k)^n}$

Cross-multiply by $\dfrac{(1 + k)}{(1 + g)}$

c) $P_0\left[\dfrac{1 + k}{1 + g}\right] = D_0 + \dfrac{D_0(1 + g)}{(1 + k)} + \dfrac{D_0(1 + g)^2}{(1 + k)^2} + \ldots + \dfrac{D_0(1 + g)^{n-1}}{(1 + k)^{n-1}}$

Subtract equation (b) from (c)

d) $P_0\left[\dfrac{1 + k}{1 + g}\right] - P_0 = D_0 - D_0\left[\dfrac{(1 + g)^n}{(1 + k)^n}\right]$

If $k > g$, as n becomes infinitely large $D_0(1 + g)^n/(1 + k)^n$ approaches zero.

e) $P_0\left[\dfrac{1 + k}{1 + g}\right] - P_0 = D_0$

Rearranging,

f) $P_0 = \dfrac{D_0(1 + g)}{k - g}$

$$P_0 = \frac{D_0(1 + g)}{k - g} \tag{5-20}$$

Where D_0 is the most recent annual dividend; k is the required rate of return on the stock; and g is the constant growth rate in dividends expected forever.[14]

Note that the forecast growth rate must be less than the discount rate for the model to be useful. Later in this chapter, we will see how this and other restrictive assumptions can be relaxed.

Example

Assume that the Artic corporation has just paid a cash dividend of $1 per share. The dividend is expected to grow at a rate of 6 percent per year forever. The required rate of return on the stock is 16 percent.

The intrinsic value of the stock using Equation 5-20 is $10.60 per share:

$$P_0 = D_0(1 + g)/(k - g)$$

$$= (\$1.00)(1.06)/(.16 - .06)$$

$$= \$10.60$$

Stocks With Zero Growth

A stock with a zero growth rate in cash dividends is a perpetuity, similar to the preferred stock we valued previously. Note that, if the growth rate, g, is zero, then Equation 5-20 becomes:

$$P_0 = \frac{D_0}{k} \tag{5-21}$$

Example

Assume that the Bach Corporation's dividend of $1.00 per share is not expected to increase or decrease during the life of the corporation. Investors require a return of 10 percent from the company's stock.

With this information, the company's stock is worth $10 per share.

$$P_0 = \frac{D_0}{k}$$

$$= \$1.00/.10$$

$$= \$10.00$$

---

[14]Dividend growth rates often are estimated by examining historical growth rates and then extrapolating into the future. For a review of how growth-rate estimates can be developed using the tables in the Appendix, see Chapter 4.

Stocks With Variable Growth

The Gordon model has to be modified when evaluating stocks whose dividends will grow at a variable rate before settling down to a constant, sustainable growth rate. For example, a company in a rapidly growing industry might have very rapid growth in earnings and dividends for a few years, then have slower, though above-average, growth in earnings and dividends for a few years, and finally settle into a longer-term sustainable growth rate for the foreseeable future.

The constant-growth model can be applied only to the last stage of such a pattern. However, the dividends of the first two stages also represent cash flows to shareholders and must be included for a complete estimate of stock value.

To value a stock with variable growth, first take the present value of dividends to be received during the nonconstant periods, then add the value of cash dividends during the constant-growth period. The constant growth dividends are valued by using the Gordon model at the beginning of the constant growth period. The value derived is then discounted back to time 0.

Example

The Ace Company recently paid a dividend of $1.00 per share. This dividend is expected to grow at a rate of 20 percent for five years (First Stage), then to grow at a rate of 10 percent for three years (Second Stage), and thereafter to grow at a rate of 5 percent indefinitely (Steady State). The projected dividends are shown in Table 5-13.

TABLE 5-13   Variable Growth Rates

	Year	Formula	Dividend
First Stage Growth = 20%/yr	1	$D_0(1 + g)$	($1.00)(1.20) = $1.20
	2	$D_1(1 + g)$	($1.20)(1.20) = $1.44
	3	$D_2(1 + g)$	($1.44)(1.20) = $1.73
	4	$D_3(1 + g)$	($1.73)(1.20) = $2.07
	5	$D_4(1 + g)$	($2.07)(1.20) = $2.49
Second Stage growth = 10%/yr.	6	$D_5(1 + g)$	($2.49)(1.10) = $2.74
	7	$D_6(1 + g)$	($2.74)(1.10) = $3.01
	8	$D_7(1 + g)$	($3.01)(1.10) = $3.31
Steady State years 9-∞	9	$D_8(1 + g)$	($3.31)(1.05) = $3.48
	.	.	. . .
	.		. . .
	.	.	
	∞	.	. . .

First Stage. The dividends in each of the first five years are estimated by simply increasing the previous year's by 20 percent, the assumed growth rate in the first period. For example, the year-one dividend is forecast to be 20 percent higher than the previous dividend of $1.00. The year-two dividend, $1.44, is 20 percent higher than the year-one dividend, and so on.

Second Stage. The dividend in year six is only 10 percent higher than the dividend in year five, due to the slowdown in growth. The year-seven dividend is 10 percent greater than the year-six dividend, and the year-eight dividend is 10 percent greater than the year-seven dividend.

Steady-State Stage. Finally, the year-nine dividend increases at only 5 percent, reflecting the decline to the company's long-term, sustainable, growth rate. Since we can now apply the Gordon model to value all dividends from year 9 onward, it is not necessary to calculate these individually.

Each of the dividends must now be discounted at the required rate of return, estimated to be 10 percent in this case (see Table 5-14). The dividends to be received in years one to eight are simply discounted and added up. The present value of dividends for years nine and thereafter is calculated by using the constant-growth valuation model. However, this value is calculated as of year eight. To find the present value at time 0, we must further discount the year-eight value. The value of the stock is $43.64.

TABLE 5-14   Dividend Discount Model Variable Growth

Year	Forecast Dividend	PVIF$_{10\%}$	Present Value
1	$1.20	.909	$1.09
2	1.44	.826	1.19
3	1.73	.751	1.30
4	2.07	.683	1.41
5	2.49	.621	1.55
6	2.74	.564	1.55
7	3.01	.513	1.54
8	3.31	.467	1.55

Value of stock at end of year 8:

$$P_8 = \frac{D_8(1 + g)}{k - g} = \frac{(\$3.31)\,(1.05)}{.10 - .05} = \$69.51$$

Present value of stock at time 0:

$$(\$69.51)\,(.467) = \underline{\underline{32.46}}$$

$$P_0 = \$43.64$$

Stocks That Do Not Currently Pay Dividends

While the dividend valuation model may appear to be irrelevant in the valuation of stocks which currently pay no dividends, such stocks can be viewed as a version of the variable-growth case. Instead, dividends are zero until the company begins paying dividends in the future. The point to keep in mind is that dividends are the only cash flows paid to common stock-holders. A share of stock represents the right to receive dividends when they are ultimately paid.

Common Stock Yields

Financial managers need to know what rate of return investors require from the company. In large, widely-held companies, it is impossible to ask shareholders directly. Chapter 6 explores several other ways this can be done; but as one alternative, financial managers sometimes examine the price at which their common stock is trading to gain insights into the yields, or rates of return, required by shareholders. The method employed is similar to that used in determining preferred stock and bond yields: the common stock yield is the rate of return which makes the present value of expected cash flows equal to the actual stock price. This relationship is most apparent in the Gordon version of the dividend discount model. By re-arranging Equation 5-20, one can solve for k, the required rate of return implied by the company's stock price. This is shown in Equation 5-22.

$$P_0 = D_0(1 + g)/k - g$$

$$\text{Since} \quad D_0(1 + g) = D_1$$

$$\text{then} \quad P_0 = D_1/(k - g)$$

$$\text{and} \quad k = \frac{D_1}{P_0} + g \qquad (5\text{-}22)$$

Equation 5-22 states that the required rate of return on a company's stock is equal to the dividend yield plus the expected constant growth rate in dividends per share.[15]

---

[15]This chapter does not show it, but through trial and error, k can also be estimated from the variable-growth model as well.

SUMMARY

This chapter has extended the present value idea to the valuation of specific types of investments: financial securities. This was intended to stress the generality of the valuation model and to key in on its main variables: cash flow estimates and discount rates. The cash flow estimates for bonds and preferred stocks are readily determined since these are specified in the terms of the security issue. This is not the case with common stocks because the cash flows from stock are not specified in advance. For this reason, the dividend valuation model is often employed to value common stocks on the assumption that dividends will grow at a constant rate. The dividend valuation model can be adapted to deal with companies exhibiting supernormal growth rates, zero-growth rates, and companies that pay no dividends.

MULTIPLE CHOICE QUESTIONS

1. A bond's yield to maturity is the same as its coupon rate when:
   a) The bond is not callable
   b) The bond is a zero-coupon bond
   c) The bond's price equals its face value
   d) There is no risk of default

2. The price of preferred stock can be estimated by dividing its specified dividend by:
   a) The estimated dividend growth rate
   b) The stock's P/E multiple
   c) The stock's par value
   d) Its dividend yield

3. A stock's value reflects both the present level of dividends as well as:
   a) Earnings per share
   b) Previous dividends
   c) Its par value
   d) Expected future dividends

4. A call premium means that the borrower must:
   a) Pay a penalty to prepay the borrowing
   b) Be ready to repay bonds if called
   c) Permit bonds to be cashed in at any time
   d) Call the bonds or pay a penalty

5. The cumulative feature of preferred stock means that:
   a) Preferred stock dividends are automatically reinvested in the company
   b) Preferred stock dividends not paid in one period must be made up in subsequent periods
   c) New preferred stock is entitled to all dividends previously paid on outstanding preferred stock
   d) No preferred stock dividends can be paid until all outstanding debt is repaid

6. Using the Gordon model of stock valuation, the yield on common stock is equal to:
   a) The current yield plus the term to maturity
   b) The dividend yield plus par value
   c) The stock's P/E multiple
   d) The dividend yield plus expected growth in dividends

7. The Gordon model of stock valuation:
   a) Cannot be used if the company does not pay dividends
   b) Can be used only if the expected growth rate in dividends is greater than the required rate of return
   c) Cannot be used if the company's growth rate in dividends is zero
   d) Can only be used with stocks exhibiting variable dividend growth rates

8. When a bond sells at a premium:
   a) The coupon rate must be greater than the yield to maturity
   b) The coupon rate must be less than the yield to maturity
   c) The coupon rate must be equal to the yield to maturity
   d) Investors are willing to pay more for a bond than it is worth

9. Reinvestment rate risk can be avoided by investing in:
   a) British Consols
   b) Zero-coupon bonds
   c) Preferred stock
   d) Coupon paying bonds

10. When a bond is selling at a discount, the current yield will:
    a) Underestimate its yield to maturity
    b) Overstate its yield to maturity
    c) Equal its yield to maturity
    d) Equal its coupon rate

DISCUSSION QUESTIONS

1. What are the determinants of investment value, according to the valuation equation?

2. Identify and discuss the main steps in the valuation process.

3. Why is investment valuation of critical importance to financial managers?

4. Explain and compare interest rate risk and reinvestment rate risk.

5. What is a *Consol?* In what way is it similar to preferred stock?

6. Describe the process by which an increase in interest rates always produces a decline in bond prices.

7. In what ways is preferred stock like a bond? In what ways does it resemble common stock?

8. What is the rationale for the dividend discount model?

9. What are the principal assumptions of the Gordon model?

10. How must the dividend discount model be adjusted in valuing stocks with supernormal growth rates in dividends? Stocks with zero dividend growth? Stocks that currently pay no dividends?

SOLVED PROBLEMS

bond valuation

SP-1. Exeter Company's bonds will mature in 20 years. The bonds have a face value of $1,000 and carry a coupon rate of 10 percent. Assume interest payments are made semiannually.

    a) Identify the cash flows provided by the bonds. Indicate the amount and timing of each cash flow.

    b) Determine the present value of the bonds' cash flows assuming a required rate of return of 12 percent.

preferred stock valuation

SP-2. The Exec Company's preferred stock pays a dividend of $3.00 per share annually. Assuming a required rate of return of 14 percent, calculate the value of Exec's preferred stock.

common stock valuation

SP-3. The Best Company earned $2.00 per share and paid a dividend of $1.00 per share in the year just ended. Earnings and dividends per share are expected to increase indefinitely at a rate of 8 percent per year. What is the value of the stock assuming a return of 12 percent is required?

common stock-variable growth

SP-4. Ace paid a common stock dividend of $1.00 per share in the year just ended. This dividend is expected to increase by 20 percent per year for the next three years, after which it will grow at a constant rate of 8 percent indefinitely. Assuming a required rate of return of 15 percent, calculate the value of the stock.

PROBLEMS

1. Wickam Company's bonds will mature in 10 years. The bonds have a face value of $1,000 and carry a coupon rate of 15 percent. Assume interest payments are made semiannually. *bond valuation*

   a) Identify the cash flows provided by the bonds. Indicate the amount and timing of each cash flow.
   b) Determine the present value of the bond's cash flows assuming a required rate of return of 12 percent.

2. The Artic Company's preferred stock pays a dividend of $4.50 per share annually. Assuming a required rate of return of 16 percent, calculate the value of Artic's preferred stock. *preferred stock valuation*

3. The Banby Company earned $1.60 per share and paid a dividend of $0.20 per share in the year just ended. Earnings and dividends per share are expected to increase indefinitely at a rate of 5 percent per year. What is the value of the stock, assuming a return of 9 percent is required? *common stock valuation*

4. MiltCo. paid a common stock dividend of $1.50 per share in the year just ended. This dividend is expected to increase by 18 percent per year for the next four years, after which it will grow at a constant rate of 6 percent indefinitely. Assuming a required rate of return of 12 percent, calculate the value of the stock. *common stock valuation-variable growth*

5. Acme bonds have the following characteristics. Face value is $1,000, coupon rate is 8 percent and term to maturity is 10 years. The required rate of return on the bonds is 14 percent. Calculate the bonds' value assuming semiannual interest payments. *bond valuation*

6. The Jem Company issued 20-year bonds on January 1, 1988. The bonds were sold at par ($1,000), with a 12-percent coupon. Interest is paid semiannually (on June 30 and December 31). *bond yields*

   a) What was the yield to maturity of the bonds on January 1, 1988?
   b) What will be the price of the bonds on January 1, 1993—five years later—assuming that the bonds are selling to yield 10 percent? Assume semiannual compounding.
   c) Assume that the bond may be called on January 1, 1991 at a premium of one year's interest. Use the approximation method to calculate the yield to call at the time of issue (i.e., January 1, 1988). Assume annual compounding. (Note: use Equation 5-11 in footnote 10.)
   d) Use the approximate-yield-to-maturity formula to estimate the yield to maturity on the bond as of January 1, 1993 if the bond is selling for $900. Assume annual interest payments. (Note: use Equation 5-10 in footnote 8.)

7. The Magic Company bond has the following characteristics. Face value is $1,000, coupon rate is 8 percent, and term to maturity is 10 years. The required rate of return on the bond is 12 percent.

   a) Calculate the bond's value assuming annual interest payments.
   b) Calculate the bond's value assuming semiannual interest payments.

8. A British Consol has a coupon rate of 5 percent and a face value of $1,000. What is its value, given a required rate of return of 10 percent?

9. The Bish Corporation has decided to issue $1 million worth of 20-year bonds in order to finance an expansion. The current rate of return on bonds similar to Bish's is 14 percent. What coupon rate must the new bonds carry in order for the bonds to be sold at par?

10. Assume that the Chuzit Company issues 10-year bonds with a coupon rate of 12 percent when investors want a yield of 14 percent. What must the total face value of bonds issued be in order to raise $1 million in cash? (Ignore costs associated with issuing the bonds.) Assume annual compounding.

11. Drexel bonds have a maturity of 10 years, a coupon rate of 12 percent and a face value of $1,000.

    a) Under what conditions will the bonds sell at par? Discount? Premium?
    b) Assume that the required rate of return on the bonds is 10 percent and that actual price of the bond is $1,200. Is the bond overpriced? Underpriced? If so, by how much? (Assume annual compounding.)

12. The Finkel Company's preferred stock has a par value of $50 and pays a 10-percent dividend. What is the value of the preferred stock, assuming investors require a return of 15 percent on the stock?

13. The Grip Company's preferred stock pays a dividend of $10 annually. The stock is selling for $50 a share. You require a 20-percent rate of return on the stock. Would you conclude the stock is overpriced? Underpriced? Accurately priced? Why?

14. The Newix Company's common stock is expected to pay a dividend of $1.00 next year. The dividend is expected to grow at a rate of 5 percent per year indefinitely. If investors require a rate of return of 15 percent on the stock, calculate the stock's value.

15. Assume that you are analyzing the common stock of the Grid Company. You expect the stock to pay a dividend of $1.00 per share next year and that the dividend will increase at a rate of 6 percent per year indefinitely. You think that the stock should provide a return of 16 percent.

    a) Calculate the value of the stock according to your estimate.
    b) If the stock is actually selling for $12 a share, what is the actual yield on the stock?

16. The Paultz Company is expected to pay a dividend of $1.28 per share   *common stock valuation*
in 1988. Dividends it has paid for the last five years are shown below:

Year	Dividend Per Share
1983	1.00
1984	1.05
1985	1.10
1986	1.20
1987	1.22

a) Estimate the stock's past growth rate in dividends per share.
b) Estimate the value of the stock if the dividend growth rate is expected to stay constant and the required return on the stock is
12 percent.

17. The Quark Company is expected to pay a dividend of $1.50 per share   *common stock valuation — variable growth*
next year. You expect the dividend to increase at a rate of 20 percent for
the following four years; then 10 percent for the next five years; and
then stabilize at a growth rate of 5 percent per year indefinitely. If the
required rate of return is 15 percent, calculate the value of the stock.

SOLUTIONS TO SOLVED PROBLEMS

SP-1. a) Since the bond will pay interest of $50 each six months until it
matures in 20 years, the interest payments are a 40-period annuity. At maturity, Exeter will also pay the bondholder the face
value of the bond, $1,000. An easy way to identify and list the
bond's returns is shown in the following table

Type of Return	Amount	Period Received
Interest	$ 50	1-40
Face value	$1000	40

b) The table in part (a) can be expanded to show the calculations
involved in determining the bond's value.

Type of Return	Amount	Period	Present Value Factor	Present Value
Interest	$ 50	1-40	15.046	$752.30
Face value	$1000	40	.097	97.00
			Total	$849.30

Step 1: Calculate the present value of the interest payments. The interest payments are an annuity lasting 40 (semiannual) periods at a semiannual required rate of return of 6 percent (i.e., half the annual rate). From Appendix Table 4, it is found that the Present Value Interest Factor of an Annuity (PVIFA) for a 6-percent 40-period annuity is 15.046. Thus the present value of the interest payments is:

$$\$50 \times 15.046 = \$752.30$$

Step 2: Calculate the present value of the principal or face value amount. Remember that the semiannual rate (6 percent) and 40 semiannual periods are used even though the face value is received in 20 years.

$$\$1000 \times .097 = \$97.00$$

Step 3: Add the present values:

The value of the bond = $\$752.30 + 97.00$

$$= \$849.30$$

SP-2.
$$P = \text{Dividend}/k$$

$$= \$3.00/.14$$

$$= \$21.43$$

SP-3. The value of the stock can be calculated using the Gordon model. Since the company's dividend is increasing at a rate of 8 percent per year, next year's dividend will be 8 percent higher than last year's.

$$D_1 = D_0(1 + g) = D_0(1.08)$$

$$= \$1.08$$

The required rate of return, k, is given as 12 percent and the constant dividend growth rate, g, equal to 8 percent is also given. The value of the stock is $27 per share.

$$P_0 = D_1/(k - g)$$

$$= \$1.08/(.12 - .08) = \$27$$

SP-4.

Year	Dividend*	Discount Factor @ 15%	PV @ 15%
1	$1.20	.870	$ 1.04
2	1.44	.756	1.09
3	1.73	.658	1.14
3	$26.71	.658	17.58
		Total:	$20.85

*Increase by 20 percent years one to three and at 8 percent in year four and thereafter.
**$P_3 = 1.73(1.08)/[.15 - .08] = 1.87/.07 = \$26.71$

The total value of the stock is the present value of dividends during the non-steady-state period plus the present value of dividends during the steady-state period. The value of the steady-state dividends as of the end of year 3 can be estimated with the Gordon model.

$$P_3 = \frac{D_3(1 + g)}{k\text{-}g} = \frac{1.73(1.08)}{.15 - .08}$$

The steady-state value must now be discounted back to time 0. The present value (at time 0) of the steady-state dividends is:

Present value of steady-state dividends = \$26.71 (.658) = 17.58

This present value is added to the present values of dividends for years 1 to 3 to produce the total value of the stock (\$20.85).

REFERENCES

Basu, Sanjoy. "The Information Content of Price-Earnings Ratios." *Financial Management,* Summer 1975, pp. 53–64.

Gordon, Myron J., and L. I. Gould. "The Cost of Equity Capital: A Reconsideration." *Journal of Finance,* June 1978, pp. 849–861.

Gordon, Myron J., and Eli Shapiro, "Capital Equipment Analysis: The Required Rate of Profit." *Management Science.* October 1956, pp. 102–110.

Williams, John B. The Theory of Investment Value. Cambridge, MA: Harvard University Press, 1938.

CASE EXERCISE

Wilbur Grey

Wilbur Grey had an interesting problem in early 1988. He was trying to determine the value of common stock shares for the WBG Company in 1929. His problem was difficult because the stock in question had never been traded and was still closely held. In addition, virtually no financial information was available prior to 1958, the year a fire burned the company's headquarters to the ground.

The stock was owned by Wilbur's grandmother, Elma Grey. Elma had recently sold it for $10,000 per share and asked Wilbur to help her figure out the amount of taxes she would have to pay on the sale. Since she would have to pay taxes on the difference between the fair market value of the stock at the beginning of 1929 when she had received the stock as a gift and the selling price of $10,000, Wilbur wanted to justify as high a fair market value as possible.

Through discussions with older relatives and his grandmother, Wilbur gradually assembled some key information. The company was founded in 1909 by three physicians, White, Black, and Grey, to sell medical supplies. Each of the founders donated cash and property equal to $10 per share. Drs. Black and White each received 450 of the 1000 original shares and Dr. Grey received 100. As the years passed, the shares were passed from generation to generation through gifts and estates. They were never sold, and the number of shares never changed. In early 1929, Elma Grey received 60 shares from her father's estate and her brother, Jeb, received the other 40. At that time, the book value of the stock was $164 per share.

The founders had had no desire to withdraw dividends from the company, but among later generations the firm's policy of not paying dividends became an intense issue. The Black family wanted the company to pay dividends, while the White family was firmly opposed. Since both families had equal ownership, Elma and Jeb Grey, with 10 percent of the shares always cast the crucial vote, which was against payment of dividends. In 1975, however, Jeb Grey encountered financial difficulties. While he refused to sell the 40 shares he had, Jeb was able to convince Elma to vote with the Black family in favor of very large dividends (See Exhibit C-1). The White family thought the dividend payments were ruinous and tried, unsuccessfully, to purchase the Grey shares. In early 1988, Elma, following Jeb's death, decided to sell her shares in the company. The best offer she received from the Black family was $9,000 per share, and she accepted the White offer of $10,000 per share.

In establishing a value for the stock as of 1929, Wilbur's first intent was to apply the dividend discount model, since he knew this model was theoretically well supported and might be easier to defend in the event the IRS were to challenge his estimate of fair market value. His plan was to discount the dividends paid per share and the selling price all the way back to 1929. However, when he raised this idea with his grandmother, she

Year	Dividend Per Share
1975	$400.00
1976	$448.00
1977	$474.88
1978	$503.37
1979	$533.58
1980	$565.59
1981	$599.53
1982	$635.50
1983	$673.63
1984	$714.04
1985	$756.89
1986	$802.30
1987	$850.00

EXHIBIT C-1
WBG Company
Dividend History

chuckled. "Until 1975," she noted, "there were no dividends and no prospect of any. I only voted for them because old Jeb wouldn't sell. No, the value of that stock in 1929 had nothing to do with dividends," she concluded.

In dealing with the valuation problem, several things bothered Wilbur. First, his grandmother was probably right that, in 1929, dividends were not very important to the owners. "In any case," he thought, "the dividend discount model hadn't even been invented!" Second, while he did know the exact amount of dividends paid, could he assume that these were the dividends that would have been expected as of 1929? Third, what discount rate should he use? Considering the number of years that had passed, he thought that the discount rate used could be the most important number in the model. Fourth, he thought the IRS would argue that the fair market value in 1929 was equal to its book value ($164 per share). But he thought this ignored the value of any possible future growth potential of the company. Fifth, even if he could apply the dividend discount model, he thought the IRS would claim that the current price of $10,000 per share was affected by struggle for control over the small company, with the result that the current price and, by extension, the discounted value would be fair market value.

Case Questions

1. Evaluate the arguments for and against using the dividend discount model to value the WBG stock in 1929. Evaluate the arguments for and

161

against using a book value approach. Which would you recommend to the Tax Court if you were called to testify as an expert witness?

2. Assuming the dividend discount model is used, how would you attempt to estimate an appropriate discount rate?

3. Determine the value of the stock as of the beginning of 1929 given the dividends paid, the selling price of the stock, and the following discount rate assumptions:

   a) 6 percent
   b) 8 percent
   c) 10 percent

   How sensitive is the estimated value of the stock to the discount rate?

CHAPTER 6

RISK AND THE RATE OF RETURN

**W**e saw, in Chapter 5, that an investment's value is jointly determined by its future cash flows and the rate of return it must offer investors. However, an investment's cash flows are, in practice, subject to uncertainty. This uncertainty is commonly referred to as *risk*. Most investors are *risk averse*, which means they take such risk into account by requiring higher rates of return. In particular, the greater an investment's risk level the higher its *risk adjusted* rate of return must be. Since virtually all business investments involve an element of risk, an understanding of the risk-return relationship is of great importance to the firm's management.

The idea that an investment's required rate of return should be adjusted to reflect its risk level is certainly not a recent discovery. Indeed, for centuries, investors who have failed to grasp this notion have gone broke. Nonetheless, until the 1960s there was no practical method for quantifying an investment's risk level or, more importantly, determining how much the rate of return should be adjusted to reflect an investment's risk. While many important issues of implementation need to be resolved, this risk-return model, known as the Capital Asset Pricing Model (CAPM) has found such wide applicability that it is now of central importance in the study of finance. The CAPM was invented to explain the risk-return relationship among common stock investments, and it has had its greatest success in that application. However, subsequent chapters will show that the CAPM can also provide many important insights into investment, operating, and financing decisions made by the firm's managers.

● Objectives and Organization of this Chapter

This chapter has two principal objectives. First, it will carefully examine the nature of investment risk. Since all business investments have at least some risk, the finance manager needs to evaluate risk properly and find ways effectively to incorporate such evaluations in the firm's investment decisions. Moreover, while operating and financing decisions differ from investment decisions, they too may affect the overall risk and return profile of the firm and influence its stock price. Thus, an understanding of risk provides useful insights into the risk and return consequences of operating and financing decisions.

The second principal objective of this chapter is to illustrate the systematic relationship between an investment's risk and the rate of return it should provide investors. This risk-adjusted rate of return can then be used to value investments that differ ir. risk levels. Thus, we will be able to apply the valuation methods of Chapter 5 much more generally. In that chapter, recall that required rates of return were simply assumed in determining investment value. Chapter 6 will illustrate how such rates of return vary according to risk differences.

The first section of the chapter considers the concept of the rate of return. It shows what the rate of return means and how it is estimated when it is unknown. The second section addresses the meaning and measurement of investment risk. This requires a brief review of statistical probability. With probability ideas as background it becomes possible to develop estimates of investment returns and risks. The third section examines the nature of risk. It shows that risk determinants are many but that they can be classified into three principal groups: company risks, industry risks, and market risks. This classification helps explain the important idea of portfolio risk in section four. Section four shows that, when many diverse investments are combined in a portfolio, company and industry risks are eliminated and the only remaining investment risk is market risk. Section five presents the Capital Asset Pricing Model. This model relates an investment's market risk to the rate of return the investment should provide investors. Section six illustrates how the risk-return relationship changes over time and what these changes imply for stock prices. Section seven examines the idea of market equilibrium and shows how stock prices change to produce the returns required given their relative risk levels. Finally, section eight addresses the relevance of the CAPM to management decision making and discusses problems of implementation.

 ## THE RATE OF RETURN

Few ideas in finance turn up with so many different names as the *rate of return*. For example, in Chapter 4, we referred to the interest rate (of return) when discussing savings accounts and the discount rate (of return) when discussing the present value of future cash flows. In Chapter 5, we referred to bond and stock *yields* in discussing the returns such investments provide investors. Yet, all of these terms really refer to the same thing — the rate of return produced by the investment. This chapter introduces even more synonyms for the rate of return. The broad variety of synonyms is due, in large part, to the historical development of financial practices in which specialized areas of finance have adopted their own names for the same idea. Although it would seem simpler to have one name for the rate of return, this would obscure many subtle and important nuances and practices.

What is the Rate of Return?

The rate of return is a percentage indicating how much an investor's wealth increases per dollar of investment made. The increase in wealth is equal to the sum of any cash received plus any change in the value of the investment.

Using this definition, the rate of return can be expressed algebraically as:

$$R = ([P_1 - P_0] + CF_1)/P_0 \qquad (6\text{-}1)$$

Where R is the rate of return, P_0 is the beginning investment value; P_1 is the value one period later; $[P_1 - P_0]$ is the change in investment value; and CF_1 is the cash flow to be received at the end of the period. When applied to stocks, CF_1 usually means any cash dividends received.

Example

Assume that an investor purchases a share of the Wide Company's common stock for $100. The investor expects to receive a cash dividend of $1.00 at the end of one year and expects the stock price to be $112 at the end of the year. In this case the investor's expected rate of return is 13 percent.

$$R = ([P_1 - P_0] + CF_1)/P_0$$
$$= ([\$112 - \$100] + \$1)/\$100 = \$13/\$100 = .13, \quad \text{or} \quad 13\%$$

RISK

We know from Chapter 5 that an investment's cash flows are received in the future. In general, this introduces an element of uncertainty or risk in the investment. That is why we refer to an investment's *expected* rate of return. For example, the 13 percent expected rate of return on the Wide stock calculated above is based on the expectation of a cash dividend of $1 and a stock price of $112 at the end of a year. However, if the forecast turns out to be wrong, the actual rate of return could be much more or much less than the 13 percent the investor expected at the time the investment was made.

expected rate of return

Many factors could affect the forecast returns from the Wide stock. For example, in Chapter 3 we examined the impact of business cycles on a company's profits and stock price. Let us now examine the impact of the economic environment on the future returns from the Wide Company stock investment. It will be assumed that the dividend of $1.00 will be paid regardless of the economic environment but that the company's stock price may vary.

Assume, for example, that, if the overall economy experiences a recession during the coming year, Wide's profits will be lower than expected and the company's stock price will drop to $90. Alternatively, if the economy expands rapidly, Wide's profits will be higher than anticipated, and its stock price will rise to $134 per share. Finally, assume that, if the normal economic conditions prevail, Wide's profits will increase as expected and the stock price will rise to $112 per share. Table 6-1 summarizes these three possible outcomes for 1988 and the resulting rates of return that would be earned by investors in the Wide stock.

Probability Distributions, Risk and Return

The three possible price and return forecasts for Wide may not be equally likely. For example, there may be only a slight chance that the economy will experience a recession or expansion during the year. This is important information to an investor. To understand this point more clearly, consider the following analogy to a weather report. It is of interest to know that it might rain, but it is important to know whether the probability of rain is, say, 10 percent or 90 percent. Likewise, an investor needs to incorporate the probability of a particular return when more than one return is possible.

Accordingly, Table 6-2 indicates a probability associated with each possible economic environment along with the resulting return for Wide stock during 1988.

TABLE 6-1 Wide Stock Prices and Rates of Return for 1988

Economic Condition	Stock Price	Rate of Return
Recession	$ 90	$([90 - 100] + 1)/100 = -9\%$
Normal	$112	$([112 - 100] + 1)/100 = 13\%$
Expansion	$134	$([134 - 100] + 1)/100 = 35\%$

TABLE 6-2 Wide Common Stock Rate of Return Forecasts and Probabilities

(1) Economic Environment	(2) Probability	(3) Forecast Return on Wide Stock
Recession	.20	-9%
Normal	.60	13%
Expansion	.20	35%
Total	1.00	

Note that the probabilities must add up to 1.00, meaning that it is certain that one of the three outcomes will occur. Also note that only the three returns are considered. In other words, according to Table 6-2, a return of, say, 10 percent is not possible (i.e., has a zero probability of occurring). This is obviously unrealistic, and we will relax this assumption later.

The set of possible returns and their associated probabilities can be described graphically as shown in Exhibit 6-1.

The horizontal axis shows the range of possible returns, and the vertical axis shows the probability of each return. The height of each bar indicates the probability of that return being realized. Again, note that any other return, except for the three indicated, has a zero probability of occurring.

The Expected Rate of Return

There are now three possible forecast returns for Wide in 1988. Which is the "right" one? The best estimate of the "true" rate of return should incorporate information about the possible returns and their probabilities. This is known as the *expected* rate of return.

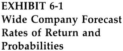

expected rate of return

The expected rate of return is a weighted average of the possible rates of return. Each possible return is weighted by the probability of that return

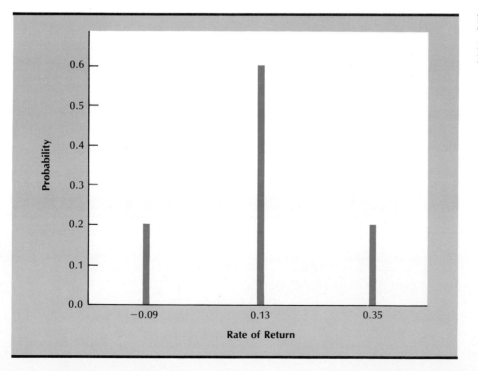

EXHIBIT 6-1
Wide Company Forecast Rates of Return and Probabilities

occurring. Algebraically, this is shown as:

$$\hat{R} = \sum_{i=1}^{n} p_i R_i \qquad (6\text{-}2)$$

Where $\hat{R}$ is the expected rate of return on the stock, the hat ˆ indicates that it is an estimate; "$\sum_{i=1}^{n}$" is the summation of each forecast return, R_i times its probability, "p_i" for all possible returns, 1 through n.

Table 6-3 shows how the expected return is calculated for the Wide stock. Column (1) indicates the possible economic environment; column (2) is the associated probability of each environment. Column (3) is the forecast rate of return given that environment; and column (4) is the product of column (2) times column (3). The sum of column (4) is the probability weighted average (expected value) rate of return.

Continuous Probability Distributions

So far we have considered only one risk factor, the business cycle, with three possible economic environments, prices, and returns for the Wide stock. In reality, of course, many other economic environments are possible. For example, there may be moderate or deep recessions, mild or rapid expansions, or anything in between. Likewise, in a severe recession Wide's stock price might actually drop below $90, producing a return much lower than expected. Or, in a very rapid expansion, it might rise above $134, producing a return much higher than expected. Or it might fall anywhere in between. If one could specify every possible return and its associated probability, the distribution would resemble a curved or continuous figure such as the one shown in Exhibit 6-2.

Exhibit 6-2 has the familiar "bell" shape of the Normal distribution, the most common continuous probability distribution. Note that the horizontal axis indicates the possible returns that Wide stock may produce in 1988 and the vertical axis shows the probability of each return. Note also that returns greater than expected seem as likely as returns less than expected.

Unlike Exhibit 6-1, the continuous distribution in Exhibit 6-2 shows that a 10 percent rate of return, for example, does have some probability of

TABLE 6-3 Wide Common Stock Expected Rate of Return in 1988			
(1)	(2)	(3)	(4) = (2) × (3)
Economic Environment	Probability	Forecast Return on Wide Stock	Weighted Return
Recession	.20	−9%	−1.8%
Normal	.60	13%	7.8%
Expansion	.20	35%	7.0%
Total	1.00	Expected rate of return:	13.0%

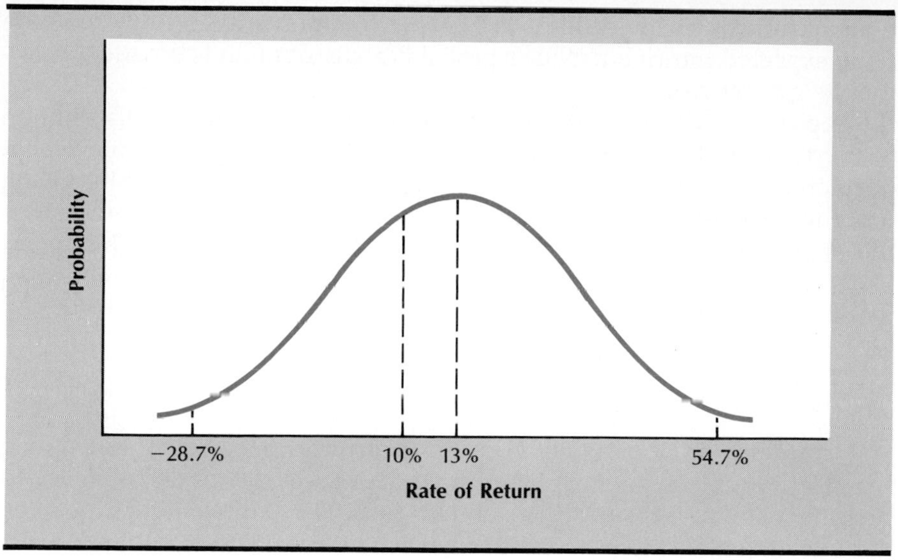

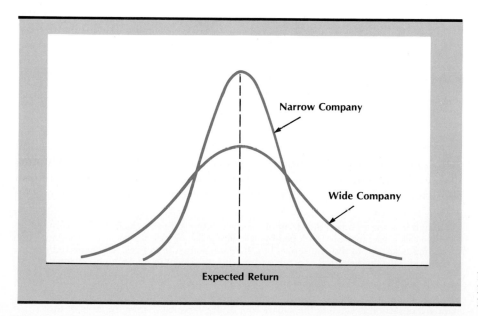

EXHIBIT 6-2
Wide Company,
Continuous Probability
Distribution

occurring. In summary, while the expected return for Wide stock in 1988 is still 13 percent, the stock may produce a broad range of possible returns. However, the farther the possible return is from the expected return, the lower its probability. For example, the probability of a return less than −28.7 percent or more than +54.7 percent is very low.

In general, the broader the probability distribution of returns the greater the total risk an investment has. Exhibit 6-3 shows the probability distribu-

EXHIBIT 6-3
Probability Distribution
Reflects Risk

tions of returns for the Wide and Narrow common stocks. Both have the same expected return but Wide's probability distribution is broader, reflecting its greater risk.

A picture such as that in Exhibit 6-3 shows clearly how the distribution of the Wide and Narrow returns compare. However, it is not practical to develop graphic comparisons for investments as is done in Exhibit 6-3 in order to evaluate their relative risks. A much more convenient measure is the standard deviation, or dispersion, of expected returns. This quantitative measure can yield many useful insights into the nature and behavior of investment risk.

Standard Deviation (σ)

The standard deviation of expected returns is a measure of how broad the distribution of possible returns is. The greek letter for *s, sigma,* is typically used to represent the standard deviation. For example, the standard deviation for stock *x* might be written as σ_x, which would be read as "sigma x." For any given expected return, the larger the standard deviation (or average amount of deviation from that return), the broader the distribution of returns. Hence, the greater the total risk an investment has.

Table 6-4 shows how the expected return and standard deviation of returns are calculated for the Wide stock.

First calculate the expected return by multiplying each forecast return (Column 1) by its probability of occurrence (Column 2) and summing (Column 3). As has already been determined, the expected return for the Wide stock is 13.00%. Next, calculate the deviation of each possible return from the expected return (Column 4). For clarity, note that the % signs have been left off the calculations. Then square each deviation (Column 5) and multiply by the probability of the forecast return and sum (Column 6). This gives the variance. Finally, calculate the standard deviation of the Wide stock's expected returns by taking the square root of the variance. The standard deviation is 13.91 percent.[1]

Using the Standard Deviation

The standard deviation provides much useful information about the distribution of returns. If the distribution of returns is approximately normal (i.e., bell shaped) there is approximately a 68-percent probability that the actual return will be within plus or minus one standard deviation from

---

[1]Although it is the standard deviation of expected *future* returns which is of concern, an estimate can sometimes be developed by calculating the historical standard deviation. The procedure is similar to the one above, but there are some differences. The expected return is replaced with the historical average return, and the deviation of each observation is related to the historical average. Each deviation is then squared and summed. The average squared deviation (i.e., the variance) is calculated by dividing by the number of observations minus 1, reflecting a correction for the loss of a degree of freedom. The standard deviation is equal to the square root of the variance. For an example of the calculation, see Solved Problem 2.

TABLE 6-4   Wide Company: Calculation of Standard Deviation

(1) Forecast Return	(2) Probability	(3) = (1) × (2) Weighted Return	(4) Deviation	(5) Deviation Squared	(6) Weighted Deviation
−9	.2	−1.8	(−9 − 13) = −22	484	96.80
13	.6	7.8	(13 − 13) = 0	0	0
35	.2	7.0	(35 − 13) = 22	484	96.80
Expected return (R)		13.00		Variance:	193.60
				Standard deviation:	$\sqrt{193.60}$
					= 13.91%

the mean (i.e., the expected return). There is approximately a 95-percent probability that the actual return will be within plus or minus two standard deviations from the expected return and approximately a 99.7-percent probability that the actual return will be within plus or minus three standard deviations from the expected return. These return intervals are illustrated in Exhibit 6-4.

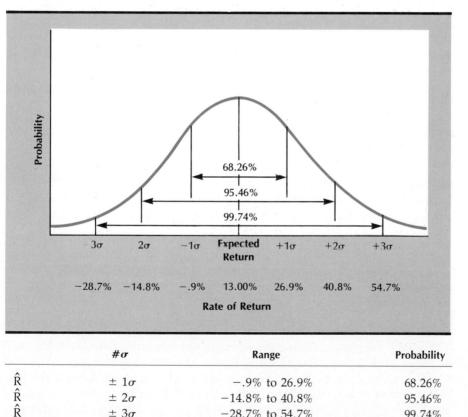

EXHIBIT 6-4
Wide Company
Probability Distribution of Returns

	#σ	Range	Probability
$\hat{R}$	± 1σ	−.9% to 26.9%	68.26%
$\hat{R}$	± 2σ	−14.8% to 40.8%	95.46%
$\hat{R}$	± 3σ	−28.7% to 54.7%	99.74%

As we have seen, the Wide stock has an expected return of 13 percent with a standard deviation of 13.9 percent. If the distribution of returns is approximately normal, there is approximately a 68-percent probability that the actual return will be between −.9 percent and 26.9 percent (i.e., minus and plus one standard deviation). There is approximately a 95-percent probability that the actual return will be between −14.8 percent and 40.8 percent. There is approximately a 99 percent probability that the actual return will be between −28.7 percent and 54.7 percent. Although the large range of possible outcomes (i.e., −28.7 to 54.7 percent) associated with minus and plus three standard deviations may seem too great to provide meaningful information, it is a virtual certainty that an investor will not a) lose everything nor b) double his or her money within a year.

 ## RISK AND RETURN DETERMINANTS

So far we have examined the returns and risk produced by only one factor, the business cycle. In reality, of course, this is an oversimplification. Stock returns are determined by an infinite number of factors, each of which has an unlimited number of possible outcomes. For example, a rise in interest rates may reduce stock prices, but large rises will affect stocks more than small rises. Moreover, the industry in which a company operates might be depressed, even though the overall economy may be expanding rapidly. If so, stock prices and returns of most companies in the industry will be depressed, while stock prices and returns overall might be rising. In addition to all these factors, there may be problems unique to each company which will affect its stock price (and returns) adversely while not affecting other companies. For example, if a company has a labor dispute, introduces unpopular products, or experiences some other setback, its stock price might drop even though both the general economy and other companies in its industry are doing well.

Company-Specific Risk

A dramatic example of company-specific risk occurred on March 28, 1979 at Three Mile Island. The General Public Utilities Company experienced a failure in one of its two nuclear reactors. The potential for a nuclear disaster caused widespread alarm throughout the country. The company's stock price began a steep decline, from almost $18 per share the day

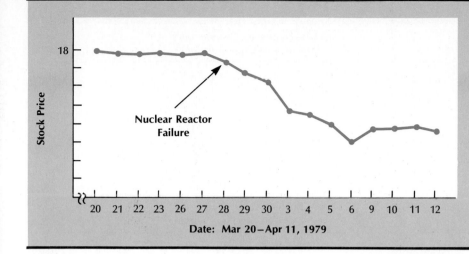

**Nuclear Reactor
Failure**

Stock Price

Date: Mar 20–Apr 11, 1979

20 21 22 23 26 27 28 29 30 3 4 5 6 9 10 11 12

**EXHIBIT 6-5
General Public Utilities'
Stock Price Decline**

before the disaster to less than $9 per share six weeks later. Exhibit 5 shows how quickly the stock price decreased almost entirely as a result of the crisis.

The many different factors that combine to determine a company's future stock price, and returns, can be grouped into three primary categories. These are *marketwide* factors; *industrywide* factors; and *company-specific* factors. One authoritative study of these factors estimated that about 20 percent of the fluctuation in a company's stock price can be attributed to company-specific factors; another 49 percent of the variation could be attributed to industrywide factors; and the remaining 31 percent could be attributed to marketwide factors.[2] Table 6-5 presents a descriptive listing of the kinds of factors included in each of these categories.

market factors
industry factors
company factors

PORTFOLIO RISK AND RETURN

When any investment, such as the Wide Company stock, is considered in isolation, all of the risk factors identified in Table 6-5 will have some effect on its returns. However, some of these risks can be reduced or eliminated by investing in a portfolio, or collection of investments. When investors own portfolios with many diverse investments, the expected returns and risk factors of the individual investments are averaged across all investments in the portfolio.

---

[2]See B. J. King. "Market and Industry Factors in Stock Price Behavior." *Journal of Business,* January 1966, pp. 139–190.

TABLE 6-5   Representative Risk Factors

Company-Specific Risk Factors
(20% of stock price variation)

1. Labor strike
2. Management incompetence
3. Product failure
4. Regulatory violations
5. Lawsuits
6. Loss of key personnel
7. Loss of patent protection
8. Natural disaster

Industry-Wide Risk Factors
(49% of stock price variation)

1. Regulation
2. Industry-wide labor problems
3. Foreign competition
4. Substitute products
5. Changing consumer tastes
6. Excess productive capacity

Market-Wide Risk Factors
(31% of stock price variation)

1. Business cycle
2. Interest rates
3. Inflation
4. Energy prices

Portfolio Expected Return

portfolio return

The expected return from a portfolio is equal to the weighted average of the expected returns from investments in the portfolio. This can be defined as shown in Equation 6-3.

$$\hat{R}_p = \sum_{I=1}^{n} w_I \hat{R}_I \qquad (6\text{-}3)$$

$$= w_1\hat{R}_1 + w_2\hat{R}_2 + w_3\hat{R}_3 + \ldots + w_n\hat{R}_n$$

where $\hat{R}_p$ is the expected return on the portfolio; $\sum_{I=1}^{n}$ is the summation operator; w_I is the proportion of the total portfolio invested in asset I; and $\hat{R}_I$ is the expected return from asset I.

Assume that there are two stocks in a portfolio. Forty percent of the portfolio is invested in stock A, which has an expected return of 25 percent; and 60 percent of the portfolio is invested in stock B, which has an expected return of 12 percent. The expected return of the portfolio is 17.2 percent.

$$\hat{R}_p = w_A \hat{R}_A + w_B \hat{R}_B$$
$$\hat{R}_p = .40(25\%) + .60(12\%)$$
$$= 17.2\%$$

Portfolio Risk

Unlike the portfolio expected return, the determination of portfolio risk is more complex due to the interactions among investments within the portfolio. For example, we have determined that the riskiness of any single investment can be measured by its standard deviation. However, the standard deviation of a portfolio is *not* the weighted average of the individual standard deviations of investments in the portfolio. This is because company-risk and industry-risk factors present in one investment can be offset by other investments in the portfolio, thereby reducing the impact on the portfolio. In portfolios that are well diversified, the only risks that cannot be eliminated are marketwide risks. Any risk that can be eliminated in a portfolio is known as *diversifiable risk.* Any risk which cannot be diversified in a portfolio is known as portfolio risk, nondiversifiable risk, or market risk.

portfolio risk

diversifiable risk

Example

Assume that an investor buys stock in both the Wide and Narrow companies. During the year, the Wide Company experiences a labor dispute and its profits, stock price, and returns to shareholders all decline. However, no such misfortune befalls the Narrow Company. Indeed, if the Narrow Company is a competitor of the Wide Company, Wide's labor dispute may actually increase Narrow's sales, profits, stock price, and returns above what were expected. Thus, the adverse effect of the labor strike in the Wide Company will be averaged across two investments rather than just one. The more investments added to the portfolio, the smaller the effect of the Wide Company's labor dispute.

To illustrate the principle of portfolio risk reduction, let us reconsider the effect of the business cycle on stock returns. To simplify the discussion, consider a portfolio including only two stocks.

| Example |

Portfolio Risk Reduction

Consider the Wide and Narrow companies. Unlike the Wide Company, the response of the Narrow Company to economic conditions is countercyclical. That is, the Narrow Company suffers in expansions and thrives in recessions. The sales, profits, and stock price of a countercyclical company would drop with expansions and rise with recessions.[3] Table 6-6 contains the expected returns under each economic outcome for both the Wide and Narrow companies. Note that probability distributions are now similar.

TABLE 6-6 Expected Rate of Return in 1988 for Portfolio Containing One-Half Wide Stock and One-Half Narrow Stock

(1)	(2)	(3) Expected Return Wide	(4) Expected Return Narrow	(5) Expected Return 1/2 Wide + 1/2 Narrow
Economy	Probability			
Recession	.20	−9%	35%	.5(−9%) + .5(35%) = 13%
Normal	.60	13%	13%	.5(13%) + .5(13%) = 13%
Expansion	.20	35%	−9%	.5(35%) + .5(−9%) = 13%
Total	1.00			

Note that if two such stocks as these are combined in a portfolio, with each having a weight of 50 percent in the portfolio, the weighted average forecast return is the same, 13 percent, for all economic conditions. Expansion, recession, or normal economic conditions will affect each of the stocks in the portfolio differently but have no effect on the portfolio. In particular, note that the standard deviation of the portfolio is *not* equal to the weighted average of the Wide and Narrow standard deviations. The standard deviation of the portfolio is zero because there is no deviation from the expected return of the portfolio. This portfolio has no risk at all!

---

[3]An example of a countercyclical investment might be a lower-cost, lower-quality substitute product. When the economy is expanding and consumers have more income, they tend to buy the higher-priced, higher-quality item. When the economy is in recession, consumers have less money and tend to buy the lower-price, lower-quality item.

The Correlation Coefficient (r)

To see how portfolio risk has been diversified away, let us examine the behavior of the returns for the two stocks. Note that, if an economic expansion occurs, the Wide stock's returns will be higher (35 percent) than expected (13 percent), while the Narrow stock's returns will be lower (−9 percent) than expected. Conversely, if an economic recession occurs, Wide's returns will be lower (−9 percent) than expected and Narrow's will be higher (35 percent) than expected. In other words, relative to their expected returns, the forecast returns for each stock move in exactly opposite directions, offsetting one another's deviations away from the expected return.

The degree and direction of the relationship between the Wide and Narrow stock returns is measured by the *correlation coefficient*. The correlation coefficient can range from −1.00 to + 1.00.

correlation coefficient

When the returns of two investments—such as those of the Wide and Narrow stocks—always move in exactly opposite directions, they are said to be *perfectly negatively correlated*. Perfect negative correlation is indicated by a correlation coefficient of −1.00. When two investments are perfectly negatively correlated, it is possible to create a portfolio of the two that has zero risk. Perfect negative correlations are rare, however, because the stocks of most companies tend to rise and fall together to some extent in response to marketwide forces.

negative correlation

If the returns from two stocks always change in the same direction, they are said to be *perfectly positively correlated*. This is also rare, however, because the returns for a given stock are heavily influenced by unique factors (which were referred to as *company-specific* factors in Table 6-5). Most stocks are positively correlated but not perfectly positively correlated. Thus some opportunities for risk reduction in a portfolio can be realized.

positive correlation

Portfolio Risk and the Number of Investments

Since risk reduction depends on the offsetting interactions of investments, portfolios which contain many diverse investments produce more opportunities for risk reduction than portfolios that are less diversified. For example, a portfolio that includes two shares of the Wide stock will have more risk than a portfolio that includes one Wide share and one Narrow share.

Exhibit 6-6 illustrates the risk reduction process as the number of investments in a portfolio increases. The addition of the first few investments reduces the portfolio standard deviation quickly, yet much diversifiable risk remains that can be eliminated by adding still more investments. Finally, reduction in diversifiable risk becomes more gradual. The dashed line indicates what the standard deviation would be with maximum diversification. The standard deviation remaining after the maximum diversification represents *market risk*, i.e., risk that cannot be diversified away.

market risk

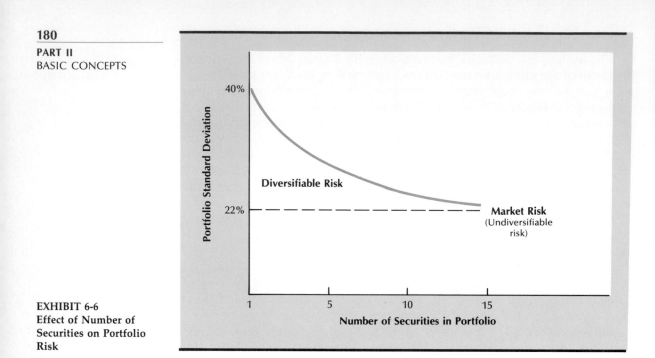

EXHIBIT 6-6
Effect of Number of
Securities on Portfolio
Risk

The Market Portfolio

market portfolio

The most diversified portfolio available at a given time is known as the *market portfolio*. Since it is maximally diversified, all possible opportunities for risk elimination have been exploited. In other words any stock included in the market portfolio has all of its company and industry risks eliminated, leaving only its market risk. The Standard & Poor's Index of 500 common stocks is generally considered to be representative of the market portfolio. Almost any large, diversified collection of stocks will resemble the market portfolio.

Measuring Market Risk

In a portfolio, only a security's market-risk factors remain. Company and industry factors still affect each stock in the portfolio, but they are eliminated for the portfolio as a whole. Recall that, when the Wide and Narrow Companies stocks were combined in a portfolio, the returns for each stock were still affected by economic conditions. For the portfolio as a whole, however, economic conditions had no effect.

An investment's sensitivity to market risk is revealed by the correlation coefficient of its returns with the market portfolio. One authoritative study of stocks determined that, on the average, the correlation coefficient between a stock's returns and the market portfolio is approximately 50 percent[4].

The correlation coefficient between the stock and the market portfolio is defined as shown below:

$r_{x,M}$ = Correlation of security X's return with the market portfolio return

The risk of the market portfolio is measured by the standard deviation of the portfolio:

$$\sigma_M = \text{standard deviation of the market portfolio}$$

THE CAPITAL ASSET PRICING MODEL (CAPM)

*capital asset
pricing model (CAPM)*

The capital asset pricing model provides a mechanism for measuring an investment's portfolio risk and relating this risk measure to the rate of return it should provide investors. Although the specific assumptions underlying the model are quite stringent and the statistics involved in applying it can be involved, the CAPM is based on a relatively simple idea: an investment's rate of return should reflect its relative risk level. Investments that are riskier than the market portfolio should offer more return than the market portfolio; investments which are less risky than the market portfolio should offer less return than the market portfolio; and investments that are just as risky as the market portfolio should offer just as much return as the market portfolio.

Assumptions Underlying the CAPM

In its strict form, the CAPM depends on several important assumptions which we will detail below. However, keep in mind that the CAPM is a "robust" model, meaning that even if all assumptions are not exactly met, it still provides a reliable framework for evaluating the relationship between risk and return.

A Single-Period Model.   The CAPM assumes that the investment horizon is only one period long. This period is typically interpreted to mean one year but in practice could cover any time horizon. The requirement is only that no new information comes into the investment market during that period. Thus, if the model is applied to a 10-year investment, the single period covers 10 years, and it is assumed that there are no changes in investors' expectations about the risks and returns of available investments during that time. Multi-period models have been developed to relax this assumption, but they are quite complex.

---

[4]See Marshall Blume. "On the Assessment of Risk." *Journal of Finance*, March 1971, p. 4.

Utility Maximization. Investors are assumed to attempt to maximize the utility of their wealth position. Utility increases with the expected return and decreases with risk, measured as the variance of expected returns.

Homogeneous Expectations. All investors share the same information on expected returns and variances among investments. This means that all information is immediately available and free to all investors and that all investors interpret that information in the same way.

Risk-Free Rate. All investors can borrow or lend at the same riskless rate of return.

Frictionless Markets. Investment markets are perfectly efficient, meaning that there are no transactions costs, no taxes, perfect divisibility of investments, and the transactions of one individual do not affect prices.

The Beta Coefficient

The assumptions underlying the CAPM allow the development of an internal market equilibrium in which an investment's expected rate of return is determined by its relative risk measured by its *beta*.[5]

beta coefficient

The beta of an investment can be estimated with regression analysis of historical returns. Typically, monthly-returns data for the stock and for the market portfolio for the previous 60 months are used. The monthly stock returns are then regressed against the monthly market returns. The slope of the regression line indicates the sensitivity of the security returns to market factors and is known as the *beta coefficient*. Regressions using daily data are also widely used to estimate beta. An example of such a regression estimate is shown in Exhibit 6-7.

covariance

More formally, beta is equal to the covariance of returns between the security and the market divided by the variance of the market returns.

$$\text{Beta}_x = \text{Cov}_{x,M}/\text{Var}_M = r_{x,M}\,\sigma_x\sigma_M/\sigma_M^2$$

The beta coefficient indicates how much the stock's return will change for a given change in the market portfolio return. For example, a stock with a beta of 2.00 will be twice as volatile as the market portfolio. If the return on the market portfolio goes down 1 percent, the return on the stock will go down 2 percent, twice as much. A stock with a beta of .50 will be only half as volatile as the market portfolio. If the return on the market portfolio goes down 1 percent, the return on the stock will go down only .5%, half as much.

---

[5]Beta is the Greek symbol for b.

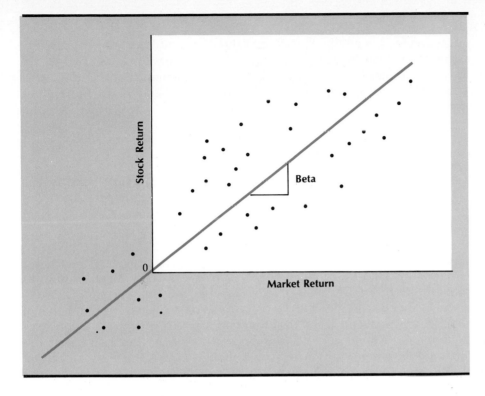

EXHIBIT 6-7
Regression Estimate of
Stock Beta

Stocks with betas less than 1.00 are considered "defensive" because *defensive stocks*
their returns are, on the average, less volatile than the market portfolio.
Stocks with betas greater than 1.00 are considered "aggressive" in- *aggressive stocks*
vestments because they fluctuate more than the market. Betas of exactly 1.0
indicate that the stock's returns are equally as risky as the market portfolio.

TABLE 6-7	Interpretation of Beta
Beta	Interpretation
>1.00	Investment is riskier than the market and should provide a greater return than the market.
=1.00	Investment is as risky as the market and should provide the same return as the market.
<1.00	Investment is less risky than the market and should provide less return than the market.

Published Betas

Nowadays, many firms such as Value Line and Merrill Lynch provide estimates of betas for a large number of U.S. corporations. (See Exhibit 6-8 for an example. Note that the "risky" stock, General Public Utilities, of Three Mile Island fame, is actually quite well behaved in the market portfolio.)

A Simple Way To Calculate Beta

If one knows the standard deviation of an investment's returns, the standard deviation of the market portfolio's returns, and the correlation coefficient ($r_{x,M}$) between the investment and the market portfolio, beta can be calculated as shown in Equation 6-5.[6]

$$\text{Beta}_x = r_{x,M}(\sigma_x/\sigma_M) \tag{6-5}$$

Note that, if a stock's correlation coefficient is 1.00, Equation 6-5 indicates that all of security X's risk is market risk and, thus, in a portfolio none of it will be diversified. However, if the correlation coefficient is .50, then half of X's risk is market risk and the other half will be diversified in a portfolio. Equation 6-5 should also make it apparent that a security with a high standard deviation might have a low beta if its correlation with the market is low.

EXHIBIT 6-8
A Sample of Value-Line Betas

Company	Estimated Beta
Chrysler Corporation	1.20
Church's Fried Chicken	0.90
Coca-Cola	0.85
Coleco	1.10
General Public Utilities	0.85
Mattel, Inc.	1.20
McDonald's Corporation	1.10
Quaker Oats	0.75
Toys 'R' Us	1.25
Wheeling-Pittsburgh Steel	1.15

Source: Value Line Investment Survey, April 18, 1986.

---

[6]Recall that beta is equal to the covariance of returns between the security and the market divided by the variance of the market returns.

$$\text{Beta}_x = \text{Cov}_{x,M}/\text{Var}_M = r_{x,M}\sigma_x\sigma_M/\sigma_M^2$$

Dividing numerator and denominator by σ_M gives Equation 6-5:

$$\text{Beta}_x = r_{x,M}(\sigma_x/\sigma_M)$$

Example		**185**
		CHAPTER 6 RISK AND THE RATE OF RETURN

The standard deviation of expected returns for the Waverly Company is 22 percent. The standard deviation of expected returns for the S&P 500 stocks is 20 percent. The correlation of Waverly's returns with the market is .50. With this information, Waverly's beta can be determined as: Beta (Waverly) = .5(.22/.20) = .55

The Security Market Line

Although the beta of an investment provides insights into its relative risk level, it has a much more powerful role. The beta can be used to estimate the investment's required rate of return given its relative risk. This relationship is expressed in the Security Market Line, as shown in Exhibit 6-9.

Security Market Line

Note that, for an investment with a beta of 1.00 (i.e., risk level equal to that of the market portfolio) the required return is equal to the expected return on the market portfolio ($\hat{R}_m$). Also, note that, for an investment with a beta of zero, the expected return is equal to the risk-free rate (R_f). The higher the beta, the higher the required return.

$\hat{R}_m$ = *market return*

R_f = *risk free rate*

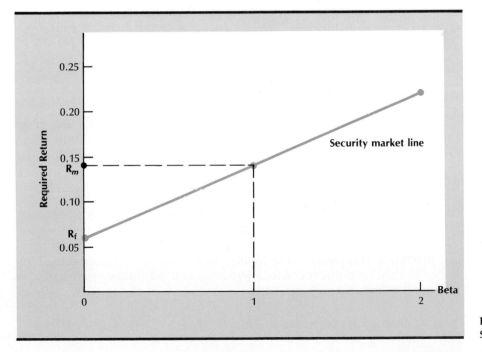

EXHIBIT 6-9
Security Market Line

Market Risk Premium

The market risk premium is equal to the expected return on the market in excess of the risk-free rate.

$$\hat{R}_p = \hat{R}_M - R_f \tag{6-6}$$

market risk premium

One authoritative study estimates that the historical risk premium on the market portfolio has been 8.3 percent.[7] The market risk premium is a measure of investor risk aversion, meaning the reluctance of investors to accept risk.

The Security Market Line Equation

The graphic relationship between an investment's beta and its required rate of return can also be expressed algebraically. Note that the symbol, k_i is being used to indicate the required rate of return from investment i given its risk level. When markets are efficient, k_i is the same as "$\hat{R}_i$." However, when markets are not efficient, k_i and $\hat{R}_i$ are not equal. Students often

required return vs.
expected return

become confused when the *required return* is referred to as the *expected return*. Whenever the terms are used interchangeably, it is assumed that the investment is fairly priced and the market is efficient.

$$k_i = R_f + (\hat{R}_m - R_f)B_i \tag{6-7}$$

The risk-free rate (R_f) and the expected market return ($\hat{R}_m$) are the same for all investments. Thus the difference in required rates of return among investments at any point in time is due solely to differences in beta. Note that, when beta is equal to 1.00, the required return is equal to $\hat{R}_M$, and when beta is zero the required return is R_f.

CHANGES IN THE SECURITY MARKET LINE (SML)

In practice, the Security Market Line changes continuously as a result of changes in the risk-free rate and in the market risk premium. Consequently, the required rates of returns on all stocks are also continuously changing, sometimes increasing (and thereby reducing stock prices), and sometimes decreasing (and thereby increasing stock prices).

Changes in the Risk Free Rate (R_f)

In the U.S. economy, 90-day United States Treasury Bills are considered to be risk-free investments, since there is no risk that investors will get less (or more) return than promised by the Treasury at the time the bills are

[7]Roger G. Ibbotson, and Rex A. Sinquefield. *Stocks, Bonds, Bills, and Inflation: 1926–1978.* Charlottesville, VA: Financial Analysts Research Foundation, 1979.

purchased if they hold the bills until maturity.[8] The federal government guarantees the yield on the Treasury Bills. If the government had to, it would print enough new money to pay off its Treasury Bills as they come due or it would raise the necessary taxes. Yields on newly issued Treasury Bills are regularly published in financial pages of most daily newspapers.

The risk-free rate of return varies over time as interest rates in general fluctuate. Note that, even though the risk-free rate can vary from time to time, it is known with certainty over the immediate future. A move up or down in the risk-free rate will shift the SML up and down in parallel, assuming no change in the market risk premium. Exhibit 6-10 shows how the SML can shift solely from a change in the risk-free rate.

The SML can also shift due to changes in the market risk premium or from a combination of changes in both the risk-free rate and the market risk premium. Naturally, any change in the SML changes the required rates of return for all investments.

risk-free rate

Changes in the Market Risk Premium (R_p)

The market risk premium, like the risk-free rate, also changes over time. While the main influence on the risk-free rate is the general level of

CHAPTER 6
RISK AND THE RATE
OF RETURN

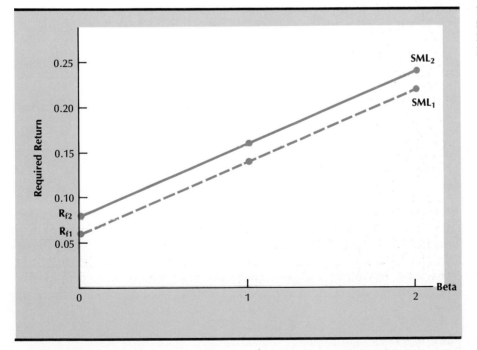

EXHIBIT 6-10
Security Market Line Increase In Risk-Free Rate

---

[8]We are ignoring purchasing power risk.

interest rates, the main determinant of the market risk premium is attitudes toward bearing risk (sometimes referred to as *investor psychology*). When investors are pessimistic or anxious about the future, they demand greater rewards for bearing risk and the market risk premium increases. When investors are optimistic and feel secure about the future, they become more willing to take risks and the market risk premium decreases. Changes in the market risk premium cause the SML to shift even if the risk-free rate does not change, as shown in Exhibit 6-11.

Assume that SML_1 is the original SML. If investors want more return for bearing risk, the slope of the SML becomes steeper, as reflected in SML_2. As investors become more willing to bear risk and demand less of a risk premium, the slope of the SML becomes flatter, as indicated in SML_3. Note that the risk-free rate is assumed not to change. In reality, both the risk-free rate and the market risk premium may change simultaneously, as shown in Exhibit 6-12.

Assume that SML_1 is the original situation. If interest rates should rise and investors fear that higher interest rates will lead to an economic recession, R_f will increase and so will the market risk premium, resulting in both a higher and steeper SML, as indicated by SML_2.

MARKET EQUILIBRIUM

When investments are priced accurately, the required rate of return is all that one can expect to receive from investments. While it would be desirable to find investments which are expected to provide more than the minimum return required, this can happen only by sheer luck—something like winning a lottery—or if investment markets are inefficient.[9]

market equilibrium

efficient markets

Markets that can be characterized as efficient always tend toward equilibrium, even though there may be periods of transition involving disequilibrium.

Efficient Markets: Required rate of return=Expected rate of return

$$k_i=\hat{R}_i$$

The New York Stock Exchange is a good example of a relatively efficient market—in this case, the market for common stocks. Salient features of an efficient market are that full information pertaining to all investments is completely, quickly, and inexpensively available to everyone; that transactions for buying and selling can be executed readily and economically; and that there are many participants, without significant barriers to entry or exit.

---

[9]We are using the term *inefficient* in its economic sense. This is based on the assumption that efficiency of the market increases with the degree of competition. Mispricing is more likely to occur when markets are not competitive.

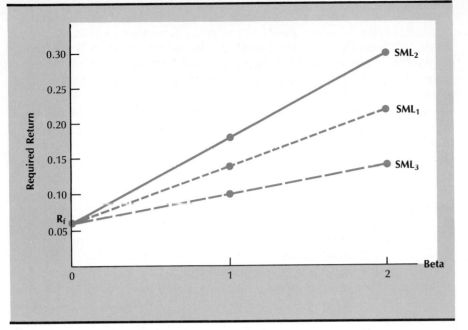

EXHIBIT 6-11
Security Market Line
Change in Investors
Attitudes Toward
Risk-Taking

EXHIBIT 6-12
Security Market Line
Combined Effects of
Changes in Risk-Free
Rate and Investors'
Attitudes Toward
Risk-Taking

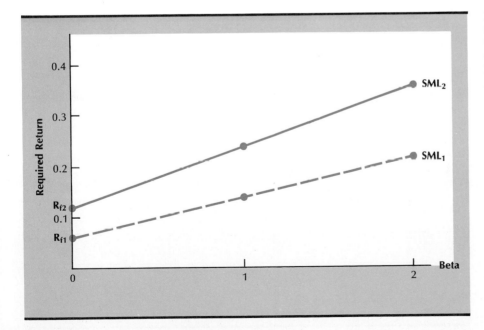

Equilibrium Mechanics

In Exhibit 6-13, the *expected* ($\hat{R}$) rates of return and betas for investments, A, B, and C, have been plotted. The fact that each of these investments, though they differ in respect to risk level, lies on the Security Market Line indicates that their expected returns are equal to their required rates of return.

Thus the returns investors are projecting for investments A, B, and C are no more nor no less than they should be. Even so, note that the returns from investment C are expected to be higher than those from investment B. Does this mean that the investment C is better? Not at all, because investment C has greater risk and, according to the SML, is providing just enough of a bonus over investment B to compensate for its greater risk level. Restating, when the market for the stock is in equilibrium, the stock's expected rate of return is equal to its required rate of return.

A measure of market efficiency is how quickly disequilibrium returns are corrected. Perfectly efficient markets adjust instantaneously. Two disequilibrium stocks have been plotted on the SML shown in Exhibit 6-14.

Stock D's expected return (25 percent) is well in excess of its required rate (11 percent), given its beta (.625). In an efficient market, this would be instantly recognized and everyone would try to buy stock D. As demand for D's stock increases, its stock price will rise until, at the margin, its expected returns become equal to the required return. Let us examine how this occurs.

EXHIBIT 6-13
Security Market Line Equilibrium Returns for Investments A, B, C

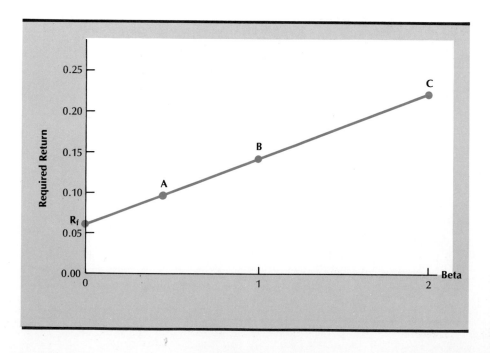

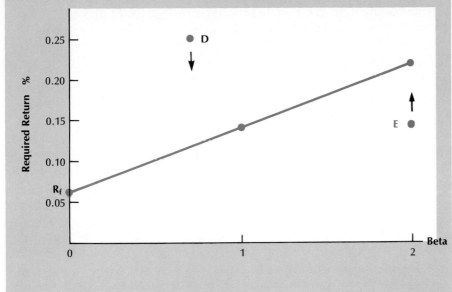

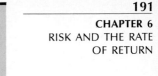

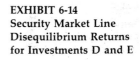

EXHIBIT 6-14
Security Market Line
Disequilibrium Returns
for Investments D and E

Table 6-8 shows the original equilibrium situation for stock D, the disequilibrium situation, and the new equilibrium.

In the original situation, assume the price and dividend forecasts shown. The price one year later is expected to be $110 and a dividend of $1.00 is expected. Given its current price, the expected rate of return from stock D is 11 percent. Given its risk level, the SML indicates that stock D should provide a return of 11 percent, thus it is at equilibrium.

Now, assume that gold is discovered on land that the company owns. As the gold is mined and sold, future profits and dividends will be higher, raising the price of the stock. Assume that the expected price, $\hat{P}_1$, is now $120 and the expected dividend rises to $5.00. At its current price, $100, the expected rate of return jumps to 25 percent. Stock D has become a "hot stock," and everyone rushes to buy it. As the demand for stock D increases, its price begins to rise until it reaches $112.61, the new equilibrium situ-

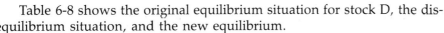

TABLE 6-8   Adjustment Process for Stock D

	Original Equilibrium	Disequilibrium	New Equilibrium
$\hat{P}_1$	$110	$120	$120
$\hat{D}_1$	$ 1	$ 5	$ 5
P_0	$100	$100	$112.61
$\hat{R}_1$	11%	25%	11%

ation. At $112.61, stock D, gold and all, is no longer a "hot stock," because anyone buying it for $112.61 will only get an expected return of 11 percent, the minimum required rate of return, given its risk level. Of course, the "lucky" investors who had bought it at a lower price would have realized higher returns. The rate of return given the market price of $112.61, can be checked using Equation 6-1:

$$\hat{R} = ([\hat{P}_1 - P_0] + \hat{CF}_1)/P_0$$
$$= ([\$120.00 - 112.61] + \$5)/\$112.61$$
$$= .11, \quad \text{or} \quad 11\%$$

The results for stock D can be restated in the following manner. When an investment's expected returns are greater than its required return, it is underpriced, meaning that the value of the stock is greater than its current price. In other words, it is a "bargain." When markets are efficient, bargains do not last long. Investors lucky enough to be "first in line" earn high returns, but consistently having such good luck is rare. Table 6-9 shows the reverse situation for stock E.

Assume that, originally, the price, $\hat{P}_1$ is expected to be $112 one year from now and that a dividend of $2.00 is also expected. At its current price of $100, stock E is offering a 14 percent rate of return, which is the equilibrium rate given its beta.

Now assume that the company reports unfavorable profit forecasts and stock E's expected price one year from now drops to $105 and expected dividends drop to $1. At its current price of $100, the stock is now offering an expected return of only 6 percent, much below its required rate. In this case, the "unlucky" investors sell their ownership of stock E. Since no one wants to buy at $100, the current stock price drops to $93, at which the stock offers potential stock investors the requisite 14 percent, bad news and all. At a 6-percent rate of return, stock E was overpriced; it cost more than it was worth.

MANAGEMENT AND THE CAPM

When investment markets are imperfect, the expected rate of return is rarely equal to the minimum required rate of return. Thus, in such markets,

TABLE 6-9   Adjustment Process for Stock E

	Original Equilibrium	Disequilibrium	New Equilibrium
$\hat{P}_1$	$112	$105	$105
$\hat{D}_1$	$ 2	$ 1	$ 1
P_0	$100	$100	$ 93
$\hat{R}_1$	14%	6%	14%

there is a significant possibility of finding extremely profitable investments as well as making disastrous ones. Imperfect investment markets are like "high-stakes" poker: not a place for the naive or unlucky investor.

Fortunately, or unfortunately, many investments made by business firms are in investment markets that are imperfect from the rate-of-return standpoint. At one extreme, for example, monopoly markets are very imperfect in that expected returns can far exceed or fall short[10] of the rates dictated by their risk levels.

Highly competitive markets tend to be more efficient because, as other investors recognize the above-required rates of return, they enter and compete the excess away.

Example

The Fun-Tek Corporation has developed and marketed a popular new video game. Due to its popularity, the game is expected to produce returns well in excess of those required, given its level of risk. Two months after its introduction, five very similar games are introduced by Fun-Tek's competitors. Fun-Tek's higher-than-required rate of return is protected to some degree by patents, trademarks, copyrights, brand image, and distribution system, all of which tend to weaken the ability of its competitors. Yet, through competition Fun-Tek's sales, profits, and expected returns gradually become lower than first expected, tending toward equilibrium.

Limitations of the CAPM Approach

In applying the CAPM to business investments, numerous practical obstacles must be addressed. First, estimating the investment beta is difficult because there may be little or no historical experience or reliable forecasts on which to base estimates of market risk.[11] Second, the business investment market typically departs significantly from the market efficiency assumptions underlying the CAPM. Third, while investments in stocks are easily reversed (i.e., can be liquidated), business investments are not readily liquidated. Often this can be done only at substantial economic loss.

Fourth, the very concept of a "market portfolio," which is so critical to the CAPM, may be completely alien to the analysis of investment risk from the standpoint of management. For example, the project manager re-

---

[10]A regulated monopoly such as the U.S. Postal Service may produce returns well below what would be required under competitive conditions.

[11]In Chapter 16 and elsewhere, we will examine some alternatives for dealing with these problems of implementation.

sponsible for the performance of one investment does not have the benefit of project diversification. To him or her, the relevant investment risk is more accurately measured by the total risk of the investment rather than by only its market risk as indicated by the CAPM. This can lead to serious overestimates of risk, higher-than-required rates of return from investments, and reduced innovation.

Example

Assume that the Acme Company produces many different products. Joe Smith, product manager, is considering whether to propose that the company manufacture a new product which he has labeled Product #19. Joe knows that, if he proposes the investment and it is adopted, he will be assigned to manage it. As far as Joe is concerned, Product #19's performance will reflect company-specific risks, industrywide risks, and marketwide risks. He knows that any of these could turn the product into a dismal failure. Since he will be rewarded or penalized for the performance of Product #19, Joe sees considerable risk in the new idea.

Let us assume that Joe has estimated the expected return from Product #19 to be 25 percent with a standard deviation of 60 percent. The expected return on the market portfolio is 14 percent with a standard deviation of 20 percent. Finally, assume that the correlation coefficient of Product #19's returns with the market is .50 and that the risk-free rate of return is 8 percent.

As far as Joe is concerned, he will reap no benefits from diversification because Product #19 will be his only responsibility. Joe might well conclude that the beta for Product #19 is 3.0 (i.e., 60%/20%) With this perspective, Joe thinks that Product #19 should produce a return of 26 percent. Thus, Joe would reject the Product proposal.

$$\text{Joe's perspective: } k = 8\% + (14\% - 8\%)3$$

$$= 26\%$$

However, a shareholder in Joe's company would view Product #19 as much less risky because half of its risk could be diversified. From a shareholder's perspective, Product #19's beta is only 1.5 [(60% × .50)/20%], indicating a required return of 17%.

$$\text{Shareholder perspective: } k = 8\% + (14\% - 8\%)1.5$$

$$= 17\%$$

As far as the shareholder is concerned, Product #19 would be a very good investment and should be undertaken. However, before Joe can be talked into evaluating investments the way shareholders would want him to, the reward system at Acme will have to be revised.

The CAPM assumes that the shareholders' perspective should dominate, yet getting managers to adopt this perspective when evaluating investment risks is a serious practical obstacle. Such violations of the CAPM assumptions require, at the least, higher rates of return than implied by the CAPM. Just how such premiums for departures from the CAPM assumptions should be determined is as yet unknown.

All of the serious limitations involved in employing the CAPM to business investment decisions notwithstanding, managers cannot ignore the fact that shareholders' expectations of future returns all reflect assessments of business investments undertaken by the firm.

Since current and prospective shareholders, through the equilibrating mechanism of the market, determine the price of the company's common stock, shareholders' expectations must be incorporated in investment decisions made by the firm if stock price is to be maximized. This suggests two important implications for managers. First, managers must seek to improve the profitability of existing investments through effective operating activities and decisions. By improving the profitability of existing investments, operating managers can raise shareholders' expectations of future returns without necessarily increasing risks and, thus, increase stock price. Second, management must seek investments whose expected returns exceed their required returns as carefully estimated as possible, as this too will raise shareholder's expectations of future returns and maximizes share prices. Third, managers must seek to minimize the costs of financing the company's operating and investment activities without unduly exposing the firm to new risks. Those are the basic themes of this text.

SUMMARY

This chapter has dealt with the importance of risk in determining the minimum returns which should be produced by investments and, thus, the value of investments. Much progress has been made in this area since the development of the Capital Asset Pricing Model, which has not only provided an objective, quantifiable measure of risk but also a general framework for relating risk and return. This is because the Capital Asset Pricing Model, through the Security Market Line, provides a competitive benchmark for investments which may differ widely with respect to both risk and return features. To date, the Capital Asset Pricing Model has been most applicable to determining the required rates of return for common stock investments. Yet, it provides management many important insights into the rates of return which shareholders require from the firm. This information can be used to guide the evaluation of operating, financing, and investment decisions.

MULTIPLE CHOICE QUESTIONS

1. The rate of return is a percentage indicating:
   a) How much risk an investment has
   b) The increase in stock price
   c) The increase in wealth per dollar of investment
   d) The variance in investment value per dollar of investment

2. The expected rate of return is determined by:
   a) Business cycles
   b) Probability forecasts of returns
   c) Industry risk factors
   d) Diversifiable risks

3. The standard deviation:
   a) Is the same for all investments
   b) Varies continuously as investor risk aversion changes

c) Measures the degree of association between the stock and the market portfolio
d) Is the square root of the variance

4. If the distribution of returns is approximately normal (i.e., "bell shaped") there is approximately a 68-percent probability that:

a) The expected return will not occur
b) The actual return will be less than zero
c) The actual return will be within one standard deviation from the expected return
d) The actual return will be greater than zero

5. One authoritative study of these factors estimated that about 30 percent of the fluctuation in a company's stock price can be attributed to:

a) Mismanagement
b) Insufficient diversification
c) Company-specific factors
d) Marketwide factors

6. In portfolios that are well diversified:

a) The only risks that cannot be eliminated are marketwide risks
b) The standard deviation is zero
c) There is no market risk
d) The expected return is zero

7. The degree and direction of the relationship between two stocks is indicated by:

a) The standard deviation
b) The beta coefficient
c) The correlation coefficient
d) The variance

8. One authoritative study of stocks determined that, on the average:

a) The correlation coefficient between a stock and the market portfolio is .50
b) Market factors account for 50 percent of the variation in a company's stock price
c) Industry factors account for 30 percent of the variation in a company's stock price
d) Individual stocks are riskier than the market portfolio

9. The beta coefficient indicates:

a) Investors' attitudes toward bearing risk
b) How much the stock's return will change for a given change in the market portfolio return
c) The relationship between two stocks
d) The dispersion of returns for a stock

10. The market risk premium is equal to:
   a) Beta times the risk-free rate
   b) The standard deviation of the security
   c) The expected return on the market in excess of the risk-free rate
   d) The expected return on the security in excess of the risk-free rate

DISCUSSION QUESTIONS

1. Why do investment discount rates vary from one investment to another?

2. Draw and label the Security Market Line graph, making your own hypothetical assumptions about the risk-free rate and the market risk premium.

3. What is the appropriate measure of risk for an investment considered in isolation? How does this differ from portfolio risk?

4. When it is said that the returns from two investments are negatively correlated, what is being said about the behavior of their returns?

5. Why does the portfolio effect reduce investment risk?

6. What is the meaning of the market portfolio? Give an example of it.

7. What is meant by market risk? Give some examples of market risk. Why can't they be diversified away?

8. Describe the Security Market Line equation. Define each of the variables in the equation and explain how you might develop numerical estimates for the variables in applying the model to a single stock's required rate of return.

9. Define the market risk premium.

10. Why is the intercept of the SML the risk-free rate of return?

SOLVED PROBLEMS

beta calculation

SP-1. Assume that you are analyzing the behavior of stock A relative to the market portfolio (M). They have the following distributions of possible future returns:

Probability	Stock A	M
0.2	−5%	10%
0.1	0%	5%
0.3	25%	20%
0.4	5%	13.75%

   a) Calculate the expected rate of return, $\hat{R}$, for stock A and the market, M.

Year	Return (percent)
1	(30.20)
2	12.10
3	9.36
4	4.58
5	(10.32)
6	(6.48)
7	25.00
8	19.37
9	14.61
10	(12.00)

7. The Fluge Company is expected to pay a dividend of $1.28 per share in 1988. Dividends it has paid for the last five years are shown below: *stock valuation with CAPM*

Year	Dividend per share
1983	1.00
1984	1.05
1985	1.10
1986	1.20
1987	1.22

The stock's beta is estimated to be 1.5. The rate of return on Treasury Bills is 6.8 percent per year, and the market-risk premium is expected to be 8.3 percent.

a) Estimate the stock's growth rate in dividends per share.
b) Estimate the required rate of return on the stock.
c) Estimate the value of the stock.

8. Investment A has the following possible cash flow outcomes in year one.   *expected value and standard deviation*

a) Calculate the expected cash flow.
b) Calculate the standard deviation.

Cash flow Outcome (year 1)	Probability
$1,000	.3
1,200	.4
400	.1
800	.2
	1.0

SOLUTIONS TO SOLVED PROBLEMS

SP-1.   a) Expected returns.

$$\hat{R}_A = (0.2 \times (-5\%)) + (0.1 \times 0\%) + (0.3 \times 25\%) + (0.4 \times 5\%) = 8.5\%$$

$$\hat{R}_M = (0.2 \times (10\%)) + (0.1 \times 5\%) + (0.3 \times 20\%) + (0.4 \times 13.75\%) = 14\%$$

b) Standard deviation of stock A.

(1) Forecast Return	(2) Probability	(3) = (1) × (2) Weighted Return	(4) Deviation	(5) Deviation Squared	(6) Weighted Deviation
−5	.2	−1.0	$(-5 - 8.50) = -13.5$	182.25	36.45
0	.1	.0	$(0 - 8.50) = -8.5$	72.25	7.225
25	.3	7.5	$(25 - 8.50) = 16.5$	272.25	81.675
5	.4	2.0	$(5 - 8.50) = -3.5$	12.25	4.90
	Expected return (R)	8.50		Variance:	130.25
				Standard deviation	$\sqrt{130.25}$
					= 11.41%

b) Standard deviation of the market portfolio.

(1) Forecast Return	(2) Probability	(3) = (1) × (2) Weighted Return	(4) Deviation	(5) Deviation Squared	(6) Weighted Deviation
10	.2	2.0	$(10 - 14) = -4$	16	3.2
5	.1	.5	$(5 - 14) = -9$	81	8.1
20	.3	6.0	$(20 - 14) = 6$	36	10.8
13.75	.4	5.5	$(13.75 - 14) = -.25$	.0625	.025
	Expected return (R)	14.00		Variance:	22.125
				Standard deviation	$\sqrt{22.125}$
					= 4.70%

c) Beta for stock A.

$$\beta_A = r_{A,M}(\sigma_A/\sigma_M)$$

$$= .50(11.41\%/4.70\%)$$

$$= 1.21$$

d) $\hat{R}_M = 14$ percent; $R_F = 6$ percent Plot SML. Should look like Exhibit S-1.

e) A's rate of return should be about 16 percent (from graph). Using the CAPM equation:

$$k_A = R_F + (\hat{R}_M - R_F)\beta_A$$

$$= 6\% + (14\% - 6\%)1.21$$

$$= 15.68\%$$

f) See the graph in exhibit S-1 for the plot of the expected return. The required return using the CAPM approach is 15.68 percent, much higher than expected. Stock A should drop in price until the stock offers the required return of 15.68 percent.

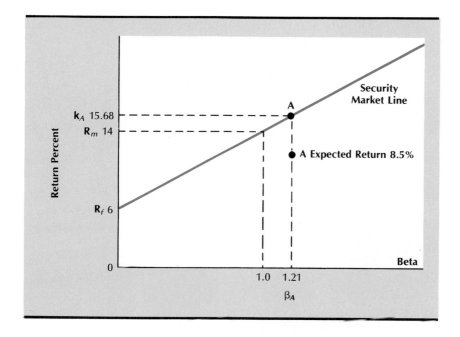

EXHIBIT S-1
Security Market Line and Required Return for Security A

SP-2. a) Calculate the return for each period using the formula:

$$R_1 = ([P_1 - P_0] + D_1)/P_0$$

For example, for 1981:

$$R_{1981} = ([P_{1981} - P_{1980}] + D_{1981})/P_{1980}$$

$$= ([\$16.00 - \$20.00] + \$2.00)/\$20.00$$

$$= -\$2.00/\$20.00 = -.10 \quad \text{or} \quad -10\%$$

In table form, returns for Acme stock in each year and the average for the seven years are shown below:

Year	Stock A's return R_a
1981	−10.00%
1982	26.25%
1983	24.44%
1984	−2.00%
1985	22.35%
1986	38.89%
1987	10.23%
$R_{Average}$	15.74%

b) The standard deviation of returns is estimated using the equation:

$$\sigma = \sqrt{\frac{\sum_{i=1}^{n}(R_i - R_{Avg})^2}{n-1}}$$

For stock A, the estimated standard deviation is as follows:

$$\sigma_A =$$

$$\sqrt{\frac{(-10.00 - 15.74)^2 + (26.25 - 15.74)^2 + \ldots + (10.23 - 15.74)^2}{7-1}}$$

$$= \sqrt{\frac{662.55 + 110.46 + 75.69 + 314.71 + 43.69 + 535.92 + 30.36}{6}}$$

$$= \sqrt{295.56} = 17.19\%$$

REFERENCES

Lintner, J. "The Valuation of Risk Assets and the Selection of Risky Investments in Stock Portfolios and Capital Budgets." *Review of Economics and Statistics,* February 1965, pp. 13-37.

Markowitz, H. Portfolio Selection: Efficient Diversification of Investments. Cowles Foundation Monograph 16, New Haven: Yale University Press, 1959.

Sharpe, W. F. "Capital Asset Prices: A Theory of Market Equilibrium under Conditions of Risk." *Journal of Finance,* September 1964, pp. 425–442.

PART

EVALUATION AND FORECASTING

CHAPTER

7

ANALYSIS OF
FINANCIAL STATEMENTS

nformation contained in the income statement and balance sheet, while limited in detail and subject to variations in financial accounting practice, can provide valuable insights into the profitability and risk of a company. These financial statements represent management's official report to "outsiders" on the results of policies, decisions, and activities undertaken by the company. For the most part, the statements are the principal sources of information to which creditors and investors have access. Decisions creditors make about extending credit to the company or investors make about the value of the company's stock are heavily influenced by the information contained in these statements. Since the financial manager must rely on creditors and investors to provide financing for the firm and since the financial manager is ultimately concerned with maximizing the long-run value of the company's stock, he or she must understand how financial statements will be interpreted by outsiders.

Internally, the financial manager can use information from the financial statements to identify areas of strength and weakness relative to competitors and to advise top management on functional areas that need detailed examination.

Finally, since companies typically grow or deteriorate gradually rather than in radical jumps, an analysis of a series of financial statements over time can help both insiders and outsiders identify important trends and forecast future results.

Several techniques can be employed in analyzing financial statements. This chapter will deal primarily with the most common and productive technique, called *ratio analysis*. Ratio analysis involves relating two pieces of financial information in order to standardize the information, permit comparisons, and produce insights on their joint effects.

Objectives and Organization of this Chapter

The first objective of this chapter is to illustrate the use of ratio analysis. The chapter will identify the major types of financial ratios, show how they are calculated, and illustrate how they may be interpreted. A second objective is to show how the financial manager can organize financial ratios into an overall system, popularly known as the *Du Pont* system, which provides insights into the contributions of management functions to the overall profitability of the firm.

This chapter has three principal sections. The first briefly reviews the features of the income statement and balance sheet, including a "managerial" interpretation of the statements. The second section presents the main categories of ratios and indicates how each ratio is calculated and how it may be interpreted. The second section also demonstrates the use of a type of ratio analysis called percentage of sales, or common size statements. The ratios will all be based on information in the financial statements for the Brendle Manufacturing Company. The third section of the chapter presents a managerial system of ratio analysis commonly known as the Du Pont system because it was developed by the Du Pont Corporation to assess managerial performance.

 ### PRINCIPAL FINANCIAL STATEMENTS

As was noted in Chapter 2, corporations periodically report their financial results and the condition of the company to shareholders. For example, the company's annual report conveys information about operating, investing, and financing activities during the year. This information is presented in the firm's *income statement* and *balance sheet.*

income statement

balance sheet

statement of cash flows

statement of changes in retained earnings

Most, if not all, corporations also prepare a *statement of cash flows* (as of this writing, expected to replace the *statement of changes in financial position*) and a *statement of changes in retained earnings,* both of which are derived from the income statement and balance sheet. An important supplement to the financial statements are the *notes to the financial statements,* which explains major events affecting the financial results and any significant changes in accounting procedures during the reporting period. They also provide details on items of special importance, such as repayment schedules of major debts or acquisitions of other companies. The notes are valuable to the financial analyst in interpreting the financial statements.

Balance Sheet

The balance sheet is a summary of all things owned by the company (assets) and all sources of financing being used (liabilities and shareholders' equity) at a particular point in time. For this reason, it is considered a "snapshot" of the firm. The balance sheet is a cumulative statement in that it is a continuing record of asset, liability, and shareholder account transactions. For example, when assets are purchased, the company's total assets increase. When assets are sold or wear out, the asset total decreases. Correspondingly, if money is borrowed, the liabilities amount increases; if debts are paid, the liabilities amount decreases. If profits are earned, the shareholders' equity account increases; if losses are incurred, the shareholders' account decreases. A key feature of the balance sheet is that total assets must equal the total of liabilities plus shareholders' equity. In other words, *the balance sheet must balance.* A balance sheet for the Brendle Manufacturing Company as of 12/31/86 and 12/31/87 is shown in Table 7-1.

Assets. Assets are classified on the balance sheet as either *current* or *noncurrent.* Current assets include cash, marketable securities (i.e., short-term securities), accounts receivable, and some miscellaneous "prepaid"[1]

current assets

TABLE 7-1 Brendle Manufacturing Company Balance Sheet as of December 31 (8000)

Assets	1987	1986
Current assets:		
Cash	$ 19	$ 25
Marketable securities	56	66
Accounts receivable	293	239
Inventories	253	190
Total current assets	$ 621	$ 520
Fixed Assets:		
Gross fixed assets	$1,036	$ 967
Less: accumulated depreciation	337	327
Net fixed assets	699	640
Total assets	$1,320	$1,160
Liabilities and Stockholders Equity		
Current liabilities:		
Accounts payable	$ 149	$ 118
Notes payable	50	50
Accrued expenses	122	91
Total current liabilities	321	$ 259
Long-term debt	$ 220	$200
Deferred income taxes	140	123
Total liabilities	$ 681	$ 582
Stockholder's equity		
Common stock—$2.00 par, 50,000 shares outstanding in 1986 and 1987	100	100
Paid-in surplus	288	288
Retained earnings	251	190
Total stockholder's equity	$ 639	$ 578
Total liabilities and equity	$1,320	$1,160

[1]Such as prepaid insurance or prepaid rent. These are items paid for but not yet expensed ("written off") on the income statement.

items. By definition, current assets include cash and other assets that will be converted to cash within the year. For example, accounts receivable represent sales made on credit which the company expects to collect within the year, generally in 30 to 60 days. *Inventories* may include raw materials, work in process, and finished goods.[2] Again, it is expected that the raw materials and work in process will be converted to finished goods and sold within the year.

inventories

Noncurrent assets, by definition, include all assets with lives in excess of one year. *Fixed* assets are the most important type of noncurrent asset; they include such things as land, buildings, machinery, and equipment. In an accounting sense, a portion of such long-term investments is recovered each year through *depreciation expense.* The total amount of depreciation recovered from the assets listed is shown as *accumulated depreciation. Net fixed assets* are equal to *gross fixed* assets less accumulated depreciation.

fixed assets

depreciation expense
accumulated depreciation
net fixed assets

Liabilities. As with assets, liabilities are listed on the basis of maturity. *Current* liabilities are debts that must be paid within one year. *Accounts payable* are debts owed to suppliers. *Notes payable* generally represent bank loans but may also be short-term loans from other sources. *Accrued expenses* are miscellaneous debts which must be paid within one year. An example of an accrued expense would be employee wages that have not been paid simply because the payroll period does not coincide with the date of the balance sheet.

current liabilities

Long-term liabilities are loans that will be due beyond one year. Some long-term loans require partial payment each year. In such cases, the portion due within the year is shown in the *current liabilities* part of the balance sheet, listed as "current portion of long-term debt." Another item that frequently appears on a balance sheet is *deferred income taxes.* These are tax liabilities that result from the difference in depreciation methods used in tax reporting and financial reporting.[3]

Stockholders' Equity. Stockholders' equity represents money that the corporations' owners (Stockholders) have invested in the company since its creation. There are three accounts that comprise stockholders' equity. The *common stock account* represents the number of shares issued times the par value per share. The par value is an arbitrary number that establishes the maximum financial responsibility of a shareholder should the firm become insolvent. The Brendle Corporation common stock has a par value of $2.00, and there are 50,000 shares outstanding. Thus, the common stock account is $100,000.

common stock account

---

[2]A manufacturer would have all of these. A retailer or wholesaler would typically only have finished-goods inventories.

[3]As noted in Chapter 2, "Business Organization and Taxes," accelerated depreciation used in the tax report reduces income and income taxes. Straight-line depreciation used in the published financial statements shows higher income and higher income tax liability. The difference between the two is known as *deferred income taxes.*

The *paid in surplus account* is closely related to the common stock account. An example best explains this relationship. Assume that, upon incorporation, Brendle sold 50,000 shares at $7.76 per share. Of the total, $2.00 per share would be recorded in the common stock account and $5.76 per share would be recorded in the paid in surplus account. Since 50,000 shares were sold, the common stock account would show $100,000 (50,000 shares × $2.00 per share) and the paid in surplus account would show $288,000 (50,000 shares × $5.76 per share). In other words, the "surplus" per share is the selling price, $7.76 less the par value, $2.00.

paid in surplus account

The *retained earnings account* is the accumulated profits earned by the company since its creation less any cash dividends paid to shareholders. It is a common misconception to think that the retained earnings account represents a pool of cash being held for shareholders. The only cash the firm has is shown in the cash account on the asset side of the balance sheet. When shareholders' profits are retained and reinvested, these funds go not only into the cash account, but also into all other investments the firm makes. Thus, the Brendle Company has retained earnings of $251,000 at the end of 1987. But the company only has $19,000 in cash. Where did the rest go? It went toward the purchase of inventory, machinery, equipment, and all the other assets listed on the balance sheet.

retained earnings account

The stockholders' equity account is sometimes known as the *shareholders' equity,* or *net worth* account. Since the balance sheet must balance, notice that stockholders' equity must be equal to total assets minus total liabilities.

$$\text{Net worth} = \text{Total assets} - \text{total liabilities} \qquad (7\text{-}1)$$

Since the retained earnings account changes only as a result of profits earned (less dividends paid), it provides the formal link between the balance sheet and the income statement. Because of this relationship with the retained earnings account, the income statement could be viewed as a detailed listing of transactions affecting the retained earnings account during the year. Sales increase retained earnings. Expenses and taxes decrease retained earnings.

Income Statement

The basic purpose of the income statement is to measure the results of operations during the period. Income statements for the Brendle Manufacturing Company for the years 1986 and 1987 are shown in Table 7-2.

Net income is equal to sales (sometimes called revenues) less costs (the terms *costs* and *expenses* are used interchangeably) of producing sales and income taxes. Costs are generally categorized in three ways. *Cost of goods sold* represent costs that can be attributed directly to specific goods or services sold. For example, the raw material and labor that go into producing widgets would be included in the cost of goods sold when the widgets are sold

cost of goods sold

TABLE 7-2 Brendle Manufacturing Company Income Statement, Year
Ended December 31 ($000)

	1987	1986
Sales	$1,479	$1,436
Less: Cost of goods sold	1,062	1,031
Gross profits	417	405
Less Operating expenses:		
General and administrative	141	141
Marketing	50	50
Depreciation	10	10
Total operating expenses	201	201
Earnings before interest and taxes	216	204
Less: Interest expense	26	24
Earnings before taxes	190	180
Less: Income taxes	76	72
Net income	114	108
Earnings per share	$2.28	$2.16
Dividends per share	$1.06	$1.00

operating expenses

(and part of inventory on the balance sheet until sold).[4] If a piece of equipment was used in producing widgets, the depreciation on this equipment along with other *factory overhead,* such as utilities, would be included in the cost of goods sold. These types of costs are also called *direct* costs or *product* costs because they are not shown on the income statement as costs until the products with which they are associated are actually sold. *Operating expenses* represent expenses incurred in the normal operation of business, but which cannot be assigned to particular products. For example, executive salaries, general expenses of the marketing organization (such as advertising), and general depreciation expenses (such as depreciation on the factory and office buildings) cannot be assigned to particular products. Operating expenses are also sometimes known as *period* expenses because they are to be charged or written off during the accounting period regardless of what products might or might not be sold.

nonoperating expenses

A third category of costs is known as *nonoperating expenses.* These are general expenses not associated with the production and distribution of products. A typical example of a nonoperating expense is interest expense that must be paid on loans and that reflects the financing of the company rather than the results of operations.

gross profit

The three categories of expenses make possible the determination of four types of profit. *Gross profit* is simply net sales less cost of goods sold. This is sometimes considered a "fundamental" profit figure because it mea-

---

[4]Either as *work in process* or *finished goods.* For a retailer or wholesaler, costs of goods sold are the costs of goods purchased for resale.

sures the spread between selling prices and direct costs of producing the products. If this spread is not large enough, the firm is in danger of poor financial performance and risks being overtaken by more efficient competition. *Earnings before interest and taxes (EBIT)* is a second level of profits. This profit figure represents the spread between gross profit and operating expenses. Since EBIT is profits after direct production costs and operating expenses, it is considered a basic measure of the underlying profitability of the entire company. EBIT is also known as *operating profit.* Financial analysts are particularly concerned with EBIT because it is a profit measure unaffected by differences in the ways in which firms are financed (which would affect the interest expense), special events (such as income from the sales of assets), or wide differences in tax rates.[5]

earnings before interest and taxes

Earnings before taxes is equal to EBIT less interest expenses. It is calculated in order to determine tax liability. Taxes are determined by multiplying earnings before taxes times the company's tax rate.

earnings before taxes

Net income represents profits earned for stockholders net of all expenses associated with producing those profits. Net income is often referred to as *the bottom line* both because it is the last formal item on the income statement and also because it indicates to stockholders just how much money was earned for them from all activities during the year.

net income

Earnings per share and dividends per share, while not part of the income statement itself, are often presented after the net income figure as informational items. Earnings per share are calculated by dividing the number of common stock shares outstanding into the net income figure.[6] Dividends per share are equal to total dividends paid divided by the number of common stock shares outstanding.

earnings per share

The Statement of Cash Flows

In Chapter 1, we noted that all active organizations share three activities: operating, investing, and financing. Viewed from a financial perspective, each of these activities involves cash flows. The relationships among the various activities are shown in Exhibit 7-1.

As Exhibit 7-1 indicates, the cash and marketable securities balance is the focal point of the cash inflows and outflows produced by the company. The cash and marketable securities balance is depicted as a reservoir that rises with inflows and drops with outflows. For example, the operating activity of a business corporation involves producing goods and services for sale. The sales of these goods and services increase the reservoir while the

---

[5]For example, if a firm has had losses in prior years, it may carry them forward and reduce its taxable income and, hence, taxes in the current year. This is discussed more fully in Chapter 2, "Business Organization and Taxes." Firms may also show nonoperating income, which may be received from interest earned on short-term investments. Such income will increase profits but is not the direct result of operations.

[6]If the company has preferred stock, the dividends on the preferred must be deducted from net income before calculating earnings per share.

costs of producing the goods and services decrease the reservoir. Likewise, investing activities involve cash outflows for the purchase of plant and equipment, buildings, and other long-term assets. Conversely, sales of long-term assets produce cash inflows. Finally, financing activities including borrowing or the sale of common stock produce cash inflows while the repayment of debt, repurchase of stock, or payment of dividends all produce cash outflows related to financing activities. In short, the cash flows within the company are complex and continuous.

Much can be learned about a company by analyzing the pattern of its cash flows over a period of time. The statement of cash flows combines information from the income statement and balance sheet in order to provide a description of the cash flows within the company during a period of time.[7]

The statement contains three main parts: cash flows from operating activities, cash flows from investing activities, and cash flows from fi-

EXHIBIT 7-1
Cash Flow Relationships

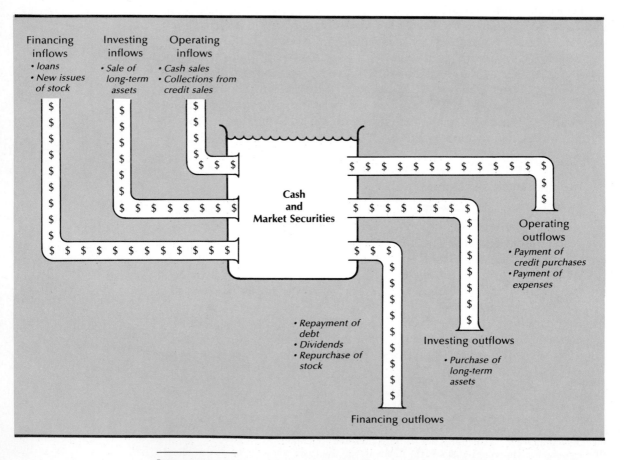

---

[7]The statement is very similar to the statement of changes in financial position and (as of this writing) is expected to replace it in the annual report.

TABLE 7-3 Brendle Manufacturing Company Statement of Cash Flows for the Period 1986–1987 ($000)

Cash flows from operating activities:		
Net income	$114	
Depreciation	10	
Increase in deferred income taxes	17	
Increase in accounts receivable	(54)	
Increase in inventory	(63)	
Increase in accounts payable	31	
Increase in accruals	31	
Net cash flows from operations		$86
Cash flows from investing activities:		
Increase in gross fixed assets	($69)	
Net cash outflows for investing activities		($69)
Cash flows from financing activities:		
Increase in long-term debt	20	
Dividends paid	($53)	
Net cash flows from financing		($33)
Net increase (decrease) in cash		($16)

nancing activities.[8] A statement of cash flows for the Brendle Company is shown in Table 7-3.

Cash Flows From Operating Activities.   The income statement matches sales and expenses to compute net income. If all sales and expenses were on a cash basis, the net income figure would represent the cash from operations. However, if any sales or expenses are not cash, net income will not be equal to the cash flow from operations. In order to determine the cash flows from operations, the net income figure must be adjusted to reflect noncash sales and expense transactions. Information about noncash sales and expense items is shown on the balance sheet.

By examining the changes in balance sheet accounts from one period to the next, the net income figure can be converted to a net cash flow from operations. This has been done for the Brendle Company in Table 7-3. Note that, since depreciation and deferred taxes reduce net income but do not affect the cash account, they are added back. Second, changes in current asset and current liability accounts may absorb or provide cash in the normal course of operations, and these changes must be reflected if the cash flows are to be complete. The impact of balance-sheet changes on the cash account can be determined by the following relationships:

---

[8]In Chapter 8 we will show in more detail how the statement of cash flows is constructed.

Sources of cash

Decrease in any asset account
Increase in any liability or equity account

Uses of cash

Increase in any asset account
Decrease in any liability or equity account

For example, if a company sells on credit, its accounts receivable will increase but not its cash account. Thus, an increase in accounts receivable is shown as a use of cash. A decrease in accounts receivable, on the other hand, represents a collection from customers and is a source of cash. Liabilities are just the reverse. An increase in borrowing is a source of cash while a repayment (i.e., decrease) of debt would be a use of cash. Note that only changes in current assets and current liabilities are included in the cash-flow-from-operations computation. Changes in long-term assets and liabilities are shown as investing or financing cash flows.

Investing Cash Flows. Increases in long-term assets represent a use of cash for investment purposes. For example, purchase of a machine would be treated as a use of cash for an investing activity. Conversely, a sale of equipment or other long-term asset would be a source of cash. Investment expenditures are reflected in the gross fixed assets figure on the balance sheet. An increase of $69,000 in this item indicates that this amount of cash was used for investments.

Financing Cash Flows. Changes in long-term liabilities and equity accounts affect the cash and marketable securities balance. For example, an increase in long-term debt will generate a cash inflow, while the payment of dividends to shareholders will be a use of cash related to the firm's financing methods.

Net Increase (Decrease) in Cash. The net cash flows from each of the business activities are combined to produce the net impact on the firm's cash and marketable securities balance. The net change should be the same as the change indicated by the comparative balance sheets. Thus, the computed net decrease in cash of $16,000 for the Brendle Company is the same as the change in cash and marketable securities on the balance sheet.

The Statement of Retained Earnings

The Statement of Retained Earnings is a brief summary of transactions that affected the retained earnings account during the period. Typically, this statement indicates the amount and disposition of any profits earned.

TABLE 7-4 Brendle Manufacturing Company Statement of Retained Earnings for the Year Ended December 31, 1987	
Retained earnings, Jan. 1, 1987	$190,000
Add net income for 1987	114,000
Less dividends	−53,000
Retained earnings, Dec. 31, 1987	$251,000

The statement of retained earnings for the Brendle Company for the year ended December 31, 1987 is shown in Table 7-4.

A MANAGERIAL VIEW OF THE FINANCIAL STATEMENTS

One theme of this text is that the financial manager requires an understanding of, and interaction with, other functional areas of management in the firm. This is because his or her major responsibility is to illuminate the financial consequences of marketing, production, and administrative policies, decisions, and performance. Nowhere is this more evident than in the analysis of financial statements. While these statements are "financial" in that they are based on financial accounting records and principles, it is important to recognize that they summarize the financial consequences of *managerial* activities throughout the company. Indeed, the analysis of financial statements is of value principally for the information it provides on the effectiveness of marketing, production, and administration. Thus, the financial analyst must "translate" financial data in terms of these management functions to determine what is going on within a company.

Students of finance have a natural tendency to focus on the numbers of financial statements and to overlook the fact that the numbers simply summarize in economic terms the actions and decisions of hundreds, perhaps thousands, of employees. The analysis of financial statements becomes vastly richer when interpreted in these managerial terms.

Example

The *Sales* figure on the income statement reflects the revenues generated by the firm over a period of time. Yet, since sales are generated by the efforts of the entire marketing organization, the analysis of sales performance reflects the effectiveness with which the marketing organization carried out its tasks. Sales is the product of volumes of goods and services the marketing organization sold and the prices at which they could be sold. If financial analysis indicates that sales are too low, for example, the explanation will have to come from the marketing manager. Perhaps the company's competitive market position has eroded. Perhaps the company is not emphasizing the right products. Perhaps prices are out of line with those of competitors. Or, more generally, perhaps the economy was depressed. Whatever the explanation, the point is that financial analysis helps focus attention quickly on the right managers and the right questions.

Financial Analysis and the Marketing Group

Marketing activities are also reflected on the balance sheet. The level of accounts receivable is determined by the credit policies of the firm and the degree of control exercised over credit. This topic will be covered in detail later. Financial analysis helps determine whether credit is being managed effectively. In its effort to sell products competitively, it is in the interest of the marketing department to grant liberal credit terms and to avoid offending credit customers who might be slow in paying. However, from the company's overall perspective, any build-up in accounts receivable must be financed by borrowing, retaining shareholders' profits, drawing down the cash account, or selling other assets. Remember, the balance sheet must balance. What is good for the marketing department may not be in the best overall interests of the company.

Financial analysis not only helps identify managerial practices that seem to be out of line. It also helps guide decision making by managers in the overall interest of the company. Managerial "tunnel vision" can easily result in unbalanced corporate performance. Financial analysis helps coordinate individual decisions toward a common goal.

Financial Analysis and the Operations Group

The cost-of-goods-sold figure on the income statement reflects the volume of goods and services sold as well as the cost per unit of producing them. Thus, this figure indicates the effectiveness of the company's production activities. Financial analysis helps determine whether the company's production costs are too high. If production is inefficient or relatively costly, the cost-of-goods-sold figure will be higher than it should be. Is production scheduling inefficient? Are production labor costs excessive? Is technology outmoded? Is the purchasing department paying more for raw materials than is necessary? These are the types of questions that only a close inspection of production activities can answer. But the financial manager has made an important contribution by simply identifying an area, production in this case, that should be examined by management in order to improve results.

The previous applications have tried to demonstrate the fact that financial statements encompass all functional areas of the firm. For this reason they represent a "report card" on management. The income statement reports the most recent review period; the balance sheet represents the cumulative results of policies, decisions, and performance as of a single point in time. The relationship between the financial statements and various management functions is suggested in Exhibit 7-2. For example, "sales" and "selling expenses" on the income statement and "accounts receivable" on the balance sheet primarily reflect the activities of the marketing organization. "Cost of goods sold" on the income statement and "inventory" on the balance sheet reflect the activities of the production function. "General and administrative" expenses and "depreciation" on the income statement reflect the costs of overall management of the company. "Interest expense" on the income statement and "cash," "debt," and "shareholders' equity" on the balance sheet reflect on the finance function of the company. Naturally, in each of these areas there are overlapping responsibilities; and more detailed internal analysis will reveal them.

USE OF FINANCIAL RATIOS

In order to be interpreted meaningfully, financial ratios must be compared against some benchmark. Three principal ways to compare ratios are: *cross-sectional* comparisons, *time series* comparisons, and comparisons against management *targets*. Wherever possible, a combination of all three methods should be used in evaluating ratios.

*cross sectional
comparisons
time series comparisons
comparisons against
management targets*

Cross Sectional Comparisons

Cross-sectional comparisons involve comparing a firm's ratios with those of other firms of about the same size in the same industry. A cross-

EXHIBIT 7-2
Relationship Between
Financial Statements and
Management Functions

Management Function	Income Statement	Balance Sheet
MARKETING	Sales Selling expenses	Accounts receivable
		Inventory
PRODUCTION	Cost of goods sold	Fixed assets
ADMINISTRATION	General & administrative Depreciation	
FINANCE	Interest expense	Cash Debt Shareholders' equity

sectional comparison may also involve comparing a firm's ratios with some *industry average* or directly against the firm's main rivals.

profit margin ratio

Example

The *profit margin ratio* is calculated by dividing net income by sales. Assume that the Jones Company had sales of $100,000 and net income of $10,000 in 1987. This means the profit margin for the Jones Company was 10 percent in 1987. In other words, the Jones Company made a profit of 10 cents on each dollar of sales. If one knows that the industry average profit margin was 7 percent in 1987, one can say that the Jones Company appeared to have above-average profit performance in 1987. If Jones' main competitor, the Drew company, had a profit margin of 8 percent, it appears that Jones' profitability on sales was competitively strong.

All such comparisons, of course, must be made with care. Differences among firms on the basis of size, accounting practices, product mix, level of integration in production or distribution, extent of diversification, and other factors can result in significant differences in ratios. The effective financial analyst never jumps to conclusions on the basis of ratios alone; for him or her, ratios provide clues, not answers.

Times Series Comparisons

A second standard which the financial manager should use to evaluate ratios is the past record of the company. This type of analysis, also known as *trend analysis*, has two principal advantages. First, it compares a company's recent ratios against its own past performance. When comparisons with other firms or industry averages are not helpful, this may be the most relevant standard for comparison. Second, by examining a company's ratios over a period of time, trends can be more readily detected.

trend analysis

Example

The Jones Company's profit margin was 10 percent in 1987, 8 percent in 1986, 6 percent in 1985, and 6 percent in 1984. Over time, the Company's profitability on sales has steadily increased. Again, there are many possible reasons for the pattern, but the trend suggests that the Company's relative performance in 1987, when compared to the industry average, does not appear to have been a "fluke."

Like cross-sectional comparisons, time series comparisons are not completely reliable. For example, a firm might alter its own accounting practices significantly from one year to the next; or, it might alter its product mix substantially over time; or, it might diversify to a significant extent by acquiring other firms. Additionally, the economic environment might change dramatically as the economy moves through a business cycle, or the company's competitive environment might change dramatically. Any of these factors can influence ratios over time. However, good judgment along with industry and trend analyses should allow the financial manager to develop an accurate profile of how the firm performed in the past and to assess the current operating and financial position more accurately.

Management Targets

A third basis of comparison is the internal management targets the firm may set for itself. These financial ratio targets reflect efforts by management to control and guide performance so that strategic objectives will be realized.

Example

Jones' top management had set a profit margin target of 9 percent for 1987. The Company's actual profit margin of 10 percent was above the target and, hence, the firm was "successful" in this area.

Management targets are useful in helping a firm improve its financial performance over time. In many respects, management targets represent the most meaningful standards of comparison because, if realistic, they measure the company's performance on the basis of what it *should* be doing rather than what it has done in the past (time series analysis) or what other companies, which might be quite different, are doing (cross-sectional comparisons). Although some firms do publicly state their performance goals or targets in some areas (e.g., a firm's president may announce the company's intention of producing a 15-percent return on equity on average), such information is primarily internal.

A Composite Picture

Wherever possible, all three types of benchmarks should be used to avoid improper comparisons. An example of such a composite is shown in Exhibit 7-3. The industry average or norm for profit margin is shown as a horizontal line. The dashed line shows the company's trend over six years, while the unbroken line represents management targets.

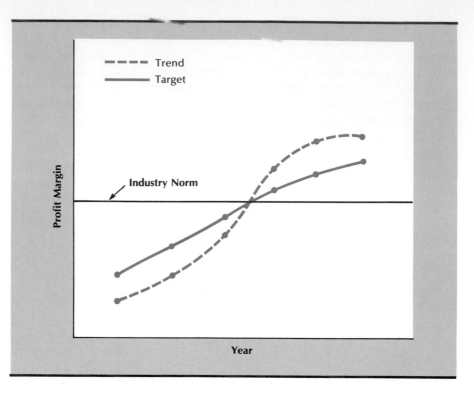

EXHIBIT 7-3
Composite Trends

TYPES OF FINANCIAL RATIOS

The quantity and variety of ratios that may be calculated are limitless. However, ratios tend to fall into five main types.

liquidity ratios

1. *Liquidity ratios* indicate the ability of the firm to meet short-term obligations as they come due.

activity ratios

2. *Activity, or utilization, ratios* indicate the efficiency or productivity with which assets were managed.

leverage ratios

3. *Financial, or leverage, ratios* indicate the extent to which borrowed or debt funds are used to finance assets.

profitability ratios

4. *Profitability ratios* indicate the firm's effectiveness in terms of profit margins and rates of return on investment.

market-value ratios

5. *Market-value ratios* reflect the value which investors place on the company.

Liquidity Ratios

Liquidity ratios measure the firm's ability to meet obligations to short-term creditors when such obligations mature or come due. The less liquid the firm, the greater the risk. Debt obligations are paid with cash, and thus the firm's cash flows ultimately determine solvency.[9]

It is possible, however, to estimate the firm's liquidity by examining several balance-sheet items. This type of liquidity analysis centers on the relation of current assets to current liabilities and the rapidity with which receivables and inventory turn into cash in the normal course of the business.

The *current ratio* and *quick ratio* are used to gauge the firm's liquidity position.[10] It is also useful to assess the firm's credit payment practices, as reflected in the *payables turnover ratio* and the *average payment period ratio*.

current ratio
quick ratio

payables turnover ratio

average payment period ratio

Current Ratio. The current ratio is a measure of a company's ability to meet its current debts. It is calculated by dividing current assets by current liabilities. An unusually low current ratio indicates that a company may face some difficulty in meeting its bills; an unusually high current ratio suggests that funds are not being used economically within the firm. For example, there may be excessive amounts of inventory on hand, some of which may be obsolete or slow moving. The amounts of accounts receivable may be excessive, or there may be large idle cash balances. By the use of the quick ratio described below, additional analysis of the company's current position may be obtained. The liquidity of the Brendle Company declined between 1986 and 1987 when examined in terms of the current ratio as shown below. Also, since Brendle's 1987 position was below the industry average, the financial manager should be interested in exploring why this occurred.

<u>1987</u>   <u>1986</u>

Current Ratio:

$$\frac{\text{Current assets}}{\text{Current liabilities}} = \frac{\$621,000}{\$321,000} = 1.93:1 \qquad \frac{\$520,000}{\$259,000} = 2.01:1$$

$$= 1.93 \text{ times} \qquad = 2.01 \text{ times}$$

Industry average $= 2.00:1 = 2.00$ times

Quick, or "Acid Test," Ratio. Strictly speaking, this is computed by dividing the sum of cash, marketable securities, and accounts receivable (these three are called "quick" assets) by current liabilities. More typically,

---

[9]Thus, the best way to assess the firm's liquidity is to project its actual cash flows via a cash budget. Typically, however, outsiders do not have access to sufficiently detailed data to prepare meaningful cash budget projections. The statement of cash flows along with liquidity ratios are often the best alternatives.

[10]While difficult to compare meaningfully, it is very useful to examine the firm's net working capital level. Net working capital is equal to current assets minus current liabilities. The current ratio is an attempt to standardize this relationship so that it may be compared on a cross-sectional or time-series basis. Again, these may be the only readily available indicators of the firm's liquidity. But they can be misleading and must be used with care.

the ratio is calculated by simply dividing current assets less inventory by current liabilities. Since this comparison eliminates the inventories from consideration, it serves as another check on the adequacy of the current ratios.[11] It is a measure of the extent to which cash and "near cash" (including accounts receivable) cover the current liabilities. The change between the two years also indicates a decline in Brendle's liquidity position to a level slightly below the industry average.

	1987		1986	

Quick Ratio:

$$\frac{\text{Current assets} - \text{Inventory}}{\text{Current liabilities}} = \frac{\$368,000}{321,000} = \frac{1.15}{\text{times}} \quad \frac{\$330,000}{259,000} = \frac{1.27}{\text{times}}$$

Industry Average = 1.20 times

As with the other ratios, the trends in this measure from year to year are worth observing. Given the actual data for the Brendle Company, it probably is not of immediate concern. However, Brendle's quick ratio is moving toward 1:1; and if the current liabilities should come to exceed cash and receivables, creditors may become uneasy.

Payables Turnover and Average Payment Period. As a firm becomes less liquid, it may have difficulties in paying its trade creditors promptly. Trends in this direction may be revealed by calculating *payables turnover* or the *average payment period*. The payables turnover is computed by dividing annual credit purchases by the year-end accounts payable. An alternative computation is to determine the average daily credit purchases (annual credit purchases/360 days)[12] and then divide this average into the accounts payable outstanding to determine the *average payment period*. Adequate credit purchases information is not available from a firm's income statement.[13] Thus, unless additional information is provided, the analyst is forced to use the cost of goods sold. Brendle's ratios are based on using annual cost of goods sold; they indicate a slowing in the firm's paying habits on credit purchases. However, 1987 results were very close to the industry average.

	1987		1986	

Payables Turnover:

$$\frac{\text{Cost of goods sold}}{\text{Accounts payable}} = \frac{\$1,062,000}{\$149,000} = \frac{7.13}{\text{times}} \quad \frac{\$1,031,000}{\$118,000} = \frac{8.74}{\text{times}}$$

[11]The main reason for omitting inventory is for purposes of "conservatism." Since the inventory has not been sold, there is no guarantee that it will generate needed cash. However, by eliminating this significant current asset altogether, the firm's true liquidity may be underestimated.

[12]Following conventional practice, calculations are based on a 360-day year simply to make calculations easier.

[13]While this limits external analysis, internal financial analysis might permit identifying credit purchases to be, for example, 60 percent of cost of goods sold. Since this percentage could change from time to time and thus distort payables turnover and average payment period ratio comparisons, credit purchases should be used when possible.

Average Payment Period:

$$\frac{\text{Accounts payable}}{\text{Cost of goods sold} \div 360} = \frac{\text{Accounts payable}}{\text{Cost of goods sold per day}}$$

	1987		1986	

$$\frac{\$149,000}{1,062,000 \div 360} = \frac{\$149,000}{\$2,950} = \frac{50.5}{\text{days}} \qquad \frac{\$118,000}{1,031,000 \div 360} = \frac{\$118,000}{2,864} = \frac{41.2}{\text{days}}$$

Industry average = 50.0 days

Activity, or Utilization, Ratios

Activity, or utilization ratios indicate how well the firm is using its total assets to support sales. They also indicate how well the firm uses its fixed assets and various components of its total assets, such as accounts receivable or inventories.

Total Assets Turnover.   This is computed by dividing sales by the firm's *total assets turnover* total assets. Brendle's 1986 and 1987 total assets turnover ratios are calculated as follows:

	1987		1986	

Total Assets Turnover:

$$\frac{\text{Sales}}{\text{Total assets}} = \frac{\$1,479,000}{1,320,000} = \frac{1.12}{\text{times}} \qquad \frac{\$1,436,000}{1,160,000} = \frac{1.24}{\text{times}}$$

Industry Average = 1.20 times

Asset utilization declined to a level below the industry average. The financial manager should want to know why. This could be accomplished, at least in part, by examining some of the asset categories in greater detail.

Fixed Assets Turnover.   This is computed by dividing sales by the firm's *fixed assets turnover* long-term, or fixed, assets. It indicates whether a firm has altered its capital intensity (fixed assets) relative to sales. Brendle's fixed assets turnover declined from 2.24 to 2.12, indicating that fixed assets increased more rapidly than sales and thus account for at least part of the decline in the assets turnover ratio.

	1987		1986	

Fixed Assets Turnover:

$$\frac{\text{Sales}}{\text{Fixed assets}} = \frac{\$1,479,000}{699,000} = \frac{2.12}{\text{times}} \qquad \frac{\$1,436,000}{640,000} = \frac{2.24}{\text{times}}$$

Industry Average = 2.10 times

Receivables Turnover and Average Collection Period.   The receivables *receivables turnover ratio* turnover is computed by dividing annual sales, preferably credit sales, by the year-end accounts receivable. The purpose is to measure the liquidity of the receivables. If the annual rate of turnover is six times, this means that, on the average, receivables are collected in two months. If the turnover is four times, the firm must wait an average of three months for the return of funds invested in receivables. The average collection period ratio indicates how many days it is taking the firm to collect on its receivables. This ratio is calculated by dividing average credit sales per day (e.g., total credit sales/360 days) into accounts receivable. If adequate credit sales information is not available, the analyst is forced to use total sales. This is the case for Brendle. Thus, the following calculations are based on sales.

<u>1987</u>   <u>1986</u>

Receivables Turnover:

$$\frac{\text{Sales}}{\text{Accounts receivable}} = \frac{\$1,479,000}{293,000} = \frac{5.05}{\text{times}} \qquad \frac{\$1,436,000}{239,000} = \frac{6.01}{\text{times}}$$

Industry Average = 5.50 times

Average Collection Period:

$$\frac{\text{Accounts receivable}}{\text{Sales} \div 360} = \frac{\text{Accounts receivable}}{\text{Sales per day}}$$

<u>1987</u>

$$\frac{\$293,000}{\$1,479,000 \div 360} = \frac{\$293,000}{4,108} = 71.3 \text{ days}$$

<u>1986</u>

$$\frac{\$239,000}{\$1,436,000 \div 360} = \frac{\$239,000}{3,989} = 59.9 \text{ days}$$

Industry Average = 65.5 days

Brendle's average collection period has increased from approximately 60 days to 71.3 days. This suggests a possible future liquidity problem. This concern is reinforced by the fact that the industry's average collection period is only slightly more than 65 days.

When a company has experienced a sharp growth in sales or when its sales are seasonal, care must be used in evaluating the receivables turnover ratio. If sales have increased in the months preceding the end of a fiscal year, the year-end accounts receivables appearing on the books will reflect those enlarged sales. Comparison of these accounts receivables with sales for the entire year will be misleading because the level of sales for the entire year is not representative of the much higher rate of sales experienced in the last few months. If the figure for year-end receivables is used, the calculated receivable turnover figure will appear to be low. In this case, it would be better to compare sales to a monthly or quarterly average of accounts receivable. If sales are seasonal, such as those of a department store, it may not be objectionable to compare the receivables turnover ratio from one year to the next, so long as the fluctuations in sales occur about the same time each year. It would clearly be inappropriate to compare the receivables turnover ratio of one department store as of July 31 with that of another store as of January 31.[14]

As with the other ratios, this one may also be too high or too low. An unusually high turnover of accounts receivables for a particular line of business may indicate an unnecessarily tight credit policy that is hurting sales by driving away slow-paying customers. The firm may be selecting only the best customers or may be insisting on unusually strict payment terms. If this situation exists, it may also be reflected in a low turnover of inventory and in a low ratio of sales to operating assets. In contrast, an unusually low turnover of accounts receivable would indicate a congestion of funds that would cut down on the available flow of funds for reinvestment in inventory.

The relationship between a firm's average collection period (the financing terms it provides to customers) and its average payment period (the financing it receives from suppliers) is very important to its cash cycle and liquidity position. Ideally, a firm wants at least as good credit terms from suppliers as it gives to its customers. In the case of the Brendle Company, the 1986 average collection period was about 60 days, compared with about 41 days for the average payment period. Since Brendle must meet its short-term creditor obligations more frequently than it receives payment from its customers, plans must be made for financing this difference. An increase in the average collection period occurred in 1987. However, Brendle was able to offset this largely by slowing its own payments to suppliers.

Inventory Turnover. Inventory turnover is computed by dividing the cost of goods sold by the year-end inventory.[15]

Here one is seeking to determine how rapidly funds flow through the inventory pool and how current that inventory is. This turnover figure *inventory turnover* indicates whether the inventory is deficient or excessive in relation to the level of sales. Brendle's annual inventory turnover has declined from 5.43 to 4.20 times, to a level somewhat below the industry average. It should be of concern to the financial manager.

---

[14]This is a real limitation from the standpoint of external financial analysis. Internal analysis would allow the financial manager to determine more exactly the accounts receivable collection pattern and the mix between cash and credit sales. Other techniques of credit analysis are discussed in Chapter 11.

[15]When a firm's sales level changes greatly from one period to the next, this ratio should be calculated using average inventory in the denominator. Average inventory is equal to beginning inventory plus ending inventory, divided by two. Also, this ratio is sometimes calculated by dividing total sales by ending (or average) inventory. This tends to overstate the turnover rate because inventory is usually recorded at cost rather than at sales prices.

<table>
<tr><td></td><td>1987</td><td>1986</td></tr>
</table>

| | 1987 | 1986 |

Inventory Turnover:

$$\frac{\text{Cost of goods sold}}{\text{Inventory}} = \frac{\$1,062,000}{253,000} = \frac{4.20}{\text{times}} \qquad \frac{\$1,031,000}{\$190,000} = \frac{5.43}{\text{times}}$$

Industry Average = 4.35 times

An unusually low or declining inventory turnover suggests various possibilities. Every firm makes a compromise between being out of stock on occasion and tying up funds in inventory. A decline in inventory turnover indicates that, in making this compromise, the firm has been leaning more toward keeping a full stock on hand. When the turnover is unusually low, it also suggests that there may be obsolete or slow-moving stock on hand.

An unusually high turnover is not necessarily ideal. In a manufacturing concern, efforts to maintain an especially high turnover of raw materials may be penalized by running out of items so that production lines are shut down. A high turnover of finished goods may indicate that the company is losing profitable sales by being out of stock too frequently. It is even possible that a high turnover may be the result of a reduction in the selling price to increase sales (but also resulting in a decrease in profitability). Whether or not this policy is in the long-term interests of the firm depends on the operating performance achieved.

Financial Leverage Ratios

The use of borrowed funds to purchase assets affects both the income statement and the balance sheet. The financial manager should be interested in the firm's ability (as indicated by income-statement data) to meet or service its interest and principal repayment obligations on the borrowed funds. This safety factor is reflected in interest coverage and fixed charge coverage ratios and also by the amount of total debt carried by the firm.

debt ratio

Total Debt to Total Assets (Debt Ratio). This is computed by dividing the total debt or liabilities of the business by the total assets. This ratio is also commonly known as the *debt ratio*. It shows the portion of the total assets financed by the creditors. Brendle's total debt ratio increased slightly during 1987 but still remained somewhat lower than the industry average.

| | 1987 | 1986 |

Total Debt to Total Assets:

$$\frac{\text{Total debt}}{\text{Total assets}} = \frac{\$681,000}{\$1,320,000} = .516 \qquad \frac{\$582,000}{\$1,160,000} = .502$$

$$= 51.6\% \qquad\qquad = 50.2\%$$

Industry Average = 52.4%

A debt-to-assets ratio that is too high tells the financial manager that the chances of securing additional borrowed funds are slight, or that additional funds will cost more. Indeed, pressure from creditors may soon restrict the firm's activities in many other respects as well. For example, investments in fixed assets, as well as dividend payments, may be restricted by creditors. It is also possible to have too low a ratio of debt to total assets, since there are tax benefits associated with the use of debt.

Equity Multiplier. The *equity multiplier* is computed by dividing total assets by the firm's common equity or net worth. It provides an alternative way of looking at the firm's use of total financial leverage. Brendle's equity multiplier changed little between 1986 and 1987 and remained a little under the industry average.

equity multiplier

	1987	**1986**

Equity Multiplier:

$$\frac{\text{Total Assets}}{\text{Common equity}} = \frac{\$1,320,000}{639,000} = \frac{2.07}{\text{times}} \qquad \frac{\$1,160,000}{578,000} = \frac{2.01}{\text{times}}$$

$$\text{Industry Average} = 2.10$$

Brendle's financial leverage appears to have increased but is still below the industry average.

Cash Flow to Total Debt. This ratio measures the cash flow produced by the firm relative to total debt. It is a rough estimate of how long it would take the company to pay off all its debts if all of its cash flows were simply used to pay its debts each year. Obviously, a company's cash flows will be allocated to making investments in assets as well as paying some debts each year if the company is to grow. However, it does measure a company's burden of debt relative to its ability to generate cash. A company's cash flow is estimated by adding net income and depreciation. The calculations for Brendle are shown below.

cash flow to total debt

Cash flow to total debt:

$$\frac{(\text{Net income} + \text{Depreciation})}{\text{Total debt}}$$

	1987	**1986**

$$= \frac{(\$114,000 + 10,000)}{\$681,000} \qquad = \frac{(108,000 + 10,000)}{\$582,000}$$

$$= 18.2\% \qquad\qquad = 20.3\%$$

$$\text{Industry Average: } 11.5\%$$

Brendle's cash flow relative to total debt has deteriorated slightly in 1987 but is still above the industry average. To see how this ratio may be interpreted, consider that, if Brendle's cash flow is about one-fifth of its total debt, it would take Brendle about five years to pay off all its debts if all cash flows were used for this purpose, continued at that level, and if Brendle did not borrow more money.

We have seen, however, from the statement of cash flows, that the cash flow from operations must also be adjusted for working capital changes as well as depreciation. Thus, the actual cash flow from operations generated in 1987 was more like $86,000 (see Table 7-3) than the $124,000 calculated above. This produces a cash-flow-to-total-debt ratio of only 12.6 percent rather than the 18.2 percent indicated:

$$\text{Cash Flow from Operations to Total Debt} = \frac{\$86,000}{\$681,000} = 12.6\%$$

The ratio is much lower, but in order to evaluate it properly one would have to compute the figures for 1986 and the industry in the same fashion. It is likely that the same pattern as the net-income-plus-depreciation method would be indicated.

interest coverage

Interest Coverage (Times Interest Earned). *Interest coverage,* or *times interest earned,* is calculated by dividing the earnings before interest and taxes (EBIT) by the annual interest charges. Brendles' interest coverage remains well above the industry average.

	1987	**1986**

Times Interest Earned:

$$\frac{\text{EBIT}}{\text{Interest Expense}} = \frac{\$216,000}{26,000} = \frac{8.30}{\text{times}} \qquad \frac{\$204,000}{24,000} = \frac{8.50}{\text{times}}$$

Industry Average = 7.00 times

The interest coverage figure indicates the extent to which the EBIT level could decline before the margin of protection for the long-term creditors will be impeded. If a new bond issue is contemplated, it is desirable to add the interest charges already carried to those that will be added by the proposed bond issue to judge its safety.[16]

fixed charge coverage

Fixed Charges Coverage. In addition to interest payments there may be other *fixed charges,* such as rental or lease payments and sinking-fund payments on debt. The latter are periodic payments that are required to

---

[16]A number of statistical models have been developed in recent years for purposes of predicting possible corporate bankruptcy and for purposes of conducting credit analysis. These techniques employ various types of ratios that, when taken together, provide a basis for evaluating business firms. For example, see Edward I. Altman. "Financial Ratios, Discriminant Analysis and the Prediction of Corporate Bankruptcy." *Journal of Finance,* September 1968, pp. 589–609; and Edward I. Altman, R. G. Haldeman, and P. Narayanan. "ZETA Analysis: A New Model to Identify Bankruptcy Risk of Corporations." *Journal of Banking and Finance,* June 1977, pp. 29–54.

reduce the principal amount of the debt. While frequently required on corporate bond issues, a more familiar example of sinking-fund payments may be found in installment loans and most home mortgages. These are customarily arranged so that part of each payment is for interest and the remaining part serves to reduce the outstanding balance of the principal. The latter portion of the payment is a sinking-fund payment.

Since the sinking fund is merely a repayment of debt, it is *not* a deductible expense for income tax purposes. Because the times-fixed-charges-earned calculation is to be on a before-tax basis, the sinking-fund payment must be adjusted to a before-tax basis as well. To do this, one must ask: What must be the amount of earning before interest and taxes that is just sufficient to cover the after-tax sinking fund payment? Any figure, including a sinking fund, that is on an after-tax basis can be restated on a before-tax basis by dividing the after-tax amount by one minus the tax rate.

Sinking-fund payments and rental or lease payments generally are indicated in footnotes[17] to a firm's annual report. While footnotes to Brendle's balance sheets are not provided, let us assume that the company had no lease payments, that sinking fund obligations were $10,000 in each year, and that its tax rate was 40%. This makes it possible to calculate fixed charge coverage for Brendle as follows:

Fixed Charge Coverage:

$$\frac{\text{Earning-before interest, lease payments and taxes}}{\text{Interest} + \text{Lease payments} + [(\text{Sinking-fund payment})/(1 - \text{tax rate})]}$$

1987

$$\frac{\$216,000}{\$26,000 + (\$10,000/.60)} = \frac{5.06}{\text{times}}$$

1986

$$\frac{\$204,000}{\$24,000 + (\$10,000/.60)} = \frac{5.02}{\text{times}}$$

Industry Average = 4.60 times

Again, there is a slight deterioration in 1987 relative to 1986; but the company is still above average in fixed charge coverage.

Alternatively, this calculation may be based upon annual cash flow generated before taxes rather than just earnings before interest, lease payments, and taxes (EBIT). The addition in the numerator of the ratio would come mainly from noncash charges against income, such as amortization and depreciation expenses. This form of the calculation matches an estimate of the cash inflows to the required cash outflows for interest, lease payments, and pre-tax cost of sinking fund payments.

---

[17]I.e., the "Notes to Accompany Financial Statements."

Calculation of coverage ratios is made more complex when preferred stock is present in the financial structure. Preferred stock is an ownership interest, but annual dividend payments are usually limited to a stated level. Dividends on the preferred stock must be paid before any share of earnings is paid to the common stockholders who are, of course, the residual owners. Since preferred stock dividends are paid out of after-tax dollars, they are best handled just like sinking fund payments. That is, the preferred dividend amount would be divided by one minus the effective tax rate, with the resulting amount being added to the denominator of the fixed charges coverage ratio.

Profitability Ratios

profit margin ratios
rate of return ratios

There are two principal types of profitability ratios. *Profit margin* ratios focus on different parts of the income statement. *Rate of return* ratios are more inclusive and examine the relationship between profits and the investment needed to generate the profits.

gross profit margin

The *gross profit margin* is calculated by dividing gross profits by sales. The calculations for the Brendle Company are shown below:

	1987	1986

Gross Profit Margin:

$$\frac{\text{Gross profit}}{\text{Sales}} = \frac{\$417,000}{\$1,479,000} \qquad \frac{\$405,000}{\$1,436,000}$$

$$= 28.2\% \qquad\qquad 28.2\%$$

Industry Average: 27.5%

The gross profit margin sheds some light on the firm's cost/price structure. The gross profit margin reflects the effectiveness of the production activities, the strength of selling prices, and the input costs of labor and materials. Importantly, the gross profit margin may also simply reflect a change in the product sales mix. If a firm moves from a low-margin/high-volume product mix to a high-margin/low-volume product mix, the change in the gross profit margin could be significant. There has been no change in Brendle's gross profit margin, even though sales have increased. Brendle is slightly more profitable in this ratio than the industry average.

operating profit margin

The *operating profit margin* is calculated by dividing operating profits (EBIT) by sales. For Brendle, the operating profit margin is calculated as:

	1987	1986

Operating Profit Margin:

$$\frac{\text{EBIT}}{\text{Sales}} = \frac{\$216,000}{\$1,479,000} = .146 \qquad \frac{\$204,000}{\$1,436,000} = .142$$

$$= 14.6\% \qquad\qquad = 14.2\%$$

Industry Average = .130 = 13.0%

The operating profit margin reflects both the cost of goods sold as a percentage of sales and all other operating expenses as a percentage of sales. Brendle's operating profit margin has increased slightly in 1987 and was above the industry average in both 1986 and 1987.

net profit margin

The *net profit margin* was introduced earlier. It is calculated by dividing net income by sales. The calculation for Brendle is shown below:

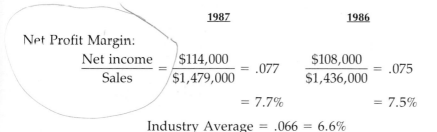

	1987	1986
Net Profit Margin:		
$\dfrac{\text{Net income}}{\text{Sales}} =$	$\dfrac{\$114,000}{\$1,479,000} = .077$	$\dfrac{\$108,000}{\$1,436,000} = .075$
	$= 7.7\%$	$= 7.5\%$

Industry Average $= .066 = 6.6\%$

Brendle's net profit margin is above the industry average and shows a slight improvement in 1987 over 1986. Thus, Brendle seems to be doing well controlling expenses relative to sales in terms of a two-year trend and industry comparisons.

operating profit rate of return

The *operating profit rate of return* is calculated by dividing operating profit (EBIT) by total assets. This calculation is shown below for the Brendle Company. Notice that this return, while declining for Brendle, still exceeded the industry average in 1987.

	1987	1986
Operating Profit Return:		
$\dfrac{\text{EBIT}}{\text{Total assets}} =$	$\dfrac{\$216,000}{\$1,320,000} = .164$	$\dfrac{\$204,000}{\$1,160,000} = .176$
	$= 16.4\%$	$= 17.6\%$

Industry Average $- .150 = 15.0\%$

return on assets ratio

The *return on assets* ratio is typically calculated by dividing net income by total assets. A difficulty with this method of calculating the ratio is that it does not measure all the returns produced by management. Net income is the return to shareholders only. If the firm has debt, the return provided to debtholders (i.e., interest) should be shown. In order to adjust for this, analysts add interest payments after taxes to the numerator.[18]

The return on assets ratio for Brendle has been calculated in two ways, as shown below:

---

[18]After-tax interest, rather than actual interest, paid should be used to avoid introducing another bias; namely, the fact that the interest is tax-deductible and thus the firm that uses debt pays less taxes than otherwise.

Return on Assets:

$$\frac{\text{Net income}}{\text{Total assets}} = \frac{\$114,000}{\$1,320,000} = .086 \qquad \frac{\$108,000}{\$1,160,000} = .093$$

$$= 8.6\% \qquad\qquad = 9.3\%$$

$$\text{Industry Average} = .076 = 7.6\%$$

Or,

Return on Assets:

1987

$$\frac{\text{Net income plus interest } (1 - \text{tax rate})}{\text{Total assets}} = \frac{\$114,000 + \$26,000(1 - .4)}{\$1,320,000}$$

$$= 9.8\%$$

1986

$$= \frac{\$108,000 + \$24,000(1 - .4)}{\$1,160,000}$$

$$= 10.6\%$$

$$\text{Industry Average: } 8.5\%$$

A similar pattern is revealed in both forms of calculation. Brendle's overall return on assets has declined in 1987 but is still above the industry average.

return on equity

The *return on equity* ratio is typically calculated simply by dividing net income by common equity. From the standpoint of shareholders, this is the most important profitability ratio because it measures the profitability with which management used their money. If the company has preferred stock outstanding, then not all of the net income will go to the common shareholders. Thus, the numerator should be adjusted by subtracting preferred stock dividends from net income. Since Brendle does not have any preferred stock outstanding, this is not necessary. The return on equity calculations for Brendle are shown below:

1987   1986

Return on Equity:

$$\frac{\text{Net income}}{\text{Common equity}} = \frac{\$114,000}{639,000} = .178 \qquad \frac{\$108,000}{578,000} = .187$$

$$= 17.8\% \qquad\qquad = 18.7\%$$

$$\text{Industry Average} = .159 = 15.9\%$$

Brendle continued to out-perform the industry average, even though its return on equity declined from 18.7 percent in 1986 to 17.8 percent in 1987.

This group includes additional ratios investors commonly calculate in assessing the value of a company's stock. Since they influence investors, these ratios are of natural concern to the financial manager as well.

Earnings Per Share. *Earnings per share* is calculated by dividing net income by the number of common stock shares outstanding. If preferred stock is outstanding, the amount of preferred dividends is subtracted from the net income figure. The earnings-per-share figures for Brendle are calculated below:

earnings per share

	1987	1986

Earnings Per Share:

$$\frac{\text{Net income}}{\text{Common shares outstanding}} = \frac{\$114,000}{50,000} \quad \frac{\$108,000}{50,000}$$

$$= \$2.28 \quad = \$2.16$$

The earnings-per-share figure is a popular ratio among investors. In a sense it is a profitability measure because it measures the profits earned on each share. The earnings-per-share figure is only meaningful if compared for the same company over time (time series analysis).[19] This is because the denominator, number of shares outstanding, varies considerably among firms and has no relationship to economic value. For example, if a company repurchases some of its outstanding stock, earnings per share can be increased immediately.

The *price/earnings multiple,* sometimes called the P/E ratio, relates the company's earnings per share to the market price of the stock. The P/E multiple reflects investor expectations about the prospects for the company's earnings. Relatively high P/E multiples may indicate investors' expectations for significant future growth in profits per share; a relatively low multiple suggests reduced expectations. When analysts calculate a firm's price/earnings multiple, they often take a simple average of the firm's high and low prices during the year. Assuming an average stock price of $16.00 in 1987 and $14.00 in 1986, Brendle's P/E ratios:

price/earnings multiple

	1987	1986

Price/Earnings Multiple:

$$\frac{\text{Average market price per share}}{\text{Earnings per share}} = \frac{\$16.00}{\$2.28} \quad \frac{\$14.00}{\$2.16}$$

$$= 7.0 \text{ times} \quad 6.5 \text{ times}$$

---

[19]Assuming the number of shares stays constant. If the company has changed the number of its shares outstanding through stock splits, the earnings-per-share calculations should be adjusted accordingly. For example, if Brendle split its stock on a "two-for-one" basis in 1987, its common stock shares outstanding would double to 100,000 and EPS would only be $1.14. To be comparable, the 1986 EPS should also be based on 100,000 shares.

Price/earnings multiples are susceptible to broad changes in stock market conditions. Rising stock markets tend to raise all P/E multiples: declining markets lower them.

dividend payout ratio

The *dividend payout ratio* is calculated by dividing the total dividends paid during the year by the amount of net income earned. It may also be calculated on a per-share basis. It indicates the percentage of net income paid out as dividends. The ratios for Brendle are calculated below.

Dividend Payout Ratio:

	1987	**1986**
$\dfrac{\text{Dividends per share}}{\text{Earnings per share}} =$	$\dfrac{\$1.06}{\$2.28}$	$\dfrac{\$1.00}{\$2.16}$
	$= 46\%$	46%

The dividend payout ratio often reflects management's internal assessment of the investment prospects for the company. For example, low payout ratios suggest that numerous profitable investments are available. In certain cases, however, low ratios may indicate financial constraints imposed by creditors, significant financial setbacks, or simply management's reluctance to part with cash. High payout ratios, on the other hand, may reflect a mature product line, few profitable investment opportunities, or the desire of managment to maintain the historical dividend even though earnings have declined.

dividend yield

The *dividend yield* is calculated by dividing dividends per share by the stock price per share. In a sense, it represents the cash return on investment in the company until the investor sells the stock.

The dividend yield for Brendle is calculated below:

Dividend Yield:

	1987	**1986**
$\dfrac{\text{Dividends per share}}{\text{Market price per share}} =$	$\dfrac{\$1.06}{\$16}$	$\dfrac{\$1.00}{\$14}$
	$= 6.6\%$	7.1%

liquidation value

Book Value Per Share. The company's book value per share is a base line or *liquidation* value of the common stock on the assumption that all asset values can be liquidated at their book-value equivalents. Since book values usually understate market values of the company's earnings potential, market prices per share normally exceed book value per share.

	1987	**1986**
Book Value Per Share:		
$\dfrac{\text{Total shareholders' equity}}{\text{Common shares outstanding}} =$	$\dfrac{\$639,000}{50,000}$	$\dfrac{\$578,000}{50,000}$
	$= \$12.78$	$\$11.56$

Market Value to Book Value Ratio. It is not meaningful to compare market prices per share among companies because the number of shares outstanding affects the market price per share. For the same reason, comparing book values per share is not meaningful across companies. However, the *market-value-to-book-value ratio* standardizes these comparisons in the same way that the P/E ratio standardizes market prices and earnings. The market-value-to-book-value ratio reflects the value that investors place on the firm's ability to earn profits with its assets. The market-value-to-book-value ratio is calculated for Brendle below. In perfectly competitive economies, the market-value-to-book value ratio approximates 1.00.

market value to book value ratio

	1987	1986

Market Value to Book Value Ratio:

$$\frac{\text{Market price per share}}{\text{Book value per share}} = \frac{\$16}{\$12.78} \quad \frac{\$14}{\$11.56}$$

$$= 1.25 \quad 1.21$$

SUMMARY OF FINANCIAL RATIOS FOR THE BRENDLE COMPANY

Table 7-5 is a summary of the financial ratios we have calculated for the Brendle Company, along with industry comparisons grouped into the five types of ratios.

Sources of Industry Ratios

There are numerous sources of standard industry ratios to use as a basis for comparison. Dun and Bradstreet, Inc. publishes 14 ratios for each of 125 lines of business activity annually in *Dun's Review*. The ratios are also available in booklet form from Dun and Bradstreet. These ratios are particularly useful because they represent a large sample of companies and are given for the upper quartile, median, and lower quartile of a variety of measures. Some selected ratios for a recent year are shown in Table 7-6. Note the wide variation among industries and among firms within the same industry.

Other sources include the Robert Morris Associates, an association of bank loan officers that publishes annually. The Standard and Poor's Corporation provides aggregate composite balance-sheet and income-statement data for a variety of industry groups. Many trade associations prepare detailed profit and loss statements and balance-sheet ratios. For example, the National Retail Furniture Association provides extensive balance-sheet and income-statement analyses for its members.

TABLE 7-5 Summary of Financial Ratio Profile for the Brendle Manufacturing Company

Ratio	Formula	1987	1986	Industry Average
1. Liquidity ratios				
Current ratio	$\dfrac{\text{Current assets}}{\text{Current liabilities}}$	1.93 times	2.01 times	2.00 times
Quick ratio	$\dfrac{\text{Current assets} - \text{inventory}}{\text{Current liabilities}}$	1.15 times	1.27 times	1.20 times
Average payment period	$\dfrac{\text{Accounts payable}}{\text{Cost of goods sold} \div 360}$	50.5 days	41.2 days	50.0 days
2. Activity or utilization ratios				
Total assets turnover	$\dfrac{\text{Net sales}}{\text{Total assets}}$	1.12 times	1.24 times	1.20 times
Fixed assets turnover	$\dfrac{\text{Net sales}}{\text{Fixed assets}}$	2.12 times	2.24 times	2.10 times
Average collection period	$\dfrac{\text{Accounts receivable}}{\text{Net sales} \div 360}$	71.3 days	59.9 days	65.5 days
Inventory turnover	$\dfrac{\text{Cost of goods sold}}{\text{Inventory}}$	4.20 times	5.43 times	4.35 times
3. Financial leverage ratios				
Total debt to total assets	$\dfrac{\text{Total debt}}{\text{Total assets}}$	51.6%	50.2%	52.4%
Equity multiplier	$\dfrac{\text{Total assets}}{\text{Common equity}}$	2.07 times	2.01 times	2.10 times
Times interest earned	$\dfrac{\text{Earnings before interest and taxes}}{\text{Interest expense}}$	8.30 times	8.50 times	7.00 times
4. Profitability ratios				
Operating profit margin	$\dfrac{\text{Earnings before interest and taxes}}{\text{Net sales}}$	14.6%	14.2%	13.0%
Net profit margin	$\dfrac{\text{Net income}}{\text{Net sales}}$	7.7%	7.5%	6.6%
Operating profit return	$\dfrac{\text{Earnings before interest and taxes}}{\text{Total assets}}$	16.4%	17.6%	15.0%
Return on assets	$\dfrac{\text{Net income}}{\text{Total assets}}$	8.6%	9.3%	7.6%
Return on equity	$\dfrac{\text{Net income}}{\text{Common equity}}$	17.8%	18.7%	15.9%

TABLE 7-5 cont.

Ratio	Formula	1987	1986
5. Market value ratios			
Earnings per share	$\dfrac{\text{Net income}}{\text{Common shares outstanding}}$	2.28	2.16
Price/earnings multiple	$\dfrac{\text{Average market price per share}}{\text{Earnings per share}}$	7.0 times	6.5 times
Dividend payout ratio	$\dfrac{\text{Dividends per share}}{\text{Earnings per share}}$	46%	46%
Dividend yield	$\dfrac{\text{Dividends per share}}{\text{Market price per share}}$	6.6%	7.1%
Book value per share	$\dfrac{\text{Total shareholders' equity}}{\text{Common shares outstanding}}$	$12.78	$11.56
Market value to book value ratio	$\dfrac{\text{Market price per share}}{\text{Book value per share}}$	1.25	1.21

Another useful source is the *Quarterly Financial Report for Manufacturing Corporations,* published by the Federal Trade Commission. This sample survey provides income statements and balance sheets for all manufacturing corporations, classified by both industry and asset size.

PERCENTAGE OF SALES AND COMMON SIZE STATEMENTS

Percentage-of-sales and common-size statements standardize the information in the income statement and balance sheet to allow rapid comparison of each statement item in terms of either cross-sectional or time-series bases. To perform this type of analysis, each item in the statement is simply divided by a common number, such as sales or total assets. In this way, of course, percentage-of-sales analysis is simply a form of ratio analysis. This adjusts for differences in the scale of operations when comparing different companies or the same company over a period of years. For example, Table 7-7 presents a percentage-of-sales analysis of the income statement for the Brendle Company for 1986 and 1987.

An advantage of the percentage-of-sales statement is that the analyst can focus quickly on the items that result in differences in profit performance. The analyst tries to find which items on the income statement resulted in the difference. An examination of Table 7-7 indicates that the

TABLE 7-6 Selected Dun and Bradstreet Quartile Figures

Line of Business (and Number of Businesses)	Current Assets to Current Debt (Times)	Average Collection Period (Days)	Net Sales to Inventory (Times)	Total Debt to Tangible Net Worth (Percent)	Net Profits on Net Sales (Percent)	Net Profit on Tangible Net Worth (Percent)
Manufacturing lines:						
Motor vehicle parts	3.61	53	13.4	143.2	8.71	43.69
and accessories	2.21	39	7.4	76.8	4.94	24.03
(325)	1.47	25	4.8	33.3	2.48	12.78
Meat packing plants	3.91	19	55.1	211.8	2.61	26.95
(234)	1.79	14	32.9	92.2	1.04	13.75
	1.25	9	18.1	32.2	.43	4.39
Soft drinks: bottled	4.04	29	23.0	134.8	7.54	29.34
and canned	2.33	21	15.3	53.5	4.30	17.31
(162)	1.36	13	11.8	18.1	1.81	10.25
Canned fruits and	2.90	33	7.9	261.5	5.21	26.08
vegetables	1.64	22	4.6	117.0	3.13	12.38
(108)	1.20	16	3.1	48.5	.89	2.75
Office, computing	3.13	89	10.1	206.4	10.50	40.67
and accounting	1.98	64	5.0	106.4	6.24	21.38
machines	1.51	38	3.3	44.1	2.62	11.73
(276)						
Wholesale lines:						
groceries	3.50	27	18.5	245.1	2.75	26.01
(874)	2.04	15	12.1	105.7	1.10	12.92
	1.40	8	8.1	41.9	.41	5.73
Lumber, plywood,	3.33	50	20.7	242.6	4.76	34.75
and mill work	1.99	35	9.5	107.7	2.29	18.60
(1,359)	1.39	23	5.8	46.8	.99	9.69
Retail lines:						
grocery stores	6.78	7	21.8	171.4	5.00	40.26
(4293)	2.81	2	15.0	67.4	2.05	19.49
	1.50	0	10.0	21.2	.87	8.85
Lumber and other	4.45	51	10.3	178.3	6.24	32.49
building materials	2.50	35	6.2	79.8	3.49	17.08
dealers	1.62	20	4.1	32.3	1.62	7.89
(3739)						

Note: Figures shown are for upper quartile, median quartile, and lower quartile. These are determined by first ranking the figures or ratios by industry from highest to lowest. Then figures are selected at points one-fourth, one-half, and three-fourths down the list.
Source: *Dun's Review*, November, 1980.

cost of goods sold was the same as a percentage of sales in both years. Thus, this item does not explain the difference in net profit margins. General and administrative expenses declined by .3 percent and marketing expenses declined by .1 percent. This improved cost performance was offset slightly by an increase in interest expense, which increased by .1 percent and an increase in taxes as a percentage of sales, .1 percent. The net effect explains why profits increased by .2 as a percentage of sales in 1987. These results can be summarized in brief form, as shown in Table 7-8.

TABLE 7-7   Brendle Manufacturing Company Percent of Sales Income Statement for the Year Ended December 31

Earnings	1987	1986
Net sales	100.0%	100.0%
Less: Cost of goods sold	71.8%	71.8%
Gross profits	28.2%	28.2%
Less: Operating expenses		
General & administrative	9.5%	9.8%
Marketing	3.4%	3.5%
Depreciation	.7%	.7%
Total operating expenses	13.6%	14.0%
Earnings before interest and taxes	14.6%	14.2%
Less: Interest expense	1.8%	1.7%
Earnings before taxes	12.8%	12.5%
Less: Income taxes (40% rate)	5.1%	5.0%
Net income	7.7%	7.5%

TABLE 7-8

Decrease in general and administrative expenses	.3%
Decrease in marketing expenses	.1%
Total decrease in expenses	.4%
Increase in interest expenses	(.1%)
Increase in taxes	(.1%)
Increase in profits	.2%

Cost control seems to have been effective in 1987 for the Brendle Company. Although the improvement in profits as a percentage of sales is relatively small, the fact that this improvement has been produced on larger sales volume is a good sign.

Common-size balance sheet. Table 7-9 presents a common-size balance sheet statement for the Brendle Company. In this case, all of the balance-sheet items are calculated as a percentage of total assets. A primary purpose of this type of analysis is to reveal shifts in the composition of assets and methods of financing.

The proportion of current assets has increased in 1987, from 44.8 percent of total assets to 47.0 percent. However, among the current assets it is evident that the most liquid assets, cash and marketable securities, have decreased relative to total assets while accounts receivable and inventory have increased. The firm has shifted its investment profile, deliberately or not, toward marketing and production. For example, the build-up in accounts receivable could reflect more aggressive credit policy or, alternatively, lax control of credit. The build-up in inventory could represent sales below expected levels or slow moving items. The interrelationship between

TABLE 7-9 Brendle Manufacturing Company Percent of Assets Balance Sheet as of December 31

	1987	1986
Current Assets		
Cash	1.4%	2.2%
Marketable securities	4.2%	5.7%
Accounts receivable	22.2%	20.6%
Inventories	19.2%	16.4%
Total current assets	47.0%	44.8%
Fixed Assets		
Gross fixed assets	78.5%	83.4%
Less Accumulated depreciation	(25.5%)	(28.2%)
Net fixed assets	53.0%	55.2%
Total assets	100.0%	100.0%
Current Liabilities		
Accounts payable	11.3%	10.2%
Notes payable	3.8%	4.3%
Accruals	9.2%	7.8%
Total current liabilities	24.3%	22.3%
Long-term debt	16.7%	17.2%
Deferred income taxes	10.6%	10.6%
Total liabilities	51.6%	50.2%
Stockholders' Equity		
Common stock	7.6%	8.6%
Paid-in surplus	21.8%	24.8%
Retained earnings	19.0%	16.4%
Total stockholders' equity	48.4%	49.8%
Total liabilities and equity	100.0%	100.0%

marketing and production is revealed by the possibility that sales have not kept pace with the production schedule *and* more liberal credit terms are considered necessary to bring sales into line with production.[20]

Among its liabilities, the common-size statement reveals that only accounts payable and accruals have increased as a percentage of total assets. Overall, total liabilities have increased as a percentage of total assets from 50.2 percent in 1986 to 51.6 percent in 1987, indicating that the firm is relying more heavily on debt, primarily suppliers (i.e., as reflected in accounts payable).

---

[20]Of course, a more reasonable approach might be to bring production into line with sales.

THE DU PONT MODEL

The Du Pont model is a framework for organizing related financial ratios to reveal the determinants of a firm's overall rate of return. This model was developed by the Du Pont corporation to monitor management performance. There are many versions of the model, but we will present only the *return-on-equity* version because it is the most comprehensive rate-of-return measure. An example of this model is shown in Exhibit 7-4.

The model has a "pyramid" shape, with the return on equity at the top of the pyramid. Below the return-on-equity figure are several levels of increasing detail. Each level determines the ratio above. For example, the return on equity is equal to the return on assets times the equity multiplier. The next level down shows that the return on assets is determined by the net profit margin on sales times the total asset turnover. The next level shows that the net profit margin is equal to sales less expenses and taxes (all stated as a percentage of sales to permit comparison). Total asset turnover is determined by the amount in each asset category. The efficiency of asset use can be determined by comparing the activity ratios computed earlier. For example, the efficiency of fixed-asset investment is indicated by the fixed-asset turnover figure.

In preparing the model for analysis, the various ratios are computed for each item. Exhibit 7-4 includes Brendle's ratios for 1986 and 1987. The 1987 figures are shown in brackets.

Analyzing Results

Begin by comparing the return on equity at the top of the pyramid. The return on equity has declined from 18.7 percent in 1986 to 17.8 percent in 1987. Was the decline due to a decline in return on assets, a decrease in the equity multiplier, or a combination of the two? The return on assets declined in 1987. However, the equity multiplier increased. Thus the decrease in the return on equity can be attributed to a decrease in the return on assets.

The return on assets reflects operating management's ability to generate profits with the assets under its management. On the other hand, the equity multiplier is primarily determined by the Board of Directors and, in that sense, does not reflect directly on the effectiveness of operating management. The more debt a company uses in its financial structure, the larger the equity multiplier and, for a given return on assets, the higher the return on equity. Of course, more debt usage results in more interest expense and thus lower profits, which will depress the return on assets. In general, whenever the after-tax cost of debt (interest rate) is less than the return on assets, debt usage will result in higher return on equity (this is known as positive leverage). The Du Pont model helps separate these two factors — operating performance and financing policy — in terms of their effect on return on equity.

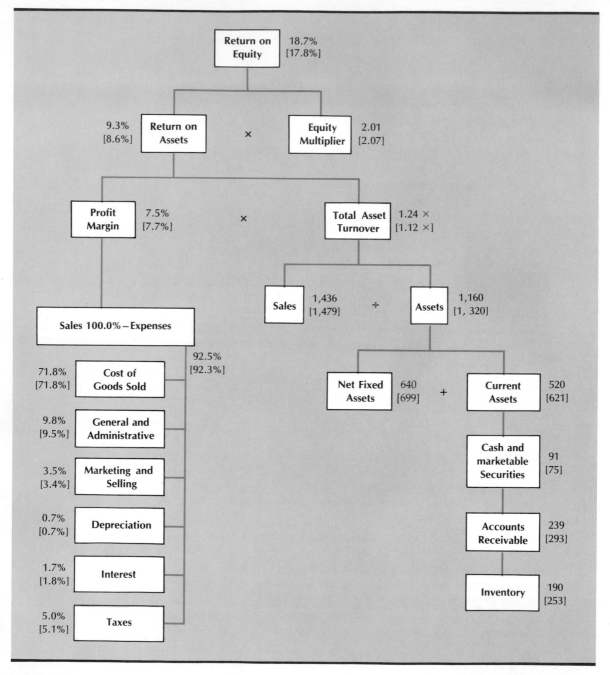

EXHIBIT 7-4
The Du Pont Model

Now the decrease in return on assets needs to be explained. Was it due to a decrease in the net profit margin, the total asset turnover, or both? Since the net profit margin actually increased slightly, the decline in return on assets must be attributed entirely to weaker asset management, as indicated by the decrease in total asset turnover.

The determinants of the net profit margin can be examined with the percentage-of-sales comparisons.[21] Since the changes are only minor, in this case, the analyst will be primarily concerned with the determinants of the total asset turnover. By examining each major asset category in terms of a utilization ratio, it is easy to determine which asset items were responsible for the decline in asset utilization. It is apparent that the levels of accounts receivable, inventory, and fixed assets all contributed to the reduced total asset turnover.

The information can now be summarized as follows. The decline in the return on equity in 1987 was due primarily to excessive build-up in accounts receivable, inventory, and fixed assets. Of course, there may be perfectly good reasons for this build-up but the important point is that it resulted in lower return on equity in 1987.

LIMITATIONS OF RATIO ANALYSIS

Now that you have seen how ratios are used, you should take notice of the following limitations. First, no matter how sound the techniques may be, if the data analyzed are inaccurate the results are not going to be reliable. The numbers contained in the financial statements of a company are subject to wide differences in the accounting interpretation of events.

Second, even large differences in ratios are meaningless unless the basic reasons for the differences can be found. For example, the ratio of net profit to sales may change because of a shift in the product mix or changes in the overall economy rather than from changes in the firm's operating performance.

Third, rarely will all ratios yield a consistent pattern. Typically some favorable differences as well as unfavorable differences will be indicated by ratios. The effective analyst weighs these contrary signals in developing an overall assessment of the risk and profitability of a company.

Fourth, inflation also has an effect on both the comparability of ratios and how they should be interpreted.

INFLATION AND RATIO ANALYSIS

Inflation does not have a uniform impact on the company's financial statements and consequently can bias the results of ratio analysis. To see how inflation affects ratio analysis, let us consider the financial statements in Table 7-10. Assume that these statements reflect the company's operations and financial condition before any inflation.

---

[21]The analyst might want to do this in any case because even if the net profit margin overall is fine, some expense items might be seriously above-average while others are significantly below-average. He or she should also check to see whether the difference is due to a change in tax rates.

TABLE 7-10   Financial Statements Before Inflation ($000)

Income Statement

Sales	$1,000
Cost of goods sold	600
Gross profit	400
Operating expenses	60
Depreciation	20
EBIT	320
Interest	20
Earnings before taxes	300
Taxes (50%)	150
Net income	150

Balance Sheet

Cash	20	Accounts payable	$300
Accounts receivable	80	Current liabilities	$300
Inventory	600	Long-term debt	200
Current assets	700	Total liabilities	500
Net fixed assets	200	Equity	400
Total	$900	Total	$900

Common shares outstanding: 100,000. Earnings per share: $1.50.

Impact on Income Statement

Now, let us assume that unexpectedly, inflation causes all prices and costs to increase by 10 percent. Sales and operating expenses may increase immediately by 10 percent each; but cost of goods sold, depreciation, and interest expenses may not increase right away if these expenses reflect pre-inflation transactions. For example, if the company's cost-of-goods-sold figure reflects inventory purchased at pre-inflation costs, it will not reflect inflation at all. Likewise, the depreciation on equipment purchased at pre-inflation prices will not rise. And interest expense on debt negotiated before inflation was anticipated will not reflect the impact of inflation. In other words, these items will reflect historical rather than current costs of doing business. As a result, the income statement will show an increase in net income and earnings per share due to the nonuniform impacts of inflation rather than to any fundamental improvement in management performance. This is shown in Table 7-11.

For example, because of the 10-percent inflation alone, profits have increased by $47,000, an increase of 31 percent. But taxes have also increased by 31 percent from a 10-percent inflation.

Impact on Balance Sheet

The impact of inflation also extends to the balance sheet. For example, cash needed for transactions will increase because operating costs have

TABLE 7-11   Income Statement After 10-Percent Inflation ($000)

Sales (+10%)	$1,100
Cost of goods sold[§]	600
Gross profit	500
Operating expenses (+10%)	66
Depreciation[§]	20
EBIT	414
Interest[§]	20
Earnings before taxes	394
Taxes (50%)	197
Net income	197

[§]Reflects historical, pre-inflation cost (Common shares outstanding: 100,000. Earnings per share: $1.97)

increased. Accounts receivables balances will also increase, reflecting the higher prices of goods sold. Moreover, new inventory purchased at inflated prices will reflect the higher prices caused by inflation. Similarly, the costs of replacing or adding fixed assets will also reflect the inflation impact. Finally, the interest costs of new debt will now be higher because of inflation. However, because of different lags, the balance sheet will not automatically reflect all of these higher costs of doing business. Cash, accounts receivable, inventory, and accounts payable may show the inflation effects quickly, but the fixed-asset and debt accounts will take longer to reflect the impacts of inflation. The short-run effects are shown in the balance sheet in Table 7-12.

Impact on Ratios

The variable effects of inflation on the financial statements will bias ratios and may lead to overstating financial performance. This is illustrated in Table 7-13, which shows some key ratios calculated before and after the impact of inflation.

TABLE 7-12

Balance Sheet			
Cash (+10%)	22	Accounts payable	$330
Accounts receivable (+10%)	88	Current liabilities	$330
Inventory (+10%)	660	Long-term debt	200
Current assets	770	Total liabilities	530
Net fixed assets	200	Equity	440
Total	$970	Total	$970

TABLE 7-13

Ratio	Before Inflation	After Inflation
Gross profit margin	40%	45%
Net profit margin	15%	18%
Total asset turnover	1.1 times	1.13 times
Return on assets	16.7%	20%
Return on equity	38%	45%
Earnings per share	$1.50	$1.97

S U M M A R Y

The principal financial statements of the company are the income statement and the balance sheet. From these statements are also derived the statement of cash flows and the statement of retained earnings. The income statement reflects primarily the results of operations during an accounting time period. The balance sheet conveys information about the firm's level and composition of investments as well as the mix of financing it is employing at a selected point in time. The statement of cash flows combines information from the income statement and balance sheet and provides a glimpse of the sources and uses of cash during the period. The statement of retained earnings indicates what changes occurred in the shareholders' investment, including the level of profits produced and dividends paid during the accounting period.

The company's financial statements convey valuable information to management as well as to creditors and shareholders about financial performance and condition. For the most part these statements are the principal sources of information to which creditors and shareholders have access. Internally, the financial manager can use information from financial statements to identify areas of strength and weakness relative to competitors.

Several major techniques can be employed in the analysis of financial statements. This chapter dealt primarily with the popular technique known as ratio analysis. It also examined the use of a financial model of performance known as the Du Pont model. While ratios and financial models are only as good as the information that goes into them, with skill and care a financial analyst can learn much about a company with their use.

MULTIPLE CHOICE QUESTIONS

1. Comparing the firm's performance with the industry average is a form of:
   a) Time-series analysis
   b) Cross-sectional analysis
   c) Regression analysis
   d) Marginal analysis

2. Return on assets is equal to:

   a) Return on equity times total assets turnover
   b) Profit margin on sales times return on equity
   c) Profit margin on sales times total assets turnover
   d) Profit margin on sales divided by total assets turnover

3. Liquidity ratios indicate:

   a) The amount of fixed assets a company has
   b) The liquidation value of the company
   c) The ratio of current assets to net worth
   d) The amount of current assets relative to current liabilities

4. Activity ratios indicate:

   a) The scope of business lines
   b) Percentage of capacity utilization
   c) Financings undertaken during the year
   d) Efficiency of asset use

5. The quick ratio does not include:

   a) Cash
   b) Accounts receivable
   c) Inventory
   d) Accounts payable

6. The average payment period indicates:

   a) How long it takes the company to collect accounts receivable
   b) The average maturity of the company's accounts payable
   c) The size of the average cash payments made per period
   d) The average maturity of overdue receivables

7. The debt ratio measures:

   a) The ratio of debt to cash
   b) The average maturity of outstanding long-term-debt
   c) The ratio of debt to total assets
   d) The ratio of debt to current assets

8. Which of the following represents a use of cash?

   a) Sale of inventory
   b) Increase in accounts receivable
   c) Increase in accounts payable
   d) Decrease in fixed assets

9. Which of the following represents a source of cash?

   a) Sale of inventory
   b) Payment of bank loan
   c) Increase in fixed assets
   d) Increase in accounts receivable

10. The average collection period is equal to:

   a) Accounts receivable divided by sales per day
   b) Accounts receivable multiplied by sales per day

c) Accounts receivable divided by cost of goods sold

d) Accounts receivable divided by 360

DISCUSSION QUESTIONS

1. How might financial ratios be used to evaluate a firm's operating and financial performance?

2. Explain why financial managers must be cautious when using ratios.

3. The return on equity (ROE) ratio can be expressed in financial model form. Identify the components of the model and explain how they are related to each other.

4. Describe the five principal categories of financial ratios.

5. What ratios would you use to measure a firm's liquidity position?

6. How would you measure the performance of a firm in terms of asset utilization?

7. What is meant by *common-size* financial statements?

8. When conducting a composite ratio analysis, what ratios might be useful in assessing financial leverage and profitability?

9. Financial analysis may be aided by the preparation of a statement of cash flows. When examining balance-sheet changes, which general item changes are sources and which are uses of cash?

10. Some industries are characterized by high total assets-turnover ratios and low net profit margins, and vice versa. Give some examples and explain why such differences exist.

SOLVED PROBLEM

SP-1. Using the financial statements below, calculate the indicated financial ratios for the Blitz Company and compare them with the industry norms. Assume a 360-day year.

ratio analysis

Blitz Company	
Balance Sheet	
Assets	
Cash & marketable securities	$144,000
Accounts receivable	288,000
Inventory	432,000
Total	864,000
Net fixed assets	936,000
Total	$1,800,000

Liabilities and Shareholders' Equity

Accounts payable	$144,000
Notes payable	72,000
Other current liabilities	198,000
Total	414,000
Long-term debt	414,000
Total liabilities	828,000
Shareholders' equity	972,000
Total	$1,800,000

Income Statement, Year Ended 12/31/88

Sales	$2,200,000
Cost of goods sold	1,496,000
Gross profit	704,000
Selling, general, and administrative expenses	440,000
Depreciation expense	44,000
Earnings before interest and taxes (EBIT)	220,000
Interest expense	22,000
Profit before taxes	198,000
Taxes on income	79,200
Net income	$ 118,800

Industry Norms

Current ratio	2.0	
Quick ratio	1.0	
Total asset turnover	1.6	times
Fixed asset turnover	2.9	times
Average collection period	30.0	days
Average payment period	30.0	days
Inventory turnover (based on cost of goods sold)	5.0	times
Total liabilities to total assets	.33	
Equity multiplier	1.49	times
Times interest earned	20.0	times
EBIT/sales	.12	
Net profit/sales	.066	
Return on assets	.106	
Return on equity	.158	

PROBLEMS

ratio analysis

1. Following are income statements and selected balance-sheet items for the Trace Manufacturing Company.

Trace Manufacturing Company Income Statements, Years Ending December 31 ($000)

	1986	1987
Net Sales	$1,000	$1,200
Less: cost of goods sold	700	840
Gross profit	300	360
Less: operating expenses*	176	176
Earnings before interest and taxes	124	184
Less: interest expense	24	24
Earnings before taxes	100	160
Less: income taxes (34% rate)	34	54
Net income	$ 66	$ 106

Selected Balance Sheet Items as of December 31 ($000)

	1986	1987
Total assets	$860	$920
Total liabilities or debt	552	552
Total stockholders' equity	308	368

*includes general and administrative, marketing, and depreciation expenses

a) Calculate the return on assets and the return on equity in each of the two years.

b) What seems to have caused the changes in the rate-or-return results between the two years?

c) The following 1987 ratios are available for the industry: equity multiplier = 2.00 times; total assets turnover = 1.5 times; net profit margin = 7.00 percent; and operating profit margin = 12.00 percent. How does Trace Manufacturing compare?

2. The long-term sources of funds of two corporations are shown below. If a corporate income tax rate of 34 percent is assumed, what is the return on equity in each case, when earnings before interest and taxes (EBIT) is as follows: 1986, $25,000; 1987, $40,000.

leverage

        Corporation A: 15-percent bonds, $35,000
              Common equity,   65,000
        Corporation B: Common equity $100,000

3. The following financial statements, covering calendar years 1986 and 1987, were prepared for the Sand Company. You have recently been hired by the firm and are presently in its management training program. The President of Sand has just asked you to prepare a brief financial analysis of the firm's recent performance. You are to apply a Du Pont model approach in preparing your analysis.

Du Pont model

a) Calculate the return on assets and the return on equity in each of the two years.
b) Decompose each of the financial ratios calculated in Part (a) into its major component parts and express each in terms of the Du Pont model.
c) Compare the results for 1986 and 1987 and provide a brief summary of your findings.

Sand Company

Income Statement, Year Ended December 31 ($000)

	1986	1987
Net sales	$859	$871
Less: Cost of goods sold	576	584
Gross profit	283	287
Less: Operating expenses		
Selling and administrative	110.4	105.3
Depreciation	39	44
Total operating expenses	149.4	149.3
Earnings before interest and taxes	133.6	137.7
Less: Interest expense	25.8	27.4
Earnings before tax	107.8	110.3
Income taxes (34%)	36.7	37.5
Net income	$ 71.1	$ 72.8

Balance Sheet as of December 31 ($000)

	1986	1987
Current Assets:		
Cash	$30	$15
Marketable securities	15	18
Net accounts receivable	150	189
Inventory	129	170
Prepaid expenses	36	15
Total current assets	360	407
Fixed Assets:		
Land	50	50
Buildings	417	450
Less: Accumulated depreciation	(168)	(177)
Machinery and equipment	718	747
Less: Accumulated depreciation	(460)	(495)
Total net fixed assets	557	575
Total assets	$917	$982

Current liabilities:		
Accounts payable	$73	$91
Bank loan (8%)	60	60
Accrued expenses	33	38
Total current liabilities	166	189
Long-term debt (10%)	210	217
Total liabilities	376	406
Stockholder's Equity:		
Common stock—$5 par, 38,000 shares authorized and outstanding	190	190
Paid-in surplus	165	165
Retained earnings	186	221
Total stockholders' equity	541	576
Total stockholders' equity and liabilities	$917	$982

4. The Sand Company wants to compare its 1987 operating and financial performance against industry norms. Make use of the 1987 financial statements in Problem 3 for Sand.

   ratio analysis

   a) Calculate selected financial ratios for Sand so that they may be compared with the industry norms provided below.
   b) Comment on the weaknessses and strengths exhibited by Sand relative to the industry norms.

Ratio	1987 Industry Norms	1987 Sand
Current ratio	2.50 times	————
Quick ratio	1.00 times	————
Total assets turnover	1.00 times	————
Fixed assets turnover	2.00 times	————
Average collection period	60.00 days	————
Inventory turnover (cost)	3.00 times	————
Total debt to total assets	50.0%	————
Times interest earned	6.0 times	————
Operating profit margin	16.0%	————
Net profit margin	7.5%	————
Return on assets	7.5%	————
Return on equity	15.0%	————

5. Make a comparison of Grid Plastics with industry data.

   ratio analysis

Grid Plastics

Balance Sheet, as of December 31

	1986	1987
Cash	$ 76,500	$ 35,700
Accounts receivable	306,000	346,800
Inventories	382,500	637,500
Total current assets	765,000	1,020,000
Land and buildings, net	60,000	73,000
Machinery, net	188,000	208,000
Other fixed assets	37,500	40,500
Total assets	$1,050,500	$1,341,500
Notes payable, bank (12%)	—	127,500
Accounts payable	122,500	195,000
Accruals	61,000	71,000
Total current liabilities	183,500	393,500
Long-term debt (10%)	300,000	300,000
Common stock (50,000 shares)	359,000	359,000
Retained earnings	208,000	289,000
Total	$1,050,500	$1,341,500

Income Statement

	1986	1987
Net sales	$3,315,000	$3,442,500
Cost of goods sold	2,652,000	2,754,000
Gross operating profit	663,000	688,500
General and administrative expenses	275,000	300,500
Depreciation	102,000	120,700
Interest	43,500	30,000
Net income before taxes	242,500	237,300
Taxes (34%)	82,450	80,682
Net income	$160,050	$156,618

Industry Data (1987)

Current ratio:	2.8
Return on net worth:	22.2%
Inventory turnover (cost basis):	7.0 times
Average collection period:	45 days
Net profit margin	4.0%
Total assets turnover:	3.0 times
Operating profit margin	8.5%
Return on total assets:	12.0%
Total debt to total assets ratio:	46%

a) Compare the performance of Grid Plastics relative to industry averages on the basis of the Du Pont model. Assume industry ratios remain constant between 1986 and 1987.

b) Briefly indicate why Grid's performance relative to the industry changed between 1986 and 1987.

6. The following are the financial statements of the Javits Company.

ratio analysis

Javits Company

Balance Sheet, as of December 31, 1987

Cash		$ 60,000
Accounts receivable		230,000
Inventories		170,000
Property and equipment	$600,000	
Less allowance for depreciation	190,000	410,000
Total assets		$870,000
Accounts and notes payable–trade		$ 95,000
Notes payable — bank		24,000
Accrued liabilities		16,000
Estimated federal income tax liability		21,000
First mortgage, 8% bonds, due in 2000*		150,000
Second mortgage, 8% bonds, due in 1995		50,000
Common stock — $5 par value, issued and outstanding 50,000 shares		250,000
Paid-in-surplus		25,000
Retained earnings		239,000
Total liabilities and equity		$870,000

*Sinking fund payments of $12,000 per year are paid on the bonds

Income Statement, Year ended December 31, 1987

Net sales*		$1,072,000
Cost of sales:		
Inventory of finished goods — 1/1/87	94,000	
Cost of goods manufactured	780,000	
Inventory of finished goods — 12/31/87	(103,000)	771,000
Gross profit on sales		$301,000
Selling expenses	160,000	
General expenses	73,000	233,000
Net operating profit		$68,000
Interest expense		16,000
Net income before Federal income tax		$52,000
Federal income tax (34%)		17,680
Net income		$34,320

*All sales were on credit

a) Calculate the following ratios for the Javits Company:

- Current ratio
- Quick ratio
- Payables turnover
- Average payment period
- Inventory turnover
- Receivables turnover
- Average collection period
- Total debt to total assets
- Interest coverage
- Equity multiplier

- Fixed charge coverage
- Total debt to net worth
- Fixed assets turnover
- Total assets turnover
- Operating profit margin
- Net profit return
- Return on assets
- Return on equity
- Interest coverage

b) Given the following information for the industry, explain why Javits' return on equity is higher (or lower) than the industry's:

Total assets turnover = 1.20 times

Net profit margin   = 6.6%

Equity multiplier   = 2.1 times

ratio analysis

7. The following is a condensed balance sheet for the Marx Corporation.

Current assets	$700,000	Current liabilities	$200,000
Fixed assets	800,000	Long-term liabilities	500,000
		Net worth	800,000
	$1,500,000		$1,500,000

Income before interest and taxes, $80,000
Interest charges on long-term liabilities, $16,000

a) How much additional fixed assets could be financed with short-term credit before reducing the current ratio to 2:1?
b) How much additional inventory could be purchased on trade credit before reducing the current ratio to 2:1?
c) How much cash would need to be applied to the reduction of current debt to increase the current ratio to 5:1?
d) How much additional long-term debt could be issued at an annual interest cost of 10%, if it is desired to cover fixed charges by at least three times and to have a total liabilities-to-net-worth ratio not in excess of 1:1?

forecasting with ratios

8. The GRT Manufacturing Corporation is planning to form a subsidiary to manufacture ball-point pens. The firm will establish the subsidiary with an $800,000 investment in the subsidiary's common stock. The vice-president of finance wishes to prepare a *pro forma* balance sheet for the subsidiary based upon various average ratios for this type of busi-

ness derived from published sources. Using the limited information that is available (shown below), complete the balance sheet below. Show computations.

Assets		Liabilities and Capital	
Cash	_____	Notes and accounts payable	_____
Accounts receivable	_____	Common stock	$800,000
Inventory	_____		
Plant and equipment	_____		

Total assets turnover: 1.2 times
Average collection period (based on 360-day year): 40 days
Gross profit margin: 30 percent
Inventory turnover (based on cost of goods sold): 4 times
Debt to net worth: 0.5:1
Quick ratio: 0.8:1

9. The Colton Company operates in the "widget" industry, which has the following characteristics, on average. Industry balance sheet accounts are:

forecasting with ratios

Assets		Liabilities and Capital	
Cash	_____	Current liabilities	_____
Accounts receivable	_____	Long-term debt	_____
Inventory	_____	Common stock	_____
Fixed assets	_____	Retained earnings	_____

Complete the "average" balance sheet by using the following data:

- Current assets are $1,000,000, and net profit after taxes is $100,000 on average for the industry.
- The average collection period is 60 days, and the inventory turnover is five times (based on net sales). Credit sales are 50 percent of net sales.
- The current ratio is 2:1, retained earnings are $300,000, and total debt to total assets is 50 percent.
- The rate of return on total assets averages 6.67 percent, and the average turnover of total assets for the industry is two times.

10. The Watts Electronics Corporation has been a successful manufacturer of small electronic components for computers and other sophisticated electronic equipment since its incorporation in 1976. Following are financial statements for the two most recent years of operation.

common size statements

Watts Electronics, Inc.

Balance Sheet, as of December 31

	1986	1987
Cash	$ 24,000	$ 20,000
Accounts receivable	231,000	300,000
Inventories	425,000	500,000
Total current assets	680,000	820,000
Fixed assets, net	220,000	380,000
Total assets	$900,000	$1,200,000
Bank loan, 10%	80,000	80,000
Accounts payable	134,000	260,000
Accruals	48,000	65,000
Total current liabilities	262,000	405,000
Long-term debt, 11%	200,000	200,000
Common stock, $10 par	300,000	350,000
Paid-in-surplus	58,000	145,000
Retained earnings	80,000	100,000
Total liabilities and equity	$900,000	$1,200,000

Income Statements, Year Ended December 31

	1986	1987
Net sales	$2,300,000	$2,500,000
Cost of goods sold	1,840,000	2,000,000
Gross profit	460,000	500,000
General administration and selling	200,000	200,000
Depreciation	20,000	40,000
Interest	30,000	30,000
Earnings before taxes	210,000	230,000
Taxes paid (34%)	71,400	78,200
Earnings after taxes	$138,600	$151,800

a) Prepare common-size balance sheets and income statements for both 1986 and 1987 for Watts Electronics.

b) Based on the common-size financial statements, evaluate Watts' operating and financial performance in 1987 compared with 1986.

Du Pont analysis

11. The management of Watts Electronics, Inc. desires a financial analysis of the firm's performance during 1986 and 1987. The data in problem 10 are to be used to conduct the financial analysis.

a) Prepare a Du Pont analysis for 1986 and 1987.

b) Develop a financial ratio profile that summarizes Watt's performance over the two years.

c) Provide a brief comparative analysis of firm performance over the two years.

12. Construct financial statements for the Jones Company, from the jumbled financial data below. In addition, indicate the earnings per share and price of the company's stock.

financial accounting

General administration and selling:	$1,020,000
Current ratio:	2.0
Average collection period (360-day year):	90 days
Cash:	?
Cost of goods sold:	75% of sales
Depreciation expense:	$100,000
Fixed assets turnover:	5.0 times
Notes payable (current):	$915,000
Interest expense:	$130,000
Long-term debt:	?
Tax rate:	34%
Cost of goods sold/inventory:	5.0 times
Total assets turnover	1.55 times
Average payment period*:	36 days
Equity multiplier:	2.0 times
Total shareholders' equity:	$2,000,000
Common shares outstanding:	100,000 shares
P/E multiple:	10 times

*Purchases equal cost of goods sold. Assume 360-day year

SOLUTION TO SOLVED PROBLEM

SP-1. Current ratio = Current assets ÷ Current liabilities
$$= 864,000 \div 414,000 = 2.1$$

Quick ratio = (Current assets − Inventory)/Current liabilities
$$= (864,000 - 432,000)/414,000 = 1.0$$

Total asset turnover = Net sales ÷ Total assets
$$= 2,200,000 \div 1,800,000 = 1.2 \text{ times}$$

Fixed asset turnover = Net sales ÷ Fixed assets
$$= 2,200,000 \div 936,000 = 2.4 \text{ times}$$

Average collection period = Accounts receivable ÷ (Net sales/360)
$$= 288,000/(2,200,000/360) = 47.1 \text{ days}$$

Average payment period = Accounts payable ÷ (Cost of of goods sold/360)
$$= 144,000/(1,496,000/360) = 34.7 \text{ days}$$

Inventory turnover (cost basis) = Cost of goods sold ÷ Inventory
$$= 1,496,000 \div 432,000 = 3.5 \text{ times}$$

Total liabilities to total assets = Total debt ÷ Total assets
$$= 828,000 \div 1,800,000 = .46$$

Equity multiplier = Total assets ÷ Stockholders' equity
$$= \$1,800,000 \div 972,000 = 1.85 \text{ times}$$

Times interest earned = EBIT ÷ Interest expense
$$= 220,000 \div 22,000 = 10.0 \text{ times}$$

EBIT/sales = EBIT ÷ Sales
$$= 220,000 \div 2,200,000 = .10$$

Return on assets = Net income ÷ Total assets
$$= 118,800 \div 1,800,000 = .066$$

Return on equity = Net income ÷ Stockholders' equity
$$= 118,800 \div 972,000 = .122$$

	Comparison		
	Blitz Co.	*Industry Norm*	*Assessment*
Current ratio	2.1	2.0	OK
Quick ratio	1.0	1.0	OK
Total asset turnover	1.2 times	1.6 times	Weak
Fixed asset turnover	2.4 times	2.9 times	Weak
Average collection period	47.1 days	30.0 days	Very weak
Average payment period	34.7 days	30.0 days	Weak
Inventory turnover	3.5 times	5.0 times	Very weak
Total liabilities to total assets	.46	.33	Weak
Equity multiplier	1.85 times	1.49 times	High
Times interest earned	10.0 times	20.0 times	Weak
EBIT/sales	.10	.12	Weak
Net income/sales	.054	.066	Weak
Return on assets	.066	.106	Weak
Return on equity	.122	.158	Weak

The Blitz Company is weak relative to the industry norms in virtually all respects. Major problems are evident in the operating profit margin, inventory turnover, and accounts receivable collections.

REFERENCES

Altman, Edward I. "Financial Ratios, Discriminant Analysis and the Prediction of Corporate Bankruptcy." *Journal of Finance,* September 1968, pp. 589–609.

Altman, Edward I., R. G. Haldeman, and P. Narayanan. "ZETA Analysis: A New Model to Identify Bankruptcy Risk of Corporations." *Journal of Banking and Finance,* June 1977, pp. 29–54.

Beaver, William H. "Financial Ratios as Predictors of Failure." *Empirical Research in Accounting: Selected Studies in Journal of Accounting Research,* 1966, pp. 71–111.

Benishay, Haskell. "Economic Information in Financial Ratio Analysis." *Accounting and Business Research,* Spring 1971, pp. 174–179.

Horrigan, James C. "A Short History of Financial Ratio Analysis," *Accounting Review* April 1968, pp. 284–294.

CASE EXERCISE

The Newton Company

Nick, controller of the Newton Company, strode confidently down the hall toward the president's office. When president Toby Reynolds wanted a "private word," you could count on a challenge.

"Nick," began Toby, "I had breakfast with Mark from Collier's Bank. Mark told me that Martinco has run into severe financial problems and the company may be available for acquisition."

"I'm familiar with the company," interjected Nick. "In fact, they use our Fox assembly in their Trunck work stations. I thought the Trunck was a big success story for them. What happened?"

"Too much success, I think; but I'd like to get your opinion once you've had a chance to go over the financials. Mark says they're falling over each other trying to get those Truncks out the door. There's been a complete breakdown of financial controls; they've had something like three controllers in the last two years. Still, I think there is a good fit with us from a product-line standpoint and, frankly, I'm impressed with their technical know-how and the forward integration potential we could gain through their distribution network."

"Anyway, Nick, could you look over these statements? That's all Mark is authorized to provide at this point," Toby said, handing Nick a thin folder (see Exhibits C-1 and C-2). "I promised to give Mark an idea as to whether we'd be interested in a closer look. Can you let me know in about an hour?"

EXHIBIT C-1
Martinco Income Statement for the Year Ending 12/31/87 ($000)

Sales	$12,400
Cost of goods sold	9,440
Gross profit	2,960
Selling, general & administrative	2,040
Operating profit	920
Interest expense	620
Profit before taxes	300
Federal taxes (34%)	102
Net income	198

Assets		Liabilities & Equity	
Cash & marketable securities	$ 260	Accounts payable	$ 900
Accounts receivable	3,100	Notes payable	2,760
Inventory	2,380	Other current	560
Total current	$5,740	Total current	$4,220
Net fixed assets	2,260	Long-term debt	1,760
		Shareholders' equity	2,020
Total	$8,000	Total	$8,000

Industry ratios

Current ratio	2.2 times
Total debt/assets	50%
Sales/inventory	7.00 times
Average collection period	52 days
Fixed assets turnover	3.25 times
Total asset turnover	1.85 times
Net profit/sales	3.19%
Return on assets	5.90%
Return on equity	10.80%
Gross margin	18.00%
Selling, general & administrative	12.30%

EXHIBIT C-2
Martinco Balance Sheet as of 12/31/87 ($000)

Case Questions

1. Apply a financial analysis to the Martinco financial statements using the Du Pont model.

2. Identify the apparent strengths and weaknesses, if any, in the Martinco performance.

3. What is your assessment of the company's financial potential?

CHAPTER 8

FINANCIAL PLANNING
AND FORECASTING

I n Chapter 7, we used financial ratios to develop insights into a company's financial performance and condition. Financial ratios can also be used to forecast financial results and to develop financial plans that maximize a firm's stock price.

For most large firms, financial forecasting and planning are closely interrelated. They are carried on continuously and involve the entire management team. From a financial perspective, the main results of these activities are their effects on the firm's future profits and financing requirements. Numerous techniques for forecasting future profits and financing requirements are used in practice, differing principally in their levels of detail and sophistication. This chapter explores several of these techniques.

Objectives and Organization of this Chapter

The primary objective of this chapter is to illustrate the techniques of financial forecasting and planning. To do so, it describes the preparation of a comprehensive set of financial statements based on a company's forecasts and plans. It also shows that these statements form an integrated package of projections and that the assumptions underlying the statements must be mutually consistent.

The first section of the chapter describes the overall process of financial forecasting and planning. The second section describes the procedures for developing profit projections. Profit projections are determined by sales and cost projections. Thus, as background to the discussion of profit projections, there is included a brief description on sales forecasting methods and the analysis of a firm's cost structure. This background information is used to illustrate the preparation of the firm's *pro forma* income statement. Then the chapter shows how a financial model of the income statement can be put together for computer applications, including multiyear forecasts and sensitivity analyses of the underlying assumptions.

The third section of the chapter examines how a firm estimates its financing requirements with the use of the *pro forma* balance sheet. Again, the importance of the firm's sales level on its asset and financing requirements is shown. The fourth section describes the preparation of the cash budget and shows how it supplements the *pro forma* balance sheet in revealing the firm's financial requirements. The fifth section shows how the *pro forma* statement of cash flows can provide insights into the firm's financing requirements. The final section of the chapter presents two financial planning models that can be used for longer-term financial forecasting.

THE FINANCIAL FORECASTING AND PLANNING PROCESS

The activities of financial forecasting and planning are so closely inter-related that precise delineations are not meaningful. After all, a financial plan necessarily represents a forecast of anticipated results.

Generally, financial forecasts represent the "if this, then that," consequences of assumptions about the firm's environment, operating characteristics, and financial policies. Financial forecasts come in many varieties; but the most important information they produce is the firm's projected sales, profits, and financing requirements.[1] Given an initial forecast of these items, management designs its responses in the form of operating and financial plans that may, if necessary, indicate needed changes in operating and financial policies. For example, an adverse financial forecast might stimulate plans for aggressively increasing sales, changing the product mix, drastically cutting costs, deferring capital expenditures, or arranging additional bank financing. In final form, the financial plans become *the* plan which the entire company is committed to achieving.

In an important sense, the plan becomes the firm's official forecast and, as such, represents a standard for performance. Plans must be implemented and controlled if they are to be realized. This is accomplished by the use of a system of budgets. Budgets break out plans into subperiods such as quarters, months, weeks, and possibly days and assign managerial responsibilities.[2] For example, the cost-of-goods-sold forecast in the plan becomes the responsibility of the production manager, to make sure costs do not exceed their planned levels. In addition to the operating budget, there must be a capital expenditure budget indicating the amount and timing of cash outlays for the acquisition of new capital equipment. The

---

[1]In Brendle's case, the most important forecast is the annual forecast because this is keyed to the annual reporting cycle as well as to the overall planning and budgeting exercise for the company. Brendle also develops a five-year forecast based on the firm's fundamental operating and financial relationships as well as on financial policies currently in place.

[2]The diversity and detail of a company's budget system depends on the company's size as well as management requirements. Generally, the more complex the budget system the greater its data requirements and the longer it takes to prepare. These factors, of course, involve costs that must be compared to the benefits expected. In any event, the activities of forecasting, planning, and budgeting should be continuous if they are to stay relevant. The firm's operating environment is always changing, and management must recognize such changes while there is time to deal with them.

marketing manager is responsible for developing a budget to achieve the planned sales level. This budget is composed of advertising and selling expense budgets to control the costs of marketing the company's goods and services. The financial manager develops a cash budget to make sure the company has enough cash on hand to meet operating requirements and other financial obligations (such as loan repayments and dividends) and to provide for emergencies in the event the cash forecasts are incorrect. The timing and amounts of additional cash requirements (or excesses) allow the financial manager to develop plans to raise the needed funds or invest the cash excesses in the best possible way.

Budgets allow management to monitor progress closely, and they provide a basis for evaluating and controlling performance. In addition they permit quick corrective action in the event a firm begins to stray off course.

The financial manager's direct responsibilities in the overall forecasting, planning, and budgeting process vary from firm to firm depending on, among other things, the size of the firm. However, there are two essential responsibilities in the overall process. The financial manager's most immediate responsibility is to forecast and plan competently for the firm's financing requirements in the near future as well as over the long term. The second responsibility is to forecast competently the profits for the firm given its sales forecasts and operating characteristics.

The critical determinant of both profits and financing requirements, given the firm's financial characteristics and policies, is its sales level. For this reason, all financial forecasts are based on a sales forecast. If there is considerable uncertainty surrounding the forecast, the financial manager should consider a range of sales levels, examine their financial implications, and develop contingency plans. By using selected financial ratios organized into simple financial models, such projections can be developed and revised quickly.

The Financial Plan

The financial consequences of the forecasting, planning, and budgeting process are gathered together in the financial plan. This plan reviews the assumptions about the firm's environment, operating characteristics, and financial policies adopted by its management. These assumptions are then used to project a set of financial statements that represent the company's financial plan. The plan serves as the negotiating basis for arranging additional financing, if necessary, in the form of debt and/or new stock issues.

Typically, the financial plan includes a set of *pro forma* income statements (i.e., forecast income statements) covering the next few years; *pro forma* balance sheets and *pro forma* statements of cash flow covering the same time periods; and detailed cash budgets for the next year or two. The immediate, or short-term, projections are of particular importance because of their greater probable accuracy and because they reflect the firm's intended short-term operating plans. Moreover, management's performance against immediate projections sheds light on the validity of longer-term projections. The longer-term forecasts, while much more suspect in terms of specific accuracy, are intended to reveal emerging trends or important financial requirements that will require longer lead times for preparation. Financial planning models are useful for these longer-term projections.

THE PROFIT EQUATION

Profits are equal to sales revenues minus expenses and taxes.[3] Thus, profit forecasts are developed by forecasting sales and costs. The general form of this profit relationship is shown in Equation 8-1.

$$\text{Forecast profits } (P) = \text{Forecast sales } (S) - \text{Forecast costs } (C) \quad \text{(8-1)}$$

Complicating this relationship, however, is the fact that a firm's sales and costs are closely related. The exact nature of this relationship depends on the firm's cost structure and is one of the most distinguishing characteristics across firms and industries.

In order to use the profit equation, sales forecasts and assumptions about the behavior of costs relative to sales must be developed.

Sales Forecasts

In this section, we will briefly describe several different, though complementary, approaches that can be used to develop sales forecasts. These approaches are bottom-up forecasts, top-down forecasts, trend forecasts, and probabilistic forecasts.[4]

bottom-up forecasts

Bottom-Up Forecasts. The bottom-up method involves an internally generated forecast. Management asks the sales department to develop an estimate of monthly sales for the next year. Each product manager is asked to determine how much she or he will be able to sell during the period, with the estimate often supported by major-customer and product-line projections. By accumulating these individual reports, the sales manager is able to prepare an estimate of sales by product line and in total.[5]

---

[3]For convenience, we will use the terms *expenses* and *costs* interchangeably.
[4]Detailed descriptions of forecasting methods are outside the scope of this book.
[5]Since sales personnel will likely be evaluated on the basis of how well they meet projections, this potential bias and others should be taken into account by the user of the sales forecast. Ideally, the sales forecast should include a forecast of unit sales for each product or service and the selling price per unit for each. An important benefit from this breakdown is the greater precision possible in estimating costs and, hence, profits.

Top-Down Forecasts. The top-down method bases the forecast upon an analysis of external economic factors.[6] For example, the forecast might begin with a projection for the overall economy, taking into consideration federal fiscal and monetary policies, the business cycle, the expected rate of inflation, and other factors. From these projections forecasts for major sectors of the economy are made; and from these, forecasts of total sales are developed for industries and subindustries within which the firm operates. Finally, given the subindustry projections and the firm's anticipated market share, a sales forecast for the firm is developed. Because of the complexity and data relationships of such forecasts, computerized econometric models are typically used. The top-down forecast is used to check the reasonableness of the bottom-up or other forecast methods.

top-down forecasts

Trend Forecasts. A much simpler forecast method employs historical sales information to detect a pattern or trend in sales growth. This trend may be stated in dollar or percentage terms. For example, if sales are increasing by $200,000 per year, next year's forecast can simply be set $200,000 above the current year's actual sales. Alternatively, if sales growth has averaged 5 percent per year over the past five years, next year's sales estimate might be set at 5 percent above the current year's actual sales. Trend forecasts must be realistic to be of value. This means they should be modified to take into account top-down information such as the state of the economy, industry conditions, and other factors. In addition, such bottom-up factors as the addition or loss of a major customer should be considered in modifying trend estimates.

trend forecasts

Probabilistic Forecasts. Probabilistic forecasts explicitly recognize the uncertainty that exists in all forecasts. Probabilistic forecasts may simply contain a range of outcomes such as "high," "low," and "best-guess" estimates; or "optimistic," "pessimistic," and "most likely," estimates. For example, the high estimate might be based on the assumption that all favorable circumstances materialize and that sales are as high as possible. The low forecast might be based on the assumption that the marketing environment turns out to be unfavorable in all major respects.

probabilistic forecasts

Typically, each outcome specified is related to some state of the overall economy. For example, the high forecast might be linked to rapid growth in the overall economy. By assigning probabilities to each of the possible outcomes, the relative importance to be given in planning for that outcome

---

[6]The level and detail and sophistication employed varies widely from firm to firm. Some use full-scale econometric models or subscribe to a service such as DRI, Inc. or Chase Econometrics, while others simply rely on a qualitative assessment such as "favorable" or "unfavorable" forecasts. Both approaches are externally oriented.

TABLE 8-1 Brendle Manufacturing Company Sales Forecast — 1988 ($000)			
State of National Economy	Probability of State Occurring	Sales Forecast	%Δ to 1987
Recession	.2	$1,331	−10%
Moderate Growth	.6	$1,553	+5%
Rapid Growth	.2	$1,775	+20%

can be determined.[7] An example of a probabilistic sales forecast for Brendle Manufacturing Company's 1988 sales level is shown in Table 8-1.

Other Methods. When more explicit analysis of the forecast uncertainty is desired, computer simulation may be necessary. With such procedures, probability distributions for many critical variables (such as product selling prices, advertising expenditures, and state of the economy) are estimated. By repeatedly combining estimates randomly selected from each distribution hundreds of times, a full probability distribution of estimated sales can be developed.

An obvious shortcoming of the simulation method is that it requires considerable specialized data which are costly and time consuming to develop and analyze. Moreover, relationships among the variables, such as the relationship between selling price and sales, need to be specified. If they are mis-specified, the error or bias may be difficult to detect in the mass of data generated. Nonetheless, a major benefit of such analyses is that management objectively specifies critical assumptions and allows them to be examined for realism and consistency.

Selecting the Sales Forecast

Each of the forecast methods supplements the others, but it is unlikely that they will all be in agreement. For planning purposes, at some point management must decide on a specific forecast that represents a reasonable compromise among the estimates. This reconciliation forms the basis of the management sales target. In addition to the reconciliation of other forecasts, the management sales target should also incorporate sales goals or objectives set by the chief executive officer of the company.

---

[7]By multiplying each outcome times its probability and summing, the expected sales forecast can be determined (i.e., (.2)(1,331) + (.6)(1,553) + (.2)(1,775) = 1.553). To minimize unnecessary numerical complexity, we have designed Brendle's forecast so that the expected value is equal to the moderate-growth sales level of $1,553,000.

Cost Forecasts

Cost forecasts require an analysis of the firm's cost structure as reflected on the income statement. In particular, each of the cost items must be examined to determine how it will behave relative to changes in sales volume.

The firm's cost structure reflects three types of cost behavior: variable costs, fixed costs, and semivariable costs. We will first define each type of cost and then discuss how the analysis can be applied to Brendle's 1987 income statement. A graphic illustration of the three types of cost behavior is shown in Exhibit 8-1.

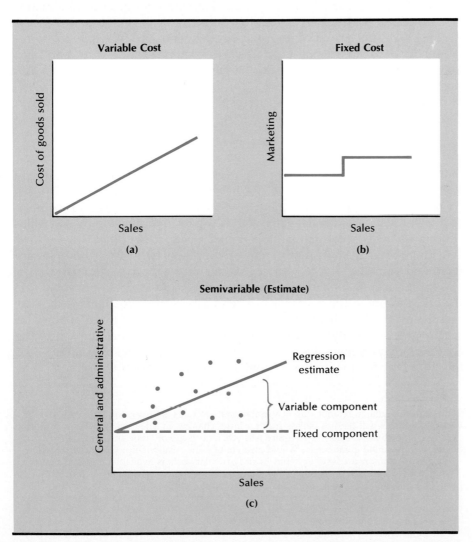

EXHIBIT 8-1
Brendle Mfg. Company:
Relationship of Selected
Costs to Changes
in Sales

variable costs

Variable Costs.   Variable costs are costs that change in direct proportion to variations in sales.[8] For example, when sales increase by 10 percent, total variable costs also rise by 10 percent. Examples of variable costs are direct labor and raw materials used in producing a company's products. For example, the relationship between Brendle's cost of goods sold and sales level is shown in panel (a) of Exhibit 8-1.

fixed costs

Fixed Costs.   Fixed costs do not change with short-run variations in sales. In the long run, of course, all costs must be considered variable with respect to sales.[9] It is useful to distinguish between fixed operating costs and fixed financial costs. As the name suggests, fixed operating costs are the fixed costs incurred in the production, marketing, and administrative functions of the firm.[10] Brendle's only fixed financial cost is interest expense. All other fixed costs are operating costs. An example of the relationship between fixed costs, in this case fixed marketing costs, and sales volume is shown in panel (b) of Exhibit 8-1. Note that marketing costs maintain a long-term relationship to sales (i.e., over time marketing expenses are increasing as sales increase) but do not vary with short-run changes in sales.

semivariable costs

Semivariable Costs.   Semivariable costs contain both variable and fixed-cost elements. That is, some portion of these costs changes directly with changes in sales volume while the remainder does not. For purposes of analysis, semivariable costs must be split into their fixed and variable-cost elements. Considerable judgment is involved in developing such allocations and, when substantial uncertainty exists, it is prudent to see how sensitive the analysis is to different assumptions as to what portions are fixed and variable.

To split semivariable costs into their fixed and variable portions, it is useful to examine the behavior of such costs relative to changes in sales volume over time. This may be done with either simple trend analysis or with regression analysis. With either technique, the actual amount of the cost is plotted against sales volume, as shown in panel (c) of Exhibit 8-1. A line that best fits the scatter of points is drawn through the points.[11] The

regression analysis

---

[8]Although the general relationship of variable costs to sales is linear, for any particular variable cost this will tend to be less true for large changes in sales volume. For example, very large increases in sales may require less efficient usage of labor and materials. A price decrease to promote greater sales would also change the relationship. Of course, if more exact information on the level or behavior of particular costs is available it should be used.
[9]Fixed costs can and do change over the short run in response to changes in inflation, periodic expansion, changes in production, marketing, administration, or financing methods—but not in a systematic response to short-run changes in sales. Otherwise they would be, to that extent, variable costs.
[10]Lease payments could be considered fixed financial costs.
[11]With trend analysis, this line may simply be "eye balled." With regression analysis, it is determined mathematically.

intercept of the line represents the fixed-cost component, and the slope of the line represents the variable-cost component. The slope of the line represents the percentage relationship between variable costs and sales.

Brendle's financial manager estimates that general and administrative expenses, though primarily fixed ($121,000) have a variable component equal to 1.4 percent of sales.

Table 8-2 shows a breakdown of Brendle's 1987 income statement organized into fixed and variable components.

TABLE 8-2 Brendle Manufacturing Company Cost Analysis of 1987 Income Statement ($000)

		Variable Cost $	Variable Cost %	Fixed Cost $
Sales	$1,479			
Cost of goods sold	1,062	$1,062	71.8%	—
Gross profits	417			
General and administrative	141	20	1.4%	121
Marketing	50	—	—	50
Depreciation	10	—	—	10
EBIT	216			
Interest	26	—	—	26
Profit before taxes	190			
Taxes	76			
Net income	$114			
Total		1,082	73.2%	207

Note that cost of goods sold is treated as completely variable. Marketing, depreciation, and interest expense are completely fixed for the next year. General and administrative expenses, however, are considered to be semivariable, and Brendle's financial manager has split the total into variable and fixed components. In other words, of the total general and administrative expenses of $141,000, $20,000 is considered variable and $121,000 is considered fixed.

As indicated in Table 8-2, Brendle's total fixed costs were $207,000 and total variable costs were $1,082,000, representing 73.2% of sales in 1987.

THE *PRO FORMA* INCOME STATEMENT

Combining the set of sales forecasts and the analysis of Brendle's cost structure, *pro forma* income statements can be readily developed for each sales forecast. This is shown in Table 8-3.

TABLE 8-3   Brendle Manufacturing Company Pro-Forma Income
Statements — 1988 ($000)

	State of Economy		
	Recession	Moderate growth	Rapid growth
Sales	1,331	1,553	1,775
Cost of goods sold	956	1,115	1,274
Gross Profits	375	438	501
General & administrative	140	143	146
Marketing	50	50	50
Depreciation	10	10	10
EBIT	175	235	295
Interest	26	26	26
Profit before taxes	149	209	269
Taxes (40%)	59	83	108
Net income	90	126	161

To see how the figures are derived, let us examine the cost of goods sold, general and administrative expenses and depreciation.[12]

The cost of goods sold figure is calculated by simply multiplying the forecast sales level by 71.8 percent. Thus, cost of goods sold, at the sales forecast of $1,331,000 is $955,658 (i.e., $1,331,000 × .718). The general and administrative expenses figure is equal to 1.4 percent times the forecasted sales level plus the fixed-cost component of $121,000. Thus at the forecast sales level of $1,331,000, the figure of $139,634 is equal to $1,331,000 times .014 (= $18,634) plus $121,000. The depreciation figure, $10,000, does not change regardless of the forecast sales level, indicating its status as a fixed cost.

According to the *pro forma* income statement, net income may vary considerably next year. If recession occurs, the company will produce profits of $90,000, or about 21 percent below the 1987 level of $114,000. A decline in profits will adversely affect the company's stock price and diminish funds for expansion, employee raises, marketing programs, renovation of production facilities, product development, and other activities.

Because of the unfavorable consequences of a sales decline, the company's top management will develop contingency plans to deal with an overall economic recession. These plans will include more aggressive marketing efforts, rigid cost controls, and deferral of discretionary expenditures. Thus financial plans represent management's responses to the

---

[12]Since Brendle's 1987 income statement is rounded to the nearest thousand dollars, we have also rounded off the calculations based on the statement to tie the estimates more closely to the *pro forma* income statements, which are also rounded to the nearest thousand dollars.

financial forecast in order to pursue the maximization of the company's stock price.

If rapid growth materializes, the company will earn a large (41 percent) increase in profits relative to 1987. Management will expect a rise in the company's stock price. Funds will be available for product development, expansion, increased shareholder dividends, and so on. Nonetheless, financial planning will be needed to make sure the favorable sales and profit opportunity is not wasted. Production will have to be increased to insure the availability of finished goods to meet sales demand. Sales and cost budgets will still be needed, and they will have to be monitored to achieve the firm's full profit potential.

A Financial Model of the Income Statement

Once the company's cost structure has been evaluated, the financial manager has effectively created a financial model of the income statement. Such a model can be applied easily to the financial spreadsheets programs commonly available for personal computers. Financial spreadsheet programs such as *MultiPlan* and *Lotus* 1-2-3, for example, permit rapid construction of *pro-forma* income statements and readily allow for instantaneous sensitivity analysis of alternative sales forecasts or changed assumptions about cost behavior.

Exhibit 8-2 shows how the financial relationships in Brendle's income statement could be modeled.

The net income relationship is of particular interest. This is the after-tax profit equation. If the financial manager is simply interested in a quick projection of profits given the assumed cost structure and a sales forecast,

EXHIBIT 8-2
Brendle Manufacturing Company

Item	Relation
Sales:	Given
Cost of goods sold:	.718(sales)
Gross profit:	sales $-$ CGS $=$ .282(sales)
General & administrative:	.014(sales) $+$ 121,000
Marketing:	50,000
Depreciation:	10,000
EBIT:	Sales $-$ .732(sales) $-$ 181,000
Interest:	26,000
Profit before taxes	.268(sales) $-$ \$207,000
Taxes (40%):	.107(sales) $-$ 83,000
Net income (60% $\times$ PBT):	.161(sales) $-$ 124,000

the profit equation can be used directly without having to project the entire income statement.

In applying sensitivity analysis, however, the user will be interested in projecting the entire statement to see how various components are affected by a change in one or more of the assumptions behind the model. Table 8-4, for example, shows a partial sensitivity analysis of assumptions underlying Brendle's forecast. For example, the projection in part (a) of Table 8-4 shows what net income will be in 1988 if sales decline by as much as 20 percent from their 1987 level. Part (b) of Table 8-4 shows the effect on net income if cost of goods sold increases to 75 percent of sales in 1988, given the projected sales level of $1,553,000. Part (c) shows the effect of a rise in fixed marketing costs to $75,000, given the projected sales level of $1,553,000.

TABLE 8-4 Brendle Manufacturing Company Sensitivity Analysis of Selected Pro Forma Income Statement Assumptions ($000)

(a) Assumes 1988 sales decline 20 percent to $1,183
(b) Assumes cost of goods sold rises to 75 percent of sales; sales are $1,553
(c) Assumes fixed marketing costs increase to $75,000; sales are $1,553

	(a)	(b)	(c)
Sales	1,183	1,553	1,553
Cost of goods sold	849	1,165	1,115
Gross profit	334	388	438
General and administrative	138	143	143
Marketing:	50	50	75
Depreciation:	10	10	10
EBIT	136	185	210
Interest	26	26	26
PBT	110	159	184
Taxes	44	64	74
Net income	66	95	110

Of the three changes in assumptions examined, the most adverse impact on net income would come from a 20 percent sales decline.

THE *PRO FORMA* BALANCE SHEET

Just as expenses must be incurred to generate sales revenues, assets must also be employed to support sales. In some cases, this relationship might seem obvious. For example, a manufacturer needs machinery and other equipment to produce goods for sale. Perhaps less obvious, though no less essential, extension of credit to customers will require additional investment in accounts receivable. Inventories are likewise needed for production and sales. Cash balances for meeting maturing obligations, and normal operating transactions will also vary with sales.

Thus, as sales levels rise and fall, asset requirements rise and fall. However, the key point is that any change in assets must be matched by a corresponding change in financing. In other words, the balance sheet must balance. Sales forecasts heavily determine asset requirements, and asset requirements determine financing requirements. Similarly, *changes* in sales heavily determine the *changes* in asset requirements, and the *changes* in asset requirements determine the *changes* in financing requirements.

Constructing the *Pro Forma* Balance Sheet

The *pro forma* balance sheet can be developed using an analytical method similar to the one used for the *pro forma* income statement. In other words, each asset and liability account is examined to see how it behaves relative to changes in the level of sales. Current asset and current liability accounts tend to respond more quickly to changes in sales than fixed-asset and long-term liability accounts. Accounts receivable and inventories, for example, will increase in proportion to sales if the average collection period and inventory turnover are expected to stay constant.

Let us assume that Brendle's financial manager has estimated the following current asset relationships. We have also shown the dollar amounts, assuming a sales level of $1,553,000.

Asset	% of Sales	$ Amount
Cash and marketable securities	5%	$ 78,000
Accounts receivable	20	310,000
Inventories	16	248,000

Certain liabilities also may be expected to vary with sales. For example, purchases of materials to be used in the production process are likely to vary with sales. Purchases made on credit become accounts payable, and thus accounts payable can be expected to vary with sales. Of course, if the percentages to sales are expected to change, the projected percentages must be used. For example, if accruals were 9 percent of sales in 1987 but are expected to be 8 percent in 1988, then 8 percent should be used.

Let us assume that Brendle's financial manager has estimated the following liability relationships for 1988:

Liability	% Of Sales	$ Amount
Accounts payable	9%	$140,000
Accruals	8%	124,000
Deferred income taxes	9%	140,000

Other balance-sheet items do not increase very much or at all in response to short-term changes in sales levels. For example, long-term debt tends to maintain a long-term rather than short-term relationship to sales. Thus, for short-term projections, these accounts must be forecast directly. Likewise, notes payable (e.g., bank loans) and new common stock sales represent external financing sources that have to be negotiated and, in that sense, do not change automatically with sales. Since the 1988 amounts for these items is what we are attempting to determine, we temporarily assume that they will stay at their 1987 levels.

Brendle's financial manager has estimated the following balance-sheet items directly:

Gross fixed assets: to increase by $100,000

Accumulated depreciation: to increase by $10,000

Net fixed assets: $699,000 in 1987 (to increase by $90,000 in 1988)

Notes payable: $50,000 in 1987 (1988 to be determined)

Long-term debt: $220,000 in 1987 (1988 to be determined)

Common stock: $100,000 in 1987 (no change in 1988)

Retained earnings: $251,000 in 1987 (to increase by net income minus dividends of $56,000 in 1988)

Once the balance sheet relationships to sales have been estimated, they are grouped into the *pro forma* balance sheet.

Brendle's *Pro Forma* Balance Sheets

The *pro forma* balance sheet reveals the amount of additional external financing (i.e., borrowing or sales of stock), if any, that will have to be raised to achieve the forecast sales level. Table 8-5 contains *pro forma* balance sheets developed for 1988 under different sales growth assumptions.

For example, assuming a sales level of $1,553,000 for Brendle, total assets required are projected to be $1,425,000. However, projected financing sources (before additional external financing) will be only $1,383,000. The balance sheet will not balance. Another $42,000 of financing will have to be arranged to pay for the needed assets.

Note, furthermore, that the balance-sheet financing requirement is as of the end of 1988. However, the actual financing need during the year may be substantially more. The balance sheet only indicates what it will be on

TABLE 8-5   Brendle Manufacturing Company Pro Forma Balance Sheets—1988 ($000)

	Recession	Moderate Growth	Rapid Growth
Sales	$1,331	$1,553	$1,627
Assets			
Cash and marketable securities	67	78	81
Accounts receivable	266	310	325
Inventories	213	248	260
Current assets	546	636	666
Net fixed assets	789	789	789
Total assets	$1,335	$1,425	$1,455
Liabilities and Shareholders' Equity			
Accounts payable	$ 120	$ 140	$ 146
Notes payable	50	50	50
Accruals	106	124	130
Current liabilities	276	314	326
Long-term debt	220	220	220
Deferred income taxes	120	140	146
Total liabilities	616	674	692
Common stock	100	100	100
Surplus	288	288	288
Retained earnings	285	321	356
Total	$1,289	$1,383	$1,436
Net financing required: Total assets − total liabilities and shareholders' equity:	$46	$42	$19

December 31, 1988. A better estimate of financing requirements during the year can be developed by either shorter-term (e.g., monthly) balance sheets or by developing cash budgets on a quarterly, monthly, or even shorter time interval.

THE CASH BUDGET

The cash budget allows the financial manager to examine financial requirements closely, usually by focusing on time intervals within a year. For example, the financial manager might develop the cash budget on a quarterly, monthly, or even daily time-period basis. Major corporations forecast their cash daily, with the aid of computerized cash management systems.

Table 8-6 contains the cash budget prepared by Brendle's financial manager on a quarterly basis for the year 1988, assuming the moderate-growth sales projection of $1,553,000. Notice that the cash budget has three principal parts:

- Cash receipts
- Cash disbursements
- Financing

As indicated by the "Financing required" line on the cash budget, as of the end of the fourth quarter the net financing required, $42,000, exactly matches the financing requirement estimated with the *pro forma* balance sheet. This should always be the case if the statements are prepared consistently. However, the cash budget also reveals that, during the second quarter, financing required will soar to a peak of $234,000! This type of information reveals vividly the need to examine shorter time segments when the firm's

TABLE 8-6   Brendle Manufacturing Company Quarterly Cash Budget — 1988

	Q1	Q2	Q3	Q4
I. Receipts				
Collections from sales	293	290	500	452
II. Disbursements				
Payment for purchases	149	174	140	133
Labor	131	131	131	127
General & administrative	35	36	36	36
Marketing	12	13	12	13
Interest	6	7	6	7
Taxes		42	21	20
Dividends	14	14	14	14
Capital expenditures	25	25	25	25
Total	372	442	385	375
III. Financing				
Net inflow (outflow)	(79)	(152)	115	77
Beginning cash & marketable securities	75	(4)	(156)	(41)
End cash	(4)	(156)	(41)	36
Desired cash	(78)	(78)	(78)	(78)
Cumulative Financing required (surplus)	82	234	119	42

sales are seasonal.[13] If Brendle's financial manager had planned to meet only the $42,000 financing requirement indicated by the *pro forma* balance sheet, he or she would have been embarrassed to discover that this was inadequate as early as the first quarter, with the financing requirement already up to $82,000. The company would have been in deep trouble by the end of the second quarter.

Frequently, though not in this case, the cash budget will reveal anticipated cash surpluses. If so, the financial manager should be prepared to use the surplus, even if temporary, to repay bank lines of credit and, if surplus still remains, to invest in short-term, high-quality investments such as U.S. Government securities. Such cash management practices are dealt with in more detail in Chapter 10.

Cash Receipts

As previously stated, accurate sales forecasts are important to the ability to project profits and external financing requirements. Accurate sales forecasts are equally important to the preparation of cash budgets or cash flow forecasts. However, the annual sales projection must be broken down into the same time periods for which the cash budget will be prepared.

To see how the cash budget is developed, let us assume that Brendle's moderate-growth sales forecast is based on the following sales forecast.

1988 Quarterly Sales Forecast ($000)
(Assuming Annual Sales of $1,553,000)

	Q1	Q2	Q3	Q4	Total
Sales	290	500	453	310	$1,553

Collections from Sales.   Note that sales are lowest in the first quarter and peak in the second quarter. To translate these sales estimates into cash flows, some assumptions must be made about the collection pattern of accounts receivable.

The lag between the time of sale and the receipt of cash is determined by the credit terms granted by the company and the promptness with which credit customers make payments. A good guide for estimating the collection time for credit sales is past experience. Two methods for esti-

---

[13]For certain firms, such as capital goods manufacturers, this seasonal build-up of cash requirements can easily extend into cycles as long as 18 months. For such firms, the minimum budget horizon should be longer than one year.

mating collections from credit sales are the *percentage of sales method* and the ending receivables method.

With the percentage method, the company may expect to get a certain percentage of the credit sales collected in the month of sale; another portion collected in the month following sale, and so on. For example, all of Brendle's sales are made on credit terms; and, on the average, Brendle may expect to get 30 percent of sales in the first month following sale, another 50 percent in the second month following sale, and the remaining 20 percent in the third month following sale.

With the *ending receivables method*, cash collections are equal to sales in the period (whether for cash or credit) plus the change in receivables. The The change in receivables is calculated by subtracting the ending accounts receivable from the beginning accounts receivable for the period. Of course, the ending accounts receivable for one period is the same as the beginning accounts receivable for the following period. Thus, only ending accounts receivable need to be calculated for each period. To determine the ending receivables for each period, the financial manager can just assume an average collection period based on past experience.[14]

Brendle's financial manager estimates that the company's average collection period will be 90 days. Thus, ending accounts receivable represent the last 90 days of sales, assuming that credit sales and collections are approximately uniform throughout the quarter. For clarity, we will ignore such complicating factors as bad debts and late payments. Table 8-7 shows how the ending accounts receivable estimate can be used to forecast cash collections from sales. Note that the beginning accounts receivable for the first quarter of 1988 is equal to the ending accounts receivable as of December 31, 1987.

TABLE 8-7 Brendle Manufacturing Company Forecast Cash Collections from Sales — 1988

	Q1	Q2	Q3	Q4
Sales	290	500	453	310
+Beginning accounts receivable	293*	290	500	453
Total	583	790	953	763
−Ending accounts receivable	290	500	453	310
=Cash collections	293	290	500	453

*From balance sheet of 12/31/87

---

[14]In forecasting accounts receivable, it is usually assumed that sales are made uniformly throughout the period and that months have 30 days. For example, Brendle's cash budget and sales forecast are in 90-day periods. If the financial manager expected the average collection period to be 45 days, the ending accounts receivable estimate would be one-half (i.e., 45/90) of the quarter's sales. Likewise, a collection period of 30 days would mean accounts receivable would be one third (i.e., 30/90) of the quarter's sales.

Other Receipts.   Since the cash budget must be a comprehensive forecast of all cash inflows and outflows, it should include all other expected cash receipts. Thus, for example, if the company planned to sell off a piece of equipment or other asset, the expected cash receipts, after taxes, should be included. In our example, no other receipts are expected.

Cash Disbursements

To be valid, the cash budget should include all cash disbursements that are expected to occur during the cash budget period. These disbursements will typically include payments for materials, labor, and other operating costs. Other cash disbursements for capital expenditures, taxes, dividends, and scheduled debt payments should also be included. However, the cash budget should *not* include expenses that do not represent an actual cash outflow, such as depreciation.

Payments for Purchases.   Purchases of raw materials and other supplies are typically made on credit terms. This creates a delay between the time of purchase and the actual cash disbursement. The extent of this delay depends on the types of credit terms received by the firm and the promptness with which the firm pays its bills.

The pattern of purchases during the year is determined by the sales forecast and the production policy the company has adopted. For example, Brendle's sales are not uniform during the year. Should the company's production schedule also vary as its sales projections vary? Or, should production be at a uniform rate during the year? The latter alternative will result in more inventory costs but substantially lower production costs. Let us assume that Brendle has chosen a policy of relatively uniform production during the year.

Brendle's financial manager expects to pay for purchases 90 days after purchase. Until paid, credit purchases are shown as accounts payable on the balance sheet. Thus, purchases for the fourth quarter of 1987 (i.e., the $149,000 accounts payable at 12/31/1987) will be paid for in the first quarter of 1988. Disbursements for purchases in each quarter are shown below:[15]

	Actual 1987	Forecast for 1988			
	Q4	Q1	Q2	Q3	Q4
Purchases	$149	$174	$140	$133	$140
+ Beginning accounts payable		$149	$174	$140	$133
− Ending accounts payable	($149)	($174)	($140)	($133)	($140)
= Cash payments		$149	$174	$140	$133

---

[15]This same procedure should be employed to deal with any other payment delays. For example, if some portion of wages is accrued each period, the actual cash payment for wages during the period will be equal to the wage expense plus the beginning accrued amount minus the ending accrued amount.

Other Disbursements.   Production operations involve other cash outflows besides raw materials purchases. Payments for direct labor and factory overhead must also be made. For clarity, assume these other payments are made as indicated in the cash budget.

Similarly, assume that general and administrative expenses and marketing expenses are incurred uniformly throughout the forecast period and paid for in the quarter incurred.

Interest expense will be paid quarterly during the year. The estimated tax liability for the year, $83,000, is scheduled to be paid in the second, third, and fourth quarters. Dividends of $14,000 per quarter will be paid. Additional expenditures for capital equipment, totalling $100,000 for the year, are projected to be disbursed uniformly during the year. These other cash disbursements are shown in Table 8-8.

Financing

Once the total cash receipts and disbursements for each quarter have been estimated, their financing implications can be examined.

Net Cash Inflow (Outflow).   The net cash flow for each quarter is calculated by subtracting total cash disbursements from total cash receipts. In the first and second quarters the net cash flows are negative; but in the third and fourth quarters the cash flows are positive, as indicated in Table 8-6, which we discussed earlier and which is reproduced on page 289. This pattern of cash flows is due to the fact that sales peak in the second quarter but cash is not collected from these sales until the third quarter. In the third and fourth quarters, collections from previous sales exceed cash disbursements; some of the temporary financing requirement is relieved.

Brendle's cash flow pattern is heavily influenced by the fact that its sales are seasonal while its production and operating expenditures are uniform. If Brendle tailored its production and operating activities to match its sales pattern, its net cash flows would not fluctuate as much. However, its costs of production would be much higher. The effects of seasonal sales patterns

TABLE 8-8   Other Cash Disbursements

	Q1	Q2	Q3	Q4
General & administrative	35,000	36,000	36,000	36,000
Marketing	12,500	12,500	12,500	12,500
Interest	6,500	6,500	6,500	6,500
Taxes		42,000	21,000	20,000
Dividends	14,000	14,000	14,000	14,000
Capital expenditures	25,000	25,000	25,000	25,000

TABLE 8-6   Brendle Manufacturing Company Quarterly Cash Budget — 1988

	Q1	Q2	Q3	Q4
I. Receipts				
Collections				
from sales	293	290	500	452
II. Disbursements				
Payment				
for purchases	149	174	140	133
Labor	131	131	131	127
General & administrative	35	36	36	36
Marketing	12	13	12	13
Interest	6	7	6	7
Taxes		42	21	20
Dividends	14	14	14	14
Capital expenditures	25	25	25	25
Total	372	442	385	375
III. Financing				
Net inflow				
(outflow)	(79)	(152)	115	77
Beginning cash				
& marketable securities	75	(4)	(156)	(41)
End cash	(4)	(156)	(41)	36
Desired cash	(78)	(78)	(78)	(78)
Cumulative Financing				
Required (surplus)	82	234	119	42

on cash flows are an important reason why cash budgets covering a full year should be undertaken.

   Beginning Cash and Marketable Securities.   The company's current cash balance plus marketable securities (which can be converted to cash quickly) are available to meet net cash outflows. The beginning cash and marketable securities for the first quarter ($75,000) is necessarily the ending balance shown on the balance sheet for 12/31/1987. However, even though this amount of cash is available to meet cash outflows, such a use will seriously deplete the cash balance for the company and put the company below its desired cash balance. For example, in light of Brendle's higher expected level of activity in 1988, Brendle's financial manager wants to keep $78,000 in cash at all times. But, if its opening amount of $75,000 is used up by the first quarter cash requirement of $79,000, Brendle will not have a penny in the bank.

   Ending Cash and Desired Cash.   To make sure the company's cash balance does not drop below its minimum desired level, Brendle's financial manager first calculates the company's ending cash balance (negative $4,000) as if there were no additional financing. This ending cash balance is then compared with the desired cash balance. In the first quarter, the company's cash balance will be a negative $4,000 without any additional financing. The ending cash balance, before additional financing, in the first quarter is carried over as the beginning cash balance for the second quarter. In order to get the balance up to the desired minimum of $78,000, the financial manager will have to raise $82,000 in the first quarter.

Cumulative Financing Required (Surplus). From the financial manager's standpoint, the most important information on the cash budget is contained in the *bottom line*. This is an estimate of the firm's cumulative financing requirement over the year. As a matter of conventional practice, the amount needed, such as the $82,000 in the first quarter, is shown as a positive number rather than in parentheses. A negative number on this line represents a cash excess. By the end of the year, the cash budget indicates an external financing requirement of $42,000.

It is important to recognize that the financing required on the cash budget is *in addition* to any borrowing or other funds of which the company has use.

Relationship of Cash Budget to *Pro Forma* Balance Sheet

The additional financing indicated by the cash budget should equal the projected financing requirement produced by the *pro forma* balance sheet. Recall from Table 8-5 that, at a projected sales level of $1,553,000, the external financing required is forecast to be $42,000 at the end of 1988. This is the same requirement indicated by the cash budget at the end of the fourth quarter, 1988.

 ### *PRO FORMA* STATEMENT OF CASH FLOWS

It is a common misconception that a company making profits has plenty of cash and should not need additional financing. The cash budget, together with the *pro forma* income statement, reveals that this is not the case. For example, according to the *pro forma* income statement for 1988 (Table 8-3) Brendle is forecasting $126,000 in profits given the moderate-growth scenario. Yet, as we have just seen from the forecast cash budget (Table 8-6), Brendle will have to raise a minimum of $42,000 and a maximum of $234,000 from external sources during the year.

The relationship of profits to cash flow can be more clearly seen by developing the *pro forma* statement of cash flows.

In order to prepare the statement of cash flows, the analyst first calculates the change in each balance-sheet item from one period to the next. Since this is a *pro forma* statement, it is necessary to compare the actual balance sheet at December 31, 1987 against a forecast balance sheet as of December 31, 1988. The *pro forma* balance sheet selected corresponds to the moderate-growth scenario, with a projected sales level of $1,553,000. The comparative balance sheets are shown in Table 8-9.

The change in each item is classified as to whether it is a source or a use of cash. The classification is based on the following decision rules:

Sources of cash:

- A decrease in any asset account
- An increase in any liability account

Uses of cash:

- An increase in any asset account
- A decrease in any liability account

Table 8-9 shows the balance-sheet changes for the Brendle Company between 1987 and 1988 classified as to whether each change represents a source or use of cash.

Since the balance sheets are in balance, total sources must be equal to total uses of cash.

TABLE 8-9   Brendle Manufacturing Company Changes in Balance Sheets as of December 31

	1988*	1987	Source ($)	Use ($)
Cash & marketable securities	78	75		3
Accounts receivable	310	293		17
Inventory	248	253	5	
Current assets	636	621		
Gross fixed assets	1,136	1,036		100
Less: accumulated depreciation	(347)	(337)	10	
Net fixed assets**	789	699		
Total assets	$1,425	$1,320		
Accounts payable	$140	$149		9
Notes payable***	92	50	42	
Accruals	124	122	2	
Current liabilities	356	321		
Long-term debt	220	220		
Deferred income taxes	140	140		
Common stock	100	100		
Paid-in-surplus	288	288		
Retained earnings	321	251	70	
Total	$1,425	$1,320	$129	$129

*Forecast based on moderate growth and sales level of $1,553,000.
**Net fixed assets is equal to gross fixed assets less accumulated depreciation. The change in net fixed assets is not calculated, in order to avoid double counting.
***Assumes financing required ($42,000) is met with an increase in notes payable.

After the changes in the balance-sheet items have been calculated and classified, the following adjustment to the information should be made: replace the change in retained earnings with net income (treat this as a source of cash) and dividends paid (treat this as a use of cash). The reason for this adjustment is to avoid *double counting,* since the change in retained earnings is, by definition, equal to net income less dividends.

After the adjustment has been made, the main items of the Statement of Cash Flows can be organized.

Cash Flows from Operating Activities. Generally, this includes net income and changes in current assets (except cash and marketable securities) and current liabilities. Sources of cash are shown as positive numbers, and uses of cash are shown as negatives.

Net income	$126
Depreciation	10
Increase in accounts receivable	(17)
Decrease in inventory	5
Decrease in accounts payable	(9)
Increases in accruals	2
Increase in notes payable	42
Net cash flows from operations	$159

Cash Flows from Investing Activities. This includes all noncurrent asset transactions.

Increase in gross fixed assets	($100)

Cash Flows from Financing Activities. This includes all noncurrent liability (and equity) accounts.

Dividends paid	($56)

After the cash flows are grouped by type, the Statement of Cash Flows can be prepared, as shown in Table 8-10.

Interpretation of the *Pro Forma* Statement of Cash Flows

Note that the *pro forma* statement of cash flows is consistent with both the cash budget and the *pro forma* balance sheet for 1988. For example, the

TABLE 8-10 *Pro Forma* Statement of Cash Flows For the Period 1987–1988

Cash flows from operating activities:	
Net income	$126
Depreciation	10
Increase in accounts receivable	(17)
Decrease in inventory	5
Decrease in accounts payable	(9)
Increase in accruals	2
Increase in notes payable	42
Net cash flows from operations	$159
Cash flows from investing activities:	
Increase in gross fixed assets	($100)
Net cash flows from investing	($100)
Cash flows from financing activities:	
Dividends paid	($ 56)
Net cash flows from financing	($ 56)
Net increase (decrease) in cash	$3

increase in notes payable of $42,000 is equal to the projected financing requirement as of the end of 1988. Also, the net increase in cash reflects the rise in the desired cash balance from $75,000 in 1987 to $78,000 in 1988. Further examination of the statement reveals the effect of the planned capital expenditures and dividends on the company's cash position. By year end, the severe impact of the accounts receivable build-up due to the seasonality of sales has dissipated. In fact, by year-end, the investment in accounts receivable will have tied up only $17,000 of cash. The real cash drain in 1988 will be the $100,000 expansion; but, even ignoring that, Brendle's financial manager may look a little covetously at the dividend outflow of $56,000. Since dividends will exceed the amount of new bank borrowing (i.e., $42,000), one could argue that the company will be borrowing to pay dividends. Indeed, if Brendle's borrowing begins to rise precipitously, this point will almost certainly be raised by the firm's banker.

LONG-RANGE FINANCIAL PLANNING MODELS

The basic objective of a long-range financial plan is to anticipate future financial requirements. Basically, long-range planning involves making estimates of a series of future balance sheets in order to see what financial requirements remain unfulfilled over and above planned short-term debt, expected retention of earnings, and existing long-term debt and equity. The shortfall must be met with additional long-term debt, new issues of common stock, and reduction in cash dividends. If these sources are still insufficient, planned sales and plant expansion must be curtailed to fit the expected availability of financial resources.

As sales increase over time, so must the dollar amount of assets. This is because larger investments in assets are needed to support higher sales levels, whether the higher sales levels result from more units sold or inflation in prices. We previously used the asset turnover ratio to illustrate the relationship between sales and assets. While it is possible to alter or change asset turnovers, such changes are limited by the characteristics of the business activity or the industry in which the company operates.

The ability to project or forecast sales is critical to determining future financial requirements. Many firms prepare several long-range sales forecast possibilities to reflect different possible economic, industry, and firm developments. Then they modify their forecasts as new information becomes available. Accordingly, the financial manager often must estimate financial requirements under several possible sales developments that could occur in the future. Let us examine two types of financial planning models that can be used to forecast the financial consequences of sales growth. These are the financial requirements model and the sustainable growth model.

The Financial Requirements Model

The financial requirements model is used to estimate the amount of financing that will have to be raised from interest-bearing debt or the sale of common stock over the planning horizon. This model is based on the underlying relationship between sales, assets, and certain liability accounts. To use the model, each balance-sheet item is calculated as a percentage of the firm's sales. Table 8-11 shows the 1987 balance sheet for the Gateway Manufacturing Company, expressed in dollar amounts and as a percentage of the $1 million in net sales for 1987. Total assets were 80 percent of sales in 1987, which can also be viewed as an asset turnover of 1.25 times ($1,000,000/$800,000).

Next, those balance-sheet items are likely to move or vary with sales during the forecast period are identified. Let us turn to Table 8-11. Accounts receivable and inventories will vary directly with sales if the average collection period and inventory turnover ratio are expected to remain constant. To see whether this is true, the financial manager would want to examine whether Gateway's asset items to sales held about the same percentage relationships in prior years. Cash necessary to carry on day-to-day transactions also might be expected to vary with sales.

The relationship between fixed assets and sales tends to be more irregular or "lumpy," and thus must be examined more closely. In the short run, if the firm has excess production capacity, fixed assets may not move directly with sales. Over a long time, however, a more constant relationship might be expected. For Gateway, if all assets are expected to vary directly with sales, then for each $1 increase in sales, we would expect $.80 increase in assets.

Certain current liabilities also may be expected to vary with sales and thus serve to reduce future financial requirements. For example, purchases

TABLE 8-11 Gateway Manufacturing Company Balance Sheet as of December 31, 1987

	($000)	% of Sales*
Assets		
Cash	$ 50	5
Accounts receivable	150	15
Inventories	200	20
Net fixed assets	400	40
Total assets	$800	80%
Liabilities		
Accounts payable	150	15
Accruals	50	5
Long-term debt	200	20
Common stock	250	25
Retained earnings	150	15
Total liabilities and equity	$800	80%
Financial Requirements Model		
Total assets as a percent of sales		80.0%
Less current liabilities that increase as a percent of sales**		20.0
Percent of sales increase that needs to be financed		60.0%

*Based on 1987 sales of $1 million.
**Only accounts payable (15%) and accruals (5%) would be expected to change directly with sales.

of materials to be used in the production process would be expected to vary with sales. These purchases are an important element in a firm's cost of goods sold. Purchases made on credit become accounts payable, and thus accounts payable would be expected to vary with sales. In a similar fashion, accrued wages would be expected to vary with sales, since higher labor inputs are required to increase production output. Other accruals, such as income tax obligations, also might be expected to increase with sales. Thus, as was the case with current assets, levels of accounts payable and accruals are maintained to support sales. These dollar amounts can be referred to as forms of *spontaneous financing*. In contrast, notes payable, bank loans, long-term debt, or new stock issues must be negotiated and will not automatically increase with sales. As noted earlier, the purpose of the financial requirements model is to estimate the amount of negotiated financing that will be needed over the planning horizon.

    One item that is important in reducing the need for negotiated external financing is the retention of profits in the firm. For example, assume that Gateway's net income for 1987 was $80,000, which, when compared to $1,000,000 in sales, resulted in a net profit margin of 8 percent. If Gateway has a policy of paying out 50 percent of its net income in the form of cash

spontaneous financing

dividends, the firm can be expected to retain 4 percent of each year's sales in the business. This increase in retained earnings serves to reduce external financial requirements.

The external financing requirements model can be expressed in equation form as follows:

$$\text{External Funds Needed(EFN)} = A(\Delta S) - C(\Delta S) - M(R)(S_1) \qquad (8\text{-}2)$$

Where A = assets as a percentage of sales; ΔS = change in sales; C = spontaneous financing as a percentage of sales; M = net income as a percentage of sales; R = profit retention rate, which is the percent of net income that is expected to be retained in the firm; and S_1 = forecasted dollar amount of sales.

We can now apply the percent-of-sales equation to estimate Gateway's 1988 external financing needs. Sales in 1988 are expected to increase by 15 percent to $1,150,000, and the firm does not presently have any excess production capacity. This, plus the 1987 data and relationships, can be used to estimate Gateway's needs as follows:

$$\text{EFN} = .80(\$150,000) - .20(\$150,000) - .08(.50)(\$1,150,000)$$

$$\text{EFN} = \$120,000 - \$30,000 - \$46,000$$

$$\text{EFN} = \$44,000$$

This indicates that Gateway will need to obtain $44,000 in additional external funds during 1988 in order to finance assets that are necessary to support a 15-percent increase in sales. These funds will have to be acquired through bank loans, debt issues, or common stock sales.

The Sustainable Growth Model

Many firms rely almost exclusively on debt to meet financing requirements rather than on new sales of common stock. Since debt financing is not unlimited, they attempt to grow at rates that can be sustained by available debt and increases in profit retentions. The sustainable growth model helps managers determine the amount of sales growth they can finance assuming no new stock is sold and that the amount of total debt (including all liabilities) that can be raised is some fixed proportion of equity. For this reason, the sustainable growth model is a useful supplement to the external financing requirements model. The similarity of the sustainable growth model to the financing requirements model is indicated by Equation 8-3.

$$G = \frac{M(R)(E)}{[A - (M)(R)(E)]} \qquad (8\text{-}3)$$

$$= \frac{.08(.50)(2.5)}{[.80 - (.08)(.50)(2.5)]}$$

$$= .1429 \quad \text{or} \quad 14.29\%$$

Where G = maximum sustainable sales growth rate; A = assets as a percentage of sales = .80; M = net income as a percentage of sales = .08; R = profit retention rate = .50; and E = equity multiplier (equal to total assets divided by shareholders' equity) = 2.5.

The model incorporates the effects of operating characteristics and financial policies on the firm's sustainable growth rate. For example, the asset-to-sales ratio and the profit margin on sales are determined by the firm's ability to use assets efficiently and to produce profits. Better asset management and profitability will both help the firm to grow more quickly. The two financial policies are the firm's dividend policy and its debt policy. The more dividends the firm pays out per dollar of profits, the slower its growth rate will be. The firm's debt policy affects growth through the equity multiplier. Firms that rely heavily on debt to finance assets will have a higher equity multiplier and grow faster than firms that are more conservative.

The sustainable growth estimate of 14.29% indicates that, given the firm's operating characteristics and financial policies, it can increase sales by only 14.29% per year. In order to grow faster than this, something has to change. Assuming that the firm is operating as efficiently and profitably as possible, the faster growth will have to come from a reduction in the dividend payout ratio or an increase in debt, or both.

SUMMARY

This chapter has presented several techniques for estimating a firm's future profits and financing requirements. The documents illustrated comprise the firm's financial plan. This plan will serve as the negotiating basis for arranging additional financing. Thus, the financial plan must be realistic, accurate, and comprehensive. A financial plan comprised of a *pro forma* income statement, *pro forma* balance sheet, cash budget, and *pro forma* statement of cash flows can provide the necessary information for assessing the firm's earnings potential and future financing needs. For longer-range financial planning, simple financial models based on relationships of sales, assets, and liability accounts can provide valuable insights into the magnitude and proper mix of long-term financing. Such models also provide valuable insights into the relationship between a firm's operating characteristics and financial policies and its sustainable sales growth.

MULTIPLE CHOICE QUESTIONS

1. Over time, an increase in sales is accompanied by:
   a) A decrease in assets
   b) An increase in shareholders
   c) A decrease in profitability
   d) An increase in assets

2. Which of the following items should not appear on the cash budget?
   a) Tax payments
   b) Repayments of debt
   c) Sales of fixed assets if less than book value
   d) Depreciation expense

3. Longer accounts receivable terms have which of the following impacts on the cash budget?
   a) Decrease financing requirements
   b) Increase the cash balance

c) Increase inflows relative to outflows

d) Decrease inflows relative to outflows

4. Delaying payment of bills has which of the following impacts on the cash budget?

   a) Increases outflows relative to inflows
   b) Decreases outflows relative to inflows
   c) Does not affect the cash budget
   d) Decreases inflows relative to outflows

5. Which of the following will increase financing requirements on the cash budget?

   a) A sale of fixed assets
   b) A sale of common stock
   c) An increase in profits
   d) An increase in dividends

6. Which of the following will decrease financing requirements on the cash budget?

   a) A purchase of fixed assets
   b) A decrease in the average collection period
   c) A decrease in profits
   d) A repurchase of common stock

DISCUSSION QUESTIONS

1. Briefly summarize why it is important for a business to prepare financial plans.

2. What is a cash budget? What time period should a budget cover?

3. Identify and briefly explain the basic methods that are generally used to estimate future financing needs, given a sales forecast or projection.

4. What methods do firms employ in making long-range sales forecasts?

5. What questions should the financial manager be able to answer once a cash budget has been prepared?

6. Identify and briefly explain the types or kinds of assumptions that represent important aids in the preparation of the cash budget.

7. Briefly summarize the usefulness of cash budgets for planning purposes.

8. What are *pro forma* financial statements? How are they related to the cash budget?

9. Do the estimated net profits after taxes for a fiscal year represent the net addition to the cash balance for the period? Discuss in detail.

10. Of seasonal and cyclical fluctuations in business, which do you believe is the easier to forecast with reasonable accuracy a year in advance? Why?

SOLVED PROBLEMS

cash budget

SP-1. James Smith has decided to start a company to sell and distribute a micro-processor-controlled electronic automotive device, the Engine-Ear. Mr. Smith has developed the following sales and cost estimates.

"The Engine-Ear": Summary of Financial Estimates

Month	Estimated Sales
April, 1988	$600,000
May	800,000
June	700,000
July	540,000
August	360,000
September	680,000
October	800,000
November	1,100,000
December	640,000
January, 1989	800,000

Sales credit terms: Net 45 days. All sales will be on credit, and no bad debts are expected. Assume that all months have 30 days and that credit sales are collected evenly throughout the month.

Purchases: Purchases average 70 percent of sales and are made in the month prior to sale. Purchase terms are net 30 days.

Selling, general and administrative expenses: Expected to be semi-variable. The fixed portion will be $30,000 per month, and the variable portion—sales commissions—will be 1 percent of sales. One-fourth of the monthly expense is accrued ("wages payable") at the end of each month.

Other expenses: Other expenses will average 3 percent of sales. One-half of each month's expenses will be accrued ("other current liabilities").

Depreciation: Depreciation expenses will be $40,000 per month.

Taxes: Tax payments of $100,000, $150,000, and $150,000 will be made in June, September, and December, respectively.

Desired cash balance: The minimum cash balance desired is $100,000.

Prepare a cash budget for the nine months April through December, 1988.

integrated pro forma statements

SP-2. The Locoste Corporation is a retailer. The company adds a markup on goods it purchases for resale. The company president is preparing for a meeting with a banker to review financing requirements during the next three months. After discussion among the various managers, the forecasted sales over the next three months

were developed. The forecasts and a recent balance sheet are
shown below:

Month	Sales Forecast
April, 1989	$600,000
May	800,000
June	700,000

Balance Sheet as of March 30, 1988 ($000)

Cash	$ 20	Taxes payable	$ 70
Accounts receivable	400	Notes payable	450
Inventories	480	Long-term debt	150
Net fixed assets	100	Total liabilities	670
		Equity	330
Total assets	$1,000	Total	$1,000

All sales are made on credit terms of net 30 days. Assume
30-day months, no bad debts, and that collections are spread evenly
throughout the month. Thus, the accounts receivable on the balance
sheet at the end of March will be collected in April. The April sales
will be collected in May, and so on. Inventory on hand represents
safety stock that the company intends to maintain. Cost of goods
sold averages 80 percent of sales. Goods are purchased in the
month of sale and paid for in cash. Other cash expenses average
8 percent of sales. Depreciation is $8,000 per month. Taxes are
40 percent. Tax liabilities are accrued until paid. Tax payments are
made in April and June. Assume that April tax payment will be for
taxes accrued at the end of March and that June's tax payment will
be for any tax liabilities generated in April, May, and June.

No payments on outstanding debt or notes payable are
planned. There are no capital expenditures planned during the
period, and no dividends will be paid. The company's desired cash
balance for the period is $30,000. The president hopes to meet any
cash shortages during the period by increasing the firm's notes
payable to the bank.

a) Prepare monthly *pro forma* income statements for April, May,
   and June and a quarterly total ending June 30.
b) Prepare monthly *pro forma* balance sheets as of the end of April,
   May, and June.
c) Prepare monthly cash budgets for April, May, and June.

SP-3. A balance sheet and other financial information for the All Purpose
Mirror (APM) company's most recent fiscal year are shown below.
Sales next year are expected to total $1,200,000.

   a) Use the financial requirements model to determine how much
      external funding will be required next year to support sales

financial planning models

growth. (Assume that accounts payable and accruals are spontaneous liabilities).
b) Use the sustainable growth model to estimate the growth rate in
sales that can be supported given the firm's operating characteristics and financial policies as of 1987.

All Purpose Mirror Company

Balance Sheet at 12/31/1987

Assets		Liabilities and Equity	
Cash	20,000	Accounts payable	150,000
Accounts receivable	140,000	Accruals	50,000
Inventory	280,000	Notes payable	50,000
Total current assets	440,000	Total current liabilities	250,000
Net fixed assets	360,000	Long-term debt	150,000
		Equity	400,000
Total	$800,000	Total	$800,000

Other Financial Data

1987 sales:	$1,000,000
1987 net income:	100,000
1987 dividends:	40,000

statement of cash flows

SP-4. Balance sheets for the Hanson Cast Company are shown below.
Sales in year two were $1,500,000, producing $109,000 of net income. Dividends of $30,000 were paid.

a) Calculate the change in each balance-sheet item.
b) Indicate whether the change in each balance-sheet item represents a source or use of cash.
c) Prepare a statement of cash flows covering the years one to two.
d) What information do these changes provide about the activities
of the corporation during year two?

Hanson Cast Company

Assets	Year 1	Year 2
Cash and marketable securities	16,000	8,000
Accounts receivable	112,000	170,000
Inventory	168,000	250,000
Current assets	296,000	428,000
Gross fixed assets	650,000	685,000
Less accumulated depreciation	146,000	160,000
Net fixed assets	504,000	525,000
Total assets	800,000	953,000

Accounts payable	112,000	130,000
Notes payable	80,000	132,000
Other current liabilities	32,000	16,000
Total current liabilities	224,000	278,000
Long-term-debt	40,000	60,000
Common stock	300,000	300,000
Retained earnings	236,000	315,000
Total	800,000	953,000

PROBLEMS

1. The "Soul Searcher" is a small, durable device that attaches to the back   *cash budget*
of a shoe and starts beeping at the sound of hands clapping. A company has been organized to market the product, but the owners are unsure of financing required. As a novelty item, the Soul Searcher is not expected to generate sales for more than nine months. To determine financing needs for the nine months, April through December, the owners have decided to develop a cash budget based on the following sales and cost estimates. The product will be manufactured by others. The Soul Searcher company will be responsible only for selling and distributing the finished product.

"The Soul Searcher": Summary of Financial Estimates	
Month	*Estimated Sales*
April, 1988	$ 800,000
May	900,000
June	1,000,000
July	940,000
August	800,000
September	700,000
October	600,000
November	600,000
December	600,000
January, 1989	800,000

Sales credit terms: Net 45 days. All sales will be on credit and no bad debts are expected. Assume that all months have 30 days and that credit sales are collected evenly throughout the month.

Purchases: Purchases average 70 percent of sales and are made in the month prior to sale. Purchase terms are net 30 days.

Selling, General and Administrative expenses: Expected to be semi-variable. The fixed portion will be $30,000 per month, and the variable portion — sales commissions — will be 1 percent of sales. One-fourth of the monthly expense is accrued ("wages payable") at the end of each month.

Other expenses: Other expenses will average 3 percent of sales. One-half of each month's expenses will be accrued ("other current liabilities").

Depreciation: Depreciation expenses will be $40,000 per month.

Taxes: Tax payments of $100,000, $150,000, and $150,000 will be made in June, September, and December, respectively.

Desired cash balance: The minimum cash balance desired is $100,000.

Prepare a cash budget for the nine months April through December, 1988.

integrated pro forma statements

2. The Biggs Corporation is a retailer. The company adds a markup on goods it purchases for resale. The company president is preparing for a meeting with a banker to review financing requirements during the next three months. After discussion among the various managers, the forecasted sales over the next three months were developed. The forecasts and a recent balance sheet are shown below:

Month	Sales Forecast
April, 1988	$1,200,000
May	1,400,000
June	2,000,000

Biggs Corporation			
Balance Sheet as of March 30, 1988 ($000)			
Cash	$ 40	Taxes payable	$ 140
Accounts receivable	800	Notes payable	800
Inventories	480	Long-term debt	300
Net fixed assets	680	Total liabilities	1,240
		Equity	760
Total assets	$2,000	Total	$2,000

All sales are made on credit terms of net 30 days. Assume 30-day months, no bad debts, and that collections are spread evenly throughout the month. Thus, the accounts receivable on the balance sheet at the end of March will be collected in April. The April sales will be collected in May, and so on. Goods on hand represent safety stock, which the company intends to maintain. Costs of goods sold average 80 percent of sales. Goods are purchased in the month of sale and paid for in cash. Other cash expenses average 8 percent of sales. Depreciation is $16,000 per month. Taxes are 34 percent. Tax liabilities are accrued until paid. Tax payments are made in April and June. Assume that the April tax payment will be for taxes accrued at the end of March and that June's tax payment will be for any tax liabilities generated in April, May, and June.

No payments on outstanding debt or notes payable are planned. There are no capital expenditures planned during the period, and no dividends will be paid. The company's desired cash balance for the period is $50,000. The president hopes to meet any cash shortages during the period by increasing the firm's notes payable to the bank.

  a) Prepare monthly *pro forma* income statements for April, May, and June and a quarterly total ending June 30.
  b) Prepare monthly *pro forma* balance sheets as of the end of April, May, and June.
  c) Prepare monthly cash budgets for April, May, and June.

3. A balance sheet and other financial information for the Fabu-Plastics company's most recent fiscal year are shown below. Sales next year are expected to total $1,600,000.

  a) Use the financial requirements model to determine how much external funding will be required next year to support sales growth. (Assume that accounts payable and accruals are spontaneous liabilities).
  b) Use the sustainable growth model to estimate the growth rate in sales that can be supported given the firm's operating characteristics and financial policies as of 1987.

financial planning models

Fabu-Plastics

Balance Sheet as of 12/31/1987

Assets		Liabilities and Equity	
Cash	20,000	Accounts payable	150,000
Accounts receivable	140,000	Accruals	150,000
Inventory	280,000	Notes payable	50,000
Total current assets	440,000	Total current assets	350,000
Net fixed assets	460,000	Long-term debt	350,000
		Equity	200,000
Total	$900,000	Total	$900,000

Other Financial Data

1987 sales:	$1,200,000
1987 net income:	80,000
1987 dividends:	40,000

---

4. Balance sheets for the Cork Company are shown below. Sales in year two were $2,750,000, producing $250,000 of net income. Dividends of $100,000 were paid.

statement of cash flows

a) Calculate the change in each balance-sheet item.
b) Indicate whether the change in each balance sheet item represents a source or use of cash.
c) Prepare a statement of cash flows covering the years one to two.
d) What information do these changes provide about the activities of the corporation during year two?

Cork Company		
Assets	*Year 1*	*Year 2*
Cash and marketable securities	4,000	8,000
Accounts receivable	180,000	170,000
Inventory	300,000	250,000
Current assets	484,000	428,000
Gross fixed assets	300,000	685,000
Less accumulated depreciation	100,000	160,000
Net fixed assets	200,000	525,000
Total assets	684,000	953,000
Liabilities and Shareholders' Equity		
Accounts payable	100,000	130,000
Notes payable	50,000	132,000
Other current liabilities	8,000	16,000
Total current liabilities	158,000	278,000
Long-term-debt	61,000	60,000
Common stock	300,000	300,000
Retained earnings	165,000	315,000
Total	684,000	953,000

financial planning models

5. The Karet Corporation anticipates a 15 percent increase in sales for 1988 over its 1987 level of $15 million. Karet is currently operating at full capacity and thus anticipates having to increase its investment in assets. Following is Karet's 1987 balance sheet.

Karet Corporation Balance Sheet as of December 31, 1987 ($000)			
Cash & marketable securities	$ 785	Accounts payable	$ 1,650
Accounts receivable	2,250	Bank loan	523
Inventory	2,550	Accrued liabilities	1,200
Total current assets	5,585	Total current liabilities	3,373
Fixed assets, net	4,800	Long-term debt	450
Total assets	$10,385	Common stock	4,752
		Retained earnings	1,810
		Total liabilities and equity	$10,385

a) Karet Corporation expects to maintain its 1987 total assets turnover ratio in 1988. Estimate the firm's 1988 total assets. How much financing of additional assets will be required during 1988?

b) Express Karet's 1987 balance sheet as a percentage of 1987 sales. Indicate which items on the balance sheet are likely to move with sales. How much of the asset financing requirement indicated in Part (a) is likely to be met by spontaneous liability increases?

c) The Karet Corporation had a net profit margin of 6 percent of sales in 1987 and anticipates a comparable rate of profitability in 1988. A 35 percent dividend payout policy also is administered by the firm. Given this additional information, estimate the internally generated funds that will be available to help meet Karet's asset financing needs.

d) Indicate the amount of external financing for 1988 the Karet Corporation will need. Applying the external funds needed (EFN) equation.

6. Assume that you have been hired by the Karet Corporation discussed in Problem 5. You are independently to estimate the firm's external financing needs. If 1988 is a year of economic downturn, you anticipate Karet's sales will decrease by 10 percent from the $15-million 1987 level. A moderate increase in economic activity is likely to be associated with a 5 percent increase in Karet's sales. Rapid economic expansion is expected to result in a 15 percent sales increase over the firm's 1987 level. The likelihood of each economic condition occurring is: downturn (30 percent), moderate growth (30 percent), and rapid growth (40 percent). *financial planning models*

a) Estimate Karet's expected sales level for 1988. What dollar amount of assets would have to be financed if Karet's total assets turnover ratio remained constant? Use the balance-sheet data provided in problem 5.

b) Construct a *pro forma* balance sheet for December 31, 1988 for the Karet Corporation. Assume that accounts payable and accruals will move spontaneously with sales and that additional financing needs (if any) can be met with an increase in the bank loan. In estimating the amount of internally generated funds, assume a net profit margin of 6 percent and a dividend payout ratio of 35 percent.

c) Use the external funds needed (EFN) equation to estimate Karet's financing requirements under each of the three economic conditions forecast for 1988. What assumptions were necessary?

d) How would your estimate of external financing needs have been altered in Part (b) if Karet had excess production capacity and did not anticipate increasing its fixed assets?

7. Following are the 1986 and 1987 income statements and selected balance sheet items for the Trace Manufacturing Company. Management expects net sales to increase by 10 percent in 1988. The 1987 total assets to net sales relationship is expected to hold for 1988. *pro forma income statment*

a) Prepare a *pro forma* income statement for 1988 for the Trace Manufacturing Company. If the increase in total assets is expected to be financed totally from profits, will the company be able to meet its financing requirements?

b) Now assume that instead of financing all increases in total assets with equity funds, one-half of the increase will be financed with debt funds carrying a 12 percent interest rate. Prepare a revised *pro forma* income statement for Trace Manufacturing that incorporates this new information.

TRACE MANUFACTURING COMPANY

Income Statements for Years Ending December 31 ($000)

	1987	*1986*
Net Sales	$1,200	1,000
Less cost of goods sold	(840)	(700)
Gross profit	360	300
Less operating expenses*	(176)	(176)
Earnings before interest and taxes	184	124
Less: interest expense*	(24)	(24)
Earnings before taxes	160	100
Less: income taxes (34% rate)	(54)	(34)
Net income	$106	$66

*Fixed expenses.

Selected Balance Sheet Items as of December 31 ($000)

	1987	*1986*
Total assets	$920	$860
Total Liabilities or debt	552	552
Total stockholders' equity	368	308

---

cash budget

8. The Furloin Company wishes to prepare a two-month cash budget covering January and February. Net sales in January are forecast to be $35,000, and net sales for February are estimated at $30,000. Purchases are expected to be $20,000 in each of the two months. Both sales and purchases were made 50 percent on credit (net 30-day terms) in the past, and this percentage is expected to continue in the future. Accounts receivable outstanding at the end of December were $15,000, and accounts payable were $8,000 at the end of December. Depreciation was $5,000 per month, and income taxes of $20,000 were to be paid during January. Cash on hand at the end of December was $8,000, with

a desire on the part of Furloin to carry a minimum cash balance of $7,000 during each month.

a) Prepare a two-month cash budget for the Furloin Company.
b) What are the maximum cash needs, if any, that Furloin must finance?
c) How would Furloin's financing needs change if sales continue to be made as described above, but with purchases in January and February being made on a cash basis?

9. Prepare a cash budget for the Jones Corporation by using the following projected information.   *cash budget*

	Cash Sales	Credit Sales (Net 60-Day Terms)	Cash Expenses	Credit Purchases (Net 30-Day Terms)
July	$40,000	$ 70,000	$30,000	$ 70,000
August	50,000	80,000	40,000	100,000
September	60,000	100,000	40,000	120,000
October	60,000	150,000	50,000	100,000
November	40,000	100,000	20,000	90,000
December	20,000	60,000	20,000	50,000

At the end of June the firm has cash on hand of $5,000 and desires to maintain an $8,000 level during each subsequent month. Accounts receivable at the end of June are $100,000, with one-half expected to be collected in each of the next two months. Accounts payable at the end of June are $50,000 and are to be paid in July.

a) What are the maximum cash needs for the Jones Corporation?
b) What type of financing, if any, seems to be indicated by your cash flow forecast?

10. Assume you have been asked to prepare a cash budget for the Blunt Company for the period August 1 to January 31. In estimating the firm's cash requirements, make the following assumptions: *cash budget*

● Sales are 40 percent for cash, 60 percent on credit.

● Of the credit sales, 75 percent are collected in the first month following the sale and 25 percent in the second month following the sale.

● Cost of goods sold average 80 percent of sales.

● All inventory purchases are paid during the month in which they are made.

● A basic inventory of $10,000 is constantly maintained. Purchases each month equal the following month's cost of goods sold.

● A minimum cash balance of $2,000 is to be maintained by the firm.

● "Accrued wages and salaries" and "other current liabilities" remain unchanged.

● Total estimated tax liability ($4,000) for August to January to be paid in December.

Balance Sheet as of July 31

Cash		$ 6,100	Accrued wages	
Accounts receivable		14,700	and salaries	$ 1,600
Inventory (cost)		26,000	Other liabilities	12,000
Furniture			Equity capital	59,200
& fixtures	$35,000			
Allowance for depreciation	9,000	26,000		
		$72,800		$72,800

Sales Actual and Forecast

June (actual)	$18,000		
July (actual)	20,000	November	40,000
August	20,000	December	50,000
September	22,000	January	18,000
October	24,000	February	18,000

Monthly Expenses

Wages and salaries:			
August	$1,400	November	2,000
September	1,500	December	2,000
October	1,600	January	1,400

Rent: $400 per month
Depreciation: $150 per month
Other expenses: 1% of sales

a) Prepare a work sheet and cash budget.
b) Indicate clearly the maximum amount of necessary borrowings. When will it be possible to repay the loan?
c) Prepare a cumulative *pro forma* income statement and balance sheet as of January 31.
d) Various simplifying assumptions have been made. Identify some of these and explain how, if they were removed, planning by the management of this company would become more complicated?

statement of cash flows   11. Following are two consecutive balance sheets for the Muse Corporation. Net income after taxes was $80 million in 1987, with $13 million being paid in cash dividends.

Muse Corporation

Balance Sheet as of December 31 ($000,000)

	1987	1986	Balance Sheet Changes Sources	Uses
Cash	$ 6	$ 30	_____	_____
Marketable securities	0	18	_____	_____
Accounts receivable	80	51	_____	_____
Inventories	210	144	_____	_____
Total current assets	296	243	_____	_____
Gross fixed assets	310	210	_____	_____
Less accumulated depreciation	(133)	(93)	_____	_____
Net fixed assets	177	117	_____	_____
Total assets	$473	$360	_____	_____
Accounts payable	$ 50	$ 30	_____	_____
Bank loan	12	30	_____	_____
Accrued liabilities	23	6	_____	_____
Long-term debt	15	9	_____	_____
Common stock	120	99	_____	_____
Retained earnings	253	186	_____	_____
Total liabilities and stockholders' equity	$473	$360	_____	_____
Total sources			=======	
Total uses				=======

a) Calculate the dollar amount of each balance-sheet change between 1986 and 1987 and indicate whether it was a source or use of cash by placing the amount in the appropriate column next to the Muse Corporation's balance sheets.
b) Prepare a statement of cash flows for the period 1986 to 1987 for the Muse Corporation.
c) Provide a brief analysis of the statement of cash flows.

12. Watts Electronics, Inc. is anticipating continued growth next year. Sales in 1988 are forecast to be $2,800,000. Following are income statements and balance sheets for the past two years of operation.

financial planning models

Watts Electronics, Inc.

Balance Sheets as of December 31

	1987	1986
Cash	$20,000	$24,000
Accounts receivable	300,000	231,000
Inventories	$500,000	425,000
Total current assets	820,000	680,000
Fixed assets, net	380,000	220,000
Total assets	$1,200,000	$900,000
Bank loan	80,000	80,000
Accounts payable	260,000	134,000
Accruals	65,000	48,000
Total current liabilities	405,000	262,000
Long-term debt	200,000	200,000
Common stock	350,000	300,000
Paid-in-surplus	145,000	58,000
Retained earnings	100,000	80,000
Total liabilities and equity	$1,200,000	$900,000

Income Statements, Year Ended December 31

	1987	1986
Net sales	$2,500,000	$2,300,000
Cost of goods sold	2,000,000	1,840,000
Gross Profit	500,000	460,000
General, administrative, & selling	200,000	200,000
Depreciation	40,000	20,000
Interest	30,000	30,000
Earnings before taxes	230,000	210,000
Taxes paid (34%)	78,200	71,400
Earnings after taxes	$151,800	$138,600

a) Use the external funds needed (EFN) equation to estimate Watts' external financing requirements for 1988. The 1987 total assets turnover ratio is expected to hold for 1988. Current liabilities, with the exception of the bank loan, are expected to change spontaneously with sales. Watts anticipates that the 1987 net profit margin will hold for 1988 and expects to retain one-half of its 1988 earnings after taxes.

b) Use the percent-of-sales method, and the information contained in Part (a), to prepare a 1988 *pro forma* balance sheet for Watts Electronics. Any external financing requirements are to be met by an increase in long-term debt.

c) Prepare a 1988 *pro forma* income statement for Watts Electronics. Depreciation expense is expected to increase by $20,000 over the 1987 level, and interest expense is expected to rise by an additional $12,000 in 1988.

13. Watts Electronics, Inc. is concerned about its ability to meet its financing needs for 1988. As noted in Problem 12, Watts expects 1988 sales to be $2,800,000.

   a) Based on the financial statements and other information provided in problem 12, how would the external financing requirements be affected if Watts could reduce its average collection period to the 1986 level?

   b) How would the external financing requirements for 1988 be affected if Watts is able to achieve an inventory turnover (cost basis) equal to its 1986 level instead of its 1987 level?

   c) Indicate the impact of an average payment period (based on the use of cost of goods sold) for 1987 equal to the 1986 calculation on Watts's external financing needs for 1988.

SOLUTIONS TO SOLVED PROBLEMS

SP-1. *Step 1:* Use a worksheet to convert sales into cash collections. The ending accounts receivable represent 45 days of sales. At the end of April, the first month of sales, receivables will be equal to April's sales. At the end of May, receivables are equal to May's sales (30 days) plus the last 15 days of April's sales. Of course, the ending accounts receivable in April is the beginning accounts receivable in May, and so on.

Cash Budget Worksheet: Cash Collections

Month	Sales	+	Beginning accounts receivable	−	Ending accounts receivable	=	Cash collections
April	$ 600,000		$ -0-		$ 600,000		$ -0-
May	960,000		600,000		1,260,000		300,000
June	700,000		1,260,000		1,180,000		780,000
July	540,000		1,180,000		890,000		830,000
August	360,000		890,000		630,000		620,000
September	680,000		630,000		860,000		450,000
October	800,000		860,000		1,140,000		520,000
November	1,100,000		1,140,000		1,500,000		740,000
December	640,000		1,500,000		1,190,000		950,000

Step 2: Use a worksheet to convert credit purchases into cash disbursements. Purchases are made in the month prior to sale. Thus, April's sales requirements are purchased in March. Purchases are 70 percent of sales. Accounts payable equal the last 30 days of purchases. To calculate cash disbursements for purchases, use the following format:

Month's purchases + Beginning accounts payable
— Ending accounts payable = Cash for purchases in month

In March, purchases are $420,000 (70 percent of April's sales of $600,000). The purchases are the ending accounts payable at the end of March (and, of course, the beginning accounts payable in April).

Cash Budget Worksheet: Cash Payments for Purchases

Month	Purchases	+	Beginning accounts payable	—	Ending accounts payable	=	Cash payments
March	$420,000		$ -0-		$420,000		$ -0-
April	672,000		420,000		672,000		420,000
May	490,000		672,000		490,000		672,000
June	378,000		490,000		378,000		490,000
July	252,000		378,000		252,000		378,000
August	476,000		252,000		476,000		252,000
September	560,000		476,000		560,000		476,000
October	770,000		560,000		770,000		560,000
November	448,000		770,000		448,000		770,000
December	560,000		448,000		560,000		448,000

Step 3: Use a worksheet to convert selling and general & administrative expenses to cash disbursements, using the format below:

Selling, general and administrative expenses
+ Beginning wages payable
— Ending wages payable
= Cash for selling, general and administrative expenses

Selling, general and administrative expenses are semivariable, equal to $30,000 plus 1 percent of sales for the month. One-fourth of the month's expenses are accrued as "wages payable."

Cash Budget Worksheet: Cash for Selling, General & Administrative Expenses (SG & A)

Month	SG & A Expense	+	Beginning wages payable	−	Ending wages payable	=	Cash payments
April	$36,000		$ -0-		$ 9,000		$27,000
May	39,600		9,000		9,900		38,700
June	37,000		9,900		9,250		37,650
July	35,400		9,250		8,850		35,800
August	33,600		8,850		8,400		34,050
September	36,800		8,400		9,200		36,000
October	38,000		9,200		9,500		37,700
November	41,000		9,500		10,250		40,250
December	36,400		10,250		9,100		37,550

Step 4: Use a worksheet to convert "other expenses" to cash disbursements. Other expenses are 3 percent of the month's sales. One-half of the month's expenses are accrued as "other current liabilities." Use the following format:

Other expenses + beginning other current liabilities
  − Ending other current liabilities = Cash for other current liabilities

Cash Budget Worksheet: Cash for Other Expenses

Month	Other Expenses	+	Beginning accrued other expenses	−	Ending accrued other expenses	=	Cash payments
April	$18,000		$ -0-		$ 9,000		$9,000
May	28,800		9,000		14,400		23,400
June	21,000		14,400		10,500		24,900
July	16,200		10,500		8,100		18,600
August	10,800		8,100		5,400		13,500
September	20,400		5,400		10,200		15,600
October	24,000		10,200		12,000		22,200
November	33,000		12,000		16,500		28,500
December	19,200		16,500		9,600		26,100

Step 5: When all collections and payments have been determined from the worksheets, prepare the cash budget. Do not forget to include any cash collections or payments made on a cash basis and which are not included on the worksheets.

Cash Budget

	April	May	June
I. Receipts			
Collections	$ -0-	$300,000	$780,000
II. Disbursements			
Purchases	420,000	672,000	490,000
SG & A	27,000	38,700	37,650
Other expenses	9,000	23,400	24,900
Tax payments			100,000
III. Financing			
Net cash flow	(456,000)	(434,100)	127,450
+ Beginning cash	-0-	(456,000)	(890,100)
= Ending cumulative cash balance	(456,000)	(890,100)	(762,650)
− Minimum desired cash balance	100,000	100,000	100,000
= Financing required (excess)	556,000	990,100	862,650

Cash Budget

	July	August	September
I. Receipts			
Collections	$830,000	$620,000	$450,000
II. Disbursements			
Purchases	378,000	252,000	476,000
SG & A	35,800	34,050	36,000
Other expenses	18,600	13,500	15,600
Tax payments			150,000
III. Financing			
Net cash flow	397,600	320,450	(227,600)
+ Beginning cash	(762,650)	(365,050)	(44,600)
= Ending cumulative cash balance	(365,050)	(44,600)	(272,200)
− Minimum desired cash balance	100,000	100,000	100,000
= Financing required (excess)	465,050	144,600	372,200

Cash Budget

	October	November	December
I. Receipts			
Collections	$520,000	$740,000	$950,000
II. Disbursements			
Purchases	560,000	770,000	448,000
SG & A	37,700	40,250	37,550
Other expenses	22,200	28,500	26,100
Tax payments			150,000
III. Financing			
Net cash flow	(99,900)	(98,750)	288,350
+ Beginning cash	(272,200)	(372,100)	(470,850)
= Ending cumulative cash balance	(372,100)	(470,850)	(182,500)
− Minimum desired cash balance	100,000	100,000	100,000
= Financing required (excess)	472,100	570,850	282,500

SP-2. a) *Pro forma* income statements.

Pro Forma Income Statements

	April	May	June	Quarter
1. Sales	$600,000	$800,000	$700,000	$2,100,000
2. Cost of goods sold	480,000	640,000	560,000	1,680,000
Gross profit	120,000	160,000	140,000	420,000
3. Other expenses	48,000	64,000	56,000	168,000
4. Depreciation	8,000	8,000	8,000	24,000
Profit before taxes	64,000	88,000	76,000	228,000
5. Taxes	25,600	35,200	30,400	91,200
Net income	$ 38,400	$ 52,800	$ 45,600	$ 136,800

1. Given; 2. 80 percent of sales; 3. 8 percent of sales; 4. given; 5. 40 percent rate.

b) *Pro forma* balance sheets.

Pro Forma Balance Sheets

Assets	April	May	June
1. Cash	$ 30,000	$ 30,000	$ 30,000
2. Accounts receivable	600,000	800,000	700,000
3. Inventory	480,000	480,000	480,000
Current assets	$1,110,000	$1,310,000	$1,210,000
4. Net fixed assets	92,000	84,000	76,000
Total	$1,202,000	$1,394,000	$1,286,000
Liabilities and Shareholders' Equity			
5. Accrued taxes	$ 25,600	$ 60,800	$ 0
6. Notes payable	658,000	762,000	669,200
Current liabilities	683,600	822,800	669,200
7. Long-term debt	150,000	150,000	150,000
Total liabilities	833,600	972,800	819,200
8. Shareholders' equity	368,400	421,200	466,800
Total	$1,202,000	$1,394,000	$1,286,000

1. Minimum desired balance; 2. Terms are 30-days, thus balance is last 30 days of sales. Assumes 30-day months. Accounts receivable end of April is equal to April's sales; 3. Safety stock inventory. equal to safety stock end of March; 4. $100,000 end of March, decreases by depreciation of $8,000 per month; 5. Accrued until paid. April balance represents April's tax liability; May's balance is accrued liability for April and May. June's balance reflects payment of all accrued taxes (plus June's) at end of June; 6. Designated plug figure. Equal to total assets less total liabilities (except notes payable) and equity. As a check for accuracy, this figure should equal notes payable at the end of March plus the cumulative financing required indicated on the cash budget for that month. Thus April's balance is equal to $450,000 plus the $208,000 financing required on the cash budget for April (shown below); 7. Long-term debt will not change, since no long-term borrowing or repayment is scheduled; 8. Equal to equity at the beginning of the month plus net income minus dividends. No dividends are planned. Thus April's equity ($368,400) is equal to March's equity ($330,000) plus net income of $38,400.

c) Cash budgets.
Step 1: Start by calculating the cash inflows from sales with a worksheet.

	April	May	June
1. Sales	$600,000	$800,000	$700,00
2. Add Beginning accounts receivable	400,000	600,000	800,000
3. Subtract Ending accounts receivable	600,000	800,000	700,000
= Collections from sales	400,000	600,000	800,000

1. Given; 2. equal to accounts receivable end of previous month. April's beginning accounts receivable are equal to the accounts receivable at the end of March as indicated on the March 30 balance sheet. May's beginning accounts receivable are equal to ending accounts receivable for April; 3. equal to the last 30 days of sales. Assuming 30-day months, the ending balance for each month is equal to that months' sales. April's ending accounts receivable (i.e., on April 30th) is equal to April's sales.

	April	May	June
4. Purchases	$480,000	$640,000	$560,00
5. Other cash expenses	48,000	64,000	56,000
6. Tax payments	70,000	-0-	91,200
Total outflows	$598,000	$704,000	$707,200

4. Purchases are equal to 80 percent of sales and are made in the month of sale. Thus, April's purchases are equal to 80 percent of April's sales; 5. Equal to 8 percent of sales for the month; 6. April's payment is for taxes accrued as of the end of March ($70,000). June's payment is equal to total tax liabilities generated in April, May, and June ($91,200). Note that this is also equal to the quarterly total for taxes on the *pro forma* income statement.

Step 3: Determine financing requirements.

	April	May	June
7. Net cash flow	(198,000)	(104,000)	92,800
8. Beginning cash	20,000	(178,000)	(282,000)
Cumulative cash balance	(178,000)	(282,000)	(189,200)
9. Desired cash balance	30,000	30,000	30,000
10. Financing required (surplus)	$208,000	$312,000	$219,200

7. Equal to total collections minus total outflows; 8. Equal to cash balance at end of prior month. April's beginning cash balance is equal to the cash balance at the end of March; 9. Given; 10. Notice the sign change. This row is labeled "financing required" and is shown as a positive number. A negative number indicates that the company has generated excess cash which can be used to repay debt or invest elsewhere. The financing required is cumulative and represents the additional financing needed over and above the financing in place at the end of March. The sum of financing required and the notes payable at the end of March should equal the notes payable on the *pro forma* balance sheet since the company plans to meet its financing requirements by borrowing from the bank.

SP-3. a) The financial requirements model is based on the following equation:

$$EFN = A(\Delta S) - C(\Delta S) - M(R)(S_1)$$

To use the EFN equation, each of the variables must be estimated from available information: $A = \$800,000/\$1,000,000 = .80$; $C = (150,000 + 50,000)/1,000,000 = .20$; $M = 100,000/1,000,000 = .10$; $R = 1.00 -$ payout ratio $= 1.00 - .40 = .60$; $S_1 = \$1,200,000$

$$EFN = .80(\$200,000) - .20(\$200,000) \quad .10(.60)(\$1,200,000) = \$48,000$$

b) The sustainable growth model is based on the following equation:

$$G = M(R)(E)/[A - (M)(R)(E)]$$

Using the variables defined in part (a) plus the equity multiplier (E) of 2.5 times (i.e., $\$800,000/\$400,000$) gives:

$$G = \frac{.10(.60)(2.0)}{[.80 - (.10)(.60)(2.0)]} = .1765 \quad \text{or} \quad 23.08\%$$

SP-4. a), b), c)

	Use	Source
Cash		8,000
Accounts receivable	58,000	
Inventory	82,000	
Gross fixed assets	35,000	
Accumulated depreciation		14,000
Accounts payable		18,000
Notes payable		52,000
Other current liabilities	16,000	
Long-term debt		20,000
Retained earnings		79,000
Total	$191,000	$191,000

Hanson Cast Company Statement of Cash Flows

Cash from operating activities	
Net income	109,000
Depreciation	14,000
Increase in accounts payable	18,000
Increase in notes payable	52,000
Increase in accounts receivable	(58,000)
Increase in inventory	(82,000)
Decrease in other current liabilities	(16,000)
Net cash from operating activities	$37,000
Net cash from investing activities	(35,000)
Cash from financing activities	
Dividends	(30,000)
Increase in long-term debt	20,000
Net cash from financing activities	(10,000)
Net increase (decrease) in cash	(8,000)

d) The principal uses of cash were expansion of two working-capital items: inventory and accounts receivable. These two items accounted for uses of $140,000. Net income provided the bulk of cash sources ($109,000), with bank borrowings (i.e., notes payable) a significant ($52,000) further source.

REFERENCES

Francis, Jack Clark, and Dexter R. Rowell. "A Simultaneous Equation Model of the Firm for Financial Analysis and Planning." *Financial Management,* Spring 1978, pp. 29–44.

Higgins, Robert. "How Much Growth Can A Firm Afford?" *Financial Management,* Fall 1977.

Maier, Steven F., and James H. Vander Weide. "A Practical Approach to Short-Run Financial Planning." *Financial Management,* Winter 1978, pp. 10–16.

Pan, Judy, Donald R. Nichols, and O. Maurice Joy. "Sales Forecasting Practices of Large U.S. Industrial Firms." *Financial Management,* Fall 1977, pp. 72–77.

CASE EXERCISE

MijiMite

Things were getting down to the wire at FABU-PLASTICS as the top-management group struggled to forecast the impact on the company's operations from its new product, MijiMite. The MijiMite was a three-foot tall robot with a vocabulary of 55 phrases and 600 words that it could fit into the phrases in speaking. Although the robot had received a very favorable reaction from consumers, the management group at FABU-PLASTICS was experienced enough to realize that its popularity could vanish as soon as the novelty wore off.

FABU-PLASTICS's president, Bill Jones, was primarily concerned about the impact on the company's financial situation, since the company was already close to its borrowing limits at the bank. When Mr. Jones asked the manager of finance, Mr. Ames, to develop a forecast of financial requirements, Mr. Ames suggested a meeting of the management group to identify the key operating assumptions that would dictate financial requirements. Since Mr. Jones had made plans to have dinner with the company's banker that evening, he immediately agreed to the meeting. By 3:30 the information in Exhibits C-1 and C-2 had been collected by Mr. Ames. After the meeting broke up, the president took Mr. Ames aside. "Give me your best shot at the figures by 6:30, okay? Just give me the figures for the next six months. Is there anything else you think you need?"

"I've got a better feel now for the operating requirements," responded Mr. Ames. "Of course, I've already got the capital expenditure schedules in my office. But, let me check a couple of things with you. I suppose the $100,000 dividend in March is firm. . . ."

The president nodded his head vigorously. "Absolutely."

"And," continued Mr. Ames, "I would like to increase our cash buffer to $100,000."

"Fine," responded the president.

EXHIBIT C-1
FABU-PLASTICS, Inc.
Balance Sheet as of 12/31/87

Cash	$ 80,000	Accounts payable	$672,000
Accounts receivable	900,000	Note payable	200,000
Inventory	772,000	Accrued marketing expenses	9,000
Total current assets	$1,752,000	Accrued general & administrative expenses	18,000
		Total current liabilities	$ 899,000
Gross fixed assets	2,048,000	Long term debt	500,000
Less accelerated depreciation	(800,000)		
Net fixed assets	1,248,000	Common stock	1,200,000
		Retained earnings	401,000
Total Assets	3,000,000	Total liabilities and equity	$3,000,000

322

Mr. Ames went back to his office and started on the forecasts. He was determined to prepare Mr. Jones as well as possible for the dinner meeting with the banker.

- Sales

EXHIBIT C-2
FABU-PLASTICS, Inc.
Forecasting Assumptions

November 1987 (Actual)	$600,000
December 1987 (Actual)	600,000
January 1988 (Estimate)	960,000
February	700,000
March	540,000
April	360,000
May	680,000
June	800,000
July	1,000,000

- Accounts receivable: all sales on credit. Average collection period is 45 days.
- Marketing expenses: 3 percent of sales; one-half accrued at the end of each month.
- Purchases: 70 percent of sales; purchases made in month prior to sale; terms 30 days.
- Cost of goods sold: 70 percent of sales.
- Depreciation expense: $40,000 per month.
- Capital expenditures: $50,000 each in January, February, April, and June; $100,000 each in March and May.
- General and administrative expenses: $30,000 per month plus 1 percent of sales; half accrued at the end of each month.
- Taxes: tax rate is 40 percent; $150,000 is to be paid in April, and $78,160 is to be paid in June.
- Dividends: $100,000 to be paid in March.
- Interest expense: $10,000 per month.

Case Questions

1. Prepare monthly *pro forma* income statements for the six months and a cumulative income statement for the six months ending June 30, 1988.
2. Prepare monthly *pro forma* balance sheets for the six months January through June 30, 1988.
3. Prepare a monthly cash budget for the six-month period.
4. Prepare monthly *pro forma* statements of cash flows and a cumulative statement covering the six months ending June 30, 1988.

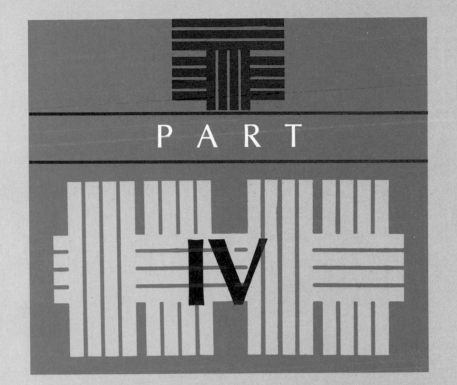

PART

IV

WORKING CAPITAL MANAGEMENT

C H A P T E R

9

WORKING CAPITAL MANAGEMENT

hapter 1 noted that the financial manager must coordinate and direct the flow of cash into and out of the firm's operating, investing, and financing activities in order to maximize stock price. This chapter and those which follow focus on operating activities as reflected in working-capital management. The effective management of working capital is important to the financial success of a firm. Without carefully developed policies, working-capital decisions tend to reduce profitability and increase risk exposure, the worst of all possible risk-return situations.

A company's working capital includes all of its current assets such as cash, marketable securities, accounts receivable, and inventories. These assets are constantly being "turned over" or "worked" in the normal operating cycle of the business. For example, inventory is sold and replaced; accounts receivable are collected and replaced by others; cash is spent and replenished.

The amount and composition of a company's current assets are the result of many factors, such as industry trade practices and competitive conditions; the firm's sales level; liquidity, credit, and production policies; past practices; and daily operating decisions made throughout the firm. For example, decisions the financial manager makes about the amounts of cash needed to meet anticipated as well as unanticipated cash transactions, decisions the marketing manager makes about extending credit to customers, and decisions the production manager makes about the amounts and types of raw materials inventories needed to support the production schedule all determine the amounts and types of current assets on the balance sheet.

Since current assets, like all other assets, must be financed, the amounts of current assets the firm holds have immediate consequences for the amounts, costs, and maturities of financing raised. These represent important decision variables for the financial manager.

• Objectives and Organization of this Chapter

This chapter has three principal objectives. First, it establishes a framework that integrates the working-capital material in the following chapters. It shows that individual working-capital decisions cumulatively affect the risk-return profile of the firm so that working-capital policies that guide decision making in the proper direction are necessary. The second objective of the chapter is to present the role of liquidity policy in working-capital management. The firm's liquidity position is its "first line of defense" against unexpected cash drains. Each of the firm's current assets is, at least potentially, a source of liquidity; but the primary resources are cash and marketable securities. This chapter explores a firm's overall liquidity policy in regard to its risk-return tradeoff. The third objective of the chapter is to present and explain the important financial idea known as the *maturity matching principle.* This principle, also known as the *hedging principle,* addresses considerations that should be taken into account in financing working-capital investments. When companies follow the matching principle, they achieve a reasonable tradeoff between risks and return. When firms violate the matching principle, they incur unnecessary risks or costs.

 ## WORKING CAPITAL AND OPERATING DECISIONS

The relationship between working-capital and operating decisions is most clearly reflected in the firm's cash balances. To see this more clearly, consider the operating decisions or policy changes that might cause the firm's cash balance to rise or to fall.

Marketing.   A change in marketing policies might affect the rate or timing of cash inflows and outflows. For example, a large advertising campaign will require an immediate cash outflow, but it may be some time before the effects of the campaign are felt in the form of an increased cash inflow from sales. The addition of new products to the company's line may mean more sales and profits in the long run, but to the financial manager it also means larger amounts of cash tied up in inventories and accounts receivable. A decision to pay sales personnel on a commission basis will tend to match the cash outflow on their salaries to the cash inflow from collections. If they are paid a flat monthly rate, the firm will be faced with a cash outflow for salaries that may not be adequately balanced by an inflow from sales during slack seasons. Of course, it may well be desirable from the point of view of the sales manager to pay regular salaries in order to keep the staff. The only point to be made is that this policy has an effect on the firm's cash balance.

Production.   Production decisions also affect cash flows. For example, management might consider leveling out seasonal peaks in production by manufacturing for inventory during the slack seasons. However, the drain on the cash balance might be severe unless inflows can be accelerated during the slack period. The risk of larger cash drains must be weighed against the lower costs and greater returns that might be obtained by level production.

Purchasing.   Purchasing decisions also affect the cash balance. For example, the purchasing agent may be able to obtain a substantial quantity discount by buying three months' supply at a time rather than one month's supply. However, the financial manager must be consulted to see whether or not the additional two months' worth of inventory can be financed. The final decision should be made in light of factors such as the cost of funds versus the savings to be gained from quantity discounts.

Personnel.   Routine personnel decisions also may affect the inflow and outflow of cash. For example, if employees are paid twice a month instead of once a month, cash will flow out more rapidly. Higher wage rates or fringe benefits will cause more rapid cash outflows, and other adjustments will have to be made to restore the cash balance.

Accounting.   In general, accounting decisions are probably the least likely to affect the flow of cash through the business, except when they affect the amount of Federal income taxes and other taxes to be paid. For example, a decision to treat an expenditure as a current expense rather than as an investment in an asset may slightly lower the amount of the income tax for the current year, but there is no immediate effect at the time upon the cash flow in the business. However the accountant treats the expenditure on the books, it is a cash outflow to the financial manager, and it correspondingly reduces the level of cash in the company.

Policy decisions in practically every area of operations affect the amount and timing of cash inflows and outflows of a firm. Consequently, these decisions should not be reached without the assistance of the financial manager. The more strapped the company is for funds, the greater weight must be given his or her advice. Unfortunately, while such a situation restricts freedom of action in marketing, production, purchasing, and other functions, it also limits the ability of the financial manager to obtain funds on reasonable terms.

WORKING CAPITAL MANAGEMENT POLICIES

A firm's working capital policies encompass the following major decisions: (1) the level of cash and marketable securities the firm should maintain; (2) the amount, if any, of credit the firm should extend to customers; (3) the appropriate levels of inventory the firm should carry to support production and sales efforts; and (4) the amounts and types of short-term financing the firm should secure. The policies and daily decisions made with respect to these questions produce important financial consequences.

In order to demonstrate the financial consequences of alternative working-capital policies, let us examine three types of policies as pursued by three otherwise identical firms (see Table 9-1).

TABLE 9-1   Effects of Alternative Working Capital Policies ($000)

	Lax	Optimal	Lean
Cash and marketable securities	$ 75	$ 50	$ 25
Accounts receivable	225	150	75
Inventories	300	200	100
Total current assets	600	400	200
Net fixed assets	400	400	400
Total assets	$1,000	$ 800	$ 600
Current liabilities	$ 200	$ 200	$ 200
Long-term debt, 12%	300	200	100
Total liabilities	$ 500	$ 400	$ 300
Shareholders' equity	500	400	300
Total liabilities and stockholders' equity	$1,000	$ 800	$ 600
Sales	$1,000	$1,000	$1,000
EBIT	180	180	180
Interest expense*	46	34	22
Profit before taxes	134	146	158
Income taxes (50%)	67	73	79
Net income	67	73	79

*Equal to 5% times current plus 12% times Long-Term Debt

Firm #1 is characterized by very lax, even nonexistent, working-capital policies. Accordingly, we will call this firm "Lax." A look at its current assets reveals lush cash and marketable securities balances, which the financial manager considers necessary to meet every possible cash requirement no matter how remote and without regard to the cost. Accounts receivable, likewise, are larger than necessary because credit is extended to support sales even though the costs of providing credit may exceed the benefits of increased sales. Similarly, the inventory levels are sizeable in order to insure that there will always be enough raw materials, work in process, and finished goods to meet production and sales quotas—even though the costs of holding such large quantities of inventories may far exceed the benefits of ready supplies. A look at Lax's financing policies reveals proportionally little reliance on short-term debt and heavy reliance on long-term debt. This spreads loan repayments over a longer period of time, which makes the company's top management happy even though the company may be paying for funds it does not need as well as paying higher interest costs than necessary.

In contrast to Lax, firm #3, which we will call "Lean," follows aggressive working-capital policies. This firm has relatively little in the way of cash and marketable securities, accounts receivable, and inventory. In addition, it relies heavily on short-term debt. As we shall see, Lean is

attempting to maximize its return on investment by minimizing investments in current assets and also by relying heavily on short-term financing.
In doing so, Lean is exposing itself to the risk of not being able to repay
its short-term obligations.

Somewhere between "Lax" and "Lean" we find "Optimal." Optimal's
working-capital policies and practices represent a compromise between the
safe (but costly) policies of Lax and the profitable (but risky) policies of
Lean. Each of Optimal's working-capital policies has been established with
regard to the risk-return tradeoff. As a consequence, Optimal avoids the
costly over-investment that typifies Lax as well as the unnecessary risks to
which Lean is exposed.

In order to demonstrate more concretely the relationship between
working-capital management and financial performance, let us build upon
the data for the three companies. Let us further assume, for the time being,
that each firm has the same sales volume, $1,000,000, and operating profits
(EBIT), $180,000. Each firm also has $400,000 invested in net fixed assets.
Finally, for simplicity, let us assume that current liabilities have an average
cost of 5 percent[1] to each firm but that long-term debt has an average cost
of 12 percent per year.

Comparison of Working Capital Policies

As mentioned previously, these three firms differ substantially in their
working-capital policies. These differences are reflected in their individual
risk-return profiles. Evidence of this can be seen in Table 9-2.

Optimal has a current ratio of 2:1. Its current assets represent 50 percent of total assets, and its current liabilities represent 25 percent of total
assets. Finally, Optimal's return on equity is 18.3 percent. Lax, in contrast,
has a current ratio of 3:1. Its current assets represent 60 percent of total
assets, and current liabilities are 20 percent of assets. Lax's return on equity
is 13.4 percent, the lowest of the three. At the other extreme, Lean illustrates an overly rigid working capital policy. Its current ratio is only 1:1.

TABLE 9-2   Working Capital Policies and Financial Performance

	Lax	Optimal	Lean
Current ratio	3:1	2:1	1:1
Current assets/total assets	.60	.50	.33
Current liabilities/total assets	.20	.25	.33
Return on equity	13.4%	18.3%	26.3%

---

[1]This is an average based on noninterest bearing liabilities such as trade credit and
accruals, as well as interest bearing bank debt.

Its current assets represent only 33 percent of total assets, and current liabilities represent 33 percent of assets. Lean's return on equity is 26.3 percent, the highest of the three firms. Lean operates in a more precarious liquidity environment.

Notice that, although Lax has the lowest rate of return on shareholder's equity, it has the highest liquidity as measured by its high current ratio and high ratio of current assets to total assets. To some extent, Lax's working-capital policies are more conservative than those of the other firms because they provide a greater margin of safety in the form of increased liquidity. However, such policies also introduce unnecessary risks insofar as the large receivables balances might increase bad debt losses, or the larger inventory positions might increase the losses from such problems as obsolescence and deterioration. Lax also has a "conservative" financing policy in that its current liabilities are a small proportion of total debt. Thus, the firm is spreading its debt repayment over longer periods of time. However, since Lax is relying more heavily on long-term debt, its financing costs are also higher, as shown in the "interest expense" figure on the company's income statement.

Lean's working-capital policies reflect relatively little liquidity, as indicated by its low current ratio and low ratio of current assets to total assets. In addition, the firm has a relatively risky financing policy, since all short-term financing (including, of course, bank debt) must continually be renewed. Lean's financial manager will have to be especially alert in the event new financing sources have to be developed on short notice. Accompanying Lean's riskier position is a relatively high return on equity. The return on equity is greater not only due to the lower investment in assets but also because of the interest saved by not using as much long-term debt as the other firms.

Some Qualifications

A few words of caution are in order. Up to this point (for illustration purposes), we have assumed sales and operating expenses were not sensitive to the working-capital policies used by the three manufacturing firms depicted in Table 9-1. This is somewhat unrealistic. For example, Lean's restrictive credit policy, while reducing accounts receivable and therefore not granting as much credit to customers as its competitors do, is going to make it more difficult for the firm to reach $1,000,000 in sales. Potential credit customers are likely to be turned away, with profitable credit sales lost. At the very least, higher marketing costs (due to increased selling and advertising efforts) are likely to be necessary for Lean to reach $1,000,000 in sales. In a similar fashion, excessively tight inventory controls are likely to result in *stock-outs* and lost sales.

In contrast, it might be possible for Lax to correct its working capital deficiencies by tightening its credit and inventory policies without affecting its sales volume or profit margins. It is the responsibility of the financial manager to determine the sensitivity of the firm's sales to different working-capital strategies. This can be done by examining working capital-to-sales relationships for other firms in the industry, by examining the historical sensitivity of a firm's sales to changes in various working-capital policies, or by computer simulations of the sensitivity of sales to alternative working-capital strategies. Only then can the financial manager develop an overall working capital management policy.

Industry Influence on Working Capital

Before leaving this overview of working-capital management, it is necessary to recognize that total current assets, as well as the various current-asset components, vary greatly across industry groupings. Thus, it is important to examine working capital policies in light of industry "norms" or standards. Table 9-3 illustrates some of these wide differences.

Current assets as a percent of total assets range from over 60 percent in the wholesale trade industry to less than 15 percent for utilities. Management of receivables is particularly significant in construction and the wholesale trades. And, naturally, inventories are a large proportion of assets in the wholesale and retail trades.

The manufacturing industry category is characterized by current-asset investments representing about 40 percent of total assets. Accounts receivable represents the most important working capital item and is closely followed by investment in inventories. Although cash and marketable secu-

TABLE 9-3 Composition of Assets by Major Industrial Groups

	Percent of Total Assets			
Industry	Cash and Government Securities	Receivables	Inventories	Fixed and Other Assets
Agriculture, forestry & fishing	6.3%	8.4%	10.0%	75.3%
Mining	3.7	18.2	4.8	73.3
Construction	10.2	25.6	15.3	49.3
Manufacturing	3.5	21.7	14.7	60.1
Electric, gas and sanitary services	2.0	8.8	3.8	85.4
Wholesale trade	7.6	24.6	29.8	38.0
Retail trade	7.4	18.6	31.3	42.7
Services	10.0	16.7	5.2	68.1
All industries	12.3	25.7	6.9	55.1

Source: Department of the Treasury, Internal Revenue Service, *Statistics of Income*, 1981, *Corporation Income Tax Returns*, Publication 16 (July, 1984)

rities represent, on average, less than 4 percent of total assets, the financial manager's efforts in this area can significantly influence the firm's liquidity and profitability.

To summarize, working-capital policies involve managing the firm's:

1. Investments in each current asset category
2. Liquidity, as measured by the relationship of current assets to current liabilities and current assets to total assets
3. Financing mix between current liabilities and long-term sources

 ## THE MATURITY MATCHING PRINCIPLE

The maturity matching principle is based on the following idea: short-term assets should be financed from short-term sources; long-term assets should be financed from long-term sources. Matching derives its popularity from the fact that, in general, it results in a reasonable compromise between financial safety and costs. Before demonstrating this, let us examine the important assumptions underlying the matching principle.

Important Assumptions Behind the Matching Principle

The matching principle assumes that certain "normal" characteristics of asset-liability relationships will continue. These assumptions and their rationales are discussed below:

Current Assets Are more Liquid than Fixed Assets. By definition, current assets are primarily in the forms of cash, short-term securities, accounts receivable, and inventories. All of the noncash assets are expected to be turned into cash in a year or less. Thus the opportunity to redeploy the funds from these assets to alternative uses (and, hence, their liquidity) is much greater than it is for fixed assets such as plant and equipment. The greater a firm's current assets (especially cash and marketable securities) the greater its liquidity. While this liquidity may offer security to a firm that needs to make rapid changes of direction for strategic reasons, it may also be dangerous for a firm to maintain high liquidity for long periods. During the late 1980s, many such high-liquidity firms became attractive targets to hostile takeovers by investors eager to acquire assets that could be sold quickly.

Profitability Is Lower on Short-term Investments than on Long-term Investments. An obvious example is cash, which has little, if any, earning power (in the form of interest bearing checking accounts) compared to fixed investments made to produce goods. Of course this is what one would expect in an efficient market, since the investments in fixed assets necessarily involve greater risks than, say, investments in the form of cash balances.

Typically, marketable securities also produce lower rates of return than fixed investments (one should not be mislead by short-term aberrations when interest rates, or yields, on marketable securities are unusually high).

Short Term Financing Is Riskier than Long Term Financing.   This is due primarily to the fact that, given the same financing need, short-term loans will have to be renegotiated ("rolled over") more often than long-term loans. For example, assume that a company needs financing for three years. If the company gets a one-year loan, it will have to pay off the loan every year and reborrow immediately. If circumstances change and the firm cannot reborrow, it has a liquidity crisis on its hands, possibly forcing immediate sales of assets at a loss or even bankruptcy. However, if the same firm negotiates a three-year loan, this financing uncertainty is eliminated. If circumstances change, the firm's financial manager has time to develop much more acceptable alternatives before the loan is due.

Short Term Financing Is Less Expensive than Long Term Financing.   Although not always true of interest-bearing debt, current liabilities generally will have an average financing cost lower than long-term debt. There are three principal reasons for this. First, as discussed in Chapter 3, interest rates on short-term securities tend to be lower than interest rates on long-term securities, everything else being equal. This relationship, known as the term structure of interest rates, is shown in Exhibit 9-1.

Second, a large portion of the firm's current liabilities, such as trade credit[2] and various tax, wage, and other accruals, do not have explicit interest costs. Thus, on a weighted-average basis, ignoring any term structure influence, current liabilities will have a lower average cost than long-term liabilities.

Third, even ignoring the first and second reasons, short-term financing tends to cost less than long-term financing because the firm avoids "redundant" financing, i.e., borrowing more and for longer periods than necessary. Short-term financing allows the firm to tailor its borrowing much more closely to its requirements with respect to both the amount and duration.

The Matching Matrix

Given the above assumptions, management faces several fundamental risk-return tradeoffs. First, the greater the firm's proportion of short-term assets to long-term assets, the greater the firm's liquidity but the lower its average rate of return on total assets; and conversely, the smaller the firm's proportion of short-term assets to long-term assets, the smaller its liquidity but the higher its average rate of return on total assets.

On the liability side, the greater the firm's reliance on short-term rather than long-term financing, the lower its average cost of financing but the

---

[2]It is assumed the firm takes trade discounts.

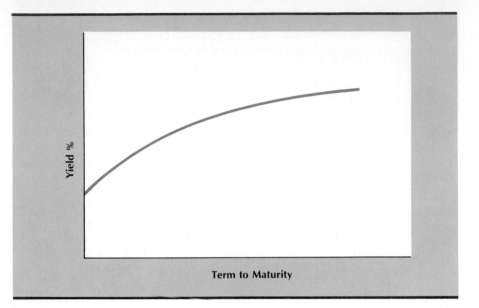

EXHIBIT 9-1
Term Structure of
Interest Rates

greater its financing risk; and the smaller the firm's reliance on short-term rather than long-term financing, the higher its average cost of financing but the lower its financing risk.

In selecting among these combinations, the financial manager is simultaneously picking an investment strategy and a financing strategy, as indicated by a cell in Exhibit 9-2.

Cell #1 in Exhibit 9-2 represents a matching strategy because the relatively lower returns of its short-term investments are matched by relatively low financing costs. And, the relatively greater risk of short-term financing is matched by greater liquidity from its short-term investments. Alternatively, cell #2 depicts a minimum-risk/minimum-return strategy because it involves relatively greater short-term investments and relatively heavy long-term financing. However, the return on investment would be lower and financing costs would be higher than usual and, thus, this strategy would produce minimum net returns.

Cell #3 represents a violation of the matching principle. By investing in long-term assets, the firm is pursuing high returns. Moreover, it is financing these assets with short-term debt. The high investment return coupled with the low financing costs result in the highest expected returns of all the investment/financing combinations. However, this combination is also the riskiest, because the firm has low asset liquidity and high financing risk.

Cell #4, like cell #1, represents a matching strategy. In this case the profitable but risky long-term investments are matched by relatively expensive but safer long-term financing.

Financing

Short-term   Long-term

	Match	Expensive
Short-term	①	②
Long-term	③ Risky	④ Match

Investments in Assets

EXHIBIT 9-2
The Matching Matrix

To summarize, in pursuing a liquidity-financing profile that is optimal from the standpoint of shareholders, the financial manager should be guided by the matching principle reflected in cells #1 and #4. Generally, if the financial manager matches the maturity (i.e., short-term or long-term) of the firm's investments with a financial source of the same maturity, the firm will hedge its financing risk while not foregoing profitable investments.

WORKING CAPITAL AND THE MATCHING PRINCIPLE

In applying the matching principle to working-capital management, it is necessary to revise the definitions of *short term* and *long term*. For example, in reality, even though a company's accounts receivable are collected every 90-days and thus clearly qualify as short-term investments, the fact is that, as one receivable is collected, another is generated in the normal course of business. In other words, there is a minimum level of investment in current assets that the firm never falls below. This minimum level is called the firm's *permanent current asset investment*. Similarly with respect to the firm's current liabilities. For example, in the normal course of business, as the firm pays its suppliers for one shipment of merchandise, it simultaneously reorders and hence generates a new account payable. Thus, there is a level of accounts payable and other liabilities that the firm never drops below. These levels are called the firm's *permanent current liabilities*. In accordance with the matching principle, permanent current assets should be treated as long-term or fixed, and thus should be financed from long-

permanent current asset investment

permanent current liabilities

term sources. Similarly, permanent current liabilities resemble long-term financing and can be used to finance permanent current assets. Finally, temporary increases in current assets are, in fact, short-term and should be financed with short-term sources. The matching principle as applied to working capital and other assets is illustrated in Exhibit 9-3.

Fixed assets and a portion of permanent current assets are to be financed with long-term debt and equity funds. This is an attempt to match average maturities. A level dollar amount of fixed and permanent current assets will always be outstanding (even though individual machinery, inventory, and accounts receivable items will change) to support nonseasonal sales. Thus these assets should be financed with similarly long-term or perpetual debt and equity funds.

The financial manager also should plan to finance a portion of the firm's permanent current assets with permanent short-term debt or current liabilities. In the event of seasonal sales patterns, the need for investment in temporary current assets would be offset in part by a temporary increase in accounts payable and accruals as a result of the step up in production that is necessary to meet the seasonal sales demand.

Short-term loans, both secured and unsecured, provide another major source of short-term debt or current liabilities. Commercial banks provide the primary source of such loans. This is supplemented by some firms with nonbank short-term loans or credit in the form of commercial paper sales, finance company loans, loans from customers and suppliers, and even the sale or factoring of accounts receivable. Unlike trade credit and accru-

EXHIBIT 9-3
Illustration of the
Matching Principle

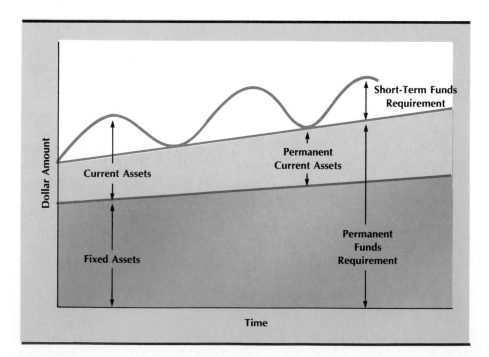

als, however, short-term loans do not change spontaneously with oper-ations and thus are better categorized as temporary rather than permanent sources of short-term debt. While it is true that there are many examples of firms that are able to roll over or refinance their short-term loans con-tinually, there are also many instances where firms have become insolvent and bankrupt because of the failure to meet loan repayment due dates.

Illustration: Working Capital and the Matching Principle

In order to focus more closely on the matching principle as it applies to working-capital management, consider the Baxter Box Company. The com-pany's financial manager has observed that the company's current assets average 70 percent of sales, and current liabilities (not including short-term debt) average 30 percent of sales. The financial manager projects the sales, current asset, and current liability figures shown in Table 9-4 for the next four quarters.

Current assets and "spontaneous" current liabilities, such as accounts payable and trade credit, rise and fall with sales. For example, current assets are $700,000 at the end of the first quarter, then peak at $1,050,000 at the end of the third quarter. Similarly, spontaneous liabilities are $300,000 at the end of the first quarter and peak at $450,000 at the end of the third quarter.

The difference between current assets and spontaneous liabilities must be made up of a combination of short-term bank debt and long-term funds. The question the financial manager must resolve is: "What mix of funds should be used?" Let us see how Baxter's financial manager might resolve this question.

Baxter has two principal financing options: a 90-day bank loan and a two-year term loan. Because of its lower cost, the financial manager is temp-ted to use the 90-day loan. If this option is used, borrowing will go from $400,000 (first quarter) to $600,000 (third quarter) and back to $400,000 (fourth quarter). However, this would have some undesirable consequen-

TABLE 9-4   Permanent Versus Temporary Working Capital ($000)

	Quarter			
	Q1	Q2	Q3	Q4
Sales	$1,000	$1,200	$1,500	$1,000
Current assets (70%)	700	840	1,050	700
Current liabilities (30%, not including debt financing)	300	360	450	300
Net financing required	$ 400	$ 480	$ 600	$ 400

ces. For example, Baxter never really pays the bank off. If Baxter gets into financial difficulties, the banker will be reluctant to keep renewing the borrowing. Thus Baxter will lose financing at the worst possible time. In addition, if money becomes "tight," the banker may prefer to lend its funds to someone else and Baxter's financial manager will have to try to find an alternative at a time when funds are scarce all over.

Alternatively, Baxter's financial manager could take out the two-year term loan and thus not have to worry about renewing the debt each 90 days. But how much should the manager borrow? If Baxter borrows $600,000, then most of the time the company has cash it does not need. For example in the first quarter, the company would have excess cash of $200,000. Moreover, this financing option is more costly on an interest-rate basis, making the excess cash even more costly.

The solution in this simplified situation has, however, general relevance: The financial manager should finance the "permanent" portion (i.e., $400,000) from permanent sources. Temporary current asset requirements should be financed from temporary sources. Thus, the financial manager would borrow $400,000 on a term loan arrangement and secure a line of credit from its bank for the remaining $200,000. This is an application of the matching principle.

SUMMARY

There are several possible working-capital management strategies or policies. The financial manager may take a very conservative approach to the management of current assets or net working capital (current assets less current liabilities) if there is a desire to emphasize lower liquidity risk over possible higher returns. From an overall working-capital viewpoint, this would be associated with a relatively high current ratio but low current assets turnover and debt mix ratios. An aggressive strategy, in contrast, would attempt to improve equity returns by maintaining these ratios at less conservative levels and thereby accepting higher liquidity risk. Of course, an overly aggressive working-capital policy might actually result in lower profitability. Sales may be lost due to stringent credit policies and/or inventory shortages or stock-outs, and profits may suffer as a consequence.

The maturity matching principle requires the financial manager to establish a policy concerning the desired balance between maturities of assets and liabilities. More aggressive financial managers will choose to finance larger proportions of permanent current assets with current liabilities (instead of long-term debt or equity). This increases liquidity risk but also tends to result in higher returns because the cost of financing is typically lower for short-term than for long-term funds.

MULTIPLE CHOICE QUESTIONS

1. Working capital refers to:
   a) Net fixed assets
   b) Long-term debt
   c) Shareholder's equity
   d) Current assets and current liabilities

2. A very high current ratio would suggest:
   a) Overly conservative financial management
   b) Overly aggressive financial management
   c) Good asset utilization
   d) High risk to short term lenders

3. A rapidly expanding business can expect:

    a) Low asset requirements
    b) Low financing requirements
    c) High financing requirements
    d) Low profits

4. Working capital management pertains primarily to the firm's:

    a) Operating activities
    b) Investing activities
    c) Financing activities
    d) None of the above

5. According to the maturity matching principle:

    a) A firm should keep no short-term debt
    b) The maturity of a firm's short-term debt should match that of its long-term debt
    c) The maturity of a firm's debt should match the maturity of its common stock
    d) The maturity of a firm's financing should match that of its assets

6. Which of the following would not reflect a working-capital decision:

    a) The amount of cash to keep in the bank
    b) Whether to grant credit to a group of potential customers
    c) Whether to invest in a new machine
    d) The amount of inventory to keep on hand

7. A firm that finances long-term assets with short-term financing:

    a) Follows a conservative working capital policy
    b) Is risky
    c) Is spending too much on financing
    d) Is observing the matching principle

8. One of the assumptions of the matching principle is that:

    a) Short-term debt is more expensive than long-term debt
    b) Short-term debt is safer than long-term debt
    c) Short-term assets are safer than long-term assets
    d) Long-term assets are less profitable than short-term assets

9. One of the assumptions of the matching principle is that:

    a) The term structure of interest rates is upward sloping
    b) The term structure of interest rates is downward sloping
    c) Interest rates are constant
    d) The actual term structure of interest rates is not important

10. Permanent current assets:

    a) Include plant and equipment
    b) Are related to the firm's sales level
    c) Are always equal to the firm's permanent current liabilities
    d) Should be financed entirely by short-term debt

11. The matching principle means:

   a) Minimizing the amount of liabilities
   b) Matching the maturities of assets and liabilities
   c) Maximizing the maturities of liabilities
   d) Maximizing the maturities of assets

12. Spontaneous financing refers to:

   a) Borrowing impulsively
   b) Financing that is not needed
   c) Creating new securities
   d) Automatic financing

DISCUSSION QUESTIONS

1. What factors determine the amount and composition of a company's current assets?

2. Discuss the relationship between working capital and operating decisions as they are reflected in the firm's cash balances.

3. What major decisions must be made in designing the firm's working-capital policies?

4. Discuss the maturity matching principle. What problems can arise when it is not observed?

5. What are the important assumptions behind the matching principle? Discuss the rationale for each assumption.

6. What is the matching matrix? Explain what each cell in the matrix represents about the firm's working capital policies.

7. Distinguish between spontaneous current liabilities and negotiated current liabilities.

8. What is meant by the terms *permanent current assets* and *permanent current liabilities*?

SOLVED PROBLEMS

SP-1. The Minx company's balance sheet and income statement for 1987 are shown below: *liquidity management*

Minx Company

Balance Sheet As of 12/31/87

Cash	80,000	Accounts payable	200,000
Accounts receivable	300,000	Other current liabilities	25,000
Inventory	520,000	Total current liabilities	225,000
Total current assets	900,000	Long-term debt	400,000
Net fixed assets	350,000	Total liabilities	625,000
Total assets	$1,250,000	Stockholders equity	625,000
		Total	$1,250,000

Sales	$1,500,000
Cost of goods sold	922,000
Gross profit	578,000
Selling expenses	80,000
General and administrative	150,000
Depreciation	50,000
EBIT	298,000
Interest	48,000
Profit before taxes	250,000
Taxes (34% rate)	85,000
Net income	$165,000

a) Restate Minx's balance sheet and income statement to show the effects of a current asset to sales ratio of 50 percent. Assume that the debt *ratio* will stay the same and that any debt paid off saves interest expense of 12 percent. Do not attempt to restate each of the current asset items — just the total current asset figure.

b) Calculate Minx's ROE on the basis of its actual statement and on the basis of your restated statement.

working capital policies

SP-2. The management of Michelson Company wishes to evaluate three alternative policies with regard to the current asset level of the firm: (1) an aggressive policy requiring current assets at 30 percent of projected sales; and (2) an average policy with current assets at 45 percent of projected sales; and (3) a conservative policy with current assets at 60 percent of projected sales. Expected sales for next year are set at $3.5 million. Net fixed assets are projected to be $1.75 million. Management considers the firm's 40-percent total debt to total assets ratio as optimal. The current cost of long-term debt, which makes up 15 percent of the total debt structure, is 10 percent. Management expects earnings before interest and taxes to be 22 percent of sales.

a) Determine the current ratio for each alternative. What is the turnover of current assets for each policy?

b) Using the return-on-equity financial model, illustrate how the different policies affect the firm's profitability. Assume that interest is computed only for the long-term debt and that the firm has a 34-percent tax rate. Give a brief explanation of your results.

c) Based on your results in parts (a) and (b), what do each of these policies mean in terms of risk to the firm?

1. The Fluge Company's balance sheet and income statement for 1987 are shown below:

Fluge Company			

Balance sheet As of 12/31/87

Cash	80,000	Accounts payable	200,000
Accounts receivable	200,000	Other current liabilities	25,000
Inventory	320,000	Total current liabilities	200,000
Total current assets	600,000	Long-term debt	425,000
Net fixed assets	650,000	Total liabilities	625,000
Total assets	$1,250,000	Stockholders equity	625,000
		Total	$1,250,000

Income Statement, Year Ending 12/31/87

Sales	$1,500,000
Cost of goods sold	922,000
Gross profit	578,000
Selling expenses	80,000
General and administrative	150,000
Depreciation	50,000
EBIT	298,000
Interest	48,000
Profit before taxes	250,000
Taxes (34% rate)	85,000
Net income	$165,000

a) Restate Fluge's balance sheet and income statement to show the effects of a current asset to sales ratio of 20 percent. Assume that the debt *ratio* will stay the same and that any debt paid off saves interest expense of 14 percent. Do not attempt to restate each of the current asset items—just the total current asset figure.

b) Calculate Fluge's ROE on the basis of its actual statement and on the basis of your restated statement.

2. The management of Devon Brothers wishes to evaluate three alterna- *working capital policies* tive policies with regard to the current asset level of the firm: (1) an aggressive policy requiring current assets at 25 percent of projected sales; (2) an average policy with current assets at 35 percent of projected sales; and (3) a conservative policy with current assets at 50 percent of projected sales. Expected sales for next year are set at $6 million. Net fixed assets are projected to be $4 million. Management considers the firm's 50 percent total debt to total assets ratio as optimal.

The current cost of long-term debt, which makes up 20 percent of the total debt structure, is 10 percent. Management expects earnings before interest and taxes to be 5 percent of sales.

a) Determine the current ratio for each alternative. What is the turnover of current assets for each policy?

b) Using the return-on-equity financial model, illustrate how the different policies affect the firm's profitability. Assume that interest is computed only for the long-term debt and that the firm has a 34-percent tax rate. Give a brief explanation of your results.

c) Based on your results in parts (a) and (b), what do each of these policies mean in terms of risk to the firm?

liquidity management

3. The Ensign Company is experiencing severe working capital problems. Its bank notes payable level is approaching the limit agreed upon previously by the company's management and the bank. Based on the company's total asset structure as shown below, and using the following comparative industry ratios, briefly explain the sources of the company's problems.

Ensign Company	
Asset Structure	
Cash	$10,000
Marketable securities	9,000
Accounts receivable	290,000
Inventory	95,000
Fixed assets	576,000
Intangible assets	20,000
Total assets	$100,000

Comparative Industry Ratios	% of Total Assets
Cash and marketable securities:	4.5%
Accounts receivable:	21.5
Inventory:	5.2
Fixed and other long-term assets:	68.8

working capital policies

4. The Alpha Company and the Beta Company both operate in the same industry. Following are their respective balance sheets and income

statements for 1987. You have been asked to evaluate their working capital management policies.

Balance Sheets

	Alpha	Beta
Cash and marketable securities	$80,000	$40,000
Accounts receivable	520,000	360,000
Inventory	800,000	600,000
Total current assets	1,400,000	1,000,000
Fixed assets, net	1,000,000	500,000
Total assets	$2,400,000	$1,500,000
Accounts payable	300,000	150,000
Accrued liabilities	400,000	200,000
Total current liabilities	700,000	350,000
Long-term debt, 10%	500,000	350,000
Common equity	1,200,000	800,000
Total liabilities and equity	$2,400,000	$1,500,000

Income Statements

	Alpha	Beta
Net sales	$3,000,000	$1,500,000
Cost of goods sold	2,400,000	1,200,000
Gross profit	600,000	300,000
Operating expenses	200,000	100,000
Interest expense	50,000	35,000
Earnings before taxes	350,000	165,000
Income taxes paid (34% rate)	119,000	56,100
Net income	$231,000	$108,900

a) Calculate each firm's current ratio and current liabilities to long-term debt ratios. Which firm has the more aggressive working-capital policy? Explain.

b) Use the Du Pont financial model to evaluate the return on equity of the Alpha and Beta firms. (The DuPont model is discussed in chapter 7.) Explain, in a working-capital context, why one firm performed better than the other.

SOLUTIONS TO SOLVED PROBLEMS

SP-1. a) The Minx Company. If current assets = 50 percent sales,

Current assets	750,000	Current liabilities	225,000
Net fixed assets	350,000	Long-term debt[1]	325,000
Total assets	$1,100,000	Total liabilities	550,000
		Stockholders' equity[2]	550,000
		Total	$1,100,000

[1] "Plug figure." Total liabilities stay at 50 percent of total assets, or $550,000. Since current liabilities are 225,000, long-term debt needed is only $325,000. Notice that the company actually needed $400,000 with its high current asset to sales ratio. Thus, $75,000 of borrowing would have been avoided. Since this borrowing cost 12 percent, the savings on interest expense would have been $9,000 (i.e., $75,000 × .12). This should be reflected in the income statement.

[2] Total assets are $1,100,000, half of which are financed with liabilities, leaving needed equity financing of $550,000 instead of the $625,000 actually used. Thus, a current asset to sales ratio of 50 percent would have "freed up" $75,000 of equity financing that could have been paid out in dividends.

Impact on Income Statement. The only effect here is on the interest expense, which would have been $9,000 less than actual (see footnote 1 above). This would have increased net income by $5,940 (i.e., $9,000 × .66) after taxes. The additional profits could also have been paid out in dividends.

Sales	$1,500,000
Cost of goods sold	922,000
Gross profit	578,000
Selling expenses	80,000
General and administrative	150,000
Depreciation	50,000
EBIT	298,000
Interest	39,000
PBT	259,000
Taxes (34%)	88,060
Net income	$170,940

At the industry average 50-percent current asset to sales ratio, dividends could have been paid totalling: $75,000 + $5,940 = $80,940.

b)

	Return on Equity (ROE)
Actual	165,000/625,000 = 26.4%
At 50% Current asset to sales ratio	170,940/550,000 = 31.08%

The company's actual ROE of 26.4 percent is very good, but it could have been even higher if current assets relative to sales had met the industry average.

Michelson Company

Balance Sheet Computations

	Aggressive	Average	Conservative
Current assets	$1,050,000	$1,575,000	$2,100,000
Fixed assets	1,750,000	1,750,000	1,750,000
Total assets	$2,800,000	$3,325,000	$3,850,000
Total debt (.4)	$1,120,000	$1,330,000	$1,540,000
Common equity (.6)	1,680,000	1,995,000	2,310,000
Total liabilities and equity	$2,800,000	$3,325,000	$3,850,000
Long-term debt (.15)	$ 168,000	$ 199,500	$ 231,000
Current liabilities (.85)	952,000	1,130,500	1,309,000
Total liabilities	$1,120,000	$1,330,000	$1,540,000

Income Statement Computations

	Aggressive	Average	Conservative
Sales	$3,500,000	$3,500,000	$3,500,000
Expenses	2,730,000	2,730,000	2,730,000
EBIT (.22)	$ 770,000	$ 770,000	$ 770,000
Interest expense	16,800	19,950	23,100
Profit before taxes	753,200	750,050	746,900
Income taxes (34%)	256,088	255,017	253,946
Net income	$ 497,112	$ 495,033	$ 492,954

Assumption: interest only on long-term debt.

a) Aggressive Policy:
   Current ratio: $1,050,000/$952,000 = 1.10
   Turnover of current assets: $3,500,000/$1,050,000 = 3.33
   Average Policy:
   Current ratio: $1,575,000/$1,130,500 = 1.39
   Turnover of current assets: $3,500,000/$1,575,000 = 2.2
   Conservative Policy:
   Current ratio: $2,100,000/$1,309,000 = 1.60
   Turnover of current assets: $3,500,000/$2,100,000 = 1.67

b)

   ROE = Asset turnover $\times$ Profit margin $\times$ Equity multiplier

   = (S/A) $\times$ (NI/S) $\times$ (A/E)

Aggressive Policy:

ROE = ($3,500,000/2,800,000) × (497,112/3,500,000)
        × (2,800,000/1,680,000)

    = 1.25 × 14.20% × 1.67

    = 29.65%

Average Policy:

ROE = (3,500,000/3,325,000) × (495,033/3,500,000)
        × (3,325,000/1,995,000)

    = 1.05 × 14.14% × 1.67

    = 24.79%

Conservative Policy:

ROE = (3,500,000/3,850,000) × (492,954/3,500,000)
        × (3,850,000/2,310,000)

    = .909 × 14.08% × 1.67

    = 21.38%

From a profitability standpoint, although the conservative policy reduces risk through high liquidity, this is expensive. Not only is the asset turnover low, but the net profit margin is also smaller than the other alternatives. Additional interest expense due to more long-term debt in the capital structure caused a lower profit margin.

c) The conservative policy bears the least amount of risk, with a current ratio of 1.60. However, profitability and asset turnover are lowest under this policy, and the financial manager must weigh the trade-off between risk and return.

REFERENCES

Knight, W. D. "Working Capital Management: Satisficing versus Optimization." *Financial Management,* Spring 1972 pp. 33-40.

Mehta, Dileep. Working Capital Management. Englewood Cliffs, NJ: Prentice-Hall, 1974.

Smith, Keith V. Readings on the Management of Working Capital, 2nd Ed. New York: West Publishing Co., 1980.

CASE EXERCISE

The Taking of Miss Lucy

Brian had only been out of college one year and was thrilled to be in on the kind of financial wheeling and dealing he had only been able to read about before. He listened in awe as the plan for the takeover of Miss Lucy's Steamboat Company was detailed to a group of bankers by his uncle, Ivan String. "I tell you, they're ripe for the plucking. You'll have most, if not all, of your cash back within a year. And, at the yields I'm offering, you're all going to look like geniuses," exhorted Mr. String. Brian could tell that the bankers were tempted but that they needed to hear the plan again to be sure.

The Plan

Ivan's plan had two phases. Phase one was to acquire 60 percent ownership of the company. Phase two was to acquire the remaining 40 percent. It was phase one that Ivan was now trying to arrange with the bankers. His plan was to buy 60,000 shares of Miss Lucy's common stock by offering to pay $7 per share, or $2 more than its current stock price of $5 per share. Ivan would raise the needed funds by securing short-term loans from the bankers in the room. The second phase of Ivan's plan would be to borrow long-term against Miss Lucy's remaining assets and use the funds to purchase the remaining 40,000 shares of stock, leaving Ivan with 100% of the company.

The success of the plan rested on several important elements. First, Miss Lucy's was top heavy in liquidity, most of it in cash, marketable securities, and accounts receivable. (See Exhibit C-1). While the industry ratio of current assets to sales was 50 percent, Miss Lucy's was 60 percent. Privately, Ivan was convinced that a ratio of current assets to sales as low as 40 percent was possible with aggressive management. By reducing the levels of these assets, the company would be overflowing with cash. As majority shareholder, Ivan could insist that this cash would be paid out to shareholders as dividends. Second, the company was generating over $200,000 in operating cash flows (net income plus depreciation) per year. This excess cash could also be paid out to shareholders in the form of dividends. Third, the excess liquidity made the company's return on equity much lower than it could be, and this was depressing the company's stock price to a level only about half of what Ivan thought it was worth. Fourth, the steamboat company had a number of river-front real estate properties that were listed on the balance sheet at $100,000 but which he believed could be sold quickly for $200,000

Balance Sheet as of 12/31/87

Cash	280,000	Accounts payable	200,000
Accounts receivable	400,000	Accruals	25,000
Inventory	220,000	Current liabilities	225,000
Total current assets	900,000		
Net fixed assets	350,000		
Total assets	$1,250,000	Stockholders' equity	1,025,000
		Total	$1,250,000

Income Statement, Year Ending 12/31/87

Sales	$1,500,000
Cost of goods sold	922,000
Gross profit	578,000
Selling expenses	78,000
General and administrative	250,000
Depreciation	150,000
PBT	100,000
Taxes (34% rate)	34,000
Net income	$66,000

Assumptions
 # shares: 100,000
 Earnings per share: $0.66
 Stock price $5.00 per share

EXHIBIT C-1
Miss Lucy's Steamboat Company

Case Questions

1. Evaluate phase one of Ivan's plan. Assume that sales stay at $1,500,000 and that current assets can be reduced to 50 percent of sales. Assume that the reduction in current assets is used to repay the short-term borrowings and that the river-front properties can be sold at the prices stated by Ivan.

2. Do the same (as in question 1) assuming that current assets can be reduced to 40 percent of sales.

3. Assume that Ivan accomplishes phase one, do you think phase two could also succeed? Assume that the remaining 40,000 shares would cost $9 per share. Show how it might or might not work.

4. If you were one of the bankers in the case, would you go along with Ivan's proposal?

CHAPTER

10

CASH AND MARKETABLE SECURITIES

s shown in the previous chapter, financial managers are responsible for establishing policies in regard to the amounts of cash and marketable securities the firm will hold. Such policies reflect management's attitude concerning the trade-off of risk (as indicated by the amount of liquidity contained in cash and near-cash balances) and return. Returns from investments in marketable securities usually are less than returns generated from the firm's investments in other assets. Thus greater liquidity results in lower profitability, and vice versa.

Once general or overall cash and near-cash policies are established, financial managers can direct efforts toward managing cash and marketable securities more efficiently in light of those policies. Insofar as possible and desirable, financial managers should speed cash flows into the firm and delay cash flows out of the firm. And in the event that they have the use of idle cash, they should attempt to make it as productive as possible by investing in short-term marketable securities consistent with an acceptable level of risk.

Objectives and Organization of this Chapter

This chapter has several objectives. First, it shows the vital importance of a firm's cash flows to all operating decisions. Second, it shows that "excess" cash balances, while making management feel more secure, have important costs that should be considered. Third, it suggests ways in which cash balances may be used more efficiently. Fourth, it examines ways in which temporary cash excesses can be used more profitably.

The first section of the chapter discusses the principal determinants of a firm's cash balances. Section two describes the firm's operating cash cycle and the effects of working-capital policies on it. Section three describes ways in which the firm can accelerate its cash collections and thereby save financing costs or increase liquidity. Section four describes practices firms employ to slow down disbursements in order to conserve cash. Section five describes the relationship between cash management and short-term investments in marketable securities. The final section shows how a firm can manage its marketable-securities investments in order to maximize returns while not exposing the firm's liquidity position to unnecessary risks.

MOTIVES FOR HOLDING CASH AND MARKETABLE SECURITIES

There are four basic motives or reasons for holding cash balances and marketable securities. First, cash balances are necessary for routine payments of payrolls and other bills, and they are needed to conduct other day-to-day transactions. Transactions balances are sometimes called *working balances*. This *transactions motive* also includes planned purchases of inventory and certain fixed assets. In this case, funds are usually held in marketable securities (instead of in idle cash balances) until the planned purchases are made.

transactions motive

The second reason for holding cash and marketable securities is referred to as the *precautionary*, or safety, *motive*. These funds are available to meet situations where realized cash receipts and disbursements differ from the forecasted or projected mix. For example, there might be a slowdown in the collection of accounts receivable, production delays due to raw material shortages, or equipment breakdowns. In these instances, the firm will need more funds. Such uncertainties make it necessary to hold a safety stock of cash and marketable securities.

precautionary motive

The third motive is the *speculative motive*. While this is generally considered to be the least significant motive, it occasionally can lead to added profits. For example, a rapid increase in the supply of certain raw materials (e.g., oil) might temporarily depress the price of such materials so as to make it profitable to stockpile additional supplies. Marketable securities might be sold in order to take advantage of such situations. Occasionally attractive land and fixed-asset opportunities also may develop. Undoubtedly, funds held for this motive would be in the form of marketable securities.

speculative motive

The fourth motive relates to the holding of *compensating balances* at commercial banks. Banks provide a number of services, including collecting, clearing, and transferring of funds as well as short-term borrowing privileges to business firms. While some of these services involve direct fees, others are paid for indirectly by requiring firms to hold compensating balances, usually in the form of minimum checking-account balances at the banks. Such balances earn little or no return and may even be loaned by the banks to other customers. Compensating balances are often the major reason why businesses hold large cash balances.

compensating balances

The amount of cash and marketable securities held as a percentage of assets differs substantially across industry categories. This is because some industries require more cash and marketable securities due to greater variability and uncertainty in their cash inflow and outflow patterns. Thus the industry within which the firm operates substantially influences the financial manager's decision to hold cash and marketable securities balances to meet transaction and safety needs (and possibly even compensating-balance requirements).

However, cash management policies also can differ substantially within industries, depending upon management attitudes toward risk versus re-

356

turn. Conservative managers would opt for higher proportions of assets to be held in cash and marketable securities relative to the industry's average policies. This would lower firm risk (because of increased liquidity) and lower profitability. More aggressive managers would sacrifice liquidity for the possibility of higher returns. Thus, even though industry characteristics partially dictate cash management policies, the financial manager still has plenty of opportunity to set the firm's balance between risk and return in terms of the amount of cash and marketable securities to be held. Once basic cash management policies have been established, efforts should focus on improving the efficiency of cash and marketable securities management within the constraints set by these policies.

THE CASH OPERATING CYCLE

In order to understand how cash may be managed more efficiently, one should focus on the day-to-day cash flows associated with a firm's normal operations. This short-term cash operating cycle is depicted for a typical manufacturing firm in Exhibit 10-1.

Exhibit 10-1 illustrates the flow of cash to purchase raw materials, to cover the production process and the carrying of finished goods, and to carry accounts receivable (because of credit sales) until they are collected in the form of cash. Since the purchases also are made on a credit basis, the time required between purchases and payments is depicted.

Notice that cash purchases and cash sales have been omitted from the illustration, as well as short-term accruals such as wages, leases, and tax obligations.[1] Cash purchases would result, of course, in more rapid cash outflows, whereas cash sales would reduce the time-to-conversion from cash back into cash. Policies and contractual requirements associated with accruals allow little opportunity for alteration. Thus, while they influence liquidity ratios and total cash flows, accrual payment periods, once established, generally are out of the financial manager's control. Of course, there are many examples of firms in financial distress choosing to delay obligations to pay wages to their employees.

Time to Conversion Method

Exhibit 10-2 illustrates a linear version of the short-term cash operating cycle for the Brach Products Company.

By focusing on working-capital components, the average age or average time it takes to convert from one stage in the cycle to the next stage is observed. This is sometimes referred to as the time-to-conversion method for examining and managing a firm's short-term cash operating cycle.

---

[1] This is done for the sake of simplicity, so that we may focus on major cash management strategies. Recognize, though, that the amounts and patterns of such flows can be very important in the preparation of formal cash budgets, as was demonstrated, in Chapter 8.

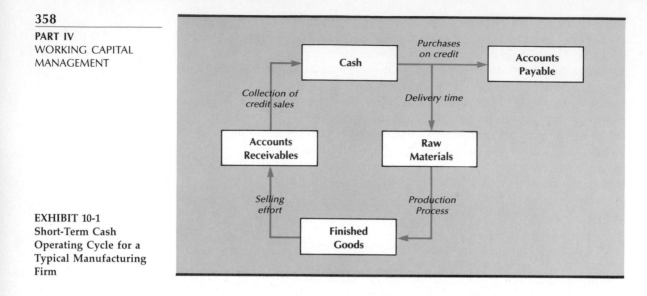

EXHIBIT 10-1
Short-Term Cash
Operating Cycle for a
Typical Manufacturing
Firm

EXHIBIT 10-2
Working Capital
Components of the
Short-Term Cash
Operating Cycle for the
Brach Products Company

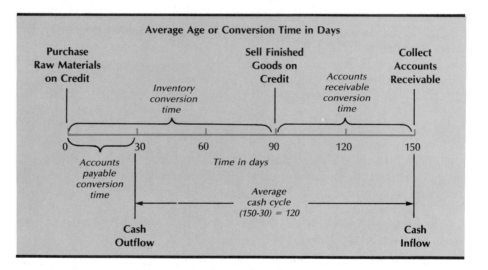

Accounts Payable Conversion Time. Each cycle is initiated with the placement of a purchase order for raw materials. Since Brach Products' purchases are on credit, we are interested in the time period available between the placement of the purchase order and the payment for the materials ordered. This is important because it reduces the length and thus the time period over which the working capital must be financed. The average age or conversion time for Brach's accounts payable is 30 days and can be estimated by calculating the average payment period ratio as was defined in Chapter 7.

Inventory Time to Conversion.   The second step in estimating the average time that is required to complete one cash operating cycle involves estimating the average age or conversion time associated with the firm's inventory. Start with the average time required between the placement of a purchase order and delivery of the materials. This takes, on average, five days for Brach Products. Next, it is important to estimate the average time required to complete the production process. That is, how long does it take to move from raw materials through work-in-process and finally to finished goods inventory? This production process takes Brach Products, on average, 50 days to complete. The final element involves estimating the average time required for finished goods to be converted into sales. This average of 35 days, coupled with delivery and production time, results in an average age or conversion time of 90 days.[2]

Accounts Receivable Conversion Time.   The third step requires an estimate of the average age, or conversion time, associated with the firm's accounts receivable. This can be determined by calculating the average collection period as was described in Chapter 7. For Brach Products the accounts receivable are outstanding for an average of 60 days.

Average Cash Cycle.   The average cash cycle is equal to the inventory plus accounts receivable conversion times minus the accounts payable conversion time:

Average cash cycle = Inventory conversion time + Accounts receivable
conversion time − Accounts payable conversion time

Exhibit 10-2 shows that the total time from cash-to-cash conversion for Brach Products is 150 days on average. However, since the average conversion time on accounts payable is 30 days, the average cash cycle for Brach is 120 days. In other words, Brach Products turns over its cash cycle approximately three times a year (i.e., 360 days divided by 120 days). The length and variability of this cash cycle turnover affect the level of cash and marketable securities needed by the firm. In general, higher cash cycle turnovers are associated with lower average cash needs and lower working-capital financing requirements (and would also be reflected in formal cash budgets). Further, the greater the variability in the conversion times of accounts payable, inventory, and accounts receivable, the higher the level of liquidity needed by the firm.

---

[2] The financial manager, having access to internal financial data, should be able to provide a fairly accurate estimate of the average age or conversion time of the firm's inventory. From an external standpoint, only a rough estimate of the inventory conversion time can be made. This is done by calculating the average inventory turnover defined in Chapter 7 and then dividing the ratio into a 360-day year. Such an approach, however, should be used with caution because it tends to underestimate the inventory time-to-conversion requirement.

Some firms choose to relate their cash and marketable securities balances to sales. For example, a cash turnover (sales/cash and marketable securities) measure can be examined over time and in comparison with other firms in the same industry. The target cash turnover ratio depends on management's attitudes toward liquidity risk versus profitability. Higher cash turnover ratios, like higher cash cycle turnover ratios, improve the profitability of firms. This is because there is an opportunity cost (the foregoing of a return) associated with holding idle cash balances; and even marketable securities generally provide returns lower than can be made from other asset investments. Thus the objective of efficient cash management is to minimize the amount of cash required for transaction and compensating-balance purposes while still maintaining adequate safety in the form of marketable securities balances.

The financial manager should strive to minimize, given acceptable operating constraints or limitations, the firm's short-term cash operating cycle. For example, Brach Products might be able to extend its accounts payable conversion time to 40 days without jeopardizing its trade credit rating,[3] reduce its inventory-production time requirements to 80 days, and lower its average collection period on accounts receivable to 50 days. This would produce an average cash operating cycle of 90 days (based on a cash-to-cash conversion of 130 days less the 40-day accounts payable period). Idle cash needs also may be reduced if the cash cycle reduction is accompanied by less variability in cash flows.

 ## ACCELERATING CASH COLLECTIONS

Even if a company cannot persuade its customers to pay their accounts more rapidly, it can often shorten the period that elapses between the time a customer signs a check and the moment it has the use of the funds. That is, the short-term cash operating cycle depicted in Exhibit 10-2 did not directly consider the time required between when a customer writes a check to pay his or her account and when the funds are available to Brach Products for disbursement. Reduction of such collection time represents another method for improving cash management efficiency.

Lock-Box Collection System

Collection time associated with a customer's payment of a bill with a check is comprised of three elements—mailing time, processing time, and clearing time. The use of a lock-box collection system is designed to reduce

---

[3] Or, as we shall see, without passing up valuable discounts.

all three elements associated with collection time. To understand this, let us assume that Brach Products Company is located in New York City and sells to a customer in Phoenix, Arizona. After the customer deposits a check for payment in the mail in Phoenix, it takes about four days to arrive in New York. Then it takes another day to process the check. Brach does not have the use of the check funds (the bank calls these *uncollected funds*) until the check is "cleared" (deposits from cleared checks are called *Federal funds*) through the Federal Reserve banking system to the bank of the customer in Phoenix. Thus Brach has to wait about a week between the time the check is mailed and funds are usable from the payment. This lag between disbursement and collection is known as *float*. Meanwhile, if Brach's customer is alert to the existence of the float, its financial manager may play the float by, in essence, not depositing the funds for the check until the check is presented for payment. In this case, Brach has *negative float,* since it cannot use the funds for a week. The customer, on the other hand, has *positive float,* since the customer has longer use of the funds. Of course, if the customer does not play the float, the bank has the benefits of the positive float.

float

negative float
positive float

The financial manager should try to reduce negative float in the firm's collection system (and increase positive float in making payments, as we shall see). One procedure would be for Brach to have the checks deposited to a bank account before the payments are processed by Brach, rather than afterwards. This is known as a *lock-box* arrangement. For example, Brach might have its customers forward checks to a lock-box in a post office in New York and arrange with a New York bank to pick up these checks, credit them to its account, and forward any enclosed billing information (such as the name of the payer, the amount of the check, and any other necessary information). Brach would then begin processing the payment after, not before, the check was on its way through the clearing process.

lock-box arrangement

An alternative would be to move the lock-box out west. For example, Brach could establish a lock box in the post office in Tucson, Arizona for all of its accounts in the Southwest. Customers in this area would then be instructed to send their payments on account to Brach's lock box in Tucson, where a bank selected by Brach would remove the checks two or three times a day and credit them to Brach's account. Brach could instruct the Tucson bank to remit balances over a certain amount by *wire transfer* to its New York bank. This procedure might reduce the time interval from the mailing of the check to the availability of funds from seven to two days. In other words, Brach would reduce the float by five days. The optimal number and locations of lock boxes may be estimated by computer simulation, computer programming, or by other analytical techniques.

wire transfer

Reducing the float means freeing up funds that are otherwise in the pipeline. The savings from such reductions can be calculated by multiplying the amount of cash float eliminated times the opportunity cost of funds (e.g., the cost of funds the company will not have to borrow) and subtracting the cost of the lock-box services provided by the bank.

Savings From Reduction of Float

To illustrate the possible savings from one lock box, assume that Brach's annual sales amount to $36 million, and average daily collections amount to about $100,000. An average reduction of float by five days would free a gross amount of $500,000 annually for use elsewhere in the business (or to repay bank borrowing). Brach's opportunity cost of funds is 12 percent, and the cost of the lock-box services is $40,000. By using the lock-box service, Brach will save a net amount of $20,000 per year.

Total funds freed	$500,000
Times: opportunity cost of funds @ 12%	
Equals pre-tax savings from collection system	$ 60,000
Less: cost of lock-box services	$ 40,000
Equals: annual net savings before taxes from lock box	$ 20,000

There are other benefits to be derived from this system in addition to the reduction in float. Because checks are collected faster, Brach learns of bad checks and weak credit situations sooner. A considerable portion of Brach's own check-handling procedures is transferred to the Tucson bank. Because of the size of its operations, the Tucson bank may be able to handle the task more efficiently than Brach can. Furthermore, Brach achieves better control over incoming cash and considerably reduces the chances of fraud. There are other intangible benefits obtained through use of the regional bank for credit information and as a possible source for loans. The disadvantages of the system lie in the charges made by the bank for its services and the costs and problems of converting to the system. However, if net pre-tax profits increase by as much as $20,000, the system is worth adopting.

Concentration Banking

concentration banking

If the Tucson bank is instructed to forward all funds over a certain amount to Brach's New York bank, the New York bank is called a *concentration bank.* Since most firms have a number of separate checking accounts, cash balances are reduced if all, or many, of those accounts are concentrated in only a few banks. While the bank in Tucson only receives deposits, disbursements are made out of the New York concentration bank. Alternatively, a regional concentration bank might be established in Denver, Colorado in addition to the central bank in New York City.

Other Arrangements

Of course the variety of collection systems is limitless. The main factors are the geographical distribution of payers and their relative importance (i.e., average check size). For example, in the event that a single customer was paying a very large bill, Brach might even send a representative by plane to pick up the customer's check and provide special handling so as to expedite the cash collection process.[4]

DELAYING DISBURSEMENTS OF CASH

While the financial manager attempts to reduce the collection time involved when accounts receivable payments are made, efficient cash management suggests that attempts should be made to lengthen the collection time when disbursing funds. Such stretching of disbursement float has been discussed widely in recent years. The object is to lengthen both mailing time and check clearing time. To illustrate, let us return to Brach Products Company. Brach purchases on credit from a major supplier located in Boston, Massachusetts. However, rather than making payments from its New York City bank, Brach Products may opt to write a check on an account it has in a Denver, Colorado bank. This is known as *remote disbursement banking* and results in a longer clearing time for Brach's check. While it is technically illegal to write checks on accounts with insufficient funds, many corporations rely on *overdraft* arrangements with their commercial banks to avoid the possibility of "bouncing" checks.

remote disbursement banking

Remote disbursement banking can be used to lengthen the mail time to the extent that the postmark date on a letter is accepted as constituting the legal payment date. Under such circumstances, Brach Products could make arrangements to have its check drawn on its Denver, Colorado bank to be mailed in Denver for payment to its supplier located in Boston.

Electronic Funds Transfer Systems (EFTS).   As the development and use of electronic funds transfer systems (EFTS) continues and the nation moves closer to a "checkless" society, major changes will occur in cash management policies and procedures used to improve cash management efficiency. Major changes certainly will occur in both the collecting and disbursing of cash.

---

[4] A survey of some of the largest U.S. industrial corporations indicated that the lock-box collection system was the most frequently used method to speed the collection of checks. Second in importance was the use of concentration banking systems. This was followed by systems designed for special handling of large remittances. See: Lawrence J. Gitman, Edward A. Moses, and I. Thomas White. "An Assessment of Corporate Cash Management Practices." *Financial Management,* Spring 1979, pp. 35-36.

MARKETABLE SECURITIES

Instead of permitting temporarily idle funds to remain in a checking account, the financial manager should invest those funds in money market securities that are easily convertible into cash. Recall from Chapter 3 (see Table 3-1) that the money market is comprised of instruments and securities with lives of one year or less. In addition to having relatively short lives, an active secondary money market must also exist for marketable securities to qualify as near-cash securities. Thus the ease of cash convertibility indicates their degree of marketability. Safety of principal is another important ingredient. It does little good to have marketability if, for example, a security purchased for $1,000 can only be sold for $800 a short time later. The issuer must be of very high quality (and thus have a very low probability of default on the issue) in order for the marketable securities to be an acceptable investment. Furthermore, in order to provide added protection of principal, shorter maturities should be emphasized. This is because changes in interest rates affect the market prices of long-term debt securities much more than market prices of short-term securities.

To summarize, marketable securities that qualify as acceptable liquid or near-cash assets should have an active or ready resale market and provide for safety of principal by being of high quality and relatively short maturity.

Types of Marketable Securities

There is actually a wide variety of securities that would be suitable for a near-cash investment portfolio. An indication of recent yields available on several marketable securities investments is provided in Table 10-1.

U.S. Treasury Bills and Notes. Probably the most useful securities for temporary investment of idle funds are U.S. Treasury Bills. They are issued weekly by the Treasury, with maturities ranging from 91 days to one year. They are readily marketable, even in very large amounts.

Treasury Notes have initial maturities of one to five years, although needs for shorter maturities can be met by purchasing notes in the market as they approach maturity (e.g., after four years, a five-year note will have one year left before maturity). Occasionally the yields on notes may be slightly lower than on bills with about the same maturity date because holders usually receive rights to exchange their present securities for a new issue at maturity.

TABLE 10-1 Comparative Yields on Three-Month Money Market Securities

U.S. Treasury Bills	5.21%
Commercial Paper	5.57%
Bankers' Acceptances	5.60%
Certificates of Deposit	5.71%

Commercial Paper.   A second alternative is the purchase of high-grade commercial paper, i.e., promissory notes issued by large, established corporations. Beginning in 1964, some large commercial banks led by the First National Bank of Boston also began to issue short-term unsecured promissory notes, generally in denominations of $1 million or more. More recently, the large bank-holding companies have also issued commercial paper.

Among the most useful forms of commercial paper for large corporate investors are the notes sold by the major finance companies. Since these are available for any maturity up to 270 days, the purchaser can time their maturity in relation to its needs for funds very precisely. Thus one can arrange to buy paper that will mature just a day before a payment is due on corporate income or social security taxes. The yield on high-grade commercial paper is usually somewhat above that available on short-term government securities.

Negotiable Certificates of Deposit (CDs).   Commercial banks issue negotiable certificates of deposit, or CDs. Designed to recapture corporate deposits, these represent receipts for time deposits and offer yields that vary according to maturity and the size and financial reputation of the issuing bank. Banks offer CDs for time periods of from less than 90 days to 365 days in denominations of $100,000 and up.

Bankers' Acceptances.   An importer of goods is usually not required to pay for them immediately. The seller may send the buyer an order to pay, a draft, with, say, a three-month maturity. If the seller wishes to be particularly certain of being paid, he or she may ask that the buyer have the draft *accepted* by a commercial bank. By this process the bank guarantees the payment of the draft at maturity, and the buyer gains ready access to credit (after payment of an appropriate fee to the banker for the service). Once accepted by the bank, the draft becomes a *banker's acceptance.* If the seller does not wish to wait for the funds for three months, he or she can readily sell it in the marketplace.

With the growth in international trade, the volume of bankers' acceptances outstanding has grown rapidly. Bankers' acceptances generally offer somewhat higher yields than Treasury Bills, but they are a very safe form of short-term investment.

Repurchase Agreements.   Generally referred to as "Repos," repurchase agreements are arrangements whereby a corporation buys a large amount of Treasury obligations from a bond dealer for a few days (frequently over a weekend), with the understanding that the dealer will repurchase the securities at an agreed price. Thus the corporation aids the dealer in carrying his or her inventory of bonds and obtains in return a yield that usually is slightly above the available yield on a Treasury obligation of similar maturity.

Other Marketable Securities. Federal agencies, such as the Federal Land Banks and Federal Home Loan Banks, are authorized to issue securities. Although these securities are not guaranteed by the U.S. Government, they are highly regarded as short-term investments. Yields offered are slightly higher than those on Treasury bills of similar maturity, but the spread has narrowed in recent years.

Still other possible media for short-term investment of idle funds are the securities issued by state and local governments. Since these have the added advantage of being exempt from Federal corporate income taxes, the market yields are somewhat lower than on Treasury bills. However, the yield after taxes may be higher.

Some corporate treasurers also have occasionally invested in short-term Eurodollar (deposits in foreign countries denominated in U.S. dollars) time deposits and even in time deposits denominated in foreign currencies. However, because of possible greater default risks and fluctuations in currency exchange rates, there may be less safety of principal in such investments.

DEVELOPMENT OF A MARKETABLE SECURITIES PORTFOLIO

Assume that a financial manager has cash balances available for investment in marketable securities as shown in Table 10-2.

An analysis of the cumulative net flows indicates that, in the first six months, excess cash will not drop below $800,000. Depending on the reliability of these estimates, the financial manager might decide to invest $800,000 in six-month securities. Assume that the $800,000 is invested in six-month commercial paper yielding an 8-percent annual rate. Note that another $100,000 could be invested during the first three months. Assume that this is invested in three-month CDs paying 7 percent. Finally, note that another $100,000 of the original $1 million can be invested for 30 days before it will be needed. Assume that this $100,000 is invested in 6-percent Treasury Bills. The portfolio in the first month is shown in Table 10-3.

TABLE 10-2 Forecast of "Excess" Cash Balances ($000)					
Jan.	Feb.	Mar.	Apr.	May	June
$1,000	$900	$900	$800	$800	$800

TABLE 10-3 Planned Marketable Securities Portfolio			
Security	Maturity	Annual Yield	$ Amount
Commercial paper	180 days	8%	$800,000
Certificates of deposit	90 days	7%	100,000
Treasury bills	30 days	6%	100,000

In February, the one-month Treasury Bills mature and the cash is used for requirements. In April, the CDs mature and are used for requirements. In June, the commercial paper matures and is used for requirements.

From this example, it is easy to see that the cash budget is crucial to the proper program of investment in marketable securities. Errors in the cash budget can have adverse consequences on security selection. Furthermore, the greater the uncertainty contained in the cash budget statement, the more limited marketable securities investment must be. For example, if the cash budget were substantially unreliable, virtually any investment in six-month commercial paper would not be advisable.

The preceding example should also have suggested that there are optimal strategies for shifting among maturities and securities for any expected cash flow pattern. Thus the preparation of reliable cash forecasts should be a high priority for the financial manager.

SUMMARY

Once general or overall cash and near-cash policies are established, financial managers can direct efforts toward managing cash and marketable securities more efficiently in light of those policies. Insofar as possible and desirable, financial managers should speed cash flows into the firm and delay cash flows out of the firm. In the event that they have the use of idle cash, they should attempt to make it as productive as possible by investing in marketable securities consistent with an acceptable level of risk.

MULTIPLE CHOICE QUESTIONS

1. Which of the following best characterizes the transactions motive for holding corporate cash?
   a) Paying accounts payable
   b) Hedging against a downturn in sales
   c) Compensating the bank for a line of credit
   d) Buying extra inventory in anticipation of a price rise

2. Which of the following best characterizes the speculative motive for holding corporate cash?
   a) Payment of wages and salaries
   b) Protection in the event of unexpected cash requirements
   c) Taking advantage of bargain purchases of raw materials
   d) Compensating the bank for a line of credit

3. Compensating balances are:
   a) A method of indirect remuneration to banks for credit services
   b) Illegal
   c) Frowned on by bankers
   d) Usually insignificant

4. The major reason for companies holding large cash balances is:
   a) Speculative purposes
   b) Transactions

c) Compensating balances

d) Safety buffer

5. In a lock-box system:

   a) The company picks up payments directly from a post office box several times a day
   b) Banks telegraph deposits regularly to the company
   c) Customers mail payments directly to the company's headquarters
   d) Customers mail payments to an address serviced several times a day by a bank

6. Bank A only receives deposits and regularly forwards them to bank B, which is used for disbursements. This is an example of:

   a) Lock-box banking
   b) Concentration banking
   c) Float
   d) Compensating balances

7. Company A is headquartered in Boston. The company purchased materials in Boston and paid with a check drawn on its bank in San Diego. This is an example of:

   a) Negative float
   b) Correspondent banking
   c) Concentration banking
   d) Positive float

8. A certificate of deposit is:

   a) A short-term security issued by commercial banks
   b) A short-term security issued by major industrial firms
   c) A receipt given by insurance companies
   d) A capital market security

DISCUSSION QUESTIONS

1. Indicate and briefly explain the reasons that business firms have for holding cash balances and near-cash securities.

2. Briefly describe a typical short-term cash operating cycle that would be characteristic of a firm that manufactures and sells products. Illustrate the process with a diagram.

3. What is meant by a "cash cycle turnover" ratio? Why is the length and variability of the cash cycle turnover important to the financial manager?

4. Identify and briefly describe several methods whereby a firm can speed up the collection of cash from its customers. Why do these methods improve cash management efficiency?

5. How might a firm delay the disbursement of cash when paying its bills?

6. Identify the important characteristics that marketable securities should have. What are some of the types of marketable securities that are acceptable for business firms to hold as near-cash investments?

7. Why should a business firm have a portfolio of marketable securities?

SOLVED PROBLEMS

cash cycle

SP-1. The American Basket Company has an average collection period of 60 days, an average payment period of 30 days, and inventory turnover of 10 times.

a) Based on a 360-day year and assuming that operating activity is level throughout the year, calculate the company's average short-term operating cycle.

b) Calculate the company's cash cycle turnover.

c) Assume that the company decides to take advantage of a discount from its suppliers by paying its bills in 10 days rather than 30 days. What will be the impact on the cash operating cycle and cash cycle turnover?

cash cycle

SP-2. Maggie's Taffy Co. has the balance sheet shown below. Sales were $12,000,000.

a) Calculate the company's short-term cash operating cycle.

b) Calculate the cash cycle turnover.

c) Assume that the company goes to a "cash only" sales policy. Calculate its cash operating cycle and cash cycle turnover on this assumption.

Maggie's Taffy Company

Balance Sheet ($000)

Assets		Liabilities and Net Worth	
Cash	420	Accounts payable	900
Accounts receivable	2,055	Notes payable	1,050
Inventory	2,475	Other current liabilities	300
Total	4,950	Total	2,250
Net fixed assets	3,300	Long-term debt	1,500
Total	8,250	Common stock	750
		Retained earnings	3,750
		Total	8,250

PROBLEMS

cash cycle

1. The Oscar Company has an average collection period of 90 days, an average payment period of 45 days, and inventory turnover of 10 times.

   a) Based on a 360-day year and assuming that operating activity is level throughout the year, calculate the company's average short-term operating cycle.
   b) Calculate the company's cash cycle turnover.
   c) Assume that the company decides to take advantage of a discount from its suppliers by paying its bills in 10 days rather than 45 days. What will be the impact on the cash operating cycle and cash cycle turnover?

2. TuneyCo. has the balance sheet shown below. Sales were $15,000,000.   *cash cycle*

   a) Calculate the company's short-term cash operating cycle.
   b) Calculate the cash cycle turnover.
   c) Assume that the company goes to a "cash only" sales policy. Calculate its cash operating cycle and cash cycle turnover on this assumption.

TuneyCo.			
Balance Sheet ($000)			
Assets		*Liabilities and Net Worth*	
Cash	420	Accounts payable	900
Accounts receivable	2,055	Notes payable	1,050
Inventory	2,475	Other current liabilities	300
Total	4,950	Total	2,250
Net fixed assets	3,300	Long-term debt	1,500
Total	8,250	Common stock	750
		Retained earnings	3,750
		Total	8,250

3. Shelley Shoelace Company is considering the adoption of a system to speed up cash collections from its customers. The new system will speed up overall collections an average of three days.   *cash collection system*

   a) Assuming that sales are $25,000,000 per 360-day year, calculate the total cash "freed up."
   b) To implement and monitor the cash system, the company's banker will require compensating balances of $100,000 and an annual fee of $20,000. If the firm can earn 15% on cash freed up, should it adopt the system?

4. The Mt. St. Helens Ashtray company's cash budget indicates an excess of cash of $100,000 for the next 30 days. No short-term debt is outstanding, and the treasurer would like to invest the cash in a high-yielding money market fund. The fund is expected to earn 15 percent per year. Transactions costs are $1,000 plus 1/2 percent of the principal amount. Assume 360 days per year.

    a) Compare expected earnings and costs of the investment for one month.

    b) Assume that the annual earnings rate and the fee structure do not change. What is the minimum length of time the cash should be invested before profits of $1,000 are earned?

5. Michele Shipping is concerned about improving its management of working capital as reflected in the firm's short-term cash operating cycle. On average, Michele Shipping collects its accounts receivable in 50 days after credit sales are made and pays its accounts-payable obligations 35 days after credit purchases are placed. The firm's inventory conversion time averages 70 days.

    a) Calculate the time it takes Michele Shipping to complete an average short-term cash operating cycle.

    b) Assuming a 360-day year, calculate the firm's cash cycle turnover.

    c) Now assume Michele is able to slow its payments to creditors to an average of 40 days after its credit purchases are made by using a new, but distant, supplier. However, if the new supplier is used, resulting slower delivery of materials will lengthen the average inventory conversion time by three days. Should Michele switch to the new supplier?

6. Assume that the Michele Shipping Company described in Problem 5 has the opportunity of selecting one of the following plans. Which plan—x, y, or z—will alter its short-term cash operating cycle?

Working Capital Plan	Accounts Receivable	Inventory	Accounts Payable
x	+ 15 days	− 12 days	− 18 days
y	− 12 days	− 7 days	+ 8 days
z	+ 5 days	− 12 days	+ 3 days

    a) Which of the three plans would you recommend to Michele? Why?

    b) What are some of the basic assumptions that underlie your choice of working capital plan in part (a)?

7. The Jurado Manufacturing Corporation annually calculates a number of turnover ratios involving several of its working-capital accounts. Operating activity is level throughout the year. Based on a 360-day year, the firm calculates the average turnover of three of its accounts to be: accounts receivable = nine times, inventory = six times, and accounts payable = 12 times.

a) Calculate the time it takes Jurado to complete its average short-term cash operating cycle.
b) Calculate Jurado's cash cycle turnover.
c) How would the cash cycle turnover for Jurado be affected if the turnover ratios for the accounts receivable and accounts payable accounts were reversed?
d) What assumptions underlie the use of the above turnover ratios when estimating short-term cash operating cycles?

8. The Lester Bach Company of Buffalo, NY, is considering using a lock-box system for its customers in California. At present its credit sales to that area amount to about $21,600,000 per year. Establishment of a lock box in San Francisco would enable the company to reduce its collection float from eight days to three days. The bank in San Francisco will expect the company to maintain a minimum balance of $70,000. The net additional annual cost of adopting the system will be $1,500. Base any calculations on a 360-day year.

lock-box system

a) What is the net amount of cash that will be freed for use elsewhere in the business?
b) If the firm can earn 10 percent on funds released from the float, should it adopt the proposed system?

9. Following are three firms with excess cash that could either be held as idle cash balances or be invested in marketable securities.

marketable securities portfolio

Firm	Excess Cash Funds	Available Investment Period
A	$100,000	30 days
B	50,000	90 days
C	60,000	60 days

Transaction costs of buying and selling the marketable securities amount to $500 plus 1 percent of the dollar amount of funds invested. The marketable securities will yield 10 percent annually. Assume a 360-day year.

a) Calculate the dollar amount each firm will earn if it invests its excess cash in marketable securities.
b) When taking transaction costs into consideration, would you recommend purchase of marketable securities by each of the three firms? Why?

c) Under the above conditions, if a firm plans to invest in marketable securities for 45 days, what minimum amount must be invested in order at least to cover the associated transaction costs?

10. The Schuler Company and the FormAlloy Company both operate in the same industry. Following are their respective balance sheets and income statements for last year. You have been asked to evaluate their working capital management policies.

Balance Sheets

	Schuler	FormAlloy
Cash and marketable securities	$ 80,000	$ 40,000
Accounts receivable	520,000	360,000
Inventory	800,000	600,000
Total current assets	1,400,000	1,000,000
Fixed assets, net	1,000,000	500,000
Total assets	$2,400,000	$1,500,000
Accounts payable	300,000	150,000
Accrued liabilities	400,000	200,000
Total current liabilities	700,000	350,000
Long-term debt, 10%	500,000	350,000
Common equity	1,200,000	800,000
Total liabilities and equity	$2,400,000	$1,500,000

Income Statements

	Schuler	FormAlloy
Net sales	$3,000,000	$1,500,000
Cost of goods sold	2,400,000	1,200,000
Gross profit	600,000	300,000
Operating expenses	200,000	100,000
Interest expense	50,000	35,000
Earnings before taxes	350,000	165,000
Income taxes paid (34% rate)	119,000	56,100
Net income	$ 231,000	$ 108,900

a) Calculate each firm's: (1) cash turnover, (2) fixed assets turnover, and (3) total debt to total assets ratios. What are your observations?
b) Calculate each firm's (1) operating cash cycle and (2) cash cycle turnover. Assume 360-day years and calculate conversion times on the basis of sales. Explain the differences.

c) Use the return on equity (ROE) financial model to evaluate the performances of the Schuler and FormAlloy firms. Explain, in a working-capital context, why one firm performed better than the other.

11. You have been asked to examine the short-term cash operating cycle characteristics for the Schuler and FormAlloy companies. In addition to the financial statements data provided in Problem 10, the following information is available for last year:

cash cycle

	Schuler	FormAlloy
Credit sales	$3,000,000	$1,500,000
Cost of goods sold	2,400,000	1,200,000
Credit purchases	2,000,000	1,000,000

Accounts receivable and accounts payable are related to credit sales and credit purchases, respectively. Inventory turnovers are calculated on a cost basis. Both firms also use a 360-day year for purposes of calculating financial ratios.

a) Calculate the inventory conversion time, average collection period, and the average payment period for both Schuler and FormAlloy.
b) Indicate the time it takes for each firm to complete its average short-term cash operating cycle. What assumptions are you making?
c) Calculate the cash cycle turnovers for both Schuler and FormAlloy. Why do they differ?
d) How do the short-term cash operating cycle findings in this problem compare with the working-capital policies identified in Problem 10?

SOLUTIONS TO SOLVED PROBLEMS

SP-1. a) Convert the inventory turnover to an inventory conversion time figure. If inventory turnover is 10 times in 360 days, it must be turning over once in every 36 days. If it takes 36 days to convert inventory to sales and another 60 days to convert sales to cash collected, a total of 96 days are needed to complete the conversion. However, since the average payment period is 30 days, this is deducted from the cash-to-cash conversion. The short-term operating cash cycle is thus 66 days.

b)
$$\text{Cash cycle turnover} = \frac{360}{\text{Cash operating cycle}}$$

$$= \frac{360}{66}$$

$$= 5.45 \text{ times}$$

c)
$$\text{Cash operating cycle} = 36 + 60 - 10$$

$$= 86 \text{ days}$$

$$\text{Cash cycle turnover} = \frac{360}{86}$$

$$= 4.19 \text{ times}$$

SP-2. a) $\text{Inventory to sales conversion} = \dfrac{360 \text{ days}}{\text{Inventory Turnover}}$

$$= \frac{360 \text{ days}}{[\text{sales/inventory}]}$$

$$= \frac{360 \text{ days}}{[12,000/2,475]}$$

$$= 74.25 \text{ days}$$

$$\text{Sales to cash conversion} = \text{ACP}$$

$$\text{ACP} = \frac{\text{Accounts receivable}}{[\text{sales/360}]}$$

$$= \frac{2,055}{[12,000/360]}$$

$$= 61.65 \text{ days}$$

$$\text{Payables to cash conversion} = \text{APP}$$

$$\text{APP} = \frac{\text{Accounts payable}}{[\text{sales/360}]}$$

$$= \frac{900}{[12,000/360]}$$

$$= 27 \text{ days}$$

$$\text{Short-term cash operating} = 74.25 \text{ days}$$
$$+ 61.65 \text{ days} - 27 \text{ days}$$
$$\text{cycle} = 108.9 \text{ days}$$

b) $$\text{Cash cycle turnover} = \frac{360}{\text{Cash operating cycle}}$$

$$= \frac{360}{108.9}$$

$$= 3.31 \text{ times}$$

c) Cash operating cycle = 74.25 days
$$+ \ 0 \text{ days} - 27 \text{ days}$$

$$= 47.25 \text{ days}$$

$$\text{Cash cycle turnover} = \frac{360}{47.25}$$

$$= 7.62 \text{ times}$$

REFERENCES

Baumol, William J. "The Transaction Demand for Cash: An Inventory Theoretic Approach." *Quarterly Journal of Economics,* November 1952, pp. 545–556.

Gitman, Lawrence J., Edward A. Moses, and I. Thomas White. "An Assessment of Corporate Cash Management Practices." *Financial Management,* Spring 1979, pp. 32–41.

Nauss, Robert M., and Robert E. Markland. "Solving Lock Box Location Problems." *Financial Management,* Spring 1979, pp. 21–31.

Richards, Verlyn D., and Eugene J. Laughlin. "A Cash Conversion Cycle Approach to Liquidity Analysis." *Financial Management,* Spring 1980, pp. 32–38.

CASE EXERCISE

Brill, Inc.

Morgan James took over as Treasurer of the Brill Company in early 1988. His first priority was to investigate the company's cash management system, in particular the procedures employed in handling cash collections. The overall cash management system was administered by Brill's controller, Mr. Jones. When Mr. James asked Mr. Jones about the firm's cash collection system, he was informed that it was integrated into the company's overall credit monitoring system to minimize the chance of billing errors. Mr. Jones added that the company had developed its system 15 years earlier and had found it to work well.

Cash Collection System

Payments were received in the mailroom, where they were sorted and forwarded to the accounts receivable department. There the payment was analyzed and payments were posted to ledger accounts. The ledger was updated and the checks were sorted for delivery to the bank. The internal processing time averaged two days although, in some cases where billing questions arose, processing might take a week. After processing, the checks were deposited in Brill's local bank, Santa Fe First. Each month the bank statement indicated the total of deposits made, the total of checks cleared, and the amount of funds available for withdrawal. Mr. Jones personally reconciled this statement each month.

Mr. James inquired as to whether any thought had been given to a bank-administered check processing system that could reduce the float in the check collection process. Many such systems were available for a fee from banks. Mr. James mentioned an article he had recently read, which indicated that a bank-administered lock-box system could typically reduce collection float by two days. Mr. Jones responded that such systems had indeed been considered though never examined in depth. There were several reasons for this, Mr. Jones noted. First, the current system had worked well and had grown with the company. Although Brill's annual sales now totalled $360 million, the system had been installed when the company's sales were only $50 million. Second, the company's president was concerned that the company might become too dependent on its bankers and that the bankers would get intimately familiar with the company's business affairs. Third, the costs of such systems were often higher than anticipated, while the benefits of faster collections were too dependent on the level of interest rates. Finally, when the idea of collecting checks more quickly had been raised at a management meeting, the marketing manager had voiced strong concerns that ill will might be created among customers, many of whom were small and thinly capitalized. Aggressive check collection procedures could actually cause many checks to bounce. Mr. James acknowledged these concerns but believed he should at least attempt to determine how much could be saved with a faster collection system.

Case Questions

1. Assume that the Brill Company's sales of $360 million are spread uniformly throughout the year. How much could the company save for each day of float it cuts off its collection system, given an opportunity cost of 12 percent on the funds?

2. Identify the sources of delay in the current collection system. How many days of float do you think could be cut off the system if the company employed a bank-administered lock-box system?

3. Assume that a bank-administered lock-box system would cost Brill $100,000 per year and that the opportunity cost of collection float is 12 percent. How much could be saved with such a system?

4. Evaluate the other concerns raised about an aggressive collection system? What would you recommend?

C H A P T E R

11

ACCOUNTS RECEIVABLE MANAGEMENT

C ollectively, a firm's credit policies serve as one of its principal competitive instruments. In many ways, the extension of credit has the same effect on demand for a company's products as a price reduction. Not surprisingly, a firm's credit policies are closely related to its pricing policies. For example, by offering credit, retailers may be able to attract customers away from competitors who do not offer credit. Noncredit providers, on the other hand, must reduce prices in order to compete with credit providers. As a result, the prices and gross profit margins for credit providers tend to be higher than those of noncredit providers. Similarly, the prices and gross profit margins of companies that provide liberal credit terms tend to be higher than those of less liberal credit providers. However, firms that offer credit must absorb costs which noncredit firms do not have to, such as the costs of a credit department which screens credit applicants and bills and processes payments. There are also collection costs associated with non-payers and slow payers, as well as bad-debt losses. Finally, there are costs of financing the credit extended, since accounts receivable, like all other assets of the company, must be financed.

Because of the close relationship between a firm's credit policies and its sales level, the firm's marketing management has a strong interest in how credit policies are set. Unless carefully developed, these policies can generate friction between the marketing and financial groups. This is due to the fact that the marketing manager is primarily responsible for generating sales and is typically evaluated on his or her ability to do so. Thus, the marketing manager would prefer liberal credit policies, particularly if the demand for the company's products is weak. However, to the financial manager, maximizing sales is not an end in itself but only a means to a broader aim: maximizing the value of the firm. Thus, if the costs associated with extending credit exceed the benefits of increased sales (i.e., gross profits), the credit should not be extended even if the sale is lost. Such decisions can clearly lead to disagreement between the marketing and financial managers. Yet much of this disagreement can be avoided if both managers collaborate in setting credit policies.

• Objectives and Organization of this Chapter

The primary objective of this chapter is to illustrate the importance of credit management to the firm's financial well-being (i.e., its risk-return profile). To do this, the chapter first defines the scope of credit management in terms of the credit policies that must be established. It then demonstrates how the financial manager should evaluate these credit policies from the perspective of risk and return. Next, it describes methods for implementing and administering the firm's credit policies.

SCOPE OF CREDIT MANAGEMENT

credit standards

credit terms

collection policies

A firm's credit management encompasses three distinct policies. Policies with respect to *credit standards* determine who shall be eligible for credit. For example, the firm may decide that only customers with impeccable credit records will be extended credit. Policies governing *credit terms* determine the conditions on which credit will be extended. For example, the firm may decide to extend credit terms of "net 60 days," meaning that the full amount of the invoice must be paid in 60 days or sooner. *Collection policies* determine how aggressively the firm should pursue nonpayers or late payers. For example, the firm may decide that any bill more than three months overdue will be turned over to a collection agency.

Risk-Return Considerations

Each credit policy or proposed change in credit policy must be carefully evaluated with regard to the risks and benefits that will flow from it. For example, liberal credit standards will result in higher risks of bad debts and unusually high collection and financing costs. Unless the increased profits generated by such credit standards exceed the costs, the firm's stock price will suffer. Alternatively, if the firm's credit terms are set too stringently, as in requiring payment within 30 days while competitors extend 60-day terms, this will result in reduced sales and profits along with the reduced costs and risks of credit. Unless the savings from reduced credit costs exceed the profits lost, the firm's economic value will be reduced. Finally, collection policies that are too lenient may produce benefits in the form of good will, increased sales, and increased profits; but they will also increase the risks and costs of the credit program. Again, a financial manager must weigh the benefits against the costs that will result from the firm's collection policies in order to maximize the economic value of the firm.

Dynamic Considerations

A financial manager's role in the management of accounts receivable is dynamic in that it involves frequent adjustment of credit standards, credit terms, and collection policies in conjunction with changing economic conditions. Ideally, credit policies should be managed so that the firm's sales match production capacity so long as "marginal" accounts add to firm profitability. Credit policies often need to be relaxed to stimulate sales when the economy is in a downturn and the firm has excess capacity. When the economy is expanding rapidly and the firm is operating at full capacity, financial managers might move to tighten credit policies (particularly if additional sales demand is being projected). Thus, appropriate credit policies change with the level of economic activity over time.

Other Considerations

In establishing or altering credit policies, financial managers must be careful to consider all important consequences. For example, a change in credit policy that is intended to attract new customers might well change the credit behavior of existing customers, resulting in substantially increased costs and other undesired effects. Similarly, a change in credit policy designed to attract new customers may provoke a comparable response from competitors, thus resulting in none of the expected benefits while incurring all of the expected costs. Finally, a change in credit policy may have important undesirable effects on company operations. For example, a change in credit policy to stimulate sales may require substantial revision of production schedules and inventory levels as well as of production and distribution capacities. If any of these considerations are not properly addressed in strategic planning, credit policies that look good on paper may turn out to be very unsuccessful.

CREDIT STANDARDS

At any time, the firm has available a pool of potential customers to which credit sales could be made. Within this pool there are undoubtedly many credit risks. The financial manager's responsibility is to decide to which groups the firm should extend credit. This is done by setting credit standards for the firm.

In selecting its credit standards, the firm must weigh costs against expected benefits. When a firm relaxes credit standards, the expected benefits are in the form of higher sales and profits. The expected costs are in the forms of higher financing costs resulting from greater investment in receivables and possibly higher costs for the credit-department, collection, and bad-debt expenses. Conversely, when a firm tightens credit standards, less credit is extended. In this case, the benefits are in the forms of reduced financing costs (because accounts receivable are lower) and possibly lower costs for the credit department, collection, and bad debt expenses. However, in such cases, the firm expects sales and profits to be lower.

Example

Relaxing Credit Standards

The Ace Company currently has annual sales of $600,000, all of which are made on credit terms of "net 30" days. Since all customers pay on time, Ace's average collection period is 30 days.[1] By multiplying its average collection period (ACP) times annual credit sales per day (SPD), Ace's accounts receivable balance of $50,000 can be determined, as shown below:

$$\text{Accounts receivable} = \text{ACP} \times \text{SPD}$$

$$= 30 \text{ days} \times \$600,000/360$$

$$= \$50,000$$

Ace's bad-debt loss on its current credit standards averages 1 percent of credit sales. Variable costs are 75 percent of sales, and the company's required rate of return from its investment in accounts receivable is 20 percent before taxes.

Due to weak sales demand, the company is considering a reduction in its credit standards to extend credit to an entirely different market segment. The marketing manager believes annual sales from this new group could total $36,000 per year. However, the group will tend to pay much more slowly than current customers. Thus, even with the same credit terms of "net 30 days," the average collection period will be substantially longer, perhaps as long as 60 days. In addition, bad debt expense of the new group will be 2 percent of credit sales. Should management adopt the proposal?

Given an average collection period of 60 days and sales per day of $100 ($36,000/360), the firm's accounts receivable will increase by $6,000, as shown below:

$$\Delta \text{ Accounts receivable} = \text{ACP} \times \Delta \text{ SPD}$$

$$= 60 \text{ days} \times \$100$$

$$= \$6,000$$

The calculation of incremental costs and benefits from the proposed change in credit standards is shown in Table 11-1.

Incremental Benefits. Incremental benefits are equal to the increased sales of $36,000 times the contribution margin percentage (i.e., 1 − variable cost percentage) of 25 percent, which increases profits by $9,000.

---

[1] Unless cash discounts are offered, very few, if any, firms would pay their credit bills early (this is because it is very costly to pay prior to due dates, as will be shown in Chapter 13). In contrast, some credit customers (particularly those of lower credit quality) will undoubtedly pay after due dates. Thus, in actual practice a firm's average collection period is likely to be longer than the firm's net period selling terms unless discounts are offered. For illustration purposes, we are assuming that the Ace Company's net credit period and average collection period are the same.

TABLE 11-1   Incremental Evaluation of Relaxed Credit Standards

Incremental Benefits		
1. Increase in sales	$36,000	
2. Increase in profits before taxes (1-Variable cost %) × (line 1)		$ 9,000
Incremental costs		
3. Increase in A/R (Increase in sales per day × ACP)	6,000	
4. Increase in accounts receivable investment (line 3 × variable cost %)	4,500	
5. Incremental financing costs (Line 4 × opportunity cost)		900
6. Incremental bad debt losses (Line 1 × bad debt %)		720
7. Net incremental benefit (Line 2 − line 5 and 6)		$7,380

Incremental Financing Cost.   As noted, the proposed credit change will increase accounts receivable by $6,000. However, the firm's incremental investment will only be the variable cost, or "out-of-pocket" cost of producing these receivables.[2] Since variable costs are 75 percent of sales, the increased investment in accounts receivable will be $4,500. Assuming a required rate of return of 20 percent from its accounts receivable investment, the increased financing cost will be $900.

Incremental Bad Debt Losses.   Bad debt expense will be 2 percent of the credit sales to the new group. Since current customers are not affected by the relaxing of credit standards, bad-debt expense from sales to current customers is not affected. Thus, the incremental bad debt expense is 2 percent of the incremental sales of $36,000, or $720.

Net Incremental Benefits.   Since profits before taxes will increase by $9,000 while costs will only increase by $1,620 (i.e., $900 plus $720), the change in credit standards will produce a net increase in profits before taxes of $7,380. The proposal should be adopted.

---

[2]Some authors argue that an opportunity cost should be applied to accounts receivable at their sales values (which includes both the cost of the products sold plus the profit in the sale). For further discussion of the opportunity cost versus explicit cost approaches, see Edward A. Dyl. "Another Look at the Evaluation of Investment in Accounts Receivable"; Joseph C. Atkins and Yong H. Kim. "Comment and Correction: Opportunity Cost in the Evaluation of Investment in Accounts Receivable"; and Tirlochan S. Walia. "Explicit and Implicit Cost of Changes in the Level of Accounts Receivable." All in *Financial Management,* Winter 1977, pp. 67–78.

CREDIT TERMS

Credit terms specify the conditions on which credit is extended. These conditions typically involve three factors: the length of the credit period; the amount of discount, if any, for early payment; and, the length of the discount period. Of course, a package of credit terms may incorporate many combinations of these factors. For example, companies that want to accelerate cash inflows from credit sales will offer bigger discounts for early payment. Naturally, such discounts reduce the profitability of sales. Alternatively, a company may offer a small discount for early payment but offer a longer discount period.

Example

The Jones Company sells to the Arendt Company $100,000 worth of aluminum sheathing on terms of "1/15, n45." According to the credit terms, the Arendt Company has the choice of paying the full $100,000 in 45 days (the net credit period) or paying within 15 days (the discount period) and taking a 1 percent discount (i.e., $1,000) off the invoice. In other words, if the Arendt Company pays within the discount period, it will send a check for $99,000, otherwise it must pay the full $100,000.

Although the length of the credit period and the size of the cash discount are frequently set by the customs of an industry, there is no reason to follow custom blindly. For example, by increasing the cash discount, a company might possibly shorten the collection period and attract new customers. Offsetting these advantages is the higher discount on invoices — a cash loss on existing as well as new accounts. Again, the decision should rest on a comparison of the expected incremental benefits and costs.

Example

Increasing the Discount

The Bennett Company currently has annual sales of $15,000,000. All sales are made on credit terms of net 60 days. On the average, Bennett's customers pay on time, so that the company's average collection period is also 60 days. With an average collection period of 60 days and sales per day of $41,667 ($15,000,000/360), Bennett's average accounts receivable balance is $2,500,000, as shown below:

$$\text{Accounts receivable} = \text{ACP} \times \text{SPD}$$

$$= 60 \times \$41,667$$

$$= \$2,500,000$$

In response to competition from a foreign manufacturer, the firm is considering offering a cash discount of 2 percent for payments made within 10 days of the invoice date (i.e., 2/10, n60). If the discount is offered, the financial manager expects that existing customers, accounting for half of the company's credit sales, will take the discount. The remaining half will continue to pay in 60 days. If so, the company's average collection period will drop to 35 days. The reduction in accounts receivable will save the company financing costs of 20 percent before taxes. Table 11-2 shows how the incremental benefits and costs from the proposed change in credit terms may be evaluated.

TABLE 11-2   Incremental Analysis of Increasing Discount

Incremental Benefits

1. Current level of accounts receivable (SPD × ACP)	$2,500,000	
2. New level of accounts receivable (SPD × New ACP)	1,458,333	
3. Reduction in accounts receivable investment	$1,041,667	
4. Savings of accounts receivable financing costs (line 3 × opportunity cost of funds)		$208,333
Incremental Costs		
5. Discounts granted (.02 × .50 × $15,000,000)		150,000
6. Net Incremental Benefits (line 4 minus 5)		$58,333

Incremental Benefits.   In this case, the proposed change in credit terms is not expected to increase sales but, rather, to decrease the level of accounts receivable being carried by the firm. Thus, the incremental benefits from the change will come from a reduction in financing costs. The firm currently has accounts receivable of $2,500,000. If the discount offer reduces the average collection period to 35 days, accounts receivable will drop to $1,458,333, a reduction of $1,041,667. The financing costs saved will total $208,333.

Incremental Costs.   The incremental cost of the discount offer will be equal to the discount times the portion of credit sales on which the discount will be taken. Given the discount of 2 percent and the assumption that half of all sales will be discounted, the incremental cost of the policy change will be $150,000.

Incremental Net Benefit.   Since the incremental benefits of $208,333 exceed the incremental costs of $150,000, the discount proposal seems desirable.

Lengthening the Credit Period.

Instead of changing its discount terms, the Bennett Company is considering lengthening its credit period from net 60 days to net 70 days. If the company does this, it expects to attract more customers and expects sales to increase by $600,000 annually. The company's variable costs average 85 percent of sales and, thus the contribution margin on sales is 15 percent. In this case, the firm will have to offer the same credit terms to its existing customers. Existing customers will slow down their payments to take advantage of the 70-day terms and, as a consequence, the accounts receivable balance from existing sales will increase. Of course any new sales generated by the proposed policy will also result in more receivables. The increase in receivables investment, in turn, will result in increased financing costs. Bennett's financial manager does not expect any increases in other credit costs such as billing, collections, or bad debts. The comparison of incremental benefits and costs is shown in Table 11-3.

TABLE 11-3   Incremental Analysis of Lengthening Credit Period

Incremental Benefits		
1. Incremental sales	$600,000	
2. Incremental profits		$90,000
Incremental Costs		
3. Incremental A/R from existing sales	416,667	
4. Incremental A/R investment from existing sales		416,667
5. Incremental A/R from new sales	116,667	
6. Incremental A/R investment from new sales		99,167
7. Total incremental A/R investment		515,834
8. Incremental A/R financing costs		103,167
Net Incremental Benefits		(13,167)

Incremental Benefits.   The expected incremental profits ($90,000) are calculated by multiplying the incremental sales ($600,000) by the contribution margin (15 percent).

Incremental Costs.   The incremental costs are the costs of financing the increased receivables investment. In calculating the increased receivables investment, it is necessary to distinguish between receivables generated from existing sales and receivables generated from new sales. As shown in Table 11-3, the receivables from existing sales will increase by $416,667. All of this increase, since it comes from existing sales, is considered part of the incremental investment in receivables. The new sales will generate another $116,667 in accounts receivable. However, only the variable-cost portion (.85 × $116,667 = $99,167) of these receivables is treated as incremental investment. The rationale is that existing sales cover fixed costs and that incremental sales only need to cover incremental variable costs.

Thus, the total incremental investment in receivables is equal to the $416,667 from existing sales plus $99,167 from new sales, or, $515,834. The increased financing costs will be $103,167.

Net Incremental Benefits. In this case, the incremental costs ($103,167) will exceed the incremental benefits ($90,000) by $13,167. Thus the change in credit period should not be adopted.

COLLECTION POLICIES

In addition to establishing policies concerning the setting of credit standards and terms, the firm must develop collection policies and procedures for handling accounts receivable when they become overdue. For example, if a firm sells on "net 60-day" terms, what should it do if a bill has not been paid by the 61st day? Collection policies, like other credit policies, may be restrictive or lenient, depending on how they are enforced. By monitoring accounts receivable over time, the credit manager can develop an idea of the effectiveness of his or her collection efforts. Financial software is available that keeps track of this type of information.

Collection policies should be based on the principle of not throwing good money after bad. As an illustration, suppose a firm is owed $1,000 by FlyByNight Furniture Company. Assume that, without any collection effort, the probability of collecting the amout owed is 0.05, but that, with collection effort, the probability will rise to 0.15. The expected increase in the amount collected through the added effort is $100, [(.15 − .05) × $1,000]. Clearly, it would not be worthwhile to spend more than $100 to attempt to collect the account. Even that is a maximum amount, since that would be spending the $100 currently to receive a payment that will, at best, be delayed. Firms offering consumer credit have also developed scoring systems based on characteristics of their debtors and their payment records. These systems help them determine how much collection effort to spend on delinquent accounts.

Collection Techniques and Efforts

A variety of collection techniques can be used to improve collection of past-due accounts. Letters and telephone calls are the least expensive forms of collection techniques. For example, a business might sell on "net 60-day" terms. When an account becomes 10 days overdue, the credit department might send a polite letter reminding the customer that the account is overdue. At 90 days, or even before, the credit manager might follow with a strong letter demanding payment and/or a telephone call, possibly by an attorney. Depending on the amount owed, it might be worthwhile for a salesperson to call on the customer in the hope that the personal visit might encourage payment.

After 120 days or so, it is becoming more common for firms to turn over delinquent accounts to commercial collection agencies. Dun & Bradstreet operates the largest of about 80 commercial collection firms. These so-called "dunning" firms charge 20 to 25 percent of the amount they collect on past-due accounts as their fee. It is interesting to note that, while such collectors are under pressure to collect past-due accounts, they also must do it diplomatically so as to not create ill will. Formal legal action is usually a last resort undertaken to attempt to collect past-due accounts.

Past-due accounts may be declared bad debts at the time they are turned over to a commercial collection firm, or when legal action is taken. Then if a portion of such accounts is ultimately collected, the bad-debt write-offs are adjusted accordingly.

Credit Insurance

Credit insurance is designed to protect manufacturers, wholesalers, and other types of businesses from unexpected credit losses. If a bank extends a loan secured by accounts receivable, it may require that the borrower insure those accounts and name the bank as beneficiary.

primary loss

Because selling prices should be adequate to cover normal credit losses, credit insurance is not designed to protect against that normal, or *primary loss*. Since it is virtually certain that a given percentage of sales on credit will prove to be uncollectible, a firm cannot obtain insurance against this loss. Thus, if the experience of the industry and the firm's experience indicate that credit losses will normally amount to 1 percent of sales, this amount is established by the credit insurance company as the primary loss. Should that be, say, $11,000, the contract with the insurance company would specify that the firm must bear the first $11,000 of total credit losses during the year.

coinsurance

With respect to the transfer of abnormal credit losses to the insurance company, there are two limiting features. To prevent the reckless granting of credit, the insurance company will require that the firm participate in 10 to 20 percent of the net loss suffered, depending upon the risk involved. This is called *coinsurance*. Second, the insurance company will also limit its coverage on individual accounts to an amount related to the credit rating of the customer at the time of shipment. For example, the credit insurance company may limit its coverage to $10,000 on each of the accounts receivable with a D & B rating of "EE2" (a low rating) at time of shipment.

Example

391

CHAPTER 11
ACCOUNTS RECEIVABLE
MANAGEMENT

Assume that the primary loss is $11,000; and losses and coverage on three accounts were as follows:

	A	B	C	Total
Coverage	$10,000	$5,000	$2,500	$17,500
Loss	8,000	7,000	2,000	17,000

With these limits the amount of loss admitted (i.e., allowed by the insurance company) on these accounts would be as follows:

A	$8,000
B	5,000
C	2,000
	$15,000

Notice that for account B, even though the loss was $7,000, only $5,000 was covered and thus the admitted loss is only $5,000. If the coinsurance were 10 percent, $1,500 would be deducted from the $15,000, leaving $13,500. Since the primary loss of $11,000 would be deducted from this amount the firm would collect $2,500 from the insurance company:

Total loss	$15,000
− coinsurance (10%)	1,500
− primary loss	$11,000
Due from insurance company	$ 2,500

The desirability of credit insurance depends upon an individual company's circumstances. When sales are largely to uninsurable risks, credit insurance may be unavailable or overly expensive. To sell only to insurable accounts or only within the limits provided on insurable accounts may mean an uneconomical restriction of credit sales. If accounts are widely diversified and the company soundly financed, some financial managers may not use credit insurance, although premiums are smaller when the risk is smaller. However, if the company is not in a strong financial position or is selling a relatively few large accounts, credit insurance may be especially desirable. To put it another way, the greater the risk that failure of a few important accounts could cause financial downfall, the more attractive is credit insurance.

CREDIT ADMINISTRATION

credit analysis

Once credit policies are in place, the firm must establish procedures for evaluating credit applicants and monitoring accounts to insure that payments are made on time. *Credit analysis* is performed to determine the eligibility of credit applicants. This evaluation may take many forms, depending primarily on the amount of credit being requested. Generally, the greater the amount of credit requested, the more detailed the credit analysis. Once credit has been granted, *monitoring* accounts receivable balances becomes of critical importance. For example, the firm must know as soon as possible whether a particular credit customer has "turned bad" in order to restrict future credit and minimize possible losses. Likewise, slow payers increase the costs of financing credit and, possibly, make otherwise profitable credit policies unprofitable. The following sections discuss how the firm can undertake credit analysis and the methods that can be used to monitor accounts receivable.

monitoring

CREDIT ANALYSIS

Credit analysis traditionally involves the "five Cs" of credit:

- Character
- Capacity
- Capital
- Conditions
- Collateral

character

The analysis begins with *character,* which is an assessment of the willingness to pay credit bills. In the case of credit sales made to business firms, this involves judging the willingness of the firm's management to pay its bills, since one company's accounts receivable are, of course, another's accounts payable. *Capacity* represents the ability of the firm to meet its accounts payable obligations out of operations. Here financial managers are interested primarily in the credit customer's liquidity ratios and cash flows (as noted in Chapter 7). It also is important to assess the credit customer's *capital* in the event the customer has difficulty in meeting credit obligations. Debt to assets and other ratios that indicate the customer's net worth or equity position are analyzed in evaluating capital.

capacity

capital

Two additional factors sometimes play an important role when conducting credit analysis. As might be expected, *conditions* that exist and are

conditions

expected in terms of economic activity may be very important when investigating credit applicants. Bad debts increase and more firms fail during recessions than when the economy is booming, making it important for financial managers to be aware of economic conditions when conducting credit analyses. However, something of a paradox exists in that financial managers might be inclined to lower credit standards (that is, accept lower-quality credit customers) during economic downturns in order to maintain sales volume. *Collateral* in the form of assets pledged as security by the credit customer behind extended credit represents the fifth "C" in credit analysis.

collateral

Financial statements and other information are necessary for financial managers to conduct credit analysis adequately. Time and cost are two factors that limit the extent of a financial manager's search for credit information. Within limits, the more that is spent, the more information that is obtained, although there is probably a diminishing marginal return from such expenditures. Also, it takes time to gather more information, and credit decisions must usually be made promptly. Thus, there comes a point when the incremental costs of credit investigation and analysis exceed the possible reduction in credit losses.

Discriminant Analysis

Creditors who deal with large numbers of relatively small accounts cannot afford the time or expense of evaluating each applicant in detail. Such creditors may base most of their credit decisions on computerized methods such as *credit scoring* systems. By applying a statistical method known as discriminant analysis to the credit histories of the company's customers, creditors identify the most important characteristics of debtors (such as annual income, length of employment, or profession) that seem to distinguish good accounts from bad accounts. The common credit card application form, usually no more than a page in length, is an example of credit scoring based on discriminant analysis. The most important characteristics are then given weights, or *points,* by a statistical model, which can then be applied to new applicants for credit. For example, in the case of consumer credit, an applicant may receive eight points for having been with his or her current employer for one to three years, but 13 points for having been employed three to six years, and so on. The sum of these points yields a credit score. If the score is high enough, credit is granted; if the score is too low, the applicant is rejected. The accept/reject cut-off scores are determined by the firm's credit standards. Typically, there is a "gray-area" score between immediate acceptance and rejection. Applicants whose scores fall in the gray area are reviewed by a skilled credit analyst who may order a credit report on the applicant. Using this or other information, the analyst decides whether credit should be extended.

credit scoring

Sources of Credit Information

Many sources of information are available from credit reporting organizations to assist in making credit analysis decisions. Their use will depend upon the nature of the business, amount of credit involved, and credit investigation costs.

Dun & Bradstreet, Inc.   Among D&B's many services, two are of primary importance to the credit manager, the *Reference Book* and written *credit reports*. Close to three million business firms of all types are listed alphabetically according to state and town in the Reference Book.

Exhibit 11-1 shows an excerpt from the Dun & Bradstreet Reference Book along with a key to the D&B ratings.

Notice the reference to Beaumont & Hunt, Inc. The numbers to the left of the name in the Reference Book indicate the firm's industry. To the right of the firm name is the three-character D&B rating, where the letters indicate the firm's estimated financial strength (as measured by net worth) and the number indicates the composite credit appraisal. The highest credit rating is denoted "1." Other ratings include good, fair, and limited.

Should a financial manager desire additional information, he or she could order a D&B credit report, such as the one shown in Exhibit 11-2 for the Beaumont & Hunt firm.

Notice that the report contains credit payment records and financial statement information. Although not shown, the second page of the report would include a brief history of the firm and its operations plus information concerning the firm's relations with its banker.

National Credit Interchange System.   The National Association of Credit Management sponsors a national network of credit information, which is available to firms conducting credit analysis. This network is known as the National Credit Interchange System, and it receives accounts receivable data containing customer payment information from major U.S. business firms. Such trade experience records are gathered on a quarterly basis and are immediately made available to National Association of Credit Management members via computer terminals. Trade credit analysis has been enhanced tremendously by the development of a national credit information network.

Specialized Credit-Reporting Agencies.   Some credit-reporting agencies specialize in credit information for specific industries. For example, industry or trade associations often collect and distribute credit information on credit customers to their members. Such information also may be made available to firms operating in other industries on a reciprocal exchange-of-information basis.

Bank Credit Data.   A bank may provide valuable credit information. For example, if a company was located in Chicago, it could request its bank

Key to Ratings

ESTIMATED FINANCIAL STRENGTH		COMPOSITE CREDIT APPRAISAL			
		HIGH	GOOD	FAIR	LIMITED
5A	$50,000,000 and over	1	2	3	4
4A	$10,000,000 to 49,999,999	1	2	3	4
3A	1,000,000 to 9,999,999	1	2	3	4
2A	750,000 to 999,999	1	2	3	4
1A	500,000 to 749,999	1	2	3	4
BA	300,000 to 499,999	1	2	3	4
BB	200,000 to 299,999	1	2	3	4
CB	125,000 to 199,999	1	2	3	4
CC	75,000 to 124,999	1	2	3	4
DC	50,000 to 74,999	1	2	3	4
DD	35,000 to 49,999	1	2	3	4
EE	20,000 to 34,999	1	2	3	4
FF	10,000 to 19,999	1	2	3	4
GG	5,000 to 9,999	1	2	3	4
HH	Up to 4,999	1	2	3	4

GENERAL CLASSIFICATION

ESTIMATED FINANCIAL STRENGTH		COMPOSITE CREDIT APPRAISAL		
		GOOD	FAIR	LIMITED
1R	$125,000 and over	2	3	4
2R	$50,000 to $124,999	2	3	4

EXPLANATION

When the designation "1R" or "2R" appears, followed by a 2, 3 or 4, it is an indication that the Estimated Financial Strength, while not definitely classified, is presumed to be in the range of the ($) figures in the corresponding bracket, and while the Composite Credit Appraisal cannot be judged precisely, it is believed to fall in the general category indicated.

"INV." shown in place of a rating indicates that the report was under investigation at the time of going to press. It has no other significance.

"FB" (Foreign Branch). Indicates that the headquarters of this company is located in a foreign country (including Canada). The written report contains the location of the headquarters.

ABSENCE OF RATING, expressed by two hyphens (--), is not to be construed as unfavorable but signifies circumstances difficult to classify within condensed rating symbols. It suggests the advisability of obtaining a report for additional information.

EMPLOYEE RANGE DESIGNATIONS IN REPORTS ON NAMES NOT LISTED IN THE REFERENCE BOOK

	KEY TO EMPLOYEE RANGE DESIGNATIONS		
Certain businesses do not lend themselves to a Dun & Bradstreet rating and are not listed in the Reference Book. Information on these names, however, continues to be stored and updated in the D&B Business Information File. Reports are available on such businesses and instead of a rating they carry an Employee Range Designation (ER) which is indicative of size in terms of number of employees. No other significance should be attached.	ER 1	1000 or more	Employees
	ER 2	500 - 999	Employees
	ER 3	100 - 499	Employees
	ER 4	50 - 99	Employees
	ER 5	20 - 49	Employees
	ER 6	10 - 19	Employees
	ER 7	5 - 9	Employees
	ER 8	1 - 4	Employees
	ER N		Not Available

38	Am...stone		
17 61	Asendorf Tin Shop		FF2
76 22	Austen Wes TV Service		EE2
55 41	Backers Service Station		HH2
57 12	Barber Furniture Co Inc		CC1
50 13	Beasleys Automotive	0	FF4
53 11	Beaumont & Hunt, Inc.		BB1
59 41	Bedlans Sporting Goods		DC3
51 91	Bervin Distrg Inc of Beatrice		– –
51 91	Bervin Distributing Inc		CC2
15 21	Blackwell Trenching Service		DD2
15 21	Boeckner Brothers Inc		DC2
54	Boogaarts Fairbury Inc		

EXHIBIT 11-1
Excerpt from a Dun &
Bradstreet Reference
Book and the Key to Its
Rating System

to ask one of its correspondent banks in New York state to check on the credit standing of a customer located there. Although it would obviously not do this for a $100 order, it might very well do so for a large, important order. Bank credit information is especially useful if a firm wishes a particular question answered, such as whether or not the customer has pledged inventory or receivables to secure a loan.

Financial Statements. While financial statements are usually available in the credit reports of Dun and Bradstreet and similar sources, a firm may desire more detailed or more recent information. Often the credit applicant

EXHIBIT 11-2   Example of a Dun & Bradstreet
Consolidated Report

© *Dun & Bradstreet, Inc.*

This report has been prepared for:

**BE SURE NAME, BUSINESS AND
ADDRESS MATCH YOUR FILE**

**ANSWERING
INQUIRY**

SUBSCRIBER: 008-001042

THIS REPORT MAY NOT BE REPRODUCED IN WHOLE OR IN PART IN ANY MANNER WHATEVER

CONSOLIDATED REPORT

DUNS: 00-647-3261	DATE PRINTED	SUMMARY
BEAUMONT & HUNT, INC.	OCT 15, 197-	RATING BB1
120 LEMOINE AVE.	DEPARTMENT STORE	STARTED 1956
AUGUSTA, GA. 30901		PAYMENTS DISC-PPT
TEL 404 872-9664	SIC NOS.	SALES $1,600,000
	53 11	WORTH $261,791
DANIEL T. BEAUMONT, PRES.		EMPLOYS 20
		HISTORY CLEAR
		CONDITION STRONG
		TREND UP

SPECIAL EVENTS
09/10/7-   Kevin Hunt, Sec/Treas, reported a $3,000 merchandise
            loss in Sept 8 burglary. Loss is fully insured.

PAYMENTS   {Amounts may be rounded to nearest figure in prescribed ranges}

REPORTED	PAYING RECORD	HIGH CREDIT	NOW OWES	PAST DUE	SELLING TERMS	LAST SALE WITHIN
09/7-	Disc	17000	6000	-0-	2 10 30	1 mo.
08/7-	Ppt	6800	300	-0-	30	2 mos.
	Ppt	5000	2500	-0-	30	1 mo.
07/7-	Disc	12000	2500	-0-	30	2-3 mos.
	Ppt	2500	1000	-0-	30	2-3 mos.
	Ppt	1000	-0-	-0-	EOM	2-3 mos.
02/7-	Disc	10000	500	-0-	2 10 30	1 mo.
	Ppt	3000	500	-0-	2 10 30	1 mo.
	Ppt	1500	-0-	-0-	30	2-3 mos.

CHANGES
05/17/7-   Subject recently expanded its line of merchandise with the
            addition of sporting goods.

UPDATE
08/10/7-   Aug 10, 197-, Beaumont, Pres. said nine months sales through
            July 31 were up 10%, profits rising. Concern now employs 20.

FINANCE
02/15/7-   Fiscal statement dated October 31, 197-.

Cash	$ 75,000		Accts Pay	$ 140,510
Accts Rec.	110,746		Accruals	48,636
Inventory	285,465		Fed. & other taxes	26,714
Prepaid	1,240			
	----------			----------
Current	472,451		Current	215,860
Fixt & Equip	5,200		Capital Stock	50,000
			Retained Earnings	211,791
	----------			----------
Total	477,651		Total	477,651

            Annual sales $1,600,000; net income $48,000; monthly rent
        $2,500. Lease expires 198-. Fire insurance on mdse & fixt $300,000.
        {Above figures from statement provided by Accountant: Fred Mitchell,
        Augusta, Ga. Prepared from books without audit.}
                                    {CONTINUED}

Source: Reports—Reference Books, Dun & Bradstreet, Inc.

is asked directly for a current balance sheet and income statement. Some credit managers refuse credit to any concern that does not provide its financial statements upon request.

Other Sources of Information.   If the expected value of the information warrants the added time and expense, additional insights may also be obtained by personal interviews and visits by a firm's salespeople to the credit applicant. Occasionally, information may also be sought from trade associations, better business bureaus, chambers of commerce, attorneys, and credit references. Collection experience with a given customer is an especially valuable basis for reassessing creditworthiness. In a sense, each grant of credit is a means of buying information about a customer's payment habits. With each timely collection, the probability of the customer's continuing to be an acceptable credit risk is greater.

Retail concerns are involved not with trade credit, but with consumer credit. This form of credit includes direct loans to consumers extended by financial institutions such as commercial banks and personal finance companies, as well as credit extended to individuals for the purchase of consumer goods. Because the amounts involved are frequently small, costs of investigation must be limited. The growth of regional and national credit agencies providing consumers' credit records from computers has been a logical accompaniment to the rapid growth of consumer credit. If the amount involved is fairly large, a firm might also check with the customer's bank to obtain a general idea of the size of her or his deposit balances or whether the relationships with the bank have been satisfactory.

MONITORING ACCOUNTS RECEIVABLE

After the financial manager has set up acceptable credit standards and credit terms, attention then focuses on the performance of the collection effort. The financial manager must set acceptable average collection periods (ACP) or, equivalently, days sales outstanding (DSO) levels, as well as acceptable ratios of bad debt to credit sales. Of course, if credit standards or terms are changed, it should be recognized that collection policy "targets" also need to be changed. Otherwise, the collection department might be unduly penalized because other credit policies were changed. For example, if a firm started to sell to a lower-quality group of credit customers, it would expect the average collection period to increase and bad debts and collection costs to rise. This should be reflected in collection policy expectations.

Two frequently used methods for monitoring collection patterns associated with credit sales and resulting accounts receivable are *changes in days sales outstanding,* (or average collection period) *levels,* and *changes in the accounts receivable aging schedule.*[3]

Days Sales Outstanding (DSO) Method

To calculate the number of days credit sales are outstanding, on average, divide the accounts receivable balance at some point in time by credit sales per day. In Chapter 7, where this procedure was explained, we concentrated on ratios calculated on an annual basis. In contrast, when monitoring accounts receivable collection patterns, it is necessary to consider quarterly or even monthly time periods so as to be able to observe possible changes. The aging schedule, as we will see, can also be used for shorter time intervals.

accounts receivable aging schedule

Assume that one is interested in monitoring the accounts receivable balances arising from credit sales made by the Seaside Seasonal Sales Company, using the DSO method. Since the firm's management has not altered credit standards or credit terms, the focus is on collection performance. For purposes of illustration, Table 11-4 shows monthly credit sales and accounts receivable dollar amounts outstanding at the end of each of three calendar quarters for Seaside. Monthly credit sales were level for the first quarter, rose during the second quarter, and declined during the third quarter — although credit sales for each quarter amounted to $180,000. Also note that the end-of-quarter dollar amounts of receivables were: $78,000, $102,000, and $54,000, respectively. Should Seaside be concerned about possible collection problems?

Traditional receivables analysis might begin by focusing on possible changes in days sales outstanding. When monthly sales are level, the DSO will be the same whether it is based on a monthly (30-day) period or a quarterly (90-day) period. For example, if sales per day are based on credit sales for March, they are $2,000 ($60,000/30 days). Likewise, sales per day for the first quarter are $2,000 ($180,000/90 days). And since the receivables outstanding at the end of March is $78,000, the days sales outstanding will be 39 days under both sales period calculations.

However, when DSOs are calculated as of the end of June, the DSO based on credit sales of $90,000 in June falls to 34 days, while the 90-day based DSO rises to 51 days. Thus, one DSO calculation suggests that the collection pattern has worsened while the other suggests an improvement. DSO calculations made at the end of September show just the opposite pattern, with DSOs of 54 days and 27 days, respectively. Clearly both DSO calculations provide misleading signals about receivable collection patterns. This is known because receivables outstanding at the end of each

---

[3]A survey of 150 firms indicated that the days sales outstanding measure often was used to forecast receivables, while the aging schedule provided the primary basis for monitoring or controlling receivables. See Bernell K. Stone. "The Payments-Pattern Approach to the Forecasting and Control of Accounts Receivable." *Financial Management,* Autumn 1976, pp. 70–71.

TABLE 11-4 Traditional Methods for Monitoring Accounts Receivable for Seaside Seasonal Sales Company

					DSO Based on Sales, Period of:	
	Credit Sales	Dollar Amount	Percent of Sales	Percent of Total	30 days	90 days
Month	(1)	(2)	(3)	(4)	(5)	(6)
Jan.	$60,000	$ 6,000	10%	7.7%		
Feb.	60,000	18,000	30	23.1		
Mar.	60,000	54,000	90	69.2		
End of 1st Q.		$ 78,000		100.0%	39.0 days	39.0 days
April	30,000	3,000	10%	2.9%		
May	60,000	18,000	30	17.7		
June	90,000	81,000	90	79.4		
End of 2nd Q.		$102,000		100.0%	34.0 days	51.0 days
July	90,000	9,000	10%	16.7%		
Aug.	60,000	18,000	30	33.3%		
Sept.	30,000	27,000	90	50.0		
End of 3rd Q.		$54,000		100.0%	54.0 days	27.0 days

Receivables Outstanding at End of Quarter

quarter reflect the same percentage of previous monthly credit sales, as shown in Column 3 of Table 11-4. Thus one is observing in the changing DSOs the impact of changes in credit sales patterns, and not changes in collection patterns.

Aging Schedule Method

The use of the accounts receivable aging schedule method for monitoring receivables also can provide misleading signals, given certain conditions. Column 4 in Table 11-4 provides an aging schedule as of the end of each quarter. An alternative way of expressing the aging schedule as of the end of March would be:

Period Outstanding	Accounts Receivable Outstanding	Percent of Total Receivables
60 to 90 days	$ 6,000	7.7%
30 to 60 days	18,000	23.1
0 to 30 days	54,000	69.2
Totals	$78,000	100.0%

This means that 69.2 percent of the $78,000 in receivables outstanding at the end of March are less than 30 days old, 23.1 percent are 30 to 60 days old, and 7.7 percent are 60 to 90 days old. Seaside might have a policy of writing off any account as a bad debt when it becomes outstanding more than 90 days. Such bad debts, of course, would not show up in an aging schedule and thus would have to be monitored separately as a percentage of credit sales.

Column 4 of Table 11-4 shows what seems to be an improved collection pattern at the end of June, because accounts receivable are more current (i.e., 17.7 percent are 30 to 60 days old and only 2.9 percent are 60 to 90 days old). In contrast, the aging schedule prepared at the end of September suggests a worsening collection pattern. These misleading signals are, as was the case for the DSO method, due to changing credit sales patterns. Thus, in the event that a firm is characterized by: (1) a pattern of *seasonal credit sales*, or (2) a significant *credit sales trend*, both the DSO and aging schedule methods should be used with caution when examining receivable collection patterns.

Receivable Balance/Collection Pattern Method

When credit sales trends or seasonal patterns exist, a firm's accounts receivable may be monitored effectively by examining either the receivable balance pattern or the collection pattern.[4] This is concerned with the proportion of any month's credit sales that remains outstanding (or conversely has been collected) at the end of each following or subsquent month. On a cumulative basis, one would expect a decay pattern in outstanding receivables associated with a given month's credit sales as one moves through time. In contrast, cumulative collection percentages would be expected to grow over time.

Table 11-5 illustrates how accounts receivable might be monitored on a monthly basis for Seaside Sales.

Assume that one begins by monitoring Seaside's credit sales in the month of March. Based on past experience, Seaside collects, on average, 10 percent of its credit sales during the month in which they were made. At the end of one subsequent month, a cumulative 70 percent traditionally were collected. Ninety percent of credit sales were collected after two months, and 99 percent by the third month after the month of sale. Receivables outstanding longer than three months are written off as bad debts by Seaside Sales. Note that credit sales made in March adhere to the firm's normal past experience.

---

[4]For further discussion, see Wilbur G. Lewellen and Robert W. Johnson. "Better Way to Monitor Accounts Receivable." *Harvard Business Review,* May-June 1972, pp. 101–109; and Bernell K. Stone. "The Payments-Pattern Approach to the Forecasting and Control of Accounts Receivable." *Financial Management,* Autumn 1976, pp. 65–82. Also, a "weighting" approach for overcoming traditional monitoring problems is suggested in Michael D. Carpenter and Jack E. Miller. "A Reliable Framework for Monitoring Accounts Receivable." *Financial Management,* Winter 1979, pp. 37–40.

TABLE 11-5   Receivable Balance or Collection Pattern Methods for Monitoring Accounts Receivable for Seaside Seasonal Sales Company

			Percent of Receivables Outstanding at End of:				
Credit Sales Period	March	April	May	June	July	Aug.	Sept.
Month of sale	90%	90%	89%	92%	90%	90%	89%
one month before		30	31	32	29	30	29
two months before			9	12	13	8	10
three months before				1	2	3	0

			Percent of Sales Collected at End of:				
Credit Sales Period	March	April	May	June	July	Aug.	Sept.
Month of sale	10%	10%	11%	8%	10%	10%	11%
one month before		70	69	68	71	70	71
two months before			91	88	87	92	90
three months before				99	98	97	100

The receivable balance method is, of course, a mirror image of the collection pattern. Ninety percent of the credit sales made during March were outstanding in the form of receivables at the end of March. By the end of April, the receivables remaining outstanding from March credit sales dropped to 30 percent. Only 9 percent remained outstanding at the end of May, with 1 percent of the original receivables recorded from March being classified as bad debts at the end of June.

Further examination of Table 11-5 suggests a possible deterioration in the collection pattern of receivables related to credit sales made in April and May. Remaining receivable proportions are declining or decaying at a slower-than-normal rate, and the collection rate is also slowing. However, by analyzing patterns for subsequent monthly credit sales periods, no directional change from past experience is apparent in the collection of receivables (as was the case when Column 3 in Table 11-4 was examined). There seem to have been random variations around the normal experience for Seaside. Such variation is to be expected. Thus, it is important to use these monitoring methods over time. The receivable balance or collection pattern methods consequently offer an additional basis for monitoring accounts receivable.

SUMMARY

The management of accounts receivable involves several complex and interrelated decisions. Credit analysis must be conducted and overall credit policies established. Potential credit customers are analyzed on the basis of character (willingness to pay), capacity (ability to pay), the firm's capital, the prevailing economic conditions, and whether collateral will be involved. A pool of potential credit customers then can be identified, along with several different degrees of quality within the pool. Firms might be grouped, for example, into high-, good-, and low-credit quality categories. Credit standards then can be set on the basis of an evaluation of incremental benefits and costs associated with alternative credit standards. The objective is to manage credit policy in such a way that the firm's sales match production capacity, so long as marginal or lower-quality accounts add to the firm's total profitability.

The size of the pool of potential credit customers as well as the mix within the pool can be expected to change with changes in the level of economic activity. This means that the financial manager must be willing and able to adjust credit standards when such actions are in the best interest of the firm. When there is rapid economic expansion, the financial manager might move to a policy of more restrictive credit standards because of excess sales demand. In contrast, during recessionary periods, more lenient credit standard policies may prove to be more profitable due to otherwise unused production capacity.

Policies also need to be established concerning credit terms. As with credit standards, credit terms can be restrictive or liberal in support of the firm's sales efforts. Principal credit terms involve the length of the credit period; the amount of discount offered, if any, for early payment; and the length of the discount period. Each of these features will produce incremental benefits as well as costs and should be evaluated accordingly.

Management of accounts receivable also involves the development of procedures for screening credit applicants and monitoring credit balances. Collection procedures must be established and decisions made as to whether to use commercial collection firms and when to take legal action against past-due accounts. Careful monitoring of accounts receivable through the use of aging schedules and receivables balance or collection pattern methods will help the financial manager evaluate the collection effort. Finally, the financial manager should consider the use of credit insurance to protect against possible extraordinary bad debts, such as default by a major credit customer.

MULTIPLE CHOICE QUESTIONS

1. The five "Cs" of credit are character, capital, conditions, collateral, and:

   a) Cash
   b) Potential
   c) Convenience
   d) Capacity

2. *Capital* refers to a customer's:

   a) Head
   b) Connections
   c) Cash
   d) Net worth

3. Discriminant analysis is a technique for:

   a) Affirmative action
   b) Credit analysis
   c) Managing the cash conversion cycle
   d) Aging receivables

4. Extending longer accounts receivable terms will:

   a) Decrease the cash operating cycle
   b) Increase the cash operating cycle
   c) Not affect the cash operating cycle
   d) Always decrease sales

5. An aging schedule is used for:

   a) Monitoring the seniority of management
   b) Deciding which bills will get paid
   c) Monitoring accounts payable
   d) Monitoring accounts receivable

6. A primary loss refers to:

   a) The losing politician
   b) Credit losses assumed 100% by the insured company
   c) Credit losses due to fire
   d) Credit losses assumed 100% by the insurance company

7. The average collection period can be misleading as an indicator of credit management when:

   a) Customers are late in paying
   b) Customers take discounts
   c) Credit sales are uniform
   d) Credit sales have a strong seasonal trend

DISCUSSION QUESTIONS

1. It is sometimes said that the financial manager's role in the management of accounts receivable is "dynamic." Explain.

2. Briefly summarize the significance of accounts receivable in the operation of business firms.

3. What financial management decision areas are involved when overall credit policies are established? Should credit guidelines be rigid or flexible? Explain.

4. If credit analysis is conducted to identify a pool of potential credit customers, what is involved in setting acceptable credit standards? Under what conditions would a financial manager change the firm's credit standard policies?

5. Explain the average collection period implications of a change in credit terms on a firm's short-term cash operating cycle. How might such a change affect firm profitability? (If necessary, review Chapter 10.)

6. It is sometimes said that collection policies should be based on the principle of not throwing good money after bad money. Explain.

7. Indicate two traditional methods that are used to monitor accounts receivable. Under what conditions might misleading results occur?

8. Explain how the receivable balance or collection pattern methods may be of use when monitoring a firm's collection efforts.

9. Explain the potential value of credit insurance.

SOLVED PROBLEMS

SP-1. Jericho, Inc. has sales of $20,000,000. Variable costs average 65 percent. Fixed costs are $4,000,000. The company is operating considerably below capacity. To boost sales, the marketing manager has suggested extending credit to a group of lower-quality credit risks. Sales to this group could total $2,000,000. Bad debt expenses typically average 10 percent of credit sales to this group, and collection costs will average 6 percent of credit sales to the group. The average collection period on the lower-quality account is expected to be 90 days. Jericho's financing cost is 30 percent pre-tax.

  a) Calculate the incremental benefits of the proposed credit policy.
  b) Calculate the marginal cost associated with the credit policy.
  c) Compare the benefits and costs from the proposed policy.

SP-2. The American Company expects sales of $20,000,000, of which 80 percent are made on credit. Terms are currently net 45, but experience has shown that the average collection period is actually 60 days. The president asks the finance manager to explore the advisability of offering a 2-percent discount for payment of invoices within 15 days. If offered, approximately 15 percent of credit customers would take the discount. Variable costs of production are 75 percent of sales, and the actual average collection period would be 50 days. The company's pre-tax financing cost is 20 percent.

a) Calculate and compare the benefits and cost of the president's suggestion.

SP-3. The Maret Company has a credit insurance policy providing for a primary loss of $100,000 and coinsurance of 10 percent. Coverage on each risk class is limited, as shown below.

Risk Class	Coverage Limit
1	$250,000
2	$150,000
3	$ 80,000
4	$ 50,000

Assuming the following credit losses occur, how much will the company collect from its insurance company?

Risk Class	Loss
1	$ 80,000
2	$100,000
3	$110,000
4	$100,000

PROBLEMS

1. Jones, Inc. has sales of $10,000,000. Variable costs average 70 percent. Fixed costs are $3,000,000. The company is operating considerably below capacity. To boost sales, the marketing manager has suggested extending credit to a group of lower-quality credit risks. Sales to this group could total $3,000,000. Bad-debt expenses typically average 10 percent of sales to this group, and collection costs will average 6 percent of sales to the group. The average collection period on the lower-quality account is expected to be 90 days. The proposed credit policy will not affect existing customers. Jones' financing cost is 20 percent, pre-tax.

a) Calculate the incremental benefits of the proposed credit policy.
b) Calculate the incremental costs associated with the credit policy.
c) Compare the benefits and costs of the proposed policy.

2. The Ace Company expects sales of $20,000,000, of which 70 percent are made on credit. Terms are currently net 60, but experience has shown that the average collection period is actually 90 days. The president asks the finance manager to explore the advisability of offering a 2 percent discount for payment of invoices within 30 days. If offered, approximately 20 percent of credit customers would take the discount. Variable costs of production are 70 percent of sales, and the actual average collection period would be 50 days. The company's pre-tax financing cost is 20 percent.

   a) Calculate and compare the benefits and cost of the president's suggestion.

3. The Wilks Company has a credit insurance policy providing for a primary loss of $200,000 and coinsurance of 20 percent. Coverage on each risk class is limited as shown below.

Risk Class	Coverage Limit
1	$ 50,000
2	$150,000
3	$ 90,000
4	$110,000

Assuming the following credit losses occur, how much will the company collect from its insurance company?

Risk Class	Loss
1	$ 80,000
2	$100,000
3	$ 90,000
4	$ 80,000

4. The Apex Furniture Company reported the following financial information for the past two years.

	1987	1986
Annual credit sales	$7,000,000	$5,000,000
Average accounts receivable	$1,500,000	$1,000,000

Assume a 360-day year for calculation purposes.

   a) Calculate the average collection period for each year.

b) Calculate the accounts receivable turnover for each year.
c) Estimate the average accounts receivable for 1987 if the 1986 receivables turnover ratio had been maintained in 1987.
d) What might have caused the changes in receivables relative to sales from 1986 to 1987?

5. The Trock Furniture Company is presently operating at less than full capacity and expects flat sales next year unless it lowers its credit standards to include a lower-quality group of credit customers. The current sales level is $7,000,000, variable costs in the form of cost of goods sold are 70 percent of sales, and fixed costs (including collection costs for existing customers) are expected to remain at $1,500,000 next year. A lowering of credit standards will increase sales by 10 percent. Collection costs are expected to be 6 percent of the credit sales made to the lower-quality credit group, with bad debts expected to be $14,000 along with an average collection period of 70 days for the proposed group of "marginal" accounts.

a) Calculate the marginal impact of the proposed group of credit customers in terms of pre-tax profit.
b) Calculate the marginal increase in average investment in accounts receivable that would be required if credit sales are made to the new group.
c) Would you recommend that Trock Furniture lower its credit standards next year if the firm expects a 15 percent pre-tax return on such investments?

6. The sales manager for International Crafts, Inc. estimates that sales could be increased 10,000 units by selling to a group of less-creditworthy customers. The credit manager estimates that credit losses from this group will amount to 7 percent of sales and that additional collection effort attributable to the group will cost $5,000. The plant is operating at about 60 percent of capacity, producing 120,000 units. Accounts receivable from the marginal accounts will average $20,000.

   The accountant prepares the statement shown below and advises against selling to this additional group. Do you agree? Support your position.

Selling price per unit		$ 7.00
Cost of goods sold:		
Materials	$1.75	
Direct labor	2.15	
Factory overhead*	1.40	5.30
Gross margin		1.70
Selling expenses**	.60	
Administrative expenses**	.55	1.15
Profit per unit		.55
Profit on 10,000 units		$5,500

Credit losses	$2,965	
Additional collection costs	4,000	6,965
Net loss by selling to poorer grade of customer		($1,465)

*Heat, light, power, salaries of supervisors, and other indirect labor. Production could rise substantially before these costs would be affected.
**Sales personnel are paid salaries, not commissions. No change is contemplated in other fixed selling expenses, such as advertising and administration.

7. The Timely Manufacturing Corporation produces an inexpensive clock. Sales are at a level of $325,000 per year but could be more than doubled with current production facilities. The suggestion has been made that the firm be more lenient on its credit policies. It is currently selling to risks categorized as A, B, and C. The credit manager has prepared the information shown below for higher-risk classes. The data shown are for each class by itself, that is, the $40,000 increase in sales to class E would be over and above the sales made to class D. The credit manager estimates that the company should earn at least 20 percent on a before-tax basis from its credit policy.

Risk Class	Estimated Increase in Sales ($)	Estimated Average Collection Period (Days)	Expected Rate of Default and Collection Costs (%)
D	30,000	60	5
E	40,000	72	7
F	45,000	80	9
G	40,000	90	11
Selling price per unit		$2.00	
Variable costs per unit		$1.75	

What additional risk classes, if any, should the credit manager add to present sales?

8. The Solomon Corporation estimates that credit sales for next year will be $2,250,000. Management must decide on credit standards to maximize the firm's profitability. The company's credit pool consists of four classes of customers: AA = superior quality; AB = good quality; AC = marginal quality; and AD = poor quality.

a) Based on the information given below, determine for each class: (1) the incremental profits; (2) marginal accounts receivable investment; (3) net incremental benefits.

b) What credit standards should the company plan to establish for next year?

						CHAPTER 11
Annual credit sales	$1,237,500	$562,500	$337,500	$112,500		ACCOUNTS RECEIVABLE
Average collection period	30 days	45 days	75 days	100 days		MANAGEMENT
Collection costs	1%	2%	5%	8%		
(% of sales)						
Bad debt costs	1%	3%	10%	15%		
(% of sales)						

Variable costs of sales: 85%

Required Pre-Tax return: 20%

9. The management of the Carter Company plans to tighten its current credit policy so that its average collection period will be reduced from 65 days to 58 days. Under the old 65-day policy, average accounts receivable were expected to be $1,755,000. Annual credit sales were expected to remain at the same $9,720,000 level for the 65-day or 58-day plans.

   a) Calculate average accounts receivable outstanding with the 58-day average collection period.
   b) How much in financing costs is Carter likely to save by reducing its average collection period by seven days? Assume that financing costs are 12 percent before taxes.
   c) In order to achieve a reduction in average collection period for its receivables, Carter will have to offer a 3-percent cash discount on credit sales paid within 15 days. Cash discounts are expected to be taken on 10 percent of the credit sales by Carter's customers. Calculate the costs associated with a seven-day reduction in average collection period.
   d) Would you recommend that Carter Company retain the 65-day collection period or adopt the 58-day plan?
   e) To what extent, if any, would your answer in Part (d) change if the new cash discount policy causes the average collection period to decline 15 days instead of just seven days from the 65-day level? Show your calculations.

10. The Brich Company is considering whether to tighten its current credit policy so that its average collection period will be reduced from 72 days to 62 days. Based on a 360-day year, and a 72-day average collection period, year-end (and average) accounts receivable are estimated at $720,000. Assume all sales are credit sales and the firm's variable costs are expected to remain at 60 percent of sales.

    a) Calculate the annual credit sales based on the average collection period of 72 days.
    b) Credit sales to existing customers are expected to fall by 10 percent if the credit policy is tightened to achieve a 62-day average col-

lection period. Calculate the average amount of accounts receivable that will be outstanding under this policy.

c) Brich's accounts receivable financing costs are 12-percent. Should Brich tighten its credit terms even though some credit sales would be lost?

11. The Spinner Corporation plans to boost next year's sales by changing its credit terms from 2/15, net 30 to 3/10, net 45. Credit sales are expected to increase from $625,000 to $700,000. Variable costs, in the form of cost of goods sold, amount to 70 percent of sales. Currently, 80 percent of Spinner's customers take advantage of the discount, but this is expected to fall to 70 percent under the new credit terms. The average collection period is expected to increase from 18 days to 22 days.

a) Calculate the incremental earnings before interest and taxes (EBIT) level for the Spinner Corporation.

b) Calculate the incremental investment in accounts receivable under the assumption of sales of $700,000.

c) If Spinner requires an 18-percent pre-tax return on receivable investments, should the new credit terms be adopted?

12. The Larimer Cable Corporation is concerned about possible deterioration in its credit department collection efforts. Accounts receivable balances were: end of June, $44,000; end of September, $59,000; and end of December, $69,000. The following information also was available:

		Remaining Receivables by Month of Sale at End of:		
Month	Monthly Credit Sales	June	Sept.	Dec.
April	$30,000	$ 3,000		
May	30,000	9,000		
June	40,000	32,000		
July	$40,000		$ 4,000	
August	50,000		15,000	
Sept.	50,000		40,000	
Oct.	40,000			$4,000
Nov.	50,000			20,000
Dec.	50,000			45,000

a) Calculate the days sales outstanding (or average collection period) based on sales periods of 30 and 90 days as of the end of June,

September, and December. What seems to have been occurring in terms of Larimer Cable's collection efforts?

b) Prepare accounts receivable aging schedules as of the end of June, September, and December. What do they seem to be suggesting about the firm's collection effort?

c) Although adequate data are not available in order to apply the receivable balance or collection pattern methods to monitor Larimer's accounts receivable, a percent-of-sales analysis can be made. Express remaining receivables as a percent of the sales in the month in which they originated as of the end of June, September, and December. What does this approach seem to indicate about Larimer Cable's collection efforts?

d) From an overall credit policy standpoint, what kinds of credit policy changes might account for the changes in accounts receivable levels noted by the Larimer Cable Corporation? Consider more than just the firm's collection effort.

13. Your company has a credit insurance policy that provides for a primary loss of $23,000 and a coinsurance feature of 10 percent on rated accounts. Coverage on each account in the following classes is limited as follows:

CC	$25,000
DC	20,000
DD	15,000
EE	10,000

During the year four accounts become insolvent. The D&B rating at the time of shipment and the amount of loss is shown below:

CC	$13,000
DC	3,000
DD	20,000
EE	16,000

How much will you collect from the insurance company on the basis of this information?

14. The Child Company and the Volk Company both operate in the same industry. Following are their respective balance sheets and income statements for last year.

Balance Sheets

	Child	Volk
Cash and marketable securities	$ 80,000	$ 40,000
Accounts receivable	520,000	360,000
Inventory	800,000	600,000
Total current assets	1,400,000	1,000,000
Fixed assets, net	1,000,000	500,000
Total assets	$2,400,000	$1,500,000
Accounts payable	300,000	150,000
Accrued liabilities	400,000	200,000
Total current liabilities	700,000	350,000
Long term debt	500,000	350,000
Common equity	1,200,000	800,000
Total liabilities and equity	$2,400,000	$1,500,000

Income Statements

	Child	Volk
Net sales	$3,000,000	$1,500,000
Cost of goods sold	2,400,000	1,200,000
Gross profit	600,000	300,000
Operating expenses	200,000	100,000
Interest expense	50,000	35,000
Earnings before taxes	350,000	165,000
Income taxes paid	140,000	66,000
Net income	$ 210,000	$ 99,000

a) Asuming all sales were credit sales and a 360-day year, estimate the average collection period for each firm.

b) Calculate the accounts receivable turnover for each firm, assuming sales were level throughout the year.

c) If Volk were able to adjust its average collection period to the level being achieved by Child, what would be its year-end accounts receivable balance?

d) Identify the differences in year-end receivables balance between Volk and Child due to sales differences and credit-policy differences.

15. The Acme Company had the following monthly credit sales:

Month	Monthly Credit Sales
January	$40,000
February	$50,000
March	$60,000
April	$50,000

Month	Monthly Credit Sales	**413**
		CHAPTER 11
May	$50,000	ACCOUNTS RECEIVABLE
June	$50,000	MANAGEMENT
July	$80,000	
August	$50,000	
September	$20,000	

Accounts receivable balances at the end of March, June, and September, were $50,000; $50,000; and $50,000, respectively.

a) Calculate the average collection period based on sales periods of 30 and 90 days as of the end of March, June, and September.

b) Compare the results.

SOLUTIONS TO SOLVED PROBLEMS

SP-1. a) Incremental benefits:

1. Increase in sales	2,000,000
2. Increase in profits before taxes $(1 - VC\%)\,(\text{line 1})$	700,000

b) Incremental costs:

3. Increase in A/R $\left(\dfrac{2,000,000}{360}\right)(90)$	500,000
4. Increase in A/R investment (line 3) (.65)	325,000
5. Increase in financing cost (line 4) (.30)	(97,500)
6. Increase in bad debt expenses (line 1) (.10)	(200,000)
7. Increase in collection costs (line 1) (.06)	(120,000)
8. Total incremental costs (line 5 + line 6 + line 7)	(417,500)

c) Incremental benefits

(line 2)	700,000
− Incremental costs (line 8)	(417,500)
Net incremental benefits	282,500

SP-2. Benefits:

$$\text{Accounts receivable (current policy)} = \frac{(\$20,000,000)(.8)}{360} \times 60$$

$$= \$2,666,667$$

$$\text{Accounts receivable (new policy)} = \frac{(\$20,000,000)(.8)}{360} \times 50$$

$$= \$2,222,222$$

Reduction in accounts receivable =	$ 444,445
Financing costs	×.20
Savings from policy	$88,889

Accounts receivable would decrease by $444,445. At a pre-tax cost of 20 percent, the reduction in investment saves financing costs of $88,889.

Costs of New Policy:

$$(20,000,000)(.8)(.15)(.02) = 48,000$$

Sales will total $20,000,000, of which 80 percent will be on credit. Of credit sales, 15 percent will take the discount of 2 percent. The cost of the discount will thus be $48,000. Since benefits outweigh the costs, the president's idea seems to be a good one.

SP-3.

Risk Class	Loss	Coverage Limit	Claim
1	$ 80,000	$250,000	$ 80,000
2	$100,000	$150,000	$100,000
3	$110,000	$ 80,000	$ 80,000
4	$100,000	$ 50,000	$ 50,000
			$310,000
		Less primary loss	−100,000
			$210,000
		Less coinsurance	21,000
		Net claim	$189,000

REFERENCES

Atkins, Joseph C., and Yong H. Kim. "Comment and Correction: Opportunity Cost in the Evaluation of Investment in Accounts Receivable." *Financial Management*, Winter 1977, pp. 67–78.

Carpenter, Michael D., and Jack E. Miller. "A Reliable Framework for Monitoring Accounts Receivable." *Financial Management,* Winter 1979, pp. 37–40.

Dyl, Edward A. "Another Look at the Evaluation of Investment in Accounts Receivable." *Financial Management,* Winter 1977, pp. 67–78.

Hill, Ned C., and Kenneth D. Riener. "Determining the Cash Discount in the Firm's Credit Policy." *Financial Management,* Spring 1979, pp. 68–73.

Kim, Yong H., and Joseph C. Atkins. "Evaluating Investments in Accounts Receivable: A Wealth Maximizing Framework." *Journal of Finance,* May 1978, pp. 403–412.

Lewellen, Wilbur G. and Robert W. Johnson. "Better Way to Monitor Accounts Receivable." *Harvard Business Review,* May-June 1972, pp. 101–109.

Sachdeva, Kanwal S., and Lawrence J. Gitman. "Accounts Receivable Decisions in a Capital Budgeting Framework." *Financial Management,* Winter 1981, pp. 45–49.

Stone, Bernell K. "The Payments-Pattern Approach to the Forecasting and Control of Accounts Receivable." *Financial Management,* Autumn 1976, pp. 70–71.

Walia, Tirlochan S. "Explicit and Implicit Cost of Changes in the Level of Accounts Receivable." *Financial Management,* Winter 1977, pp. 67–78.

CASE EXERCISE

Karen, Inc.

Karen, Inc. sold lawn furniture on terms of 45 days, consistent with industry practice. Considerably different from industry practice, however, was the company's policy of not granting discounts for early payment. While competitors typically offered discounts of 2/10, net 45, Karen sought to compete by being more patient with slow payers, as evidenced by its average collection period of 60 days compared with an average collection period of 30 days for the industry overall. Karen Barnes, the company president, felt that a more tolerant credit policy not only offset the absence of a discount for early payment but also helped sales to poorly capitalized customers who would otherwise not be able to buy as much — although the sales impact of this policy had never been estimated.

In early 1988, Karen's financial manager, John Ball, convinced the president that an analysis of the credit policy was warranted. Mr. Ball noted that the level of receivables was now $85 million and was forcing the company to use up large amounts of its borrowing available from banks. In addition, the company's principal banker had just raised the interest rate on the company's line of credit to 15 percent. Finally, Mr. Ball argued that the existing policy was too broad. Many of the firm's customers were financially weak and did need longer payment terms; but other, financially strong, customers had no incentive to pay early or even to pay on time. Mr. Ball believed that offering discounts similar to those of Karen's competitors would actually save the company money while simultaneously reducing its use of short-term debt. When Ms. Barnes asked Mr. Ball how many of the firm's customers could be expected to take the discount, if offered, he replied that he was not sure but that a rough estimate could be developed by considering the experience of others. When asked to elaborate, he said, "I'm assuming that those who take the industry discount pay on the 10th day and those who don't take the discount pay on the 45th day, as a rough approximation. Now, if the collection period averages 30 days, we could estimate what percentage would be taking the discount and what percentage wouldn't, assuming we offer the same terms and have the same experience."

Case Questions

1. Using the method described by Mr. Ball, estimate the percentage of Karen's customers who might be expected to take the discount if offered. Assume that the credit terms would be the same as the industry, 2/10, net 45, and that all sales are made on credit.

2. Evaluate the costs and benefits associated with changing Karen's credit policy to the industry terms.

CHAPTER

12

INVENTORY MANAGEMENT

nventory is an asset the firm holds to make sales. There are several different types of inventory: *supplies, raw materials, goods in process,* and *finished goods.* Supplies are usually defined as items that are used in the operation of the business but do not go into or become incorporated in the final product. Raw materials are the materials, subassemblies, or other items brought in from other plants or purchased from suppliers, that become part of the final product. Goods in transit from raw materials to finished goods are considered goods in process, while the completed product is termed finished goods.

The levels and composition of inventories a firm holds can generate significant costs and risks that affect the economic value of the firm. For example, the costs of carrying inventory may be as much as 30 percent of the value of the inventory. While the financial manager does not have direct responsibility for inventory management, he or she does have the responsibility for making sure that inventory policies and practices do not unnecessarily increase inventory costs and risks. In carrying out this responsibility, the financial manager must work closely with the production and sales managers, as their inventory preferences may not coincide. For example, the production manager will prefer abundant raw material inventories to insure against any interruption in production schedules, and the sales manager will prefer abundant finished goods inventories to be able to meet all possible sales opportunities. To the financial manager, abundant inventories involve greater costs and risks, which may not be justified. The financial manager must help the firm steer a course between excessive and inadequate inventory investment by developing decision rules governing such choices as the quantity of inventory to order, the amount of safety or *anticipatory* stocks to hold, when to reorder new supplies, and so on. In general the financial manager's perspective will be that of trying to minimize inventory costs and risks while not impairing the production or sales efforts.

● Objectives and Organization of this Chapter

The primary objective of this chapter is to illustrate the financial consequences of a firm's inventory policies and practices. In the first section, the chapter briefly discusses the determinants of the firm's inventory level. In the second section, it identifies inventory costs, then shows how these costs can be estimated and minimized given the firm's production and sales plans. In the third section, it explains the role of safety stocks as a way of minimizing interruptions in production or sales schedules. Finally, it shows how the company may use anticipation stocks to attenuate the effects of fluctuations in product supplies or demands on production and sales plans.

DETERMINANTS OF INVENTORY INVESTMENT

finished goods inventory

work-in-process inventory

raw materials inventory

The principal determinant of a firm's inventory level is its anticipated sales level. For example, the higher the firm's anticipated sales, the more finished goods it must have on hand. For manufacturing firms, increased finished goods requirements generate increased work-in-process and raw materials inventories.

Business cycles affect the sales of most firms. When sales levels decline rapidly, as in a recession, inventory levels may quickly become excessive and generate unnecessary costs and risks by freezing corporate funds in unsold inventories, increasing inventory carrying costs, and increasing the dangers of product obsolescence or changes in consumer tastes. Conversely, a rapid business expansion may rapidly increase sales demand. If the company is unprepared, inventory will be unable to keep up with sales, resulting in lost sales and market share and, for manufacturing firms, chaos in production schedules. As discussed in chapter 3 the financial manager must help identify turning points in business cycles to enable the firm properly to adjust inventory levels by altering production and purchasing schedules.

Sales volatility also affects a firm's inventory levels. For example, if sales are highly unpredictable or highly seasonal, firms will hold larger safety stocks and anticipation stocks than if sales are stable and uniform throughout the year. When sales are volatile, a firm's inventory becomes an important mechanism for stabilizing production operations. Larger inventories, of course, produce larger costs and risks of their own. Here too the financial manager must help determine the costs and benefits of excess inventory investment.

The variety and levels of inventories a firm carries also depend greatly on its type of business. For example, wholesale and retail businesses mainly carry only finished goods inventories; and these account for a large proportion of their total assets, since they need relatively little investment in fixed assets. Manufacturing firms carry a full range of inventories, including supplies, raw materials, goods in process, and finished goods. While significant in their dollar amounts, manufacturing inventories represent a smaller proportion of the companies' total assets than is true for wholesale and retail firms. This is due to the fact that manufacturing firms must make large investments in other assets such as plant and equipment.

Within a given line of business, the levels and composition of a firm's inventories are also closely related to its competitive strategies. For example, firms that offer broad product lines serving all major market segments maintain larger and more varied inventories per dollar of sales than firms that focus their sales efforts on narrow market segments.[1] Examples of such competitive choices are readily evident in all types of businesses. For instance, in the food service business, a "full-menu" restaurant needs to maintain larger and more varied inventories than a "fast-food" restaurant of similar revenue size. A record store carrying a wide selection of music needs to carry larger and more varied record inventories than a store of similar size specializing only in rock music.

The motives behind such competitive choices are clear: full-product-line firms attempt to attract a much broader portion of the market and, by offering the convenience of broader product selections, achieve higher profits than firms that specialize and carry narrow product inventories. However, full-product-line firms have larger inventory costs and risks than do specialized firms. Narrow-product-line firms reduce the costs of inventory financing and thus can offer lower prices in the hope that sales will be significantly greater. For both types of firms, however, poorly controlled inventory investments can turn profitable strategies into unprofitable ones.

INVENTORY ACCOUNTING METHODS

Accountants record the cost of a firm's inventory usage and holdings in one of three basic ways:

1. First-in-first-out (FIFO)
2. Last-in-first-out (LIFO)
3. Average cost

Under FIFO, a firm's cost of goods sold reflects the cost of the oldest inventory items on hand during an accounting period. Items remaining in inventory at the end of the accounting period consequently reflect more recent costs when the FIFO method is used. In contrast, the LIFO method includes the costs of more recently purchased items in the period's cost of sales,

FIFO

LIFO

[1]If large amounts of commodities are carried in inventory, it may be possible to reduce losses from price fluctuations by hedging. Briefly, this is a process of entering futures contracts to sell the commodity or some product derived from the commodity at a certain price. Theoretically, when a flour miller buys wheat, he or she might at the same time enter into a futures contract to deliver wheat at a given price in the future. Should the price of the wheat decline, the miller is likely to lose on the value of wheat in inventory but will offset that loss through a gain on the futures contract. Although practice seldom coincides with theory, the miller will probably have smaller annual inventory losses (and profits) from hedging than not hedging. In some cases a bank may require that the inventory be hedged before it grants a loan to a company that carries large amounts of inventory.

while the inventory value at the end of the period reflects the costs of older inventory items. As one might expect, the average-cost method considers a weighted average of the prices paid for both old and recent inventory items. This results in the same average costs being applied to cost of materials used to produce revenues and to record end-of-period inventory values.

Valuation Method	Income Statement (Cost of Goods Sold)	Balance Sheet (Inventory)
FIFO	Oldest costs	Most recent costs
LIFO	Most recent costs	Oldest costs
Average	Weighted average of costs	Weighted average of costs

Let us now examine the impact of these three inventory accounting methods on both the income statement and balance sheet for the Erin Electronics Corporation. Assume for illustrative purposes that Erin Electronics starts with no inventory on hand at the beginning of the year. One thousand microprocessors are purchased in early January at a cost of $14 per unit. Later during the year, Erin purchases an additional 1,000 units at $16 per unit. These microprocessors are used in the manufacture of Erin "Fly-Byes" on a unit-by-unit basis (one microprocessor per "Fly-Bye").

Table 12-1 shows that Erin Electronics sells 1,500 "Fly-Byes" during the year at a price of $20 each, resulting in revenues of $30,000. However, the cost of materials used in producing the "Fly-Byes" differs depending on which inventory accounting method is used. Under the FIFO method, Erin uses 1,000 microprocessors at a cost of $14 per unit plus 500 units at a cost of $16 per unit, for a total cost of $22,000. The LIFO method records usage of 1,000 microprocessors at a per unit cost of $16 plus 500 units at $14 each for a total cost of materials of $23,000. The average-cost method results in a cost of materials of $22,500, based on 1,500 units having an average cost of $15 each.

Table 12-1 further shows that the choice of inventory accounting method also affects the firm's income tax liability and net income. During periods of rising prices or costs for materials, as was illustrated for Erin Electronics, the FIFO method produces lower cost of sales, lower income tax payments, and higher net income. In contrast, usage of the LIFO method during periods of rising costs produces higher cost of sales, lower income tax payments, and lower net income. Just the opposite relationships will occur during periods of falling costs of materials. The average-cost method will produce costs in between the FIFO and LIFO figures whether prices are rising or falling.

Table 12-2 shows the effect of the three inventory accounting methods on Erin's balance sheet when prepared at the end of the year. Remaining inventory on hand at the end of the year is $8,000 if the FIFO method is used. This is based on 500 units in stock at a cost of $16 per unit. Inventory

TABLE 12-1   Impact of Alternative Inventory Accounting Methods on the Income Statement: Erin Electronics, Inc.

Income Statement, Year Ending December 31

	FIFO	LIFO	Average Cost
Revenues (1500 units @ $20)	$30,000	$30,000	$30,000
Less cost of materials			
(1000 units @ $14 + 500 units @ $16)	22,000		
(500 units @ $14 + 1000 units @ $16)		23,000	
(1500 units @ $15)*			22,500
Less other costs of production	2,000	2,000	2,000
Gross profit	6,000	5,000	5,500
Less operating expenses	3,000	3,000	3,000
Earnings before taxes	3,000	2,000	2,500
Less income taxes (34%)	1,020	680	850
Net income	$1,980	$1,320	$1,650

*Average cost per unit ($14 + $16)/2

TABLE 12-2   Impact of Alternative Inventory Accounting Methods: Erin Electronics, Inc.

Balance Sheet, December 31

Assets	FIFO	LIFO	Average Cost
Cash and receivables	$ 6,000	$ 6,000	$ 6,000
Inventory			
500 units @ $16	8,000		
500 units @ $14		7,000	
500 units @ $15*			$ 7,500
Total current assets	14,000	13,000	13,500
Fixed assets	10,000	10,000	10,000
Total assets	$24,000	$23,000	$23,500

Liabilities and Equity			
Current liabilities	$10,000	$ 9,000	$ 9,500
Equity	14,000	14,000	14,000
Total	$24,000	$23,000	$23,500

is valued at $7,000 under the LIFO methods, since the cost of the remaining 500 units would be $14 each. The average-cost method results in an ending inventory valued at $7,500. For the sake of simplicity we also have allowed the current liabilities to vary with the inventory value recorded under the three methods. It is obvious that, during periods of rising prices, ending inventory balances are higher under FIFO and lower under LIFO. The reverse occurs during periods of falling prices.

INVENTORY CONTROL

The inventory control function, while not under the direction of the financial manager, involves financial costs. Thus it is important to control inventory at the least cost. Adequate inventory control is necessary to provide for smooth and orderly production and distribution processes and to avoid costly shrinkages and stock-outs.

Many business firms must stock and monitor thousands of different items of inventory. This is particularly true for manufacturing firms, and it leads to the question: which items should be more tightly controlled? Ordinary screws and bolts, for example, warrant only loose control because more would have to be spent to control the waste-associated costs of these items than could be saved by controlling them. Other inventory items undoubtedly warrant tighter control.

The ABC Inventory Control System

ABC inventory control

The ABC system of inventory control is one method for assigning different degrees of control to inventory items. Inventory items are divided into three categories on the basis of their investment values relative to the firm's total inventory value. Exhibit 12-1 illustrates an ABC inventory control system.

Items classified as "A" are very costly and constitute 70 percent of the total inventory investment amount but only 20 percent of the items numerically. These items should be tightly controlled. "B" items constitute 30 percent of the items but only 20 percent of the investment and thus warrant only an average control effort. The "C" category includes 50 percent of the inventory items but only 10 percent of the value. Thus these items deserve only loose control. It is important to recognize that exceptions are sometimes necessary in applying the ABC system. For example, low-cost items that are critical for maintaining a smooth production process require added attention and thus deserve treatment as "A" items. Inventory management involving cost-balancing considerations is particularly applicable to "A" and some "B" items, as will be discussed later in this chapter.

INVENTORY MANAGEMENT AND THE CASH CYCLE

Chapter 10 described the cash operating cycle of the Brach Products Company. We determined that Brach has an average cycle of 120 days, as shown in Exhibit 12-2.

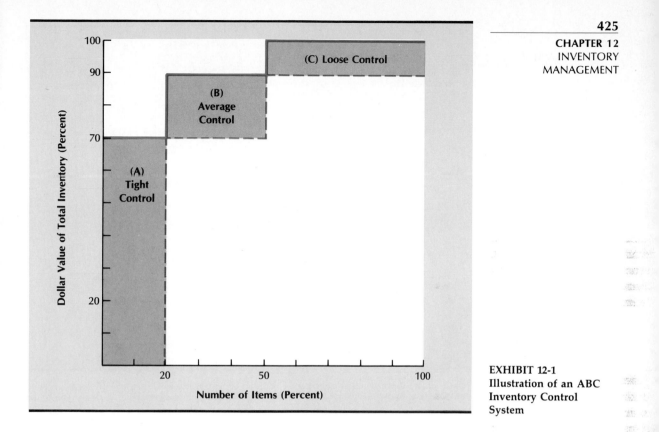

EXHIBIT 12-1
Illustration of an ABC
Inventory Control
System

Exhibit 12-2 indicates that a manufacturing firm's inventory conversion *inventory conversion time* time or average age, can be broken down into three elements. The first element is the delivery time required between the placing of an order and the actual receipt of raw materials. While the financial manager probably has limited responsibility in this area, it should be recognized that shorter delivery times are likely to be associated with higher raw materials turnover ratios. This is because less inventory backup or safety stock would be needed if delivery can be counted on to occur quickly. Increased efficiency in inventory control also may help to increase the turnover of raw materials.

The second element focuses on the length of the production process, or what might be termed the production cycle. Improved production planning *production cycle* and scheduling, along with production control methods, might be implemented so as to reduce production time from raw materials through work-in-process to finished goods. Such efforts would be associated with higher work-in-process turnover ratios. Of course, while management efforts in this area are important to the financial manager, they are largely under the domain of the production function.

The third element in the inventory time to conversion period is the average time required between when products are available as finished

Brach Products Company

Average Age or Conversion Time in Days

EXHIBIT 12-2
Inventory Conversion
Impact on the Cash
Operating Cycle

Cash Cycle Components	Current	Projected
Inventory Conversion Time*	90 days	80 days
Accounts Receivable Conversion Time	60	60
	150	140
Accounts Payable Conversion Time	−30	−30
Average Cash Cycle	120 days	110 days

*The inventory conversion time currently is comprised of: raw materials delivery time (five days), production process or cycle time (50 days), and finished goods inventory carrying time (35 days). The 10-day projected reduction is based on a new 45-day production cycle and a 30-day finished goods carrying time.

goods inventory and when they are sold. Improved forecasting of sales demand and coordination of production with sales forecasts will lead to an improvement in the turnover of finished goods and thus contribute to a reduction in the inventory conversion time period. In this area, the financial manager can make a substantial contribution. Sales forecasts must be as accurate as possible. These forecasts then must be coordinated with the other plans and budgets, as discussed in Chapter 8. Finally, tight control must be exercised by the financial manager so that, when actual sales deviate from forecasted sales, necessary adjustments are quickly made in terms of purchasing, inventory, and production.

In the operating cash cycle illustration of the Brach Company, assume that the financial manager (with the aid of the production manager) is able to achieve a five-day reduction in the production cycle time and a five-day reduction in the finished goods carrying time. If this is accomplished, the inventory conversion time will be reduced from 90 days to 80 days, which, in turn, causes the average cash cycle to decline to 110 days. The benefit of a shorter cash cycle arises because average inventory balances will be lower and, as a result, fewer funds will be required to finance the firm's assets.

Information pertaining to raw materials delivery time, the length of the production cycle, and detailed inventory mix is essential to making an accurate estimate of a firm's inventory conversion time period. In lieu of such detailed information, however, it is possible to develop a rough (usually low) estimate of the inventory time to conversion by using the inventory turnover ratio initially defined in Chapter 7.

Assume that Brach Products' annual cost of goods sold is $12 million and the firm's year-end inventory is $3 million. One can estimate the average inventory turnover for Brach as follows:

$$\text{Inventory turnover} = \text{Cost of goods sold/inventory}$$

$$= \$12,000,000/3,000,000 = 4.0 \text{ times}$$

The 4.0 inventory turnover ratio divided into a 360-day year yields 90 days as the average age of Brach's inventory and our estimate of the inventory time to conversion period.

A direct way of calculating the inventory average age (IAA) would be:

inventory average age (IAA)

$$\text{IAA} = \text{Inventory/[annual cost of goods sold/360]}$$

$$= \text{Inventory/cost of goods sold per day}$$

$$= \$3,000,000/[\$12,000,000/360]$$

$$= \$3,000,000/33,333 = 90 \text{ days}$$

In the event that beginning-of-period inventory amounts had differed substantially from ending amounts, we would have used average inventory (beginning inventory plus ending inventory divided by two) to estimate the IAA or inventory conversion time.

An increase in the inventory turnover ratio will result in a decline in the inventory average age and thus in the inventory time to conversion period. This will also lower the firm's average inventory balances that are outstanding throughout the year.

Assume that Brach's average inventory is the same as the ending inventory of $3 million. More efficient inventory management by Brach, however, might have resulted in the average inventory age being reduced from 90 days to 80 days. The average inventory level, given the same sales, then would be:

$$\text{Average inventory} = \text{Cost of goods sold per day} \times \text{inventory average age}$$

$$= [\$12,000,000/360] \times 80$$

$$= \$2,667,000$$

This would produce a reduction of $333,333 in average inventory levels for Brach Products. If the cost of carrying or financing average inventory amounts is, say, 20 percent, there is the possibility for savings amounting to $66,667 ($333,333 × .20). At the same time, a reduction in inventory conversion time might result in additional costs in the form of higher ordering costs, fewer quantity discounts, and possible production or distribution-related interruption costs. In some cases, sales might even be lost due to stock-outs. These added costs must be compared against the expected savings to determine whether a net benefit would result.

Cost-balancing approaches also are available to aid in minimizing the total costs associated with the management of inventory. These are particularly useful for relatively large-investment "A" and some "B" items identified on the basis of an ABC inventory control system.

INVENTORY COSTS

carrying costs

ordering costs

total inventory costs

Inventory costs include: *carrying costs* and *ordering costs*. The behaviors of these costs are peculiar in that reducing one type of cost has the effect of increasing the other. *Total inventory costs* are the sum of carrying costs and ordering costs. As we shall demonstrate, total inventory costs are minimized when carrying costs are just equal to ordering costs for a given level of unit sales.

Inventory Carrying Costs

Inventory carrying costs include such things as financing costs, storage and warehousing costs, insurance, property taxes, physical deterioration, and shrinkage (euphemism for theft). The larger a firm's inventory, the higher its carrying costs will be. Estimates of total carrying costs range from 15 to 30 percent of inventory value. Carrying costs are often stated on a *per unit* basis. Costs per unit are equal to inventory value per unit times the carrying cost per dollar.

Carrying cost per unit = Inventory cost per unit × Carrying cost per dollar

> **Example**
>
> Zenons cost $160 per unit. Carrying costs are 25 percent of inventory value. Thus, carrying costs per Zenon are $40.

Total carrying costs can be calculated by multiplying average inventory investment by carrying costs per dollar of inventory value—or, equivalently, by multiplying average number of units in inventory times carrying costs per unit. Average inventory units is equal to the quantity (Q) ordered (or produced) divided by two:

$$\text{Average inventory units} = Q/2 \qquad (12\text{-}1)$$

Example

Average Inventory

Assume that a company buys 7 units of a product. It then sells one unit per day. The average number of units the company will have is 3.5 per day.

Beginning of Day	Number of Units
1	7
2	6
3	5
4	4
5	3
6	2
7	1
8	0
Total 8 days	28 units

Average: 28 units/8 days = 3.5 units per day

Exhibit 12-3 shows, graphically the relationship between inventory levels and time, assuming uniform usage. Notice that, at the beginning of the 8th day, inventory has dropped to zero (assuming no buffer or safety stock) and a new shipment of seven units arrives.

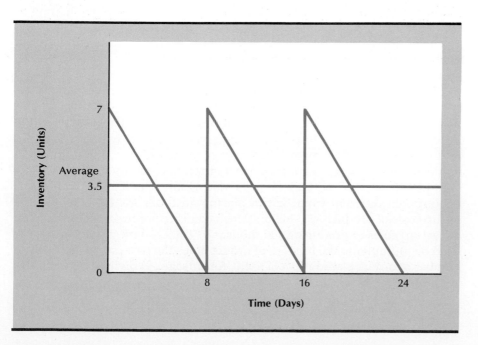

EXHIBIT 12-3
Average Inventory Levels

Example

Total Carrying Costs

Ace Company is a large electronics manfacturer that produces personal computers, rocket belts, robots, and other electronic products.

The company produces 10,000 computers per production run (in the context of a manufacturing firm, the firm "orders" goods for sale by scheduling a production run). Sale of the computers is uniform, and the company keeps no safety stocks. Inventory carrying costs are $100 per unit. Total carrying costs of the computers are $500,000 per year, as calculated below:

$$\text{Total carrying costs} = \text{Average inventory units} \times \text{carrying cost per unit}$$

$$= 10,000/2 \times \$100$$

$$= \$500,000$$

Inventory Ordering Costs

If a firm orders inventory frequently, it can reduce its average inventory size and, thus, inventory carrying costs. For example, if a retail firm places orders each week, the quantity ordered or lot size and average inventory will be much lower than if it orders quarterly. If a firm manufactures a product only once a year to meet sales demand, the quantity produced in each run and average inventory will be much higher than if it schedules production runs six times a year.

Of course there are also costs associated with ordering inventory. However, these "ordering" costs do not include the actual cost of the merchandise, but rather all the other costs of acquiring inventory. These may include the clerical costs a retail firm incurs when placing orders with a wholesaler or the "set-up" costs a manufacturer must incur when switching production from one product to another. Most ordering costs are fixed, since, for example, the clerical work involved in placing an order for 1,000 umbrellas is not much different from that in placing an order for 10. Likewise the set-up costs of producing 1 million salt shakers are not much different from the set-up costs of producing 100 thousand. Total ordering costs are calculated by multiplying the number of orders times the cost per order (O). The number of orders placed is equal to the total usage (S) divided by the order quantity (Q).

$$\text{Total ordering costs} = S/Q \times O$$

Example	

Ace expects to sell 160,000 personal computer units in 1988. Production set-up costs for the computer units are approximately $20,000 per run. If the company schedules ("orders") runs of 8,000 units per run, the company will need 20 production runs per year. The company will have 20 orders during the year at a cost of $20,000 per order. Total ordering costs will be $400,000.

$$\text{Total ordering costs} = 160,000/8,000 \times \$20,000$$

$$= \$400,000$$

ECONOMIC ORDER QUANTITY (EOQ)

The EOQ is the lot size or order quantity that will minimize total inventory costs for a given sales level. Total inventory costs are the sum of carrying costs plus ordering costs. At the EOQ level, inventory carrying costs will be equal to ordering costs. For this reason, the EOQ approach to minimizing inventory costs is also known as the *cost-balancing* method. The relationships of ordering costs, carrying costs, and total inventory costs to the quantity ordered are shown in Table 12-3 for Ace Company, based on the following assumptions:

cost balancing

- Total annual sales: 160,000 units
- Production set-up costs/run: $20,000
- Computer inventory cost/unit: $100

The table shows that, if Ace schedules 20 production runs of 8,000 per units per run, total inventory costs will be minimized (column 6) at a level of $800,000, given the estimated sales volume of 160,000 units. Thus, the

TABLE 12-3   Relationship of Inventory Costs to Order Quantity

(1) Orders	(2) Order Quantity	(3) Order Cost	(4) Average Inventory	(5) Carrying Costs	(6) Total Inventory Cost
5	32,000	100,000	16,000	1,600,000	1,700,000
10	16,000	200,000	8,000	800,000	1,000,000
15	10,667	300,000	5,333	533,333	833,333
20	8,000	400,000	4,000	400,000	800,000
25	6,400	500,000	3,200	320,000	820,000
30	5,333	600,000	2,667	266,667	866,667

EOQ is 8,000 units. Not coincidentally, notice that at this level of inventory ordering costs will just equal carrying costs. If fewer but longer runs are scheduled, say 10 runs of 16,000 units, ordering costs will be lower but carrying costs will be much higher, and total inventory costs will be higher.

EOQ Formula

The EOQ formula provides a more exact and direct way of determining the EOQ:[2]

where:

Q = order quantity (in units)

S = anticipated usage requirements for the period (in units)

O = cost of ordering

C = carrying cost per unit

economic order quantity (EOQ)

Then, the economic order quantity (Q^*) is:

$$Q^* = \sqrt{\frac{2SO}{C}} \qquad (12\text{-}2)$$

With the figures for the Ace Company,

$$Q^* = \sqrt{\frac{2(160{,}000)\,(20{,}000)}{100}}$$

$$= 8{,}000$$

Exhibit 12-4 shows the more general relationship between inventory costs and quantity ordered. Notice that, where the order cost curve intersects the carrying cost line (Q^*), both costs are equal. In addition, the "saucer-shaped" total inventory cost curve is at its minimum point at Q^*. At order quantities less than Q^*, order costs are greater than carrying costs; the firm should carry more and order less. When the order quantity is greater than Q^*, carrying costs are greater than ordering costs; the firm should carry less inventory and order more frequently.

---

[2]The formula is easily derived. At the economic order quantity, total carrying costs are equal to total ordering costs. Thus, one simply solves for the quantity, Q, at which both are equal.

$$\text{Total carrying costs} = (Q/2) \times C$$

$$\text{Total ordering costs} = (S/Q) \times O$$

then set,

$$(Q/2) \times C = (S/Q) \times O$$

$$Q^2 = (2SO)/C$$

$$Q^* = \sqrt{\frac{2SO}{C}}$$

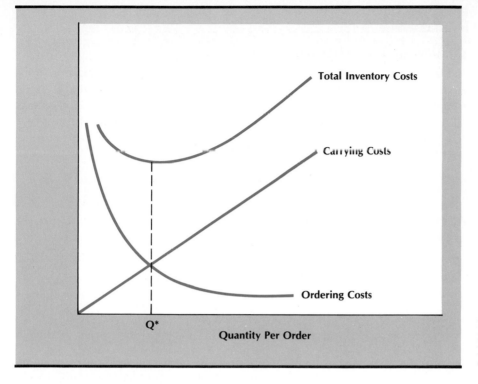

Total Inventory Costs

Carrying Costs

Ordering Costs

Q*

Quantity Per Order

EXHIBIT 12-4
Relationship of
Inventory Costs to
Order Quantity

Quantity Discounts and the EOQ

The EOQ method is a useful framework for analyzing the trade-offs between order frequency and inventory size, but it contains many restrictive assumptions in the form it has been presented. One of these assumptions is that product costs are not affected by the quantity ordered. This is not realistic. The cost per unit of large orders tends to be lower than for small orders. For example, when Ace's production manager can schedule a longer run, labor productivity will be higher and material usage will be more efficient than for shorter runs, and costs of production will decrease. Similarly, if Ace buys a million semiconductors from Japan Data, Ace is likely to get a price discount. Discounts on large orders reflect the fact that selling costs on a one-million unit order will be a lot lower for Japan Data than they will be on, say, 10 orders of 100,000 each. Japan Data passes some of the savings on to Ace. If the discount quantity size is larger than the EOQ size, then Ace will not minimize inventory costs. However, the savings from the price discount may more than offset the higher inventory costs. To evaluate properly whether the company should ignore the EOQ and buy in larger discount quantities, the financial manager must consider the incremental costs and benefits. If the incremental savings on price exceed the incremental inventory costs, the company should ignore the EOQ level and take the discount.

quantity discounts

Example

Quantity Discounts and the EOQ

Let us assume that Ace expects to use 1 million specialty microchips in its production of computers. The nondiscounted cost of the chips is $1.00 each. Order costs are $1,000 per order, and carrying costs are 20 percent of inventory acquisition cost, or 20 cents per unit. With this information, the EOQ formula indicates that the optimal order quantity is 100,000 units, as shown below:

$$Q^* = \sqrt{\frac{2 \times 1,000,000 \times 1,000}{.20}} = 100,000 \text{ units}$$

At the indicated EOQ, inventory carrying costs ($10,000) will equal ordering costs and total inventory costs will be $20,000, as shown below:

(1)	(2)	(3)	(4)	(5)	(6)
			Average	Carrying	Total
Quantity	No. Orders	Ordering Costs	Inventory	Costs	Inventory Cost
100,000	10	10,000	5,000	10,000	20,000

Now let us assume that Japan Data offers Ace a discount of two cents per chip on orders of 200,000 units or more. At this order level Ace's inventory costs will not be minimized and will total $25,000, as shown below,

(1)	(2)	(3)	(4)	(5)	(6)
			Average	Carrying	Total
Quantity	No. Orders	Ordering Costs	Inventory	Costs	Inventory Costs
200,000	5	5,000	100,000	20,000	25,000

Inventory costs will be $5,000 higher than necessary, but the firm will save $20,000 on the purchase of microchips (two cents per unit),

Savings per unit × Number of units purchased = Savings from discount

$$.02 \times 1,000,000 = \$20,000$$

In this case, Ace should take advantage of the quantity offer even though inventory costs will not be minimized, because the firm will increase profits by $15,000 ($20,000–5,000).

REORDER POINT (*RP*)

Since there is a lag, or delay, between the placing of an order and the receipt of the materials, the firm must have a procedure for signalling management when it is time to place a new order. Assuming that inventories are used at an even rate, the relation of new orders (or production runs) and the safety stocks of raw materials (or finished goods) might be diagramed as shown in Exhibit 12-5.

reorder point

Assume that the safety stock for an inventory item is 100 units and that the EOQ is 1,000 units. If the company uses 50 units per week and two weeks normally elapse from the time the order is placed to delivery, the reorder point should be set at 200 units. When the inventory reaches 200 units, an order would be placed for 1,000 units.[3] By the time that order arrives two weeks later, the inventory will be reduced to 100 units. If the order does not arrive on time, the firm can dip into its safety stocks for two weeks. In general, the reorder point when a safety stock is involved can be expressed as follows:

$$RP\text{(units)} = \text{(Lead time in weeks} \times \text{Weekly usage)} + \text{Safety Stock}$$

$$(12\text{-}3)$$

The reorder point for the above example would be at 200 units [i.e., (2 × 50) + 100]. Of course, the reorder point also could be expressed in terms of daily usage.

SAFETY STOCKS

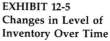

A portion of inventory is maintained as a safety stock to absorb random fluctuations in purchasing, production, or sales. Thus, even though Ace

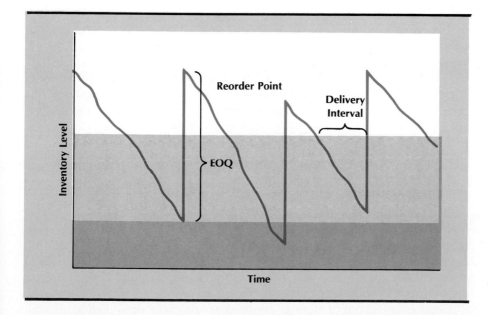

**EXHIBIT 12-5
Changes in Level of
Inventory Over Time**

_____

[3]An alternative procedure is to order at regular intervals and adjust the size of the order to the rate of usage.

orders 200,000 microchips at a time, the company would not time its orders so that it runs out of one shipment just as the next is arriving. Instead, Ace will keep some stock to use in maintaining an even flow of production in case Japan Data's microchips do not meet specifications or delivery of the chips is delayed. Safety stocks in the form of goods in process provide a continual flow of materials through the machines in spite of occasional delays at one stage or another in the process. Finally, safety stocks would also be maintained in finished goods to avoid making customers wait for delivery in the event of production problems or unexpected sales demand.

In determining the appropriate sizes of safety stocks, the firm's financial manager should consider, principally, the risk of running out of stock, the relationship of inventory size to stock-outs, and the relation of the costs of carrying inventory to the costs of being out of stock.

Risk of Stock Outs

When a firm has unexpectedly large sales demands, it may run out of inventory stock. Then some shipments will have to be delayed or "back-ordered." If customers want prompt delivery or if competitors have ample supplies, these *stock outs* will mean lost sales, profits, and, possibly, market share. Safety stocks of finished goods are intended to meet fluctuations in demand. Other things being equal, the larger the safety stock, the smaller the risk of being out of stock. However, the relationship is not linear. Although the number of stock-outs can be reduced by increasing the inventory of finished goods, they are not reduced in proportion to the increases in inventory.

Experience indicates the relationship between inventory size and stock-outs is somewhat as shown in Exhibit 12-6. As indicated in Exhibit 12-6, an increase in inventory investment from $50 to $100 effects a marked reduction in the percentage of stock-outs, from about 44 percent to 24 percent. However, a corresponding improvement is not obtained by increasing the investment further. An inventory investment of $300 results in a stock-out rate of 5 percent, whereas an investment of $500 is required to reduce stock-outs to 2 percent.

Stock Out Costs

In the case of raw materials, the costs of being out of stock may be the costs of shutting down the production line. In some continuous-process industries, such as a steel mill, this may be very high. In late 1986 a General Motors plant that produces auto electronics in Indiana went on strike. In a matter of days, 11 other GM plants were forced to shut down due to running out of electronics parts.

Costs of being out of stock of finished goods show up in lost sales and emergency production orders. The cost of these lost sales is the profits they

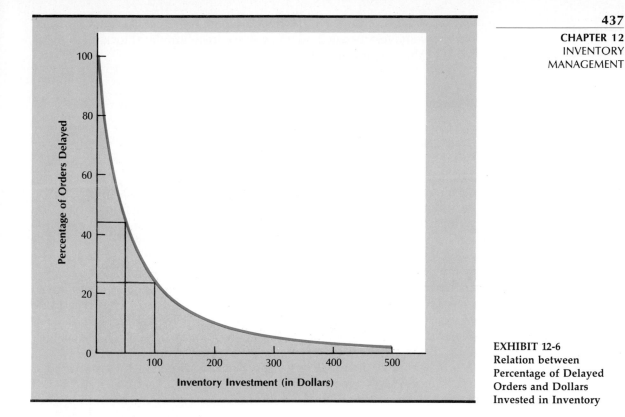

EXHIBIT 12-6
Relation between
Percentage of Delayed
Orders and Dollars
Invested in Inventory

would have added as well as the incremental production and other costs. There are also "hidden" costs. For example, it is impossible to tell what future sales will be lost if the firm acquires a reputation for being out of stock or slow on delivery. Customers may gradually drift away without making their reasons explicit. Nonetheless, an important first step is the recognition by management that there are costs of being out for stock and that these costs may be considerable.

ANTICIPATION STOCKS

anticipation stocks

In addition to safety stocks, firms may need anticipation stocks in order to carry them through a seasonal bulge in purchasing, production, or sales. Many business concerns cannot aim to have fairly constant levels of inventory throughout a year but must build up inventories because of seasonal factors. Steel mills around the Great Lakes must accumulate inventories of iron ore during the summer months to keep production going during the winter when the lake freighters cannot bring in ore. Because canners and other food processors must pack when the crops are harvested, they build up large stocks of finished goods. Manufacturers of toys, lawn mowers, and snow shovels usually find it necessary to accumulate stocks well in advance of their selling seasons.

Size of Anticipation Stocks

The first step in the determination of anticipation stocks is to prepare a forecast of sales by period. Incorporated in this forecast should be an estimate of the probable degree of error in the forecast. It is often useful to compare past forecasts with actual results to estimate the probable error. Assume that (1) experience has shown that estimates of seasonal movements in sales are often wide of the mark; (2) the lead time from production to finished product is six weeks; and (3) the industry practice is to provide immediate delivery to customers. If a firm errs in estimating sales, as is likely, it will have little opportunity to overcome any inventory shortage by rushing through a production order in time to provide the desired level of customer service. About the only way out of this situation may be to maintain rather large anticipation stocks of finished goods. However, to do so increases both the costs and risks of excess inventory investment. For some firms, such decisions are equivalent to "betting the firm." If the decision turns out to be wrong, the firm will go bankrupt.

On the other hand, if production can be adjusted to sales rapidly, anticipation stocks need not be as high. Consider a fast-food franchise. It maintains very little in the way of an inventory of finished goods but relies on a hot griddle to bring finished goods into line with demand. In other industries, customers do not expect immediate delivery, so that adjustments of production to demand may be made by expanding or contracting the delivery time. This situation is true, in large part, of the machine tool industry.

The guiding principle in planning the level of anticipation stocks is to minimize the combined cost of being out of stock and the costs of carrying excess inventory. The concept may be illustrated by using some basic figures for the White Manufacturing Company, which appear in Table 12-4. Assume that one has made an estimate of the units of sales (demand) for each period. The word "period" is used to indicate that estimates of sales and production must be prepared not by months but by production days. This takes into account the fact that production days in March exceed those in February. To simplify the illustration, planned production, sales, and inventories for only six periods are shown.

> **Example**

Sales for the White Manufacturing Company vary from 20 to 80 units per period. By using inventories to uncouple production from sales, the ad-

TABLE 12-4 Determination of Level of Anticipation Stocks for the White Manufacturing Company

Period	1	2	3	4	5	6	Total
Planned sales (units)	50	40	20	50	80	60	300
A. Level production							
Planned production	50	50	50	50	50	50	300
Inventory (end of period)*	10	20	50	50	20	10	
Safety stocks	10	10	10	10	10	10	
Inventory in excess of safety stocks	0	10	40	40	10	0	100 unit-periods
Cost of carrying one unit each period = $1							
Cost of anticipation stocks for level production = $100							
B. Variable production							
Planned production	50	40	40	50	60	60	300
Inventory (end of period)*	10	10	30	30	10	10	
Safety stocks	10	10	10	10	10	10	
Inventory in excess of safety stocks	0	0	20	20	0	0	40 unit-periods
Cost of carrying one unit one period = $1							
Cost of anticipation stocks for variable production = $40							

*Assuming opening balance of 10 units.

vantages of level production can be obtained at the cost of carrying additional inventory. If the company plans to produce 50 units every period, inventories will rise as high as 50 units (in periods three and four), or 40 units in excess of the assumed safety stocks of 10 units. Over the entire six periods, the company will carry a total overstock of 100 units or, to put it another way, will maintain an inventory of 100 unit-periods in excess of the safety stocks. On the assumption that it costs $1 per unit to carry it in inventory for one period, the inventory carrying cost of the level production plan is $100.

At the other extreme, a manager might plan to produce strictly in accordance with the sales pattern. Under this system there would be no overstock. If actual sales follow planned sales, each period should end with a minimum safety stock of 10 units. This production pattern may be undesirable for several reasons. It may even be impossible if a firm does not have the capacity to produce 80 units per period (the maximum level of demand). As a compromise between level production and the full seasonal production, a firm might adopt the production and inventory schedule shown in the lower half of Table 12-4. In this case, production varies from 40 to 60 units per period, and the anticipation inventory is reduced to 40 unit-periods. Against the carrying cost of inventory ($40), the added costs of the fluctuations in production must be balanced. With variable rather than level production, there may be costs such as overtime, layoffs, or training. Should these costs exceed the $60 saving in inventory carrying cost that resulted from adopting the variable production plan, it would be unwise to accept this proposal. Intangible considerations concerning morale and relations with the union might also enter into the decision. By experimenting with various alternative production plans (or by more elaborate mathematical calculations), a production pattern may be developed that will meet seasonal demand with the desired degree of safety and keep combined production and inventory carrying costs at a minimum.

Once production and inventory schedules have been adopted, the plans must constantly be checked against actual experience. Should sales rise above expectations, safety stocks may be drawn down and production schedules increased. Again, it should be emphasized that the safety stocks should be used rather than allow the full impact of the higher sales to be felt by the production schedule. The object is to permit a relatively smooth adjustment in production schedules. If action is taken too quickly, or if the adjustment in production schedules is too large, inventory may build up so rapidly that production schedules must be cut back sharply. With a poor inventory control system, it is possible to magnify, rather than minimize, the fluctuations of sales on production schedules.

When lead time is long and the season short, there may be no opportunity to replenish stocks if there is an error in estimates of sales. Orders lost then are lost forever. (This was the case of the manufacturer of "Cabbage Patch Kids" in its first year.) Moreover , if one errs on the other extreme and overstocks, prices will probably have to be reduced sharply to clean out the inventory after Christmas. Although this is sometimes termed a "crash problem," it represents only a more extreme version of the general problem of determining anticipation stocks. In these crash problems, the penalties of substantial errors on either side are usually greater than in industries with a less intense seasonal movement in sales.

S U M M A R Y

Inventory investment is costly as well as risky. It is the least liquid of all the firm's current assets, and thus errors in inventory management can have particularly adverse consequences for a firm's economic value. The financial manager has an important responsibility for making sure that inventory costs and risks are minimized. This chapter presented a model the financial manager can use in identifying, assessing, and minimizing the costs of inventory investment. Although rigid in its assumptions, the model can be modified to incorporate more realistic considerations. Minimizing inventory costs will result in smaller levels of inventories than the production or marketing managers will want. The financial manager must consult with them to insure that all important tangible as well as intangible factors are considered before recommending changes to existing policies and practices.

The smaller a firm's inventories, the greater the risks of stock-outs. Stock-outs can be extremely costly in both production and marketing terms. By investing in safety stocks, the probability of stock-outs can be reduced. While carrying safety stocks large enough to eliminate all stock-outs is not cost-effective, the financial manager should try to gauge what level of stock-outs is reasonable by balancing the costs of safety stock investments against the costs associated with stock-outs.

When a firm's sales are highly seasonal or unpredictable, anticipation stocks may be held in order to stabilize production or exploit fully the sales opportunities that may arise. Again, the financial manager must attempt to balance the increased costs of carrying anticipation stocks against the costs associated with variable production or lost sales.

MULTIPLE CHOICE QUESTIONS

1. FIFO inventory valuation requires:
   a) Excellent timing
   b) Cost of goods sold reflects cost of oldest inventory purchases
   c) Cost of goods sold reflects inflation
   d) Cost of goods sold reflects cost of most recent inventory purchases

2. LIFO inventory valuation requires:

   a) Cost of goods sold reflects cost of most recent inventory purchases
   b) Cost of goods sold reflects cost of oldest inventory purchases
   c) Larger investments in assets
   d) Bigger tax liabilities

3. A five-day reduction in the production process time will:

   a) Lead to unemployment
   b) Reduce inventory conversion time
   c) Increase inventory conversion time
   d) Increase the cash operating cycle

4. An ABC inventory control system is based on the idea that:

   a) Warehousemen are not bright
   b) Only three items, at most, are important in any inventory
   c) Letters are easier to handle than numbers
   d) Only three classes of inventory are needed for most inventory management

5. The inventory average age is calculated by:

   a) Counting the number of candles in stock
   b) Dividing inventory by cost of goods sold
   c) Dividing inventory by cost of goods sold per day
   d) Dividing inventory by 360

6. The EOQ formula is that order quantity at which:

   a) Inventory is minimized
   b) Inventory carrying costs are minimized
   c) Inventory order costs are zero
   d) Inventory carrying costs equal inventory ordering costs

7. The reorder point is affected by:

   a) Sales price per unit
   b) Inventory usage rates
   c) The method of inventory valuation used
   d) Average inventory age

8. In the ABC inventory control system, C items:

   a) Account for most of the inventory value
   b) Account for least of the inventory value
   c) Account for most of the inventory cost
   d) Account for least of the inventory quantity

DISCUSSION QUESTIONS

1. Identify the three basic methods used to record inventory values. How are financial statements affected by inventory values recorded under these methods during periods of rising prices?

2. How are safety and anticipation stocks affected by level versus variable production schedules?

3. Explain the time-to-conversion implications of a change in inventory turnover on a firm's short-term cash operating cycle. How might such a change affect profitability?

4. Explain how the inventory average age (IAA) is calculated. Compare the IAA and the inventory conversion time period.

5. Identify some of the major costs associated with the carrying of inventory.

6. What costs must be balanced when trying to minimize total inventory costs?

7. Describe the economic order quantity formula.

8. Explain the role of safety stocks in the management of inventory.

9. Describe some of the trade-off considerations involved in the costs of carrying inventory relative to the costs of being out of stock.

10. Explain the use of anticipation stocks in the management of inventory involving seasonal operations.

SOLVED PROBLEMS

SP-1. Flit Corp. is a retail food store. During the coming year it expects to sell 50,000 cans of green beans. The corporation currently has 25,000 cans in stock, purchased at 15 cents per can. In six months a shipment of 25,000 more cans will be received at a cost of 18 cents per can. At year end, next year, another 25,000-can shipment will be received, at a cost of 20 cents. The corporation has decided to set one price — 24 cents per can — for all sales during the coming year.

inventory valuation

a) Ignore the other sales activities of the store. Prepare three different statements showing the sales, cost of goods sold, and gross profits on the bean sales on the basis of FIFO, LIFO, and Average-cost inventory valuation methods.

b) Calculate the gross profit margin under each alternative.

c) Show the effect of each inventory valuation on the inventory account of the year-end balance sheet.

SP-2. X Corporation maintains an inventory of five items. These items, costs per unit, and the number of units carried in inventory are shown below. Set up an ABC inventory control system.

ABC inventory system

Item	Cost/Unit	Quantity
X1	$ 0.001	10,000
X2	5.000	20
X3	.150	313
X4	40.000	5
X5	1.000	168

SP-3. Sales for Watt Co. are expected to be $1,200,000. Cost of goods sold will average 70 percent of sales.

   a) Calculate the average age of Watt's inventory, assuming an average inventory level of $168,000.
   b) Calculate the firm's average inventory if the average inventory age is reduced by one day.
   c) Assuming a 20-percent cost of carrying and financing inventory, how much will Watt Co. expect to save for each day it can reduce its average inventory age?
   d) Watt Co. can cut its average inventory age by ordering smaller amounts more frequently. Assume that the firm can decrease its inventory average age by 15 days if it is willing to pass up quantity discounts of 1 percent on its annual raw materials purchases (these total $600,000 out of total cost of goods sold). In addition, ordering costs will rise by $1,500. Should the firm change its inventory policy?

PROBLEMS

1. Jet Inc., a food retailer, expects to sell 100,000 cans of tomato soup during the coming year. Assume that the soup will cost an average of 15 cents per can and that this is the cost for inventory valuation. Inventory carrying and financing costs average 20 percent of inventory dollar value. Ordering costs are $100 per order.

   a) Calculate the annual carrying costs, ordering costs, total inventory costs, and order size in units which result from placing one order, two orders, three orders, four orders, and five orders annually. From the information you develop, determine the least-cost order option.
   b) Use the EOQ formula to determine the optimal order quantity. How many orders should be placed each year?
   c) Based on the result in (b) above, what will total inventory costs be? How often should orders be placed (assume a 360-day year)?

2. Assume that Jet's supplier offers a discount price of 14 cents per can on orders of 50,000 cans or more.

   a) Calculate the cost savings if the firm buys in lots of 50,000 cans.
   b) Calculate total inventory costs if Jet buys 50,000 cans at 14 cents per can.
   c) Should the firm buy in lots of 50,000 cans instead of its EOQ order size of 5,820?

3. Wizard Electronic Games, Inc. manufactures and sells hand-held electronic games and toys. The firm expects to sell 10,000 units during the year at an average price of $25 per unit. A pre-assembled core part for each unit must be purchased by Wizard from a supplier. Wizard has on hand 2,000 core parts at a cost of $15 per unit. In the near future,

Wizard expects to purchase 5,000 core parts at $18 each. Later during the year, 5,000 more parts will be purchased at an anticipated $20 price per unit. Other costs of production are expected to be $20,000, with operating expenses also projected at $20,000. The income tax rate is 34 percent.

a) Prepare an income statement for Wizard using the FIFO inventory accounting method.
b) Prepare an income statement for Wizard using the LIFO inventory accounting method.
c) Prepare an income statement for Wizard using the average cost inventory accounting method.
d) Compare the gross profit margins and net profit margins under the three inventory accounting methods for Wizard Electronics.
e) Calculate the year-end inventory values that would be shown on Wizard Electronic's balance sheet under each inventory accounting method.

4. The Wizard Electronic Games company described in Problem 3 expects that, due to economies of scale, its cost for pre-assembled core parts to be used in producing electronic games and toys will decline next year. Assume the first 5,000 core parts purchased will cost $19 each, with the second 5,000 having a $17 per unit price. Given the same sales, other production costs, and operating costs anticipated for this year in Problem 3, estimate the net income and year-end inventory balances for next year for Wizard Electronics under each of the three inventory accounting methods. If one method must be used for both years, which one would you recommend? Why?

inventory valuation

5. You have been asked to establish an ABC inventory control system for the Smither Company, which has 10 items that are carried in inventory. Following is the average price per unit and the average number of units carried, listed by item code:

ABC inventory system

Item Code	Average Cost Per Unit	Average Number of Units
100	$15.00	50
110	5.00	80
120	.175	1144
130	25.00	20
140	.10	700
150	45.00	10
160	40.00	10
170	.15	900
180	36.00	20
190	60.00	6

a) Calculate the average investment in each item.
b) Express for each item its average investment as a percentage of the total inventory investment.
c) Express for each item its average number of units as a percentage of the total number of units in inventory.
d) Classify the items into groups, indicating the need for: tight control (A items), average control (B items), or loose control (C items). Explain the basis for your ABC inventory classification system.

inventory turnover

6. The management of Green Manufacturing Company requests a study of alternative inventory policies for next year. Forecasted sales are $20.3 million, with beginning and ending inventories projected at $4.1 million and $4.9 million, respectively. Cost of goods sold is estimated to be 75 percent of sales.

a) Determine the average inventory turnover for next year. Estimate the average age of the inventory.
b) If the production process could be revised so that the beginning and ending inventories would be $3.9 million and $4.3 million, respectively, what will be the average inventory turnover if no sales are lost? Also calculate the new estimate of the inventory average age.
c) If the cost of carrying or financing average inventory amounts is 20 percent, estimate the potential savings associated with the new policy.

inventory conversion time

7. The management of the Black Company plans to tighten its inventory control policy so that the inventory conversion time will be reduced from 80 days to 72 days. Under the old 80-day policy, average inventory was expected to be $2,000,000. Annual sales were expected to remain at the same $12,000,000 level for the 80-day or 72-day conversion time plans. Cost of goods sold are expected to continue at the 75 percent of sales level.

a) Calculate the average inventory outstanding under the 72-day conversion time alternative.
b) The Black Company currently incurs carrying and financing costs on its inventory holdings amounting to 25 percent of average inventory. How much is it likely to save by reducing its inventory conversion time by eight days?
c) In order to achieve a reduction in conversion time for its inventory, Black will lose purchase quantity discounts amounting to .3 percent of its $6,000,000 in annual material purchases. Ordering costs are also expected to increase by $14,000 annually. Calculate the total costs associated with an eight-day reduction in inventory conversion time.
d) Would you recommend that Black retain the 80-day conversion time or adopt the 72-day plan?

e) To what extent, if any, would your answer in Part (d) change if the new inventory control policy achieves only a six-day reduction in conversion time instead of the anticipated reduction of eight days? Show your calculations.

8. The ARC Company is a manufacturer of toys. Management closely controls the relation of the dollar value of finished goods inventory to sales. Comparison with similar companies indicates that ARC's inventory of finished goods is somewhat higher in relation to sales than is typical for the industry. Yet ARC has experienced a number of stock-outs and has had to dispose of some items at distress prices in late December. What is wrong? What improvements can you suggest?

inventory control

9. The Lark Company is considering whether to tighten its current inventory control policy so that its inventory average will be reduced from 85 days to 75 days. Based on a 360-day year and an 85-day inventory average age, year-end (and average) inventory is estimated at $800,000. The firm's gross profit margin is 25 percent of sales.

inventory average age

   a) Calculate the annual cost of goods sold and annual sales level based on the inventory average age of 85 days.
   b) Sales are expected to fall by 10 percent due to production and distribution interruptions and stock-outs if the inventory control policy is tightened to achieve a 75-day inventory average age. Calculate the average amount of inventory that will be outstanding under this policy.
   c) The carrying and financing costs on the firm's average inventory is 20 percent. Should Lark tighten its inventory control policy even though ordering costs will increase by $2,000 and some sales will be lost?

10. Byer Plastics pays $2 per unit of materials ordered from a supplier and uses 10,000 units per year. The firm's inventory carrying cost amounts to 25 percent per year of the average inventory dollar value. Each time an order is placed with the supplier, Byer incurs an ordering cost of $20.

economic order quantity

   a) Estimate the annual carrying costs, ordering costs, and total inventory costs associated with placing one order, five orders, 10 orders, and 20 orders annually. Also indicate the order size in units for each number of orders.
   b) Prepare a graph of the cost in dollars (y-axis) versus the size of order in units (x-axis) and plot the appropriate information from Part (a). Estimate the economic order quantity from your graph.
   c) Use the EOQ formula to calculate the economic order quantity for Byer Plastics.

11. Assume that Byer Plastics in Problem 10 is offered quantity purchase discounts by its supplier. If Byer places an order for 500 units, the price per unit would be $2. Other order sizes and prices per unit include:

quantity discounts

1,000 units ($1.80 each), 2,000 units ($1.70 each), and 10,000 units ($1.50 each).

a) Estimate the total inventory costs associated with each of the four order sizes based on the carrying costs and ordering costs provided in Problem 10.
b) Which order size in units would you recommend?
c) To what extent has the economic order quantity identified in Problem 10 been affected by the opportunity for taking purchase quantity discounts?

level vs. variable production

12. The Bentley Manufacturing Company buys large quantities of raw material X at $2.00 per unit. The company's bookkeeper has determined the following costs associated with carrying the inventory of this product. Item X constitutes about 10 percent of the raw material inventory, and there is little variation in its use from week to week. Estimated carrying costs of inventory are 18 percent of inventory value. Depreciation and property taxes on space occupied are $4000 annually (based on floor space; there is no alternative use for the space at present). Estimated direct costs per purchase order are $9.00. Estimated requirements for one year are 90,000 units.

a) What is the economic order size and number of orders, assuming that a safety stock of 950 units of this item is desired?
b) If it takes about one week to secure delivery, at what level of inventory should a reorder be placed? Show your calculations.

13. Based on the information given below:

a) Draw up complete schedules showing the determination of the carrying costs that result under level and variable production alternatives.
b) What is the cost of anticipation stocks for each alternative?
c) If the added costs of variable production (for overtime, employee training, etc.) are estimated to be $100, what recommendation would you make to management?

	Periods						
	1	2	3	4	5	6	
							Total
Projected sales (units)	32	48	56	60	76	58	330
Variable production	40	50	60	70	60	50	330

Carrying cost/unit/period = $1.65
Desired safety stock level = 15 units
Inventory at beginning of period one = 15 units

SP-1. a)

Inventory Valuation Method

	FIFO	LIFO	Average
Sales	$12,000	$12,000	$12,000
CGS			
25,000 cans @ .15 = 3,750		.20 = 5,000	.177 = 4,417
25,000 cans @ .18 = 4,500		.18 = 4,500	.177 = 4,417
	8,250	9,500	8,833
Gross Profit	$3,750	$2,500	$3,167

b)

	FIFO	LIFO	Average
Gross Profit Margin	$\dfrac{\$3750}{\$12,000} = 31.25\%$	$\dfrac{\$2500}{\$12,000} = 20.8\%$	$\dfrac{\$3167}{\$12,000} = 26.4\%$

The FIFO method is "best" in the sense of showing higher profits and profitability than the other inventory methods. However, higher taxes will have to be paid with the FIFO method than with the LIFO method. If you want to minimize taxes, LIFO is "best."

c)

FIFO inventory: 25,000 cans @   .20 = $5,000
LIFO inventory: 25,000 cans @   .15 =   3,750
Average inventory: 25,000 cans @ .1767 −   4,417

SP-2. First, calculate the average investment in each item.
Average investment = (Cost/Unit) × (Quantity)

X1	= $ 10
X2	= 100
X3	= 47
X4	= 200
X5	= 168
Total	$525

Second, calculate the percentage of total investment for each item.

Item	% of Total Investment
X1 = $ 10/525	.02
X2 = 100/525	.19
X3 = 47/525	.09
X4 = 200/525	.38
X5 = 168/525	.32

Third, group into classes A, B and C.

Class	Items	% of Total
A (70% of Total Investment)	X4	.38
	X5	.32
		.70
B (20% of Total Investment)	X2	.19
C (10% of Total Investment)	X1	.02
	X3	.09
		.11

SP-3. a)

$$\text{Inventory average age} = \frac{\text{Inventory}}{\text{Annual Cost of Goods Sold}/360}$$

$$= \frac{\$168,000}{\$(1,200,000)(.70)/360}$$

$$= 72 \text{ days}$$

b)

$$\text{Average inventory} = \frac{\text{Annual Cost of Goods Sold}}{360/\text{inventory average age}}$$

$$= \frac{840,000}{360/71 \text{ days}}$$

$$= \$165,667$$

Notice that we are assuming an average inventory age of 71 days rather than the expected 72 days (i.e., a reduction of one day).

c)

$$\text{Average inventory (72 day-age)} = \$168,000$$

$$\text{Average inventory (71 day-age)} = \$165,667$$

$$\text{Reduction in average inventory investment} = \$\ \ 2,333$$

$$\text{Annual Savings at 20\%} = \$\ \ \ \ \ 467$$

By reducing its average inventory age by one day, inventory investment can be reduced by $2,333 resulting in savings of $467.

d) Savings of $467 are realized for each day average inventory age is reduced. With a 15-day reduction, savings would be $7,005.

Savings per day reduction = $467

times 15 days   15

Total annual savings $7,005

Costs of the new inventory policy consist of lost discounts and high ordering costs.

$$\text{Lost purchase discounts} = (1\%) \times (\$600,000)$$
$$= \$6,000$$

Increased ordering costs = 1,500

Total costs of new
inventory policy $7,500

At this point, the costs of the inventory policy change outweigh the gains, so Watt Co. should not change. However, as sales volume increases, a 15-day policy will increase savings and the proposed inventory policy may become advantageous.

REFERENCES

Beranek, William, "Financial Implications of Lot Size Inventory Models," *Management Science*, 13, April 1967, pp. 401-408.

Brooks, L. D. "Risk-Return Criteria and Optimal Inventory Stocks," *Engineering Economist*, Summer 1980, pp. 275-299.

Magee, John F. "Guides to Inventory Policy," I-III, *Harvard Business Review*, 34, January–February 1956, pp. 49-60; March–April 1956, pp. 103-116; and May–June 1956, pp. 57-70

Snyder, Arthur, "Principles of Inventory Management," *Financial Executive* 32, April 1964, pp. 16-19.

CHAPTER

13

SHORT TERM FINANCING

orking capital management requires the effective use of short-term financing sources as well as the management of short-term assets. Short-term financing constitutes an important source of operating funds for most companies. This type of financing, by definition, must be repaid in a year or less and, thus, is reflected on the firm's balance sheet as a current liability.

Short-term financing can be categorized as *spontaneous* or *negotiated*. Spontaneous financing is generated automatically during the firm's operating cycle and usually is noninterest bearing. For example, accounts payable are created automatically as soon as the company purchases raw materials on credit. Negotiated financing, on the other hand, must be arranged personally, is typically limited in amount, and bears interest charges. A short-term bank loan is an example of this type of financing.

Most firms have several short-term financing choices. For example, a firm may engage in secured forms of financing, such as pledging of accounts receivable, factoring of receivables, and inventory-secured financing. Each financing type has its own costs and borrowing conditions and should be analyzed carefully because these costs and conditions are not always obvious. This chapter illustrates procedures for analyzing common forms of short-term financing.

● Objectives and Organization of this Chapter

This chapter has two principal objectives. First it surveys the broad range of short-term financing resources available. Second it shows how the particular features of financing media impose different costs and constraints on the firm. In the first section, the chapter describes spontaneous forms of short-term credit and how they may be evaluated in terms of costs and other features. In the second section, it discusses major forms of negotiated financing, such as commercial paper and unsecured bank credit. In the third section, it describes some of the many types of secured financing.

The principal form of spontaneous financing is trade credit extended by a supplier to a buyer of its goods and services. Practically every firm has some form of trade credit.

The most common form of trade credit is the *open account*. The process is usually set in motion when the buyer sends the seller a purchase order. At the time the order is shipped, the seller sends an invoice that describes the items shipped, their selling price, and the terms of sale. The credit extended becomes an account receivable to the seller and an account payable to the buyer. In some cases, a seller who finds that a customer is well overdue on an account may request a promissory note in order to obtain a formal acknowledgment of the debt and a commitment as to the date when it will be paid.

Net Period Credit Terms

The most frequently used type of trade credit term is the net period due date and is stated as "net 30 days," "net 45 days," or over some longer period. Once the credit period has begun, the credit account must be paid in full within the stated net period. Such net period terms also may include cash discount provisions. A typical example would be the credit terms of 2/10, n/30 offered by many wholesalers of plumbing and heating supplies. This means that if the bill is paid within 10 days of the date of the invoice (compliance with the time limit is usually determined by the postmark date on the payment envelope) 2 percent can be taken off the bill. If the cash discount is not taken, the full amount of the bill must be paid within 30 days. It is not uncommon for customers to pay even later than 30 days and still try to take the discount. If the customer is an important source of business, the supplier will often overlook this; if the customer is not so important, the discount will not be allowed. This selective enforcement of terms is, of course, a form of price discrimination, which is illegal according to the Wright-Patman Act.

net period

cash discount

Some credit terms really provide no credit at all. For example, terms of cash on delivery (C.O.D.) require immediate payment to the shipper at the time of receipt. In such cases, the possibility exists that the buyer will not accept the goods or will not have sufficient funds to pay the required amount. If so, the seller has to pay round-trip shipping and handling costs. For such reasons, some sales are made on a cash-before-delivery basis (C.B.D.), meaning that payment must be received by the seller before the goods are delivered.

cash on delivery C.O.D.

cash before delivery C.B.D.

Seasonal Dating

These credit terms are designed to encourage buyers to send in orders for seasonal goods before the period of peak sales so that the seller can judge his or her market and level out production and shipping activities as much as possible. It also allows the seller to avoid significant inventory carrying costs as, in essence, the buyer is providing warehousing services to the seller. Seasonal dating arrangements are found on sales of toys and holiday greeting cards.

seasonal dating

Consignments

Under this arrangement the seller ships goods but retains title to them while they are held for sale. When the goods are sold, the buyer sends the supplier the amount realized on the sale, less gross profit; or the buyer might send the gross amount from sales until he or she has paid for all the goods consigned. The buyer has the right to return any unsold goods to the supplier. Consignment selling is common when the seller desires to get a new product on display or to put on a big sale of some item. These terms are common in the magazine publishing business.

consignment

Why Credit Terms Vary

The variations in trade credit are understandable. First, the period of credit granted is related to the nature of the commodity. Items having a high turnover, such as meats, groceries, and cigarettes, are sold on fairly short credit terms. Merchandise that is in the nature of a fad may carry fairly short terms because the supplier is not willing to bear the risk of obsolescence.

Second, the credit risk involved is reflected in the terms. Retail clothing stores are characterized by a rather high rate of failure. This may explain in part the rather large cash discount allowed; it represents an effort by the supplier to get money in as quickly as possible. Credit applicants who are particularly weak may be forced to buy on C.B.D. or C.O.D. terms.

Third, the nature of competition among suppliers is expressed in credit terms as well as in price and service. Buyers will probably obtain better credit terms from a large group of sellers than from a small group of sellers. When the product or the seller is new, easier credit terms than are customary may be one of many methods used to gain a foothold in the market. During a recession, sellers may ease their credit terms in an effort to maintain sales.

Finally, the financial strength of the seller relative to that of the buyer is also a determinant of credit terms. In some trades, the retailers must be carried along by their financially stronger suppliers. On the other hand, if the supplier is especially weak, credit terms may have to be restricted by the supplier in order to speed the inflow of cash, even at the sacrifice of sales and profits.

Trade Credit As a Source of Funds

Trade credit should be taken on purchases whenever possible, even though it may be offered only for a few days. In general, the firm should try to purchase from sellers who offer the best credit terms, giving consideration to the price, quality, and delivery of the goods purchased. Also, the financial manager should not pay trade credit bills prior to their due dates or net period dates (except to gain cash discounts).

Stretching Accounts Payable. The impact of stretching out the credit period can be examined in conjunction with a firm's short-term cash operating cycle. Let us return to the Brach Products Company example used in Chapter 10. Exhibit 13-1 illustrates Brach's time-to-conversion requirements for completing its cycle. The accounts payable conversion time averages 30 days; and along with an inventory conversion time of 90 days and an accounts receivable conversion time of 60 days, the average cash cycle requires 120 days to complete. However, if the financial manager is able to lengthen the trade credit period on purchases to 40 days (by finding more lenient suppliers or slowing payments), the average cash cycle can be reduced to 110 days. Because accounts payable will be larger, lesser amounts of other short-term and long-term funds will be needed to finance the firm's working capital.

The financing benefits of longer credit terms are easily seen in the following example. Assume that Brach's annual purchases on credit from suppliers total $6 million and year-end accounts payable are $500,000. This information can be combined in the form of the average payment period

EXHIBIT 13-1
Trade Credit Policy Impact on the Cash Operating Cycle for Brach Products Company

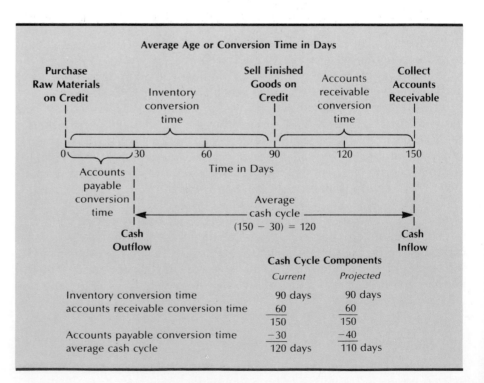

	Average Age or Conversion Time in Days	

Cash Cycle Components		
	Current	*Projected*
Inventory conversion time	90 days	90 days
accounts receivable conversion time	60	60
	150	150
Accounts payable conversion time	−30	−40
average cash cycle	120 days	110 days

(APP) discussed in Chapter 7. The APP is equal to accounts payable divided by credit purchases per day (i.e., annual credit purchases divided by 360).

average payment period
A.P.P.

$$\text{APP} = \text{Accounts payable/Credit purchases per day}$$

$$= \$500,000/\$16,667 = 30 \text{ days}$$

A lengthening of Brach's APP or accounts payable time-to-conversion to 40 days, given the same annual purchases, then would be:

$$\text{Average payables} = \text{Annual credit purchases per day} \times \text{APP}$$

$$= \$16,667 \times 40 = \$666,680$$

This would produce an increase of $166,680 in average payable levels for Brach. If the cost of financing current assets is, say 15 percent, an increase in average payables will reduce such financing costs and provide an increase in pre-tax profits of $25,000 ($166,667 × .15). Of course, this form of analysis assumes no costs are connected with a 10-day increase in the APP. In actual practice, there may be costs associated with the use of trade credit.

Trade Credit Costs

When cash discounts are available, an explicit cost arises when a firm fails to pay on time so that it loses the cash discount. Assume that credit terms are 2/10, net 30. If the invoice is for $100, the real cost of the goods is $98, and $2 is added to the cost as a finance charge if the firm fails to pay by the 10th day.[1] If the buyer would normally pay on the 30th day, it has paid a $2.00 fee for the use of $98 for 20 more days. The effective rate for those days is 2/98, and there are eighteen 20-day intervals in the year.[2] Algebraically, the effective cost of missing discounts can be calculated using Equation 13-1.

Effective cost of missing discounts:

$$= \frac{\text{Discount \%}}{100\% - \text{Discount \%}} \times \frac{360}{\text{Net period} - \text{Discount period}} \quad (13\text{-}1)$$

$$= \left(\frac{.02}{.98}\right) \times \left(\frac{360}{20}\right)$$

$$= .3673, \quad \text{or,} \quad 36.73\%$$

---

[1]The cost of purchase discounts missed is often incorporated in "Purchases" and carried through to "Cost of Goods Sold" on the income statement. In other cases, a separate expense, "Purchase Discounts Missed," may be shown.

[2]We are assuming a 360-day year (360/20 = 18) to be consistent with common practice in calculating ratios. A precise calculation would use a 365-day year, as required for disclosure of the annual percentage rate (APR) under the Consumer Credit Protection Act of 1968. The use of a 365-day year would result in a true APR of 37.24 percent.

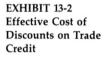

annual percentage rate (APR)

The size of the effective annual percentage interest rate (APR) associated with missing cash discounts means that, for most firms, it would be less costly to finance with other sources of funds. For example if Brach were offered 2/10, net 30 day terms on all its purchases, it would probably be advantageous to reduce its accounts payable time-to-conversion to 10 days and thus increase its average cash cycle to 140 days. The 20-day loss in accounts payable financing could be offset through a bank loan that would cost less than 37 percent.

effective cost of missing discounts

As indicated by Equation 13-1, the effective cost of passing up discounts depends in part on (a) the amount of the discount and (b) the length of the discount period. The larger the discount for early payment and the shorter the discount period, the higher the effective annual percentage interest rate (APR) will be. For example, Exhibit 13-2(a) shows the relationship between the effective interest rate and the discount percentage. Panel 13-2(b) shows the relationship between the effective interest rate (APR) and the discount period.

Other Spontaneous Financing

accruals

In addition to trade credit, firms get significant spontaneous financing from various accruals. Accruals are recurring short-term liabilities and have no explicit financing costs. Examples of accruals are wage and tax accruals. Wage accruals are generated when a company has not paid employees all the money they have earned. If employees are paid once a month, for example, the wages earned would be accrued until paid at the end of each month. Tax accruals are created when the firm has generated, but not paid, a tax liability.

EXHIBIT 13-2
Effective Cost of Discounts on Trade Credit

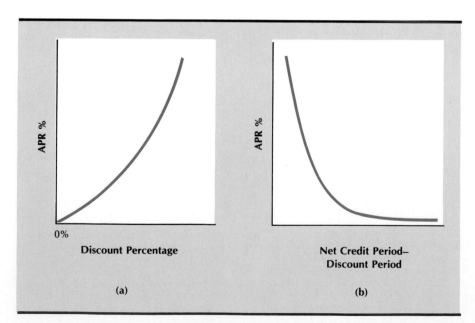

NEGOTIATED FINANCING

In contrast to spontaneous financing, negotiated financing is not automatically available to the buyer. It must be arranged, usually from a third party, such as a bank. Other sources of negotiated financing are the issue of commercial paper and loans from suppliers.

Bank Credit

Short-term financing from banks may be either secured or unsecured. Let us first discuss unsecured credit and later take up secured arrangements.

Short-term bank loans typically are established for one year or less and take the form of either a credit line or single loan arrangement. A special case of the line of credit, known as a *revolving credit* agreement, can actually be rolled over or extended for more than a year.

revolving credit

Line of Credit

A line of credit usually involves an agreement between the borrower and the bank concerning the maximum amount of credit that will be extended during any one period. Under this form of arrangement, the bank is not legally obligated to provide the credit in the amount agreed upon, an important difference from revolving credit, discussed below. However, most banks will honor their informal commitment rather than develop the reputation of being unreliable.

line of credit

Credit lines are customarily established for only a year at a time. The bank's officers usually review the line yearly and may adjust it to the changed creditworthiness of the borrower. This borrowing arrangement explains why the bank expects to be informed promptly of any change in the borrower's financial position during the year.

The most common use of credit lines is with seasonal borrowing. On the basis of a cash budget, a firm would estimate its maximum borrowings and arrange a credit line for that amount. Because the line is to meet seasonal needs, the firm should not have to use the line for one or more months out of each year (in bank parlance, the firm should be "out of the bank" for some minimum period of each year).

seasonal borrowing

Revolving Credit

Revolving credit is a formal line of credit that involves lending against a pool of accounts receivable or inventory, with those assets serving as collateral, or security for the loan. These loan arrangements frequently extend for a period of more than a year and often involve a firm commitment on the part of the bank to supply the credit, subject to certain

459

limitations. The firm may be in debt to the bank for the duration of the agreement, although the level of the debt fluctuates with the need for credit.

 ## COST OF LOANS

The cost of a bank loan (or loan from another lender) depends on how the interest rate is calculated, whether a minimum or compensating balance (to be defined) is required, the credit quality of the borrower, and the prevailing supply and demand for loans at the time of the loan request.

Lenders may determine interest charges in a number of ways. Since each method produces a different effective cost, it is important to calculate the "true" interest rate being levied so that comparisons can be made with the costs of alternative sources of funds. In general, the "true" interest rate on a loan can be estimated by dividing the dollar amount of interest by the amount of money actually used. This general relationship is shown in Equation 13-2.

$$\text{Effective interest rate} = \text{Interest charged/Money used} \qquad (13\text{-}2)$$

Simple Interest

Under this method, the stated interest rate is the same as the true or effective rate. For example, a borrower may take out a one-year loan with an interest rate of 9 percent. At the end of the year, the borrower pays $1,000 plus interest of $90. Since the borrower actually got the use of $1,000 for a full year and paid $90, the effective interest rate would be 9 percent.

$$\text{Effective interest rate} = \text{Interest charged/Money used}$$
$$= \$90/1000 = .09 \quad \text{or} \quad 9\%$$

Discount Method

discount loan

This procedure is commonly used by commercial banks. The borrower signs a note promising to pay, for example, $1,000 in one year. In contrast to a simple-interest loan, the bank takes the agreed interest charge out in advance, and thus the borrower (assuming the bank charges "9 percent, discounted") receives only $910 dollars ($1000 − $90). At the end of the year the borrower repays $1,000. Thus, the borrower has paid $90 for the use of $910 for one year. The effective rate of interest is not the stated rate of 9 percent, but 9.89 percent, as shown below:

effective interest rate

$$\text{Effective interest rate} = \$90/910 = .0989 = 9.89\%$$

Of course, the borrower who actually needs the use of $1,000 has to borrow more. The amount he or she has to borrow (B) is equal to the amount needed (N) plus the discount interest (I). Since the interest is 9 percent of the borrowing ($I = .09B$), the following general formula can be used to determine the total amount that has to be borrowed:

$$B = N + I \qquad (13\text{-}3)$$

$$= \$1,000 + .09B$$

$$.91B = \$1,000$$

$$B = \$1,000/.91 = \$1,099$$

To check: Interest of (.09 × \$1,099) \$99 is paid in advance, leaving the \$1,000 needed.

Installment Loans

Installment loans usually require monthly payments to reduce the principal. Under the "add on" method, the interest is added on to the principal and the total is repaid in equal installments. With this method, the bank would give the borrower \$1,000, but the borrower would agree to repay \$1,090 in 12 installments of \$90.83 (i.e., \$1,090/12) each. The effective rate is about twice the stated rate because the borrower is making monthly payments on the principal of the loan throughout the year and, thus, the average borrowing is less than \$1,000. In fact, the average borrowing is about half of the initial loan or, in this case, \$500 (\$1,000/2).

installment loan

The effective interest rate on installment loans can be estimated using Equation 13-4.[3]

$$i = \frac{2mD}{P(n+1)} = \frac{2(12)(90)}{1000(13)} = 16.6\% \qquad (13\text{-}4)$$

Where i = the effective annual interest rate; m = the number of payments per year (usually 12); D = the total interest charge in dollars; P = the loan principal; and n = the total number of payments.

Compensating Balances

Commercial banks frequently require that borrowers maintain deposit balances in some relation to the amount they are borrowing or the amount of the line of credit. These are called *compensating balances* because they are a form of compensation to the bank.

Compensating balances vary from bank to bank and from time to time. Sometimes the requirement is informal and not specified precisely. For example, banks may expect borrowers to maintain deposits equal to 15 to

compensating balances

---

[3]This method is only an approximation of the calculation method required by the Federal Reserve Board under the Truth in Lending section of the Consumer Protection Act of 1968 (the regulation for putting this into effect is known as Regulation Z).

20 percent of the line of credit. Some banks requiring compensating balances permit customers to average the requirement, generally over a year, in order to adjust to seasonal fluctuations in cash balances.

Effect of Compensating Balances on Loan Costs

The minimum-balance requirement adds to the costs only if the required balance is higher than the firm would normally keep in the bank. If the required balance is higher, the effect is to reduce the amount of the bank loan that can be used and to raise the effective cost of the loan. In this respect, the compensating balance is similar to a discounted loan, since interest is computed on the total borrowed but the borrower does not have use of all the funds.

Example

Assume a company obtains a loan for $100,000 at 9 percent per annum, and the bank requires a minimum deposit balance of 20 percent, or $20,000. If the borrower would not normally keep any deposits at the bank, it has use of only $80,000 of the loan although it is paying for $100,000. Consequently, the effective annual cost of the money is $9,000/$80,000 or 11.25 percent.

In general, if a company is required to keep compensating balances (and assuming the company would not normally keep other balances at the bank), the effective interest rate can be calculated with Equation 13-5.

$$\text{Effective interest rate} = \frac{\text{Interest}}{\text{Loan} - \text{compensating balance}} \quad (13\text{-}5)$$

$$= \frac{(.09)\,(100,000)}{100,000 - 20,000}$$

$$= .1125 = 11.25\%$$

Dividing the numerator and denominator of Equation 13-5 by the loan amount produces a more direct calculation of the effective interest rate:

$$\text{Effective interest rate} = \frac{\text{Interest/Loan}}{1 - \dfrac{\text{Compensating balance}}{\text{Loan}}} \quad (13\text{-}6)$$

$$= \frac{\text{Stated interest rate}}{1 - \text{Compensating balance percentage}}$$

$$= \frac{.09}{1 - .20}$$

$$= .1125 = 11.25\%$$

Working Balances.   If the company normally keeps some deposits at the bank for operating or "working" purposes, these balances can be used to offset the compensating balance requirements. For instance, in the example above, if the company normally has working balances of $15,000, it will only need to set aside $5,000 from the $100,000 loan. Thus it will have use of $95,000, and effective cost of borrowing will drop to 9.47 percent.

working balances

$$\text{Effective interest rate} = \text{Interest charges/Available funds} \quad (13\text{-}7)$$

$$= \$9{,}000/95{,}000 = 9.47\%$$

Or, more generally, let N = the amount actually needed; WB = normal working balances; cb% = compensating balance percentage; and, r = stated interest rate.

$$\text{Effective interest rate} = \left(1 - \frac{WB}{N}\right)\left(\frac{r}{1 - cb\%}\right) \quad (13\text{-}8)$$

Commercial Paper

Large, financially strong firms often have access to commercial paper funds in addition to short-term bank credit. Commercial paper consists of short-term promissory notes. These debt obligations are issued in denominations of $100,000 or more and often exceed $1 million in size. The maturity is seldom for more than 270 days.

Commercial paper may be sold through dealers (known as commercial paper houses) or sold directly to investors. Finance companies are the dominant issuers of commercial paper and directly place over three-fourths of their paper. Nonfinancial companies usually sell their paper through dealers, who typically receive a "spread" of 1/8 to 1/4 of 1 percent for their marketing services.

commercial paper

Commercial paper is sold at a discount (like U.S. Treasury Bills) from its maturity or face value instead of carrying a stated interest rate.

Example

Cost of Commercial Paper

Assume that a firm sells $1 million of commercial paper with a 180-day maturity. If the firm receives $950,000, then the effective interest rate is determined by dividing the $50,000 difference, or discount, by the available net proceeds of $950,000. This amounts to a 5.26 percent rate for one-half year. The effective interest rate is annualized by multiplying 5.26 percent by two (360 days/180 days) to determine an annual rate of 10.52 percent. The calculations are shown in Equation 13-9.

$$\text{Effective interest rate} = \frac{\text{Discount (\$)}}{\text{Face value} - \text{discount (\$)}}$$
$$\times \frac{360}{\text{Maturity term (days)}} \quad (13\text{-}9)$$

$$= \frac{50,000}{1,000,000 - 50,000} \times \frac{360}{180}$$

$$= .1052 = 10.52\%$$

Corporations willing to sell their commercial paper usually must first have lines of credit at leading commercial banks. For corporations other than large finance companies, unused lines (open-to-borrow arrangements) should equal outstanding commercial paper. This backstop by bank lines is deemed necessary because of the highly impersonal nature of the commercial paper market.

Loans from Suppliers

Occasionally suppliers provide credit to buyers in addition to trade credit. For example, a beer distributor may provide a cooler to a tavern so long as the owner continues to purchase the required brand. Although this is not cash, it relieves the owner of the necessity of using cash to buy one. The large oil companies usually finance the sales made by their outlets on credit cards by crediting the charge slips held by dealers against deliveries of gasoline. In a sense the supplier buys the accounts receivable of the service station operator. Such arrangements are most common among small businesses.

SECURED LOANS

A secured loan is a loan protected by a security interest. Secured loan arrangements are sometimes referred to as "asset-based financing" or "securitization" since the loan is backed by specific assets of the firm. Under the Uniform Commercial Code, a security interest is "an interest in personal property or fixtures that secures payment or performance of an obligation." The term *collateral* refers to "the property subject to a security interest." If the borrower does not fulfill the obligations, the creditor may seize the collateral. If the assets are more than enough to satisfy the claims of the secured creditors, the excess realized from their sale must be applied to settle the claims of any unsecured creditors before any payments are made to the owners. Should the pledged assets be insufficient to satisfy the claims of the secured creditors, they share and share alike in any remaining assets with the unsecured creditors to the extent of their unsatisfied claims.

collateral

Lenders do not "reach for security," as they put it, because they think that a loan will not be repaid. If they thought that, they would not make the loan in the first place. Bankers may ask for security on marginal loans rather than turn down the applications on an unsecured basis, but they hope that they do not have to seize—and "get stuck" with—the assets pledged.

Let us now consider the various assets that might serve as collateral. Since we are considering only short-term loans, it is understandable that the desired collateral is correspondingly liquid, such as accounts receivable and inventory.

RECEIVABLE LOANS

Accounts receivable can be used to secure short-term financing either by a pledging or factoring arrangement. In a pledging arrangement, the borrower keeps ownership of the receivables. In a factoring arrangement, ownership of the receivables is transferred to the factor (a financial institution).

Pledging of Receivables

A business firm may give a security interest to a lender in all or a portion of its accounts receivable. In essence, a pool of accounts receivable is assigned to a lender. Feeding into the pool are newly created accounts receivable resulting from sales. Reductions in the pool result from customers' payments on account, returns and allowances, bad debts, and overdue accounts. If the pledged accounts receivable are not paid, the borrower takes the loss. The lending procedures are designed to limit borrowings to some fixed percentage of the receivables in the pool.

pledging of receivables

Since security agreement documents used are relatively standard, the negotiating between lender and borrower centers on the percentage of the dollar amount advanced in relation to the dollar amount of receivables pledged or assigned, and the interest or service charges. A firm willing to be satisfied with a low-percentage advance may obtain a slight reduction in the cost of the funds advanced, because of the lender's greater margin of protection.

In determining the amount to advance, the lender must judge the possible decline in value of the accounts receivable pledged. Failure of customers to pay their accounts, returns of defective merchandise, and demands for reductions in price because of poor quality reduce outstanding receivables. Consequently, the lender will check not only the borrower's credit rating but may also check that of the borrower's major customers with a credit agency, such as Dun and Bradstreet. The borrower must also provide the prospective lender with an aging of receivables and a record of past bad debt and returns and allowances.

To illustrate a typical receivable-based financing arrangement, assume that a firm is borrowing from a commercial finance company. The borrower retains responsibility to decide on the creditworthiness of its customers. Once the firm has sold goods on credit to a customer, the firm assigns the account to the finance company. The borrower must certify that its customer is solvent, that the accounts are genuine, that the amounts owed are not being disputed by the customer, and that the borrower does not owe its customer any money that can be offset against the amount owed on the account.

non-notification financing

Since the lender does not notify the borrower's customers that accounts have been assigned, this arrangement is termed *non-notification financing*. This feature may be desirable, because in some lines of business it is still regarded as a sign of financial weakness to "hock" accounts receivable. Under this form of financing, it is the borrower's responsibility to make all collections on the receivables. As checks come in from customers, it lists them and forwards them intact to the finance company to credit its account.

Because of the detailed handling costs involved, a firm should expect to pay more for this form of credit than on an unsecured loan from a commercial bank. The charges are determined mainly by the average size of the accounts receivable, the amount and turnover of receivables, and the quality of the receivables. Small accounts with a high turnover require more servicing, and the lender will pass on these costs in one form or another. Low-quality receivables are likely to be reflected in a high finance charge and low percentage of advance.

Factoring Accounts Receivable

In a factoring arrangement, the receivables are sold *without recourse;* that is, the factor cannot require the seller to make good on any *bona fide* accounts if the balance owed cannot be collected. When a company pledges its accounts receivable, all of the receivables will be recorded on its balance sheet as an asset, with a note to the effect that some portion has been pledged. In a factoring arrangement, none of the factored receivables are shown on the balance sheet.

factoring of receivables

The agreement made with the factor is usually written for a year and renewed annually. The factor typically makes the decisions on credit sales. On the invoice to an approved customer, the seller states that the account has been sold to a factor and that all payments are to be made directly to the factor. Duplicate copies of invoices are sent promptly to the factor.

maturity factoring

Maturity Factoring.   Under the factoring function known as maturity factoring, the factor provides a credit and collection service for the seller's accounts, handles the necessary bookkeeping, and absorbs any bad-debt losses that may occur. The factor pays the seller in full on the maturity date of the invoice, whether or not the cash has been collected.

Discount Factoring. Under the arrangement known as discount factoring, the seller may draw against the receivables purchased by the factor prior to their maturity. In essence, this means the seller is borrowing from the factor.

discount factoring

Factoring, as opposed to other forms of borrowing, is especially desirable when the seller needs the range of credit services that the factor provides. For example, in highly seasonal businesses, it is frequently uneconomical to maintain a credit department that will work overtime during a portion of the year and be idle the rest of the time. Because a factor serves many different industries, it is able to operate more economically without wide seasonal swings in volume of activity. In addition, in certain industries, such as textiles, the risks of credit loss are fairly high and credit extension takes considerable skill. Because factors are in a better position to assess the risks than an individual company, a firm may be able to increase sales more than if it carried the risk of bad debts itself. This is especially true in the export business. Thus evaluation of the desirability of factoring receivables should balance any expected added revenues from sales, less the incremental costs of added sales and less the charges for factoring, against the costs of maintaining a credit department and the risk of losses on bad debts.

Factoring is not characteristic of many lines of business, in which it would be a mark of weakness to be found factoring receivables. However, this traditional bias has been breaking down. When money is scarce and expensive, many concerns turn to factoring and find it a very satisfactory means of financing.

Example

Cost of Factoring

The Sunrise Plastic Company is having serious liquidity problems, and the treasurer believes that a factoring arrangement should be evaluated. A local factor offers to assume a majority of credit checking functions. By turning these activities over to the factor, the company will save approximately $15,000 per month. For this service, the factor will charge a fee of 2 percent. In addition, the factor will advance the company up to 100 percent of the face value of receivables purchased. For its lending services, the factor will charge 1 percent per month on funds received (payable in advance—i.e., discount basis). The treasurer expects credit sales to average $1,000,000 per month. The effective annual cost of this arrangement can be estimated as follows:

Costs of Factor

Cost of credit service (2%) (1,000,000)	= $ 20,000
Less savings	−15,000
Net	$ 5,000
Net receivables available	$995,000
Less interest @ 1%	9,950
Costs (net credit department costs plus interest charges)	= $ 14,950
Proceeds	= $985,050
Interest rate	= .015
Annual interest rate	= 18.21%

INVENTORY FINANCING

inventory lien

Inventory financing involves the pledge of all or a portion of the borrower's inventory as security for a loan. The lender must determine what percentage of the cost or market value of the pledged inventory can be lent; through what legal device the claim, or lien, on the inventory will be enforced; and the charge to be made for the money.

A margin of safety is required by the lender to protect against a possible decline in the market value of the goods pledged and to cover any costs that will be involved in selling the goods. The amount of loan that can be acquired from most lenders varies from 50 to 90 percent of the cost or market value of the inventory, whichever is lower. Although it might appear from this that the lender is relying wholly on the collateral pledged, the bank or other lender looks first to the credit strength of the borrower. The borrower who cannot repay the loan in the normal course of operations should not expect to obtain one.

There are two basic methods for using inventory as collateral for a loan. The borrower may maintain possession of the inventory, or place it in the hands of a responsible third party. A borrower may indicate a preference for one or another security device, but the ultimate decision will probably be made by the lender. Among other things, the lender will consider the nature of the inventory, the use to which it is put, and the borrowing firm's reliability and integrity.

When loans are based on inventory retained by the borrower, the interest charge may include a service charge for the costs of checking inventory and assuring compliance with the agreement. The more difficult and time-consuming this task, the higher the combined charge.

Because of the initial costs of establishing such an agreement, a firm would not ordinarily undertake to pledge its inventory unless it planned to continue this arrangement for an extended period of time.

Chattel Mortgage (Floor Planning)

Sometimes the collateral for a loan is clearly identifiable, just as automobiles may be identified by their serial numbers. With this protection, lenders may be willing to advance a relatively large portion of the cost of goods sold. For example, a bank may advance an amount equal to 90 percent of the cost of a car to a dealer. This form of financing is commonly called *floor-planning* and applies to all forms of consumer durables.

chattel mortgage

floor-planning

Under this security agreement, the dealer agrees to hold the car and the proceeds from its sale in trust for the bank. The note the dealer signs is a demand note, because as soon as the car is sold, the dealer must immediately return to the bank the amount it has advanced on the car.

The bank protects its interest in the car and the proceeds of its sale by filing a financing statement with the appropriate public official. This puts the dealer's other creditors on notice that title to the dealer's stock of new cars probably rests with the bank. The bank also requires that the dealer properly insure the cars in its interest. At irregular and unannounced intervals, an agent of the bank physically checks the dealer's inventory. The serial numbers on the automobiles are compared with the numbers shown on the security agreement. Either the car should be there, or the proceeds of its sale should be in the hands of the bank. If this is not the case, the car has been sold "out of trust," and the dealer is using the cash that properly belongs to the bank. The bank will then demand immediate payment of all amounts owed by the dealer.

Floating Lien

Often the collateral for a loan is not clearly identifiable, such as women's dresses in process of manufacture. In this case, the security agreement provides for a floating charge or continuing lien on the shifting stock. The security interest applies to the raw materials, goods in process, and finished goods. The goods can be sold to a retailer, but the lien then applies to the accounts receivable generated. Again, so that other creditors can be warned that the lien has been placed on the goods and their proceeds, a financing statement must be filed with the proper state official.

floating lien

From the borrower's point of view, this form of security agreement has a number of advantages. It is much more convenient in production processes to have complete control of the goods. No great amount of paper work is required to take the raw materials out of the borrower's storage facilities and put them into production. The required periodic reports of receipts and shipments are probably no more onerous than those that would be used for the firm's own accounting procedures. Nor is there any third party involved who must be paid to act as a custodian for the goods. However, from the lender's point of view, this is less desirable because the goods are in control of the borrower and not clearly identifiable, and thus much greater reliance must be placed on the borrower's honesty. The inspections necessary to encourage honesty are time-consuming and expensive. Consequently, the lender will probably loan closer to 50 percent than 90 percent of the value of the inventory. This type of financing is restricted primarily to commercial finance companies, which have had long experience in this specialized form of lending.

Warehouse Receipt Financing

From the point of view of the lender, the security arrangements just discussed have one overriding disadvantage. The goods remain in the hands of the borrower. As a result, a good deal of policing must be done by the lender, and it is impossible to gain complete protection. A much greater measure of safety for the lender is obtained when the goods serving as collateral for a loan are placed in the hands of a third party (a warehouse concern), which then issues a document placing security interest in the goods in the hands of the bank (warehouse receipt). Under this arrangement, the warehouse may not release the goods to the borrower unless the bank authorizes the withdrawal. And the bank ordinarily will not authorize withdrawal unless the borrower pays off a corresponding portion of the debt to the bank.

warehouse receipt financing

There are two types of warehouses that may be used: terminal warehouses and field warehouses. A *terminal warehouse* is a public warehouse that rents space to the storer of the goods. More recently, *field warehouses* have come into increasing prominence. A field warehouse is set up on the premises of the borrower. The designated storage area is fenced off and placed under lock and key in the hands of the warehouse company. The field warehouse may be a storeroom, a storage tank, a pile of coal, logs in a mill pond, or lumber stacked in a lumber yard. The only requirement is that the warehouse company be in "continuous, exclusive, and notorious possession." Various signs are posted around showing the areas under the control of the warehouse company. Frequently, an employee of the borrower familiar with the storage and handling of the inventory is hired by the warehouse company, placed under bond, and put in charge of the storage area.

terminal warehouse

field warehouse

A borrower would be likely to request a field warehouse rather than a public warehouse arrangement when frequent access to raw materials or finished goods that have been pledged is needed. (Ordinarily, goods in process cannot be handled under a field warehouse, because the warehouse person could not maintain adequate control of the materials.) Such arrangements would also be required if the nature of the inventory would prohibit public or terminal warehousing. This would be true of the logs in the mill pond.

OTHER COLLATERAL

Many other types of collateral may be pledged to obtain a loan. Commercial banks frequently make loans to small businesses based on collateral that is unrelated to the business. This comes about because the business itself has no acceptable assets that may be pledged or because the owner does not wish to reveal information concerning the business. This collateral may consist of securities, savings accounts, mortgages on commercial or residential properties, and the cash surrender value of life insurance policies.

S U M M A R Y

Accounts payable and accruals play an important role in financing increases in current assets needed to support sales volume growth. Even after credit terms and accrual practices have been established, accounts payable and accruals can be expected to change proportionately with changes in production and sales. Such current liability increases serve to reduce what otherwise would be larger external financing requirements.

Next to trade credit, bank credit is the most widely used form of short-term borrowing. Large corporations often have access to other sources of funds, such as commercial paper, and very small companies may not be sufficiently creditworthy to obtain bank loans. Significant credit terms on a bank loan may include requirements for a compensating balance.

The riskier a business, the greater is the likelihood that it will find it necessary to pledge some of its assets in order to obtain a loan. From the lender's point of view, the most desirable business assets are the accounts receivable, followed by inventory.

MULTIPLE CHOICE QUESTIONS

1. Commitment fees are normally associated with:
   a) Agreements to buy the firm's products
   b) Violations of loan provisions
   c) Lines of credit
   d) Agreements to sell the firm's products

2. The most common use of credit lines is:
   a) Capital expenditures
   b) Stock dividends
   c) Seasonal borrowing
   d) Permanent working capital requirements

3. Compensating balances usually have the effect of:
   a) Decreasing the effective cost of loans
   b) Increasing the effective cost of loans

    c) Decreasing the size of the line of credit

    d) Encouraging more use of debt

4. Factors specialize in financing based on:

    a) Cash

    b) Inventory

    c) Accounts receivable

    d) Plant and equipment

5. Floor planning is a type of:

    a) Interior decorating

    b) Showroom design

    c) Inventory loan

    d) Budgeting

6. Under the discount method of borrowing:

    a) A company is allowed to borrow less than it needs

    b) Interest rates are reduced

    c) Interest is deducted at the time of the loan

    d) Compensating balances are not required

7. Maturity factoring means that the factor:

    a) Will only buy well seasoned receivables

    b) Only provides credit functions like credit analysis and collection

    c) Only lends against receivables

    d) Will only purchase receivables on collection

8. The credit terms 2/10, n/30 mean:

    a) A 10 percent discount rate if paid within two days of invoice date

    b) A 10 percent discount rate if paid within 30 days of invoice date

    c) A 2 percent discount rate if paid within 30 days of invoice date

    d) A 2 percent discount rate if paid within 10 days of invoice date

9. Consignment credit terms means:

    a) Assets are pledged as security

    b) Payment is due only when the asset is sold

    c) A loan is collateralized by a line of credit

    d) A loan is cosigned

DISCUSSION QUESTIONS

1. How does a change in the trade credit period affect a firm's short-term cash operating cycle?

2. What is commercial paper and how is it sold? Why is commercial paper issued by corporations?

3. Distinguish between a firm's compensating balances and its working balances.

4. If you are purchasing on terms of 2/10, n/30 but selling on terms of net 60, what financial problems are created? What might prevent you from changing the trade credit terms under which you purchase and sell?

5. Distinguish between simple interest and discount interest.

6. Identify and briefly explain the following terms
   a) line of credit
   b) revolving line of credit
   c) installment credit.

7. Inventory may be used as loan collateral. Sometimes this collateral remains in the possession of the borrower; at other times it is placed under the control of a third party. Explain the pros and cons of the two arrangements.

8. Explain what is meant by the statement that the effective cost of an installment loan with add-on interest may be twice the stated rate.

9. What is meant by factoring accounts receivable? How does this differ from the pledging of receivables as collateral for a bank loan?

10. Describe the difference between maturity factoring and discount factoring.

SOLVED PROBLEMS

SP-1. Clinical Laboratories has begun to experience severe cash flow problems. The Treasurer estimates that an increase of $100,000 in funds would be sufficient to overcome liquidity problems. The President wonders if the cash flow problem could be met by simply delaying payment to trade suppliers. The treasurer agrees but argues that, since the company currently takes the discount on all payables, the president's suggestion would be more expensive than simply borrowing from the bank at 15 percent per annum.

   a) Assume that annual credit purchases will total $5,400,000; average accounts payable turnover is 12 times. Calculate the expected accounts payable balance and average payment period. Calculate the new accounts payable balance and the average payment period the president's suggestion would entail.

   b) Assume that the company is receiving credit terms of 2/30, n/60 from all its suppliers and currently takes all discounts. What percentage of its total payables would have to be extended 60 days in order to generate the needed funds? What would the annual dollar cost of the passed discounts be?

   c) Compare your answer to (b) with the alternative of borrowing $100,000 from the bank at 15 percent per annum.

SP-2. The Neptune Company will sell $1,000,000 of its commercial paper for $975,000. The paper has a maturity of 72 days. Calculate the effective annualized interest rate. (Assume a 360-day year.)

SP-3. The Amica Company is having serious liquidity problems. The treasurer believes that a factoring arrangement should be evaluated. A local factor offers to assume a majority of credit checking functions. By turning these activities over to the factor, the company will save approximately $30,000 per month. For this service, the factor will charge a fee of 2.5 percent. In addition, the factor will advance the company up to 100 percent of the face value of receivables purchased. For its lending services, the factor will charge 2 percent per month on funds received (payable in advance, i.e., discount basis). The treasurer expects credit sales to average $2,000,000 per month. Estimate the effective annual interest rate of the factoring arrangement.

SP-4. The Joy Co. needs to raise an additional $100,000 for six months. Several possibilities are available. The financial manager is inter ested in identifying the least-cost option. Which will prove the right solution?

Option 1: Bank loan at 18 percent per annum

Option 2: Borrow 125,000 from the bank at 15 percent per annum plus 20 percent compensating balance. (No balances are currently kept at the bank.

Option 3: Borrow $119,048 at 16 percent per annum discounted.

Option 4: Delay payments to trade creditors. This will cause Joy Co. to miss discounts with terms of 2/10, n/45 (Assume 360 days.)

Option 5: Borrow against inventory on a warehouse receipt basis. The loan will carry an interest rate of 14 percent per annum. Warehousing charges will be $1,000 per annum plus $1\frac{1}{2}$ percent of the inventory warehoused. (Assume inventory warehoused will be 120,000.)

Option 6: Borrow against accounts receivable from a commercial finance company. Interest of 16 percent per annum will be charged against the total face value of receivables pledged. The loan value of receivables pledged will be 80 percent of face value. Total face value of receivables pledged will be $125,000.

Option 7: Sell $107,000 of six-month commercial paper at discount. Net proceeds will be $100,000. The commercial paper has to be backed 100 percent by a line of credit at Joy Co.'s bank. The line of credit is available for a committment fee of $\frac{3}{4}$ of 1 percent per annum.

Option 8: Borrow for one year (minimum term) at 13 percent. Since funds are needed for only six months, the second six months the funds can be invested in marketable securities at 10 percent per annum. The marketable securities investment will involve transaction costs of $\frac{1}{2}$ of 1 percent of the principal invested.

PROBLEMS

1. Jones Carpets has begun to experience severe cash flow problems. The treasurer estimates that an increase of $25,000 in funds would be sufficient to overcome liquidity problems. The president wonders if the cash flow problem could be met by simply delaying payment to trade suppliers. The treasurer agrees but argues that, since the company currently takes the discount on all payables, the president's suggestion would be more expensive than simply borrowing from the bank at 12 percent per annum.

   a) Assume that annual credit purchases will total $600,000; average accounts payable turnover is 36 times. Calculate the expected accounts payable balance and average payment period. Calculate the new accounts payable balance and the average payment period the president's suggestion would entail.

   b) Assume that the company is receiving credit terms of 2/10, n/30 from all its suppliers and currently takes all discounts. What percentage of its total payable would have to be extended 30 days in order to generate the needed funds? What would the annual dollar cost of the passed discounts be?

   c) Compare your answer to (b) with the alternative of borrowing $25,000 from the bank at 12 percent per annum.

2. The August Company will sell $10,000,000 of its commercial paper for $9,500,000. The paper has a maturity of 270 days. Calculate the effective annualized interest rate. (Assume a 360-day year.)

3. The Jones Company is having serious liquidity problems. The treasurer believes that a factoring arrangement should be evaluated. A local factor offers to assume a majority of credit checking functions. By turning these activities over to the factor, the company will save approximately $2,000 per month. For this service, the factor will charge a fee of 1 percent. In addition, the factor will advance the company up to 100 percent of the face value of receivables purchased. For its lending services, the factor will charge 1 percent per month on funds received (payable in advance—i.e., discount basis). The Treasurer expects credit sales to average $500,000 per month. Estimate the effective annual interest rate of the factoring arrangement.

4. Assume that Brighton Industries will pay its accounts payable on the final due date instead of paying early and taking the available dis-

counts. Calculate the implied annual percentage cost of missing discounts for the following credit terms. (Assume 360 days in the year.)

a) 2/10, n/30
b) 2/30, n/60
c) 3/45, n/120

5. The Ace Furniture Company reported the following financial information for the past two years.

	1986	1987
Annual credit purchases	$4,000,000	$6,000,000
Average accounts payable	$500,000	$900,000

Assume a 360-day year for calculation purposes.

a) Calculate the average payment period for each year.
b) Calculate the accounts payable turnover for each year.
c) Estimate the average accounts payable for 1987 if the 1986 payables turnover had been maintained in 1987.
d) What might have caused the change in payables from 1986 to 1987?

6. The Grade Company's annual credit purchases from suppliers are $7.8 million, and its accounts payable conversion time is 38 days. Inventory conversion time is currently 100 days, and accounts receivable conversion time is 65 days. Sales and purchases tend to remain level, so beginning and ending balance-sheet amounts for payables and current asset items are stable.

a) Determine the average accounts payable balance.
b) If Grade is able to find a more lenient supplier so that its accounts payable conversion time increases to 45 days, what will be the increase in accounts payable outstanding on the firm's balance sheet?
c) Show how the increase in the payables conversion time in part (b) will affect the length of Grade's average cash cycle.

7. The management of Wakers plans to slow its current payables payment policy so that the accounts payable conversion time will be increased from 47 to 51 days. Under the old 47-day policy, average accounts payable were expected to be $940,000. Annual credit purchases were expected to remain at the same $7,200,000 level for the 47-day or 51-day conversion time plans.

a) Calculate average accounts payable outstanding under the 51-day conversion time alternative.
b) Wakers currently finances its current assets through the use of a 12-percent bank loan. How much might be saved by increasing the payables conversion time by four days?
c) In order to achieve an increase in conversion time for its payables, Wakers will have to give up a 2-percent cash discount on credit purchases paid within 15 days. Cash discounts normally would be

available on 10 percent of the credit purchases made by Wakers from its suppliers. Calculate the costs associated with a four-day increase in payables conversion time.

d) Would you recommend that Wakers retain the 47-day conversion time and continue to take cash discounts, or should the firm adopt the 51-day plan?

e) In order to justify giving up the cash discounts mentioned in part (c), how many days increase in the payables conversion time would be necessary?

8. Calculate the annual percentage rate or cost of failure to take cash discounts under the following trade credit terms. Assume that the purchaser makes payment on the final due date.

   a) 2/10, n/30
   b) 2/15, n/45
   c) 6/10, n/60
   d) 8/15, n/30

9. Maxwell, Inc. is purchasing furniture on terms of 3/10, n/90. The Company will be unable to pay by the tenth day but could pay the $25,000 invoice price at the end of 60 days. Alternatively, the Company could borrow the necessary funds through a 90-day bank loan at an 18-percent annual rate.

   a) Calculate the effective interest rate or cost of paying for the furniture at the end of 60 days. Would such a payment plan be superior to payment on the final due date?

   b) Calculate the dollar costs associated with paying for the furniture at the end of 90 days versus borrowing from the bank in order to take advantage of the cash discount offer. On what basis should Maxwell purchase the furniture?

   c) Assume that, instead of a 90-day loan, the bank will offer only a 180-day loan at an 18-percent annual interest rate. Should Maxwell borrow from the bank and take the cash discounts, or should it just pay the full invoice price at the end of 90 days? Prepare necessary calculations to support your decision.

10. The Sommerville Corporation plans to issue $1.5 million of commercial paper. Sommerville will receive $1.4 million if 180-day commercial paper is sold through dealers; or, if 90-day commercial paper is sold, the firm will receive $1.445 million.

    a) Calculate the effective annual interest rate for the 180-day commercial paper issue.

    b) Should the firm issue 90-day commercial paper or borrow from a commercial bank at a 15-percent rate for 90 days? Why?

11. The Second National Bank offers you a 90-day loan for $15,000 discounted at 9 percent per annum. Also available is a $15,000, 90-day loan from the Third National Bank, which requires repayment of principal plus interest at a 9.5-percent annual rate when the loan is due.

a) What are the net proceeds that each bank would give you?

b) What is the effective rate of interest being charged by each bank?

c) Instead of a 90-day loan, assume that you can borrow for a 390-day period. How would your answers to Parts (a) and (b) be altered?

12. In order to finance the purchase of a display case, the Trophy Company signs a note for $12,000, repayable in 12 equal monthly installments. The bank quotes its rate at 12 percent "add-on" per annum. Alternatively, the bank offers a 12.5-percent "add-on" rate with quarterly payments.

a) What is the approximate effective annual rate of interest that the Trophy Company would have to pay under the two installment loan alternatives?

b) Estimate the effective annual interest rates if the above bank loans were for two years but still required monthly and quarterly installment payments, respectively.

c) How would the effective interest rates change if the two loan alternatives were for five years?

13. The Ace Cable Company charges $13.40 per month to subscribers who use its cable services. This amounts to an annual charge of $160.80.

a) What is the effective interest rate to a subscriber making these installment payments instead of making a single payment of $140 at the beginning of the year? (Use equation 13–4).

b) Redo part a) assuming subscribers are charged only $133 if they pay at the beginning of the year.

14. The Jibbit Company needs the full use of $50,000 for 12 months. Jibbit can obtain a loan of $9\frac{1}{2}$ percent without a compensating balance or one at 9 percent with a compensating balance equal to 20 percent of the amount borrowed. Both principal and interest will be paid at the maturity of the loan.

a) Which loan arrangement should Jibbit choose and how much should be borrowed if the firm would otherwise maintain no balance with the bank?

b) If Jibbit normally maintains an $8,000 balance with the bank, which loan arrangement would be preferable?

15. The Hereward Company faces a seasonal expansion of inventory of $80,000. A full $80,000 is needed for 60 days, and calculations are to be based on a 360-day year. The financial manager is interested in comparing the effective annual financing costs in dollar amount and on a percentage basis for each of several financing alternatives.

a) Calculate the dollar amount and percentage financing costs associated with a bank loan at $9\frac{1}{2}$ percent per annum.

b) Calculate dollar and percentage financing costs associated with a bank loan at an annual rate of 9 percent discounted.

    c) If Hereward purchases the inventory on terms of 2/10, n/60 and plans to pay for the purchase on the 60th day, what would be the dollar and percentage financing costs?

    d) Hereward can borrow on a warehouse receipt from a commercial finance company. Terms are 12 percent interest per annum, with the loan amounting to 75 percent of the value of the goods. Additional inventory is available to provide adequate collateral. The warehousing charge is a fixed yearly charge of $500 plus a flat charge of $1\frac{1}{2}$ percent of the value of the inventory warehoused. Calculate the dollar and percentage financing costs of this alternative.

    e) Hereward can borrow against accounts receivable from a commercial finance company at a rate of $\frac{1}{20}$ of 1 percent per day on the outstanding face value of the accounts receivable pledged. The loan value of the receivables will be 90 percent of their face value. Calculate the dollar and percentage financing costs of this alternative.

    f) Which financing alternative should the Hereward Company use to finance its seasonal expansion of inventory? Why?

16. The Fulton Company is considering the possibility of selling its accounts receivable. Although the factor will not purchase the existing accounts, new receivables will be purchased on the following terms:

Cash	$ 80,000	Notes and accounts payable	$1,000,000
Accounts receivable	400,000		
Inventory	520,000		
	$1,000,000		$1,000,000

- Factor's commission, 1 percent of value of receivables, net of returns and allowances.

- Average payment date of receivables to be considered as 20 days.

- Interest at 15 percent per annum is to be charged on amounts advanced by the factor prior to the average due date. The amount advanced by the factor is equal to gross sales, less returns and allowances, less the factor's commission. To simplify calculations, it is assumed that returns and allowances are 2% of sales.

- Annual credit sales are expected to be $6,000,000.

    a) Calculate the average receivables loan on the assumption that sales are level throughout the year.

    b) On the assumption that the firm borrows all that the factor will advance, what will be the total interest cost?

    c) What will be the total factor's commission?

SP-1. a) $\text{Expected Accounts payable} = \dfrac{\text{Annual credit purchases}}{\text{Accounts payable turnover}}$

$$= \dfrac{5,400,000}{12}$$

$$= \$450,000$$

$\text{Expected Average payment period} = \dfrac{\text{Accounts payable}}{\text{annual credit purchases}/360}$

$$= \dfrac{\$450,000}{5,400,000/360}$$

$$= 30 \text{ days}$$

$\text{New Accounts payable balance} = \$450,000 \text{ (planned)}$

$+\ 100,000$

(added fund required)

$= \$550,000$

$\text{New Average payment period} = \dfrac{\begin{array}{c}\text{new level of accounts}\\\text{payable needed}\end{array}}{\text{annual credit purchases}/360}$

$$= \dfrac{\$550,000}{15,000}$$

$$= 36.67 \text{ days}$$

b) To extend its average payment period to 36.67 days, the company has to extend only a portion of its payables to 60 days and thus miss the discount. To find the portion to be extended, set up an equation. D = Percent of payables paid in 30 days and thus eligible for the discount; $(1 - D)$ − Percent of payables paid in 60 days and, thus ineligible for the discount:

$$D(30 \text{ days}) + (1 - D)(60 \text{ days}) = 36.67$$

$$D(30 \text{ days}) = 23.33$$

$$D = \dfrac{23.33}{30} = .78$$

$$(1 - D) = .22$$

In other words, continue taking the discount on 78 percent of purchases (i.e., pay on the 30th day) and forego the discount on 22 percent (i.e., pay on the 60th day).

Annual $ cost of passed discounts $= (\$5,400,000)(.22)(.02)$

$$= \$23,760$$

c)   Bank borrowing cost $= (100,000)(.15)$

$$= \$15,000$$

Bank borrowing is much cheaper than missing discounts.

SP-2.

$$\frac{\text{Interest}}{(72 \text{ days})} = \frac{\text{cost of funds}}{\text{proceeds}}$$

$$= \frac{\$25,000}{975,000}$$

$$= 2.56\%$$

$$\text{Annualized interest rate} = (2.56\%)\left(\frac{360}{72}\right)$$

$$= 12.82\%$$

SP-3. Costs of Factor.

Cost of credit service (2.5%) ($2,000,000)	$ 50,000
Less savings	−30,000
Net	$ 20,000
Net receivables available	$1,980,000
Less interest @ 1%	39,600
	$1,940,000
Costs:	$ 59,600
Proceeds:	$1,940,400
Interest rate:	.031
Annual interest rate:	36.9%

SP-4. Option 1: Effective interest rate $= 18\%$

Option 2: $Interest − (125,000)(.15)$: $18,750

Net proceeds: 100,000

Effective interest rate: 18.75%

Option 3: $Interest − (119,048)(.16)$: 19,048

Net proceeds: 100,000

Effective interest rate: 19.05%

Option 4: Effective interest rate on unused discounts: $\frac{2}{98} \times \frac{360}{35} = 21\%$

Option 5: Interest on loan − (100,000)(.14): 14,000

Warehouse handling charges: + 1,000

Warehouse maintenance fee (.015)(120,000): + 1,800

	Total costs	16,800
	Net proceeds:	100,000
	Effective interest rate:	16.8%
Option 6:	Interest cost (125,000) (.16):	20,000
	Net proceeds:	100,000
	Effective interest rate:	20%
Option 7:	Discount cost:	7,000
	Line of credit commitment fee (.0075) (107,000):	802.50
	Total	7,802.50
	Net proceeds:	100,000
	Effective interest rate (6 mos.):	7.803%
	Effective annual interest rate:	15.606%

Recall that the commercial paper issue will be for only six months. The costs must be doubled to be stated on an annual basis.

Option 8:	Total interest cost (100,000) (.13):	13,000
	Less earnings = (100,000) (.10)/2:	− 5,000
	Plus cost of MS investing = (100,000) (.005):	+ 500
	Net interest	8,500
	Net proceeds	100,000
	Effective interest rate	8.5%

REFERENCES

Bartler, Brit, Jr., and Richard J. Rendleman, Jr. "Fee Based Pricing of Fixed Rate Bank Loan Commitments," *Financial Management,* 8, Spring 1979, pp. 13-20.

Boettcher, James H., and Fernando B. Sotelino. "A Look at the Variable-Maturity Loan," *Harvard Business Review,* 60, May–June 1982, pp. 80 86.

Denonn, Lester E. "The Security Agreement," *Journal of Commercial Bank Lending,* 50, February 1968, pp. 32-40.

Smith, Keith V. Guide to Working Capital Management. New York: McGraw-Hill, 1979.

Stone, Bernell K. "Allocating Credit Lines, Planned Borrowing, and Tangible Services over a Company's Banking System," *Financial Management,* Summer 1975, pp. 65-78.

CASE EXERCISE

Schmidt Company

Joe Smithers, recently installed as vice-president, finance for the Schmidt Company, realized he might be taking a large risk in criticizing Mr. Schmidt's credit arrangements. However, Mr. Schmidt, though near retirement, demonstrated a remarkable willingness to be second-guessed. Mr. Smithers' basic criticism was that the company's credit arrangements were excessive and costly. For example, the company's lines of credit were more than double what the firm would reasonably require. Mr. Schmidt had viewed with pride the firm's large cash balances and its ready access to credit (Exhibit C-1). Mr. Schmidt had considered banking relationships particularly crucial, because he believed they could assist the firm during an emergency. Moreover, he had thought that the credit lines might yield some strategic value in that competitors would be less inclined to provoke the company if it had sufficient reserves to undertake an extensive marketing counterattack.

The Schmidt Company currently had a revolving line of credit with a syndicate of five banks. Total commitments amounted to $80 million. The distribution of these lines among banks is shown in Exhibit C-2. Except for the Blue Bank, which had compensating requirements of 20 percent of use and 20 percent of availability (i.e., deposit balances equal to 20 percent of the amount borrowed plus 20 percent of the unborrowed credit line), Schmidt's compensating arrangement was 15 percent of use and 15 percent of availability.

Although Schmidt's bankers were willing to count the company's average normal operating ("working") balances toward the required compensating balance, no interest was paid on the balances and any shortfall by the end of the year would be treated as a *de facto* loan at the prime rate, currently averaging 15 percent.

Mr. Schmidt also had not believed in paying trade credit early to take the industry discount (2/10, n/30), because he had considered such credit a costless loan, that is, a substitute in certain cases for bank credit but one that had no interest cost. Since purchases totaled $300 million in 1987, Mr. Schmidt viewed supplier credit as equivalent to a sizeable line of credit at the bank.

Case Questions

1. Assume no change in the company's total line of credit. What will the shortfall costs total? (Assume that the year-to-date relationships are maintained during the year.)

2. Assume the company's total credit lines are reduced to $45 million. What recommendations would you make on reallocating the lines among banks? (Assume that the year-to-date relationships are maintained during the year.)

EXHIBIT C-1
Schmidt Company

Balance Sheet as of December 31, 1987 ($ Millions)

Assets		Liabilities & Stockholders' Equity	
Cash	$ 15.0	Bank debt	$ 20.0
Treasury Bills*	20.0	Accounts payable	40.7
Accounts receivable	85.0	Other current liabilities	10.0
Inventory	50.0	Current	70.7
current	170.0		
P & E (net)	213.0	Shareholders' equity	340.3
Other long-term	28.0		
Total	$411.0	Total	$411.0

*Average yield is 12%

EXHIBIT C-2
Schmidt Company

Credit Arrangements As of February 1988 ($ Millions)

	Bank					
	Total	Blue	White	Red	Yellow	Black
Line	$80	$20	$15	$30	$10	$5
Use	5	2	0	3	0	0
Average balance*	20	0	5	10	0	5

*Average daily working balance in accounts, year-to-date.

3. Evaluate the firm's trade credit policy.
4. Evaluate Mr. Schmidt's rationale for the excessive liquidity and credit arrangements.

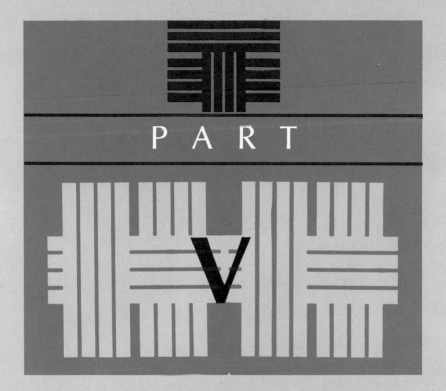

PART

V

INVESTMENT
DECISIONS

CHAPTER

14

INTRODUCTION TO CAPITAL BUDGETING

Capital budgeting decisions typically involve multiyear investments and significant amounts of a firm's available funds. Once implemented, they are difficult to reverse. Thus, careful evaluation of major capital budgeting proposals is of strategic importance. Several numerical methods are widely used in business to evaluate proposals. Some of them are theoretically unsound and can lead to biases or other errors in investment selection. Other methods are sound but more mathematical; and before the availability of computers, they were considered difficult to implement. This chapter begins the study of capital budgeting. It first examines the most widely used methods for evaluating capital budgeting proposals. Several difficulties that commonly arise in applying the methods are also discussed.

Objectives and Organization of this Chapter

The primary objective of this chapter is to describe and evaluate the principal numerical methods of capital budgeting. A second objective is to illustrate certain practical problems that arise when making capital budgeting appraisals and to provide some guidance for addressing them.

The first three sections of the chapter describe what we mean by capital budgeting and how firms organize the capital budgeting process. Section four then describes the principal techniques used in evaluating the costs and benefits of proposed investments. The final sections deal with special issues that arise in capital budgeting analyses.

WHAT ARE CAPITAL BUDGETING INVESTMENTS?

Every asset listed on the company's balance sheet represents an investment made by the company. Capital budgeting investments, often referred to as *fixed-asset investments*, represent investments that are expected to last more than one year. Obvious examples include plant and equipment expenditures. These are shown as "fixed assets" on the balance *fixed assets* sheet. Yet, current-asset investments needed to support the long-term investments are also multiyear investments, even though they show up on the "current assets" portion of the balance sheet.

Capital Expenditure Categories

Because capital budgeting investments may extend for many years, the benefit stream, measured in after-tax cash flows, is often subject to great uncertainty and volatility — poor in some (perhaps early) years, quite good in others. The risk and variability of after-tax cash flows can vary widely from one type of investment to another. For this reason, many companies sort investment proposals into several categories and apply different standards of acceptability to them.

Investment proposals generally can be classified as either mandatory investments or discretionary investments.

Mandatory	**Discretionary**
● Defensive/strategic	● Cost reducing
● Legally required	● Revenue expanding
	● New products
	● Acquisitions

Defensive Investments

defensive and strategic investments

Defensive and strategic investments represent investments that must be made if the firm is to continue in a certain line of business, such as simple replacement of worn-out machinery.

Example

Defensive/Strategic Investment

The Williams Company has a subsidiary that makes analog stopwatches. Although the demand for them has dropped dramatically since the introduction of the digital stopwatch, there is still a small but loyal market. The Williams Company subsidiary has a substantial part of this market. Even though the company has, for some time, considered withdrawing from this business altogether, no decision has yet been made. However, the stopwatch subsidiary has forwarded an urgent investment proposal requesting the purchase of an expensive precision stamping machine. The existing machine has completely worn out; and if it is not replaced, the Williams Company will simply be out of the stopwatch business. If the replacement machine is purchased, there will be no impact on either the revenues or the operating costs of the stopwatch business.

Typically, defensive or strategic investments such as the stopwatch proposal cannot be evaluated in isolation but rather must be considered in the overall context of the line of business.

Legally Mandated Investments

legally mandated investments

Many investment proposals involve cash outlays without any expectation of increased cash inflows. For example, government statutes that require antipollution equipment can involve enormous capital expenditures without generating additional cash benefits to the company. Of course if the company does not comply, existing revenues will be lost when the company is forced to shut down or pay large penalties. In that sense, the preservation of existing cash flows may be viewed as the benefits accruing to the investment. Another important type of legally mandated investments includes those made to protect the health and safety of employees and customers. Federal regulations concerning safety features in automobiles are obvious examples of legally mandated investments.

Cost Reducing

While new product and revenue expansion investments are expected to generate new sales as well as new operating expenses, cost-reducing investments generally affect only the existing level of operating expenses. *cost reducing investments* Nonetheless it should be apparent that "a dollar saved is a dollar earned." Thus cost-reducing investments are also expected to produce benefits in the form of higher after-tax cash flows.

Example

Cost Reducing Investment

Matrix has a bakery subsidiary that makes hot dog buns. It currently has a gas operated bun-making oven that can bake 5,000 buns per day. The bakery subsidiary has learned from a bun oven manufacturer that a new bun oven is available that can also produce 5,000 buns per day but has new technology that reduces the gas usage requirements by 50 percent. This type of investment will reduce operating costs but will have no impact on bun production or sales. Since the manufacturer is willing to guarantee the cost savings claimed, there is relatively little uncertainty about the benefits to be produced.

Expansion

Expansion proposals are intended to increase production and sales *expansion investments* volume of products and services in existing lines of business. This is usually done with the objective of achieving more efficient output, possibly for competitive price reduction, or in anticipation of a generally increased market.

Expansion Investment

Grenoch's principal business is clipping articles published in newspapers and magazines for clients. The Clipping Services Division has proposed the purchase of 1,000 new microfiche readers in order to meet rapidly growing demand for clipping services. The investment represents an expansion of a familiar business, yet it is not without its own uncertainties, since the market may not turn out to be as large as projected. Yet the cost estimates for machines, inventories, operating expenses, and so on can be estimated reliably from past experience.

New Products

new product investments

In order to ensure its continuing competitive position and ultimate survival, every company needs to keep developing new products to replace those that are inevitably phased out in the market. New products are expensive to develop, and only a few of them may be pursued to full production and marketing. Nevertheless, every company must apply careful scrutiny to new product ideas.

Example

New Product Investment

The DataMax Company is considering an investment proposal forwarded by its research and development division. The division has proposed the manufacture and sale of a product called the CompuShaver: an electric shaver with a microprocessor that measures the user's whisker length and texture and instantly adjusts the razor for a perfect shave. The Compu-Shaver would be considered a new product proposal because the company has never made one before. New products involve numerous risks, including the risks of unfamiliar market factors and the uncertainties of cost estimates and investment requirements.

Acquisitions

acquisitions as investments

Investment proposals to purchase another firm are perhaps the most extensive, as they involve changes in revenues and costs and, possibly, entry into unfamiliar markets—as in the case of Coca-Cola's purchase of Columbia Pictures. In addition, there are many managerial uncertainties involved since an entire business, including employees and managers, is being acquired. Although acquisitions, in principle, can and should be evaluated in the same fashion as other investments, they are discussed separately in Chapter 24.

CRITERIA FOR INVESTMENT DECISIONS

Generally, two broad criteria are established for investment proposals: economic evaluations and conformity with business strategy.

Economic Evaluation

Investments are grouped by type, largely so that different economic standards for acceptance or rejection can be established. An important influence on the stringency of economic evaluations is the level of risk perceived in the proposed investment. For example, the relatively low risk of estimation error in cost-reduction and replacement investments suggests establishing easier acceptance standards than the high risk involved in new product and acquisition proposals. Chapter 16 will systematically examine procedures for dealing with risk in capital budgeting. Surveys indicate that risk evaluation is by far the major problem faced by large firms in capital budgeting decisions.

Conformity with Business Strategy

Capital expenditure proposals must ultimately conform with the general business strategy of the company. Most companies are very reluctant to deviate from the products and markets in which they find themselves most competitive. An investment proposal, even if highly profitable, may be rejected if it takes the company into unfamiliar areas. However, as a matter of deliberate business strategy, a company's board of directors may have chosen to diversify into new areas. On this basis, management might approve a proposal that does not look profitable in the near future, believing there will be future benefits not reflected in the analysis. Even so, the board of directors is likely to set guidelines for the new business areas in which it wishes to consider investment. Significant shifts in business strategy are often brought about through mergers and acquisitions of companies in the desired areas.

ORGANIZATION AND CONTROL OF CAPITAL EXPENDITURES

The organization for carrying out capital budgeting procedures and controlling capital expenditures varies from company to company. In a small company, all proposals for capital expenditures may be submitted to the president and board of directors for consideration. Frequently, in a large company the exception principle is employed. A department head may be authorized to approve small expenditures up to, say, $10,000; a plant manager, payments up to $100,000; and the president, capital expenditures up to $1,000,000. Larger proposals might be submitted to an investment committee headed by the president. This committee evaluates the proposals in terms of their costs and benefits and in relation to the availability of funds. The final recommendation for various capital expenditures is usually submitted to the board of directors for approval.

Once a capital expenditure is approved, an appropriation may be set aside to cover that estimated expenditure. If the financial manager is charged with the control of capital expenditures, it is his or her responsibility to obtain progress reports on the project. Should the funds be draining away faster than anticipated, it may be necessary to ask for a supplemental appropriation (or a more careful director of the project). Regular progress reports are necessary in order to revise financial plans as needed. Some sort of report is customarily submitted at the completion of the project, that is, when the machine is finally in place or the building is ready for occupancy. At this point the appropriation is closed.

The Post Audit

investment post audit

Probably the most important step in the control process is an evaluation, or audit, of the results of the proposal. What was the final cost in relation to the anticipated cost? Did the benefits realized match up to the projected gains? These are difficult questions, but a firm needs a systematic review of the results of capital expenditures for two reasons. First, if department heads know their results will be checked, their original proposals are likely to be more realistic than they might otherwise be. Second, financial managers should be able to learn from past errors and so improve the capital budgeting processes. Where did we err? Why did the investment cost more than anticipated? What expenditures did we forget? Where were our assumptions wrong?

CAPITAL BUDGETING TECHNIQUES

Several methods are used for evaluating capital budgeting proposals. We will discuss the four most common techniques:

1. Payback (PB)
2. Average Rate of Return (ARR)
3. Net Present Value (NPV)
4. Internal Rate of Return (IRR)

Companies frequently modify or combine one or another of these techniques to conform more closely with their own budgeting systems. For example, many companies compute a Profitability Index (PI), which is very closely related to the Net Present Value Calculation. Hence, many variations of these basic techniques are found in practice. Nonetheless, every capital expenditure analysis involves three elements:

- Identification of all relevant costs.
- Identification of the amounts and timing of benefits.
- Procedures for evaluating the benefits relative to the costs.

The payback and average-rate-of-return methods are widely used. They are quite simple methods but significantly flawed. The net-present-value and internal-rate-of-return methods are known as discounted cash flow (DCF) methods. Discounted cash flow methods are theoretically well founded and are becoming increasingly adopted in practice. To consider and compare these methods on a consistent basis, let us assume that the Honey Dipped Company is considering an investment in a new doughnut-making machine. The machine is expected to reduce operating costs while doubling capacity. The machine will cost $19,100 and is expected to produce the net cash flows shown in Table 14-1.

discounted cash flow methods

Payback

The *payback period* is the length of time necessary for the net investment outlays to be recovered. Many companies may focus strictly on an acceptable time period for payback of their capital. The payback period method assumes that cash flows are received uniformly throughout the year.

payback period

Example

Payback Period for the Doughnut Machine

The net investment outlays for the doughnut machine are $19,100. Expected cash inflows of $6,020 will be received in each of the first three years. By the end of the third year, $18,060 ($6,020 × 3), will have been recovered, which is $1,040 short of the original investment. Thus the payback period is more than three years. Assuming that cash flows are produced at a uniform rate during the year, the $1,040 represents approxi-

TABLE 14-1 Investment Summary: Doughnut Making Machine Proposal					
Year	0	1	2	3	4
Cash inflow (outflow)	($19,100)	$6,020	$6,020	$6,020	$9,720

mately 11 percent of the cash inflows to be produced by the investment in year four ($1,040/9,720). Thus the payback period for the investment is 3.1 years.

Payback Acceptance/Rejection Decision Rule. The payback period has been calculated, but what does it mean? Companies like Honey Dipped predetermine acceptable payback periods for different types of investments. For example, Honey Dipped requires all cost-reduction investments to have payback periods of less than four years. With its payback period of 3.1 years, the new doughnut machine is considered acceptable if classified as a cost reducing investment.

If the machine had been classified as an "expansion" investment, however, it would be rejected because Honey Dipped requires payback periods of two years or less on expansion proposals. The application of these criteria could generate many hours of excitement in the capital budgeting meetings at the Honey Dipped Company, as executives try to agree whether a project is a revenue expanding project or a cost reducing project.

Weaknesses of the Payback Method. The payback method has several major deficiencies. First it ignores variations in the rate at which cash flows are realized. For example, there might be two different investments whose annual after-tax cash flows would be as shown in Table 14-2.

Although both machines are paid for in three years, the investments are not equally desirable, because of the time value of money. For example, in the first year investment X produces $7,000 in cash while Y produces only $3,000. The extra $4,000 from X can be reinvested and produce even more cash in years two and three. By ignoring the time value of money, the payback period method is not sensitive to the pattern of cash flows produced within the payback period.

A second important weakness in the payback method is that it fails to consider any cash flows *beyond* the payback period. Let us assume that one decides that any investment must pay for itself within two years, or it will not be made. On this basis, a $10,000 machine that returned $5,000 a year for only two years and nothing thereafter might be purchased. Conversely, the firm would be forced to reject a proposal to buy a $10,000

TABLE 14-2 Cash Flow Expected					
			Year		
Project	0	1	2	3	4
X	($15,000)	$7,000	$5,000	$3,000	$4,000
Y	($15,000)	$3,000	$5,000	$7,000	$4,000

machine that would return $4,000 a year for five years. Neither decision would maximize the market value of owners' equity, which is the final objective of financial management.

A third weakness of the payback method is that it simply ignores the profitability of the investment. Indeed, the payback method is not designed to measure profitability but rather liquidity (how fast is the investment recovered?). There is an implicit assumption that shorter payback projects are more profitable than longer payback projects (for example, a payback period of two years means one gets 50 percent of the original investment per year). But most people would prefer an investment that returns 25 percent of the original investment each year forever to one that returns 50 percent per year for two years only. For example, consider the two projects in Table 14-3. Project A has faster payback than B, but which would you prefer?

This type of bias becomes even more serious when all acceptable investments cannot be undertaken; a problem that will be addressed in more detail later in this chapter.

Rationale for Payback Method. The payback approach is popular among small companies without sophisticated capital budgeting procedures and which may be desperately short of cash. Also, industries characterized by instability, uncertainty, and rapid technological change may adopt the payback approach on the grounds that the future is so unpredictable there is no point in projecting differential flows of cash beyond, say, two years. This is a weak rationale, however, because it can easily involve the waste of investment cash and thereby keep the company in perpetual crisis.

Average Rate of Return

The *average rate of return* (or accounting rate of return) is the ratio of the average annual net income after taxes to the average investment over the life of the project. This is not based on cash flows, but on the reported accounting income.

average rate of return
accounting rate of return

Average annual net income is calculated by summing up all the net income to be produced and dividing by the number of years. Average investment is estimated by dividing the net investment by two. This is a

TABLE 14-3 Which Project Would You Choose?				
Project	Cost	Cash Per Year	# Years	Payback Period
A	($100,000)	$50,000	2	2 years
B	($100,000)	$25,000	10	4 years

very rough estimate, particularly when accelerated depreciation methods are used, when nondepreciating assets such as working capital are involved, and when salvage values will be realized. However, the problems with the average-rate-of-return method are much more severe than these.

$$ARR = \text{Average net income}/(\text{Investment}/2) \qquad (14\text{-}1)$$

Assume that net income will average $1,770 per year and that the average investment is calculated as $9,550 (i.e., $19,100/2). Thus the average rate of return would be calculated as 18.5%.

Acceptance/Rejection Decision Rule. Companies using the average-rate-of-return method pre-specify the minimum acceptable rates of return. If the investment's ARR exceeds the "hurdle," the investment is acceptable; otherwise it is rejected. For example, the minimum acceptable rate of return on expansion investments at Honey Dipped is 15 percent. The doughnut machine would be viewed as an acceptable investment, since its projected ARR of 18.5 percent exceeds the hurdle rate.

Weaknesses of the ARR Method. Unlike the payback method, the ARR method explicitly focuses on investment profitability. However, it is seriously flawed in at least two respects. First, like the payback method, it ignores the impact of the time value of money. Second, it ignores the timing of cost-recovery cash flows, since it looks at net income rather than cash flow.

Net Present Value (NPV) Method

present value of cash inflows (PVCI)

The net-present-value method involves comparing the present value of cash inflows (*PVCI*) with the cost of the investment (*I*). The cost of the investment is equal to the present value of cash outflows needed to undertake the investment. In this text we are assuming that all investment outflows occur at the beginning (i.e., at $t = 0$). We will use the terms "investment cost," "present value of cash outflows," and "investment outflows" interchangeably. The net present value is determined by subtracting the cost of the investment from *PVCI*. By focusing on both cash flows and the present values of these cash flows, the NPV method explicitly considers the time value of money.

required rate of return

In order to determine present values, one needs to know what the required rate of return (discount rate) from the investment is as well as the amounts and timing of cash flows. In a strict sense, the required rate of

---

[1]This is another simplification assumed by the technique since accelerated depreciation, salvage values, and working capital investments will affect the average investment in different ways.

return from capital budgeting investments is equal to the investment's *cost of capital.* The cost of capital is the rate of return investors require on the capital they supply to make the investment. Determining the cost of capital is sufficiently complex and so important to the quality of the analysis that it must be discussed in much more detail than is possible in this chapter. Therefore a full discussion is deferred to Chapter 17. Since the primary interest here is in illustrating the use of techniques, simply assume that the cost of capital, *k* is known. (However, remember that the cost of capital rate selected is very important to the proper evaluation of capital proposals.)

cost of capital

$$\text{NPV} = \text{Present value of cash inflows } (PVCI)$$

$$- \text{ Net investment outflows } (I) \qquad (14\text{-}2)$$

net present value (NPV)

If we let CF_t represent the after-tax cash inflows generated by the investment at time t, the present value of cash inflows ($PVCI$) can be calculated as follows:

$$PVCI = \sum_{t=1}^{n} CF_t/(1 + k)^t \qquad (14\text{-}3)$$

Where $\sum_{t=1}^{n}$ represents the summation of each year's discounted cash flow (discounted at the cost of capital rate k) beginning with year one ($t = 1$), then adding the present value amount for year two ($t = 2$), and continuing to add the annual present value amounts through year n.[2]

Example

Net Present Value of Doughnut Proposal

Honey Dipped has established a required rate of return of 15 percent on product expansion investments. Hence the present value of cash inflows ($PVCI$) for the investment is $19,309.52. The net investment outflows (I) are $19,100. The net present value of the investment is $209.52, as shown in Table 14-4.

TABLE 14-4   Net Present Value Calculation: Investment Proposal

Cash inflow	$6,020.00	$6,020.00	$6,020.00	$9,720.00
Discount factor @ 15%	.870	.756	.658	.572
Present value @ 15%	$ 5,237.40	$4,551.12	$3,961.16	$5,559.84
Total present value:	$19,309.52			
Less investment outlays	($19,100.00)			
Net present value	$ 209.52			

---

[2]This is consistent with the presentation and discussion of valuation in Chapter 5.

Acceptance/Rejection Decision Rule. If the value of the investment exceeds its cost, the investment is clearly a bargain and should be accepted. If the investment value is less than its cost, the investment is unacceptable. Stated differently, if the NPV is positive, accept the investment; if the NPV is negative, reject. If the NPV is equal to zero, one asset (cash) is simply being exchanged for another (permanent assets) and the firm should be, technically, indifferent as to whether to accept or reject the investment.

A Common Mistake. Students sometimes recommend rejecting even some positive net-present-value projects because "the net present values are not high enough given the risks of the project." This statement is erroneous for the following reason. If the project is properly analyzed, the true risks will be incorporated in the cash flow estimates and the discount rate used. Positive net present value means that the project is economically sound given its risk level.

Profitability Index (PI)

profitability index (PI)

The profitability index indicates the present value of cash inflows per dollar of investment. It is calculated by dividing the present value of cash inflows by the investment outflows.

$$PI = \text{Present value of cash inflows/Investment outflows} \qquad (14\text{-}4)$$

Example

Profitability Index of Doughnut Proposal

The PI for the doughnut machine investment proposal would thus be 1.01 ($19,309/19,100). If the PI is greater than 1.0, the investment should be accepted; if less than 1.0, the investment should be rejected. The PI is closely related to the NPV method and will always give the same "accept/reject" decision.

Internal Rate of Return

internal rate of return (IRR)

The internal rate of return (IRR) is the discount rate that equates the present value of the cash inflows ($PVCI$) with the investment (I). Stated differently, the IRR is the discount rate that results in a zero net present value (NPV); that is, ($PVCI - I$) = NPV = 0 at the IRR.

Recall that, with the net-present-value method, we arrived at an expected present value of cash inflows ($PVCI$), given expected annual cash inflows (CF_t), and a predetermined cost of capital k. Now we are solving for the discount rate, and we designate the internal rate of return by the letter, r.

By definition, the internal rate of return, IRR, is that discount rate, r, that makes *PVCI* equal to *I*. Substituting from Equation 14-3:

$$\text{Net investment(I)} = PVCI = \sum_{t=1}^{n} CF_t/(1 + r)^t \qquad (14\text{-}5)$$

Finding the IRR for a project is a trial-and-error process. One first must calculate the present value of the cash inflows at some selected discount rate for the project. Next one must subtract the investment outlay from the *PVCI* to determine how close the NPV is to zero. If the NPV is positive, one needs to apply a higher discount rate to the stream of cash inflows. For negative NPVs it is necessary to use a lower discount rate and repeat the cash flow discounting process. This trial-and-error process is continued until the present value of the cash inflows is approximately equal to the net initial investment. At this point, one will have found the project's internal rate of return.

Example

Internal Rate of Return for the Doughnut Proposal

Since the doughnut-making machine investment has a positive NPV at a 15 percent discount rate, the IRR must be more than 15 percent. By trial and error, one tries different discount rates above 15 percent until the NPV is approximately zero. This is shown in Table 14-5. The IRR for the doughnut machine investment is between 15 and 16 percent.

Acceptance/Rejection Decision Rule. If the investment's internal rate of return is greater than its cost of capital, the investment should be accepted: the return is greater than required. If the internal rate of return is less than the cost of capital, the investment should be rejected because

TABLE 14-5   Internal Rate of Return Calculation: Investment Proposal

Year	Cash Flow	D. F. @ 15%	PV @ 15%	D. F. @ 16%	PV @ 16%
1	$6,020	.870	$ 5,237.40	.862	$ 5,189.24
2	$6,020	.756	$ 4,551.12	.743	$ 4,472.86
3	$6,020	.658	$ 3,961.16	.641	$ 3,858.82
4	$9,720	.572	$ 5,559.84	.552	$ 5,365.44
		Total present value	$19,309.52		$18,886.36
		Less investment	($19,100.00)		($19,100.00)
		NPV	$ 209.52		−$ 213.64

the return will be less than required. If the internal rate of return is equal to the cost of capital, the company should be indifferent between accepting and rejecting the investment.

Relationship Between NPV, PI, and IRR

The algebraic structure of the NPV and IRR methods reveals the close relationship between the two methods. The NPV method addresses the question: "How much is the investment worth?" The IRR method addresses the question: "What rate of return will the investment produce?"

As noted, when calculating an investment's net present value, discounting at the cost of capital, if the NPV is positive, the IRR must be greater than the cost of capital. If the NPV is negative, the IRR is less than the cost of capital. If the NPV (again discounting cash flows at the cost of capital) is equal to zero, then the IRR must be equal to the cost of capital. This relationship is summarized in Table 14-6.

TABLE 14-6 Relationship of NPV, PI, and IRR		
NPV > 0	PI > 1	IRR > cost of capital
NPV = 0	PI = 1	IRR = cost of capital
NPV < 0	PI < 1	IRR < cost of capital

Therefore, if an investment is acceptable in terms of the NPV method, it will also be acceptable in terms of the IRR method, and vice versa. If an investment is unacceptable in terms of the NPV method, it will also be unacceptable in terms of the IRR method, and vice versa. Both methods, in other words, will give the same accept or reject verdict.

WHEN NPV AND IRR METHODS DO NOT AGREE

If *all* acceptable investments can be undertaken by the company, it makes no difference whether the NPV or IRR method is used. However, when all acceptable investments *cannot* be undertaken, it *does* make a difference which method is used. In this case, the NPV method is generally superior to the IRR method.

There are two types of situations in which all acceptable investments cannot be undertaken and, thus, in which conflicts between the IRR and NPV methods may surface. These two types of situations occur when investments are mutually exclusive and when the company employs capital rationing.

Mutually Exclusive Investments

When the acceptance of one investment will automatically imply rejection of another investment, the investments are said to be mutually exclusive. A simple example of this would be deciding which car to buy. Similarly, if a company decides to automate office work with an IBM system, it may necessarily preclude using a DEC system.

When a company has to decide between mutually exclusive investments, it may resort to ranking investments. If the NPV method is employed, the NPV of each investment is calculated and ranked. The investment with the highest NPV is ranked No 1, and so on. If the IRR method is used, the IRR for each investment is calculated and ranked. The investment with the highest IRR is ranked No. 1, and so on. The problem arises when the ranking produced by the NPV method is different from the ranking produced by the IRR method. Then how should the decision be made? Shortly, we will see why the ranking conflict arises and how it should be resolved. First let us consider another situation in which the ranking problem may arise.

mutually exclusive investments

investment rankings

Capital Rationing

Capital rationing situations arise when the total dollar investment required by acceptable projects (positive NPVs) is greater than the amount management is willing or able to budget for capital expenditures. Management may decide to ration capital in the short run in order to avoid the need to raise funds at an unfavorable time, or to maintain the current level of dividend payments. In addition, management may simply have an unreasoned fear of assuming debt or selling new stock. In fact, firms often face capital rationing; and financial managers must devise means to rank projects under such circumstances.

capital rationing

The net present value method is particularly appropriate when a company is faced with capital rationing.

To illustrate the point, consider Table 14-7, which lists a number of independent project proposals available for acceptance by the MSA Company.

TABLE 14-7   MSA Company Independent Project Proposals Available

Project	Cash Outlay	Cash Inflow End of Year	NPV @10%	IRR	Rank By: NPV	Rank By: IRR
F	$10,000	$12,000	$ 908	20%	3	1
G	10,000	11,900	817	19%	4	2
H	10,000	11,600	544	16%	5	5
I	20,000	23,400	1,271	17%	2	4
J	30,000	35,400	2,179	18%	1	3

Assume that management has limited the total capital budget to $30,000. Which projects should be selected by MSA if its cost of capital is 10 percent?

Examination of the IRRs is not very illuminating. The 18-percent return on Project J is nice, but is it as good as, say, the 20-percent return from project F, coupled with the 17-percent return from project I? A much better approach is to determine the net present values of all possible subsets of proposals that will use up the $30,000 available. For example, Projects F, G, and H could be undertaken, since they require outlays of $10,000 each and will provide a combined NPV of $2,269 ($908 + 817 + 544). All possible combinations can be grouped as shown in Table 14-8.

TABLE 14-8	
Acceptable Project Combination	Combined Net Present Values
F, G, H	$2,269
F, I	2,179
G, I	2,088
H, I	1,815
J	2,179

This array shows very quickly that the value of the firm will be raised most by investing the $30,000 in projects F, G and H. Obviously, the solution is more difficult when a very large array of projects is involved. Nonetheless, the optimal solution is attainable, especially with the aid of a computer, whereas it would not be readily accessible (or even optimal) to employ the internal rate of return under capital rationing. Thus, under conditions of capital rationing, the NPV method is preferable to the IRR for making capital investment decisions.

Why the Conflict In Rankings Occurs

There are two principal reasons why the conflict in rankings between the NPV and IRR methods arises. First large size disparities in the investments being ranked cause conflicts. Second, differences in assumptions made by both methods about the reinvestment rates of return of cash flows cause conflicts.

size disparity

Size Disparity Problem. If two or more investments differ greatly in size, the conflict in rankings between the NPV and IRR methods may arise.

Consider projects A and B shown in Table 14-9. Although both offer a rate of return greater than the cost of capital and both have positive net present values, the firm cannot accept both, either because they are mutually exclusive or because of the constraint of capital rationing.

TABLE 14-9   NPV Vs. IRR Ranking Conflict: Size Disparity

Investment	Investment Outlay	First Year Cash Flow	IRR	NPV	Rank By IRR	Rank By NPV
A	$10,000	$11,500	15%	$454	1	2
B	$22,000	$24,860	13%	$598	2	1

Note that the ranking according to the IRR method is the reverse of the ranking produced by the NPV method. In this case, the difference arises because investment B is larger than investment A. This raises the question: Is it better to have a great return on a small investment or a good return on a large investment? If you had an either-or choice between earning a 25-percent return on $1,000 for one year or a 50-percent rate of return on $1 for one year, which would you choose? Since most people would prefer ending the year with an extra $250(.25 × $1,000) as opposed to an extra 50 cents (.50 × $1.00), a decision based on the IRR would be unfortunate. Why is this so?

In the comparison of projects A and B, note that project B involves higher investment outlays and higher net cash inflows than does A. Since project B also has a higher NPV, think of project B as incorporating all of the cash flows of A plus an incremental investment, which we can call investment B-A. In other words, think of investment B as a composite of two investments: A and B-A. Then break B up into these two components, as shown in Table 14-10.

TABLE 14-10   Splitting Up Investment B

		Let: $B = B_A + B_{B-A}$		
Investment	Investment Outlay	First Year Cash Flow	IRR	NPV
B_A	($10,000)	$11,500	15.0%	$454
B_{B-A}	($12,000)	$13,360	11.3%	$144
B	($22,000)	$24,860	13.0%	$598

Note that one component of B, which is designated B_A, looks exactly like investment A. The other component, B_{B-A}, is an incremental investment that may be made by accepting B. Since B_A looks exactly like A, it has the same NPV and IRR as A does. Thus, by undertaking investment B, one is not giving up the "higher" IRR. The important question is whether the incremental investment, B_{B-A}, also is an acceptable investment. When the NPV and IRR are calculated for the incremental investment, the NPV, $144, is positive and the IRR, 11.3 percent is greater than the cost of capital. Thus if one must choose between projects A and B, B is preferable because one gets an investment exactly like A plus an incremental investment that is also desirable from both the NPV and IRR standpoints. From this example, it can be concluded that, when there is a conflict in rankings, the NPV method will result in the "right" decision.

Differences in Assumptions. Students sometimes ask if one could not do even better by taking investment A and also investing in some other project, "C" for example. However, this question assumes that the firm is rationing capital and that project C would not otherwise be accepted. We have not assumed that the firm is capital rationing, only that investments A and B are mutually exclusive. Thus, the firm should accept investment B *and* C.

Reinvestment Rate Problem. A conflict in rankings between the IRR and NPV methods may also arise, even though there is no substantial size disparity between investments. The conflicts may arise simply due to a wide disparity in the pattern of cash flows.

Example

Let us assume that one is trying to choose between the two mutually exclusive projects shown in Table 14-11.

TABLE 14-11

	Cash Flow in Year			
Investment	0	1	2	3
D	($10,000)	4,200	4,200	4,200
E	($10,000)	7,000	4,000	1,000

Note that, in contrast to the level cash inflows for project D, cash inflows decrease for project E over time. If one ignores the time value of money (i.e., assumes a zero interest rate), the net present value for project D would be $2,600 versus only $2,000 for project E based on the summing of the cash outlays and inflows for each project. However, at certain positive discount rates the preference of project D may not hold, and either project may have the higher NPV.

Present Value Profile.   The relationship between NPV and IRR for   *present value profile* projects characterized by different cash flow patterns can be illustrated by developing a present value profile of the investment, as shown in Exhibit 14-1. Note that, for a firm with a cost of capital of 10 percent or less, project D would be preferred over project E based on the size of calculated NPVs. However, between a 10-percent and 11-percent discount rate (actually 10.54 percent) there is a crossover in that, from then on, there exists an

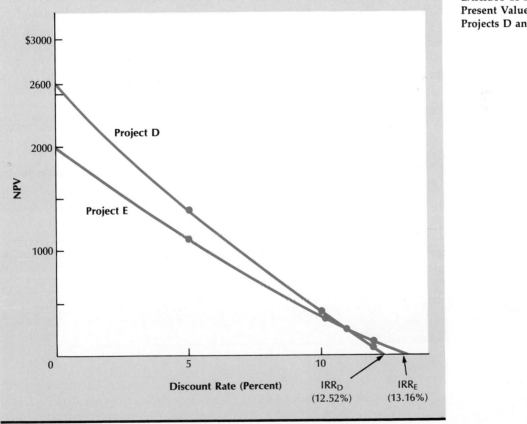

EXHIBIT 14-1
Present Value Profile for
Projects D and E

NPV preference for project E over project D. Actually the IRR from project E is approximately 13 percent, compared to about 12.5 percent for project D.

The reinvestment rate problem arises from two factors. First, in calculating the IRR for a project, there is an implicit assumption that all cash received during the course of the investment will be reinvested either in the same or similar projects. Moreover, it is assumed that the rate earned on the reinvested cash flows will be the same rate as the original project. For example, project E has an IRR of about 13 percent. This will actually be true only if the cash flows, such as the $7,000 received in year one, are reinvested at 13 percent. This is an implicit assumption. The NPV method also contains a reinvestment rate assumption. In the NPV calculation, the assumption is that all project cash flows are reinvested at the cost of capital (which is always less than the IRR for acceptable investments).

The second factor arises from the fact that, if the reinvestment rate is assumed to be higher than the cost of capital, there is a real advantage in receiving cash flows faster. This is why the pattern of cash flows becomes important. For example, in year one, project E gets $7,000 back in cash flow while project D only gets $4,200. When the cost of capital is low, this timing difference is less important; and thus the NPV calculation is not biased by it. In fact, note that project D will actually produce more dollars ($12,600) over the three years than will project E ($12,000). At relatively low discount rates, the total amount of cash is more important than the timing of cash flows. At high discount rates, the timing of cash flows becomes more important relative to the total amount of cash flows.

INVESTMENTS WITH UNEQUAL LIVES

*unequal investment
lives*

If a choice must be made between mutually exclusive investments with unequal lives, both the net-present-value and internal-rate-of-return methods can yield an incorrect selection decision. In such cases, special methods should be used to make the investments comparable as to useful life. First let us illustrate the problem that may arise when investments have unequal lives and then present two popular methods for dealing with the problem.

Example

Unequal Lives

Assume that investments A and B are mutually exclusive. Each investment will require cash outflows of $100,000 to undertake, but investment A will last only one year while B will last two years. At a 10-percent cost of capital, investment B has the higher net present value, as indicated below.

Investment	Cash Flow for Year 0	1	2	NPV at 10%
A	−$100,000	+$130,000	−0−	+$18,170
B	−$100,000	+$ 70,000	+$70,000	+$21,520

If the two investments had equal lives, the NPV rule would correctly indicate that investment B should be preferred to investment A. However, due to the unequal lives, such a comparison can lead to incorrect decisions. The reason is that investment A produces more cash flows which can be reinvested to generate more net present value in year two. By ignoring this value-creating potential, investment A is penalized relative to investment B. Two methods, *replacement chains* and *equivalent annual annuity* net present value, are commonly used to adjust for differences in useful lives.

Replacement Chains

According to the replacement chain method, investment A should be converted to a two-year investment by making a sequence of two one-year investments. Thus, at the end of year one, it is assumed that another investment A is undertaken. The two one-year investments thus become one two-year investment chain, as shown below.

replacement chain

Investment	Cash Flow for Year 0	1	2	NPV at 10%
First A	−$100,000	+$130,000	−0−	
Second A		−$100,000	+$130,000	
Net cash flows	−$100,000	+$ 30,000	+$130,000	+$34,650

Now investment A, with replacement, can be compared with investment B on a net-present-value basis since they are both two-year investments. Since investment A has a higher NPV than investment B, investment A should be selected.

The replacement chain method for comparing investments with unequal lives does not always work as smoothly as in the example. For example, if investment A actually had a six-year life and investment B had a 10-year life, one would have to evaluate a chain of five investment As (producing a total life of 30 years) compared to a chain of three investment Bs (also producing a total life of 30 years) in order to produce equal investment lives. An alternative method, the equivalent annual annuity (EAA) net-present-value method, produces a more direct solution.

Equivalent Annual Annuity (EAA) Method

The EAA method distributes each investment's net present value over the number of years needed to obtain it. This is done by converting the investment's NPV into an annuity, as shown below.

$$
\begin{array}{cc}
& A & B \\
\end{array}
$$

$$EAA = NPV/PVIFA_{k\%,n} = \$18{,}170/.909 = 21{,}520/1.736$$

$$= \$19{,}989 \qquad = \$12{,}396$$

Thus, A actually produces more net present value per year than B does, and A should be chosen. The EAA method gives the same result as the replacement chain method without having to determine the number of replacements required for each. To see the connection between the two methods, note that investment A's EAA over a two-year time period will produce the same total NPV as indicated by the replacement chain method.

$$\text{Two-year NPV}_A = EAA_A(PVIFA_{k\%,n})$$

$$= \$19{,}989(1.736) = \$34{,}709$$

which, except for rounding, is equal to the net present value of $34,650 produced by the replacement chain method.

MULTIPLE IRRs

A further problem with the internal-rate-of-return method is that investments may have more than one IRR. This situation can occur when the cash flows being evaluated have more than one sign reversal. For example, consider investment C, below.

	Cash Flows in Year		
	0	1	2
Investment C	−$100,000	+$600,000	−$550,000

Investment C actually has two different IRRs, 12.917 percent and 387.08 percent. Each of these rates will produce a zero NPV, which is the definition of the IRR. The present value profile for investment C, shown in Exhibit 14-2 reveals the existence of the two IRRs.

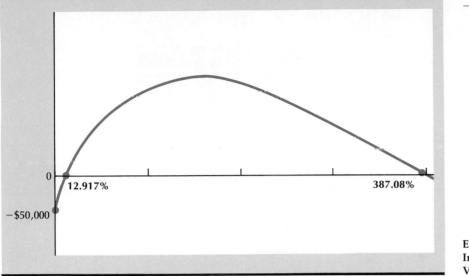

**EXHIBIT 14-2
Investment C Present
Value Profile**

In general, there may be as many IRRs as there are reversals in sign. Investment C has two such reversals and two IRRs. Not all sign reversals will produce additional IRRs. The magnitude of the reversal is also important.

The multiple IRR problem is one more reason why the NPV method is the most reliable way of making capital budgeting decisions.

SUMMARY

Capital budgeting decisions probably spell the difference between long-run success or failure for many business concerns. Regardless of the size of the company or the level at which the decisions are made, the principles should be the same. Management is committing a sum of money today in return for an expected stream of net cash benefits in the future. Evaluation of the desirability of a particular project requires that one give greater weight to income that is to be received in the near future. The time value of money must be considered.

The two methods of evaluating capital expenditures that take into account the time value of money are net present value and internal rate of return. When projects are mutually exclusive or the firm is operating under conditions of capital rationing, projects must be ranked. For this purpose, the net-present-value approach is superior to the internal-rate-of-return method. When projects are compared, net present value carries the implicit assumption that project cash flows are reinvested at the cost of capital. In addition, the change in the value of the firm may be measured directly by comparing the NPVs of various subsets of projects.

MULTIPLE CHOICE QUESTIONS

1. Capital budgeting refers to the process of:
   a) Making fixed asset investments
   b) Financing from long-term sources of capital
   c) Estimating cash requirements for operations
   d) Planning repayment of company borrowings

2. Which of the following would typically be considered a mandatory investment:
   a) Corporate acquisition
   b) New product
   c) Cost reduction
   d) Anti-pollution

3. The difference between the present value of cash inflows and the present value of investment outlays is referred to as:

   a) Net present value
   b) Internal rate of return
   c) Profitability index
   d) Net investment required

4. Two capital budgeting methods that utilize the time value of money concept are the net-present-value method and the:

   a) Net future value
   b) Average rate of return
   c) Payback period
   d) Internal rate of return

5. If two projects were alternatives for each other and both were acceptable, as indicated by positive net present values, one would select:

   a) The higher net present value
   b) The higher cost
   c) The shorter payback
   d) The higher average rate of return

6. The profitability index is closely related to the NPV method and will always:

   a) Be greater than 1.0
   b) Be greater than the payback period
   c) Give the same "accept" or "reject" decision.
   d) Exceed the required rate of return

7. The IRR is the discount rate that:

   a) Results in a positive net present value
   b) Equals the required rate of return
   c) Exceeds the minimum required rate of return
   d) Results in a zero net present value

8. If a company has ample funds available and is evaluating a single proposed project, use of net-present-value or _____ methods will give the same decision.

   a) Internal-rate-of-return
   b) Payback period
   c) Average-rate-of-return
   d) All of these

9. When the existence of mutually exclusive investments or capital rationing requires a ranking of projects, the net-present-value method is:

   a) Biased toward large investments
   b) Superior to the internal-rate-of-return procedure.
   c) Biased toward safe investment
   d) Suboptimal

10. A present value profile is used to:
    a) Estimate the cost of capital
    b) Estimate the variance of investment cash flows
    c) Adjust for risk
    d) Understand the relationship between NPV and IRR.

11. Whereas the use of internal rate of return implicitly assumes reinvestment at the calculated rate of return, net present value implicitly assumes reinvestment at:
    a) The cost of capital
    b) The risk-free rate
    c) The required rate of return
    d) The certainty equivalent rate

12. The two most commonly used non-DCF methods are payback and:
    a) Average rate of return
    b) Decision trees
    c) Certainty equivalent
    d) Simulation

13. Both the payback and the average-rate-of-return methods suffer from the fundamental deficiency that they:
    a) Ignore the time value of money
    b) Focus on profit instead of cash flow
    c) Ignore investment required
    d) Ignore depreciation

14. A major deficiency of the payback method is that it:
    a) Does not adjust for the scale of the investment
    b) Fails to consider any stream of income extending beyond the payback period
    c) Requires much data and complex calculations
    d) All of these

15. An estimate of the average investment as used in the average-rate-of-return method is:
    a) Divide annual depreciation by four
    b) Divide the investment by its economic life.
    c) Multiply the investment by two
    d) Divide the investment amount by two

DISCUSSION QUESTIONS

1. Briefly describe what is meant by the net-present-value method. How is it used in capital budgeting?

2. Describe the internal-rate-of-return method and indicate why it is referred to as a discounted cash flow capital budgeting method.

3. In certain instances, application of the net-present-value and internal-rate-of-return methods may result in a ranking conflict between projects. Explain and illustrate.

4. How do the payback period and average-rate-of-return methods differ from the discounted cash flow methods?

5. Identify possible organizational procedures for making capital budgeting decisions. Why is it important to monitor and control capital expenditures?

6. What is the difference between mandatory and discretionary types of investments? Give some examples of each.

7. Discuss the importance of the post audit in capital budgeting.

8. Describe the payback method as used to evaluate capital budgeting proposals. What are its major weaknesses? Why do firms use it?

9. Explain the relationship of the cost of capital to the minimum required rate of return from an investment.

10. Compare the net-present-value method with the internal-rate-of-return method in capital budgeting. In what respects are they similar? Different?

11. What is an investment's "present value profile?" Why is it used?

12. Under what conditions can investments have multiple IRRs?

13. What reinvestment rate assumption is made by the NPV method? The IRR method?

SOLVED PROBLEMS

SP-1. The Tulies Company is considering the purchase of a labor saving device that will last 10 years and produce after-tax cash flows of $4,640 per year for 10 years. The new device costs $20,000. Assume that the required rate of return (cost of capital) on such investments is 12 percent; and the minimum payback period is seven years.

NPV, IRR, PI, payback, interpolation

a) Calculate the investment's net present value (NPV).
b) Calculate the investment's profitability index (PI).
c) Estimate the internal rate of return (IRR) on the investment. (Use interpolation to improve your estimate. For a review of interpolation see Chapter 4 or the solution below.)
d) Calculate the payback period.
e) Based on your results in part (a), would you recommend that Tulies purchase the device?

SP-2. Jules Plumbing Company has decided to automate its accounting and billing operations. It will do so with the purchase of a central

NPV vs. IRR

minicomputer and several data terminals. After talking with various manufacturers, Jules' president has narrowed the choice down to two system manufacturers. The manufacturer for model A has offered to install a complete operating system including programming, personnel orientation, and equipment installation for a total cost of $17,000. The manufacturer of model B suggests a more gradual, phased-in computerization. For $16,000, the manufacturer will provide continuing operating support for three years, after which all the "bugs" will be out of the system and the full benefits of the computer can be realized. Both manufacturers have indicated that a five-year useful life for either system is appropriate, regardless of the model adopted by Jenkins. In other words, new technology and changes in computer programming will obsolesce either system Jules selects now. At the end of five years, Jules should assume no salvage value for either system. Jules' president has decided to evaluate the choices using a cost of capital of 10 percent; straight-line depreciation; an expected life of five years; and no salvage value. Jules' tax rate is 34 percent. The expected after-tax cash flows for each model are shown below.

Unsure of the best way to choose between the two systems, the president has asked you to rank the two models on the following bases:

a) Net-present-value method and profitability index
b) Internal rate of return.
c) Payback period.
d) Average rate of return.
e) How will you explain any differences in ranking to the president?

Investment Summary:	A	B
Net investment outlays	$17,000	$16,000
Salvage value	–0–	–0–
Economic life	5 years	5 years
After-tax cash flows:		
(Years 1-3)/year	$ 4,960	$ 2,000
(Years 4-5)/year	$ 4,960	$ 9,980

PROBLEMS

NPV, IRR, PI, payback interpolation

1. The MSA Company is considering the purchase of a labor-saving device that will last five years and produce after-tax cash flows of $20,000 per year for five years. The new device costs $50,000. Assume that the required rate of return (cost of capital) on such investments is 11 percent; and the minimum payback period is three years.

a) Calculate the investment's net present value (NPV).
b) Calculate the investment's profitability index (PI).
c) Estimate the internal rate of return (IRR) on the investment (use interpolation to improve your estimate. For a review of interpolation see Chapter 4 or the solution to Solved Problem 1).
d) Calculate the payback period.
e) Based on your results in part (a), would you recommend that MSA purchase the device?

2. Investment A has the following cash flows:

NPV IRR

	Cash Flow in Year				
	0	1	2	3	4
A	−$60,000	25,000	15,000	40,000	22,000

a) Determine the net present value of the investment given a cost of capital of 4 percent.
b) Determine the internal rate of return. (Be approximate.)

3. Investment R has the following cash flows:

NPV IRR

	Cash Flow in Year				
	0	1	2	3	4
R	−$100,000	70,000	10,000	20,000	25,000

a) Determine the net present value of the investment given a cost of capital of 10 percent.
b) Determine the internal rate of return. (Be approximate.)

NPV IRR

4. Investment T has the following cash flows:

	Cash Flow in Year				
	0	1	2	3	4
T	−$1,000,000	100,000	500,000	100,000	500,000

a) Determine the net present value of the investment given a cost of capital of 14 percent.
b) Determine the internal rate of return. (Be approximate.)

NPV IRR

5. Investment Q has the following cash flows:

	Cash Flow in Year				
	0	1	2	3	4
Q	−$75,000	30,000	30,000	30,000	30,000

a) Determine the net present value of the investment given a cost of capital of 16 percent. Note: solve it first with Table 2 in the Appendix and then with Table 4.

b) Determine the internal rate of return. (Be approximate.)

6. Investment D has the following cash flows:

	Cash Flow in Year				
	0	1	2	3	4
D	−$1,500,000	562,500	337,500	900,000	495,000

a) Determine the net present value of the investment given a cost of capital of 18 percent.

b) Determine the internal rate of return. (Be approximate.)

7. Investment G has the following cash flows:

	Cash Flow in Year				
	0	1	2	3	4
G	−$200,000	87,500	52,500	140,000	77,000

a) Determine the net present value of the investment given a cost of capital of 20 percent.

b) Determine the internal rate of return. Use linear interpolation. (For a review of interpolation see Chapter 4 or the solution to Solved Problem 1 at the end of this chapter.)

8. Investment S has the following cash flows:

	Cash Flow in Year				
	0	1	2	3	4
S	−$55,000	18,750	11,250	30,000	18,500

a) Determine the net present value of the investment given a cost of capital of 12 percent.
b) Estimate the internal rate of return. Use linear interpolation. (For a review of interpolation see Chapter 4 or the solution to Solved Problem 1 at the end of this chapter.)

9. Investment M has the following cash flows:

NPV
IRR
interpolation

		Cash Flow in Year			
	0	1	2	3	4
M	−$150,000	43,750	26,250	70,000	38,500

a) Determine the net present value of the investment given a cost of capital of 12 percent.
b) Estimate the internal rate of return. Use linear interpolation. (For a review of interpolation see Chapter 4 or the solution to Solved Problem 1 at the end of this chapter.)

10. Investment O has the following cash flows:

NPV
IRR

		Cash Flow In Year			
	0	1	2	3	4
O	−$83,935	25,000	15,000	40,000	22,000

a) Determine the net present value of the investment given a cost of capital of 6 percent.
b) Estimate the internal rate of return.

11. Investment P has the following cash flows:

NPV
IRR

		Cash Flow in Year			
	0	1	2	3	4
P	−$797,800	100,000	500,000	100,000	500,000

a) Determine the net present value of the investment given a cost of capital of 14 percent.
b) Estimate the internal rate of return.

12. Investment F has the following cash flows:

	Cash Flow in Year				
	0	*1*	*2*	*3*	*4*
F	$95,070	30,000	30,000	30,000	30,000

a) Determine the net present value of the investment given a cost of capital of 8 percent.
b) Estimate the internal rate of return.

13. Investment B has the following cash flows:

	Cash Flow in Year				
	0	*1*	*2*	*3*	*4*
B	−$115,745	70,000	10,000	20,000	25,000

a) Determine the net present value of the investment given a cost of capital of 5 percent.
b) Estimate the internal rate of return.

14. The Algo Company is considering which of two mutually exclusive investments to undertake. The cash flows of each are projected as follows:

	Cash Flow in Year					
	0	*1*	*2*	*3*	*4*	*5*
A	−$100,000	20,000	30,000	40,000	50,000	60,000
B	−$ 80,000	30,000	40,000	10,000	5,000	5,000

a) Calculate the payback for each proposal. Assume that the investment with the faster payback will be accepted. Which would be selected?
b) Assume that the cost of capital for both investments is 15 percent. Which should be adopted? Why?

15. The Hojar Company is considering two mutually exclusive investments. The projected cash flows for each are shown below:

	0	1	2	3
L	−$90,000	10,000	39,000	90,000
M	−$90,000	40,000	60,000	25,000

a) Assume that the cost of capital for both investments is 14 percent. Determine the net present value of each. Which should be selected?

b) Assume that the cost of capital for both investments is 18 percent. Determine the net present value of each. Which should be selected? Explain why your decision is altered.

c) Calculate the internal rate of return of each investment. Which should be selected on this basis? (Be approximate.)

d) Construct a present value profile for each investment on the same chart. Estimate the discount rate at which the crossover point occurs (be approximate).

e) Determine the incremental cash flows produced by investment M relative to investment L. At what discount rate will these incremental cash flows have a zero net present value (be approximate)?

16. The Raine Company has set its capital budget at $200,000 and has four capital requests which total $400,000. All of the requests are independent projects, and all have positive net present values. The projects are described below: *capital rationing*

Proposal	Investment Required	Present Value of Cash Inflows
A	−$100,000	$250,000
B	−$200,000	$400,000
C	−$ 50,000	$ 75,000
D	−$ 50,000	$ 60,000

a) Calculate the profitability index for each investment.

b) Assuming no capital rationing, by how much would the value of the firm increase if all the projects are accepted?

c) Assuming a capital budget of only $200,000, which project or projects should be accepted?

d) How much shareholder value is the Raine Company giving up as a result of its capital rationing?

17. The Park Company is considering two mutually exclusive investments. *unequal lives*
Investment C will cost $50,000 to undertake and will last three years.

Investment D will also cost $50,000 but will only last two years. The cash flows for the two investments are shown below.

	Cash Flows in Year			
	0	1	2	3
C	−$50,000	22,000	22,000	22,000
D	−$50,000	31,000	31,000	−0−

a) Determine the net present value of each, given a cost of capital of 12%. If the two investments have equal lives, which one should be accepted?

b) Use the replacement chain method of adjusting for the unequal lives of the two investments. Which one should be accepted on this basis?

c) Use the equivalent annual annuity (EAA) method to evaluate the two investments. Which one should be accepted on this basis?

unequal lives

18. The Tink Company is trying to decide between two mutually exclusive investments. Investment X will cost $60,000 to undertake and will last three years. Investment Y will cost $50,000 but will only last 2 years. The cash flows for both are shown below:

	Cash Flows in Year			
	0	1	2	3
X	−$60,000	32,000	25,000	28,000
Y	−$50,000	40,000	26,000	−0−

a) Determine the net present value of each, given a cost of capital of 15 percent. If the two investments have equal lives, which one should be accepted?

b) Use the replacement chain method of adjusting for the unequal lives of the two investments. Which one should be accepted on this basis?

c) Use the equivalent annual annuity (EAA) method to evaluate the two investments. Which one should be accepted on this basis?

multiple IRRs

19. The Jib Company is trying to evaluate a proposed investment in Product X. The difficulty is that Jib relies on the internal-rate-of-return method of evaluation and, in this case, the investment seems to have two very different internal rates of return. The cash flows are shown below.

	0	1	2
Product X	−$10,000	35,000	−26,000

a) Estimate the investment's two internal rates of return.
b) Why does the investment have more than one internal rate of return?
c) If Jib used the net-present-value method, would it have run into the same difficulty?

20. The Weeks Corporation is considering an investment in a machine costing $15,000. The after-tax inflows are estimated to be $4,000 per year for five years.

NPV
IRR
payback

a) Calculate the net present value for the machine assuming a 16-percent cost of capital for the firm.
b) Estimate the internal rate of return for the machine.
c) Calculate the payback period.
d) Based on your net present value calculation in Part (a), would you recommend that the machine be purchased?

21. The Gloob Corporation is evaluating a new piece of equipment. The equipment will require a $150,000 initial investment, with no expected salvage value at the end of its five-year life. After-tax cash flows are expected to be $50,000 per year.

NPV
IRR
payback

a) Calculate the net present value for the equipment, assuming a 16-percent cost of capital for the firm.
b) Estimate the internal rate of return for the equipment.
c) Calculate the payback period.
d) Based on your results in Part (a), would you recommend that the Gloob Corporation purchase the equipment?

22. Two conflicting proposals of equal risk have been made for the purchase of new equipment. The data on each are given below

NPV vs. IRR

	A	B
Net cash outlay	$8,500	$6,000
Estimated life	5 years	5 years
Net cash flows after taxes		
1-3 yrs.	2,500	1,500
4-5 yrs.	2,000	1,500

Assuming a cost of capital of 16 percent, rank each project in terms of:

a) Internal rate of return.
b) Net present value and profitability index.

c) Payback period.

d) How do you explain any differences in ranking?

23. Volker Associates must choose between two mutually exclusive projects having cash flows as shown below:

Project	Initial Outlay	Annual Net Cash Inflows for 5 Years
A	−$ 6,000	$2,000
B	−$10,000	3,165

a) Compute the net present value and internal rate of return for each project. Assume the cost of capital is 12 percent.

b) Compute the net present value and internal rate of return available on the incremental investment of $4,000 in project B. Assume the cost of capital is 12 percent.

c) Which project should be selected? Why? How do your findings in (b) relate to the conclusions that you draw from (a)?

24. Assume that Jacks, Inc., with a cost of capital of 10 percent, must choose between the two mutually exclusive projects having cash flows as shown below:

	Cash Flow in Year			
	0	*1*	*2*	*3*
X	$10,000	$7,000	$4,000	$2,000
Y	10,000	2,000	4,000	8,200

a) Compute the net present value and internal rate of return for each project. Why is there a difference in ranking? In the absence of capital rationing, which project should be selected? Why?

b) Management wishes to measure the sensitivity of the net present value to variations in discount rates. To provide such an analysis, prepare a present value profile for each. Plot the NPVs of projects X and Y, given discount rates of 0, 8, 12, 16, and 24 percent. What does this information convey to management?

c) On the chart prepared in (b) above, estimate the discount rate at which X and Y have the same NPV. Compare these results with those obtained in (a) above. What does this say about the relationship of NPV and internal rate of return?

25. The Oscar Manufacturing Corp. has a number of capital investment proposals available, but its capital budget is limited to $500,000.

   a) Given the information about the projects shown below, which should be selected? *capital rationing*

Project	Outlay	NPV
A	$100,000	$26,000
B	100,000	18,000
C	100,000	16,000
D	200,000	40,000
E	200,000	36,000
F	300,000	60,000

   b) Now assume that projects A and B are mutually exclusive. Which projects should be selected?
   c) Under the assumptions given in (b), how much would the value of the firm increase? How much would it have increased had it not been limited by capital rationing? How much has capital rationing cost the owners of the firm?

SOLUTIONS TO SOLVED PROBLEMS

SP-1. a) Calculation of net present value.

   Step 1: Calculate the present value of cash inflows ($PVCI$).

$$PVCI = \$4,640 \times PVIFA_{(12\%, 10 \text{ years})}$$

$$= \$4,640 \times 5.650$$

$$PVCI = \$26,216$$

   Step 2: Subtract the investment outflows to get NPV.

$$NPV = PVCI - \text{Investment outflows}$$

$$= \$26,216 - 20,000 = \$6,216$$

   The positive net present value means that the investment should be made.

   b) Profitability index (PI).

$$PI = PVCI/\text{Investment outflows}$$

$$PI = \$26,216/20,000 = 1.31$$

   c) Internal rate of return (IRR).

The cash flows are an annuity. Find the PVIFA factor that will make the annuity equal the investment (i.e., $20,000). The interest rate indicated by the PVIFA, given $n = 10$ years, is the IRR.

$$\$20,000 = \$4,640 \times \text{PVIFA}(k\%, 10 \text{ years})$$

$$\text{PVIFA}(k\%, 10 \text{ years}) = 4.310$$

Given that $n = 10$, the interest rate producing the PVIFA closest to 4.310 is 19 percent with a PVIFA of 4.339. Thus, the IRR is just slightly greater than 19 percent. A more exact estimate will require interpolation.

Notice that a 19-percent interest rate produces a PVIFA of 4.339, and a 20-percent rate has a PVIFA of 4.192. Thus, the PVIFA decreases as the interest rate increases. To interpolate in this case, calculate the difference between the investment's computed PVIFA(i.e., 4.310) and the 19-percent rate PVIFA (4.339). Next, calculate the difference in PVIFA between the 19-percent rate and the 20-percent rate. Then, take the ratio of the investment's difference relative to the total difference.

Interpolation

i) 19% PVIFA (from Table 4)	4.339
Investment's PVIFA	−4.310
difference	.029
ii) 19% PVIFA	4.339
20% PVIFA (from Table 4)	−4.192
difference	.147

iii) $\dfrac{.029}{.147} = .197$ or, .20 rounded

iv) Add the ratio to the original 19%
IRR = 19.2

d) Payback period.

Since the investment's cash flows are an annuity, simply divide the investment by the annual cash flow to get the payback period.

$$\text{Payback period} = \frac{\$20,000}{4,640}$$

$$= 4.31 \text{ years}$$

e) The machine is an acceptable investment since its NPV is positive, its IRR exceeds the required rate of return, and payback period is less than seven years.

SP-2. a) Net present value and profitability index.

Model A	1	2	3	4	5
After-Tax cash in flows	4,960	4,960	4,960	4,960	4,960

$$\text{PVCI} = \$4,960 \times (\text{PVIFA}, 10\%, 5 \text{ years})$$
$$= \$4,960 \times 3.791$$
$$= \$18,803$$
$$- \text{Investment} = -17,000$$
$$= \text{NPV} = 1,803$$
$$\text{Profitability index} = \frac{\$18,803}{\$17,000} = 1.106$$

Model B	1	2	3	4	5
After-Tax cash in flows	$2,000	2,000	2,000	9,980	9,980
× PVIF (10%)	.909	.826	.751	.683	.621
= PV	$1,818	1,652	1,502	6,816	6,198

PVCI = $17,986
NPV = $17,986 − 16,000 = $1,986
Profitability Index = 1.124

From the standpoint of selecting between the two models, the above analysis indicates that Model B is preferable because of its higher NPV and PI.

b) Internal rate of return.

Model A
Find the PVIFA that will equate the annuity cash flows with the investment. The interest rate associated with this PVIFA, given $n = 5$, is the IRR.

$$(\text{PVIFA}, k\%, 5 \text{ years}) \times \$4,960 = 17,000$$
$$(\text{PVIFA}, k\%, 5 \text{ years}) \times \$4,960 = 3.43$$

From Table 4, $n = 5$, a PVIFA of 3.43 corresponds to an interest rate of 14 percent. Thus, the IRR for Model A is 14 percent.

Model B

Since B's cash flows are not an annuity, finding the IRR will involve trial and error. A good place to start would be just above 10 percent, since in part (a) a discount rate of 10 percent resulted in positive net present value. Thus, B's IRR must be greater than 10 percent.

Year	Cash flows	PVIF (13%)	P. V. (13%)	PVIF (14%)	P. V. (14%)
1	2,000	.885	1,770	.877	1,754
2	2,000	.783	1,566	.769	1,538
3	2,000	.693	1,386	.675	1,350
4	9,980	.613	6,118	.592	5,908
5	9,980	.543	5,419	.519	5,180
		Total present value	16,259		15,730
		− Investment	−16,000		−16,000
		= Net present value	259		−270

The IRR is between 13 percent and 14 percent because these two discount rates bracket a zero net present value. With interpolation, the IRR for B is approximately 13.49 percent. On the basis of the calculated IRR, Model A is preferable to Model B, since Model A has a higher IRR.

c) Payback period.

Model A:

$$\text{Payback period} = \frac{\text{Investment}}{\text{annual cash flow}} = \frac{17,000}{4,960}$$

$$= 3.43 \text{ years}$$

Model B

	Beginning investment	Remaining investment balance
	($16,000)	
−Cash flow year 1	2,000	14,000
−Cash flow year 2	2,000	12,000
−Cash flow year 3	2,000	10,000
−Cash flow year 4	9,980	20

Model B will require slightly more than four years to recover the original $16,000 investment. In year five, cash flow will total 9,980. If it is assumed that cash flows are recovered uniformly during the year, it will take almost no time to make up the remaining $20 in year five.

$$\% \text{ of year } 5 = \frac{\$20}{\$9,980} = .002 \text{ year}$$

Payback is thus 4.002 years.

	A	B
Net present value	$1,803	$1,986*
Profitability index	1.106	1.124*
Internal rate of return	14.00*	13.49%
Payback period (years)	3.43*	4.002

*Superior.

e) The difference in cash flow patterns is responsible for the conflicting rankings given by the NPV and IRR methods. Note also that the payback and NPV rankings are in conflict. Model A's Cash flows are steady throughout, while Model B's cash flows balloon at the end of the investment life. This is important because of the implicit reinvestment rate assumptions made in the NPV and IRR methods. Model A's IRR implies that the cash benefits can be reinvested at 14 percent. Model B's IRR implies that the cash benefits can be reinvested at 13.49 percent. The NPV method implies that the cash flow benefits from both models A and B will be reinvested at the cost of capital rate (10 percent in this problem). When rankings conflict, the NPV method is preferable.

At higher discount rates (i.e., cost of capital) the value of the postponed (though larger) cash flow decreases. As noted in the text, however, the net-present-value method is the correct way to select. Payback also "penalizes" investments where the cash flows (no matter how large) come too late in the investment's life, and this is evident from the shorter payback shown for Model A.

REFERENCES

Bacon, Peter W. "The Evaluation of Mutually Exclusive Investments," *Financial Management*, 6, Summer 1977, pp. 55-58.

Bierman, Harold, Jr., and Seymour Smidt. *The Capital Budgeting Decision*, 6th ed., New York, Macmillan, 1984.

Carter, E. Eugene. "Designing the Capital Budgeting Process," *TIMS Studies in the Management Sciences*, 5, 1977, pp. 25-42.

Gitman, Lawrence J., and John R. Forrester, Jr. "Forecasting and Evaluation Practices and Performance: A Survey of Capital Budgeting," *Financial Management*, 6, Fall 1977, pp. 66-71.

_____, and Vincent A. Mercurio. "Cost of Capital Techniques Used by Major U.S. Firms," *Financial Management*, 11, Winter 1982, pp. 21-29.

Kim, Suk H., and Edward J. Farragher. "Current Capital Budgeting Practices," *Management Accounting*, June 1981, pp. 26-30.

Schall, Lawrence D., Sundem, Gary L., and Geijsbeek, William R. "Survey and Analysis of Capital Budgeting Methods," *Journal of Finance*, 33, March 1978, pp. 281-292.

CASE EXERCISE

American Fabu-Plastics, Inc.

In early 1988, George Oscar, financial consultant, was reviewing the capital budgeting procedures of a client, American Fabu-Plastics. In interviews with the company's President, Ms. Margaret, he had determined that the company's capital budgeting procedures could be summarized in one requirement: no investment was acceptable if its payback was more than six years. Ms. Margaret had mentioned to Mr. Oscar that the company's reliance on the payback method was due to the chronic cash shortages the company had experienced. For this reason, she had asked him to review the company's payback period and to advise her if it should be shortened.

The only exceptions to the payback period requirement were investments classifiable as "defensive" or "strategic." Projects classified in this group were viewed as absolutely necessary to maintain current activities. Exhibit C-1 shows the 1988 capital budget prepared by the company's financial manager.

The capital proposals for 1988 totaled approximately $43 million, of which $9 million constituted defensive expenditures. (Exhibit C-2 contains an abbreviated description of cash flow information developed for all investment proposals.) However, since the total available budget was currently set at $33.8 million (equal to the sum of net income and depreciation), not all proposals could be adopted.

Mr. Oscar thought he could make some valuable recommendations, but he was not exactly sure of the best way to proceed.

Case Questions

1. Evaluate the arguments for and against the use of the payback method in capital budgeting decisions. If you were Mr. Oscar, what recommendation would you make to Ms. Margaret on this matter? How would you try to convert her to your point of view?

Proposed Capital Investments for 1988			
Proposal	Amount ($ millions)	Type	Payback
A	$ 5.0	Strategic	n.a.
B	4.0	Defensive	n.a.
C	7.8	New	4.6
D	11.0	New	5.3
E	15.0	New	6.1
	$42.8		

EXHIBIT C-1
American Fabu-Plastics, Inc.

	Project Cash Flow Estimates ($ millions)						
Project	Year 1	Year 2	Year 3	Year 4	Year 5	Year 6	Years 7-10
A	.25	.25	.25	.25	.25	.25	.25/yr.
B	.35	.35	.35	.35	.35	.35	.35/yr.
C	1.0	1.0	2.0	2.0	3.0	3.0	1.0/yr.
D	1.0	2.0	2.0	2.5	2.5	3.0	8.5/yr.
E	1.0	2.0	2.0	2.0	2.0	5.0	10.0/yr.

EXHIBIT C-2
American Fabu-Plastics,
Inc.

2. Assume that the company's cost of capital is 15 percent for each investment in the proposal. Which investments should be accepted and rejected on the basis of NPV? Payback? Strategic/Defensive? Compare the results. Which projects would you recommend be adopted?

3. Evaluate the arguments for and against the use of the defensive/strategic category of investments. Assume that the projected investment costs and cash inflows fully incorporate their values. What impact do you think they may have on the company's value and cash problems?

4. What do you think about the company's use of capital rationing? Is it acceptable given the chronic cash shortages cited by Ms. Margaret?

CHAPTER 15

ESTIMATING CASH FLOWS

erhaps the most difficult step in the analysis of capital investments is the estimation of cash flows. More specifically, it is necessary to determine the amount, timing, and degree of risk of an investment's cash inflows and outflows.

Objectives and Organization of this Chapter

The principal objective of this chapter is to show how to identify and measure investment cash flows. In the process, the importance of incremental cash flows and the influence of tax laws on cash flows will be demonstrated. A second objective of the chapter is to apply the cash flow concepts to important types of investments. The first section of the chapter describes the major types of investment cash flows. The second section examines the impact of accelerated depreciation methods on investment cash flows and value. The third section raises other cash flow considerations, such as sunk costs and opportunity costs, which may arise in capital budgeting proposals and which must be analyzed properly. The last section applies the cash flow ideas in this chapter to the evaluation of expansion and replacement investments.

INVESTMENT CASH FLOWS

In the last chapter, it was noted that every capital expenditure proposal should contain three elements: identification of all relevant costs, identification of the amounts and timing of benefits, and procedures for evaluating the benefits relative to the costs.

In reference to capital budgeting proposals, costs and benefits should be defined in terms of cash flows. In addition, since capital budgeting investments extend beyond one year, the costs and benefits should be defined in terms of the present values of cash flows. Finally, we are concerned only with an investment's incremental cash flows: the cash flows that will change as a direct result of the investment. The correct estimation of incremental cash flows is crucial to proper investment analysis, particularly when a company considers replacing one investment with another.

incremental cash flows

Incremental Cash Flows

Let us assume that the HFX Corporation is considering an investment in a machine that costs $10,000. The machine, if purchased, will replace an existing machine that can be sold for $4,000. Thus, the incremental cash outlay will be $6,000. Since the sale of the old machine is a direct consequence of the new machine investment, these cash flows (receipts) must be incorporated in the analysis.

In all cases, a cash flow is relevant if, and only if, it will change as a result of the investment considered. When in doubt as to whether a particular cash flow is relevant to the investment decision, determine what the cash flow will be if the investment is not made and what the cash flow will be if the investment is made. The difference represents the change in cash flow attributable to the investment.

Analytically, it is useful to classify an investment's incremental cash flows into three types: *investment outflows, operating inflows,* and *terminal inflows.*

Investment Outflows

investment outflows

Investment outflows are cash outlays needed to undertake the investment. Think of these as changes produced on the asset side of the balance sheet. For example, the purchase of a machine is an investment outlay and will be reflected by a simultaneous reduction in the cash account and an increase in the fixed assets account. Likewise, an investment in working capital, such as inventory, will be reflected in an increase in inventory and a decrease in cash on the balance sheet.[1]

Investment Outflows

The Xybl Company is considering the purchase of a $15,000 forklift. If it is purchased, the company's cash balance will be reduced by $15,000, and its fixed asset account will increase by $15,000. The company's investment cash outflow will be $15,000.

If the proposed investment will replace an existing investment, further adjustments to the cash outlay amount must be taken into account.

---

[1] If such investments take place over a period of years, the present values of such outflows should be calculated. This will be addressed later in this chapter.

For example, the analyst must include the cash proceeds from the sale of the assets to be replaced and any income tax consequences.

Exhibit 15-1 contains a checklist of the most common components of investment costs.

Note that in addition to the gross investment in plant and equipment, one also should consider the possible need for increases in working capital—cash, accounts receivable, and inventory. To some extent, increases in certain current liabilities such as accounts payable will offset working capital requirements. Thus, one must finance an amount equal to the increase in net working capital (increase in current assets less increase in current liabilities).

Operating Inflows

Operating inflows are the net cash flows after taxes produced by the use or operation of the investment. In this chapter, the terms *net operating cash flows* and *cash flows after tax* are used interchangeably. Think of these as income-statement types of cash inflows.

operating inflows

Example

Operating Inflows

Assume Division A is proposing the development of a new product line and has prepared a series of *pro forma* income statements. Also assume that all sales and expenses (except depreciation) are to be made on a cash basis. The *pro forma* income statement for the first year is shown in Table 15-1. Alongside the *pro forma* are indicated the cash flows anticipated from the investment.

EXHIBIT 15-1
Checklist of Net
Investment Outlays

Gross Investment
  Invoice cost of plant and equipment
  Freight-in
  Installation costs
Net working capital
Proceeds from sale of existing assets
Tax effect on sale of existing assets

TABLE 15-1   New Product Proposal: Division A

Pro-Forma Income Statement

	Accrual Basis	Cash Basis
Sales (S)	$18,000	$18,000
Cost of goods sold (CGS)	8,000	8,000
Gross profit	10,000	10,000
Operating expenses (OE)	800	800
Operating income (EBIDT)	9,200	
Depreciation (D)	4,750	–0–
Profit before taxes	4,450	
Taxes (34%)	1,513	1,513
Net income (NI)	2,937	
+ Depreciation	4,750	
Cash flow after taxes	$7,687	$7,687

Note that the operating cash flow after taxes differs from net income only by the amount of depreciation taken. Alternatively, the cash flow produced by the investment is equal to net income plus depreciation. Keep in mind that this is true only because it is assumed that all sales and expenses other than depreciation are made on a cash basis. For convenience, this assumption is commonly adopted in evaluating capital proposals.

$$\text{Estimated cash flow after taxes } (CFAT) = \text{Net income } (NI)$$
$$+ \text{ Depreciation } (D) \qquad (15\text{-}1)$$
$$= \$2{,}937 + \$4{,}750 = \$7{,}687$$

Depreciation is an accounting expense that does not affect cash. Thus it reduces profit before taxes but has no effect on the cash balance. Strictly speaking, depreciation is not a cash inflow — it is simply not a cash outflow.

With a little algebra, cash flows after taxes can also be estimated as operating profit after taxes plus the depreciation tax shield.

$$NI = (S - CGS - OE - D)(1 - t)$$

where S is sales; CGS is cost of goods sold; OE is operating expenses; D is depreciation; and t is the tax rate. Then, Equation 15-1 can be expressed as:

$$CFAT = (S - CGS - OE - D)(1 - t) + D$$

Factoring for D, we get,

$$CFAT = (S - CGS - OE)(1 - t) - D(1 - t) + D$$

Grouping the D terms we get

$$CFAT = (S - CGS - OE)(1 - t) + Dt \qquad (15\text{-}2)$$

And, incremental *CFAT*:

$$\Delta CFAT = (\Delta S - \Delta CGS - \Delta OE)(1 - t) + \Delta Dt \qquad (15\text{-}3)$$

Applying Equation 15-2 or 15-3 (both are the same in this case, since no pre-existing cash flows are affected, it is possible to determine net operating cash flow for the new product proposal to be:

$$\Delta CFAT = (18{,}000 - 8{,}000 - 800)(.66) + (4{,}750)(.34)$$

$$= \$6{,}072 + \$1{,}615 = \$7{,}687$$

Equation 15-3 is particularly useful when only a few of the income state-ment items (such as operating expenses or depreciation) will be affected by the investment. In such cases, developing an entire income statement in order to estimate incremental cash flows would be unnecessary.

Unlevered Cash Flows.   Note that the *pro forma* income statement does not indicate any interest expense. Interest expense is a cost of financing and, thus, part of the company's cost of capital. Interest and other financing costs are incorporated in the evaluation of the proposal through the *cost of capital*, which is used to discount cash flows. Thus, if interest expense is deducted from the cash flows and they are subsequently discounted at the cost of capital, the cost of debt financing would be double-counted. Since debt is a form of leverage, cash flows that do not reflect financing costs are said to be *unlevered cash flows*.

unlevered cash flows

Terminal Cash Flows

Terminal cash inflows are produced at the end of the investment's life.[2] Generally, terminal cash inflows will be of two types; salvage value, if any, of plant and equipment; and recovery of net working capital, including cash balances, inventory stocks, and accounts receivable.

terminal cash flows

Salvage value is the estimated selling price of the plant and equipment at the termination of the investment's economic life. If the assets are sold for more or less than their book values, taxes will have to be considered.[3] The estimate of salvage value must be made at the time the investment is proposed, even though it is clearly subject to uncertainty.

salvage value

DEPRECIATION AND CASH FLOWS

The calculation of depreciation for capital budgeting purposes is often a point of confusion for students. This is because most companies employ

---

[2]These cash flows may be positive or negative, but we assume that they are typically positive.
[3]Some examples will be presented later in this chapter. For more discussion of these tax effects, see Chapter 2.

two fundamentally different depreciation concepts. These can be distinguished as *financial accounting depreciation* and *tax reporting depreciation*.

Financial Accounting Depreciation

financial accounting depreciation

The principal objective of financial accounting depreciation is to allocate the cost of depreciable assets over their useful economic lives. For example, if a machine is expected to last 10 years, a company might decide, for financial accounting purposes, to depreciate one-tenth of the cost of the machine each year. In the event the machine will have salvage value (what it could be sold for at the end of its economic life), total depreciation on the machine would equal the cost of the machine minus salvage value. In practice, many variations for computing depreciation are used. However, since more than 90 percent of all companies use the straight-line method for financial accounting purposes, only this method will be considered here.

straight-line depreciation

Financial Accounting Depreciation: Straight-Line

$$(\text{Original cost} - \text{Salvage value})/\text{Economic life} \qquad (15\text{-}4)$$

Example

Financial Accounting Depreciation: Straight-Line

Assume that the MSA Company purchases a machine costing $1,000,000. The machine has an economic life of four years and an expected salvage value of $100,000. If the company uses straight-line depreciation for financial reporting, the annual depreciation shown on its income statement will be:

$$\text{Depreciation} = (\$1,000,000 - 100,000)/4$$

$$= \$225,000 \text{ per year}$$

At the end of its useful life in four years, total depreciation taken will be $900,000 (i.e., $225,000 per year times four years), and its net book value will be $100,000.

depreciable basis

Two things in particular should be noted. First, the anticipated salvage value of the machine affects the total depreciation to be taken (known as the *depreciable basis*) and, thus, the depreciation per year. Second, the economic life of the machine is an important determinant of the annual depreciation. These two items are ignored for tax purposes.

Tax Reporting Depreciation

tax reporting depreciation

When computing its tax liability, a company is permitted to deduct depreciation as an expense. According to the 1986 Tax Reform Act, a company has little choice in the method of depreciation selected. For most business equipment, for example, a company must use either the 200-percent declining balance (i.e., double-declining-balance) method or straight-line. In both cases, however, *salvage value and economic life are both ignored.* The depreciable basis is the total cost of the depreciable asset (not the cost less salvage value as with financial accounting). Thus, all of the original cost will be depreciated. In addition, total depreciation is taken over the asset's *class life* (and not the economic life). The asset class life is specified for various types of assets.

class life

A company can still use straight-line depreciation for tax purposes. But, as noted above, salvage value is ignored and the depreciation is equal to the original cost divided by the asset's class life.

Exhibit 15-2 contains a listing of various depreciation classes and the types of property included. For example, "five-year property" pertains to autos, trucks, and computers.

Half-Year Convention.   Both the 200-percent declining balance and the straight-line depreciation methods must incorporate the *half-year convention,* meaning that, regardless of when equipment is actually acquired, it is assumed to be acquired on July 1 of that year. Thus only one-half of the first year's depreciation is permitted.

half-year convention

To facilitate calculation of depreciation charges each year, the 200-percent declining balance ACRS depreciation provisions can be converted to percentages, as shown in Table 15-2.[4] Note that depreciation percentages are smaller in the first year than in the second. This is due to the half-year convention making depreciation in the first year only half of the full-year amount. Also note that depreciation on three-year property is spread over four years, five-year property over 6 years, and seven-year property over eight years. This, too, is due to the half-year convention, since the half year omitted in the first year is made up in the extra year.

ACRS depreciation

Three-Year Property	Certain small tools, specialized manufacturing devices, tractors (over-the-road), certain horses
Five-Year Property	Autos and light trucks, research and experimentation equipment, computers, aircraft (except commercial carriers), buses, heavy trucks, construction assets, certain manufacturing assets
Seven-Year Property	Most manufacturing assets, office furniture, fixtures and equipment, certain aircraft (commercial carriers)

EXHIBIT 15-2
Examples of
Depreciation Classes

[4]The new ACRS provisions do not stipulate percentages. Table 15-2 has been constructed on the assumptions of double-declining-balance depreciation and the half-year convention.

TABLE 15-2 ACRS Percentages Based on 200-Percent Declining Balance and Half-Year Convention

Year	Three-Year Property	Five-Year Property	Seven-Year Property
1	.333	.200	.143
2	.444	.320	.245
3	.148	.192	.175
4	.075	.115	.125
5		.115	.089
6		.058	.089
7			.089
8			.045

Example

Using ACRS Percentages

Assume that the machine MSA is considering qualifies as three-year property. According to Table 15-2, the 200-percent declining balance depreciation each year would be as shown below.

Year	ACRS Percentage	ACRS Depreciation
1	.333	$ 333,000
2	.444	$ 444,000
3	.148	$ 148,000
4	.075	$ 75,000
	1.000	$1,000,000

Alternatively, if MSA chooses to depreciate on a straight-line basis for tax purposes, depreciation would be calculated as shown below.

Example

Straight-Line Tax Depreciation

The annual depreciation would be $1,000,000 divided by the class life of three years, or $333,333 per year. However, due to the half-year convention, the first year's depreciation would only be approximately $166,667 (i.e., $333,333/2). Depreciation in years two and three would be $333,333 per year, and the remaining $166,667 would be recovered in year four.

Comparison of Depreciation Methods

The financial and tax depreciation methods are compared below.

	Financial Accounting	Tax Reporting	
Year	Straight-Line	200-Percent Declining Balance	Straight-Line
1	$225,000	$ 333,000	$ 166,667
2	$225,000	$ 444,000	$ 333,333
3	$225,000	$ 148,000	$ 333,333
4	$225,000	$ 75,000	$ 166,667
Total	$900,000	$1,000,000	$1,000,000

Note that the 200-percent declining balance method tilts depreciation toward the early years relative to the straight-line method. Given the time value of money, this depreciation method will normally provide higher present values of cash flows than the straight-line method. Since most business equipment will use the 200-percent declining balance method, we will mean this method when we refer to "ACRS" depreciation.

OTHER CASH FLOW CONSIDERATIONS

At times other cash flow considerations will arise in capital budgeting proposals. Some of these should be incorporated in the analysis, while others should not.

Capital Expenditures in Later Years

In addition to initial investment requirements, occasionally other expenditures may be required in future time periods. For example, a machine may have to be overhauled or repaired some time in the future. One way of handling such expenditures, or cash outflows, would be to net them against cash inflows expected during the corresponding future time periods. Otherwise they should be discounted and added to the investment cost.

Sunk Costs

Investment proposals often involve costs that have been incurred in the past, so-called sunk costs. For example, before considering a particular investment, a company might have conducted extensive market surveys and engineering studies. These expenditures are sunk costs and should not be charged against, or as part of, the initial investment required. To see this

sunk costs

point more clearly, recall the importance of incremental cash flows. The cash flows associated with sunk costs will not be affected by the decision on the investment. For example, if the investment is accepted, cash flows will not increase from the sunk costs. If the investment is rejected, cash flows will not decrease from the sunk costs.

Opportunity Costs

opportunity costs

An investment proposal may also include opportunity costs. For example, a new machine might take up building space that could be used for other purposes, such as another type of machine or for storing inventory or equipment. These alternative uses may represent opportunity costs of using the space for the new machine, and therefore such costs should be added to the machine's initial investment.

APPLICATION OF CASH FLOW ESTIMATION

expansion investments

In the following pages, the methods of cash flow estimation are applied to two common types of capital budgeting proposals: expansion investments and replacement investments. Expansion investments are relatively less complicated in their cash flow impacts, as they usually have limited, if any, effects on existing cash flows. For example, expansion investments involve such things as increasing production capacity to capture increased sales in existing product lines. Almost all of the cash flows related to expansion investments are incremental. On the other hand, replacement investments involve changing the existing asset base and can result in complex cash flow effects.

replacement investments

EXPANSION PROPOSAL

The H. S. Company is considering an investment in a specialty fabricator to meet anticipated demand for a new product. The machine will cost $100,000 installed with a four-year useful life and zero salvage value. Investment in net working capital will total $20,000. Sales for the new product are expected to be constant at $200,000 per year over the four years and zero thereafter, as the product will be discontinued. Cost of goods sold will be $100,000 per year, and operating expenses will be $40,000 per year. Assume that the machine will qualify as three-year property for ACRS purposes. The company's tax rate is 34 percent; its required rate of return on the investment is 15 percent, and its required payback period is three years. The company's capital budgeting procedures require calculation of net present value, internal rate of return, and payback period.

Incremental Investment Outflows

Investment outflows are the cost of the machine and the increased net working capital required. Since no existing investments are affected by the proposal, these are the incremental investment outflows.

Cost of fabricating machine	$100,000
Investment in net working capital	$ 20,000
Incremental investment outflows	$120,000

Incremental Operating Inflows

Assuming that sales and expenses (except depreciation) are on a cash basis, the incremental operating inflows can be estimated by adding net income to depreciation. According to the ACRS percentages in Table 15-2, depreciation will vary from year to year. Thus, cash flows will not be constant over the four years. The projected net operating cash flows are shown in Table 15-3.

The depreciation figures are determined by multiplying the investment of $100,000 (remember that net working capital does not depreciate) times the appropriate ACRS percentage for each year. Since the new investment will have no effect on any existing sales or expenses, all of the operating cash inflows are incremental.

TABLE 15-3 Fabricating Machine Proposal: Operating Cash Inflows

	1	2	3	4
Sales	$200,000	$200,000	$200,000	$200,000
Cost of goods sold	100,000	100,000	100,000	100,000
Gross profit	100,000	100,000	100,000	100,000
Operating expenses	40,000	40,000	40,000	40,000
Depreciation	33,300	44,400	14,800	7,500
Profit before taxes	26,700	15,600	45,200	52,500
Taxes (34%)	9,078	5,304	15,360	17,850
Net income	17,622	10,296	29,832	34,650
+ Depreciation	33,300	44,400	14,800	7,500
= Operating cash inflows	$ 50,922	$ 54,696	$ 44,632	$ 42,150

Incremental Terminal Cash Inflows

There is no salvage value expected for the fabricating machine. Thus, the only terminal cash inflows will be the recovery of net working capital investment of $20,000.

Net Present Value

In order to undertake a net-present-value analysis, one can set up a table summarizing all the cash flows identified for the investment, as shown in Table 15-4.

The large, positive NPV of $30,570 indicates that the investment will be acceptable.

Internal Rate of Return

Since the NPV is positive at a 15-percent rate, the IRR must be greater than 15 percent. To estimate the IRR on a trial-and-error basis, one should set up a cash flows summary as shown in Table 15-5, which allows rapid calculation of NPVs using alternative discount rates.

TABLE 15-4   Fabricating Machine Proposal: Cash Flow Summary

	0	1	2	3	4
Cash Flow					
Investment outflow	($120,000)				
Operating inflows		$50,922	$54,696	$44,632	$42,150
Terminal inflows					20,000
Totals	($120,000)	$50,922	$54,696	$44,632	$62,150
PVIF at 15%	1.000	.870	.756	.658	.572
PV at 15%	($120,000)	$44,302	$41,350	$29,368	$24,110
NPV at 15% = $30,570					

TABLE 15-5   Fabricating Machine Proposal: Internal Rate of Return Calculation

Cash Flow	PVIF (24%)	PV @ 24%	PVIF (26%)	PV @ 26%
($120,000)	1.000	($120,000)	1.000	($120,000)
50,922	.806	41,043	.794	40,432
54,696	.650	35,552	.630	34,458
44,632	.524	23,387	.500	22,316
62,150	.423	26,289	.397	16,734
NPV		$ 6,271		($ 6,060)

At a discount rate of 24 percent the NPV is a positive $6,271; while at a 26-percent discount rate the NPV is negative $6,060, suggesting that the true IRR is somewhere midpoint, around 25 percent. With a financial calculator or computerized financial spreadsheet program, the IRR would be found to be about 24.57 percent. Since this is well above the company's required rate of return, the investment is acceptable.

Payback Period

To compute the payback period, one can set up a cash flow summary such as that shown in Table 15-6. This format treats the investment outlay as a type of loan that is to be repaid from the investment's cash inflows. As indicated in Table 15-6, the payback period is approximately 2.3 years. Since this is less than the three-year maximum payback period, the investment is acceptable according to the payback analysis.

REPLACEMENT INVESTMENTS

Replacement investments are usually more complex to evaluate than expansions, since many different cash flow consequences may result. As before, we are concerned with the incremental cash flows to be produced by the investment.

The Fabu-Plastics Corporation is considering an investment in a specialty plastics extruder ("Speedy") to save costs on the production of compact disc holders. If purchased, the new machine will replace a dilapidated hand-cranked extruder ("Cranky"), which, although still usable for five more years, is quite inefficient. Speedy will cost $160,000. Freight and installation costs for the new machine will be an additional $10,000 and $5,000 respectively. Cranky has a net book value of $50,000 but can only be sold for $40,000 due to the greater demand for the more efficient new model.

Speedy qualifies as seven-year property and will be depreciated on that basis with the ACRS method. Assume that Cranky was purchased prior to ACRS and is being depreciated over its five years of life remaining on a

TABLE 15-6 Fabricating Machine Proposal: Payback Period		
	Initial Investment	Remaining Investment Balance
Investment outflow	($120,000)	($120,000)
Cash inflow year 1	$ 50,922	($ 69,078)
Cash inflow year 2	$ 54,696	($ 14,382)
Cash inflow year 3	$ 44,632	
Payback period = 2 + 14,382/44,632 years		
= 2.32 years		

straight-line basis to a zero salvage value. For purposes of this analysis, assume that Speedy will be sold at the end of five years for an amount equal to its book value at that time. In addition, net working capital requirements will increase by $25,000 if Speedy is purchased, due to the change in raw materials stocked for the machine.

Sales are projected to be constant at $600,000 per year for the next five years. Cost of goods sold, however, will decrease from $460,000 per year to only $415,000 per year if Speedy is purchased. Fabu-Plastics' income tax rate is 34 percent. The company has assigned a 15-percent cost of capital to the investment proposal and a maximum payback period of four years.

Incremental Investment Outflows

The incremental investment outflows for Speedy are shown in Table 15-7. Note that the sale of Cranky reduces the net investment cash outflows and that there is a tax benefit received due to the sale of the old machine at a loss. If an asset is sold for less than its book value, the difference is a book loss, and a tax reduction is available equal to the book loss times the corporation's ordinary income tax rate. This is the situation that applies to Cranky. The old extruder has a book value of $50,000 but can only be sold for $40,000, producing a book loss of $10,000. This loss can be deducted from the corporation's taxable income and thus produce a tax savings of $3,400 (i.e., $10,000 × .34). Thus, the net incremental investment outflows for Speedy would be $156,600.

Incremental Operating Inflows

Now that the incremental expenditures associated with a capital budgeting proposal have been considered, attention can be turned to the estimation of incremental cash inflows to be produced by the investment. The ability to estimate such inflows accurately is critical to the success of any capital budgeting decision. The calculations are shown in Table 15-8. Part (a) of the Table shows the projected net operating cash flows assuming Cranky is kept. Part (b) shows what the cash flows would be if Speedy were purchased. Part (c) shows the incremental operating inflows if Speedy is purchased.

TABLE 15-7 Incremental Investment Outflows For Speedy	
Invoice cost of Speedy	($150,000)
Freight and installation	(25,000)
Increase in net working capital	(25,000)
Proceeds from sale of Cranky	40,000
Tax credit on sale of Cranky	3,400
Incremental investment outflows	$156,600

TABLE 15-8 Incremental Operating Inflows

(a) Operating Cash Inflows With Cranky

	Year 1	Year 2	Year 3	Year 4	Year 5
Sales	$600,000	$600,000	$600,000	$600,000	$600,000
Cost of goods sold	460,000	460,000	460,000	460,000	460,000
Gross profit	140,000	140,000	140,000	140,000	140,000
Operating expenses	40,000	40,000	40,000	40,000	40,000
EBDT	100,000	100,000	100,000	100,000	100,000
Depreciation	10,000	10,000	10,000	10,000	10,000
Profit before taxes	90,000	90,000	90,000	90,000	90,000
Taxes (34%)	30,600	30,600	30,600	30,600	30,600
Net income	$ 59,400	$ 59,400	$ 59,400	$ 59,400	$ 59,400
+ Depreciation	10,000	10,000	10,000	10,000	10,000
= Operating cash inflows	$ 69,400	$ 69,400	$ 69,400	$ 69,400	$ 69,400

(b) Operating Cash Inflows With Speedy

	Year 1	Year 2	Year 3	Year 4	Year 5
Sales	$600,000	$600,000	$600,000	$600,000	$600,000
Cost of goods sold	415,000	415,000	415,000	415,000	415,000
Gross profit	185,000	185,000	185,000	185,000	185,000
Operating expenses	40,000	40,000	40,000	40,000	40,000
EBDT	145,000	145,000	145,000	145,000	145,000
Depreciation	25,025	42,875	30,625	21,875	15,575
Profit before taxes	119,975	102,125	114,375	123,125	129,425
Taxes (34%)	40,792	34,723	38,888	41,863	44,005
Net income	$ 79,183	$ 67,402	$ 75,487	$ 81,262	$ 85,420
+ Depreciation	25,025	42,875	30,625	21,875	15,575
= Operating cash inflows	$104,208	$110,277	$106,112	$103,137	$100,995

(c) Incremental Operating Cash Inflows With Speedy

	Year 1	Year 2	Year 3	Year 4	Year 5
Δ Sales	$ -0-	$ -0-	$ -0-	$ -0-	$ -0-
Δ Cost of goods sold	− 45,000	− 45,000	− 45,000	− 45,000	− 45,000
Δ Gross profit	+ 45,000	+ 45,000	+ 45,000	+ 45,000	+ 45,000
Δ Operating expenses	-0-	-0-	-0-	-0-	-0-
Δ EBDT	45,000	45,000	45,000	45,000	45,000
Δ Depreciation	15,025	32,875	20,625	11,875	5,575
Δ Profit before taxes	29,975	12,125	24,375	33,125	39,425
Δ Taxes (34%)	10,192	4,123	8,288	11,263	13,404
Δ Net income	$ 19,783	$ 8,002	$ 16,087	$ 21,862	$ 26,020
+ Δ Depreciation	15,025	32,875	20,625	11,875	5,575
= Δ Operating cash inflows	$ 34,808	$ 40,877	$ 36,712	$ 33,737	$ 31,595

Note that there is no change in expected sales. The only changes indicated are in the cost of goods sold and depreciation expense. These result in changes in taxes and net cash flows. Depreciation for Cranky has been calculated on a straight-line basis ($50,000/five years) over a five-year life, producing depreciation expense of $10,000 per year. Speedy's depreciation has been calculated using the ACRS percentages in Table 15-2 for seven-year property. At the end of five years, a total of $135,975 will have been depreciated from Speedy, leaving a net book value of $39,025.

Terminal Inflows

At the end of five years, Speedy will be sold for book value, producing a cash inflow of $39,025. Since neither a gain nor loss will result from the sale, there will be no tax consequences. In addition, the increased investment in net working capital of $25,000 will be recovered. These terminal cash inflows are summarized in Table 15-9.

Net Present Value

In order to carry out net present value calculations, it is convenient to set up a cash flow summary like that shown in Table 15-10.

TABLE 15-9 Speedy Investment Proposal: Terminal Cash Inflows, Year Five

Salvage value = book value at end of year 5		$39,205
Original cost	$175,000	
− Accumulated depreciation	135,975	
Recovery of net working capital		25,000
Terminal cash inflows		$64,025

TABLE 15-10 Speedy Proposal; Cash Flow Summary and NPV Calculation

	Year					
	0	1	2	3	4	5
Cash Flow						
Investment outflow	($156,600)					
Operating inflows		$34,808	$40,877	$36,712	$33,737	$31,595
Terminal inflows						64,025
Totals	($156,600)	$34,808	$40,877	$36,712	$33,737	$95,620
PVIF at 15%	1.000	.870	.756	.658	.572	.497
PV at 15%	($156,600)	$30,283	$30,903	$24,157	$19,298	$35,098
NPV at 15% ($4,436)						

Since Speedy's projected NPV at a 15-percent cost of capital is negative, the investment is not acceptable.

Internal Rate of Return

The negative NPV at a 15-percent discount rate indicates that Speedy's IRR is less than 15 percent. By trial and error, the IRR is shown to be very close to 14 percent. The calculations are shown in Table 15-11. More precise methods reveal the IRR to be approximately 13.95 percent.

Payback Period

The calculation of Speedy's payback period is shown in Table 15-12. The payback is in excess of the four-year maximum for this investment and thus would be unacceptable.

TABLE 15-11 Speedy Proposal: Internal Rate of Return Calculation

Cash Flow	PVIF (14%)	PV @ 14%
($156,600)	1.000	($156,600)
34,808	.877	30,527
40,877	.769	31,434
36,712	.675	24,781
33,737	.592	19,972
95,620	.519	49,627
NPV		($ 259)

TABLE 15-12 Speedy Proposal: Payback Period

	Initial Investment	Remaining Investment Balance
	($156,600)	
Cash inflow year 1	$ 34,808	($121,792)
Cash inflow year 2	$ 40,877	($ 80,915)
Cash inflow year 3	$ 36,712	($ 44,203)
Cash inflow year 4	$ 33,737	($ 10,466)
Cash inflow year 5	$ 95,620	
Payback period = 4 + 10,466/95,620 years		
= 4.11 years		

SUMMARY

The proper estimation of cash flows is probably the most difficult and yet crucial aspect of capital investment decisions. More specifically, the amounts, timing, and certainty of an investment's cash flows can each critically affect the ultimate success or failure of investment analysis. Moreover, when considering these investment attributes, one is primarily concerned with incremental cash flows. By this is meant the changes in expected cash flows that will result as a direct consequence of the decision to accept or reject the investment proposal. For analytical purposes, it is helpful to distinguish three major types of investment cash flows. These are the investment outflows required to undertake the investment; net operating cash flows, which will result from the use of the investment; and terminal cash flows, which may be realized at the end of the investment's life.

MULTIPLE CHOICE QUESTIONS

1. First-year depreciation for a $100,000 five-year investment with $10,000 salvage value, using the straight-line financial accounting method would be:

   a) $18,000
   b) $36,000
   c) $33,000
   d) $16,500

2. First year depreciation for a $100,000 investment qualifying as five-year property under ACRS would be approximately:

   a) $33,300
   b) $20,000
   c) $16,667
   d) $40,000

3. If an investment requires an increase in net working capital, the working capital should be included in:

a) Operating inflows and investment outlays
b) Terminal inflows and investment outflows
c) Only investment outlays
d) Estimated depreciation

4. An asset with a net book value of $50,000 is sold for $100,000. If the company's tax rate is 34 percent:

a) Tax on the sale is $17,000
b) No tax liability is generated
c) Tax on the sale is $34,000
d) Tax on the sale is $33,000

DISCUSSION QUESTIONS

1. Most capital budgeting projects require estimation of initial investment outlays. Explain how increases in required net working capital might affect investment outlays.

2. What are (a) sunk costs and (b) opportunity costs when viewed in a capital budgeting context? Give an example of each. Should either type of cost be included in the capital budgeting evaluation?

3. Annual cash inflows associated with a capital investment are often estimated by adding net income plus depreciation. What assumptions are being made about sales and expenses? What advantages and drawbacks do you see in using this type of estimate?

4. Compare the 200-percent declining balance ACRS method of depreciation with the straight-line method. What effect, if any, would you expect ACRS to have on an investment's value?

5. Capital budgeting cash flows should be *unlevered*. What does this mean? Explain the rationale.

6. What is meant by the half-year convention?

7. According to the chapter, the increase in net working capital should be included in the investment outflow estimate. Why are we only concerned with the increase in *net* working capital rather than the increase in total working capital?

8. What is the difference between *operating* and *terminal* cash flows?

SOLVED PROBLEMS

SP-1. Every year the Merkle Corporation empties 10,000,000 gallons of sulfurous waste chemicals into the Ohio River. These chemicals are a by-product in the manufacture of proprietary chemicals used for purifying city water supplies. A new device has been invented that

incremental cash flows; ACRS depreciation; techniques

recovers sulfur from the waste chemicals. Though of low grade, the recovered sulfur can be sold "as is" for 10 cents per gallon (net of all costs except depreciation on the recovery device and taxes). The new device costs $2,100,000 and has an economic life of four years with no salvage value. Assume that Merkle's tax rate is 34 percent and that its required rate of return (cost of capital) on such investments is 18 percent. The maximum payback period for such investments is three years. The device will qualify as three-year property under ACRS regulations.

a) Assume that Merkle elects to depreciate the device on the straight-line method provided by tax laws. Calculate the following:

1. Incremental investment outflows
2. Incremental net operating inflows
3. Incremental terminal inflows
4. Net present value
5. Profitability index
6. Internal rate of return
7. Payback period
8. Would you recommend that Merkle purchase the device?

b) Assume that Merkle depreciates the device with the 200-percent declining balance method, using the percentages in Table 15-2. Calculate the following:

1. Incremental investment outflows
2. Incremental net operating inflows
3. Incremental terminal inflows
4. Net present value
5. Profitability index
6. Internal rate of return
7. Payback period

c) Compare the straight-line and ACRS depreciation methods in relation to NPV, PI, and IRR, and payback period. How would you explain the results?

incremental cash flows;
ACRS depreciation;
techniques

SP-2. Karen's Kountry Kandy Kompany, Inc. is considering an investment in a new chocolatizer to produce a new line of candy. The chocolatizer will cost $900,000 plus an additional $100,000 for freight and installation. The company has already spent $200,000 in market research for the new product line. According to the research, sales could total $1 million per year in each of the next 10 years. Expenses (except depreciation, interest, and taxes) will be $750,000 per year. Half of the cost of the machine will be borrowed at an interest rate of 10 percent.

The chocolatizer will be depreciated over its 10-year life to a salvage value of $100,000. Increased net working capital requirements will total $150,000 and will be provided for at the time the investment is made. The company's required rate of return on the investment is 13 percent and its tax rate is 34 percent. The maximum payback period allowed for such investments is six years.

a) Assume that Karen's depreciates the chocolatizer on a straight-line basis as seven-year property for tax purposes. Calculate the following:

    1. Incremental investment outlays

    2. Incremental net operating inflows

    3. Incremental terminal cash flows

    4. NPV of the investment

    5. PI of the investment

    6. IRR of the investment

    7. Payback period

b) Assume that Karen's depreciates the chocolatizer using ACRS percentages for seven-year property (see Table 15-2 in the chapter). Calculate the following:

    1. Incremental investment outlays

    2. Incremental operating inflows

    3. Incremental terminal cash flows

    4. NPV of the investment

    5. PI of the investment

    6. IRR of the investment

    7. Payback period

c) Compare the results you got for Parts (a) and (b) with respect to NPV, PI, IRR, and payback period. How do you explain the differences?

SP-3. The Universal Food Corporation is considering the addition of a new feature to its corn flake cereal. With a unique thermal imprinting process, each corn flake will carry a special message from outer space. The thermal process will replace equipment currently used to produce corn flakes.

incremental cash flows; ACRS depreciation; techniques

The new machine will cost $120,000 and require an additional investment of $5,000 in net working capital. Assume that the new machine will qualify as three-year property and will be depreciated according to ACRS (200-percent declining balance). At the end of four years, the machine will have a salvage value of $10,000.

The old machine has a book value of $30,000 and has four years of use remaining. Assume that the old machine was purchased before the enactment of ACRS regulations and is being depreciated on a straight-line basis of $7,500 per year to a zero salvage value. The old machine could be sold now for $35,000.

The new machine will increase earnings before depreciation and taxes (EBDT) by $35,000 in the first year, $50,000 in the second year, $40,000 in the third year, and $20,000 in the fourth year. The company's tax rate is 34 percent; its required rate of return on the investment is 20 percent; and the maximum payback allowed is two years. Calculate the following:

a) Incremental investment outflows
b) Incremental depreciation
c) Incremental net operating inflows
d) Incremental terminal inflows
e) Net present value
f) Profitability index
g) Internal rate of return
h) Payback period

replacement investment

SP-4. The Tack Corporation is considering the replacement of an existing stamper with a higher-capacity, more efficient machine. The existing stamper has a book value of $3,000 and a market value of $2,000 if sold now. The existing stamper has four years of useful life remaining and is being depreciated under pre-ACRS straight-line at $750 per year to a zero salvage value. (Note: assume it was purchased prior to ACRS.)

The new stamper will cost $90,000 installed and will have a four-year life with zero salvage value. Assume that the new stamper will be depreciated according to ACRS as three-year property using the 200-percent declining balance method.

The greater capacity of the new stamper will permit an increase in sales of $25,000 per year over existing sales during the four years. Due to the greater efficiency of the new stamper, operating expenses (other than depreciation) will *decrease* by $17,000 per year over their existing levels during the four years. Additional net working capital of $4,000 will be needed to support the larger production. The company's tax rate is 34 percent; its required rate of return on the investment is 15 percent, and its maximum payback period for the investment is 3.5 years. Calculate the following:

a) Incremental investment outflows
b) Incremental depreciation
c) Incremental net operating inflows
d) Incremental terminal inflows
e) Net present value
f) Profitability index
g) Internal rate of return
h) Payback period

PROBLEMS

1. The Pur-Air Corporation is considering an investment in a recovery boiler. The proposed boiler will distill certain chemical exhausts and allow them to be recycled. The recovery boiler will save the company $100,000 per year in raw feed stock costs. The cost of the new boiler will be $700,000. The new boiler will have an economic life of 10 years with no salvage value. Assume that Pur-Air's tax rate is 34 percent, and that the required rate of return (cost of capital) on such investments is 14 percent.

incremental cash flows; ACRS depreciation; techniques

   a) Assume that Pur-Air elects to depreciate the device as seven-year property on the straight-line method provided by tax laws. Calculate the following:

   1. Incremental investment outflows
   2. Incremental net operating inflows
   3. Incremental terminal inflows
   4. Net present value
   5. Profitability index
   6. Internal rate of return
   7. Payback period
   8. Would you recommend that Pur-Air purchase the device?

   b) Assume that Pur-Air depreciates the device with the 200-percent declining balance method, using the percentages in Table 15-2. Calculate the following:

   1. Incremental investment outflows
   2. Incremental net operating inflows
   3. Incremental terminal inflows
   4. Net present value
   5. Profitability index
   6. Internal rate of return
   7. Payback period

   c) Compare the straight-line and ACRS depreciation methods in relation to NPV, PI, IRR, and payback period. How would you explain the results?

2. Michelle, Inc., is considering an investment in a molding machine to produce a new line of vinyl furniture. The molder will cost $420,000 plus an additional $50,000 for freight and installation. The company has already spent $100,000 in market research for the new product line. According to the research, sales could total $800,000 per year in each of the next 10 years. Expenses (except depreciation, interest, and taxes) will be $600,000 per year. Half of the cost of the machine will be bor-

incremental cash flows; ACRS depreciation; techniques

rowed at an interest rate of 12 percent. Increased net working capital requirements will total $100,000 and will be provided for at the time the investment is made. The company's required rate of return on the investment is 30 percent and its tax rate is 34 percent.

a) Assume that Michelle depreciates the machine on an ACRS straight-line basis as seven-year property. Calculate the following:

1. Incremental investment outlays

2. Incremental net operating inflows

3. Incremental terminal cash flows

4. NPV of the investment

5. PI of the investment

6. IRR of the investment

7. Payback period

b) Assume that Michelle's depreciates the machine using ACRS percentages for seven-year property (see Table 15-2 in the chapter). Calculate the following:

1. Incremental investment outlays

2. Incremental operating inflows

3. Incremental terminal cash flows

4. NPV of the investment

5. PI of the investment

6. IRR of the investment

7. Payback period

c) Compare the results you got for Parts (a) and (b) with respect to NPV, PI, IRR, and payback period. How do you explain the differences?

replacement incremental cash flows; ACRS depreciation; techniques

3. The United Chemical Company is considering an investment in a new mixer. The new machine will cost $100,000 and require an additional investment of $15,000 in net working capital. Assume that the new machine will qualify as three-year property and will be depreciated according to ACRS (200-percent declining balance). At the end of four years the machine will have a salvage value of $4,000.

The old mixer has a book value of $40,000 and has four years of use remaining. Assume that the old machine was purchased prior to the enactment of ACRS regulations and is being depreciated on a straight-line basis of $10,000 per year to a zero salvage value. The old machine could be sold now for $40,000.

The new machine will increase earnings before depreciation and taxes (EBDT) by $40,000 in the first year, $60,000 in the second year, $50,000 in the third year, and $40,000 in the fourth year. The company's tax rate is 34 percent; its required rate of return on the investment is

24 percent, and the maximum payback allowed is three years. Calculate and evaluate the following:

a) Incremental investment outflows
b) Incremental depreciation
c) Incremental net operating inflows
d) Incremental terminal inflows
e) Net present value
f) Profitability index
g) Internal rate of return
h) Payback period

4. The Jones Corporation is considering the replacement of an existing *replacement*
steam press with a higher-capacity, more efficient machine. The existing press has a book value of $20,000 and a market value of $25,000 if sold now. The existing press has four years of useful life remaining and is being depreciated under pre-ACRS straight-line at $5,000 per year to a zero salvage value.

The new press will cost $150,000 installed and will have a four-year life with zero salvage value. Assume that the new press will be depreciated according to ACRS as three-year property using the 200-percent declining balance method.

The greater capacity of the new press will permit an increase in sales of $50,000 per year over existing sales during the four years. Due to the greater efficiency of the new stamper, operating expenses (other than depreciation) will *decrease* by $20,000 per year over their existing levels during the four years. Additional net working capital of $10,000 will be needed to support the larger production. The company's tax rate is 34 percent; its required rate of return on the investment is 20 percent, and its maximum payback period for the investment is 3.5 years. Calculate the following:

a) Incremental investment outflows
b) Incremental depreciation
c) Incremental net operating inflows
d) Incremental terminal inflows
e) Net present value
f) Profitability index
g) Internal rate of return
h) Payback period

5. You have been asked to evaluate a new machine being considered by the A & M Corporation. The machine will require an investment of *cash flow estimation;* $15,000. Book value will be zero at the end of five years, but the in- *techniques* vestment will have an expected salvage value of $2,000. The after-tax operating inflows are estimated to be $4,000 per year for five years.

a) Calculate the net present value for the machine assuming a 16-percent cost of capital for the firm.

b) Estimate the internal rate of return for the machine.

c) Calculate the payback period.

d) Based on your net-present-value calculation in Part (a), would you recommend that the A & M Corporation purchase the machine?

cash flow estimation; techniques

6. The Bark Corporation is evaluating a new piece of equipment. The equipment will require a $20,000 initial investment with no expected salvage value at the end of its five-year life. ACRS (200-percent declining balance) will be used, and the firm's tax rate is 34 percent. Earnings before depreciation and taxes are expected to be $5,000 per year.

a) Calculate the net present value for the equipment, assuming a 14-percent cost of capital for the firm.

b) Estimate the internal rate of return for the equipment.

c) Calculate the payback period.

d) Based on your results in Part (a), would you recommend that the Bark Corporation purchase the equipment?

NPV Vs. IRR straight-line depreciation

7. Two conflicting proposals of equal risk have been made for the purchase of new equipment. The data on each are given below:

	A	B
Net cash outlay	$8,500	$6,000
Salvage value	0	0
Estimated life	5 yrs	5 yrs
Earnings before depreciation and taxes:		
1-3 yrs.	2,500	1,500
4-5 yrs.	2,000	1,500

For simplicity, assume straight-line depreciation as computed according to *financial accounting methods* (see text Equation 5-4) and a corporate tax rate of 34 percent. Cost of capital is assumed to be 10 percent. Provide the necessary computations to rank each project in terms of:

a) Internal rate of return

b) Net present value and profitability index

c) Payback period

How do you explain any differences in ranking?

replacement

8. A machine now in use by the Rumble Company has a book value of $1,800. It can be sold for $2,500, but could be used for four more years, at the end of which time it would have no salvage value. A new machine can be purchased at an invoice price of $14,000 to replace the present equipment. Frieght-in will amount to $800, and installation cost $200. Because of the nature of the product manufactured, the proposed machine also has an expected life of four years and will have no salvage value at the end of that time. With the new machine, expected direct

cash savings amount to $8,000 the first year and $7,000 in each of the next two years.

Corporate income taxes are at an annual rate of 34 percent. Assume that the old machine was acquired prior to the ACRS regulations and is being depreciated on a straight-line basis at $450 per year. The new machine will be depreciated using ACRS 200-percent declining balance and qualifies as three-year property. Cost of capital is assumed to be 10 percent. Each question below should be considered independently.

a) On the basis of the above assumptions, compute the internal rate of return after taxes on the investment and the net present value.
b) Assume now that the prospective salvage value of the new machine at the end of the third year is estimated to be $1,800 and that straight-line depreciation is calculated on this basis. If all other assumptions remain as in (a), what would be the internal rate of return and the net present value?
c) Assume that an additional $2,000 must be invested in net working capital immediately if the new machine is used, but that this will be freed at the end of the third year. If all other assumptions remain as in (a), what would be the internal rate of return and the net present value?

9. State Utilities is presently considering a capital project with an invoice price of $40,000. Transportation charges will be $1,000, and there will be an additional $1,000 in installation costs. Net working capital is expected to increase by $2,000. The firm already spent $3,000 on research and development activities in the division of the firm in which the project will be located.

cash flow estimation

The capital project being considered is expected to produce annual cash sales of $20,000 and annual cash expenses of $12,000. These are expected to occur over the eight-year life of the capital project. The project is expected to have a $5,000 salvage value and is to be depreciated on the ACRS on the 200-percent declining balance method as seven-year property. State Utilities will recover its $2,000 increase in net working capital at the end of eight years. The firm's income tax rate is 34 percent, and its required rate of return on the investment is 12 percent.

a) Calculate State Utilities' net initial investment requirements.
b) Estimate the annual net operating cash inflows.
c) Estimate the terminal cash flows projected for the investment.
d) Determine the net present value of the investment.

10. The Alpha Corporation is contemplating the purchase of a new machine to be used in the manufacture of synthetic fibers. The machine will cost $45,000, have an expected useful life of six years, and have a terminal salvage value of $3,000. Depreciation will be ACRS 200-percent declining balance for five-year property. If the machine is purchased,

replacement

total annual earnings before depreciation and taxes are expected to be $16,000.

The new machine is being considered as a replacement for an older, less efficient machine. While the existing machine could continue in operation for an additional six years, it could be sold now for $6,000. Its current book value is $9,000. The machine was acquired prior to ACRS and is being depreciated on a straight-line basis over the next six years to a zero salvage value. Continued operation of the existing machine will produce annual earnings before depreciation and taxes of $6,000. The firm is in the 34-percent income tax bracket, and its required rate of return on the investment is 10 percent.

a) Estimate the investment outflows that will result if the new machine is purchased to replace the existing machine.
b) Estimate the incremental net operating inflows of the proposed investment.
c) Calculate the net present value of the investment.
d) Calculate the approximate internal rate of return for the investment.
e) Calculate the payback period for the machine.

SOLUTIONS TO SOLVED PROBLEMS

SP-1. a) Assuming straight-line depreciation (ACRS).

1. *Incremental investment outflows*
   The incremental investment outflows are equal to the cost of the investment, $2,100,000.

2. *Incremental operating inflows.*
   Earnings before depreciation and taxes are $1,000,000 (10 cents per gallon times 10,000,000 gallons) per year. Depreciation is calculated on a straight-line basis according to ACRS provisions assuming a three-year class life.

Straight-line depreciation (ACRS) = Original cost/Class life

$$= \$2,100,000/3$$

$$= \$700,000 \text{ per year}$$

However, due to the half-year convention, only one-half ($350,000) of the annual depreciation is permitted in the first year. Depreciation in years two and three is $700,000 per year. A final deduction of $350,000 in year four is taken to make up for the first-year shortage.

Operating Cash Inflows: Straight-Line Depreciation (ACRS)

	Year			
	1	2	3	4
Δ EBDT	$1,000,000	$1,000,000	$1,000,000	$1,000,000
− Δ Depreciation	350,000	700,000	700,000	350,000
Δ EBT	650,000	300,000	300,000	650,000
− Taxes (34%)	221,000	102,000	102,000	221,000
Δ NI	429,000	198,000	198,000	429,000
+ Δ Depreciation	350,000	700,000	700,000	350,000
Δ net operating cash flows	779,000	898,000	898,000	779,000

3. *Incremental terminal cash inflows.*
   In this case, there are none since there will be no salvage value.
4. *Net present value.*

Net Present Value Calculation Assuming Straight-Line Depreciation (ACRS)

	Year				
	0	1	2	3	4
Investment outflow	($2,100,000)				
Operating inflows		779,000	898,000	898,000	779,000
Total	($2,100,000)	779,000	898,000	898,000	779,000
PVIF @ 18%	1.000	.847	.718	.609	.516
PV @ 18%	($2,100,000)	659,813	644,764	546,882	401,964
NPV = $153,423					

The positive net present value means that the investment is acceptable.

5. *Profitability index (PI).*

$$PI = PVCI/I_0$$

$$= \$2,253,423/2,100,000 = 1.07$$

The PI more than 1.0 indicates that the investment is acceptable.

6. *Internal rate of return (IRR).*

Internal Rate of Return: Straight-Line Depreciation (ACRS)

Year	Cash Flow	PVIF @ 20%	PV @ 20%	PVIF @ 22%	PV @ 22%
0	($2,100,000)	1.000	($2,100,000)	1.000	($2,100,000)
1	779,000	.833	648,907	.820	638,780
2	898,000	.694	623,212	.672	603,456
3	898,000	.579	519,942	.551	494,798
4	779,000	.482	375,478	.451	351,329
Net present value			$ 67,539		($ 11,637)

Thus, the internal rate of return is between 20 percent and 22 percent. With a financial calculator or computer financial spreadsheet program, the actual IRR is found to be about 21.69 percent.

7. *Payback period.*

	Remaining Investment Balance
Investment outflows ($2,100,000)	($2,100,000)
+ Year 1 operating inflow 779,000	($1,321,000)
+ Year 2 operating inflow 898,000	($ 432,000)
+ Year 3 operating inflow 898,000	

Payback period = 2 + 432,000/898,000 years

= 2.47 years

Since the payback period is less than the maximum allowed (3.0) for this project, it is acceptable on this basis.

8. From a strict economic standpoint, the recovery device investment is justified because it has a positive net present value. Intangible benefits will also be realized in the recycling of waste chemicals and reduced pollution of the Ohio River.

b) Assuming accelerated depreciation (ACRS).

1. *Incremental investment outflows.*
   The incremental investment outflows do not depend on the choice of depreciation method and do not change. They are $2,100,000.

2. *Incremental operating inflows.*
   Earnings before depreciation and taxes are $1,000,000 (10 cents per gallon times 10,000,000 gallons) per year. Since these earnings are computed before depreciation, the choice of depreciation method does not affect them. Accelerated depreciation is calculated using the percentages in Table 15-2 for three-year property.

ACRS Depreciation (Three-Year Property)

Year	Depreciation Percentage	Depreciation
1	.333	$ 699,300
2	.444	932,400
3	.148	310,800
4	.075	157,500
Total	1.000	$2,100,000

Operating Cash Inflows: Accelerated Depreciation (ACRS)

	Year			
	1	*2*	*3*	*4*
Δ EBDT	$1,000,000	$1,000,000	$1,000,000	$1,000,000
− Δ Depreciation	699,300	932,400	310,800	157,500
Δ EBT	300,700	67,600	689,200	842,500
− Taxes (34%)	102,238	22,984	234,328	286,450
Δ NI	198,462	44,616	454,872	556,050
+ Δ Depreciation	699,300	932,400	310,800	157,500
Δ net operating cash flows	897,762	977,016	765,672	713,550

3. *Incremental terminal cash inflows.*
   In this case, there are none since there will be no salvage value.

4. *Net present value.*

Net Present Value Calculation: Accelerated Depreciation (ACRS)

		Year			
	0	1	2	3	4
Investment outflow	($2,100,000)				
Operating inflows		897,762	977,016	765,672	713,550
Total	($2,100,000)	897,762	977,016	765,672	713,550
PVIF @ 18%	1.000	.847	.718	.609	.516
PV @ 18%	($2,100,000)	760,404	701,497	466,294	368,192
NPV = $196,388					

The positive net present value means that the investment is acceptable.

5. *Profitability index (PI).*

$$PI = PVCI/I_0$$

$$= \$2,296,388/2,100,000 = 1.09$$

The PI more than 1.0 indicates that the investment is acceptable.

6. *Internal rate of return (IRR).*

Internal Rate of Return: Accelerated Depreciation (ACRS)

Year	Cash Flow	PVIF @ 22%	PV @ 22%	PVIF @ 24%	PV @ 24%
0	($2,100,000)	1.000	($2,100,000)	1.000	($2,100,000)
1	897,762	.820	736,165	.806	723,596
2	977,016	.672	656,555	.650	635,060
3	765,672	.551	421,885	.524	401,212
4	713,550	.451	321,811	.423	301,832
Net present value			$ 36,416		($ 38,300)

Thus, the internal rate of return is between 22 percent and 24 percent. With a financial calculator or computer financial spreadsheet program, the actual IRR is found to be about 22.97 percent.

7. *Payback period.*

	Remaining Investment Balance
Investment outflows ($2,100,000)	($2,100,000)
+ year 1 operating inflow 897,762	($1,202,238)
+ year 2 operating inflow 977,016	($ 225,222)
+ year 3 operating inflow 765,672	

Payback period = 2 + 225,222/765,672 years

= 2.29 years

Since the Payback Period is less than the maximum allowed (3.0) for this project, it is acceptable on this basis.

c) The accelerated method improves the value of the proposal relative to the straight-line method under ACRS in this case. The difference between accelerated and straight-line methods is shown below. Note that the NPV with the accelerated method is $42,965 greater than with the straight-line method.

	Straight-Line ACRS	Accelerated ACRS
NPV @ 18%	$153,423	$196,388
PI	1.07	1.09
IRR (tables)	20–22%	22–24%
IRR (calculator)	21.69%	22.97%
Payback Period	2.47 years	2.29 years

SP-2. a) 1. *Incremental investment outlays.*

Invoice cost	$ 900,000
Freight & installation	100,000
Increase in net working capital	150,000
Incremental investment outflows	$1,150,000

Note that the $200,000 spent on market research is a sunk cost and thus should not be included as part of the incremental investment.

2. *Incremental operating inflows.*

Chocolatizer Proposal—Net Operating Cash Flows: Straight-Line Depreciation (ACRS)										
	Year									
	1	2	3	4	5	6	7	8	9	10
Δ EBDT	250,000	250,000	250,000	250,000	250,000	250,000	250,000	250,000	250,000	250,000
Δ D	71,429	142,857	142,857	142,857	142,857	142,857	142,857	71,429	-0-	-0-
Δ PBT	178,571	107,143	107,143	107,143	107,143	107,143	107,143	178,571	250,000	250,000
Δ Txs	60,714	36,429	36,429	36,429	36,429	36,429	36,429	60,714	85,000	85,000
Δ NI	117,857	70,714	70,714	70,714	70,714	70,714	70,714	117,857	165,000	165,000
+ Δ D	71,429	142,857	142,857	142,857	142,857	142,857	142,857	71,429	-0-	-0-
Δ CF	189,286	213,571	213,571	213,571	213,571	213,571	213,571	189,286	165,000	165,000

$$\text{Straight-line depreciation} = \text{(Original cost)/Class life}$$

$$= (\$1,000,000)/7 \text{ years}$$

$$= \$142,857 \text{ per year}$$

Interest expense is ignored, even though the problem states that part of the financing will be borrowed. Interest expense is a financing cost, is dealt with separately (in the cost of capital), and should not be double-counted.

3. *Incremental terminal cash flows.*
   The salvage value of $100,000 will be recovered at the end of year 10. Since net book value at that time will be zero, the recovery of salvage value is taxable at the company's ordinary income tax rate (34 percent).

$$\text{Salvage value after taxes} = \$100,000(1 - .34) = \$66,000$$

In addition, the initial investment in net working capital of $150,000 will be recovered at the end of year 10.
Thus incremental terminal cash flows will be $216,000.

4. *Net present value (NPV).*

Chocolatizer Proposal — Net Present Value: Straight-Line Depreciation

Year	Cash Flow	PVIF @ 13%	PV @ 13%
0	($1,150,000)	1.000	($1,150,000)
1	189,286	.885	167,518
2	213,571	.783	167,226
3	213,571	.693	148,005
4	213,571	.613	130,919
5	213,571	.543	115,969
6	213,571	.480	102,514
7	213,571	.425	90,768
8	189,286	.376	71,171
9	165,000	.333	54,945
10	381,000*	.295	112,395
Net present value			11,430

*Operating cash flow of $165,000 + terminal cash flows of $216,000.

Since the NPV is positive, the investment is acceptable.

5. *Profitability index (PI).*

$$PI = PVCI/I_0$$

$$= \$1,161,430/1,150,000$$

$$= 1.01$$

Since the *PI* is more than 1.0, the investment is acceptable.

6. *Internal rate of return (IRR).*
The net present value is positive at a 13-percent discount rate but not by much, indicating that the internal rate of return must be slightly more than 13 percent. Try 14 percent.

Chocolatizer Proposal—Internal Rate of Return: Straight-Line Depreciation			
Year	Cash Flow	PVIF @ 14%	PV @ 14%
0	($1,150,000)	1.000	($1,150,000)
1	189,286	.877	166,004
2	213,571	.769	164,236
3	213,571	.675	144,161
4	213,571	.592	126,434
5	213,571	.519	110,844
6	213,571	.456	97,389
7	213,571	.400	85,429
8	189,286	.351	66,439
9	165,000	.308	50,820
10	381,000	.270	102,870
Net Present Value			($ 35,374)

Thus the internal rate of return is between 13 percent and 14 percent. With the aid of a financial calculator or computerized financial spreadsheet program, the internal rate of return is found to be 13.24 percent. Since the IRR is greater than the required rate of return, the project is acceptable.

7. *Payback period.*

		Ending investment balance
Investment outflow	($1,150,000)	($1,150,000)
+ Operating cash inflow year 1	189,286	($ 960,714)
+ Operating cash inflow year 2	213,571	($ 747,143)
+ Operating cash inflow year 3	213,571	($ 533,572)
+ Operating cash inflow year 4	213,571	($ 320,001)
+ Operating cash inflow year 5	213,571	($ 106,430)
+ Operating cash inflow year 6	213,571	

At the end of year five all but $106,430 of the initial investment has been recovered. Since year-six inflows will be $213,571, it will take approximately 106,430/213,571, or .50 of the year to recover the remainder (assuming cash flows are received uniformly throughout the year). Thus the payback period is 5.50 years. Since the payback period is slightly under the maximum permitted (6.0 years), the investment is acceptable on this basis.

b) Assuming ACRS depreciation.

1. *Incremental investment outlays.*

   These are the same as before since ACRS depreciation methods will have no effect on investment outlays. Investment outlays are $1,150,000. The depreciation basis is $1,000,000 since ACRS ignores salvage value and net working capital is not depreciated.

2. *Incremental operating inflows.*

   Neither sales nor cash expenses are affected by the change in depreciation methods, so the earnings before depreciation and taxes (EBDT) is still $250,000 per year.

Chocolatizer Proposal — Net Operating Cash Flows ($000): ACRS Depreciation

	Year									
	1	2	3	4	5	6	7	8	9	10
Δ EBDT	250.00	250.00	250.00	250.00	250.00	250.00	250.00	250.00	250.00	250.00
Δ D	143.00	245.00	175.00	125.00	89.00	89.00	89.00	45.00	-0-	-0-
Δ PBT	107.00	5.00	75.00	125.00	161.00	161.00	161.00	205.00	250.00	250.00
Δ Txs	36.38	1.70	25.50	42.50	54.74	54.74	54.74	69.70	85.00	85.00
Δ NI	70.62	3.30	49.50	82.50	106.26	106.26	106.26	135.30	165.00	165.00
+ Δ D	143.00	245.00	175.00	125.00	89.00	89.00	89.00	45.00	-0-	-0-
Δ CF	213.62	248.30	224.50	207.50	195.26	195.26	195.26	180.30	165.00	165.00

Depreciation is calculated by multiplying the ACRS percentage for each year times the depreciable investment ($1,000,000). The percentages are taken from Table 15-2 in the chapter. For example, depreciation in year one is $143,000, which is equal to .143 times $1,000,000.

3. *Incremental terminal inflows.*

   Terminal inflows are salvage value after taxes plus recovery of net working capital. In year 10, the net book value is zero. Thus the expected salvage value in year 10 is taxed at the company's ordinary income tax rate of 34 percent.

$$\text{Salvage value after taxes} = (\text{salvage value} - \text{book value})(1 - T)$$
$$= (1,000,000 - 0)(1 - .34)$$
$$= \$66,000$$

Net working capital is unaffected by ACRS, and the full $150,000 is shown as a terminal inflow at the end of year 10.

	Terminal cash flows (year 10)
Salvage value (after taxes)	$ 66,000
Recovery of net working capital	150,000
Total	$216,000

4. *Net present value.*

Chocolatizer Proposal — Net Present Value: ACRS Depreciation

Year	Cash Flow	PVIF @ 13%	PV @ 13%
0	($1,150,000)	1.000	($1,150,000)
1	213,620	.885	189,054
2	248,300	.783	194,419
3	224,500	.693	155,579
4	207,500	.613	127,198
5	195,260	.543	106,026
6	195,260	.480	93,725
7	195,260	.425	82,986
8	180,300	.376	67,793
9	165,000	.333	54,945
10	381,000	.295	112,395
Net Present Value			$ 34,120

Since the NPV is positive, the investment is acceptable.

5. *Profitability index (PI).*

$$PI = PVCI/I_0$$

$$= \$1,184,120/\$1,150,000$$

$$= 1.03$$

6. *Internal rate of return.*
Since the NPV is positive at 13 percent, try 14 percent.

Chocolatizer Proposal—Internal Rate of Return: ACRS Depreciation

Year	Cash Flow	PVIF @ 14%	PV @ 14%
0	($1,150,000)	1.000	($1,150,000)
1	213,620	.877	187,345
2	248,300	.769	190,943
3	224,500	.675	151,538
4	207,500	.592	122,840
5	195,260	.519	101,340
6	195,260	456	89,039
7	195,260	.400	78,104
8	180,300	.351	63,285
9	165,000	.308	50,820
10	381,000	.270	102,870
Net present value			($ 11,876)

Thus, the internal rate of return is between 13 percent and 14 percent. With a financial calculator or computer, the internal rate of return is found to be 13.73 percent.

7. *Payback period.*

	Remaining Investment Balance
Investment outflow ($1,150,000)	($1,150,000)
+ Cash inflow year 1 213,620	(936,380)
+ Cash inflow year 2 248,300	(688,080)
+ Cash inflow year 3 224,500	(463,580)
+ Cash inflow year 4 207,500	(256,080)
+ Cash inflow year 5 195,260	(60,820)

At the end of year five, all but $60,820 of the initial investment has been recovered. Year six will produce cash inflows of $195,260. Assuming they are received uniformly during the year, the remaining balance will take about ($60,820/195,260) = .31 of year six's cash flows. Thus the payback period is 5.31 years.

c) The results produced under the straight-line and accelerated ACRS methods are shown in the following table.

	Straight-line	Accelerated
NPV at 13%	$11,430	$34,120
PI	1.01	1.03
IRR (tables)	13–14%	13–14%
IRR (calculator)	13.24%	13.73%
Payback period	5.50 years	5.31 years

The NPV, PI, IRR, and payback are all more favorable with the ACRS method. The reason is that it accelerates cash inflows relative to the straight-line method. Given the time value of money, earlier cash flows are more valuable than later cash flows.

SP-3. a)   Incremental investment outflows.

Cost of new machine	($120,000)
Increased net working capital	(5,000)
Proceeds from sale of old machine	35,000
Tax liability on gain from sale of old machine (35,000 − 30,000) × .34	(1,700)
Net investment outflows	($ 91,700)

b)   Incremental depreciation charges.

Year	Depreciation new	Depreciation old	Δ Depreciation
1	.333(120,000) = $39,960	$7,500	$32,460
2	.444(120,000) = 53,280	7,500 ·	45,780
3	.148(120,000) = 17,760	7,500	10,260
4	.075(120,000) = 9,000	7,500	1,500

c)   Incremental net operating inflows.

	Year			
	1	2	3	4
Δ EBDT	35,000	50,000	40,000	20,000
Δ D	32,460	45,780	10,260	1,500
Δ PBT	2,540	4,220	29,740	18,500
Δ Taxes	864	1,435	10,112	6,290
Δ NI	1,676	2,785	19,628	12,210
+ Δ D	32,460	45,780	10,260	1,500
= Δ CFAT	34,136	48,565	29,888	13,710

d) Incremental terminal inflows.
    Salvage value of $10,000 will be realized in year four. Since book value will be zero, taxes will have to be paid at a 34-percent rate. Salvage value inflow after-taxes will be $6,600 (i.e., $10,000 × .66). In addition, net working capital of $5,000 will be received.

Salvage value after taxes	$ 6,600
Recovery of incremental net working capital	5,000
Terminal inflows	11,600

e) Net present value.

	0	1	2	3	4
Investment outflows	($91,700)				
Operating inflows		34,136	48,565	29,888	13,710
Terminal inflows					11,600
Totals	($91,700)	34,136	48,565	29,888	25,310
PVIF @ 20%	1.000	.833	.694	.579	.482
	($91,700)	28,435	33,704	17,305	12,199
NPV 20% ($57)					

Since the NPV is negative, the investment is not acceptable.
f) Profitability index (PI).

$$\$91,643/91,700 = .999$$

The PI less than 1.00 indicates a negative NPV and an unacceptable investment.
g) Internal rate of return (IRR).
    Since NPV is virtually zero at a 20-percent discount rate, there is no need to calculate IRR further. More precise methods would indicate an IRR of 19.98 percent. The IRR is less than 20 percent, and thus the investment would not be acceptable on this basis.
h) Payback period.

		Remaining Investment Balance
Investment outflows	($91,660)	($91,660)
+ Operating cash inflow year 1	37,655	($54,005)
+ Operating cash inflow year 2	41,051	($12,954)
+ Operating cash inflow year 3	31,994	

Payback period = 2 + 8,999/29,888 years = 2.30 years

Since the payback period exceeds the maximum of two years, the investment would not be acceptable on this basis.

SP-4. a) Incremental investment outflows.

Cost of new machine	($90,000)
Increased net working capital	(4,000)
Proceeds from sale of old machine	2,000
Tax credit on loss from sale of old machine (1,000) × .34	340
Net investment outflows	($91,660)

b) Incremental depreciation charges.

	Depreciation new	Depreciation old	Δ Depreciation
1	.333(90,000) = $29,970	$750	$29,220
2	.444(90,000) = 39,960	750	39,210
3	.148(90,000) = 13,320	750	12,570
4	.075(90,000) = 6,750	750	6,000

c) Incremental net operating inflows.

	Year			
	1	*2*	*3*	*4*
Δ Sales	25,000	25,000	25,000	25,000
Δ O. E.*	17,000	17,000	17,000	17,000
Δ EBDT	42,000	42,000	42,000	42,000
Δ D	29,220	39,210	12,570	6,000
Δ PBT	12,780	2,790	29,430	36,000
Δ Taxes	4,345	949	10,006	12,240
Δ NI	8,435	1,841	19,424	23,760
+ Δ D	29,220	39,210	12,570	6,000
+ Δ CFAT	37,655	41,051	31,994	29,760

*Note that a decrease in operating expenses will *increase* EBDT by that amount.

d) Incremental terminal inflows.
   The only terminal inflow will be recovery of the net working capital of $4,000.

e) Net present value.

	0	1	2	3	4
Investment outflows	($91,660)				
Operating inflows		37,655	41,051	31,994	29,760
Terminal inflows					4,000
Totals	($91,660)	37,655	41,051	31,994	33,760
PVIF @ 20%	1.000	.870	.756	.658	.572
	($91,660)	32,760	31,035	21,052	19,311
NPV 20% $12,498					

The positive NPV indicates the investment is acceptable.
f) Profitability index (PI)

$$\$104,158/91,660 = 1.14$$

The PI in excess of 1.00 signals a positive NPV and an acceptable investment.
g) Internal rate of return (IRR)

Year	Cash Flow	PVIF @ 20%	PV @ 20%	PVIF @ 22%	PV @ 22%
0	($91,660)	1.000	($91,660)	1.000	($91,660)
1	37,655	.833	31,367	.820	30,877
2	41,051	.694	28,489	.672	27,586
3	31,994	.579	18,525	.551	17,629
4	33,760	.482	16,272	.451	15,226
		NPV	$2,993		($ 342)

Thus, the internal rate of return is about 22 percent. More precise methods would produce an IRR estimate of 21.78 percent. The IRR is above the required rate of return, and thus the investment is acceptable.
h) Payback period.

		Remaining Investment Balance
Investment outflows	($91,660)	($91,660)
+ Operating cash inflow year 1	37,655	($54,005)
+ Operating cash inflow year 2	41,051	($12,954)
+ Operating cash inflow year 3	31,994	

Payback period = 2 + 12,954/31,994 years = 2.40 years

The payback period is under the 3.5 maximum and thus indicates that the investment is acceptable on this basis.

REFERENCES

Angell, Robert J., and Tony R. Wingler. "A Note on Expensing Versus Depreciating Under the Accelerated Cost Recovery System." *Financial Management*, Winter 1982, pp. 34–35.

Commerce Clearing House, Inc. "Explanation of Tax Reform Act of 1986." *Federal Tax Guide Reports*, CCH Special 8, No. 2, October 22, 1986.

Cooley, Phillip L., Rodney L. Roenfeldt, and It-Keong Chew. "Capital Budgeting Procedures Under Inflation." *Financial Management*, Winter 1975, pp. 18–27.

Coopers & Lybrand. "Tax Analysis." *Tax Reform Act of 1986*, Coopers & Lybrand, 1986.

Gurnani, C. "Capital Budgeting: Theory and Practice." *Engineering Economist*, 30, Fall 1984, pp. 19–46.

Hastie, K. Larry. "One Businessman's View of Capital Budgeting." *Financial Management*, Winter 1972, pp. 36–44.

Johnson, Robert W. *Capital Budgeting*. Dubuque, IA: Kendall/Hunt, 1977.

McCarty, Daniel E., and William McDaniel. "A Note of Expensing Versus Depreciating Under Accelerated Cost Recovery System: Comment." *Financial Management*, Summer 1983, pp. 37–39.

Petty, J. William, David F. Scott, Jr., and Monroe M. Bird. "The Capital Expenditure Decision-Making Process of Large Corporations." *Engineering Economist*, Spring 1975, pp. 159–172.

Ross, Marc. "Capital Budgeting Practices of Twelve Large Manufacturers." *Financial Management*, Winter 1986, pp. 15–22.

Schnell, James S., and Roy S. Nicolosi. "Capital Expenditure Feedback: Project Reappraisal," *Engineering Economist*, Summer 1974, pp. 253–261.

Scott, D. F., Jr., and J. W. Petty. "Capital Budgeting Practices in Large American Firms: A Retrospective Analysis and Synthesis." *The Financial Review,* 10, May 1984, pp. 111–123.

Weaver, James B. "Organizing and Maintaining a Capital Expenditure Program." *Engineering Economist,* Fall 1974, pp. 1–36.

CHAPTER 16

CAPITAL BUDGETING UNDER RISK

p to this point, the discussion of capital budgeting methods and decisions has ignored risk implications. While the cash outlay required to purchase and install a new piece of equipment might be known with reasonable certainty, the estimation of cash inflows to be generated by operation of the equipment is likely to be much less certain. Anticipated revenues might be affected by changing economic conditions. Likewise, anticipated labor costs could be altered due to start-up and retraining requirements, and even anticipated material costs are subject to fluctuations associated with changes in inflation rates and availability of supplies. Taken together, these factors are likely to result in a dispersion of possible cash flow outcomes for a given time period, such as a year.

In Chapter 6, it was noted that risk reflects uncertainty about the future. Thus, the wider the dispersion of possible outcomes, the greater the risk involved in the investment decision. Why do managers care about risk when making capital budgeting decisions? They have to be concerned, because a decision for a project using any of the major methods without some risk allowance may not, in fact, maximize the value of the owners' equity if there are significant differences in risk among projects.

Objectives and Organization of this Chapter

This chapter first reviews the basic statistical procedures for quantifying the degree of dispersion of a probability distribution, which was initially discussed in Chapter 6. The concept of total variability of outcomes is used as a measure of project risk. The chapter also considers risk in a portfolio diversification context in terms of how a project might affect the firm's overall systematic risk. This is followed by a discussion of techniques that can be used to adjust for difference in project risk.

EXPECTED VALUE AND TOTAL VARIABILITY MEASURES

Many firms, because of uncertainty associated with estimating cash inflows from a project, might begin with a form of *sensitivity analysis* — that is, a series of estimates for a project which are designed to show a number of possible cash inflow outcomes. For example, cash inflows for next year might be estimated for several states of the economy, e.g., recession, moderate growth, and rapid growth. Weights or probabilities could then be assigned to the likelihood of each state occurring. Alternately, the cost accounting department, the marketing department, and the finance department might be asked to make cash inflow projections for next year. These independent projections then might be assigned weights or probabilities, based on past experience with other projects, as to their likely accuracy. Professional managers use a number of different computer methods for this type of analysis.

Example

A Sensitivity Analysis

The United Electronic Components Corporation is in the process of comparing two mutually exclusive projects, each of which will require a net investment or initial cash outlay of $30,000. These projects are denoted by the firm as Project EXP1 and Project EXP2. Each project is expected to have a five-year life with no salvage value remaining at the end of five years. Three projections of after-tax inflows for next year have been made for each project. These estimates, denoted as pessimistic, typical, and optimistic, are as follows:

| | Cash Inflow Estimates | |
	Project EXP1	*Project EXP2*
Pessimistic	$ 6,500	$ 4,000
Typical	8,500	9,000
Optimistic	10,500	14,000

Past experience suggests that the pessimistic estimate has a 20-percent probability of occurring, the typical estimate a 60-percent probability, and the optimistic estimate a 20-percent probability. Furthermore, these cash inflow projections and assigned probabilities for each project are expected to be the same in each of the five years of operation.[1]

---

[1]Risk sometimes increases over time. That is, the dispersion or variability of cash inflows may be greater in a distant year than in a more current year even though the expected values are the same. If riskiness is expected to change over time at different rates for different projects, cash inflow projections and associated probabilities need to be prepared for each year for each project. For example, Project EXP1's possible cash inflows, which were $6,500, $8,500, and $10,500 for the first year, might have been estimated as $4,500, $8,500, and $12,500 for the fifth year of the operation.

The first step in evaluating the riskiness of the two projects for United Electronic Components is to estimate the expected value of cash inflows for the first year of the project. This is accomplished by preparing a *payoff matrix,* or display of possible cash inflow outcomes, weighted by their appropriate probability of occurrence for each project, as is shown in Table 16-1.

payoff matrix

TABLE 16-1 Payoff Matrix of Cash Inflow Calculations for Two Capital Projects

United Electronic Components Corporation

State of Nature (1)	Probability of State Occurring (2)	Expected Cash Inflow if State Occurs (3)	Expected Value (2) × (3) (4)	
Project EXP1				
Pessimistic	.2	$ 6,500	$1,300	
Typical	.6	8,500	5,100	
Optimistic	.2	10,500	2,100	
	1.0		$8,500	Expected Value
Project EXP2				
Pessimistic	.2	$ 4,000	$ 800	
Typical	.6	9,000	5,400	
Optimistic	.2	14,000	2,800	
	1.0		$9,000	Expected Value

Notice in the table that the expected cash inflow value for Project EXP2 is $9,000 compared with only $8,500 for Project EXP1. Furthermore, these expected values are anticipated in each of the five years of operation.

Application of the net-present-value method might then be used to compare the relative attractiveness of the two projects based on the annual expected cash inflows. If United's cost of capital, or "hurdle rate," is 10 percent, the present value of the cash inflow streams can be estimated by using the PVIFA factor of 3.791 at 10 percent for five years (see Appendix A, Table 4) as follows:

Project EXP1: $8,500 × 3.791 = $32,224 PVCI

Project EXP2: $9,000 × 3.791 = $34,119 PVCI

Since each project has an initial investment or present value of cash outflows of $30,000, the net present value for Project EXP2 would be $4,119, compared to $2,224 for Project EXP1. Thus, by focusing only on the expected values of the cash flow streams, a manager would conclude that United should invest in Project EXP2.

It should be recalled at this point that the practice of making capital budgeting decisions on the basis of expected values of cash inflows is consistent with the handling of the replacement and revenue expansion projects described in Chapter 15. That is, the annual cash inflows used for calculation purposes were expected values. For United Electronic Components, as long as the two projects being evaluated are of comparable riskiness, then Project EXP2 is clearly preferable to Project EXP1. As a further condition of the equal-risk situation, the firm's overall cost of capital is the appropriate "hurdle rate" to apply, assuming that the projects under consideration fall into a risk category consistent with the firm's average riskiness of an investment project.

variance standard deviation

The more uncertainty about the possible outcome of cash flows, the greater the risk involved in the investment decision. It is common practice to measure a project's risk in terms of the dispersion or variability of possible outcomes. This is accomplished by measuring the variance and standard deviation associated with each of the possible outcomes.

The procedure is to subtract expected value of cash inflow calculated in Table 16-1 from the expected cash inflow for each of the probabilities (or "states of nature") to get the deviation. Squaring the deviation and then multiplying by the appropriate probability of occurrence gives the variance for each such probability. Then, sum the variances across all the "states of nature" to get the variance of the probability distribution denoted by the symbol σ^2 (sigma squared). Since the variance is in the form of somewhat meaningless squared dollars, it is necessary to take the "square root," or standard deviation, σ, of the variance in order to convert the dispersion measure back into dollars.

TABLE 16-2 Calculation of Cash Inflow Variances and Standard Deviations for Two Capital Projects

UNITED ELECTRONIC COMPONENTS CORPORATION

State of Nature and Probability of Occurrence (1)	Expected Cash Inflow if State Occurs (2)	Expected Value of Cash Inflow (3)	Deviation (2) − (3) (4)	Squared Deviation (5)	Variance (1) × (5) (6)
Project EXP1					
Pessimistic (.2)	$ 6,500	$8,500	−$2,000	4,000,000	800,000
Typical (.6)	8,500	8,500	0	0	0
Optimistic (.2)	10,500	8,500	2,000	4,000,000	800,000
				Variance (σ^2) =	1,600,000
				Standard deviation (σ) =	$ 1,265
Project EXP2					
Pessimistic (.2)	$ 4,000	$9,000	−$5,000	25,000,000	5,000,000
Typical (.6)	9,000	9,000	0	0	0
Optimistic (.2)	14,000	9,000	5,000	25,000,000	5,000,000
				Variance (σ^2) =	10,000,000
				Standard deviation (σ) =	$ 3,163

As one might have suspected by visual examination of the cash inflow distributions for the two projects, the standard deviation of $3,163 for Project EXP2 is much greater than the $1,265 figure for Project EXP1, indicating that the former project is relatively more risky. However, it is sometimes important to standardize the risk of dispersion when there are differences in expected values as well as standard deviations. This is *coefficient of variation* done through the calculation of the *coefficient of variation*—which is the probability distribution's standard deviation divided by the distribution's expected value. The calculation of the coefficient of variation is performed in equation form by first calculating the distribution's expected value $(\overline{X})$ as follows:

$$\overline{X} = \sum_{i=1}^{n} X_i P_i \tag{16-1}$$

where X_i = outcome for the *ith* state of nature; P_i = probability of occurrence of the *ith* state of nature; and n = number of states of nature.
The second step is to calculate the distribution's standard deviation (σ) in equation form as:

$$\sigma = \sqrt{\sum_{i=1}^{n} (X_i - \overline{X})^2 P_i} \tag{16-2}$$

The coefficient of variation (CV) then is expressed in equation form as the standard deviation divided by the expected value in the following fashion:

$$CV = \frac{\sigma}{\overline{X}} \tag{16-3}$$

The previously calculated expected values and standard deviations, along with the corresponding coefficients of variation for the cash inflow distributions, allow a manager to summarize risk comparisons between the two projects.

Annual Cash Inflows	Project EXP1	Project EXP2
Expected value	$8,500	$9,000
Standard deviation	$1,265	$3,163
Coefficient of variation	.149	.351

Project EXP2 clearly has the higher coefficient of variation at .351 and thus is the riskier of the two projects, since it has more risk per dollar of return. However, Project EXP2 also has the higher expected value. Which project should United Electronic Components invest in—the one with the higher expected cash inflows or the one with the less risk in terms of variability of cash inflows? This question can only be answered after appropriate adjustments have been made to reflect risk differences. Possible risk adjustment techniques will be explored in the next section. But before doing so, some consideration should be given to how a new capital project might affect a firm's overall systematic risk due to possible portfolio diversification implications.

PORTFOLIO DIVERSIFICATION AND SYSTEMATIC RISK CONSIDERATIONS

Up to this point, we have been discussing risk only as it relates to a project's variability of cash flows for a specified time period, such as one year. The standard deviation and coefficient of variation provide ways of statistically measuring the dispersion of possible cash flows in each year of a project's life. Under this concept of risk, however, the proposed project is viewed as one that is independent of the firm's portfolio of other projects or assets. It could be short-sighted not to consider also how the stream of cash inflows to be generated by a proposed capital project will covary, or move with, the firm's overall cash-flow stream over time.

In a similar fashion, the financial manager is interested in the extent to which economic activity and the firm's cash flows covary. This interest exists because, the greater the variability in a firm's cash flows, the greater the probability of bankruptcy for the firm.

cash flow systematic risk

correlation coefficient

index of cash flow systematic risk

The extent of correlation of cash flows with economic activity over time is referred to as *cash flow systematic risk*. It can be recalled from basic statistics that the correlation between two items can range from perfect positive correlation (where the correlation coefficient is $+1.00$) to perfect negative correlation (where the correlation coefficient is -1.00). In the event that there is no correlation between two items, the correlation coefficient is zero. The financial manager also is interested in the magnitude of a change in the firm's cash flows given a change in economic activity. This degree of sensitivity indicates the *index of cash flow systematic risk*. Simple "least squares" regression analysis can be used to examine both the correlation and degree-of-sensitivity aspects of systematic risk, as was briefly described in Chapter 6.

Example

Cash Flow Systematic Risk

Assume that the General Steel Corporation's cash flows are positively correlated with an index of economic activity. For three possible states of the economy, the following relationships are expected based on past experience:

State of Economy	Index of Economic Activity	Percentage Change from Normal Activity	General Steel's Cash Flow	Percentage Change from Normal Cash Flow
Normal	100		$1,000	
Recession	90	−10%	800	−20%
Rapid growth	110	+ 10%	1,200	+20%

Based on these limited data, one might conclude that there is perfect positive correlation (+ 1.00 coefficient) between changes in General Steel's cash flows and changes in economic activity. Furthermore, the data relationships suggest an index of systematic risk of 2.00, since, when economic activity changes by 10 percent, there is a change in the same direction of 20 percent in General Steel's cash flows (this 2 to 1 ratio accounts for the index of 2.00).

General Steel is presently evaluating two mutually exclusive projects. Each project requires the same cash outlay, has the same life expectancy, the same amount of project risk, and the same positive net present value. However, Project A's cash flows are positively correlated with the firm's existing cash flow stream, whereas Project B's cash flows are negatively correlated with the firm's existing cash flow stream. Should this information influence General Steel's otherwise equal decision between Projects A and B? The answer depends on how important, in the eyes of management, it is to reduce the firm's cash flow sensitivity to changes in economic activity.

Table 16-3 illustrates the effect of the positively correlated project (A) and the negatively correlated project (B) on General Steel's existing cash flows. Each project will produce cash flows that average 10 percent of the size of the firm's existing cash flows. Larger projects in a relative cash flow context would have a greater effect on the firm's existing cash flows, and vice versa. Thus, the extent of *portfolio diversification* that can be achieved by adding additional assets depends on the degree and direction of correlation, plus the relative size of the cash flow streams being combined.

portfolio diversification

Under the normal state of the economy, the combined cash flow if Project A is accepted will be $1,100. If a recession occurs, the combined cash flow is expected to be $880. A state of rapid growth will result in cash flow of $1,320. Assume also that the probability of either a recession or rapid growth occurring is the same. Table 16-3 shows that the percentage change from the normal state for the combined cash flow if Project A is accepted is still − 20 percent (recession) or + 20 percent (rapid growth). This means that, in a portfolio of assets or projects context, Project A would not produce any diversification benefits to the General Steel Corporation. The

TABLE 16-3 Portfolio Diversification and Systematic Risk Implications of Capital Projects

General Steel Corporation

State of Economy	Existing Firm Cash Flow	Project Cash Flow	Combined Cash Flow	Percentage Change from Normal Combined Cash Flow
Project A				
Normal	$1,000	$100	$1,100	
Recession	800	80	880	−20%
Rapid Growth	1,200	120	1,320	+ 20%
Project B				
Normal	$1,000	$100	$1,100	
Recession	800	120	920	− 16.4%
Rapid Growth	1,200	80	1,280	+ 16.4%

dispersion of combined cash flows continues to be the same as that which prevails for the firm's existing cash flows. As a result, the combined cash flow of the firm would still move directly with changes in economic activity, and the index of systematic risk would still be 2.00 because a 10-percent change in economic activity would be accompanied by a 20-percent similar directional change in cash flow.

Possible benefits of portfolio diversification are illustrated by Project B, whose cash flow changes move inversely with General Steel's other cash flows. The result is a reduction in the range of possible cash flows on a combined basis. In fact, the percentage change from the normal state for the combined cash flow would range from −16.4 percent (recession) to +16.4 percent (rapid growth). This means that portfolio diversification (which will occur if projects are added together that are not perfectly positively correlated) can result in a reduction in the variability of cash flows for the portfolio of projects. While the combined cash flows still move directly with changes in economic activity in the illustration, the index of cash flow systematic risk is reduced to 1.64 because a 10-percent change in economic activity is associated with only a 16.4-percent similar directional change in cash flow.

In the example, the General Steel Corporation likely would select Project B over Project A. The firm's existing index of cash flow systematic risk is relatively high at 2.00, suggesting a higher-than-average probability of bankruptcy. By adding Project B to the firm's existing set of assets, the index of cash flow systematic risk can be reduced.

diversification and bankruptcy risk

General Steel's management would have a much more difficult decision if Project A exhibited higher expected cash flow values or less project risk. The merits of higher returns or lower project risk would have to be weighed against the possible benefits of portfolio diversification. While each situation deserves special consideration, generally a manager would place greater emphasis on selecting the project that will add the most to the value of the firm by producing relatively higher returns or lower project risk. Portfolio diversification benefits would be secondary unless the probability of bankruptcy for the firm was judged to be excessively high.

PROJECT RISK ADJUSTMENT TECHNIQUES

There are two basic ways of recognizing and then adjusting for project risk. One could adjust the rate for discounting the stream of uncertain future cash inflows. This procedure is referred to as the *risk-adjusted discount technique*. Alternatively, one could adjust the uncertain stream of cash inflows to a level whereby they would be known with virtual certainty and then discount at the risk-free rate. This procedure is known as the *certainty equivalent technique*. Discussion of these techniques will be followed by a brief description of other risk-adjustment concepts known as sensitivity analysis, simulation, and decision tree analysis.

Risk-Adjusted Discount Technique

The rate at which one discounts future cash inflows is dependent on a risk-free (R_f) component and a risk premium (Rp) component. Thus, the hurdle rate or cost of capital (k) can be stated as:

$$k = R_f + Rp \qquad (16\text{-}4)$$

This equation implies that the return to be earned on a risky project must exceed the risk-free return (e.g., the rate that can be earned on government securities with maturities equal to the project's life) and include some additional compensation for investing in a risky project. Of course, the question is: what is the proper amount of compensation for the degree of risk involved?

risk-adjusted discount technique

A firm's overall cost of capital reflects the average riskiness of all the firm's projects. In examining the variability of the firm's aggregate cash flows, one could express its riskiness in terms of the coefficient of variation.

The United Electronics Components Corporation is attempting to choose between two mutually exclusive projects, termed Project EXP1 and Project EXP2. Assume that United's cost of capital has been estimated to be 10 percent and that the variability of the firm's cash flows results in a coefficient of variation for the firm of .15 based on an expected cash flow value of $8.5 million and a standard deviation of $1.265 million (these values would be determined by a process similar to the one shown in Table 16-2). Assume also that the prevailing risk-free interest rate is 8.5 percent.

corporate risk-return tradeoff

From these data, it is possible to develop an approximate *corporate risk-return tradeoff* for United Electronic Components. Such a tradeoff is depicted as a straight line in Exhibit 16-1. The risk-free return establishes the lowest possible return that is acceptable when there is no variability in possible returns. Next, United's coefficient of variation of .15 can be plotted against its cost of capital, or the return required for the firm's risk class. This makes it possible to describe an approximate risk-return tradeoff line for United, in order to adjust discount rates for projects with risks that are higher or lower than the firm's average riskiness.

The equation representing United's risk-return tradeoff line to be used for adjusting for project risk differences can be expressed as:

$$k = R_f + 10CV \tag{16-5}$$

where the risk premium is measured as the risk-return line's slope of 10 (i.e., the change in rise over the change in run) times the coefficient of variation (*CV*) figure. Of course, the slope of United's tradeoff line is subject to changes in outlook for economic activity. A pessimistic outlook would be reflected in a steeper slope, whereas a more optimistic outlook would be associated with a flatter slope.

Earlier in the chapter, Project EXP1's coefficient of variation was estimated to be .149, or virtually the same as the firm's existing coefficient of variation of .15. EXP2's coefficient of variation was estimated to be .35. Thus project EXP1 would be in the same risk class as the firm's overall risk class and consequently should have its cash inflows discounted at a 10-percent rate.[2] In the case of Project EXP2, the appropriate risk-adjusted discount rate would be determined as:

$$k = R_f + 10CV$$

$$k = 8.5 + 10(.35)$$

$$k = 12\%$$

This risk-return relationship also is depicted in Exhibit 16-1 for Project EXP2. For the two projects being considered by United Electronic Components, estimates of their relevant risk-adjusted rates can be used to compare the projects on the basis of their risk-adjusted net present value,

---

[2]Of course, as was covered under the portfolio diversification and systematic risk discussion, the correlation and size of the project's cash flows could alter the firm's index of systematic risk. Consequently, if portfolio diversification is deemed desirable, the financial manager may select a lower discount rate for a project that is weakly (or possibly negatively) correlated with the firm's risk pattern.

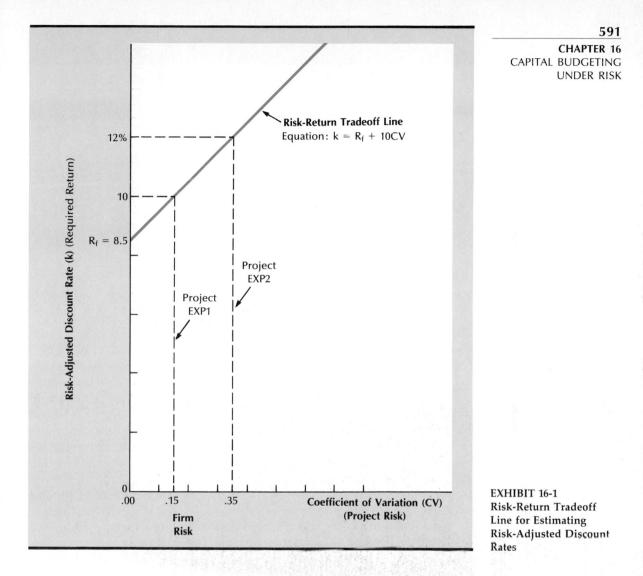

EXHIBIT 16-1
Risk-Return Tradeoff
Line for Estimating
Risk-Adjusted Discount
Rates

as is shown in Table 16-4. Based on the earlier example, Project EXP1 has an expected cash inflow of $8,500 per year for five years. The $8,500 annuity is multiplied by the 10-percent, five-year present value interest factor for an annuity (PVIFA) of 3.791 to get $32,224. Subtracting the present value cash outflows of $30,000 leaves a risk-adjusted net present value of $2,224. This is, of course, the same value that was calculated earlier, since the project's risk is the same as the firm's risk class.

Project EXP2 has a cash flow annuity of $9,000, which should be multiplied by the PVIFA factor of 3.605, representing a 12-percent risk-

TABLE 16-4 Net Present Value Comparison of Two Capital Projects Based on the Use of Risk-Adjusted Discount Rates

United Electronic Components Corporation

	Expected Annual Cash Inflow	Present Value Discount Factor	Present Value of Cash Flows
Project EXP1			
	$8,500	3.791*	$32,224 PVCI
			− 30,000 Investment
			$ 2,224 NPV
Project EXP2			
	$9,000	3.605**	32,445 PVCI
			− 30,000 Investment
			$ 2,445 NPV

*This is the present value interest of an annuity at 10 percent for five years (Appendix A, Table 4).
**This is the present value interest factor of an annuity at 12 percent for five years (Appendix A, Table 4).

adjusted rate for five years. The result is present value of cash inflows (PVCI) of $32,445 and a risk-adjusted net present value (NPV) of $2,445. Thus, even after adjusting for risk difference between the two projects, the risk-adjusted NPV is still $221 greater for Project EXP2. Of course, relative to a $30,000 investment, a $221 differential is rather small. The management of United Electronic Components might well wish to examine whether these two projects would contribute different portfolio diversification impacts on the firm's existing cash flow patterns before making a final choice. Most likely, however, portfolio diversification differences would be small, since the two projects were considered mutually exclusive. In summary, Project EXP2 contributes the higher risk-adjusted net present value and thus should be selected in order to best improve the value of the firm.

Another way of using risk-adjusted discount rate is in conjunction with independent projects. This can be demonstrated with an example comparing risk in a new product project, a replacement project, and a revenue expansion project.

Example

Comparing Projects of Varying Risk

The Savory Products Corporation is evaluating a replacement or cost reduction project and a revenue expansion project involving a new product line. A third type of project considered by Savory products might involve revenue expansion projects relating to existing product lines. Since these different types of projects are not likely to be of the same degree of riskiness, it is important to evaluate them on a risk-adjusted basis.

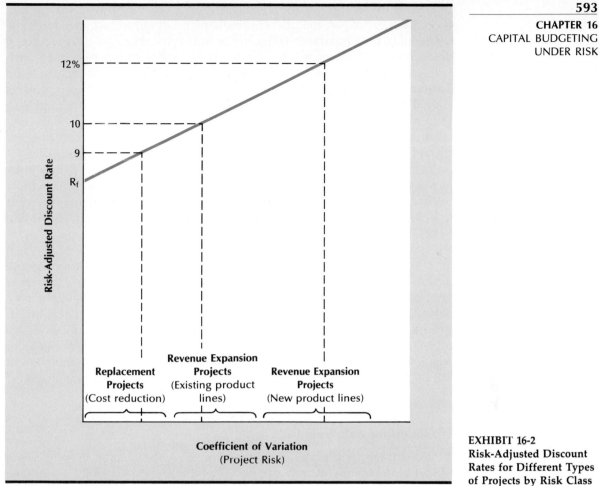

Exhibit 16-2 illustrates how Savory Products might view the relative riskiness of its three basic types of investment projects, assuming that Savory Products' cost of capital is 10 percent. The average riskiness of the firm might be established by examining the variability in the firm's cash flows. A risk-return tradeoff line for Savory Products could then be established, as was done for the United Electronic Components Corporation in Exhibit 16-1. In contrast, however, Exhibit 16-2 categorizes risk-return relationships by type of project.

Normally, one would expect replacement projects involving cost reduction efforts to be the least risky in terms of the variability of cash inflows. This expectation might lead Savory Products to discount replacement projects at a 9-percent rate, which is a rate lower than its overall cost of capital, because such projects are less risky than the firm's average risk class. Revenue expansion projects involving existing product lines might be expected to be comparable in risk to the firm's risk class and thus would be discounted at 10 percent. The variability of cash inflows associated with revenue expansion projects entering into new product lines would be greater than the firm's existing cash flow variability, and thus such projects should be associated with higher risk-adjusted discount rates, such as 12 percent for Savory Products.

In practice, it is difficult to quantify how much higher the discount rate should be in order to account adequately for increased riskiness. This is particularly true for revenue expansion projects, whereby the firm will be moving into new areas or product lines. Consequently, some firms subjectively establish hurdle, or discount, rates for projects that fall into different risk classes rather than trying actually to estimate a risk-return tradeoff line to be applied to independent projects.

It is also important to recognize that the portfolio diversification effect on a firm's cash flow systematic risk is likely to be greater for revenue expansion projects involving new product lines. For such expansion projects, the risks are higher and the cash flow streams are less likely to be perfectly positively correlated with the firm's existing cash flow stream, in contrast to the closer correlations for replacement projects and expansion projects involving existing product lines. The financial manager needs to weigh the potential trade-offs of possible increased portfolio diversification against greater project risk when evaluating expansion into new areas.

Investing with Beta

project beta

As shown in Chapter 6, which discussed the Capital Asset Pricing Model, an investment's risk can be viewed with respect to its systematic relation to the stock market as computed by its beta coefficient. Conceptually, this idea can be applied to business investments, although there are severe practical problems in implementation. The idea is to determine the investment project's required rate of return and compare it against the expected rate of return (internal rate of return). For investments in stocks traded on national exchanges, expected and required rates of return tend to be equal.

When investment markets are imperfect, however, like those in which business investments are made, the expected rate of return is often different from the required rate of return. Thus, in such markets, there is a significant possibility of finding extremely profitable investments as well as making disastrous ones.

Most of the significant investments made by business firms are in investment markets, which can be very imperfect from the rate-of-return standpoint. Generally, the less competitive markets are, the greater the likelihood is that expected and required returns will not be the same.

Highly competitive markets tend to be more efficient because, as other investors recognize the above-minimum rates of return, they enter and compete the excess away.

Example

The Fun-Tek Corporation has developed and marketed a popular new video game. Due to its popularity, the game is expected to produce returns well in excess of those required given its level of risk. Two months after its introduction, five very similar games are introduced by Fun-Tek's competitors. Fun-Tek's higher-than-required rate of return is protected somewhat by patents, trademarks, copyrights, brand image, and distribution system, all of which tend to weaken the abilities of its competitors. Yet, through competition, Fun-Tek's sales, profit margins, and expected returns become lower than first expected, tending towards equilibrium.

Application of the CAPM Approach[3]

In order to apply the Capital Asset Pricing Model to business projects, the beta of the project must be estimated along with the expected return on the "market" and the risk-free rate. With these inputs, the required rate of return on a business investment is calculated with the Security Market Line equation:

$$\text{Required rate of return, } k_{\text{project}} = R_f + (R_m - R_f)\beta_{\text{project}}$$

While investment betas can be estimated for stocks, they are much more difficult to estimate for business investments, particularly when new products are being considered.

Surrogate Betas. As a way of getting around the practical problems of estimating an individual project's beta, companies often employ the concept of surrogate betas, in which betas are estimated for divisions or major lines of business by examining the betas of publicly traded companies in those lines of business. For example, a company considering an investment in a new entertainment product, such as a compact disc player, might examine the betas of publicly traded companies heavily involved in the compact disc market. The idea is to get a better estimate of the systematic risks in such investments.

surrogate betas

---

[3]Using the CAPM to estimate the project cost of capital is discussed in more detail in Chapter 17.

Other Limitations of the CAPM Approach

In addition to the difficulty in estimating an investment's beta, other practical issues must be addressed in applying the capital asset pricing model to business investments. For example, the business investment market typically departs significantly from the market efficiency assumptions underlying the CAPM. Further, while investments in stocks are easily reversed (i.e., can be liquidated), business investments are not readily liquidated. Often they can be liquidated only at substantial economic loss.

Moreover, the very concept of a "market portfolio," which is so critical to the CAPM, may be completely alien to the analysis of investment risk from the standpoint of management. For example, the project manager responsible for the performance of one investment does not have the benefit of project diversification. To him or her, the relevant investment risk is more accurately measured by the total risk of the investment, rather than by only its market risk as indicated by the CAPM. This can lead to serious overestimates of risk, higher-than-required rates of return from investments, and reduced innovation.

Example

Assume that the Acme Company produces many different products. Joe Smith, product manager, is considering whether to propose that the company manufacture a new product, Product #19. Joe knows that, if he proposes the investment and it is adopted, he will be assigned to manage it. As far as Joe is concerned, product #19's performance will reflect company-specific risks, industrywide risks and marketwide risks. He knows that any of these could turn the product into a dismal failure. Since he will be rewarded or penalized for the performance of Product #19, Joe sees considerable risk in the new idea.

The CAPM assumes that the shareholders' perspective should dominate, yet getting managers to adopt this perspective when evaluating investment risks is another serious practical obstacle. Such violations of the CAPM assumptions require, at the least, higher rates of return than implied by the CAPM. Just how such premiums for departures from the CAPM assumptions should be determined is as yet unknown.

All of the serious limitations involved in employing the CAPM to business investment decisions notwithstanding, managers cannot ignore the fact that shareholders' expectations of future returns all reflect shareholders' assessments of business investments undertaken by the firm.

Since current and prospective shareholders, through the equilibrating mechanism of the market, determine the price of the company's common stock, shareholders' expectations must be incorporated in investment decisions made by the firm if stock price is to be maximized.

Certainty Equivalent Technique

An alternative way of recognizing and adjusting for risk differences between projects is to adjust the expected cash inflows. When the risk-adjusted discount technique is used, the discount rate includes both a time value of money component (the risk-free rate) and a degree-of-risk component (the risk premium). It is sometimes argued that the time value and risk components should be treated separately so that relative degrees of risk can be observed easily.

certainty equivalent

The certainty equivalent technique requires that the expected cash inflow values be adjusted downward to a "certain" or minimum level that management would be willing to accept in lieu of the distribution of possible cash inflow outcomes that could occur. This is done by multiplying a certainty equivalent factor (α, or alpha), which has a range between zero and 1.00, times the expected cash inflow for a particular year. If there is no variance in possible outcomes around the expected cash inflow, there would be no risk; thus a value of 1.00 would be assigned. But, as uncertainty or risk increases, a manager is likely to be indifferent between the expected cash inflow and a lesser amount that would be known with certainty. For cash flows in a given risk class, denoted by coefficient of variation measures, one might apply a certainty equivalent factor of .9. A .8 factor might be used for cash flows in the next higher risk class, and so forth. The certainty equivalent technique can best be illustrated by returning to the two mutually exclusive projects under consideration by United Electronic.

Example

A Certainty Equivalent Comparison

At United Electronic Components Corporation, Project EXP1 had an annual expected cash inflow of $8,500 with a coefficient of variation of .15. Since this project's degree of riskiness is typical of the firm's risk class, management might assign a certainty equivalent factor of, say .95 to its cash inflows. Project EXP2 has an annual expected cash inflow of $9,000 but a coefficient of variation of .35. United uses a certainty equivalent factor of .90 for projects with cash flow coefficients of variation in the .30 to .40 range.[4]

Based on this information, the risk-adjusted net present values can be calculated for each project being considered by United, applying the cer-

---

[4]In this example, we are applying the same certainty equivalent factor for cash inflows expected in each of the five years of operation. Risk, of course, sometimes will increase over time. In such cases, we would apply a lower certainty equivalent factor in, say, the fifth year than in the first year.

tainty equivalent technique. Table 16-5 shows that the expected annual cash inflows are first adjusted downward by the appropriate certainty equivalent factors in order to reflect risk differences between the two projects. Then the certainty equivalent cash inflows are discounted by the present value interest factor for an annuity (PVIFA) at 8.5 percent for five years. The risk-free interest rate is used as the discount rate to denote the time value of money. Differences in risk have been captured by adjusting the five-year expected cash inflow streams by the appropriate certainty equivalent factors.

Table 16-5 indicates a risk-adjusted net present value of $1,824 for Project EXP1. However, after using the certainty equivalent technique to adjust for risk differences, the net present value is still $98 higher for Project EXP2. This suggests that United's firm value will be maximized by selecting Project EXP2. These findings are consistent with the findings from Table 16-4, as would be expected when risk-adjusted discount rates were used to estimate risk-adjusted net present values.

TABLE 16-5 Net Present Value Comparison of Two Capital Projects Based on the Use of Certainty Equivalent Risk Adjustments

United Electronic Components Corporation

Expected Annual Cash Inflow	Certainty Equivalent Factor	Certainty Equivalent Cash Inflow	Present Value Discount Factor	Present Value of Cash Flows
Project EXP1				
$8,500	.95	$8,075	3.941*	$31,824 PVCI
				− 30,000 PVCO
				$ 1,824 NPV
Project EXP2				
$9,000	.90	$8,100	3.941*	$31,922 PVCI
				− 30,000 PVCO
				$ 1,922 NPV

*This is the present value interest factor of an annuity at 8.5 percent for five years.

By now it should be clear that implementing the certainty equivalent technique is more difficult than using risk-adjusted discount rates because of the need subjectively to assess proper certainty factors. This probably accounts for the limited use of this risk adjusting technique in actual practice by financial managers. More frequent use of risk-adjusted discount rates occurs in practice, whereby time value (risk-free) and degree-of-risk

(risk premium) components are combined to form a single discount rate for each risk class.

OTHER RISK ADJUSTMENT CONCEPTS

Earlier in the chapter, the concept of sensitivity analysis was mentioned, whereby several independent estimates of cash flows are made using different assumptions (often by different departments in the firm) or estimates are made for different states of the economy. For example, recall the pessimistic, typical, and optimistic states used for estimating cash inflows for the two projects being evaluated by the United Electronic Components Corporation. Instead of calculating expected cash inflow values for purposes of estimating a net present value for each project as was done in Table 16-1, a net present value could have been calculated for each project for each of the three economic activity scenarios. This would have provided a sensitivity analysis of possible net present value outcomes for each project. Because of the greater variability in possible cash inflows observed in Tables 16-1 and 16-2 for Project EXP2, a sensitivity analysis of net present values would also show greater variability for Project EXP2. United's management then would have to decide subjectively whether the greater dispersion in NPVs for Project EXP2 was warranted on the basis of possibly higher average NPVs relative to those expected for Project EXP1.

Some firms also use simulation techniques to develop profiles of possible net-present-value (or internal-rate-of-return) outcomes for risky projects. In order to conduct simulations, probability distributions must first be estimated for a number of variables that affect cash inflows and outflows. Included would be distributions for cash revenues and cash operating expenses, as well as distributions for the project's investment cost, its expected life, and possible salvage values. The impact of different tax rates and depreciation methods also may be incorporated in the simulations. Through the use of a computer, values are randomly selected from each relevant distribution, possibly combined with a specific tax rate and depreciation method, and then used to estimate the project's net present value. The simulation process is repeated many times until a probability distribution of possible net present values is constructed. The expected NPV, along with the distribution's dispersion for each project, can be compared against those for other projects as an aid in the management decision process.

Decision Trees

The earlier analysis of capital budgeting projects assumed that expected cash inflows in a given year were independent of the cash inflows in other years. Sometimes the cash inflows in one year are conditional or dependent on the cash inflows in a prior year. If this is the case, a decision-tree technique would be used for evaluating risk projects.

sensitivity analysis

scenarios

simulation

decision trees

Example

A Comparison of Cash Inflow Possibilities

Assume that the Rubber Tree Company can purchase a new machine for $20,000, which will help expand an existing product line. The firm plans to discount the project's cash inflows at its cost of capital of 12 percent, since the project's risk is comparable to the firm's existing risk class. Possible cash inflows for the first year, along with their associated probabilities of occurrence, are projected as follows:

Outcome	Cash Inflow	Probability of Occurrence
A	$10,000	.2
B	12,000	.6
C	14,000	.2

For each of these three possible cash inflow outcomes for the first year, the following possible outcomes and probabilities are projected for the second year:

If Outcome A		If Outcome B		If Outcome C	
Cash Inflow	*Probability*	*Cash Inflow*	*Probability*	*Cash Inflow*	*Probability*
$8,000	.4	$10,000	.4	$15,000	.4
9,000	.6	12,000	.6	18,000	.6

A decision-tree technique, as shown in Table 16-6, is applied to evaluate whether the Rubber Tree Tire Company should invest in the proposed machine. It can be seen that the worst possible outcome would be Path 1, with a cash inflow of $10,000 in the first year followed by $8,000 in the second year. In contrast, the best possible sequence would be Path 6, with $14,000 in year one and $18,000 in year two. The probability of a given path or sequence occurring is the joint probability or product of the path's associated probabilities for each year. For example, the joint probability for the worst path (No. 1) would be .08 (.2 times .4), whereas the joint probability for the best possible path (No. 6) would be .12 (.2 times .6).

In order to calculate the average or expected net present value for the machine, the net present value for each possible outcome must be calculated in the decision tree (using the same approach as applied earlier in the chapter). Then each NPV is multiplied by the joint probability for its asso-

TABLE 16-6 Decision Tree Analysis of a Capital Project

Year 0	Year 1	Year 2	Path
		.4 $8,000(.797)	(1)
	.2 $10,000(.893)		
		.6 $9,000(.797)	(2)
		.4 $10,000(.797)	(3)
−$20,000	.6 $12,000(.893)		
		.6 $12,000(.797)	(4)
		.4 $15,000(.797)	(5)
	.2 $14,000(.893)		
		.6 $18,000(.797)	(6)

Path	Net Present Value (12% Rate)	×	Joint Probability (YR. 1 × YR. 2)	=	Expected Net Present Value
1	− $4,694		.08		− $376
2	− 3,897		.12		− 468
3	− 1,314		.24		− 315
4	280		.36		101
5	4,457		.08		357
6	6,848		.12		822
			1.00		Expected NPV $121

ciated path. The final step is to sum the joint probability-weighted NPVs to arrive at an expected NPV. On the basis of the net present value of $121 shown in Table 16-6, a manager would recommend that the Rubber Tree Tire Company purchase the proposed machine.

SUMMARY

Capital budgeting probably means the difference between success and failure for many business concerns. Regardless of the size of the company or the level at which the decisions are made, the principles should be the same. A manager is committing a sum of money today in return for a expected stream of net cash benefits in the future.

Because managers and investors are averse to risk, they must consider differences in project risk (variability of possible outcomes between proposed capital projects). Capital budgeting decisions must be made in a risk-return context in order to maximize the value of owners' equity. This means that capital budgeting methods must be modified or adjusted if there exist significant differences in risk among projects.

The two basic procedures for adjusting for project risk difference are the risk-adjusted discount technique and the certainty equivalent technique. Risk-adjusted discount rates are easier to implement, and thus they are more widely used in practice by financial managers. When it is desirable to reduce the probability of bankruptcy, financial managers may also be interested in examining the extent to which proposed projects will result in portfolio diversification and possible systematic risk reductions.

MULTIPLE CHOICE QUESTIONS

1. There are two basic ways for recognizing and then adjusting for project risk: the risk-adjusted discount technique and:
   a) Compounding technique
   b) Variance
   c) The certainty equivalent technique
   d) Discounting at the risk-adjusted rate

2. The certainty equivalent technique involves:
   a) Calculating the correlation coefficient
   b) Computing the variance
   c) Adjusting the uncertain stream of cash inflows
   d) Discounting at the risk-adjusted rate

3. The risk-return tradeoff line relates an investment's coefficient of variation to:

   a) The certainty equivalent
   b) Its applicable risk-adjusted rate of discount
   c) The payback period
   d) Its net present value

4. If the cash flow outcomes in one year are conditional on results in prior years, a _____ analysis should be used:

   a) Regression
   b) Break-even
   c) Payback period
   d) Decision tree

5. An index of cash flow systematic risk of 2.0 suggests that, when economic activity changes by 10 percent, there is a change in the same direction of _____ percent in the company's cash flow after taxes.

   a) 20 percent
   b) 5 percent
   c) 10 percent
   d) 12 percent

6. By applying the firm's cost of capital as the appropriate hurdle rate, we are assuming the projects under consideration:

   a) Are uncorrelated with existing projects
   b) Are equal in risk with existing projects
   c) Have no systematic risk
   d) Are risk reducing

7. The coefficient of variation is calculated by:

   a) Expected return divided by standard deviation
   b) Correlation coefficient times standard deviation
   c) Standard deviation divided by expected return
   d) Square root of variance

DISCUSSION QUESTIONS

1. What is project risk? Identify and explain how it is measured.

2. Explain what is meant by portfolio diversification. How might increased portfolio diversification alter a firm's cash flow systematic risk?

3. One procedure for adjusting project risk difference is the risk-adjusted discount technique. Explain and describe how a firm might establish various risk-adjusted discount rates to be used in evaluating capital projects.

4. The certainty equivalent technique may be used to adjust for differences in risk between projects. Explain how this technique might be used to calculate risk-adjusted net present values.

5. Sensitivity analysis and simulation techniques can be used to identify and establish risk difference between projects. Explain.

6. Under what conditions would the use of decision trees aid in analyzing and comparing risk-adjusted net present values between projects?

SOLVED PROBLEMS

coefficient of variation

SP-1. In order to get a better handle on the actual risk in product C, the Xero Corporation has developed probability estimates of the net cash flows after taxes. These estimates are assumed to be the same in each year of the product's five-year life.

CFAT/Year	Probability
−$10,000	.20
30,000	.60
50,000	.20

The investment will cost a total of $78,000.

a) Calculate the expected cash flow in each year of the product's life.

b) Calculate the investment's expected IRR. (Be approximate.)

c) Calculate the variance, standard deviation, and coefficient of variation for the investment.

d) If Xero uses the equation: $k = R_f + 20CV$, where $R_f = 9\%$ and CV is the coefficient of variation, to estimate its risk-adjusted discount rate, calculate the project's NPV. Should the project be accepted?

e) Graph the risk-return tradeoff line. Indicate where the IRR calculated in part (b) above would appear in relation to the line. Also indicate what the investment's return should be — the required rate of return given its level of risk as calculated in part (d) above.

certainty equivalent

SP-2. The president of Acme Manufacturing Company tries to stay up to date on the most recent financial techniques. He has just finished reading an article about the theoretical superiority of the certainty equivalent method relative to the risk-adjusted rate. To try out the comparison and, at the same time, to test his intuition, he has quickly gathered the following information on a recent investment proposal. The investment proposal involved a cost reduction investment. Such proposals were normally expected to have a cost of capital of 20 percent. Alongside each of the cash flows projected, the president has jotted down his "gut feel" for what his certainty equivalent would be. The risk-free rate is 10 percent. The investment cost is $65,000.

Year	CFAT	Certainty Equivalent
1	$10,000	.90
2	20,000	.85
3	30,000	.65
4	30,000	.65
5	30,000	.65

a) Calculate the investment's net present value using the certainty equivalent method.
b) Calculate the investment's net present value using the risk-adjusted method.
c) How do your answers in (a) and (b) compare? How would you explain a difference in recommendations if the certainty equivalent method indicated an accept, for example, and the risk-adjusted method indicated a reject?

SP-3. Assume that the risk-free rate of return is expected to be 10 percent and the expected return on the market is 15 percent.   *CAPM*

a) Calculate the required returns from the following investments.

Investment	Beta
1	2.5
2	2.0
3	1.0
4	.5
5	0

b) Construct a graph showing your answer to part (a) above. On the 'x' axis put the values for beta and on the 'y' axis put the required return associated with each beta. Draw a line connecting the points.
c) Assume that the expected returns to be received from each investment are calculated as follows:

Investment	Expected Return
1	21.0%
2	19.0
3	17.0
4	14.0
5	10.0

Compare the required return with the expected returns calculated in part (a). Plot the expected returns on the graph you prepared for part (b) above. Which investments are underpriced, overpriced, or correctly priced? (Hint: an underpriced investment is one whose expected return is greater than its required return.) Which investments should be accepted? Rejected?

PROBLEMS

coefficient of variation

1. The Axion Company has developed probability estimates of the net cash flows after taxes for Product A. These estimates are assumed to be the same in each year of the product's expected five-year life.

CFAT/Year	Probability
− $50,000	.10
150,000	.70
200,000	.20

The investment will cost a total of $400,000.

a) Calculate the expected cash flow in each year of the product's life.
b) Calculate the investment's expected IRR.
c) Calculate the variance, standard deviation and coefficient of variation for the investment.
d) If Axion uses the equation: $k = R_f + 20CV$, where k is the required rate of return, $R_f = 9.6\%$, and CV is the coefficient of variation, to estimate its risk-adjusted discount rate, calculate the project's NPV. Should the product be adopted?
e) Graph the risk-return tradeoff line. Indicate where the IRR calculated in part (b) above would appear in relation to the line. Also indicate what the investment's return should be — the required rate of return given its level of risk as calculated in part (d) above.

certainty equivalent

2. The president of Amos Clamp Company tries to stay up to date on the most recent financial techniques. She has just finished reading an article about the theoretical superiority of the certainty equivalent method relative to the risk-adjusted rate method. To try out the comparison and, at the same time, to test her intuition, she has quickly gathered the following information on a recent investment proposal. The investment proposal involved a cost reduction investment. Such proposals were normally expected to have a cost of capital of 20 percent. Alongside each of the cash flows projected, the president has jotted down her "gut

feel" for what the certainty equivalent would be. The risk-free rate of
return is 8 percent. The investment cost is $130,000.

607

CHAPTER 16
CAPITAL BUDGETING
UNDER RISK

Year	CFAT	Certainty Equivalent
1	$20,000	.90
2	40,000	.85
3	60,000	.65
4	60,000	.65
5	60,000	.65

a) Calculate the investment's net present value using the certainty equivalent method.
b) Calculate the investment's net present value using the risk-adjusted method.
c) How do your answers in (a) and (b) compare? How would you explain a difference in recommendations if the certainty equivalent method indicated an accept, for example, and the risk-adjusted method indicated a reject?

3. The Jones Cycle Company is evaluating an investment project that requires a $90,000 cash outlay. Cash inflows are projected in each of the next five years as follows:

coefficient of variation

Forecast	Probability of Occurrence
$30,000	.3
25,000	.4
40,000	.3

a) Estimate the internal rate of return for the project.
b) Indicate the relative riskiness of this project compared with a coefficient of variation for another project of .35.
c) If Jones Cycle uses the equation: $k = R_f + 20CV$, where R_f is 8 percent and CV is the coefficient of variation, as its risk-adjusted discount or hurdle rate, should the project be accepted?

4. Harold's Take-Out is a small chain of short-order restaurants. Management is considering investing $50,000 either in another hot shop or in a feed and grain business. Annual cash inflows from the hot shop are estimated at $12,400, whereas annual cash inflows from the feed and grain business are estimated at $10,500—in each case for a 10-year period.

portfolio diversification

a) Initially, the firm estimates its cost of capital in the hot shop business to be 15 percent. On this basis, what is the net present value of each of the two investments, and which would be chosen?

b) However, upon reflection, management realized that the feed and grain business is less risky. Study of market data on feed and grain companies suggests that a reasonable estimate of cost of capital for this line of endeavor is 10 percent. With this added consideration of risk, which is the more attractive investment?

expected values

5. An investment proposal costing $110,000 is being examined by Sherry Foods, Inc. The investment will last 10 years. A pessimistic forecast projects cash earnings after taxes of $14,500 per year, compared with an optimistic forecast of $20,000 per year. Sherry Foods assigns a probability of occurrence of .4 for the pessimistic estimate and a .6 probability for the optimistic estimate. The firm also has a policy of using a required rate of return of 10 percent for replacement projects, 12 percent (its cost of capital) for revenue expansion projects into existing product lines, and 16 percent for projects involving new areas or product lines.

a) Calculate the annual expected cash inflows associated with the proposed equipment investment.

b) Would you recommend acceptance or rejection of this project if it involved an increase in output capacity and sales for an existing product line?

c) Would you recommend purchase of the proposed equipment if it involved expansion into a new product line by Sherry Foods?

portfolio diversification

6. The Volatile Liquids Corporation is considering three mutually exclusive projects. Calculations suggest that the projects are comparable in terms of project risk measures and expected net present values. However, the firm is concerned about possible portfolio implications, since any of the projects will increase the average asset and cash flow size of the firm by 50 percent. The firm's expected annual cash flows prior to the expansion are shown, projected by state of economic climate (with an equal probability of each state occurring), and relative to an index of economic activity, as follows:

State of Economy	Annual Cash Flow	Index of Economic Activity
Recession	$ 85,000	180
Normal	100,000	200
Rapid growth	115,000	220

Anticipated cash flows by state of economic activity for each of the three projects are as follows:

State of Economy	Project 1	Project 2	Project 3
Recession	$40,000	$50,000	$60,000
Normal	50,000	50,000	50,000
Rapid growth	60,000	50,000	40,000

a) Estimate Volatile Liquids' index of cash flow systematic risk prior to making an expansion decision. Explain the implications of your estimate.

b) Calculate the impact of each proposed project's cash flow on the firm's existing cash flow by state of economic activity. What do your findings suggest in terms of the portfolio diversification implications of each project?

c) On a combined basis (each project combined with the existing firm), indicate how each of the three alternatives will be affected by the state of the economy. How will Volatile Liquids' index of cash flow systematic risk change or be influenced by each of the three expansion alternatives?

d) Which project would you recommend that the Volatile Liquids Corporation accept if management wants to lessen the sensitivity of the firm's operations relative to changes in economic activity? Why might management have such an objective?

7. Assume that you have been asked to evaluate an investment project for *certainty equivalent* the Personal Computer Manufacturing Company. The project will require an initial investment of $120,000 and will last 6 years. Cash earnings after taxes are projected in *each* of the next six years as $34,400. The risk-free interest rate is 7 percent and the firm has a policy of assigning certainty equivalent factors of .90 to the cash inflows of projects equal in risk to the firm's risk class, such as revenue expansion projects involving existing product lines. For projects that require the firm's entrance into new product areas, certainty equivalent factors of .80 are used to adjust cash inflows.

a) Calculate the risk-adjusted net present value for the project if it involves expansion of existing product lines.

b) Would the project be acceptable on a risk-adjusted net present value basis if it involved expansion into new product areas?

c) Calculate the risk-adjusted internal rate of return based on the assumptions in Part (b). Would you recommend acceptance of the project?

8. The Toner Manufacturing Corporation is trying to decide whether to invest in a new project. Two mutually exclusive projects are available, *decision trees* with each requiring an investment of $30,000. Project XX has expected

cash inflows of $20,000 per year in each of the next two years. In contrast, it is estimated that the cash inflows for Project YY will be either $18,000 or $22,000 (each with an equal probability of .5 of occurring) next year. And, if the $18,000 occurs in the first year, cash inflow possibilities for the second year are: $15,000 (probability of .3), $18,000 (probability of .4), and $20,000 (probability of .3). In the event that the first year's cash inflow is $22,000 for Project YY, possible second-year cash inflows are: $18,000 (probability of .3), $22,000 (probability of .4), and $27,000 (probability of .3). The firm uses a 14-percent discount rate for deciding whether to invest in projects comparable in risk to the ones under consideration.

a) Calculate the risk-adjusted net present value for Project XX.
b) Calculate the worst possible net present value outcome for Project YY. Also calculate the best possible net present value outcome for Project YY.
c) Diagram the decision tree analysis that is required for evaluating Project YY.
d) Calculate the risk-adjusted expected net present value for Project YY.
e) Which project, if any, would you recommend that the Toner Manufacturing Corporation invest in? Why?

SOLUTIONS TO SOLVED PROBLEMS

SP-1. a) The expected cash flow in each year will be the same since neither the estimates nor their probabilities will change.

$$\text{Exp. CFAT/Yr} = (-\$10,000)(.20) + (\$30,000)(.60) + (\$50,000)(.20)$$

$$= \$26,000$$

b) $$(\text{PVIFA}, k\%, 5 \text{ years}) = \frac{\$78,000}{\$26,000} = 3.000$$

A PVIFA of 3.000, given $n = 5$ is closest to an interest rate of 20 percent (the PVIFA for 20 percent, five years is 2.991).

c)

CFAT/Yr. (1)	Prob. (2)	Exp. Value (3)	(4) = (1) − (3)	(4)^2	5 = (2) × (4)
−10,000	.20	26,000	−36,000	$(-36,000)^2$	259,200,000
30,000	.60	26,000	4,000	$(4,000)^2$	9,600,000
50,000	.20	26,000	24,000	$(24,000)^2$	115,200,000
				Variance	= 384,000,000
				Standard Deviation	= 19,596

The coefficient of variation is calculated by dividing the standard deviation by the expected value:

$$\text{Coefficient of variation} = \frac{\text{Standard deviation}}{\text{Expected value}}$$

$$= \frac{\$19,596}{26,000}$$

$$= .75$$

d)
$$k = R_f + 20CV$$

$$= 9\% + 20(.75)$$

$$= 24.00\%$$

For an interest rate of 24 percent and $n = 5$, the PVIFA factor is 2.745.

$$\text{PVCI} = \text{Annuity CFAT} \times \text{PVIFA}$$

$$= \$26,000 \times 2.745$$

$$= \$71,370$$

$$- \text{PVCI} = -78,000$$

$$= \text{NPV} = \$-6,630$$

Since the NPV is negative, the investment should be rejected. Note that the IRR of the investment is also lower than the 24 percent required. This would also indicate a rejection.

e) Graph not shown, refer to Exhibit 16.1.

SP-2. a) First, get the certainty equivalent cash flow by multiplying the estimated cash flow times the certainty equivalent factor. Next, take the present value of the cash flows discounted at the risk-free rate (remember, you have already adjusted for risk).

(1) Year	(2) Cash Flow	(3) Certainty equivalent	(4) = (2) × (3)	(5) PVIF (10%)	(6) = (4) × (5)
1	$10,000	.90	$ 9,000	.909	$ 8,181
2	20,000	.85	17,000	.826	14,042
3	30,000	.65	19,500	.751	14,645
4	30,000	.65	19,500	.683	13,319
5	30,000	.65	19,500	.621	12,110
			Total Present Value		$62,297
			− Investment		−65,000
			Net Present Value		−2,703

The negative net present value (−2,703) indicates that the investment should be rejected.

b) With the risk-adjusted rate, of course, one simply discounts the cash flows by the appropriate discount rate (20 percent in this case).

Year	Cash Flow	PVIF (20%)	PV (20%)
1	$10,000	.833	$ 8,330
2	$20,000	.694	13,880
3	$30,000	.579	17,370
4	$30,000	.482	14,460
5	$30,000	.402	12,060
		Total present value:	$66,100
		− Investment required	65,000
		Net present value	$ 1,100

The risk-adjusted rate method results in a positive net present value, indicating acceptance of the proposal.

c) The certainty equivalent and risk-adjusted rate methods result in different recommendations. Which one is "correct?" In principle, the certainty equivalent method is better because it forces specific assessments of attitudes towards risk. However, if properly calculated, both the risk-adjusted and certainty equivalent methods should provide the same answer. The difference in evaluations produced by the two methods in this case should motivate the president to re-examine his certainty equivalent estimates and the appropriateness of the 20-percent cost of capital arbitrarily assigned.

SP-3. a) Use the equation

$$k = R_f + (R_m - R_f)B_e$$

Investment	Beta	Required Return
1	2.5	22.5%
2	2.0	20.0%
3	1.0	15.0%
4	.5	12.5%
5	0	10.0%

b)

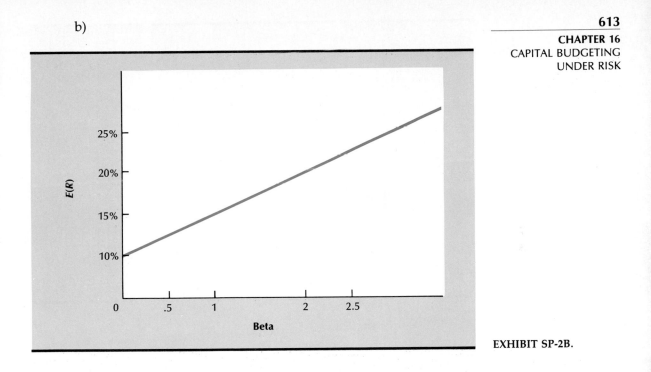

EXHIBIT SP-2B.

c)

Investment	Beta	Required Return	Expected Return	Evaluation
1	2.5	22.5%	21%	Overpriced
2	2.0	20.0%	19%	Overpriced
3	1.0	15.0%	17%	Underpriced
4	.5	12.5%	14%	Underpriced
5	0	10.0%	10%	Correctly priced

Investments three and four should be accepted because they will return more than the required amount.

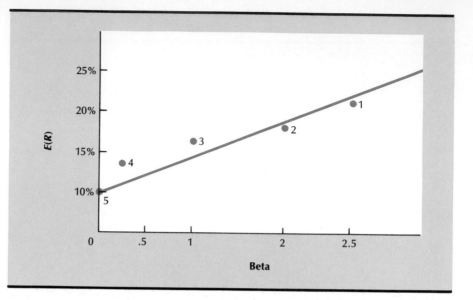

EXHIBIT SP-2C.

REFERENCES

Donaldson, Gordon. "Strategic Hurdle Rates of Capital Investment." *Harvard Business Review,* March-April 1972, pp. 50–58.

Hertz, David B. "Risk Analysis in Capital Investment." *Harvard Business Review* January-February 1964, pp. 95–106.

Lewellen, Wilbur G., and Michael E. Long. "Simulation versus Single-Value Estimates in Capital Expenditure Analysis." *Decision Sciences,* 1972, pp. 19–33.

Magee, John F. "How to Use Decision Trees in Capital Investment." *Harvard Business Review,* September-October 1964, pp. 79–96.

Osteryoung, Jerome S., Elton Scott, and Gordon S. Roberts. "Selecting Capital Projects with the Coefficient of Variation." *Financial Management,* Summer 1977, pp. 65–70.

Schall, Lawrence D., Gary L. Sundem, and William R. Geijsbeek. "Survey and Analysis of Capital Budgeting Methods." *Journal of Finance,* March 1978, pp. 281–287.

Weston, J. Fred. "Investment Decisions Using the Capital Asset Pricing Model." *Financial Management,* Spring 1973, pp. 25–33.

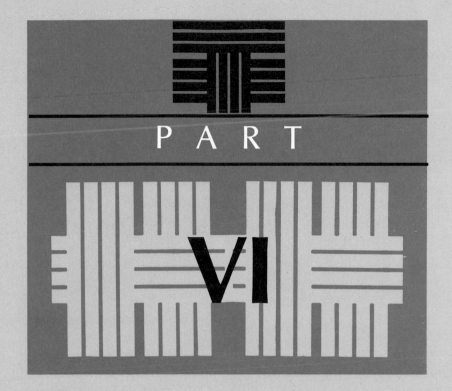

PART

VI

COST OF CAPITAL AND VALUATION

CHAPTER

17

THE COST OF CAPITAL

he cost of capital is the minimum rate of return that must be produced by investments if they are to be acceptable. This idea has been at the heart of all the discussions of investment analysis. For example, when one discounts an investment's cash flows to compute its net present value, the discount rate used is the cost of capital for the investment. Likewise, in evaluating investments in cash balances, inventory, and accounts receivable, when one refers to the opportunity cost of funds one means the cost of capital relevant to these investments.

Until now, the cost of capital for an investment was simply given, or assumed. This chapter shows how the cost of capital itself may be estimated. Already, however, three things should be apparent about the cost of capital: first, knowing the cost of capital is crucial to proper investment analysis; second, the cost of capital is investment-specific, meaning that it depends on the nature of the investment to be made and thus can vary from one type of investment to another; and third, the cost of capital is another one of those ideas in finance that shows up in many forms and has many synonyms.

Objectives and Organization of this Chapter

The objectives of this chapter are to explain the concept of the cost of capital, show how it may be estimated, and illustrate how it may be applied to investment analysis. For clarity and ease of presentation, we will first calculate the cost of capital for the firm as a whole. Then we will see how the idea may be extended to specific investments.

The first section of the chapter discusses the importance of the cost of capital idea. The second section defines the elements in the cost of capital. The third section illustrates how the component costs of major types of capital can be estimated. The fourth section explores methods for estimating the optimal mix of capital types. The fifth section extends the cost of capital methodology to specific investments.

THE COST OF CAPITAL IDEA

Capital, like labor, is needed by the firm to carry on its business (e.g., to purchase inventory, carry accounts receivable, and purchase equipment). The investors who supply debt and equity capital to a corporation expect compensation in the forms of interest income (if they supply debt to the company) and profits (if they own stock in the company), just as the employees who supply labor to the corporation expect compensation in the forms of salaries, wages, and fringe benefits.

cost of capital

The compensation to employees for labor represents a cost (e.g., salaries and wage expenses) to the corporation and, by the same token, the compensation to the suppliers of capital represents a cost (in this case the cost of capital) to the corporation. Thus the cost of capital has a dual character. These ideas, expected compensation and cost, are two sides of the same coin. Thus when an investor buys stock in a corporation, the minimum rate of return expected by the shareholder is the same thing as the corporation's cost of equity capital.

The cost of debt capital is relatively easy to estimate, but determining the cost of equity is difficult, particularly for large corporations, since there are no documents spelling out what rate of return must be earned for stockholders. Nor, can management simply ask stockholders what minimum returns they expect, for there may be thousands and even millions of individual stockholders. Nonetheless, without some idea of its cost of capital, the corporation's management will not know until it is too late whether it has satisfied stockholders or disappointed them.

When shareholders do not receive the minimum returns they expect from the corporation, stock prices fall. The corporation may be making profits, but if it is not making *enough* profits its stock price will still fall. Conversely, if the corporation produces returns for stockholders which are greater than they expect, shareholders will be pleased and stock prices will rise.

We may conclude that the cost of capital for an investment is the rate of return that will leave the company's stock value unchanged, and thus it is as important to know an investment's cost of capital as it is to know its cash flows.

The Cost of Capital Vs. the Cost of Funds

A common error is to interpret an investment's cost of capital as the cost of the specific funds to be raised to undertake the investment. This is not correct, as illustrated in the following example.

Example

Assume that a company is evaluating an investment that will cost $1 million and produce an internal rate of return of 14 percent. The company's cost of debt has been estimated to be 12 percent and its cost of equity is 15 percent. Even though the investment's rate of return is greater than its cost of debt, it would be incorrect to decide that the investment should be undertaken if the firm is going to borrow.

By borrowing, the firm increases its financial risk and, hence, the returns that shareholders will require. Thus, debt has an implicit as well as an explicit cost. By ignoring the impact on the cost of equity, the company will incorrectly estimate its cost of capital for the investment and possibly reduce the value of its stock. In order to include the implicit costs of debt, the firm needs to determine the costs of all capital sources as if they were all to be used in some pre-determined proportions to make the investment.

In addition, notice how an erroneous interpretation of the cost of capital can lead to inconsistent investment decisions. To see this, assume that the proposed investment is viewed as acceptable because the firm intends to finance it with borrowing. Since it has borrowed for this investment, assume that another investment, equivalent in all respects, will have to be financed with equity, which, according to this rule, would make the investment unacceptable.

DEFINING THE COST OF CAPITAL

The phrase, cost of capital, is really shorthand for its more formal title, *the after-tax weighted average marginal cost of capital.* Each part of this title has special significance for the manner in which the cost of capital should be estimated. Each of these features is examined in more detail in the following sections.

after-tax weighted average marginal cost of capital

After-Taxes

When one refers to the cost of capital, one means the after-tax cost. This distinction is important because the cost of one of the types of capital raised by the corporation, debt, is tax deductible. In particular, the after-tax cost of debt is less than its pre-tax cost.[1] Since investment cash flows are typically evaluated on an after-tax basis, the cost of capital should also be on an after-tax basis.

To convert the before-tax cost of debt (k_d) to an after-tax cost, multiply it by $(1 - T)$, where T is the marginal tax rate. This is shown in Equation 17-1.

$$\text{After-tax cost of debt} = k_d \times (1 - T) \qquad (17\text{-}1)$$

[1]To see why, consider the following situation. Assume that a corporation is in a 34-percent tax bracket and produces $100 of profits before taxes, the IRS gets $34 and shareholders get $66. Now assume that the corporation takes out a loan that requires an interest payment of $100. Now profits before taxes are reduced to zero, the IRS gets nothing, and shareholders get nothing. However, the amount given up by shareholders is not $100, but really $66. The other $34 was effectively paid by the IRS.

Marginal Costs

The principal purpose for computing the cost of capital is to evaluate future or proposed investments and therefore the costs of incremental capital should be considered. For example, if the company currently has bonds outstanding carrying an interest rate of 12 percent but new borrowing will cost 13 percent, the relevant cost of debt is 13 percent.

A Weighted Average

When one refers to "the" cost of capital, one means the average cost of all capital to be used. This is due to the fact that each type of capital raised by the firm has its own particular cost, and each cost should be weighted by its relative importance to the total. The weights or relative proportions of each type of capital in the capital structure should reflect the firm's optimal capital structure—meaning the financing mix that minimizes its cost of capital.

For example, assume that a company's optimal capital structure consists of a mix of 40 percent debt, 10 percent preferred stock, and 50 percent common equity. The debt has a pre-tax cost of 12 percent; the preferred, 14 percent and the common equity, 16 percent. The marginal tax rate is 34 percent. The weighted average cost of capital (k_a) would be calculated using Equation 17-2.

$$k_a = w_d k_d (1 - T) + w_p k_p + w_e k_e \qquad (17\text{-}2)$$

$$= .40(12\%)(1 - .34) + .10(14\%) + .50(16\%)$$

$$= 12.57\%$$

where w_d represents the proportion of capital raised by debt; k_d is the pre-tax cost of debt; w_p is the proportion of capital raised from preferred stock; k_p is the cost of preferred stock; w_e is the proportion of the capital structure financed with common stock; and k_e is the cost of common equity. Notice that the term $(1 - T)$ converts the pre-tax cost of debt to an after-tax basis and that neither preferred nor common stock financing costs are affected by taxes.

ESTIMATING THE COMPONENT COSTS OF CAPITAL

In order to estimate the weighted average cost of capital, the sources and costs of capital must be identified. This discussion will assume that the firm uses three generic types of capital: debt capital, preferred stock, and common equity.

Cost of Debt

cost of debt k_d

The pre-tax cost of long-term debt can be defined as the yield to maturity bondholders require. As has been shown in Chapter 5, the yield to maturity on debt is the discount rate that equates the present value of bond payments made by the firm to the price of the bond. This can be formulated as shown in Equation 17-3.

$$P_b = \sum_{t=1}^{n} \frac{I_t}{(1 + k_d)} + \frac{P_n}{(1 + k_d)^n} \tag{17-3}$$

where I_t represents interest payments at time period t; P_n is the principal payment at maturity (period n); P_b is the current market price of the bond; and k_d is the yield to maturity (i.e., cost of debt).

Example

Calculating the Marginal After-Tax Cost of Debt

Assume the Ceder Company is trying to determine its marginal cost of debt by analyzing the value of its outstanding debt. The company has $10 million of 10-percent coupon bonds issued five years ago. Each bond has a face value of $1,000. The bonds have 10 years left before maturity. The firm pays interest semiannually. The firm's financial manager notes that the bonds are being traded at a discount price of $887. Thus, the yield to maturity lenders are currently requiring from Ace Company is more than 10 percent. If Ace issues new bonds, it will have to offer this higher yield to purchasers. To determine this yield, Ace's financial manager uses equation 17-3, solving for k_d.

$$\$887 = \sum_{t=1}^{20} \frac{50_t}{(1 + k_d)^t} + \frac{1000}{(1 + k_d)^{20}}$$

$$\$887 = \$50(\text{PVIFA}_{k\%,20}) + 1{,}000(\text{PVIF}_{k\%,20})$$

$$k_d = .12 = 12\%$$

Assuming a marginal tax rate of 34 percent, Ceder's after-tax cost of debt is:

$$k_d(1 - T) = 12\%(1 - .34) = 7.92\%$$

Cost of Preferred Stock

Typically, preferred stockholders receive only cash flows from predetermined dividends. Preferred dividends must be paid before common stock dividends can be paid (thus the term *preferred*). To determine the cost of preferred stock financing, it is necessary to relate the expected annual preferred stock dividend to the market price of the preferred stock. Since preferred stock dividends are typically fixed in amount and preferred stock does not mature, as bonds do, preferred dividends represent a perpetuity. Using the preferred stock valuation model, the cost of preferred stock is the rate k_p, as shown in Equations 17-4a and 17-4b.

cost of preferred stock k_p

$$P_p = \frac{D_p}{k_p} \qquad (17\text{-}4a)$$

$$k_p = \frac{D_p}{P_p} \qquad (17\text{-}4b)$$

Where P_p is the market price of the preferred stock; D_p is the annual dividend per share; and k_p is the minimum return required by investors.

Example

Cost of Preferred Stock

Assume the Ceder Company has preferred stock outstanding with an annual dividend of $5.20. The stock is currently selling for $40 per share. Thus, the cost of preferred stock financing to the company is 13 percent, as shown below[2]:

$$k_p = \frac{5.20}{40} = .13 = 13\%$$

Note that dividends on preferred stock are not tax-deductible, hence the after-tax cost of preferred stock is the same as its pre-tax cost.

Cost of Equity

cost of common equity k_e

Estimating the cost of common equity is far more complex than estimating the costs of debt or preferred stock. An important reason is that the cash flows to common stockholders are not specified as they are, for example, with preferred stock. For this reason, several alternative, complementary methods are employed in estimating the cost of equity. Three popular methods are examined in this section: the dividend discount model, the capital asset pricing model, and the debt-premium method.

Dividend Discount Method. Recall that the dividend discount model is used to develop an estimate of the intrinsic value of common stock given a projection of dividends and the shareholders' required rate of return from the stock. This model is shown in Equation 17-5a.

$$P_s = \sum_{t=1}^{\infty} \frac{D_t}{(1 + k_e)^t} \qquad (17\text{-}5a)$$

dividend discount method

Where P_s is the intrinsic value of the firm's common stock; D_t is the expected dividend at time t; and k_e is the rate of return required by shareholders.

---

[2]We are ignoring the impact of flotation costs. Flotation costs associated with new issues of debt, preferred, and common stock should be added to the cost of the investment made.

If one makes the simplifying assumption that dividends will grow at a constant rate, g, indefinitely, the dividend discount model can be simplified, as shown in Equation 17-5b.[3]

$$P_s = \frac{D_1}{k_e - g} \tag{17-5b}$$

By substituting the actual stock price for the intrinsic value of the stock and rearranging, an estimate can be developed of the return shareholders are currently requiring from stock. This is shown in Equation 17-5c.

$$k_e = \frac{D_1}{P_s} + g \tag{17-5c}$$

In words, the cost of equity capital is the sum of the expected dividend yield (i.e., $D_1 \div P_s$) plus the expected constant rate of growth in dividends. Since the stock price and projected dividend next year for large corporations can be determined readily, the estimate of k_e depends on the estimate of growth and, particularly, whether that growth can be assumed constant. Growth rates often are estimated by examining historical growth rates and then extrapolating into the future.[4]

k_e = dividend yield plus growth

Example

Cost of Equity Using the Dividend Discount Method

The Ceder Company is expected to pay a dividend of $2.00 on common stock in the coming year. The stock is currently selling at $50 per share. Dividends are expected to increase at a rate of 12 percent per year indefinitely. Using Equation 17-5c, the cost of equity can be estimated to be 16 percent.

$$k_e = (D_1/P_s) + g$$

$$k_e = (\$2.00/\$50) + .12$$

$$= .16 \quad \text{or} \quad 16\%$$

---

[3]Of course, any variation in growth rates may be handled by using the non-constant growth version of the model and discounting each projected dividend directly. This is explained in more detail in Chapter 5.

[4]For example, if a company's cash dividends per share have increased from $.90 (1981) to $1.79 (1987), the compound growth rate of dividends can be estimated by first calculating the ratio of the ending value of $1.79 divided by the beginning value of $.90, which is 1.989. Then by turning to Appendix A, Table 1, move across the table at year 6 until you find a FVIF factor close to 1.989. The closest FVIF factor is 1.974, and it occurs at a 12-percent rate. Thus, the compound growth rate in dividends is approximately 12 percent.

Capital Asset Pricing Model (CAPM) Method. An alternative method for estimating the cost of equity capital is based on the application of the capital asset pricing model (CAPM).[5] If the market for the company's stock is efficient, the required rate of return on the stock as determined by the capital asset pricing model should be consistent with the estimate developed by the dividend discount model. Given measurement errors as well as market imperfections, one should not expect them to be exactly equal. However, if they are not reasonably close, assumptions and estimates of such things as beta, expected return on the market, and dividend growth rates should be re-examined.

In order to use the CAPM method to estimate the firm's cost of equity, it is necessary to develop estimates of the stock's beta coefficient, the expected return on the market portfolio, and the expected risk-free rate of return. These estimates are brought together in the Security Market Line Equation, shown below as Equation 17-6[6]:

$$k_e = R_f + B(R_m - R_f) \tag{17-6}$$

Example

Cost of Equity Using the Capital Asset Pricing Model

The financial manager for the Ceder Company has estimated that the company's stock beta is 1.6. He has also estimated the expected rate of return of the stock market to be 13 percent and the risk-free rate to be 8 percent. Using these estimates, he calculates the firm's cost of equity at 16 percent. Since this is equal to the estimate developed with the dividend discount model, the estimate of 16 percent for the cost of equity seems credible.

$$k_e = 8\% + (13\% - 8\%)1.6$$
$$= 16\%$$

Debt Premium Method. A third method for estimating the cost of equity builds on the relationship between a firm's bonds and its common stock. Since a firm's bondholders are in a less risky position than its shareholders, the cost of a firm's debt should be less than its cost of equity. Using *debt premium method* the debt premium method, the firm first calculates its pre-tax debt cost and adds a risk premium, say 4 percent to 6 percent, to develop an estimate of its cost of equity.

---

[5]The capital asset pricing model is discussed in considerable detail in Chapter 6.
[6]Today, many brokerage firms, such as Merrill Lynch, and advisory services, such as Value Line, provide estimates of betas for a large number of U.S. corporations.

Example

Cost of Equity Using the Debt Premium Method

Previously, it was determined that the Ceder Company's cost of debt is 12 percent. Applying a 4-percent risk premium, Ceder's cost of equity is estimated to be 16 percent. Since this estimate is equal to those developed by other methods, the firm's true cost of equity appears to be about 16 percent.

$$k_e = k_d + 4\%$$

$$= 12\% + 4\% = 16\%$$

ESTIMATING THE OPTIMAL CAPITAL PROPORTIONS

In addition to the component costs of capital, it is necessary to estimate the proportion which each type of financing will represent in the financing mix. The proper weights to use are those that reflect the optimal capital structure. As noted earlier, the optimal capital structure can be defined as one which minimizes the average cost of capital.

The theoretical development of the optimal capital structure idea is taken up in Chapter 19. Some broad guidelines, however, may be employed to determine, if only approximately, the optimal capital structure. First, insofar as taxes reduce debt costs, the use of debt tends to decrease the weighted average cost of capital. Second, the greater its use of debt, the greater the probability that the firm will become bankrupt. The spectre of bankruptcy appears to increase all financing costs at an increasing rate and thus at some point the weighted average cost of capital will begin to rise. These two ideas are reflected in Table 17-1 and Exhibit 17-1.

optimal capital structure

Table 17-2 indicates that the firm's weighted average cost of capital decreases as it begins to assume more and more debt up to a point where debt represents 40 percent of the capital structure. This occurs even though both

TABLE 17-1					
w_d	k_d	$k_d(1-T)$	w_e	k_e	k_a
0%	10%	6.6%	100.0%	13%	13.00%
20%	10%	6.6%	80.0%	14%	12.52%
40%	11%	7.3%	60%	15%	11.92%
60%	12%	7.9%	40%	20%	12.74%

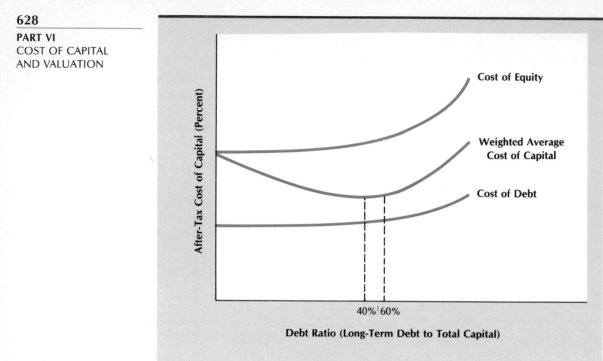

EXHIBIT 17-1

the cost of debt and the cost of equity are increasing. However, at a debt ratio of 60 percent, the jump in financing costs begins to increase the weighted average cost of capital. This same pattern is evident in Exhibit 17-1. Given the information in the table, one would conclude that the firm's optimal structure includes about 40 percent debt and 60 percent equity.

From a theoretical perspective, the optimal capital structure weights should be estimated on the basis of the relative market values of the component capital types. However, in practice, book values of capital types are often used. There are two principal approaches to measuring capital structure weights: book value weights and market value weights.

Book Value Weights

book weights

The simplest way to estimate the relative mix of financing is to use balance-sheet or book weights. With this approach, one simply examines the balance sheet of the company and calculates the percentages of each capital source relative to total long-term capital. This is demonstrated below.

Example

Using Book Weights

The Ceder Company's balance sheet shows the following capital structure[7]:

	$ Amount	Proportion of Total
Long-term debt	40,000	.40
Preferred stock	10,000	.10
Common stock	5,000	
Paid-in capital	5,000	.50
Retained earnings	40,000	___
Total capital	$100,000	1.00

Note that equity financing is comprised of common stock plus paid-in capital and retained earnings. For the Ceder company, equity financing represents 50 percent of its capital structure.

Thus, using book weights, the weighted average cost of capital would be calculated as:

$$k_a = w_d(k_d)(1 - T) + w_p(k_p) + w_e(k_e)$$

$$= .4(12\%)(1 - .34) + .1(14\%) + .5(16\%)$$

$$= .1257 \quad \text{or} \quad 12.57\%$$

There are two principal weaknesses in the book-weights method. One weakness is that book-value weights result in an inconsistent measure of the cost of capital. Recall that, when computing the costs of various types of capital, we used market values (for example, stock prices). To be consistent, market values should also be used to measure the weights. In other words, the average return required by investors represents market weights, not book weights. If book weights are very different from market weights, the book method will yield an incorrect estimate of the true weighted average cost of capital.

The second principal weakness in the book-value method is that the weights will reflect the most recent round of financing. For example, if the

---

[7]Many corporations show a long-term liability called "deferred taxes." This liability arises when a firm's tax depreciation charges exceed those on its financial reports. As long as the firm continues to generate more tax depreciation than it reports on financial statements, this liability may never have to be paid. For this reason, some financial managers include the long-term deferred taxes as part of common equity.

firm recently issued bonds, the mix of long-term debt may overstate the true mix the firm intends to use. Alternatively, if the company recently sold an issue of stock, the book value may overstate the proportion of equity the firm intends to use.

Arguments in favor of the use of book weights, in addition to ease of use, are that lenders and stock investors may rely heavily on the balance sheet in assessing the financial risk of the firm (and, hence, required returns) and that management itself may base its financing sequence on balance-sheet proportions. Moreover, barring significant changes in financial policies, if one averages the book weights over a period of years, the firm's true intended mix of capital may become more evident.

Market Weights

market value weights

Since costs are developed on the basis of market values, the use of market weights is consistent. However, a serious drawback is that these too will be affected by the company's most recent financing sequence. Whether the firm's current market proportions of capital represent its true or intended proportions is not certain. If not, neither the weights nor costs of each capital component will be accurately estimated. For example, if the firm intends to pursue a capital mix that includes only 10 percent debt but has just issued debt so that it represents 40 percent of the market value of capital, the costs of debt and equity will both be misestimated relative to the firm's desired mix.

Example

Using Market Value Weights

In using this method, the total market values of bonds and stocks and other securities issued are added up. The market value of traded bonds can be calculated by simply multiplying the number of bonds outstanding times the market price per bond. The market value of privately placed debt can be estimated by discounting the interest and principal payments to be made over the life of the debt by the required return on the firm's publicly traded debt.[8]

The market value of the firm's preferred stock is determined by multiplying the number of preferred shares outstanding by the market price per share. The market value of the firm's common stock is determined by multiplying the number of common shares outstanding by the market price per share.

---

[8]If the firm has no publicly traded debt, it may be necessary to use the required returns on debt of other firms in the same industry.

Example

Using Market Weights

Let us assume that the Merit Company has issued $1 million worth of 8-percent coupon bonds, with 10 years remaining to maturity. The bonds each have a face value of $1,000 and are currently selling for $770.60 per bond, producing a yield of 12 percent per year compounded semi-annually. In addition, the company has privately placed $1 million of debt carrying an interest rate of 10 percent per year, and five years remain before maturity. The market value of the privately placed debt at a yield of 12 percent per year compounded semiannually is $926,405. Merit also has 50,000 shares of preferred stock selling at $10 per share. Its cost of preferred stock financing is 14 percent, and the market value of its preferred stock is $500,000. Finally, Merit has 5 million shares of common stock outstanding selling for $2.50 per share. Its cost of common stock financing is 16 percent, and the market value of its common stock is $12.5 million. The company's marginal tax rate is 34 percent. Merit's market value weights are:

	Market Value	% of Total	Pre-Tax Cost
Long-term debt	1,697,005	.116	.12
Preferred stock	500,000	.034	.14
Common stock	12,500,000	.850	.16
Total	$14,697,005	1.000	

Using market value weights, the weighted average cost of capital would be:

$$k_a = .116(12\%)(1 - .34) + .034(14\%) + .850(16\%)$$

$$= 14.99\%$$

COST OF CAPITAL FOR SPECIFIC INVESTMENTS

Until now, we have focused on calculating the cost of capital for the firm as a whole. Strictly speaking, the firm's overall cost of capital can be applied to specific investments only if two important assumptions are met. First, the specific investment must possess the same risk as the firm overall. Second, the mix of financing appropriate to the specific investment must be the same as for the firm overall. In other words, the firm's cost of capital can be applied to a specific investment only if the specific investment is a microcosm of the firm overall. If either of these conditions are violated, then the firm's cost of capital is not the same as the investment's cost of capital.

investment (project) cost of capital

Example

When the Firm's Cost of Capital Cannot Be Used

The Action Company is a broadly diversified conglomerate. The firm has major activities in the energy area, including oil exploration, refining, and natural gas pipelines. Among its other businesses, the Action Company is also heavily involved in consumer products, including food, electronic equipment, and clothing.

The cost of capital for the company reflects the average business and financial risks of the firm. An investment proposal in the food business, a new breakfast cereal, for example, will differ in both business and financial risk from the company overall. In such cases, the cost of capital for the new breakfast cereal investment will not be the same as the company's overall cost of capital.

Using the firm's cost of capital in evaluating individual investments can lead to serious biases in investment selection. For example, if the firm considers investments with above-average risk, they are likely to have higher-than-average expected returns. But will they be as high as they should be? If the company uses its overall cost of capital to evaluate such investments, the company will tilt capital allocations toward riskier investments and away from safer ones. This bias can be seen clearly in exhibit 17-2.

Exhibit 17-2 overlays the firm's weighted average cost of capital onto the security market line. The exhibit also shows the rates of return (i.e., IRR) projected for investments A and B.

Notice that investment A would be accepted if the overall average cost of capital standard is used. However, given its level of risk, A will not provide a high enough return. If investment A is undertaken, the firm's stock value will actually decrease.

The opposite is true for investment B, which appears to be undesirable because its projected return is less than the firm's overall cost of capital. Yet, given B's low risk level, if it is undertaken, it will increase the firm's stock price.

What Good is the Firm's Cost of Capital?

At this point, one may wonder what difference it makes to calculate the firm's overall cost of capital if it cannot be used for specific investment proposals. First, recognize that this criticism is not always valid. For many firms whose businesses are primarily in one or two closely related industries, most of the investments they undertake are similar in business and financial risk to the company as a whole. Second, the firm's overall cost of capital provides a benchmark of the composite risk of the company. For

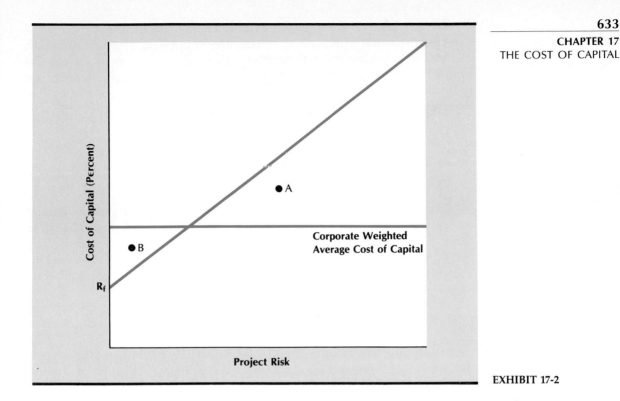

EXHIBIT 17-2

example, the Action Company's overall cost of capital can be viewed as a weighted average of the costs of capital of all its various investments. Businesses which the Company knows to be riskier than the firm overall, such as oil exploration, will have higher costs of capital. Conversely, lower-risk businesses will have lower-than-average costs of capital.

Nonetheless, the more accurately the firm estimates the true costs of capital for particular investments, the more likely it will make decisions that maximize shareholders' wealth.

Determining the Project Cost of Capital

In theory, the cost of capital for a particular project should be determined analogous to that of the firm: determine the costs of each capital component appropriate to the project and weight each cost by the project's optimal capital structure. However, this presents formidable problems in application. For example, the cost of debt for a particular project should be the cost that would be required if the project were undertaken as a separate company. Yet, determining this rate will be difficult.

Even more severe difficulties arise in estimating the project's cost of equity capital. For one thing, the project does not have its own stock, and therefore the dividend discount model cannot be directly applied. Nor, for similar reasons, can the project's beta be estimated; and thus the capital asset pricing model approach cannot be directly applied. The debt premium method also has practical difficulties, since the cost of debt for the investment may not be estimated accurately and the amount of risk premium to be applied will vary given the level of investment risk and the lack of liquidity in the investment.

Determining the Cost of Capital for Divisions

In order to preserve the spirit of the capital asset pricing model amidst such implementation problems, a compromise method employed by some firms is to estimate costs of capital on a division-by-division basis. The division's cost of capital is then applied to all projects within the division. This higher level of aggregation allows more reliable estimates of betas, capital structure proportions, and so on.

division cost of capital   A division's cost of capital can be estimated by examining the betas of publicly traded companies that operate in the same industry classification as the division itself. For example, if a company has a toy division, the beta for the division may be estimated by taking an average of betas for companies such as Mattel and Hasbro, which are primarily engaged in the toy business. The average capital structure mixes of debt and equity used by such firms could then be used as a basis for developing an estimated weighted average cost of capital for the division.

Leverage and Beta

When using betas of other companies to estimate the beta for a division, biases with respect to capital structure proportions may arise. Since a firm's beta reflects both business and financial risk, unless the capital structures of the other companies reflect the capital structure to be employed by the division, the beta will not be directly comparable.

The impact of debt on a firm's beta is estimated by Equation 17-7a. According to this equation, a firm's total beta is made up of a business risk beta plus a measure of financial leverage net of tax shields.

$$\beta_1 = \beta_u[1 + (D/E)(1 - T)] \qquad (17\text{-}7a)$$

levered beta   where β_1 is the firm's beta reflecting both financial and business risk; β_u is the firm's beta reflecting business risk alone; D/E is the debt to equity ratio; and T is the tax rate.

In order to determine the business risk beta alone, the equation can be rearranged to solve for β_u:

$$\beta_u = \beta_1/[1 + (D/E)(1 - T)] \qquad (17\text{-}7b)$$

Example

Financial Leverage and Beta

The Stretch Company is attempting to determine the cost of capital for its food products division. The firm has decided that the optimal capital structure for the division would be 17 percent debt and 83 percent equity. The cost of debt would be 12 percent, but the cost of equity is not known. The Company decides to estimate the cost of equity for the division with the capital asset pricing model. The firm expects the return on the market portfolio to be 16 percent, and the risk-free rate is expected to be 8 percent. An examination of four companies primarily involved in the food products business reveals the following betas and capital structure proportions:

Company	Beta	Debt/Equity
1	1.5	.50
2	1.2	.30
3	1.4	.40
4	1.7	.60
Average	1.45	.45

Using the averages for the four companies and equation, 17-7b, the business risk (unlevered) beta can be estimated as:

unlevered beta

$$\beta_u = 1.45/[1 + .45(.66)]$$

$$= 1.12$$

Given the estimate of the business risk beta, the Stretch Company can now adjust it for the desired capital structure for the division. Given that the firm will finance with 17 percent debt and 83 percent equity, the debt-equity ratio will be 20 percent (i.e., .17/.83). With this capital structure, the levered beta for the division would be:

$$\beta_1 = 1.12[1 + .2(.66)]$$

$$= 1.27$$

The cost of equity, $k_{e,div}$, for the division can now be calculated as:

$$k_{e,div} = 8\% + (16\% - 8\%)1.27$$

$$= 18.16\% \quad \text{or, approximately} \quad 18\%.$$

And, the weighted average cost of capital for the division can be calculated as:

$$k_{a,div} = .17(12\%)(.66) + .83(18\%)$$

$$= 16.29\% \quad \text{or, approximately} \quad 16\%$$

S U M M A R Y

The cost of capital represents the minimum rate of return that must be produced by investments. This rate varies from one investment to another on the bases of risk and financing capacity. While throughout this text we have come back to the relationship between risk and required minimum returns, the innovation in this chapter arises from the tax advantages of using debt. The tax advantages of debt have the effect of reducing the weighted average cost of capital. Thus up to a point, the more debt an investment can support, the lower its weighted average cost of capital.

Except for single-industry firms, determining the cost of capital for individual investments is extremely difficult and, at best, imprecise. Some firms address this problem by developing division-wide costs of capital that reflect the riskiness of entire industries. The estimates are made by examining the costs of capital for entire firms operating primarily in the industries of interest. Other firms calculate the cost of capital for the entire firm and then subjectively assign costs of capital to operating divisions in such a way that the average matches that for the overall firm.

MULTIPLE CHOICE QUESTIONS

1. A bond's *yield to maturity* is the same as its:
   a) Present value
   b) Coupon rate
   c) Required rate of return
   d) Discount from par value plus its coupon rate

2. The cost of preferred stock can be estimated by dividing its specified dividend by:
   a) The estimated dividend growth rate
   b) The stock's P/E multiple
   c) The stock's market price
   d) One minus the tax rate

3. The capital asset pricing model assumes that a company's relevant risk level can be estimated by its:

   a) Degree of combined leverage
   b) Beta
   c) Degree of financial leverage
   d) P/E ratio

4. The Security Market Line:

   a) Describes bargains currently available in financial markets
   b) Illustrates what securities are available and what their returns are
   c) Illustrates the current risk/return tradeoff in the market
   d) Is the minimum price at which stocks can be traded

5. A firm's optimal capital structure is one that:

   a) Minimizes its weighted average cost of capital
   b) Minimizes its cost of debt
   c) Maximizes its EPS
   d) Maximizes its return on equity

6. The highest-cost source of funds to the company is:

   a) Common stock
   b) Preferred stock
   c) Long-term debt
   d) Short-term debt

7. The weighted average cost of capital is calculated on an after-tax basis because:

   a) Preferred dividends are not tax deductible
   b) Corporate dividends are double-taxed
   c) Cash flows are calculated on an accrual basis
   d) Interest expense is tax deductible

DISCUSSION QUESTIONS

1. In what ways is capital similar to labor from the standpoint of the company's production activities?

2. What is meant by the statement, "The cost of capital has a dual character."

3. Why is it so much harder to estimate the cost of equity for a company than its cost of debt?

4. For each of the following situations, determine the impact on the firm's stock price.

Situation	Internal Rate of Return	Cost of Capital
1	25%	18%
2	18%	20%
3	20%	20%

5. Explain the importance of each phrase in the title, "after-tax, weighted average, marginal, cost of capital."

6. If the after-tax cost of debt is less than its pre-tax cost, why is the after-tax cost of equity not less than its pre-tax cost?

7. How would you define the "optimal" capital structure for a firm?

8. A company is considering an investment with an internal rate of return of 20 percent. The company will borrow at 12 percent to make the investment. Explain why the investment's marginal cost of capital is *not* 12 percent.

9. Assume that a company uses proportionately more and more debt in its capital structure. The costs of both debt and equity are increasing, and yet its average cost of capital is decreasing. Explain how this can happen.

10. A company has a bond outstanding with a coupon interest rate of 12 percent. The bond is selling at a discount. Is the cost of debt for the company more than, less than, or equal to 12 percent?

11. Describe the following methods for estimating the cost of equity capital: (a) dividend discount approach; (b) CAPM approach; (c) debt-plus-premium approach.

12. Compare the "book-value" weights against the "market-value" weights methods for calculating the weighted average cost of capital. Identify the advantages and disadvantages of each method.

SOLVED PROBLEMS

cost of capital

SP-1. The Jinques Company has the following capital structure, which it considers to be optimal:

Long-term debt	$200,000
Preferred stock	50,000
Common stock	150,000
Retained earnings	100,000
Total	$500,000

The company's outstanding bonds have 20 years remaining to maturity and carry a coupon rate of 15 percent. The bonds are currently selling for $940 per $1,000 face value. The company's outstanding preferred stock carries a dividend of $5 per share and is currently selling for $23 per share. The company's common stock is currently selling for $50 per share. Dividends next year will be about $3.50 per share and are expected to grow indefinitely at 15 percent per year. The company's tax rate is 34 percent.

a) Calculate the capital structure weights on a book-value basis given the company's existing capital structure.
b) Estimate the after-tax cost of debt capital (assume annual compounding).
c) Calculate the after-tax cost of preferred stock.
d) Calculate the after-tax cost of equity.
e) Calculate the weighted average cost of capital for the firm.

SP-2. The Acme Corporation uses no debt in its capital structure. The Company's financial manager wants to apply the capital asset pricing model to the evaluation of the five investments described below. Assume that the risk-free rate of return (R_f) is 10 percent and the expected return on the market (R_m) is 15 percent.

CAPM

a) Calculate the cost of capital, assuming all-equity financing, for each of the following investments:

Investment	Beta
1	2.5
2	2.0
3	1.0
4	0.5
5	-0-

b) Construct a graph showing your answer to part (a). On the x axis put the values for beta, and on the y axis put the required return associated with each beta. (Hint: you should be able to draw a straight line through the points, intersecting the y axis at the risk-free rate (R_f)).

c) Assume that the internal rates of return, given the investments' cash flow forecasts, are the following:

Investment	Projected Internal Rate of Return
1	21%
2	19%
3	17%
4	14%
5	10%

Plot the projected returns on the graph you prepared in part (b). Which investments should be accepted, and which should be rejected?

d) Assume that the company's overall weighted cost of capital is 15 percent. Plot the weighted average cost of capital line on your graph. Which investments should be accepted and which rejected, according to this standard? Compare your results with those in part (c). Which method would you recommend?

PROBLEMS

1. The Sparkle Company has the following capital structure, which it considers to be optimal:

Long-term debt	$400,000
Preferred stock	50,000
Common stock	150,000
Retained earnings	100,000
Total	$700,000

The company's outstanding bonds have 10 years to maturity remaining and carry a coupon rate of 12 percent. The bonds are currently selling for $900 per $1,000 face value bond. The company's oustanding preferred stock carries a dividend of $5 per share and is currently selling for $30 per share. The company's common stock is currently selling for $125 per share. Dividends next year will be about $2.50 per share and are expected to grow indefinitely at 10 percent per year. The company's tax rate is 34 percent.

a) Calculate the capital structure weights on a book-value basis, given the company's existing capital structure.
b) Estimate the after-tax cost of debt capital (assume annual compounding).
c) Calculate the after-tax cost of preferred stock.
d) Calculate the after-tax cost of equity.
e) Calculate the weighted average cost of capital for the firm.

2. The Mallera Company uses no debt in its capital structure. The company's financial manager wants to apply the capital asset pricing model to the evaluation of the five investments described below. Assume that the risk-free rate of return (R_f) is expected to be 5 percent and the expected return on the market (R_m) is expected to be 13 percent.

a) Calculate the cost of capital, assuming all-equity financing, for each of the following investments:

Investment	Beta
1	1.5
2	1.0
3	2.0
4	0.5
5	2.5

b) Construct a graph showing your answer to part (a). On the horizontal axis put the values for beta, and on the vertical axis put the required return associated with each beta. Hint: you should be able to draw a straight line through the points, intersecting the vertical axis at the risk-free rate (R_f).

c) Assume that the internal rates of return, given the investments' cash flow forecasts, are the following:

Investment	Projected Internal Rate of Return
1	21%
2	19%
3	17%
4	10%
5	20%

Plot the projected returns on the graph you prepared in part (b). Which investments should be accepted? Which should be rejected?

d) Assume that the company's overall weighted average cost of capital is 15 percent. Plot the weighted average cost of capital line on your graph. Which investments should be accepted and which rejected, according to this standard? Compare your results with those in part (c). Which method would you recommend?

3. The ABC Company generated the following earnings per share and cash dividends per share over the last six years:

cost of equity

	EPS	DPS
1987	$3.44	$1.72
1986	$3.00	$1.50
1985	$2.90	$1.45
1984	$2.50	$1.25
1983	$2.20	$1.10
1982	$1.90	$0.95

Assume that the risk-free rate of return is 10 percent, the firm's beta is 1.50, and past growth is expected to continue into the future at the same rate.

a) Estimate the annual compound growth rate of ABC's earnings and dividends.

b) Determine the firm's cost of equity using the capital asset pricing model and based on an expected return on the market of 14 percent for next year.

c) If ABC's stock price is $100 per share, estimate the cost of equity using the dividend discount model.

cost of debt

4. The Wilson Company issued a 15-year bond with a par value of $1,000 and carrying a 12-percent coupon rate. When issued last month, the bond could be sold for only $900.

a) Calculate the bond's yield to maturity assuming interest is to be paid annually.

b) If the current rate of return being demanded in the marketplace for bonds of this risk class is 14 percent, what price should the bond now be selling at, assuming interest payments are made annually?

c) If, after one year, the market rate for this risk class of bond falls to 10 percent, what would be the value then (one year from now) if interest is paid annually?

cost of capital

5. The PXD Corporation wants to estimate its weighted average cost of capital. PXD's existing capital structure, which is viewed as optimal, consists of:

Long-term debt	$2,500,000
Preferred stock	1,500,000
Common equity	6,000,000

The company pays out 50 percent of its earnings in the form of dividends, is in the 34-percent tax bracket, and has 200,000 shares of common stock currently outstanding. New 10-year debt can be sold with an 8-percent coupon rate and a discount price of $900 (par value is $1,000) per bond. Preferred stock carries a $5 dividend, and the current market price is $50. The company's common stock is also currently selling for $50 per share. Earnings and cash dividends have been growing at the same rate over time for PXD. Earnings per share figures in recent years have been: 1979, $2.33; 1980, $2.72; 1981, $2.94; 1982, $3.18; 1983, $3.43; 1984, $3.70; 1985, $3.85; 1986, $4.00; 1987, $4.32.

a) Calculate the after-tax cost of capital for debt and preferred stock.

b) Calculate the after-tax cost of capital for common stock.

c) Estimate the company's weighted average cost of capital.

6. A consultant hired by XYZ Corporation recommends that the firm estimate its cost of equity capital by applying the capital asset pricing model. The consultant estimates a beta of 1.35 for XYZ. U.S. Treasury bills are currently yielding 8 percent, and the return on the Standard & Poor's Index of 500 stocks is expected to be 13 percent over the next year. Estimate the cost of equity capital for XYZ based on the data above.

CAPM

7. The Jax Company has had the following earnings per share: 1978, $0.71; 1979, $1.00; 1980, $1.35; 1981, $1.47; 1982, $1.48; 1983, $1.80; 1984, $2.02; 1985, $1.73; 1986, $2.17; 1987, $2.50. The common stock is currently selling for $54 per share, and the firm expects cash dividends to be $1.40 for the coming year. Long-term debt can be issued at a yield to maturity of 10 percent. The company is in a 34-percent tax bracket and desires a financing mix of capital funds of 50 percent long-term debt and 50 percent common equity.

cost of capital

   a) Calculate the after-tax cost of capital for each capital source.
   b) Calculate the firm's weighted average cost of capital.

8. Trounce Company has a bond outstanding with seven years left before maturity. The coupon rate on the bond is 12 percent, and the face value of the bond is $1,000.

cost of debt

   a) If the bond is currently selling for $800, what is its yield to maturity? (Assume annual compounding. Be approximate; do not interpolate).
   b) Assume that the required yield to maturity drops to 11 percent. What would the market value of the bond be then?

SOLUTIONS TO SOLVED PROBLEMS

SP-1. a)

			% of Total
Long-term debt		200,000	40%
Preferred stock		50,000	10%
Common stock	150,000		
Retained earnings	100,000	250,000	50%

   b) Since the bond is selling at a discount, its yield to maturity must be greater than its coupon rate. To find the exact yield to maturity involves trial and error to solve for $k_\%$:

$$P_b = \text{Annuity}(\text{PVIFA}_{k\%,n}) + \text{Face value}(\text{PVIF}_{k\%,n})$$
$$\$940 = \$150(\text{PVIFA}_{k\%,20}) + \$1,000(\text{PVIF}_{k\%,20})$$

Assuming a k_b of 16 percent provides the closest approximation:

$$P_b = \$150(5.929) + 1{,}000(.051) = \$940.35$$

Thus, the pre-tax cost of debt is about 16 percent. To convert this to an after-tax cost, multiply by 1 minus the tax rate:

After-tax cost of debt $= 16\%(1 - .34) = 10.6\%$

c) Cost of preferred, k_p, is not adjusted for taxes since preferred dividends are not tax deductible:

$$k_p = D_p/P_p = \$5/\$23 = 21.7\%$$

d) Cost of equity, k_e, can be estimated with the dividend valuation model:

$$k_e = (D_1/P_s) + g$$
$$= (\$3.50/\$50) + .15 = 22.0\%$$

e) The weighted average cost of capital (k_a) can be determined with the use of a table such as the following:

Capital Type	% of Total Capital	After-Tax Cost	Weighted Cost
Long-term debt	.40	10.6%	4.24%
Preferred stock	.10	21.7%	2.17%
Equity	.50	22.0%	11.00%
			$k_a = 17.41\%$

a) Use the capital asset pricing model equation:

$$k_e = R_f + (R_m - R_f)\beta$$

Investment	Beta	Required Return (Cost of Capital)
1	2.5	22.5%
2	2.0	20.0%
3	1.0	15.0%
4	0.5	12.5%
5	-0-	10.0%

b) The Security Market Line is graphed and shown in Exhibit SP-2A.

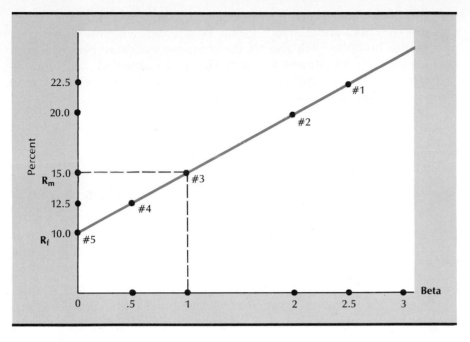

EXHIBIT SP-2A.

c) The projected internal rate of return is compared to the required
   return. All investments whose required return exceeds their projected return should be rejected. If the required return is less
   than the projected return, the investment should be accepted.
   If the required return is just equal to the projected return, the
   company should be indifferent between accepting the investment or paying the capital out to investors, since acceptance of
   the investment will not affect stock price.

Investment	Required Return	Projected Return	Recommendation
1	22.5%	21%	reject
2	20.0%	19%	reject
3	15.0%	17%	accept
4	12.5%	14%	accept
5	10.0%	10%	no recommendation

d) The weighted average cost of capital should be shown as a horizontal line in Exhibit SP-2A, since it reflects only an average
   aggregate risk and does not distinguish among investments
   within the firm.

If the weighted average cost of capital is applied across the board, investments 1 and 2, which should be rejected, will now be accepted (notice how they will also tilt the company's average beta upward). Conversely, investment 4, which should be accepted, will now be rejected. We can conclude that, whenever the overall weighted average cost of capital is applied to all investments uniformly, it will tend to favor riskier investments over safer ones.

REFERENCES

Ang, James S. "Weighted Average versus True Cost of Capital." *Financial Management,* Autumn 1973, pp. 56–60.

Arditti, Fred D., and Haim Levy. "The Weighted Average Cost of Capital as a Cutoff Rate: A Critical Analysis of the Classical Textbook Weighted Average." *Financial Management,* Fall 1977, pp. 24–34.

Beranek, William. "The Weighted Average Cost of Capital and Shareholder Wealth Maximization." *Journal of Financial and Quantitative Analysis,* March 1977, pp. 17–32.

Ezzell, John R., and R. Burr Porter. "Flotation Costs and the Weighted Average Cost of Capital." *Journal of Financial and Quantitative Analysis,* September 1976, pp. 403–414.

Gordon, M.J., and L.I. Gould. "The Cost of Equity Capital: A Reconsideration." *Journal of Finance,* June 1978, pp. 849–861.

Lewellen, Wilbur G. The Cost of Capital. Dubuque, IA: Kendall/Hunt, 1976.

Modigliani, Franco, and Merton Miller. "The Cost of Capital, Corporation Finance and the Theory of Investment." *American Economic Review,* June 1958, pp. 261–296.

Nantell, Timothy J., and C. Robert Carlson. "The Cost of Capital as a Weighted Average." *Journal of Finance,* December 1975, pp. 1343–1355.

Reilly, Raymond R., and William E. Wecker. "On the Weighted Average Cost of Capital." *Journal of Financial and Quantitative Analysis,* January 1973, pp. 123–126.

Scott, J.H. "A Theory of Optimal Capital Structure." *Bell Journal of Economics,* Spring 1976, pp. 33–54.

Wippern, Ronald F. "Financial Structure and the Value of the Firm." *Journal of Finance,* December 1966, pp. 615–634.

CHAPTER

18

FINANCIAL STRUCTURE DECISIONS

inancial structure decisions involve great potential benefits as well as risks and thus must be made carefully. Such decisions ultimately involve a choice between some form of debt and equity, and they arise whenever the firm must raise funds.

There are certain common, though at times conflicting, criteria involved in determining the methods of financing assets. Because each company's situation is different, the weight given these elements in making the decision varies according to conditions in the economy, the industry, and the company. This chapter examines the factors that are typically considered in making such decisions.

Objectives and Organization of this Chapter

The principal objective of this chapter is to identify and illustrate the factors the financial manager should consider in the choice between debt and equity financing. Most of these considerations can be incorporated in a popular acronym known as "FRICT," which stands for considerations of *FRICT* *flexibility, risk, income, control,* and *timing.*

The first section of the chapter defines the implications of financing choices on the firm's financial flexibility. In particular, it illustrates the hazard of relying too heavily on debt financing. The second section examines the effect of financing choices on the overall risk position of the firm. Here it addresses a different form of risk, one that is reflected in both the probability of bankruptcy and the volatility of earnings.

In the third section, the chapter examines the effect of financing choices on the firm's earnings per share given its anticipated EBIT level. Firms are reluctant to choose a financing method that will result in lower earnings per share and thus try to determine the impact of financing choice on it.

The fourth section discusses the impacts of financing choices on the control existing shareholders and management can exercise over the firm's destiny. Selling more stock in order to raise funds probably means bringing in new stockholders. This results in a dilution of the proportional ownership existing shareholders have. In addition, management has a larger, perhaps more diverse, group of shareholders to which it is accountable.

Alternatively, financing too heavily with debt may produce its own threats to the control positions of owners and managers.

In the fifth section, the chapter explores the effect of financial markets on the financing choice. Financial market conditions can be volatile. No firm wants to sell stock when its prices are depressed nor borrow long-term when interest rates are unusually high. By timing its financing issues to correspond with more normal conditions, the firm can benefit in many important ways.

FINANCING DECISIONS AND FLEXIBILITY

Most simply, financial flexibility means having more than one financing alternative at all times. Not only does this enable the company to use the most readily available and least expensive type of funds at any given time, but it also enhances the firm's bargaining power when dealing with prospective suppliers of funds. A firm without financial flexibility is at the mercy of financial markets.

Example

Importance of financial flexibility

The Excel Company used debt aggressively to the point where its debt was three times its net worth. The company had used these borrowed funds to finance rapid and profitable expansion of production capacity. Now, in order to continue its rapid growth, the firm needed several million dollars. This time the financial manager was unsuccessful in raising the funds. The banks not only refused more funds but informed the financial manager that they would not renew their existing loans to the company if it exceeded its present debt to equity ratio. At this point the firm's only financing option was to sell stock. Unfortunately, the stock market was in the midst of a severe downturn. The firm's stock was currently selling for about half what the firm's management thought it was worth. The firm's predicament was summed up by the president, "If we do not sell stock, we have to stop growing; and this could severely hurt our competitive position. But, if we do sell stock at its current price range, we will have a shareholder revolt!"

If the Excel Company had maintained a more reasonable mix of debt and equity, it would not be in its current predicament. The company would still have some *debt capacity*, meaning borrowing power. Notice how its financial decisions have come back to haunt it and actually threaten to derail its operating plans. And this is happening in spite of the fact that the firm is profitable and growing rapidly!

FINANCING DECISIONS AND RISK

When evaluating its financing choices, the firm should also consider the effect debt or equity will have on the overall risk profile of the company. Generally, from the standpoint of the company, debt increases overall risk while financing with equity does not.

In analyzing a firm's overall risk it is important to recognize that fluctuations in sales result in fluctuations in profits and, most important, that the variations in sales are magnified by two forces called *operating leverage* and *financial leverage*. A knowledge of the basic reasons for this magnification is important as a guide to deciding how much debt to include in the financial structure.

The leverage effect arises whenever the company employs fixed costs in its production, distribution, administrative and/or financing methods. Large fixed costs can magnify even moderate sales declines into very large declines in profits.

When analyzing a firm's leverage, it is useful to distinguish between *operating leverage*, which is produced by fixed operating costs, and *financial leverage*, which is produced by the firm's fixed financial costs. The firm's *combined leverage* is the product of its operating and financial leverages.

operating leverage
financial leverage
combined leverage

Cost Volume Profit (CVP) Analysis

The role of leverage can best be explained by use of a breakeven chart, which relates the general effect of the level of output upon income and expenses and, therefore, upon profit before taxes. Examining the costs of companies shows that some of them change in direct proportion to variations in output. When output rises 10 percent, these costs also rise 10 percent. A baby food manufacturer would probably find that the costs of fruit and vegetables are variable costs: that is, the more the firm produced, the more must be spent on these items. Other variable costs might be direct labor and the cost of the containers.

breakeven chart

Other costs are fixed costs, in that they do not change with variations in the level of output. The president of the baby food company is rather unlikely to lower her or his salary when production drops. Probably the costs of supervision, heat, light, and depreciation are also fixed costs. In addition to these fixed operating costs, the firm may incur fixed financing costs, which are the fixed borrowing costs such as interest expense or contractual financial lease payments.

Finally, there is a group of semivariable costs that do not change in direct proportion to changes in volume of production, but nonetheless do vary somewhat with output. For example, if output declines substantially, a few supervisors may be cut from the payrolls, and the remaining supervisors may manage more lines. Such mixtures of variable and fixed costs can usually be separated into variable-portion and fixed-portion components.

The general relationship between a firm's sales volume, cost structure, and profits before taxes is revealed graphically with the cost-volume-profit (CVP) chart. Exhibit 18-1 presents such a chart for the Brendle Manufacturing Company.

The horizontal axis shows various units of output or sales. The vertical axis is measured in dollars. The "TR" line is the total sales revenues that will result at each level of unit sales. The line is produced by multiplying unit sales times the selling price per unit. For purposes of illustration, assume that Brendle sells one product at $100 per unit.

The "TC" line is the total costs incurred at each sales level. It is equal to total variable costs plus total fixed costs at each sales level. Total variable costs are determined by multiplying variable costs per unit times the number of units sold. Brendle's variable costs are $73.20 per unit, and total fixed costs are $207,000.

Breakeven Point (Units)

The point of intersection of the total revenue and total cost lines has special significance. It is the point at which profits before taxes (and, of

EXHIBIT 18-1
Brendle Manufacturing
Co.: Cost-Volume-Profit
Chart

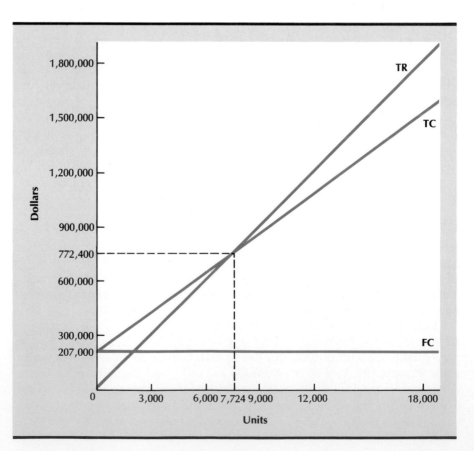

course, net income) are zero. This is the company's breakeven point in units. As sales rise above the breakeven point, profits are larger and larger. As sales fall below the breakeven point, larger and larger losses are incurred.

breakeven point

The breakeven point in units (BE_u) can be calculated directly with Equation 18-1:

$$BE_u = F_t/(p - v) \tag{18-1}$$

$$= \$207,000/(\$100.00 - \$73.20)$$

$$= 7,724 \text{ (rounded)}$$

where F_t is equal to total fixed costs; p is the selling price per unit; and v is the variable cost per unit.

Notice that the breakeven point in units, 7,724, is the same as that indicated on the CVP chart.

The breakeven point in sales dollars, BE_s, rather than units, can be calculated using Equation 18-2:

$$BE_s = F_t/cm\% \tag{18-2}$$

where F_t is the total fixed costs and $cm\%$ is the contribution margin percentage (i.e., sales price per unit minus variable cost per unit divided by price per unit). For Brendle, the contribution margin percentage is $1 - (\$73.20/\$100)$, or .268, and the breakeven point in sales dollars is:

$$BE_s = \frac{\$207,000}{.268} = \$772,388 \quad \text{or} \quad \$772,400 \text{ (rounded)}$$

Fixed costs have the effect of raising the firm's breakeven point and thus increase the possibility of losses and bankruptcy. As importantly, fixed costs also have the effect of increasing the volatility of profits. The relationship between the level of fixed costs and variability of profits is known as leverage. Since a firm has two distinct types of fixed costs (operating and financial), it is useful to separate the leverage effects into operating leverage (created by operating fixed costs) and financial leverage (created by fixed financial costs). Fixed operating costs reflect the firm's production methods. Fixed financial costs reflect the firm's financial policies. The firm's total leverage is a product of its operating and fixed leverages. The relative amount of operating, financial, and total leverage a firm has can be quantified.

fixed operating costs

fixed financial costs

Degree of Operating Leverage (DOL)

The degree of operating leverage measures the amount that a given percentage change in sales will be magnified into a larger percentage change in operating profit (EBIT). We can define the degree of operating leverage (DOL) at a point, "x", as the ratio of the percentage change in EBIT to the percentage change in output or sales. This is shown in Equation 18-3.

DOL

$$DOL_x = (\% \Delta EBIT) \div (\% \Delta Sales) \tag{18-3}$$

653

and thus,

$$\% \, \Delta \, EBIT = DOL_x \times \% \, \Delta \, Sales \tag{18-3a}$$

While Equation 18-3 refers to percentage changes in EBIT and sales on a dollar basis, the DOL can also be expressed on a unit basis, as shown in Equation 18-4.

$$DOL_x = \frac{x(p - v)}{x(p - v) - F_o} \tag{18-4}$$

Where x is the level of output in units; p is the selling price per unit; v is variable cost per unit; and F_o is the total fixed operating costs. As the equation reveals, the higher a company's fixed operating costs, the larger its DOL. Also notice that, if a company has no fixed operating costs (i.e., $F_o = 0$), it has no operating leverage and its DOL is equal to 1 (not zero). In effect, without fixed operating costs, there is no magnification effect; a 10 percent change in sales produces a 10 percent change in EBIT.

Example

Estimating the Degree of Operating Leverage

In 1987, the Brendle Company sold 14,790 electric motors (its only product) at a price of $100 per motor. Variable costs averaged $73.20 per unit, and fixed operating costs totaled $181,000. The company's EBIT in 1987 was $216,000. With this information, we can estimate Brendle's DOL as 1.84.

$$DOL \text{ at } 14,790 \text{ units} = \frac{14,790(\$100.00 - 73.20)}{14,790(\$100.00 - 73.20) - \$181,000}$$

$$= 1.84$$

This means that, for every percentage point change in sales from Brendle's 1987 level, there will be a 1.84 percentage point change in the firm's EBIT. In other words, if Brendle expects 1988 sales to increase by 5 percent over 1987, EBIT will increase by 9.2 percent (i.e., 5 percent × 1.84). The projected level of EBIT can be easily calculated. It will be 9.2 percent greater than it was in 1987.

$$EBIT_{1988} = EBIT_{1987} \times (1.092)$$

$$= \$216,000(1.092) = \$235,872$$

It is important to recognize that the leverage effect also magnifies sales declines into larger EBIT declines in a similar way. Thus, if sales in 1988 are expected to drop 5 percent, the projected decrease in EBIT would be 9.2 percent. This has particular significance for the firm's financing decisions. The greater its operating leverage, the more sensitive EBIT is to drops in sales. Of course, if EBIT decreases, the ability of the firm to cover its interest charges also drops and the prospect of defaulting on loan agreements increases. Understandably, lenders are especially cautious about loans to firms with high degrees of operating leverage and volatile sales.

It is instructive to note from equation 18-4 that the firm's DOL depends on a particular sales volume; in this case 1987. At a different sales volume, the company will have a different DOL. This will be examined more closely later.

DOL In Sales Dollars. Since the quantity sold, x, times the price per unit, p, is equal to total sales revenue, and the quantity sold, x, times the variable cost per unit, v, is equal to total variable costs, DOL may also be estimated by using Equation 18-5:

$$DOL = \frac{\text{Sales} - \text{Variable costs}}{\text{Sales} - \text{Variable costs} - \text{Fixed operating costs}} \qquad (18\text{-}5)$$

DOL in sales dollars

Moreover, since the denominator is equal to EBIT, we have:

$$DOL = \frac{\text{Sales} - \text{Variable costs}}{\text{EBIT}} \qquad (18\text{-}5a)$$

Using the 1987 data for Brendle, one can determine that total sales were $1,479,000 (i.e., 14,790 units × $100 per unit); total variable costs were $1,082,000 (i.e., 14,790 units × $73.20 per unit); and total fixed operating costs were $181,000. Thus, EBIT is $216,000. The calculated DOL of 1.84 is the same as before using data on a per-unit basis.

$$DOL = \frac{\$1,479,000 - \$1,082,000}{\$216,000}$$

$$= 1.84$$

Degree of Financial Leverage (DFL)

Financial leverage begins where operating leverage stops (i.e., EBIT). Financial leverage arises whenever a company has fixed financial costs, such as interest expenses or lease payments.

The degree of financial leverage (DFL) projects the amount by which a percentage change in operating profit (EBIT) will be magnified into a larger change in profits before taxes (PBT). In other words,

DFL

$$\% \Delta PBT = DFL \times \% \Delta EBIT \qquad (18\text{-}6)$$

The DFL can be directly calculated with Equation 18-7.

$$DFL_x = \frac{x(p - v) - F_o}{x(p - v) - F_o - F_f} \qquad (18\text{-}7)$$

where F_f represents total fixed financial costs, and the other variables are as defined previously. Since the numerator in Equation 18-7 is equal to EBIT, as we have already seen, and since the denominator is equal to profits before taxes, Equation 18-7 is equivalent to 18-7a:

$$DFL_x = \frac{EBIT}{PBT} \qquad (18\text{-}7a)$$

If the firm's tax rate does not change, the DFL will also project the amount by which a percentage change in EBIT will be magnified into a larger change in net income. If one additionally assumes that the number of common shares of stock outstanding does not change, the DFL will also project the amount by which a percentage in EBIT will be magnified into a larger change in earnings per share (EPS).

Example

Calculation of DFL for Brendle

Recall that Brendle's 1987 EBIT was $216,000. Assume that Brendle's interest expenses were $26,000 and that it had no other fixed financial costs. Thus Brendle's 1987 DFL was 1.14.

$$DFL_{14,790 \text{ units}} = 216{,}000/190{,}000$$

$$= 1.14$$

This means that for every percentage point change (up or down) in EBIT from Brendle's 1987 sales level, there will be a 1.14 percentage point change in the firm's profits before taxes, net income, and earnings per share. For example, if next year's EBIT increases by 9.2 percent (as calculated above), then profits before taxes (and net income and earnings per share) will increase by 10.5 percent (i.e., 1.14×9.2 percent). Given that 1987 profits before taxes were $190,000, the projected profits before taxes in 1988 are $209,927.

$$PBT_{1988} = PBT_{1987} \times (1.105)$$

$$= \$209{,}927$$

The existence of financial leverage makes the firm's earnings per share and return on equity more volatile: the greater the financial leverage, the greater the volatility in returns to shareholders. This is why borrowing increases the return shareholders require from the company's stock. This relationship will be discussed in more detail later by examining the impact of leverage on beta.

Degree of Combined Leverage (DCL)

The combined effects of operating and financial leverage, which can be called the degree of combined leverage (DCL) at any point, x, may be calculated directly by use of Equation 18-8.

$$DCL_x = \frac{x(p - v)}{x(p - v) - F_t} \qquad (18\text{-}8) \quad DCL$$

where x is sales volume in units; p is selling price per unit; v is variable costs per unit; and F_t is total fixed costs (i.e., the sum of fixed operating and fixed financial costs).

The DCL projects the impact of a percentage-point change in sales on profits before taxes, net income, and earnings per share. Thus,

$$\% \, \Delta \, PBT\,(net\ income,\ EPS) = DCL \times (\% \, \Delta \, Sales) \qquad (18\text{-}9)$$

Example

Brendle's DCL

With the data already gathered for Brendle, its degree of combined leverage in 1987 can be calculated using Equation 18-8.

$$DCL_{14,790\ units} = \frac{14,790(\$100 - 73.20)}{14,790(\$100 - 73.20) - \$207,000}$$

$$= 2.1$$

The degree of combined leverage can also be readily calculated by multiplying the DOL times the DFL, as shown in Equation 18-10:

$$DCL = DOL \times DFL \qquad (18\text{-}10)$$

$$= 1.84 \times 1.14$$

$$= 2.1$$

DCL Using Dollars. In the event that sales and cost data are available only in dollar amounts, the DCL at a given sales level, S, can also be calculated as shown in Equation 18-11:

$$DCL_S = (Sales - Variable\ costs)/Profit\ before\ taxes \qquad (18\text{-}11)$$

$$= (\$1,479,000 - \$1,082,000)/\$190,000$$

$$= 2.1$$

Thus, for each one percentage point change in sales from Brendle's 1987 level, there will be a 2.1 percentage point change in Brendle's profits before taxes, net income, and earnings per share so long as the company's tax rate and number of common shares outstanding do not change. For example, a 5-percent increase in Brendle's sales will result in a 10.5-percent increase in profits before taxes, net income, and earnings per share. This can be expressed in algebraic form as shown in Equation 18-12:

$$\% \, \Delta \, PBT = DCL \times (\% \, \Delta \, \text{Sales}) \tag{18-12}$$

$$= 2.1 \times (5\%) = 10.5\%$$

Leverage and Breakeven

An examination of Equation 18-9 reveals an interesting relationship between leverage and breakeven. At the breakeven point, (BE_x), total fixed costs are equal to the term, $x_{breakeven}(p - v)$. If we substitute this for F_t, we get,

$$DCL_x = \frac{x(p - v)}{x(p - v) - x_{breakeven}(p - v)} \tag{18-13}$$

which, dividing numerator and denominator by $(p - v)$, is equivalent to:

$$DCL_x = \frac{x}{x - x_{breakeven}} \tag{18-13a}$$

With Equation 18-13a, we have another shortcut for determining the degree of combined leverage at any point, given that we know the breakeven point.

Example

Brendle's DCL at Any Point

Let us assume that Brendle's breakeven point is 7,724 units. To illustrate the use of Equation 18-13a as well as the relationship between the firm's DCL and breakeven, the DCL has been calculated at three alternative sales levels: where x is equal to 7,800 units and is very close to the breakeven point; where x is equal to 14,790 units, the actual level in 1987, and where x is equal to 20,000 units, very far above the breakeven point.

	7,800 units	14,790 units	20,000 units
DCL	102.6	2.1	1.6

Close to its breakeven point, a 10-percent rise in sales would result in a 1,026 (i.e., 102.6 × 10 percent) percent increase in profits before taxes, net income, and earnings per share. At a sales level of 14,790 units, the company's actual sales level in 1987, DCL would be 2.1, which matches earlier calculations using other methods. At a sales level of 20,000 units,

DCL is only 1.6. Thus we can conclude both that Equation 18-13a provides an accurate estimate of DCL and that DCL decreases as a company moves its breakeven point.

FINANCING DECISIONS AND INCOME

When choosing a financing alternative, many companies compare the impact on earnings per share of each alternative being considered. Since the level of EBIT is not affected by the financing choice, a given level of EBIT is assumed and, for this level, profits before taxes, net income, and earnings per share are calculated under each financing option. The option producing the highest earnings per share at the assumed EBIT level is preferred on this basis.

Example

Evaluating EPS Impact of Financing Choice

The Acme Company is evaluating three alternatives for financing an $8 million expansion. Alternative #1 is an issue of 2 million shares of common stock at a net price (to the company) of $4.00 per share. Alternative #2 is an issue of 1 million common stock shares at a net price of $4.00 plus an issue of $4 million of long-term debt at an interest rate of 15 percent. Alternative #3 is an $8 million issue of long-term debt at an interest rate of 15 percent. Acme's EBIT is currently $10 million. With the expansion, EBIT is expected to be $14 million. The company's tax rate is 34 percent. Acme currently has 10 million common stock shares outstanding and has no debt or preferred stock. The company's financial manager wants to determine the EPS the company will achieve under the three alternatives given its expected EBIT of $14 million. The results are shown below in Table 18-1:

TABLE 18-1

	Alternative		
	#1	#2	#3
EBIT (000)	$14,000	$14,000	$14,000
Interest	-0-	600	1,200
PBT	$14,000	$13,400	$12,800
Taxes (34%)	4,760	4,556	4,352
Net income	$ 9,240	$ 8,844	$ 8,448
Number of shares (000)	12,000	11,000	10,000
EPS	$ 0.77	$ 0.80	$ 0.84

According to the EBIT/EPS analysis, alternative #3 (all debt) will result in the highest EPS. Though not always the case, most of the time this analysis does favor all-debt financing and hence should only be considered in combination with other factors (notably risk).

EBIT/EPS Indifference Point

When assessing the EPS impacts of various financing alternatives, financial managers often want also to determine the EBIT level at which all three alternatives would produce the same EPS. This is known as the EBIT/EPS *indifference point*. The EBIT level implied by the indifference point is significant because the preference ranking of alternatives switches depending on whether the company's actual EBIT turns out to be above or below the indifference point. To illustrate this point, let us see how the financial manager might compare alternatives #1 and #3. For any of the alternatives, Equation 18-14 can be used to determine the EPS, given some EBIT level:

EBIT/EPS indifference point

$$EPS = \frac{(EBIT - I_{\#})(1 - T)}{N_{\#}} \qquad (18\text{-}14)$$

The term $(EBIT - I_{\#})$ represents the profit before taxes of the alternative being considered. The subscript # indicates which alternative is being evaluated. The term $(1 - T)$ converts profit before taxes into net income. Net income divided by $N_{\#}$ (the number of common stock shares outstanding with the alternative considered) produces EPS. To determine the EBIT level that will produce the same EPS for two alternatives, Equation 18-14 can be used, solving for $EBIT^*$. The * indicates the indifference point EBIT level. To illustrate, in comparing alternatives #1 and #3, we have:

$$\frac{(EBIT^* - I_{\#1})(1 - T)}{N_{\#1}} = \frac{(EBIT^* - I_{\#3})(1 - T)}{N_{\#3}} \qquad (18\text{-}4)$$

$$\frac{(EBIT^* - 0)(1 - .34)}{12,000} = \frac{(EBIT^* - 1,200)(1 - .34)}{10,000}$$

$$EBIT^* = \$7,200$$

In other words, at EBIT levels above \$7,200 the all-debt alternative (#3) will produce higher EPS than the all-stock alternative (#1). At any EBIT level below \$7,200 the results are reversed (i.e., alternative #1 will produce higher EPS than #3). These relationships become clearer in an EBIT/EPS chart, as shown in Exhibit 18-2:

EBIT/EPS chart

Notice that the lines for alternatives #1 and #3 intersect at an EBIT level of \$7,200. At this point, as indicated on the EPS axis (the vertical axis), each alternative results in the same EPS (\$0.40). At all EBIT levels below \$7,200, alternative #1 produces higher EPS. At all EBIT levels above \$7,200, alternative #3 produces higher EPS. Since the expected EBIT level (\$14 million)

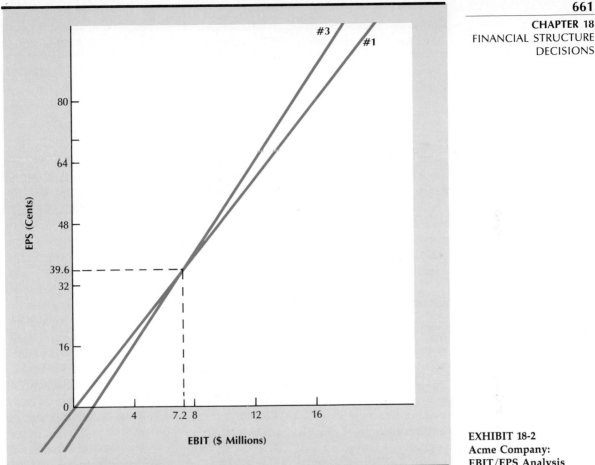

EXHIBIT 18-2
Acme Company:
EBIT/EPS Analysis

is almost double the indifference point, the superiority of alternative #3 in terms of EPS is not in doubt.

A major weakness of the EBIT/EPS analysis is that it does not properly incorporate risk. For example, just because debt financing produces higher EPS than equity financing does not mean that debt financing will maximize stock price. In fact, it is quite possible that the company's stock price will drop even though its EPS is higher. The reason is that debt financing increases the riskiness of the company and causes stock investors to insist on higher rates of return. This is usually reflected in the firm's price/earnings multiple. An increase in a company's risk level causes a decrease in the stock's price/earnings multiple. Unless EPS has increased enough, the result could be a drop in stock price. This is illustrated in Table 18-2:

Notice the EPS increase from $2.00 to $3.00, a sizeable jump; but the firm's P/E multiple has decreased due to the greater risk in the firm. The result is a decline of $2.00 in the firm's stock price.

TABLE 18-2

Stock Price	=	EPS	×	P/E Multiple
$20	=	$2.00	×	10
$18	=	$3.00	×	6

FINANCING DECISIONS AND CORPORATE CONTROL

Another consideration in planning the firm's capital structure is the desire of existing stockholders to maintain control of the company. Creditors have no voice in the selection of management, and preferred shareholders have none or very little. When the company borrows, existing shareholders sacrifice little, if any, control of management. In a corporation, each common stockholder is entitled to vote in proportion to the number of shares that he or she owns.

If the main object of the owners is to maintain control (particularly in closely held companies), it might appear advisable to raise any necessary additional funds from creditors or preferred owners. This is not always the case. As we have seen, if the company borrows more than it can safely service or repay, the creditors may seize the assets of the company to satisfy their claims. And, short of this, creditors may refuse to continue lending to the company unless granted more control over management (for example, by insisting on one or more seats on the board of directors). In this case, stockholders may lose quite a lot of control. It might be better to sacrifice a little control by some additional stock financing than to run the risk of too much debt. Companies averse to both excessive use of debt and loss of control sometimes turn to preferred stock as a kind of compromise.

FINANCING DECISIONS AND TIMING

Closely related to the factor of flexibility, is the factor of timing. An important consequence of flexibility is that it enables the firm to seize opportunities that allow it to minimize the total cost of debt and equity funds. Frequently very substantial savings may be obtained by proper timing of a security issue.

SUMMARY

When acquiring assets, firms have a choice among various methods of financing. To simplify matters, this chapter has considered only the basic features of debt and equity as related to financial *flexibility,* overall company *risk,* effects on stockholder *income,* impact on corporate *control,* and the importance of *timing.* The relative weights assigned these factors vary widely from company to company, depending upon the general economic conditions, the characteristics of the industry, and the particular situation of the company.

Subsequent chapters will discuss more thoroughly the principal types of financing available to a company. There are many variations in the financing "packages" that are made between companies seeking funds and investors. However such modifications do not change the basic distinctions between debt and equity. It is the responsibility of the financial manager to plan and manage the firm's financial structure in regard to these distinctions so as to maximize the value of the firm to the owners. Ultimately, this involves the trade-off of financial risk (in conjunction with other risks) and return.

MULTIPLE CHOICE QUESTIONS

1. A firm's DOL of 1.5 magnifies a 5-percent change in sales into:
   a) 7.5% change in net income
   b) 7.5% change in earnings per share
   c) 7.5% change in EBIT
   d) Both (a) and (b)

2. A DFL of 2.0 magnifies a 10-percent change in _____ into a 20-percent change in EPS:
   a) Sales
   b) EBIT
   c) Profit before taxes
   d) Taxes

3. A firm's EPS indifference point is the level of EBIT at which the firm's EPS:
   a) Is equal to the cost of capital
   b) Is equal to the required return on equity
   c) Is the same regardless of the financing mix
   d) Just meets investors' expectations

4. An EBIT level below the EPS indifference point usually means that:
   a) Debt financing is better than common stock financing
   b) Stock financing is better than debt financing
   c) The proposed investment should not be undertaken
   d) The firm is not minimizing its average cost of capital

5. The consideration of financial timing would suggest that, when the firm's stock price is unusually high:
   a) Sell common stock
   b) Shift from long-term debt to short-term debt
   c) Shift from short-term debt to long-term debt
   d) Repay as much debt as possible

DISCUSSION QUESTIONS

1. Explain what is meant by the acronym, FRICT, in evaluating the choice between debt and equity financing.

2. The consideration of risk is important in deciding how to finance a business firm. What is meant by operating risk and why is it important in financing decisions.

3. Explain what is meant by breakeven analysis and how a breakeven point can be found for a firm.

4. What is meant by the degree of operating leverage? What does the degree of operating leverage imply about the volatility of a firm's profits?

5. What is financial risk? How is the degree of financial leverage calculated, and how is it interpreted?

6. Explain the meaning of *combined leverage* and indicate how the degree-of-combined-leverage measure might be used to project future earnings per share figures.

7. Explain the meaning of the EBIT/EPS indifference point? Why is one financing alternative preferred above the indifference point and another preferred below it?

8. "Debt financing may produce higher EPS but lower stock price." Explain the support for this statement.

9. Discuss the relationship between the breakeven point and the degree of combined leverage.

10. In the 1960s, a group of investors got together to test an investment strategy. According to the plan, they would invest only in firms that

had high degrees of combined leverage. The 1960s produced one of the
most sustained economic expansions since the Depression. How do
you think the investors fared?

11. Discuss the importance of financial flexibility to the firm and how it
affects financing decisions. Make up an example that demonstrates
what can happen when a firm has no financial flexibility.

12. Describe the components of the cost-volume-profit chart. Explain, in
terms of the chart, why the breakeven point increases when fixed
costs increase.

13. "If a firm has no fixed costs, it has no leverage and thus its degree of
combined leverage is zero." Explain what is wrong with this statement.

14. For each of the following factors, determine what the impact on the
firm's operating or financial leverage will be (i.e., whether it will increase, decrease, or not be affected):

    a) An increase in borrowing
    b) Replacing assembly workers with robots
    c) Purchasing fabricated parts instead of making them
    d) Paying salespeople on commission instead of a salary

15. Explain the impact of each of the following on the firm's breakeven
point:

    a) A price decrease
    b) A decrease in fixed costs
    c) A decrease in variable costs

16. Discuss the following statement: "The firm's DOL depends on a particular sales volume. At a different sales volume, the company will have
a different DOL."

SOLVED PROBLEMS

SP-1. The Acme Company has sales of 300,000 units at an average price *leverage and breakeven*
of $1.40 per unit. Variable costs average $1.10 per unit and fixed
operating costs are $40,000. The firm has no fixed financial costs.

   a) Calculate the breakeven point in units.
   b) Calculate the breakeven point in sales dollars.
   c) Calculate the degree of operating leverage (DOL) at the current
   sales level.
   d) Assuming that sales increase by 12 percent, calculate the projected percentage increase in EBIT, given your answer to (c).
   e) If the company's average selling price per unit decreases by
   10 cents, calculate the impact on the breakeven point (in units).

SP-2. The Wallex Company is evaluating three alternatives for financing *EBIT/EPS analysis*
an $8 million expansion. Alternative #1 is an issue of 2 million
shares of common stock at a net (to the company) price of $4.00 per
share. Alternative #2 is an issue of 1 million common stock shares

at a net price of $4.00 plus an issue of $4 million of long-term debt at an interest rate of 15 percent. Alternative #3 is an $8 million issue of long-term debt at a rate of 15 percent. The expansion is expected to generate an increase of $4 million per year in EBIT, although the increase could be as low as $2 million or as high as $6 million. If common stock financing only is used, the company's current P/E ratio of 10 times is expected to continue. However, if alternative #2 (half stock, half debt) is used, the P/E is likely to fall to 9 times. If straight debt is used, the P/E is expected to fall to 8 times. A recent income statement for the company is shown below:

Wallex Company	
Income Statement, Year Ending 12/31/87 ($000)	
Sales	$110,000
Cost of goods sold (all variable expenses)	86,000
Gross profit	24,000
Operating expenses (all fixed)	14,000
EBIT	10,000
Interest expense	2,500
Profit before taxes	7,500
Taxes (34%)	2,550
Net income	$ 4,950

No. of common shares outstanding 10,000,000
EPS: $0.495
P/E ratio: 10 times
Market Price Per Share: $4.95

a) Calculate EPS and market price per share (MPPS) for each of the three alternatives at each of the three possible EBIT levels (i.e., $12 million; $14 million; $16 million).
b) Calculate the EBIT/EPS indifference point for each possible pair of alternatives (i.e., #1 vs. #2; #1 vs. #3; #2 vs. #3).
c) Confirm your answer to (b) with a *pro forma* calculation of EPS for the three alternatives at the indifference levels of EBIT.
d) Construct an EBIT/EPS chart. Interpret the chart in terms of your calculations in part (b).

PROBLEMS

leverage and breakeven

1. The Jakes Company has sales of 1,500,000 units at an average price of $1.00 per unit. Variable costs average $0.90 per unit and fixed operating costs are $100,000. The firm has no fixed financial costs.

a) Calculate the breakeven point in units.
b) Calculate the breakeven point in sales dollars.
c) Calculate the degree of operating leverage (DOL) at the current sales level.
d) Assuming that sales increase by 12 percent, calculate the projected percentage increase in EBIT, given your answer to (c).
e) If the company's average selling price per unit increases by 10 cents, calculate the impact on the breakeven point (in units).

2. The Bruin Company is evaluating three alternatives for financing a $16 million expansion. Alternative #1 is an issue of 2 million shares of common stock at a net (to the company) price of $8.00 per share. Alternative #2 is an issue of 1 million common stock shares at a net price of $8.00 plus an issue of 8 million of long-term debt at an interest rate of 12 percent. Alternative #3 is a $16 million issue of long-term debt at a rate of 12 percent. The expansion is expected to generate an increase of $8 million per year in EBIT, although the increase could be as low as $3 million or as high as $15 million. If common stock financing only is used, the company's current P/E ratio of nine times is expected to continue. However, if alternative #2 (half stock, half debt) is used, the P/E is likely to fall to eight times. If straight debt is used, the P/E is expected to fall to seven times. A recent income statement for the company is shown below:

EBIT/EPS analysis

Bruin Company: Income Statement For the Year Ending 12/31/87 ($000)

Sales	$200,000
Cost of goods sold (all variable expenses)	156,000
Gross profit	44,000
Operating expenses (all fixed)	24,000
EBIT	20,000
Interest expense	5,000
Profit before taxes	15,000
Taxes (34%)	5,100
Net income	$ 9,900

No. of common shares outstanding: 10,000,000
EPS: $0.99
P/E ratio: 9.1 times
Market Price Per Share: $9

a) Calculate EPS and market price per share (MPPS) for each of the three alternatives at each of the three possible EBIT levels (i.e., $23 million; $28 million; $35 million).
b) Calculate the EBIT/EPS indifference point for each possible pair of alternatives (i.e., #1 vs. #2; #1 vs. #3; #2 vs. #3).

leverage and breakeven

c) Confirm your answer to (b) with a *pro forma* calculation of EPS for the three alternatives at the indifference levels of EBIT.

d) Construct an EBIT/EPS chart. Interpret the chart in terms of your calculations in part (b).

3. We have the following information available for companies A and B:

	Company A		Company B	
Units produced and sold		25,000		25,000
Revenues		$112,500		$112,500
Variable costs	$25,000		$50,000	
Fixed costs	$50,000	$ 75,000	$25,000	$ 75,000
EBIT		$ 37,500		$ 37,500

a) What is the breakeven point for each company in units? In sales dollars?

b) What is the degree of operating leverage for each company at 25,000 units?

c) How do you explain the differences that you observe between these companies' breakeven points and degrees of operating leverage?

4. The Supreme Product Corporation manufactures only one product. Its fixed costs total $170,000, and variable costs amount to $1.65 per unit. The items are sold for $3.00 per unit.

leverage and breakeven

I.a) Prepare a chart showing the company's breakeven point.

b) Calculate mathematically the breakeven point shown in your chart.

c) Assume that the company is operating at a level of 140,000 units and that sales rise by 10 percent to 154,000 units. What is the percentage increase? Use these figures to compute the degree of operating leverage.

d) Compute the degree of operating leverage for the following levels of output: 140,000 units, 150,000 units, and 180,000 units.

II. (In this and the following sections, show all computations.) Assume that variable costs rise to 1.80 per unit, but that fixed costs and selling price remain as originally indicated.

a) What is the new breakeven point?

b) What is the degree of operating leverage at the following levels of output: 150,000 units; and 180,000 units?

c) How do you explain the differences that you observe between results in Parts 1 and II?

III. Assume that fixed costs rise to $175,000, but that variable costs and selling price remain as originally indicated in Part I.

a) What is the new breakeven point?

b) What is the degree of operating leverage at 140,000 units; 150,000 units; and 180,000 units?

c) How do you explain the differences that you observe among your results in Parts I, II, and III?

IV. Assume that the selling price is increased to $3.30 per unit, but that fixed and variable costs remain as originally indicated in Part I.

a) What is the new breakeven point?

b) What is the degree of operating leverage at 140,000 units; 150,000 units; and 180,000 units?

c) How do you explain the differences that you observe between your results in Parts I and IV?

5. The Armont Corp. is considering lowering its selling price on product Y. *breakeven* The following information is available on the costs of producing and the income from selling the product:

Sales revenue (75,000 units @ $10)		$750,000
Variable costs (75,000 units)	$412,500	
Fixed costs	$200,000	$612,500
EBIT		$137,500

To assist management in reaching a decision, the financial manager has prepared a table to show the percentage increase in volume necessary to maintain a net operating income (EBIT) of $137,500 on the item with decreases in price of 5 percent, 10 percent, and 15 percent.

	% Decrease in selling price		
	5%	10%	15%
Volume (units) necessary to produce EBIT of $137,500:			
Increase in volume (units) required:			
% Increase in volume required:			

a) Complete the table.

b) How do you explain the variations in the percentage increase in volume necessary to maintain EBIT of $137,500? (That is, why is not the percentage increase in volume required for a 10-percent decrease in price just double the percentage increase in volume required for a 5-percent decrease in price?)

6. The Bionic Manufacturing Corporation has an average selling price of $1.00 per unit. Its variable costs are $0.70 per unit and fixed operating

leverage, breakeven, EBIT/EPS analysis

costs amount to $17,000. Bionic finances all its assets by having issued 4,000 shares of common stock. Another firm in the same industry, Cryonic, has the same operating information but finances its assets with common stock consisting of 2,000 shares and debt having interest obligations of $1,600 per year. Both firms are in the 50-percent income tax bracket.

a) Determine the degree of operating leverage and the degree of financial leverage given sales of $70,000 for each firm.

b) Calculate the degree of combined leverage for each firm. Why are the measures different?

c) Considering operating fixed costs only, prepare breakeven charts and calculate the operating breakeven points for the two firms. What are your observations?

d) Prepare an EBIT/EPS indifference chart and calculate the EPS indifference point between the financial structure used by Bionic versus Cryonic. Calculate the EPS dollar amount at this comparative EPS indifference point.

EBIT/EPS analysis

7. The Racal Corporation has 12,000 shares of common stock outstanding. Last year's income statement is summarized below, along with four partial *pro forma* statements reflecting different assumptions regarding a new plant. In all instances, $1 million must be raised, and the new plant will cost $1 million dollars. Financing option #1 involves selling 8,000 shares of common stock. Option #2 involves borrowing $1 million at an interest rate of 9%.

Pro Forma

		Option #1		Option #2	
	Actual 1987	Optimistic	Pessimistic	Optimistic	Pessimistic
Sales	$500,000	$1,000,000	$650,000	$1,000,000	$650,000
Variable expenses	$150,000	$	$	$	$
Fixed operating expense	$230,000	$ 400,000	$400,000	$ 400,000	$400,000
EBIT	$120,000	$	$	$	$
Interest	$ -0-	$	$	$	$
Profit before taxes	$120,000	$	$	$	$
Taxes (50%)	$ 60,000	$	$	$	$
Net income	$ 60,000	$	$	$	$
Earnings per share	$ 5.00	$	$	$	$

Assume that you are the financial vice-president of Racal. Your assistant started the above projections using last year's financial report and projections of sales and fixed expenses sent to you by the sales and production departments.

a) Complete the tabulations. Which alternative yields a higher EPS amount?

b) Compute the EPS point of indifference between the two alternatives. If sales are most likely to be $800,000 for the period, which alternative would you recommend to the Board of Directors?

c) Assume the economic climate changes, and the optimistic sales forecast now appears to be highly probable. You and your staff expect the marketplace to attach a 16 times price/earnings multiple if debt financing is used. What alternative should be chosen from the market value point of view?

EBIT/EPS analysis

8. The Directors of the Supreme Corporation (Problem 4) are considering the methods of financing the corporation. Initially, $600,000 will be needed. Some of the directors wish to finance the needs by issuing 5,000 shares of common stock. Another group believes that the corporation should issue $300,000 of 15-percent bonds and raise the remaining $300,000 by selling 2,500 shares of common stock. Assume the company's income tax rate is 40 percent.

I.a) Calculate the EBIT/EPS indifference point.

b) Compare earnings per share (EPS) under the two proposed capital structures if EBIT is $80,000 and $100,000. How do you explain the differences in your results?

II. Assume that the 15-percent bonds are used along with the 2,500 shares of common stock.

a) Initially the company is expected to operate at a level of 192,600 units, so that EBIT will be $90,000. If EBIT should rise by 10 percent, what will be the percentage increase in earnings per share? Use these figures to compute the degree of financial leverage at EBIT of $90,000.

b) Using the formula given, compute the degree of financial leverage for the following levels of EBIT: $72,000, $90,000, and $198,000.

III. Assume that the bond-stock capital structure is to be used and that sales rise by 10 percent to 211,860 units from 192,600 units. (Selling price is $3.00 per unit; variable costs, $1.65 per unit; and fixed costs total $170,000).

a) Compute the percentage increase in EPS.

b) What is the degree of operating leverage at 192,600 units?

c) Determine the degree of combined leverage at 192,600 units. Based on the formula given in the chapter, use the degree of combined leverage figure to determine the new EPS, and show that this agrees with the result you obtained in Part (a) of this section.

EBIT/EPS analysis

9. The H Company forecasts its EBIT for the next year to be $80,000; $100,000; or $120,000, each with an equal probability of occurring. The company currently has an interest-on-debt obligation of $10,000 per year; has 10,000 shares of common stock outstanding; and is in the

40-percent tax bracket. H's EBIT forecast is based on the assumption that there will be a $200,000 expansion of the firm's plant facilities. The plant expansion can be financed by issuing 5,000 shares of common stock, by selling long-term debt with a 12-percent interest rate, or by issuing 2,500 shares of common stock and $100,000 in 12-percent bonds. If common stock is issued, the H Company anticipates a price earning ratio of 12 times. A combination of debt and equity issues is expected to result in an 11 times price/earnings multiple, while a $200,000 debt issue is likely to be associated with a 10 times multiple.

a) Calculate the EPS under each possible EBIT outcome for each of the three financing alternatives.

b) Indicate the expected EPS amount for each of the three financing alternatives. Also comment on the dispersion of possible EPS outcomes. Which financing alternative would you recommend based on your EPS calculations?

c) From a market price per share standpoint, and based on expected EPS amounts, which financing alternative would you recommend?

d) Calculate the EPS indifference point for the three financing alternatives.

EBIT/EPS analysis

10. Following are balance sheets and income statements for the Genet Corporation. The company is planning a plant and equipment expansion of $100,000 next year, and EBIT is expected to be 10 percent higher next year due to the expansion. Either of two financing alternatives are available: (a) sell common stock to net $30.00 per share (the current market price is $35.00); or (2) issue a 10-year bond at $1,000 par value per bond carrying a 12-percent interest rate. If common stock is issued, the firm's existing price/earnings ratio (based on the EPS for last year) is expected to continue; otherwise a price/earnings ratio of nine times is expected if debt financing is used. The firm currently has 35,000 shares outstanding.

a) Estimate next year's EPS under the two financing alternatives.

b) In a risk-return (market-value) context, which financing alternative would you recommend?

c) Calculate the EBIT/EPS indifference point.

Genet Corporation

Balance Sheets As of December 31

	1987	1986
Cash	$ 20,000	$ 24,000
Accounts receivable	300,000	231,000
Inventories	500,000	425,000

Total current assets	820,000	680,000
Fixed assets, net	380,000	220,000
Total assets	$1,200,000	$900,000
Bank loan, 10%	80,000	80,000
Accounts payable	260,000	134,000
Accruals	65,000	48,000
Total current liabilities	405,000	262,000
Long-term debt, 11%	200,000	200,000
Common stock, $10 par	350,000	300,000
Paid-in-surplus	145,000	58,000
Retained earnings	100,000	80,000
Total liabilities and equity	$1,200,000	$900,000

Income Statements for the Years Ending December 31

	1987	1986
Sales	$2,500,000	$2,300,000
Cost of goods sold	2,000,000	1,840,000
Gross profit	500,000	460,000
General, Administrative, & Selling	200,000	200,000
Depreciation	40,000	20,000
EBIT	260,000	240,000
Interest	30,000	30,000
Profit before taxes	230,000	210,000
Taxes (40%)	92,000	84,000
Net income	$ 138,000	$ 126,000

SOLUTIONS TO SOLVED PROBLEMS

SP-1. a) Breakeven point in units $= \dfrac{\text{Total fixed costs}}{(\text{Price} - \text{variable costs})}$

$$= \frac{\$40,000}{(\$1.40 - 1.10)} = 133,333 \text{ units}$$

One of the most common errors made in computing the break-even point is to leave out fixed financial costs when computing the total fixed costs. In this problem there are no fixed financial costs; but, if there were, they would have to be included in the numerator—otherwise the company will *not* break even at the "breakeven point."

b) *Breakeven point in sales dollars.* There are two ways to solve this. The easiest way would be simply to multiply the breakeven in units times the average selling price. Of course, this requires that you know what the breakeven in units is. That will not always be the case. The longer way to determine breakeven in sales dollars is to use the formula in the text: divide total fixed costs by the contribution margin percentage.

Step 1: Determine the contribution margin percentage ($cm\%$). This is equal to total sales minus total variable costs divided by total sales.

$$\text{Total sales} = 300{,}000 \text{ units} \times \$1.40 \text{ per unit} = \$420{,}000$$

$$\text{Total variable costs} = 300{,}000 \text{ units} \times \$1.10 \text{ per unit} = 330{,}000$$

$$cm\% = \frac{(\$420{,}000 - 330{,}000)}{\$420{,}000} = .2143 \quad \text{or} \quad .21$$

Step 2: Divide total fixed costs by the contribution margin percentage ($cm\%$)

$$\text{Breakeven point in sales} = \frac{\$40{,}000}{.21} = \$186{,}667$$

Step 3: Since, in this case, you know the breakeven point in units (133,333) and the sales price per unit, check your answer in Step 2:

$$\text{Breakeven point in sales} = \text{Breakeven point in units} \times \text{price per unit}$$
$$= 133{,}333 \times \$1.40 = \$186{,}666 \text{ (sufficiently close)}$$

c) Given the breakeven point in units (X_b), the DOL at any level of output (X) is:

$$DOL_x = X/(X - X_b)$$

$$DOL_{300{,}000 \text{ units}} = \frac{300{,}000}{(300{,}000 - 133{,}333)} = 1.80$$

d) The percentage change in EBIT will be equal to the DOL at that point times the percentage change in sales:

$$\% \, \Delta \, \text{EBIT} = DOL \times \% \, \Delta \, \text{Sales}$$

$$= 1.80 \times 12\% = 21.60\%$$

e) The new breakeven point in units, BE_u, can be found using the breakeven formula, substituting the new price per unit ($1.30) which reflects the 10-cents-per-unit price decrease:

$$BE_u = \$40{,}000/(\$1.30 - 1.10)$$

$$= 200{,}000 \text{ units}$$

Notice that what appears to be only a slight price reduction (i.e., $.10/\$1.40 = 7$ percent) produces an enormous, 50 percent, increase in the breakeven point (from 133,333 units to 200,000 units). In this light, management is going to proceed much more cautiously with the price decrease idea.

SP-2. a) The current level of EBIT is $10 million. Thus the projected EBIT levels can be $12 million; $14 million, or $16 million given EBIT increases of $2 million, $4 million, or $6 million, respectively. The easiest way to calculate EPS with each EBIT level and each financing alternative is to use the formula in the chapter:

$$EPS_\# = \frac{(EBIT - I_\#)(1 - T)}{N_\#}$$

Recall that the subscript # indicates which alternative is being considered; $I_\#$ represents the amount of interest expense which the firm will have given the financing alternative indicated; T represents the firm's tax rate; and $N_\#$ indicates the number of common stock shares outstanding given the financing alternative indicated. Since the company has existing interest payments of $2.5 million any new debt interest will be added to this. The additional interest for the stock alternative (#1) is, of course, zero; for alternative #2 ($4 million at 15 percent) the additional interest will be $600,000; and for alternative #3 ($8 million at 15 percent) the added interest will be $1.2 million. Thus, the new interest payments (in thousands) and number of common stock shares outstanding (in thousands) under each alternative are:

	Alternative		
	I_1	I_2	I_3
Total interest: (000)	$ 2,500	$ 3,100	$ 3,700
No. of shares: (000)	12,000	11,000	10,000

Regardless of the actual EBIT level, the total interest and number of shares outstanding under each alternative does not change. The only thing that varies is the assumed EBIT level. Using the formula above, the EPS for each alternative under the three EBIT levels is shown below:

EBIT (000)	12,000	14,000	16,000
EPS			
Alternative #1	.52	.63	.74
Alternative #2	.53	.65	.77
Alternative #3	.55	.68	.81
MPPS (approximately)			
Alternative #1	$5.20	$6.30	$7.40
Alternative #2	$4.77	$5.85	$6.93
Alternative #3	$4.40	$5.44	$6.48

Note that EPS is greatest with straight debt financing (alternative #3) regardless of the EBIT level outcome. However, also note that the decrease in P/E multiple more than offsets the increase in EPS under the debt alternatives. In fact, the straight common stock alternative (#1) results in the highest market price per share regardless of the EBIT outcome. Thus, alternative #1 seems best given the assumptions.

b) The EBIT/EPS indifference point can also be solved directly using the formula in the chapter:

$$\frac{(EBIT^* - I_\#)(1 - T)}{N_\#} = \frac{(EBIT^* - I_\#)(1 - T)}{N_\#}$$

$EBIT^*$ represents the level of EBIT which produces the same EPS for both alternatives; $I_\#$ represents the interest to be paid given alternative number #; T is the company's tax rate; and $N_\#$ is the number of common stock shares to be outstanding if the alternative indicated is chosen.

	EBIT* (000)
Alternative #1 vs. #2	$9,700
Alternative #1 vs. #3	$9,700
Alternative #2 vs. #3	$9,700

c) To check the accuracy of the $EBIT^*$ indifference point, EPS under each alternative is calculated below:

	Alternative (000)		
	#1	#2	#3
EBIT	$ 9,700	$ 9,700	$ 9,700
Interest	2,500	3,100	3,700
Profit before taxes	7,200	6,600	6,000
Taxes (34%)	2,448	2,244	2,040
Net income	$ 4,752	$ 4,356	$ 3,960
# shares (000)	12,000	11,000	10,000
EPS	$ 0.396	$ 0.396	$ 0.396

Thus, at an EBIT level of $9,700,000, all three financing alternatives will produce the same EPS.

d) The EBIT/EPS chart is shown below as Exhibit SP-2A. Notice that all three lines intersect at an EBIT level of $9,700,000, and thus at that level all have the same EPS of $0.396. (Note, the EBIT axis starts at $5 million.)

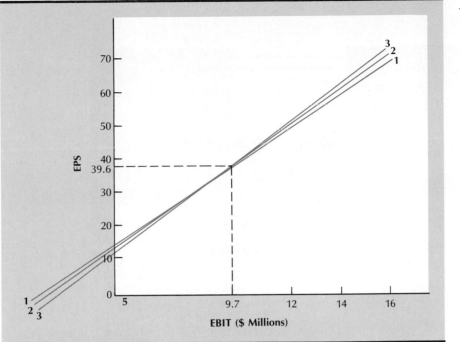

EXHIBIT SP-2A

REFERENCES

Bowen, Robert M., Lane A. Daley, and Charles C. Huber, Jr. "Evidence on the Existence and Determinants of Inter-Industry Differences in Leverage." *Financial Management,* Winter 1982, pp. 10–20.

Donaldson, Gordon. "New Framework for Corporate Debt Capacity." *Harvard Business Review,* March-April 1962, pp. 117–131.

Donaldson, Gordon. "Strategy for Financial Emergencies." *Harvard Business Review,* November-December 1969, pp. 67–79.

Gahlon, James M., and James A. Gentry. "On the Relationship Between Systematic Risk and the Degrees of Operating and Financial Leverage." *Financial Management,* Summer 1982, pp. 15–23.

Scott, David F., Jr., and John D. Martin. "Industry Influence on Financial Structure." *Financial Management,* Spring 1975, pp. 67–73.

CHAPTER 19

CAPITAL STRUCTURE
THEORY

he question to be addressed in this chapter is whether the issuance of securities other than stock has any effect on the firm's stock price. This is an important question because financing decisions and activities are central to the financial manager's role. If the composition of a firm's capital structure has no impact on the value of the firm's stock, the financial manager should not waste time considering it. However, if financing choices do affect the firm's stock price, the financial manager should try to determine how stock price is affected and pursue optimal capital-structure policies that maximize stock prices.

Objectives and Organization of this Chapter

The first section of this chapter asks the question: Why do firm's borrow money? It examines some typical responses a firm's managers might provide and the implied connection, if any, with the firm's stock price. The second section shows that most of these rationales are unfounded and that only the existence of corporate taxes and other market imperfections create a link between the firm's financing policies and its stock price. Finally, the chapter shows that even the benefits attributable to corporate taxes are diminished when the existence of personal taxes is considered.

WHY DO FIRMS BORROW?

Most businesses borrow money. If you were to ask the chief executive officer, "Why does your company borrow?" you would probably receive a surprised look — as if the answer should be obvious. But, if you persist, you might get many different answers. Let us consider some of the more common rationales for the use of debt.

"We need the money."

This answer, while certainly reasonable enough, begs the question. The question is, given that the firm needs the money, why borrow instead of, for example, selling more stock and raising the money from equity? Looking behind the "we-need-the-money" answer, one finds more basic considerations such as, "we don't want to sell stock" or "if we do not borrow, we will not be able to expand sales and profits" or "we need more capital to undertake profitable new investments." Presumably, all of these things will favorably affect stock price and would otherwise not be adopted.

However, this rationale confuses several issues. For example, an expansion in sales or addition of profitable investments may well raise the firm's stock price, but it is because the expansion in sales or new investment are economically valuable — not because they happen to be financed with debt. Moreover, if the firm will lose the benefits of expansion or new investment unless it borrows, then the firm's manager is implicitly acknowledging the existence of capital rationing.

In other words, one must be careful to avoid mixing the effects of investment and financing decisions on stock price.

"Debt increases return on equity and earnings per share."

As observed before, the firm's return on equity is influenced by the amount of financial leverage it has. Generally, the greater a firm's use of debt relative to equity, the higher its return on equity and earnings per share. According to this reasoning, higher return on equity makes the stock more attractive and should increase its market price.

Again, however, this response leaves something out. For example, as a firm uses more debt, shareholders expect to receive more compensation for the greater level of risk — this is consistent with the idea behind the capital asset pricing model. The impact on stock price is determined by the relationship between increased return on shareholders' equity and the amount of increase required to compensate for the greater risk.

"Debt is cheaper."

This rationale can mean two different things, only one of which is correct. The *wrong* reason is that the interest rate paid on debt is lower than the returns required by shareholders. What makes this argument incorrect is that it overlooks the fact that every dollar of *cheap* debt has the effect making the stock more risky and hence raises the cost of equity.

The interest rate on debt is a measure of its *explicit* cost; the effect debt use has on the returns required by shareholders is the *implicit* cost of debt. Both must be considered in evaluating the "cost of debt." What *does* make debt cheaper, even considering both its implicit and explicit costs, is the tax treatment of debt interest. Since interest expense is a tax deductible item, the existence of corporate taxes reduces the effective cost of debt relative to equity. We will discuss this idea in more detail in this chapter.

WHEN FINANCING POLICY DOES NOT MATTER

The increases in sales, profits, earnings per share, and return on equity which may accompany the use of debt are readily apparent. But the essential question is whether such increases will be rewarded by investors through an increase in the stock price of the company.

In an important article in 1958, Franco Modigliani and Merton Miller (M&M) argued that, in the absence of corporate taxes and market imperfections, the use of debt will not affect the stock price of the firm. Even though earnings per share, growth rate, and return on equity may all increase, the increases will be just sufficient to compensate investors for the increased financial risk produced by the use of debt.

Leverage in a No-Tax World

Assume that we observe two firms, U (Unlevered) and L (Levered). The U firm, by definition, uses no debt, while the L firm raises half its capital in the form of debt (on which it pays interest of 10 percent) and half from shareholders' equity. The two firms are in the same line of business, are equal in size, and have the same operating profit. All profits are paid out as dividends. There are no corporate taxes or other market imperfections. Summary income statement information for both firms is shown below:

	U	L
Sales	$1,000	$1,000
EBIT	200	200
Interest	0-	50
Profit before taxes	200	150
Taxes (0%)	-0-	-0-
Net Income	200	150

To simplify the analysis further, assume that the earnings of each firm are constant each year and thus represent perpetuities. The U firm has 100 shares of stock outstanding, and its shareholders require a return of 20 percent on their investment (K_e). Then, for the U firm, the market value per share of U's stock is $10.

	U
Earnings and dividends per share	$ 2.00
Required rate of return (k_e)	.20
Market value per share ($2.00 ÷ .20)	$10.00

In contrast to the U firm, management of the L firm has decided to employ debt financing in its capital structure. Instead of selling 100 shares, the L company has issued only 50 at $10 per share and borrowed another $500 at an interest rate of 10 percent. The following results are expected for the L company:

	L
Sales	$1000
EBIT	200
Interest	50
Profit before taxes	150
Taxes (0%)	-0-
Net income	150
Earnings per share ($150 ÷ 50 shares)	$ 3.00
Return on equity ($150 ÷ $500)	30%

With financial leverage, the L company produces noticeably higher earnings per share and return on equity. But will the L firm's stock price reflect this "superior performance?" In short, will the L firm's stock price be higher than $10 per share? According to M & M, the answer is a decisive "No!"

Why L's Stock Price Stays at $10 Per Share

There are several good reasons for arguing that L's stock price will not be higher than $10 per share. But, perhaps the simplest way to see that L is no more valuable than U is to pose this choice: If you could own either firm in its entirety, which would you prefer? If you choose the U firm, you get all the stock; if you choose the L firm you get all the stock and all the bonds. Actually, you should be indifferent between the two. Each alternative gives you exactly the same cash flow every year and, hence, neither firm is more valuable as a whole.

	Total Returns	
	U	L
Cash from bonds	-0-	$ 50
Cash from stock	$200	$150
Total cash	$200	$200

By splitting up the same EBIT ($200) into two different cash flow streams, one called equity and the other debt, the firm has created a new security but no new cash flows. Since the firm has not increased the total cash flows produced by the company, the total value of the company should not increase. This is the essence of M&M's argument, and it is often referred to as "Proposition #1."

More fundamentally, the reason the L firm's managers have not created any value by using debt is that they are not performing any service for stockholders which stockholders cannot perform for themselves. In general, any action by management that can be replicated or reversed by individual investors will not increase the value of the company's stock.[1] Since individuals can borrow, they can produce homemade leverage; hence the value of the firm will not increase simply because it is employing leverage. Let us see how this works.

Homemade Leverage

To see how homemade leverage would work, assume that L's price actually does rise above $10 per share. One could choose any number greater than $10; for example, assume that L's stock price rises to $12 per share.

homemade leverage

Rational investors should not pay $12 per share for the stock because their rate of return would be less than they could earn with homemade leverage. This argument is often referred to as the "arbitrage" support for Proposition #1.[2]

Example
_____

Homemade Leverage

Assume an investor owns five (that is, 10 percent of the total) shares of L company stock selling at $12 per share. This investor gets dividends of $3

---

[1]This argument helps explain why diversification by the firm does not increase stock price — without synergies (i.e., cost savings).
[2]Arbitrage involves the simultaneous buying and selling of identical economic goods at different prices.

per share, or $15 per year. This produces a 25 percent return on equity (i.e., $3 ÷ $12). The return on equity is higher than what is earned on the U shares (20 percent) but not high enough. With homemade leverage, an investor could get more cash and higher return on equity. To do this, the L shareholder should sell his five shares for $60, borrow $50[3] at an interest rate of 10 percent, and invest the total, $110, in 11 U shares (i.e., $110 ÷ $10 per share).

From the 11 shares, the U shareholder would earn dividends of $22 (i.e., $2 per share times 11 shares). From this, interest of $5 would be deducted (10 percent times $50), leaving net cash flow of $17. Thus, by homemade leverage, a stockholder could earn more cash ($2 in this example) than by buying stock (or holding stock) in the L company. Similarly, homemade leverage would provide a return on equity of 28.3 percent (i.e., $17 ÷ $60) compared to only 25 percent for L stockholders.

Steps In Homemade Leverage

Step #1: Sell L stock ($12 per share × 5 shares) =	$ 60
Step #2: Borrow amount proportional to company's debt/equity ratio =	$ 50
Total levered portfolio =	$110
Step #3: Buy U shares ($110 ÷ $10 per share) = 11 U shares	
Total cash received from U shares ($2 per share × 11 shares) =	$ 22
less: interest on borrowing ($50 × .10) =	($ 5)
Net cash received from U investment =	$ 17
Return on equity = $17 ÷ $60 = .283 or 28.3%	

Since greater profits could be made by selling L stock rather than owning it, L's stock price would drop. In fact, L's stock price would drop to $10 per share, the same as U's stock price. At a $10 per share stock price, L provides stockholders a 30 percent rate of return (i.e., $3 dividend ÷ $10). This rate is just enough to compensate investors for the financial risk involved, and thus shareholders will be indifferent between corporate and homemade leverage. This relationship between the required return on equity and financial leverage can be expressed as:

$$k_l = k_u + (k_u - k_d)D/E \tag{19-1}$$

---

[3]This is equal to 10 percent of the bonds issued by the L company. Since the shareholder had 10 percent of the stock, we want to keep the amount of financial risk constant by giving him the equivalent of 10 percent of the debt. We are assuming that the investor can borrow at the same interest rate as the corporation in order to keep the exposition simple.

where k_l is the required return on equity in the levered firm; k_u is the required return on equity in the unlevered firm; k_d is the cost of debt; and D/E is the ratio of debt to equity. Recall that k_u is 20 percent and k_d is 10 percent. Thus at a debt to equity ratio of 1.0, k_l is

$$k_l = .20 + (.20 - .10)1$$

$$= .30$$

A Frequently Asked Question

Students usually wonder if an investor could get even higher returns by personally borrowing and investing in the L stock, in essence getting "double" leverage.[4] The answer is that the rate of return will be higher, but only because risk has increased. Such an investor would be exposed to both corporate bankruptcy risk and personal bankruptcy risk. The increased financial risk should provide a higher rate of return. But as long as individual shareholders can match the total leverage produced by L shareholders, L's stock price will not increase. The higher risk and return from such a strategy should not disguise the fact that the L company stock is only worth $10 per share.

WHEN FINANCING CHOICES DO MATTER

Contrary to the implications of Proposition #1, most firms do include debt and other securities in their capital structures. This evidence suggests that one or more of the M&M assumptions about perfect markets does not conform to reality. Indeed, in addition to corporate taxes, there are several plausible market imperfections that may affect the value of the levered company's stock and allow it to rise above $10 per share.

Why Leverage Affects Stock Price

The fundamental question is why anyone would pay more than $10 per share for L stock. The answer is that, if L does in fact provide benefits to its shareholders that they could not receive otherwise, then L's stock might be valued at more than $10 per share. Let us examine what some of these benefits might be.

Limited Liability. An investor in a leveraged corporation has limited liability. The maximum loss exposure is the price paid for the stock. However, when an investor employs homemade leverage, the risk exposure may extend to all other assets the investor owns.

---

[4]Actually, since the L stock is levered, this compounding results in more than double leverage.

In response to this argument, however, one could argue that investors may form limited-liability investment companies organized to undertake homemade leverage yet insulate other income or assets of the investor. Such investment companies, of course, would involve costs of organization, reporting, and administration. Insofar as corporate leverage spares the investor these costs, the levered company's stock may be considered more valuable.

Transactions Costs. There are commissions and other transactions costs that may have to be incurred in carrying out the process of homemade leverage. These too will limit complete adjustment of L's price.

However, offsetting this imperfection to some extent is the fact that certain large financial institutions, may have relatively low transactions costs and thus narrow the amount by which L's price might exceed its "equilibrium" value. Remember, not all investors have to practice homemade leverage in order to exploit L's disequilibrium price. Moreover, one should recognize that the corporation itself must also incur transactions costs in arranging its financing. For example, a company issuing bonds will have many different types of flotation costs that will offset the benefits of leverage.

Borrowing Rate. To the extent individual borrowing rates on debt are higher than those of the company, there may be some additional value in corporate versus personal leverage.

This too is mitigated by the fact that large financial institutions may be able to command borrowing rates even lower than those available to industrial companies.

Amount of Leverage. If L is able to borrow more heavily than its shareholders, then it may provide something homemade leverage cannot.

However, considering the relatively low debt/equity ratios of most nonfinancial corporations, it is not likely that such companies provide significantly more leverage to investors than investors can attain themselves. For example, margin requirements on the purchase of common stock are currently 50 percent, meaning that an investor can buy $100 worth of stock with $50 — a debt to equity ratio of 100 percent. Moreover, investors may effectively produce a "pseudo-loan" by withdrawing funds from other investments they have in order to undertake homemade leverage and realize excess returns.

Corporate Taxes

When the impact of corporate taxes on a firm's value is considered, one discovers that the use of debt does increase the total returns produced by the company and hence should increase the value of the firm. However, before concluding that this is the answer as to why firms borrow, one must recall that personal taxes also exist and that the impact of the firm's borrowing on its value depends a lot on the offsetting effects of personal taxes. Let us first see how corporate taxes allow a firm to increase total returns through leverage.

How Leverage Increases Total Returns

Let us continue with our comparison of the two firms, U and L. Recall that each company has EBIT of $200 in perpetuity. Previously taxes were ignored, but now let us assume that the corporate tax rate is 34 percent.

	U	L
EBIT	$200	$200
I	-0-	$ 50
PBT	$200	$150
Taxes (34%)	$ 68	$ 51
Net income	$132	$ 99

Total Returns

	U	L
Cash to bondholders	-0-	$ 50
Cash to shareholders	$132	$ 99
Total cash	$132	$149

The net income of the U firm will be $132, compared to $99 for the L firm. However, the total returns to investors are higher from the L firm ($149) than from the U firm ($132). Now, recalling the choice posed previously, would it be better to own the U firm or the L firm in its entirety? Now one would not be indifferent, because owning the L firm one would receive more cash each year in perpetuity than if one owned the U firm.

Where the Extra Cash Comes From

The extra $17 in cash flows produced by the L company is exactly equal to the $17 reduction in taxes paid. Thus, the value "created" by using debt originates from the Internal Revenue Service. The tax deductibility of interest has reduced taxable income (i.e., provided a tax shield on income) and hence taxes. The tax shield is equal to the amount of interest (I) times the tax rate (t).

$$\text{Interest tax shield} = It$$

$$= \$50 \times .34 = \$17$$

Since the amount of interest is equal to the interest rate (r) times the amount borrowed (D), the tax shield on interest can also be expressed as:

$$\text{Interest tax shield} = rDt \qquad (19\text{-}2)$$

$$= .10 \times \$500 \times .34 = \$17$$

The interest tax shield will continue as long as the firm borrows and pays taxes. Thus, in the example, the tax shield can be considered a perpetuity (every year the L company will produce $17 more cash than the U company). Assuming, for simplicity, that the riskiness of the tax shield is roughly equivalent to the riskiness of the debt itself, the present value of the tax shield, discounted by the interest rate on debt, r, can be expressed as:

$$\text{Present value of interest tax shield} = \frac{rDt}{r} \qquad (19\text{-}3)$$

$$= Dt$$

$$= \$500 \times .4 = \$200$$

In other words, the total value of the levered company, V_{tl}, is equal to the value of the unlevered company, V_{tu}, plus the present value of the interest tax shield on debt, Dt.

$$V_{tl} = V_{tu} + Dt \qquad (19\text{-}4)$$

where V_{tl} is the total value (debt and equity) of the levered company; V_{tu} is the total value of the unlevered company; and Dt is the present value of the interest tax shield on debt.

The implication of Equation 19-4 is obvious: The more debt a firm uses, the greater its total value. But this leads to the illogical conclusion that, to maximize the value of the firm's stock, the firm should not have any (i.e., it should be financed entirely with debt). Since firms do not seem to behave according to the implications of Equation 19-4, one must consider what limits exist in practice to the use of leverage.

Limits to Leverage

It is reasonable to speculate why firms do not use extremely high levels of debt to maximize the tax shield values. In practice, there are several factors that limit the amount of debt companies are willing to assume.

bankruptcy costs

Bankruptcy Costs.   The more debt a company carries, the more likely bankruptcy becomes. In the event of bankruptcy, significant legal and administrative costs are incurred and reduce the amounts shareholders get. If assets must be liquidated, they may have to be sold at less than their true value due to the company's distressed situation. Such losses will have to be borne by shareholders. The result is that the value of the firm may increase with leverage, but only up to a point — beyond which the probability and costs of bankruptcy increase so quickly that total value actually decreases.

Agency Costs. As firms borrow more and more heavily, lenders also *agency costs* view default or bankruptcy as more probable. To protect themselves, lenders require closer monitoring of management activities. Lenders may prohibit the payment of dividends to stockholders, or the discretionary use of cash by management, or insist on slower expansion by the company. Short of liquidation, the company may lose key customers, suppliers and employees as they become fearful that the company will not survive. These higher costs of doing business come under the category of agency costs — the costs of insuring that managers acting as agents of the corporation, comply with promises made to lenders and follow policies in the best interests of shareholders. Agency costs are passed on to the company's shareholders through higher interest rates, more burdensome monitoring and reporting costs, or both.

Personal Taxes

The existence and impact of personal taxes may also offset the advantages of corporate leverage. The existence of personal taxes means that bondholders must pay taxes on interest income received by the corporation, and shareholders must pay taxes on dividends and the sale of stock. Thus, on a total returns basis, it is possible that the increase in cash realized by bondholders (after taxes) will be less than the cash given up (after taxes) by shareholders. To see this more clearly, assume that you again have the choice of owning either the U or L company in its entirety. However, considering your personal tax situation, further assume that any interest income you receive is taxed at a rate of 28 percent but any dividends you receive are not taxed at all (i.e., a tax rate of 0 percent).[5] Corporate taxes are still 34 percent.

	U	L
EBIT	$200	$200
I	-0-	$ 50
PBT	$200	$150
Tax (34%)	$ 68	$ 51
Net income	$132	$ 99

	U	L
Cash from bonds (after personal taxes)	-0-	$ 36
Cash from shares (after personal taxes)	$132	$ 99
Total cash after taxes	$132	$135

---

[5]This is unrealistically low for dividend income; but in the more general case, when dividends can be deferred and expressed as capital appreciation, the effective tax rate on equity income could be quite low.

Now notice that the amount of extra cash you get from owning the levered company is only $3 compared to the $17 extra when only corporate taxes were considered. You should still prefer the L company, but by a much slimmer margin.

The total cash you get from the U company can be expressed algebraically as:

$$EBIT(1 - t_c)(1 - t_e) \tag{19-5}$$

where t_c is the corporate tax rate and t_e is the personal tax rate on equity income.

The total cash you get from the L company can be expressed algebraically as:

$$(EBIT - I)(1 - t_c)(1 - t_e) + I(1 - t_i) \tag{19-6}$$

Which can be expanded and restated as:

$$EBIT(1 - t_c)(1 - t_e) - I(1 - t_c)(1 - t_e) + I(1 - t_i) \tag{19-6a}$$

and,

$$EBIT(1 - t_c)(1 - t_e) + I[(1 - t_i) - (1 - t_c)(1 - t_e)] \tag{19-6b}$$

Where I is the amount of interest paid and t_i is the tax rate on interest income.

Since you get $EBIT(1 - t_c)(1 - t_e)$ from both companies, the extra cash you get from the L company is equal to:

$$I[(1 - t_i) - (1 - t_c)(1 - t_e)] \tag{19-7}$$

We can check this algebra with the example where I is $50; t_i is 28 percent; t_c is 34 percent and t_e is 0 percent:

$$\$50[(1 - .28) - (1 - .34)(1 - 0)]$$

$$\$50(.72 - .66) = \$3$$

Which is the same answer we got before.

The effect of personal taxes on the value of corporate leverage is still an unresolved theoretical question. The interrelationships of corporate and personal taxes vary from firm to firm, and so the impact of leverage on particular firms is impossible to determine *a priori* without good information about the relative tax rates of individual investors. As indicated by Equation 19-7, on average, as long as the term $(1 - t_i)$ is greater than the product of terms $(1 - t_c)(1 - t_e)$, corporate leverage increases the value of the firm.

S U M M A R Y

The effect of leverage on the value of the firm is a question of vital importance. To date this has proven to be one of the most difficult questions to examine empirically. If the composition of a firm's capital structure has no impact on the value of the firm's stock, the financial manager should waste no time considering it. However, since most firms borrow and highly competent managers wrestle with financing decisions every day, our instincts must tell us that leverage affects value. While the tax treatment of debt interest at first seems to "tie up" the loose ends of theory nicely, the ends become unraveled again when the realism of personal taxes is considered. At this point, the safest thing to conclude about the relationship of leverage to value is that whether and/or how much debt affects value depends on a complex system of factors that vary in relative importance from firm to firm. These factors include, but are not limited to, the corporation's marginal tax rate and the marginal tax rates of the firm's creditors and shareholders.

MULTIPLE CHOICE QUESTIONS

1. According to M&M, in the absence of taxes, leverage will:
   a) Reduce the value of the firm by the amount of debt used
   b) Not affect the value of the firm
   c) Increase the value of the firm by the face value of the debt used
   d) Reduce the value of the firm by the amount of interest expense
2. According to M&M, given the existence of corporate taxes, leverage will:
   a) Reduce the value of the firm by the amount of debt used
   b) Increase the value of the firm by the present value of the interest tax shield
   c) Increase the value of the firm by the face value of the debt used
   d) Reduce the value of the firm by the amount of interest expense

3. According to M&M, in the absence of corporate taxes, if a firm borrows to repurchase stock:

   a) Stock price should rise by the percentage of stock repurchased
   b) Stock price should rise by the increase in earnings per share times the P/E multiple
   c) Stock price will drop
   d) Stock price will not change

4. Homemade leverage refers to:

   a) Selling the stock of an unlevered firm and buying the stock of a levered firm
   b) Avoiding commissions
   c) Selling the stock of a levered firm and buying the stock of an unlevered firm
   d) Selling the stock of a levered firm, borrowing and buying the stock of an unlevered firm

5. According to M&M, the relationship between the required return on equity and financial leverage can be expressed as:

   a) $k_1 = k_u + (k_u - k_d)D/E$
   b) $k_1 = k_d + (k_u - k_d)D/E$
   c) $k_1 = k_u + (k_d - k_u)D/E$
   d) $k_1 = k_1 + (k_u - k_d)D/E$

6. Assuming the existence of both corporate and personal taxes, corporate leverage will increase the value of the firm as long as:

   a) $(1 - t_i) > (1 - t_c)(1 - t_e)$
   b) $(1 - t_e) > (1 - t_c)(1 - t_i)$
   c) $(1 - t_i) < (1 - t_c)(1 - t_e)$
   d) $(1 - t_c) > (1 - t_e)(1 - t_i)$

DISCUSSION QUESTIONS

1. List some typical responses to the question: why do firms borrow? Examine the validity of each of these responses.

2. Distinguish between the implicit and explicit costs of debt.

3. If financial leverage increases a firm's earnings per share, dividends per share, and return on equity, how can it fail to increase the firm's stock price?

4. What is the idea behind M&M's "Proposition #1?"

5. Discuss the idea behind homemade leverage and the steps involved in implementing it.

6. How critical to homemade leverage, do you think, is the assumption that individuals can borrow at the same rate as the corporation?

7. A student wonders, "sure homemade leverage increases your rate of return from an unlevered firm, but I will bet you could do even better by using the homemade leverage to invest in the levered firm." How would you respond to this?

8. If you believe Proposition #1 holds, how much debt would your optimal capital structure contain?

9. Some people believe that even in the absence of corporate taxes, corporate leverage provides value in one or more of the following ways:

   a) Limited liability
   b) Savings on transactions costs
   c) Lower borrowing rates
   d) Greater leverage

   How would you respond to this?

10. According to theory, the value of a levered firm increases by the amount Dt, where D is the total debt the firm has and t is the marginal tax rate. What is the rationale for this conclusion?

11. If you consider only corporate taxes and ignore personal taxes, what would be the firm's capital structure? Can you think of any other limits to the use of leverage (besides personal taxes) that might become important to the company?

12. When both corporate and personal taxes are considered, according to the text, the extra cash produced by a levered firm is equal to the value of Equation (19-7):

$$I[(1 - t_i) - (1 - t_c)(1 - t_e)]$$

Explain each of the terms in the equation and what is implied about a firm's optimal capital structure.

SOLVED PROBLEMS

SP-1. Assume that there are two firms, A and B, in the same industry. They are identical in size and all other respects except one: firm A has no debt while firm B has $2,000 of debt, on which it pays interest at a rate of 12 percent. Both firms have the same EBIT ($900) every year in perpetuity. Firm A has 1,000 shares of common stock, and B has 600 shares. Neither firm pays taxes, and each pays out all net income in the form of dividends. Finally, A's shareholders require a rate of return of 18 percent.

   a) Calculate earnings per share (EPS), dividends per share (DPS), and stock price for each firm.
   b) Use Equation 19-1 and the information in part (a) above to determine the required rate of return for firm B. Check the results,

homemade leverage

given the dividends per share and stock price you determined for firm B in part (a).

c) Assume that B's stock is selling for $7 per share and that you own 1 percent of the stock (i.e., six shares). Show how you could get more cash from your investment if you used home-made leverage and invested in the A company. (Assume also that you can borrow at 12 percent and ignore commissions and other transactions costs.)

corporate taxes

SP-2. The Axt Company has net income (after taxes of 34 percent) of $30,000 every year in perpetuity. The company's stockholders require a 15-percent rate of return. The Bat Company is identical in size and in every respect except that it is borrowing $60,000 at a rate of 10 percent, while the Axt company does not borrow at all.

a) Calculate the total market value of the Axt Company.

b) Calculate the Bat Company's total market value and the market value of its equity.

corporate and personal taxes

SP-3. The firms, X and Y each have EBIT in perpetuity of $20,000. These two firms are identical in all respects, except that X has no debt but Y has bonds totalling $10,000 outstanding, on which it pays interest of 10 percent.

a) Assuming no taxes, calculate the total returns to bondholders and shareholders for each company. If you could own either firm in its entirety (i.e., all the X stock or all the Y stock and bonds), which would you prefer? Explain your answer.

b) Now assume corporate taxes are 30 percent. Calculate the total returns to bondholders and shareholders for each company. If you could own either firm in its entirety, which would you prefer? Explain your answer.

c) Assume corporate taxes are 30 percent but that personal taxes on debt income are 28 percent and personal taxes on equity income are 10 percent. Calculate the total returns to bond-holders and shareholders for each company (after all taxes). If you could own either firm in its entirety, which would you prefer? Explain your answer.

PROBLEMS

homemade leverage

1. Assume that there are two firms, A and B, in the same industry. They are identical in size and all other respects except one: firm A has no debt while firm B has $600,000 of debt on which it pays interest at a rate of 8 percent. Both firms have the same EBIT ($180,000) every year in perpetuity. Firm A has 200,000 shares of common stock, and B has 100,000 shares. Neither firm pays taxes, and each pays out all net income in the form of dividends. Finally, A's shareholders require a rate of return of 15 percent.

a) Calculate earnings per share (EPS), dividends per share (DPS), and stock price for each firm.

b) Use Equation 19-1 and the information in part (a) above to determine the required rate of return for firm B. Check the results, given the dividends per share and stock price you determined for firm B in part (a).

c) Assume that B's stock is selling for $7 per share and that you own one percent of the stock (i.e., 1,000 shares). Show how you could get more cash from your investment if you used homemade leverage and invested in the A company. (Assume also that you can borrow at 8 percent and ignore commissions and other transactions costs.)

2. The Blik Company has net income (after taxes of 34 percent) of $60,000 every year in perpetuity. The company's stockholders require a 12-percent rate of return. The Skoosh Company is identical in size and in every respect except that it is borrowing $120,000 at a rate of 8 percent while the Blik company does not borrow at all.   *corporate taxes*

a) Calculate the total market value of the Blik Company.

b) Calculate the Skoosh Company's total market value and the market value of its equity.

3. The firms G and H each have EBIT in perpetuity of $40,000. These two firms are identical in all respects, except that G has no debt while H has bonds totalling $20,000 outstanding, on which it pays interest of 12 percent.   *corporate and personal taxes*

a) Assuming no taxes, calculate the total returns to bondholders and shareholders for each company. If you could own either firm in its entirety (i.e., all the G stock or all the H stock and bonds), which would you prefer? Explain your answer.

b) Now assume corporate taxes are 34 percent. Calculate the total returns to bondholders and shareholders for each company. If you could own either firm in its entirety, which would you prefer? Explain your answer.

c) Assume corporate taxes are 34 percent but that personal taxes on debt income are 28 percent and personal taxes on equity income are 15 percent. Calculate the total returns to bondholders and shareholders for each company (after all taxes). If you could own either firm in its entirety, which would you prefer? Explain your answer.

4. I. The Clark Company has a constant level of EBIT of $180,000. Assume that there are no taxes and all earnings are paid out as dividends. Clark has 100,000 shares of common stock outstanding and is 100-percent equity financed. Clark's shareholders require an 18 percent return.   *homemade leverage; proposition #1*

a) Calculate the equilibrium market price per share.

b) Calculate earnings per share, dividends per share, and return on equity for the Clark Company.

II. Assume that Clark's top management is considering a proposal to "put some life" into the company's financial performance. According to this proposal, Clark would borrow $500,000 from its bankers at a rate of 12 percent. If the proposal is implemented,

a) How many shares would be repurchased and how many would remain?

b) What would be the new EPS, DPS, and ROE for Clark?

c) Assuming no taxes, what would the equilibrium stock price be?

corporate taxes

5. The Dash Company has a perpetual EBIT of $200,000. The company is financed entirely with 100,000 common stock shares. The shares are selling at a price of $12 each. The company's tax rate is 34 percent. Management at the company is considering a dramatic change in financial policies. The change would entail repurchasing half (50,000 shares) of the outstanding shares. Funds for the purchase would come from $600,000 of long-term debt, which is available at an interest rate of 5 percent.

a) Determine the equilibrium stock price if the plan is implemented.

corporate and personal taxes

6. Two companies, X and Y, have the same perpetual level of EBIT, $1 million. Company X has no debt, while Y is financed with $2 million of debt at a rate of 12 percent.

a) Given each of the corporate and personal tax rate situations (A, B, C, D) below, calculate the total returns for all investors (i.e., bondholders and shareholders) in each company. Compare your results. (Note these rates are assumed for purposes of illustration only.)

Situation		Tax Rate	
	Corporate	Personal Equity Income	Personal Debt Income
A	40%	-0-	-0-
B	40%	28%	28%
C	40%	28%	15%
D	25%	50%	10%

SOLUTIONS TO SOLVED PROBLEMS

SP-1. a) The earnings per share (EPS) and dividends per share (DPS) for each firm are calculated below. Since each firm pays out all its earnings, its dividends are equal to earnings per share. Note that firm B pays interest of $240 per year since it is borrowing $2,000 at 12 percent interest rate.

	A	B	697
EBIT	900	900	
Interest	-0-	240	
EBT	900	660	
Taxes	-0-	-0-	
Net income	$900	$660	
# shares	1000	600	
EPS/DPS	.90	$1.10	

Since A's stockholders require a return of 18 percent, the value of the stock is: $P_A = .90/.18 = \$5.00$. We do not yet know what rate of return B's stockholders want, but we do know that the equilibrium stock price for B is $5.00. If there are no taxes, the stock price per share is unaffected by leverage. This is one of the basic conclusions of the chapter.

b) Equation 19-1 relates the required return to the amount of leverage (measured by the debt to equity ratio):

$$k_1 = k_u + (k_u - k_d)D/E$$

We know that the required rate of return on the unlevered firm, k_A, is 18 percent and the return to bondholders in firm B is 12 percent. We also know that the value of B's debt is $2,000 and that the value of its equity is $3,000 (i.e., $5 per share times 600 shares). Thus the equilibrium rate of return for B is:

$$k_B = .18 + (.18 - .12)(2000/3000)$$

$$= .22$$

We can check this estimate of 22 percent by examining the relationship of B's dividends per share ($1.10) to stock price ($5). This reveals a return to B's shareholders of 22 percent, and thus the $5 stock price is an equilibrium value.

c) Follow the steps in homemade leverage as indicated in the chapter.

Step 1. Sell holdings in B: (six shares)($7 per share) = $42

Step 2. Borrow in the same proportion as the B firm (i.e., you owned 1 percent of the B stock, so borrow an amount equivalent to 1 percent of B's debt. This is in order to keep the risk levels constant).

Borrow = 1 percent of $2,000 = $20

Step 3. Invest in A stock. You have a total of $62 to invest, which means you can buy 12.4 shares of A stock. Since A stockholders get $.90 per share, you will receive (12.4 shares × $0.90 per share) = $11.16. Out of this, you will pay interest on the amount borrowed, assuming an interest rate of 12 percent, equal to $2.40 (i.e., $12 \times \$20$). This leaves you a net cash total of $8.76. As a stockholder in B, you only received total cash of (six shares $\times$ $1.10 per share) = $6.60. Thus, with home-made leverage, you will get more cash by selling B and buying A. This will depress B's stock price until it reaches its equilibrium value of $5 per share.

SP-2. a) The total market value of the Axt Company is determined by capitalizing the net income (since all earnings are paid out, this is the same as total dividends) by the required rate of return. The total market value of the Axt Company is $200,000:

$$\text{Market value} = \$30,000/.15 = \$200,000$$

b) Using the relationship in Equation 19-2, we know that the market value of the Bat Company is equal to the value of the Axt Company (i.e., an unlevered firm) plus the present value of its debt tax shield (Dt). Thus, the total market value of the Bat Company is:

$$\text{Market value} = \$200,000 + (\$60,000 \times .34) = \$220,400$$

Since the Bat Company has $60,000 in debt, the equity market value must be $160,400.

$$\text{Value of equity} = \text{Total market value} - \text{Value of debt}$$

$$\$160,400 = \$220,400 - \$60,000$$

SP-3. a) Total returns are indicated below:

	X	Y
Bondholders (i.e., interest income)	-0-	$ 1,000
Shareholders	$20,000	$19,000
Total return	$20,000	$20,000

Since total returns are the same for each firm, you should be indifferent in the choice of securities. The fact that Y gives you no more cash than X means that it is no more valuable (risk is certainly unchanged: since you own the bonds as well as the stock in Y, you can only default to yourself, meaning there is no financial risk to you as sole owner).

b) Corporate taxes change the results, as shown below:

	X		Y	
Bondholders		-0-		$ 1,000
Shareholders ($20,000) (.7) =		$14,000	($19,000) (.7) =	$13,300
Total		$14,000		$14,300

After corporate taxes of 30 percent, total returns are only $14,000 in firm X, but they are $14,300 in firm Y. Every year in perpetuity, firm Y will generate $300 more cash. If this is capitalized at a rate of 10 percent, the value is $3,000 (of course this is also equal to Dt). Now you would much prefer to own Y in its entirety than X because it gives you more cash.

c) The existence of personal taxes as well as corporate taxes, affects the total returns again.

	X		Y	
Bondholders		-0-	$1,000(.72)	$ 720
Shareholders $20,000(.7) (.9) =		$12,600	$19,000(.7) (.9) =	$11,970
Total		$12,600		$12,690

You would still prefer to own the levered company, since it would give you $90 more cash every year. However, the levered company is now only slightly more attractive. Thus, the existence of personal taxes can reduce the value of leverage.

REFERENCES

Bradley, Michael, Gregg A. Jarrell, and Ilan E. Kim. "On Existence of an Optimal Capital Structure: Theory and Evidence." *Journal of Finance*, May 1984, pp. 349–52.

Brennan, Michael J., and E. S. Schwartz. "Corporate Income Taxes, Valuation, and the Problem of Optimal Capital Structure." *Journal of Business*, January 1978, pp. 103–14.

DeAngelo, Harry, and Ronald Masulis, "Optimal Capital Structure Under Corporate and Personal Taxation." *Journal of Financial Economics,* March 1980, pp. 11–25.

Miller, Merton H. "Debt and Taxes." *Journal of Finance,* May 1977, pp. 261–75.

Modigliani, Franco, and Merton Miller, "The Cost of Capital, Corporation Finance and the Theory of Investment." *American Economic Review,* June 1958, pp. 261–296.

Modigliani, Franco, and Merton Miller, "Corporate Income Taxes and the Cost of Capital." *American Economic Review,* June, 1963.

CASE EXERCISE

The Marx Corporation

The Marx Corporation did not use long-term debt. This financial source, along with short-term debt, was viewed as a reserve that should be maintained to meet emergencies. Mr. Jones, Chairman of Marx, believed that the use of long-term debt increased the riskiness of the firm not only by adding fixed financial requirements but also by reducing the available borrowing power. This reasoning applied equally to the use of financial leases, which Mr. Jones believed weakened financial mobility.

According to the company's debt policy, debt and financial leases (whenever possible) were paid off if they appeared in the capital structure of an acquired company. For example, one recent acquisition entailed prepayment of $4 million in $5\frac{3}{4}$-percent debentures that had five years remaining before maturity.

Mr. Jones believed that not using financial leverage gave the company marketing and productive strength and flexibility. Nonetheless, he believed that the company could safely handle a 45-percent debt-to-assets ratio, given the going rate of 9 percent.

Case Questions

1. Evaluate the Marx Company's debt policy.

2. Assume that the Company's common stock beta is 1.0; its required return on equity with its current debt policy is 15 percent; the company's tax rate is 34 percent; the company's total assets are $100 million; and the Treasury Bill rate is 12 percent. What would the company's weighted average cost of capital be with a debt-to-assets ratio of 45 percent? (Note: use the formula for the levered beta in Chapter 17 to project the required return on equity at the higher debt level.)

3. Ignoring the personal tax shield of debt interest, how much would the value of the firm increase if the company maintained a debt-to-assets ratio of 45 percent?

4. What would you recommend to Mr. Jones regarding the company's debt policy?

CHAPTER

20

DIVIDEND POLICY:
THEORY AND PRACTICE

usiness corporations rely heavily on internally-generated cash flows to finance their firms. Depreciation-generated funds are used primarily to replace existing assets as they wear out. In order to finance asset growth, corporations find it necessary to retain earnings or obtain funds externally through debt and equity issues. Of course, any earnings retained will not be available for payment of cash dividends and vice versa. Thus, the fundamental choice posed by dividend policy is whether the firm should distribute more cash now or reinvest it to produce greater future value. In theory, this is a simple choice: the firm should retain funds that can be invested in excess of the cost of capital and pay out as dividends any funds that cannot be invested at returns in excess of the cost of capital.

Most firms do not behave in a manner completely consistent with theory. In fact firms appear to have an overriding preference for stable, gradually increasing dividends, regardless of apparent investment opportunities. This chapter examines what theory has to say about dividend policy and why firms might not follow the dictates of theory.

Objectives and Organization of this Chapter

This chapter has the dual objectives of examining dividend policy from the perspectives of theory and practice. The first section of the chapter presents dividend policy from an analytical perspective. It demonstrates under what conditions dividend policy should not be of concern to financial managers and when the "right" policy is so obvious as to be automatic.

The second section of the chapter presents counterarguments that attempt to demonstrate why dividend policy should be of importance. These counterarguments have developed in an effort to reconcile theoretical principles with the overwhelming evidence that financial managers spend a considerable amount of effort in designing and managing the firm's dividend policy.

The chapter's third section describes common features of dividend policies that may be encountered in practice.

DIVIDEND POLICY AND STOCK PRICE

The dividend policy question really boils down to the following: "By paying dividends, can the company increase its market price?" At first glance, the answer might appear to be yes. After-all, does the dividend discount model not rest on the amount and timing of dividends? Closer consideration reveals a fallacy: the more dividends a company pays out, the less cash it has for investments and growth, and growth is also part of the dividend model. Thus, the dividend question can be restated as a choice between current cash dividends and future growth.

However, by focusing on growth alone, one might conclude that the greater the growth rate, the higher the stock price. Certainly, this is also an implication of the dividend discount model. Again, there is something missing: namely, the fact that a higher growth rate means less cash dividends.

Dividend Policy: The Missing Link

Dividend policy provides the missing link between dividends and growth. By dividend policy is meant the percentage of earnings that are paid out to stockholders. What makes this the "missing link" is that dividend policy simultaneously affects both the level of dividends and the company's growth rate.

In order to demonstrate this more clearly, it is necessary to restate the dividend model in terms of dividend policy. This involves introducing a few new relationships. For example, let us follow conventional practice in representing the percentage of earnings retained by the firm with the variable, b, and the percentage of earnings paid out as 1 minus b. Thus, if the firm retains 10 percent of its earnings, then it pays out 90 percent as dividend. If earnings per share are $10, for example, the company pays a dividend of $9.00 (i.e., .90 times $10).

Furthermore, the company's growth rate, g, in dividends can be expressed as the product of its retention rate, b, times its return on equity, r. Thus, $g = br$. A simple example will demonstrate this relationship.

$g = br$

Example

$g = br$

Assume a company is initially financed entirely with $1,000,000 of shareholders' equity. The firm's return on equity is a constant 20 percent, and the firm retains a constant 40 percent of its profits. Thus, during the year, the company earns $200,000 (i.e., 20 percent times $1 million) out of which it will retain $80,000 and pay dividends of $120,000. Its equity base has increased to $1,080,000. The following year it will again earn 20 per-

TABLE 20-1

	$t = 1$	$t = 2$
1. Equity, start of period	$1,000,000	$1,080,000
2. Return on equity (%)	20%	20%
3. Net income (#1 × #2)	$ 200,000	$ 216,000
4. Retention rate (%)	40%	40%
5. Increase in retained earnings (#3 × #4)	$ 80,000	$ 86,400
6. Equity, end of period (#1 + #5)	$1,080,000	$1,166,400
7. Payout rate (%)(100% − #4)	60%	60%
8. Dividends paid (#7 × #3)	$ 120,000	$ 129,600

cent, or $216,000. Out of these profits, the firm will again retain 40 per-
cent, or $86,400 and pay dividends of $129,600 (i.e., 60 percent times
$216,000). Dividends paid have increased from $120,000 to $129,600, an
increase of 8 percent. This is the same answer we would get by multiplying the retention percentage (b = 40 percent) times the return on
equity (r = 20 percent). The calculations are shown in Table 20-1.

The Dividend Discount Model Restated in Terms of Dividend Policy

With the foregoing as background, the dividend valuation model can
be restated in terms of dividend policy as shown in Equation 20-1:

$$P = (1 - b)EPS_1/(k_e - br) \qquad (20\text{-}1)$$

The numerator is, of course, equivalent to D_1 and, in the denominator,
the term br is equivalent to g. However, in this form, the firm's dividend
policy affects both the numerator and denominator. An increase in retentions as a percentage of earnings increases growth but simultaneously decreases dividends.

Dividend policy, as reflected in Equation 20-1 appears to be a balancing
act between dividends and growth. Of course, what the financial manager
really wants to do is to maximize stock price. With one more refinement,
however, the problem disappears and, with it, the need to balance dividends against growth.

Introducing Alpha

The needed refinement is to compare the return on equity, r, with the
required rate of return, k_e. Let us define alpha as the difference between r
and k_e.

alpha

$$\alpha = r - k_e \qquad (20\text{-}2)$$

and, equivalently,

$$r = k_e + \alpha \qquad (20\text{-}2a)$$

Now, substituting in Equation 20-1, we get the full picture of the dividend policy-stock price relationship, shown as Equation 20-3.

$$P = \frac{(1 - b)EPS_1}{[k_e - b(k_e - \alpha)]} \qquad (20\text{-}3)$$

and,

$$P = \frac{(1 - b)EPS_1}{[(1 - b)k_e - b\alpha]} \qquad (20\text{-}3a)$$

When Dividend Policy Is Irrelevant: Alpha Equal to Zero

If $\alpha = 0$ (meaning, if the return on equity from investments made by the company is just equal to the required rate of return), Equation 20-3a reduces to:

$$P - \frac{(1 - b)EPS_1}{(1 - b)k_e} \qquad (20\text{-}3b)$$

$$= EPS_1/k_e$$

and the term $1 - b$, which reflects dividend policy, simply vanishes. In other words, stock price is completely unaffected by whatever decision the company makes about dividend policy.

Example

Alpha Equal to Zero

The Acton Company's required return (k_e) is 15 percent. The company's forecast earnings per share (EPS_1) are $3.00, and return on shareholders'

TABLE 20-2

	Policy No.		
	1	*2*	*3*
Return on equity, r	15 %	15 %	15%
Payout ratio	30 %	50 %	100%
Retention ratio, b	70 %	50 %	0%
Growth rate in earnings and dividends, br	10.5%	7.5%	0%
Intrinsic stock value .30($3.00)/(.15 − .105) =	$20		
.50($3.00)/(.15 − .075) =		$20	
1.00($3.00)/(.15 − 0) =			$20

equity is 15 percent. The company is considering three different dividend policies: policy #1 is a payout ratio of 30 percent; policy #2 is a payout ratio of 50 percent; and policy #3 is a payout ratio of 100 percent. Each of the policies will result in a different growth rate in earnings and dividends as indicated in Table 20-2.

Notice that the intrinsic stock value is completely unaffected by the dividend policy alternative. Thus, when a firm's return on equity is equal to the required return on equity, dividend policy has no effect on stock value.

When Dividend Policy Is Obvious: Alpha Greater Than Zero

If alpha is positive, then dividend policy does affect stock price: the higher the retention rate, b, and the lower the dividends paid, the greater stock price will be. This is evident from Equation 20-3b. As b gets larger, the term $b\alpha$ gets larger. The denominator shrinks, and P increases. At the limit, as long as alpha is positive, the firm should retain all earnings and pay no dividends.

Example

Positive Alpha

Assume that the Acton Company is again considering the three dividend policies identified earlier. However, in this example, assume that the prospective return on equity is in excess of the required return. Specifically, r is equal to 20 percent while k_e is equal to 15 percent. The results are shown in Table 20-3.

TABLE 20-3

	Policy No.		
	1	*2*	*3*
Return on equity, r	20 %	20 %	20%
Payout ratio	30 %	50 %	100%
Retention ratio, b	70 %	50 %	0%
Growth rate in earnings and dividends, br	14.0%	10.0%	0%
Intrinsic stock value .30($3.00)/(.15 − .14) =	$90.00		
.50($3.00)/(.15 − .10) =		$30.00	
1.00($3.00)/(.15 − 0) =			$20.00

Moral: Pay no dividends

When Dividend Policy Is Obvious: Alpha Less Than Zero

Finally, if alpha is negative, the firm should not invest, because the return on equity is less than the required return. But, of course, this is nothing new. It is one of the fundamental lessons about capital budgeting. We will return to this point shortly.

Example

Negative Alpha

Assume that the Acton Company is again considering the three dividend policies identified earlier. However, in this example, assume that the prospective return on equity is less than the required return. Specifically, r is equal to 10 percent while K_e is equal to 15 percent. The results are shown in Table 20-4.

TABLE 20-4

	Policy No.		
	1	*2*	*3*
Return on equity, r	10 %	10 %	10%
Payout ratio	30 %	50 %	100%
Retention ratio, b	70 %	50 %	0%
Growth rate in earnings and dividends, br	7.0%	5.0%	0%
Intrinsic stock value $.30(\$3.00)/(.15 - .07) =$	$11.25		
$.50(\$3.00)/(.15 - .05) =$		$15.00	
$1.00(\$3.00)/(.15 - 0) =$			$20.00

Moral: Pay maximum dividends

PURE RESIDUAL DIVIDEND POLICY

The argument that dividend policy is irrelevant or obvious does not mean that dividends, *per se,* are irrelevant but rather that actively managing a financial policy with regard to dividends is a waste of time. Indeed, the importance of dividends to stock price is at the heart of the dividend valuation model. Thus, it is the irrelevance of policy, not dividends, which is of concern. When theoreticians argue that dividend policy is irrelevant, they are speaking in terms of Equation 20-3a. What they are really saying is that dividend policy is determined by the firm's investment and capital structure policies. Once those are established, the amount of dividends to be paid, if any, is a mere detail—a task for the computer, not the financial manager.

pure residual policy

Dividends As a Residual

The implications of Equation 20-3a are not mysterious when one considers the idea in capital budgeting and capital structure terms. We already know that, when an investment's returns are less than required, it should not be made. That is what is behind the relationship between r and k_e.[1] If investments are not worth making, the funds should be returned to investors (e.g., in the form of dividends).[2]

Thus, once the investment proposals and financing available are determined, paying out what is left over for dividends is simply a matter of subtraction: pay out whatever remains, if anything.

Example

Dividends As a Pure Residual

Acme has several new capital investments which will increase total assets by $300,000. The firm's optimal capital structure calls for half of all assets to be financed with borrowing. The firm's net income is $200,000. Accordingly, the firm should retain $150,000 and pay dividends of $50,000. The calculations are shown in Table 20-5.

TABLE 20-5

Investment funds required		$300,000
Debt to be used (1/2 of investment)		$150,000
Equity required		$150,000
Net income	$200,000	
− Equity required	− 150,000	
Cash available for dividends	$ 50,000	

---

[1]More generally, the principle is: do not invest if the internal rate of return is less than the weighted average cost of capital. Of course, in such a case, the return on equity will also be less than the cost of equity capital. The reverse interpretation is also valid: if the return on equity capital is less than the cost of equity capital, the internal rate of return is necessarily less than the weighted average cost of capital.

[2]The message here is that, if the firm cannot earn at least as much as the cost of capital, it will at least avoid the cost by returning the capital to investors.

Studies of actual dividend policies suggest that dividend payments are not just a residual paid out after the need for retained earnings has been met. There is a strong tendency to maintain a particular level of dividend payment and to make a change in the level only when management is convinced that a new rate can be maintained for a reasonable period of time. Indeed, in practice, an overall pattern of stable and gradually increasing dividends is unmistakable. One would not expect to see such a pattern if dividend policy were simply a residual of investment and financing decisions.

Several arguments have been proposed to explain the apparent discrepancy between the theory and practice of dividend policy. The principal ones are reviewed in this section.

Information Content of Dividend Policy

information content

Dividend stability seems to reflect a desire of corporate directors to maintain a steady payment of dividends even in the face of what they may perceive to be temporary financial reverses. Such a policy may be intended to convey to shareholders an appraisal of the long-run level of earnings expectations. Reported earnings are subject to short-term influences as well as to the vagaries of accounting practices and thus, at certain times, reflect temporary financial reverses rather than long-run trends. Consequently, when the directors raise the dividend, they are signaling, or providing information to the stockholders, that they believe basic earnings have reached a new and higher level and that continued growth in EPS is expected in the future.

Investor Clienteles and Dividend Policy

dividend clienteles

The clientele argument is based on the idea that some investors rely heavily on a predictable level of dividends. These investors prefer companies that have a proven record of stable and increasing dividends. Other investors would prefer to buy stock in companies that can reinvest the money at high rates of return. These stockholders will avoid companies with high payout ratios. From the financial manager's perspective, according to the clientele argument, it is important to know the preferences of the company's investor group. By clearly identifying its dividend policy, the company hopes to attract the desired investment group. A pure residual policy is "neither fish nor fowl" from the standpoint of investor clienteles and thus will not be attractive to either investors who want stable dividends or investors who do not want dividends at all.

Legal Lists and Dividend Policy

The laws of many states prohibit institutional investors and trustees from investing in the debt and equity securities of corporations that do not maintain an unbroken record of cash dividend payments. Failure to pay some cash dividends will exclude a firm from being placed on legal lists and will result in a lack of institutional and trustee investors, which, in turn, will make it more difficult to sell additional shares of common stock and generate external equity funds. For this reason, even "growth" companies often consider it worthwhile to establish nominal dividend policies. While this results in additional flotation costs and administrative costs compared to a residual policy of zero dividends, these costs are thought to be offset by increased marketability for new common stock issues.

legal lists

TYPES OF CASH DIVIDEND POLICIES

In addition to the pure residual dividend policy described earlier, several other types of dividend policies are available to corporate directors. Let us discuss variations of the *constant* and the *target* payout ratio policies.

Constant Dividend Payout Ratio Policy

Table 20-6 illustrates and compares the application of the two policies.

TABLE 20-6

	A. *Constant Dividend Payout Ratio* Piedmont Production, Inc.			B. *Stable Dollar Amount Payout** Consolidated Manufacturing, Inc.		
Year	Earnings Per Share	Dividends Per Share	Dividend Payout Percentage	Earnings Per Share	Dividends Per Share	Dividend Payout Percentage
1978	$2.00	$1.00	50.0%	$2.00	$1.00	50.0%
1979	2.20	1.10	50.0	2.20	1.00	45.5
1980	2.40	1.20	50.0	2.40	1.20	50.0
1981	2.50	1.25	50.0	2.50	1.20	48.0
1982	1.90	.95	50.0	1.90	1.20	63.2
1983	2.20	1.10	50.0	2.20	1.20	54.5
1984	2.50	1.25	50.0	2.50	1.30	52.0
1985	2.60	1.30	50.0	2.60	1.30	50.0
1986	2.80	1.40	50.0	2.80	1.30	46.4
1987	3.00	1.50	50.0	3.00	1.50	50.0

*With a "target" dividend payout ratio of 50 percent.

In the first example, the Piedmont Corporation follows a policy of maintaining a constant dividend payout percentage of 50 percent of its earnings. Piedmont retains one-half of its earnings each year for capital investment purposes, regardless of the size of the capital budgeting opportunities available. Furthermore, when earnings fall, dividends are cut, and vice-versa, so that a firm with fluctuating earnings creates the same degree of fluctuation in its cash dividends over time. What does such a dividend policy have to offer? Not much. Little information is conveyed about the firm's capital budgeting prospects and its ability to achieve and maintain EPS growth over time.

Target Payout Ratio Policy

The Consolidated Manufacturing Company shown in Table 20-6 demonstrates a common type of dividend policy known as the "target payout ratio with stable dollar amount." Over a period of years, Consolidated intends to pay out roughly half of its profits. But, since the company intends to avoid decreases in dividends when earnings are low or investment opportunities are plentiful, it does not raise the dividend until the board feels average earnings have increased to a permanently higher level.

target payout ratio

The size of the target payout ratio offers some information to investors concerning the firm's outlook for capital budgeting investment opportunities. Firms that wish to have a stable dividend payout policy even though they may have substantial growth opportunities will set a relatively low dividend payout ratio as their target. In contrast, firms operating in mature industries will usually set relatively high dividend payout ratios as targets. In practice, the typical target payout ratio, while it varies substantially across industries and firms, most frequently has been observed in the 40-percent to 60-percent range over time for business corporations.

Extra Dividends.   Some firms make use of the combination of regular and "extra" cash dividends. For example, the directors of a firm might authorize the payment of 50 cents per share per quarter regular dividends. The implication is that, insofar as possible, these dividends will be maintained at this level through good times and bad. At the end of the year, if earnings are satisfactory, the directors may declare an extra dividend in addition to the regular one. An extra dividend thus will fluctuate with earnings and the corporation's needs for funds. The General Motors Corporation is an example of a firm that has used a policy of regular plus extra cash dividends in recent years. The cyclical nature of the automobile industry, coupled with tremendous capital investment requirements and increased foreign competition, has led to wide swings in profits and losses and makes such a dividend policy understandable.

extra dividends

PROCEDURES FOR PAYING CASH DIVIDENDS

When directors declare a dividend, they announce that all who hold common stock on a certain date in the future (the *date of record*) are entitled to receive a specified dividend on each share. Assume, for example, that on October 7, directors of Continental Energy, Inc. announced that holders of record—that is, stockholders holding the stock on October 19—would be paid dividends of $0.50 per share on November 20, (the *payment date*). Because of the time it takes to record transfers of ownership, the rules of the New York Stock Exchange and other exchanges specify that the effective date of ownership is really four full business days earlier than the date of record. Consequently, through October 15, the stock was selling *dividends-on*, and a stockholder purchasing the stock on or before that date later received the dividend. However, on the next trading day, October 16, the stock sold *ex-dividends*. On that day the stock closed below the close the previous day. Since purchasers of the stock on October 16 were not entitled to receive the dividends declared, we would expect them to pay less for the stock.

date of record

payment date

dividends-on

ex-dividends

Accounting for Dividends

Most dividends of corporations are in the form of cash. In the case of a corporation, a dividend that has been declared by the board of directors becomes a current liability (dividends payable). If one skips this intermediate step, the ultimate effect of a dividend of $2 million ($2 per share) on the pertinent accounts of the corporation is shown below:

	Before	
Cash $5,000,000	Common stock	
	(1,000,000 shares at $10 par)	$10,000,000
	Retained earnings	$15,000,000
	After	
Cash $3,000,000	Common stock	
	(1,000,000 shares at $10 par)	$10,000,000
	Retained earnings	$13,000,000

Occasionally corporations have distributed other forms of assets as dividends. When a corporation (holding company) owns stock or bonds of other corporations, it may distribute these securities to its stockholders as a dividend. This type of distribution is called a spin-off. Distillers have sometimes distributed whiskey as a dividend. The effect on the balance sheet of these dividends is the same as shown above, except that some asset (e.g., inventory) other than cash is affected.

Stock Dividends and Splits

stock dividend

A source of considerable confusion is the *stock dividend*. In fact, it is not a dividend in a true sense at all. It is really another form of *recapitalization*: that is, a change in the capital structure involving a shift in the amount or types of outstanding securities.

Ordinarily a stock dividend is payable in common stock, although preferred stock is sometimes distributed. The effect of a 10-percent stock dividend on the balance sheet and income accounts of the Vespa company is illustrated in Table 20-7. Assume that the "fair value" (usually market value) of the stock at the time of the dividend is $25 per share.

TABLE 20-7   Impact of a Stock Dividend on a Firm's Financial Statements

Vespa Company

Before 10% Stock Dividend

Current assets	$2,000,000	Total liabilities	$1,500,000
		Common stock (100,000 shares at $10 par)	1,000,000
Fixed assets	2,000,000	Capital surplus	500,000
		Retained earnings	1,000,000
Total assets	$4,000,000	Total liab. & equity	$4,000,000
	Net income	$200,000	
	Shares outstanding	100,000	
	Earnings per share	$2.00	

After 10% Stock Dividend (and when stock price is $25)

Current assets	$2,000,000	Total liabilities	$1,500,000
		Common stock (110,000 shares at $10 par)	1,100,000
Fixed assets	2,000,000	Capital surplus*	650,000
		Retained earnings	750,000
Total assets	$4,000,000	Total liab. & equity	$4,000,000
	Net income	$200,000	
	Shares outstanding	110,000	
	Earnings per share	$1.82	

*Since the stock dividend occurred when the stock was selling for $25 per share, $100,000 (10,000 shares × $10) would be added to the common stock account and $150,000 (10,000 shares × $15) to capital surplus. A corresponding total $250,000 reduction would be made in the retained earnings account.

The total value of the stock dividend, $250,000 (i.e., 10,000 shares times $25 per share) is subtracted from retained earnings and moved to the common stock and surplus accounts. The amount put into the common stock account is $100,000 (i.e., 10,000 shares times $10 par value). The remainder, $150,000 is put into the capital surplus account.

Table 20-7 indicates that, prior to the stock dividend, the Vespa Company had 100,000 shares of common stock outstanding and an EPS of $2.00. After the 10-percent stock dividend, the EPS immediately falls to $1.82 based on 110,000 shares (100,000 old shares plus the 10,000 new shares). This occurs because no additional funds have been generated through the declaration of a stock dividend, and consequently there can be no increase in net income. In other words, the firm's market total value should be the same before and after the stock dividend. On a per-share basis, we have:

	EPS		P/E Multiple		Market Price
Before stock dividend	$2.00	×	12.5	=	$25.00
After stock dividend	$1.82	×	12.5	=	$22.75

The firm's total value prior to the stock dividend was $2.5 million (100,000 shares times $25 per share), and after the stock dividend it also should be $2.5 million (110,000 shares times $22.75), ignoring a slight rounding error.

To summarize, since stock dividends represent only a form of recapitalization whereby the firm is making shifts in the common equity section of the balance sheet, there should be no increase, *per se,* in the value of existing shareholder positions. Empirical evidence supports this contention, except when stock dividends are accompanied by an increase in the firm's earnings and cash dividends.

Stock Splits

A *stock split* simply involves the dividing of the firm's common stock into a larger number of shares. For example, instead of a 10-percent stock dividend, the Vespa Company might have decided to have a "two-for-one stock split." The firm could achieve the desired stock split by merely exchanging two shares of $5 par-value common stock for each $10 par-value common stock currently outstanding. The impact of such a stock split is shown in Table 20-8. Notice that the impact on the balance sheet is minimal, since only the par value and the number of shares outstanding change in terms of the common stock account. Of course, since the number of shares is doubled after the split, with no change in the firm's net income, the EPS falls from $2.00 to $1.00.

stock split

TABLE 20-8 Impact of a Stock Split on a Firm's Financial Statements

Vespa Company

Before 2-for-1 Stock Split

Current assets	$2,000,000	Total liabilities	$1,500,000
		Common stock (100,000 shares at $10 par)	1,000,000
Fixed assets	2,000,000	Capital surplus	500,000
		Retained earnings	1,000,000
Total assets	$4,000,000	Total liab. & equity	$4,000,000
	Net income	$200,000	
	Shares outstanding	100,000	
	Earnings per share	$2.00	

After 2-for-1 Stock Split (and when stock price is $25)

Current assets	$2,000,000	Total liabilities	$1,500,000
		Common stock (200,000 shares at $5 par)*	1,000,000
Fixed assets	2,000,000	Capital surplus	500,000
		Retained earnings	1,000,000
Total assets	$4,000,000	Total liab. & equity	$4,000,000
	Net income	$200,000	
	Shares outstanding	200,000	
	Earnings per share	$1.00	

*The result of the stock split is a doubling of the number of shares of common stock that is outstanding and a cutting in half of the previous par value.

In theory, a stock split, like a stock dividend, should not alter the firm's total market value. On a per-share basis:

	EPS		P/E Multiple		Market Value
Before stock split	$2.00	×	12.5	=	$25.00
After stock split	$1.00	×	12.5	=	$12.50

Vespa's total value prior to the stock split was $2.5 million (100,000 shares times $25 per share), and after the split it also should be $2.5 million (200,000 shares times $12.50).

Why, given the above discussion, should financial managers be concerned with making stock-dividend and stock-split decisions? If the firm is successful and growing in terms of earnings (and possible cash dividends), common stock prices would be expected to rise over time. Thus, there exists a popular belief that the optimal range for stock prices is roughly $20 to $80 and that earnings multiples (price/earning ratios) will be maximized within this range. Stock splits and stock dividends may provide management a vehicle for keeping stock prices in this desired trading range. Conversely, if a firm's stock price is judged to be selling at too low a price, a *reverse split*, such as exchanging "one for two" shares, might be considered.

reverse split

Another reason cited for making stock-dividends or stock splits is to broaden the firm's equity base in terms of the number of investors (this might actually be related to an optimal stock price range). For example, Levi Strauss, which was a closely held corporation for many years, attempted to increase its number of shares outstanding in order to broaden public ownership of its stock and to improve the stock's marketability. Levi Strauss chose to do this by announcing a two-for-one stock split when its stock was trading close to $70 per share. Thus the financial manager may wish to consider stock dividends and splits if he or she feels the need to broaden public ownership in the firm and/or to achieve a certain target trading range for the common stock.

Repurchase of Common Stock

Occasionally corporations will repurchase some of their shares of common stock that are outstanding. Such actions create *treasury stock*, which is previously-issued stock that has been repurchased in either of two basic ways. It may be bought in the open market, where any investor could buy shares of the desired stock. Repurchase can also take place through the making of tender offers for a certain number of shares of common stock at a set price.

treasury stock

The most frequently cited reason for stock repurchases is that the company's stock price is too low relative to its economic value.

SUMMARY

Dividend policy involves the decision whether to retain earnings in the firm for capital investments or other purposes or to pay out the earnings in the form of cash dividends to stockholders. Many financial managers believe that a stable dollar per share dividend policy that is increased only periodically offers informational content to investors concerning management's long-run earnings levels and growth expectations. Such a policy of gradual adjustment of dividend payments frequently is coupled with a target payout ratio that management believes is appropriate for its clientele of stockholders (i.e., those preferring a certain mix in total returns between dividend yield and price appreciation).

On a purely theoretical basis, one can argue that management should first determine its capital budget investment opportunities, then determine its type of financing needs in light of an optimal capital structure, and finally view dividend policy as a residual policy. Under this approach, cash dividends would be paid only to the extent that internally generated funds remained after the capital budget-capital structure decisions had been made. While evidence does not support this pure residual dividend theory in practice, it is observed that firms with strong capital budgeting opportunities have relatively low target payout ratios, whereas firms with lower growth opportunities have relatively higher target payout ratios. Thus most financial managers tend to adhere to a stable-dollar-amount cash dividend while setting their target payout ratio in conjunction with capital investment opportunities and capital structure objectives.

MULTIPLE CHOICE QUESTIONS

1. A policy of continual adjustment of dividend payments to changes in earnings reflects a:
   a) Pure residual policy
   b) Recapitalization
   c) Target payout ratio policy
   d) Constant payout ratio policy

2. If a company has a dividend policy of a constant payout and profits fall, shareholders can expect:

 a) No change in cash dividends
 b) Stock dividends instead of cash dividends
 c) A stock split
 d) A decrease in cash dividends

3. A residual dividend policy means that dividends are paid:

 a) Only if funds are available
 b) Only when requested by shareholders
 c) Only to preferred stockholders
 d) Even if no profits are earned

4. Most companies have a dividend policy characterized as:

 a) Constant payout
 b) Pure residual
 c) Target payout
 d) Volatile

DISCUSSION QUESTIONS

1. If the intrinsic value of a firm's stock price is presumed to rest on dividends, why can theoreticians argue that dividend policy is "irrelevant?"

2. How does dividend policy affect the firm's growth rate?

3. Explain what is meant by the following: "once a firm's approved capital projects and optimal capital structure have been identified, dividend policy is a mere residual."

4. Distinguish between the two following dividend policies:

 a) Constant payout ratio
 b) Target payout ratio with stable dollar amount

5. What is meant by the *information content* of dividend policy?

6. Explain how the existence of investor clienteles might influence a company's dividend policy.

7. Why do "legal lists" motivate even "high-growth" companies to develop nominal (i.e., "token") dividend policies?

8. What are "extra" dividends? Why are they used?

9. Define the following:

 a) Date of record
 b) Dividend payment date
 c) Dividend announcement date
 d) Dividends-on
 e) Ex-dividends

SOLVED PROBLEMS

SP-1. The Acme Company has shareholders' equity of $100,000. The company expects return on equity to average 15 percent each year in the forseeable future.

growth rate

    a) Estimate the growth rate, g, in earnings and dividends per share, given the following payout ratios: i) 10 percent, ii) 100 percent.

    b) Prove, with the use of a table, such as table 20-1, that the growth rates you calculated above are correct.

SP-2. The Elm Company finances half its assets with debt and half with equity. In the past five years, the company's net income has been constant at $300,000 per year. The company's capital budgets have resulted in the increases in assets shown below.

pure residual policy

	Year				
	1	2	3	4	5
Increase in assets ($000)	$100	$200	$300	$400	$500

    a) Assuming that the company has a pure residual dividend policy, determine the dividends paid each year.

SP-3. Assuming that the Acme company follows a constant-payout-ratio dividend policy of 40 percent, determine the dividends, paid each year given the earnings shown below.

	Year				
	1	2	3	4	5
Net income (000)	$100	$50	$200	$300	$100

constant payout ratio policy

PROBLEMS

1. The Ciril Company has equity of $300,000. The company's average return on equity is 20 percent.

growth rate

    a) Estimate the company's growth rate, given the following payout ratios: i) 90 percent, ii) 80 percent.

    b) Prove that your estimates in part (a) are correct, using a summary income statement such as that shown in Table 20-1.

dividend policy

2. What dividend policy would be indicated by theory for the Ciril Company in Problem 1, assuming the following required returns on equity (k_e): i) .15, ii) .25 iii) .20?

3. A company expects earnings of $100,000 and has 50,000 shares outstanding. Determine the expected dividends per share given the following payout ratios: i) .20, ii) .40, iii) .80.

dividend policy

4. Demdi's expected earnings per share (EPS_1) are $2.50; its return on equity, r, is 18 percent, and the required return on equity, k_e, is 15 percent.

alpha and dividend policy

   a) Determine the intrinsic value of the company's stock, given each of the following payout ratios: i) 90 percent, ii) 50 percent, iii) 30 percent.

   b) What dividend policy is indicated for the company, given your answers to part (a)?

   c) How would your answers to part (b) change if Demdi's return on equity, r, were: i) .15, ii) .10.

5. The Frube Company has had net income of $200,000 in each of the past three years. The company finances half of its assets with debt. Assume that assets increased over the three years as shown below. Determine the dividends paid if the firm followed a pure residual policy.

pure residual policy

	Year		
	1	2	3
Increase in assets (000)	$150	$50	$200

6. The Grisq Company has had net income of $250,000; $150,000; and $200,000 over the past three years, respectively. If the company follows a constant-payout-ratio dividend policy of 40 percent, determine the dividends paid in each year.

constant payout ratio policy

7. The TRX Company has announced a cash dividend of $2.00 per share. Given the balance sheet accounts below, indicate the final effects of the dividend after it is paid.

dividend accounting

TRX		
Cash $1,000,000	Common Stock	$200,000
	(50,000 shares at $4 par value)	
	Retained earnings	$800,000

SOLUTIONS TO SOLVED PROBLEMS

SP-1. a) i) The growth rate can be estimated by multiplying the retention ratio, b, times the return on equity, r. The return on equity is given, but the retention ratio must be determined. Since the payout ratio is 10 percent, the retention ratio must be 90 percent. Thus, the growth rate is approximately 13.5 percent.

$$g = br$$

$$= .90 \times .15 = .135, \quad \text{or} \quad 13.5\%$$

ii) Using the procedure above, the retention ratio is zero and the growth rate is also zero.

$$g = 0 \times .15 = 0\%$$

b) i) The beginning equity is $100,000. Using this information and that given above, we can develop a table similar to Table 20-1.

	t = 1	t = 2
(1) Equity, start of period	$100,000	$113,500
(2) Return on equity (%)	15%	15%
(3) Net income (#1 × #2)	$ 15,000	$ 17,025
(4) Retention rate (%)	90%	90%
(5) Increase in retained earnings (#3 × #4)	$ 13,500	$ 15,323
(6) Equity, end of period (#1 + #5)	$113,500	$128,823
(7) Payout rate (%)(100% − #4)	10%	10%
(8) Dividends paid (#7 × #3)	$ 1,500	$ 1,702

The percentage increase in net income and dividends is the same, 13.5 percent.

ii) Assuming a payout ratio of 100 percent and, thus, a retention ratio of zero, the estimated growth rate is zero, as shown below.

	t = 1	t = 2
(1) Equity, start of period	$100,000	$100,000
(2) Return on equity (%)	15%	15%
(3) Net income (#1 × #2)	$ 15,000	$ 15,000
(4) Retention rate (%)	0%	0%
(5) Increase in retained earnings (#3 × #4)	$ −0−	$ −0−
(6) Equity, end of period (#1 + #5)	$100,000	$100,000
(7) Payout rate (%)(100% − #4)	100%	100%
(8) Dividends paid (#7 × #3)	$ 15,000	$ 15,000

Since neither net income nor dividends have increased, the growth rate of each is zero.

SP-2. Since the company finances half of its assets with debt, the remainder is financed with equity. First determine how much increased equity will be needed. Next, subtract the additional equity needed from net income. Whatever is left over (residual) is paid out as dividends.

	Year				
	1	2	3	4	5
Increase in assets (000)	$100	$200	$300	$400	$500
− Increase in debt (50%) (000)	$ 50	$100	$150	$200	$250
= Increase in equity needed (000)	$ 50	$100	$150	$200	$250
Net income (000)	$300	$300	$300	$300	$300
− Equity required (000)	$ 50	$100	$150	$200	$250
= Dividends (000)	$150	$200	$150	$100	$ 50

SP-3. Multiply the payout ratio times net income to determine dividends each year.

	Year				
	1	2	3	4	5
Net income (000)	$100	$50	$200	$300	$100
Payout ratio	.40	.40	.40	.40	.40
= Dividends (000)	$ 40	$20	$ 80	$120	$ 40

REFERENCES

Black, Fischer, and Myron Scholes. "The Effects of Dividend Yield and Dividend Policy on Common Stock Prices and Returns." *Journal of Financial Economics,* May 1974, pp. 1-22.

Elton, Edwin J., and Martin J. Gruber. "Marginal Stockholder Tax Rates and the Clientele Effect." *Review of Economics and Statistics,* February 1970, pp. 68-74.

Lintner, John. "Dividends, Earnings, Leverage, Stock Prices, and the Supply of Capital to Corporations." *Review of Economics and Statistics,* August 1962, pp. 243-69.

Miller, Merton H., and Franco Modigliani. "Dividend Policy, Growth and the Valuation of Shares." *Journal of Business,* October 1961, pp. 411-33.

Pettit, R. Richardson. "The Impact of Dividend and Earnings Announcements: A Reconciliation." *Journal of Business,* January 1976, pp. 86-96.

Stewart, Samuel S., Jr. "Should a Corporation Repurchase Its Own Stock?" *Journal of Finance,* June 1976, pp. 911-921.

Watts, Ross. "The Information Content of Dividends." *Journal of Business,* April 1973, pp. 191-211.

CASE EXERCISE

Marvell, Inc.

Marvell's dividend policy was straightforward. All earnings were retained as long as acceptable investments were available. More specifically, no dividends were paid if acceptable investment proposals exceeded or equaled profits plus depreciation. This approach led to more volatile dividends per share than was typical for the industry. (Exhibit C-1 shows comparative earnings, dividend, and stock price information for Marvell and the Crock Corporation.)

Mr. Jackson, Marvell's president, believed that it simply was not reasonable to pay out capital that could be invested profitably, and he thought it ludicrous that some firms actually had to borrow, in essence, to pay dividends. He believed such firms were trying to "have their cake and eat it too." He thought they were delaying the inevitable, since sooner or later they would have to get the money back from shareholders to repay the debt (directly through a new stock issue or indirectly through profits).

At the year-end board meeting, the estimated investible funds were compared with the set of acceptable projects. If there were more investible funds than acceptable projects, the difference was paid out as dividends. Otherwise, no dividends were paid.

	Marvell Corporation			Crock Corporation		
Year	EPS	DPS	Price*	EPS	DPS	Price*
1978	$1.03	$0.50	$ 7.00	$2.03	$1.20	$14.00
1979	1.60	-0-	5.00	2.60	1.32	21.00
1980	2.63	0.10	16.00	3.63	1.45	29.00
1981	3.48	2.00	31.00	4.48	1.60	45.00
1982	2.54	1.50	20.00	3.54	1.76	39.00
1983	2.34	1.00	12.00	3.34	1.93	33.00
1984	1.80	-0-	7.00	2.80	2.13	22.00
1985	(1.06)	-0-	7.00	(0.06)	2.34	20.00
1986	1.27	-0-	6.00	2.27	2.57	20.00
1987	2.43	-0-	17.00	3.43	2.83	34.00

*Average of annual high and low prices per share of common stock.

EXHIBIT C-1
Per Share Data for Marvell Corporation and the Crock Corporation

CASE QUESTIONS

1. How would you characterize Marvell's dividend policy? How does it compare with Crock's?

2. Estimate the average price/earnings ratios for Marvell and Crock. How might you explain the difference?

3. Which company has had more volatile earnings per share? Dividends per share?

4. What would you recommend with regard to Marvell's dividend policy?

C H A P T E R

21

INVESTMENT BANKING AND COMMON STOCK FINANCING

T he capital market is one of the most highly developed and efficient channels of distribution in the world. Business concerns that use this medium to obtain funds are almost always corporations, typically very large ones. However, since most corporations do not make frequent trips to the capital markets, financial managers may lack vital information about the best terms to offer investors and the best times to issue securities. In such cases, they rely on expert advice in these areas from investment bankers. In addition to providing such advice, the investment bankers help firms that actually sell the securities.

This chapter covers two closely related but distinct topics: the process of raising funds from the capital markets with the aid of investment bankers, and managerial relationships with shareholders of common stock. Chapter 22 will discuss managerial aspects of long-term debt; and Chapter 23 will consider still other forms of external financing.

Objectives and Organization of this Chapter

The primary objective of this chapter is to describe the mechanics of raising funds through the sale of new securities. A related objective is to describe typical features of common stock issues that must be considered by management. In the first section, the chapter discusses the role of the investment banker. The second section demonstrates how the different types of costs associated with issuing securities may be determined. The third section briefly describes important regulations governing the sale and distribution of securities.

The fourth section of the chapter describes various important features of common stock. Last, a "rights offering" is described and the chapter shows how these rights to purchase new shares of common stock should be valued.

INVESTMENT BANKING

Investment banking firms are essentially intermediaries that channel funds from those who wish to invest to those who need the funds. They purchase and resell the corporation's issue of securities. This is called underwriting. In contrast, commercial banks engage principally in short- and intermediate-term financing of business, although they do invest in corporate bonds. They are suppliers of funds and are prohibited by law from functioning as investment bankers. (As this is being written, they are asking for this right from Congress.)

Investigating Function

When an investment banking house has been selected by a company to handle the sale of its securities, it is known as the originating house. Sometimes two or three houses work together, in which case they may be called a *nucleus group*. The success of an originating house lies in its ability to effect a satisfactory compromise among the interests of the investor, other investment banking houses participating in the issue, and the corporation issuing the securities.

Since the name of the originating house will be associated with the issue, it needs to maintain the long-run good will of the investors who will buy the securities. To be sure that the issuing company is sound, the banker undertakes an exhaustive study of its financial statements, assets, and management. In drawing up recommended provisions of the security issue, the investment banker also makes certain that the necessary covenants to protect the interests of the investor are provided. (Covenants are clauses in an agreement between lender and borrower that specify obligations or promises.)

Because other investment banking houses will be asked to join in buying the issue, the originating banker must consider their interests (which correspond closely with her or his own). The originating banker is investigating the issuer for them, and thus money is riding on the quality of the findings. They will want to be sure that the issue is sound and that the time of sale and price of the issue are set so that it will sell quickly. If the originating banker performs well, the other investment bankers will be willing to participate in future issues. Better still, they may ask the originating house to participate with them when they originate issues.

Finally, the originating house has important responsibilities to the corporation issuing the security. In recommending the terms of sale, the banker must take care not to suggest covenants so restrictive that the corporation has little flexibility. He or she provides general financial advice both before and after the issue. The originating house also assists in the preparation of the documents necessary to comply with state and federal regulations governing the sale of securities to the public.

The most important service of the investment banker to the issuing corporation is in timing and pricing the issue. With respect to the timing of the issue, the investment banker's expertise is expected to show up in terms of "feel" and "judgment" for market conditions. This presumably aids the corporation in issuing securities at opportune times from cost and marketing standpoints.

The pricing of the issue is also a crucial and delicate aspect of the buying function. Even after all the preliminary investigation, which may take several months, the banker and issuer may fail to agree on these terms. On the one hand, the issuer would like to obtain as much for the securities as possible. When bonds are sold, certain claims on income and assets are sacrificed; when stock is sold, present owners may have to share future earnings, claims on assets, and rights to management with others. The issuer clearly would like to obtain as large a sum as possible in return for these sacrifices. Although the investment banker would like to have the market price of the securities rise slightly after they have been sold, he or she also does not wish to set the initial offering price too low. This would reflect on the investment banker's judgment and might cost future business.

On the other hand, the investment banker does not wish to price the issue too high. It will be difficult to sell and will sell slowly. He or she might even have to take a loss in order to move the issue. Consequently, the investment banker must have a rapid turnover of the securities handled and can ill afford to take substantial losses.

Pricing begins with the banker's estimate of what the market will pay for a public issue of new "unseasoned" securities, given the proposed features of the offering. The banker then works back from this price to determine the price that will be paid for the issue. Basically, he or she considers the current market prices of other securities of similar quality with similar features. Since these are "seasoned" securities, this new issue is likely to be priced a little lower to allow for the fact that the market will have to absorb a sudden flood of the new securities.

Exhibit 21-1 shows the first page of the prospectus relating to $1 billion in debt securities issued by IBM. Notice that the notes were offered to the public at 99.400 percent of their par values ($994 per $1,000 face amount) and the long-term bonds or debentures were offered at $996.25 per $1,000 bond on October 4, 1979. This meant that the effective yield to the public was somewhat higher than the coupon rate of $9\frac{1}{2}$ percent on the notes due in 1986 and the $9\frac{3}{8}$ percent rate on the debentures due in 2004.

From the public offering price is deducted the underwriting discount or what is sometimes referred to as the *gross spread*. This is the compensation to the investment bankers for handling the sale of the issue. For the IBM issue, the underwriting discount was .625 percent for the notes and .875 percent for the debentures and amounted to gross spreads (between the price to the public and the proceeds to IBM) of $3,125,000 and $4,375,000, respectively. Also notice that the "proceeds to company" shown in Exhibit 21-1 are before deducting legal fees, accounting fees, and printing costs estimated at about $850,000.

The gross spread amount (plus the legal, accounting, and printing charges) must cover all costs of investigating, risk-bearing, and selling the issue and still leave some profit for the investment bankers. This is because

gross spread

731

CHAPTER 21
INVESTMENT
BANKING AND
COMMON STOCK
FINANCING

Prospectus

$1,000,000,000

International Business Machines Corporation

$500,000,000
9½% Notes Due 1986

$500,000,000
9⅜% Debentures Due 2004

Interest on the Notes is payable semi-annually on April 1 and October 1 beginning April 1, 1980. The Notes are redeemable on or after October 1, 1983 at the option of the Company, in whole or in part, at their principal amount plus accrued interest.

Interest on the Debentures is payable semi-annually on April 1 and October 1 beginning April 1, 1980. The Debentures are redeemable at any time at the option of the Company, in whole or in part, at declining premiums. Prior to October 1, 1989, no such redemption may be made from or in anticipation of borrowed funds having an annual interest cost of less than 9.415%. In addition, a mandatory sinking fund beginning October 1, 1985 will be sufficient to retire at par 95% of the aggregate principal amount of the Debentures prior to maturity. The Company may increase its sinking fund payment in any year by an additional amount up to 150% of the mandatory sinking fund payment of that year.

The Notes and Debentures have been approved for listing on the New York Stock Exchange subject to official notice of issuance.

THESE SECURITIES HAVE NOT BEEN APPROVED OR DISAPPROVED BY THE SECURITIES AND EX-CHANGE COMMISSION NOR HAS THE COMMISSION PASSED UPON THE ACCURACY OR ADEQUACY OF THIS PROSPECTUS. ANY REPRESENTATION TO THE CONTRARY IS A CRIMINAL OFFENSE.

	Price to Public(1)	Underwriting Discount	Proceeds to Company(1)(2)
Per Note	99.400%	.625%	98.775%
Total	$497,000,000	$3,125,000	$493,875,000
Per Debenture	99.625%	.875%	98.750%
Total	$498,125,000	$4,375,000	$493,750,000

(1) Plus accrued interest, if any, from October 16, 1979 to date of delivery.
(2) Before deducting expenses payable by the Company estimated to be $850,000.

The Notes and Debentures are offered when, as and if accepted by the Underwriters named herein, subject to prior sale or withdrawal, cancellation or modification of the offers without notice, and subject to the approval of certain legal matters by counsel. It is expected that delivery of the Notes and Debentures will be made at the office of Salomon Brothers, One New York Plaza, New York, New York, or through the facilities of The Depository Trust Company, on or about October 16, 1979.

Salomon Brothers   **Merrill Lynch White Weld Capital Markets Group**
Merrill Lynch, Pierce, Fenner & Smith Incorporated

The date of this Prospectus is October 4, 1979.

the price to the public less the gross spread is the amount the investment bankers have promised to pay to the issuing corporation.

Final agreement on the price to the public and the gross spread is usually reached a few days or a few hours before the issue is to be sold to the public. This usually permits the banker to take into account any last-minute changes in conditions in the capital markets. In the case of the IBM issue, the bond market weakened just before the issue was to be sold to the public, and thus the notes and debentures were offered at less than 100 percent of their face amounts.

733

CHAPTER 21
INVESTMENT
BANKING AND
COMMON STOCK
FINANCING

Risk-Bearing Function

At some stage in the preliminary investigation, the originating house and issuer sign a preliminary agreement giving the banker an option to purchase the securities if they are eventually to be issued. Since no one investment banker is likely to risk buying $1 billion worth of bonds for resale, the originating house will ask other investment bankers to join together in a *syndicate* to share the burden (and commission). In the IBM issue, more than 200 other bankers joined the two firms in the nucleus group (listed in the exhibit) in underwriting the issue. Usually a certain amount of the investment bankers' commission is paid to the originating house to cover its costs of preparing the issue for the market. The balance is split among all the investment bankers according to the shares they have obligated themselves to buy and resell. As we shall see, a small portion of the commission may then be reallocated to others participating in the selling effort.

underwriting syndicate

When these bankers sign a final agreement with the issuer, they agree to *underwrite* the issue. For example, underwriters agreed to deliver to the International Business Machines Corporation $987,625,000 (for both the note and debenture issues), less about $850,000 in additional expenses, on a specified settlement date. Such settlement dates are usually set close to the public offering dates for securities. Thus, fully underwritten issues in essence shift the risk-bearing responsibility away from the issuing corporation and on to the shoulders of the participating underwriters.

underwriting

In the case of the IBM debt issues, underwriter loss estimates ranged as high as $20 million. Even with the initial selling of the notes and debentures at discounts from face values (see Exhibit 21-1), probably only about $600 million were sold initially. Substantial markdowns were required to sell the remaining $400 million of securities. These cut into, and in some cases more than totally wiped out, the underwriters' discounts.[1] The bond market was weak at the time of the IBM offering, and the Federal Reserve

---

[1]While actual underwriting losses are usually not disclosed, in part because many firms often are involved, some indication as to the magnitude of the underwriting losses associated with the IBM offer are found in two articles in the *Wall Street Journal*: October 11, 1979, p. 2 and October 12, 1979, p. 28.

best efforts basis

Board immediately afterward imposed very restrictive credit standards. Combined, these illustrate the extent of risk-bearing which may be involved in an underwriting.

In order to minimize the risk-assuming function, investment bankers sometimes will sell securities only on a *best efforts* basis rather than underwriting the securities. Under this arrangement, the selling price is fixed, but the amount of securities that will be sold at that price is uncertain. Companies that are going public for the first time often have no choice. For example, one company had its initial shares of common stock sold to the public on the following basis:

> *The first 3,920,000 shares will be offered by the Underwriter on a 'best efforts, all-or-none' basis. There is no assurance that any or all of the shares will be sold. Therefore, if 3,920,000 shares are not sold within 90 days from the date hereof (with an additional 30-day allowable extension), all the monies received will be refunded to the subscribers, without any commission or expenses and without any interest.*

At the other extreme, very large corporations have occasionally sold their securities on a best efforts, or commission, basis because they felt that the risk of not selling the securities was slight. A third alternative that is sometimes available involves direct distribution of securities by the issuing corporation.

Selling Function

The essence of the investment banker's business is turnover. When the investment banker grosses 1 percent or less on the selling price (as is common with large, high-quality debt issues), it is important to sell a large volume in order to justify the underwriting effort. If the banker cannot sell an issue before the settlement date, the issuing corporation must still be paid in full and the banker must carry the unsold securities in inventory until they can be sold. The investment banker's own funds consequently will be tied up in part of the inventory, and interest payments may be required if a portion of the unsold securities are being financed through a commercial bank. Investment bankers often use short-term commercial bank financing, secured by the securities that are being underwritten, to bridge the gap between the initial underwriting of the securities and their actual sale.

If the issue sells slowly, the underwriters may agree to reduce the selling price and take a loss rather than tie up their funds. In large part, the investment banker can avoid this predicament by buying, timing, and pricing wisely. However, it is also important to have a strong selling organization.

The formation of a syndicate is desirable not only to spread the risk but to distribute the issue widely and quickly. A large portion of the issue will be sold by the sales staff of the underwriters. On these sales, the investment banker receives the full amount of the gross spread. Some securities may be allocated to *dealers* all over the country for resale. These local security dealers perform only a selling function and do not underwrite the issue. Their role is similar to that of a broker or manufacturer's agent in marketing other products. For their selling services the dealers receive a discount from the offering price to the public. Since they perform only the selling function and do not assume any part of the investigating function or the risk of underwriting the issue, their spread is less than that of the investment bankers underwriting the issue.

735

CHAPTER 21
INVESTMENT
BANKING AND
COMMON STOCK
FINANCING

The selling effort by these underwriters and dealers begins prior to the offering date. An announcement of the forthcoming offering is made to alert the prospective investors. However, the corporation must avoid undertaking a publicity campaign. This is against SEC regulations. A copy of the first part of the registration statement (required by the SEC), called a *prospectus*, and filed with the SEC, setting forth the basic facts concerning *security prospectus* the corporation and the proposed issue, is made available to interested investors. The face of this booklet is identical to that shown in Exhibit 21-1, with some common exceptions. No price usually is shown, since that typically will be set shortly before the offering date. In addition the following statement is stamped in bright red on the face:

> *A registration statement relating to these securities has been filed with the Securities and Exchange Commission but has not yet become effective. Information contained herein is subject to completion or amendment. These securities may not be sold nor may offers to buy be accepted prior to the time the registration statement becomes effective. This prospectus shall not constitute an offer to sell or the solicitation of an offer to buy nor shall there be any sale of these securities in any State in which such offer, solicitation or sale would be unlawful prior to registration or qualification under the securities laws of any such State.*

Because of the color of the stamp and the obvious intent of the document, this booklet is referred to as a *red herring*. *red herring*

The SEC examines the material provided in the prospectus and registration statement for accuracy and adequacy; it makes no judgment as to quality or value in relation to price. When the SEC agrees to permit the sale of the securities, the members of the syndicate and dealers are notified that the registration has become *effective*. Sales personnel then notify prospective investors of the offering price of the issue and seek orders for the securities. With a good issue, proper timing and pricing, and an active selling organization, the securities may be sold within a few hours of the time their sale is permitted by the SEC.

In the prospectus for the debt issues by IBM (Exhibit 21-1) there was a statement:

> *In connection with this offering, the underwriters may overallot or effect transactions which stabilize or maintain the market prices of the notes and*

debentures offered hereby at levels above those which might otherwise prevail in the open market. Such stabilizing, if commenced, may be discontinued at any time.

This means that the managing underwriters may place orders in the open market to purchase the debt securities should the price tend to drift downward from the initial offering price.[2] Most prospectus statements for equity as well as debt offerings contain similar provisions for the possibility of stabilizing efforts by underwriters.

stabilization

Although *stabilization* is designed to prevent minor downward price fluctuations resulting from the sudden entry to the market of new issues, it is not very effective in view of the many alternative securities available. If an issue has been overpriced, eventually the underwriters will have to abandon their original offering price and let the issue seek its own level in the market.

A syndicate is formed for each issue of securities. As soon as a particular issue is sold, the syndicate is dissolved. While a company may employ the same originating house for a number of different issues, the syndicates formed by the originating house usually differ from one issue to the next.

COST OF PUBLIC ISSUES

There are two immediate costs involved in underwriting securities in a general cash offer to the public. One is the underwriters' commission, which is incorporated in the price paid by the public and is not an expense on the books of the corporation. The other is composed of various expenses (largely legal, accounting, and printing) borne by the corporation which represent deductions from the gross proceeds. Together, the two comprise total *flotation costs.*

flotation costs

Data compiled by the Securities and Exchange Commission indicate that flotation costs associated with the underwriting and distributing of new securities issues are affected by: (a) the quality of the issuer and the issue,[3] (b) the size of the issue, and (c) the type of securities issued. In addition to these factors, which will affect flotation costs at any point in time, investment banker compensation also will differ over time depending on the prevailing and expected capital market conditions.

Let us now look at the three factors that affect the size of flotation costs at any point in time. For example, higher-quality firms usually issue higher-

---

[2]In the case of the IBM notes and debentures, the debt markets continued to deteriorate rapidly after the Federal Reserve Board moved to tighten credit. Thus there was little chance for successful stabilization activities to take place.

[3]Some industry differences also seem to exist. For example, the costs of flotation are generally somewhat higher for manufacturing corporations than for corporations in telecommunications and electric and gas utilities, although differences narrow for large issues. Possibly higher flotation costs for industrial corporations reflect perceived quality differences.

quality securities and should benefit by having lower-percentage flotation costs.

737

CHAPTER 21
INVESTMENT
BANKING AND
COMMON STOCK
FINANCING

Another factor that influences flotation costs is the size of the issue. Because there are certain fixed costs associated with underwriting and distributing of new issues, smaller-dollar-amount issues will have higher percentage flotation costs. Underwriting investigation and preparation, and even other expenses such as legal and accounting fees, would not be expected to move proportionally with the size of the issue. Thus the total costs associated with the IBM debt issues described in Exhibit 21-1 would be less as a percentage of the public offering amount than if IBM had sold debt securities in the $200 to $300 million range. A $50 million debt offering would have been even more costly on a percentage flotation cost basis.

The final factor to be recognized is that percentage flotation costs are less for debt securities than for equity securities (with common stock generally being more costly than preferred stock issues). This relationship exists because the stock market historically has been more volatile than the bond market, and because the selling costs are greater for common stock issues that are typically distributed to many investors, than for bonds generally sold to relatively few large institutional investors.

SELECTION OF INVESTMENT BANKER

The investment banker who finally handles the sales of securities may be selected in one of two ways: *direct negotiation* or *competitive bid*. In the one case the issuer selects the firm; in the other case, investment bankers bid for the securities.

In direct negotiation, two factors tend to limit the degree of competition among investment bankers for issues of securities. First, a concern may allow one investment banker to handle its sales for many years, although it is under no obligation to do so. Second, there is some degree of specialization in the field. For example, some firms deal mainly in bonds of utilities, others only underwrite high-quality securities, and some prefer firms that are going public for the first time. Most offerings are made using this method.

direct negotiation

The bid method is used on standardized issues of securities by public utility holding companies (as well as by states, cities, school districts, and so on). Investment bankers form syndicates to bid on an issue. Some time before the bid date, the issuer holds a meeting to provide essential information concerning the corporation's affairs and financial position to prospective underwriters. At the appointed place, date and hour, the bids from various syndicates are opened. The securities are awarded to the highest bidder; that is, to the group whose price will give the issuer the lowest net interest cost. Often the securities may be made available for sale on the following day. Because investment bankers are skilled in judging the market, their bids are generally close.

competitive bid

DISTRIBUTION OF SECURITIES

Corporate debt and equity securities may be sold to the public or to financial institutions, particularly insurance companies and pension funds. It has already been noted that the public offering of securities may involve any of three basic methods of distribution. In contrast, the *private placement* of securities is accomplished, with or without the aid of an investment banker, by selling the securities directly to institutional investors.

Public Offerings

It is possible to distinguish two groups of public buyers. On the one hand, a company may sell its securities to the general public without requiring that purchasers have any special relationship to the company. On the other hand, the issue may be limited to those who hold securities the firm has previously issued or to other special groups, such as officers, employees, or customers.

The majority of public offerings are made to the general public rather than to special groups of investors. Most large offerings of securities to the general public are made through investment bankers.

Private Placements

The term *private placement* ordinarily applies to the direct sale of large blocks of securities by corporations to institutional investors. Because of the legal restrictions on common stock investments by these financial institutions, the bulk of private placements are long-term debt issues. Purchasers of privately placed debt issues are mainly insurance companies and pension funds and, to a lesser extent, other financial institutions.

Another differentiating characteristic between the public and private markets is in terms of the average issue size. Privately placed bond issues are, on average, substantially smaller than publicly offered bond issues. Since smaller corporations typically issue securities in smaller sizes, the private market is used more heavily by smaller corporations. A similar average size differential is not found between the two markets for common stock issues. This is due, at least in part, to the infrequent use of the private market for common stock placements.

The investment banker's role in private placements is usually to provide advice and to find a purchaser for the issue. Because the investment banker acts only as an agent for the issuing corporation and thus does not underwrite the issue, fees tend to be much smaller than those for public offerings.

GOVERNMENT REGULATION

Government regulation applies both to the sale of new issues and to the purchase and sale of previously issued securities. Regulation of transactions in existing issues is largely within the province of federal authorities, specifically the SEC, whereas both state and federal regulations may apply to the sale of new issues.

739

CHAPTER 21
INVESTMENT
BANKING AND
COMMON STOCK
FINANCING

New Issues

Interstate security sales are regulated by the Federal Securities Act of 1933. The basic philosophy of the act is that a prospective buyer should be given full, adequate, and accurate information. As noted, some time prior to the prospective offering date the issuer must file with the SEC a *registration statement*. The registration statement is a compilation of all pertinent information concerning the company and its chief officers. The *prospectus* is a summary of the significant points covered in the registration statement. Without the price and offering date, this is the "red herring" mentioned earlier. With this information, it is a statement that must be given a prospective purchaser of the securities at the time they are offered for sale. The Federal Securities Act does not tell the investor what should or should not be purchased.

registration statement
prospectus

The SEC can prevent the sale of securities until it believes that the registration statement and prospectus contain no misleading statements and omit no significant information. Most omissions or misstatements in the registration statement are dealt with by means of a letter of comment prepared by the SEC. If there are material deficiencies, the SEC may issue a *stop order* to prevent the sale of the securities until the shortcomings are corrected.

stop order

Enforcement of the act is aided by the provision of civil and criminal liabilities. In addition, purchasers of securities may sue for damages suffered as a result of untrue or materially inadequate information in the prospectus. Practically everybody connected with the issue, excluding the SEC, may be sued.

A means of evading registration with the SEC has been the use of *letter stock*. Characteristic of small and emerging businesses, letter stock is common stock issued to 25 or fewer investors who agree in an "investment letter" that they will not resell the stock to other investors within some specified period. The buyer usually cannot resell the stock unless the firm registers the issue or until another investor can be found who will similarly agree not to sell the stock in the market.

letter stock

State Regulation

Some state laws parallel the SEC approach in that they are primarily designed to prevent fraud. Others go farther and attempt to protect the investor from her or his own "poor judgment" by prohibiting the sale of securities deemed by some state commissions to be especially speculative, overpriced, or of very poor quality. It is entirely possible for a state commissioner to prevent the sale of a security within his or her state, even though the SEC has allowed its registration statement to become effective. State laws are sometimes referred to as "blue sky legislation," because they represent an attempt to prevent the sale of the "blue sky" to unwary investors. Ordinarily a corporation issuing securities may comply with these state laws by filing with the state commission information similar to that contained in its registration statement. If the securities are not to be offered in interstate commerce, the issuer need file only with the state in which the securities are offered for sale.

Existing Issues

An important aid to the original sale of new securities is the provision of fair and honest markets in which they may be subsequently sold. The Securities Exchange Act of 1934 requires the registration of security exchanges and of brokers and dealers doing business in securities traded (listed) on and outside of the exchanges. (The market in unlisted securi-*over-the-counter market* ties is called the *over-the-counter* market.) Working largely through the governing bodies of the various exchanges and the National Association of Security Dealers, the SEC attempts to prevent "fraudulent, deceptive, and manipulative acts and practices" in security transactions.

Insider Trading

Trading by corporate officers and directors in securities of their own companies is limited to some extent, and a full report of their transactions is published monthly. In an effort to speed the flow of information to the market—and thereby make it more efficient—the SEC has filed complaints against use of inside information before it became publicly available.

The U.S. Court of Appeals has "unanimously held that a corporate insider in possession of important inside information about his corporation may not trade in the corporation's stock without disclosing that information . . . This duty was unanimously held to apply to employees of the corporation, as well as to its top officers."

More recently, Dennis Levine, an executive with a major Wall Street banking firm, was sent to prison and forced to give up almost $11 million from profits generated by insider information he passed on to Ivan Boesky and others. For his illegal insider activities, Boesky agreed to pay a $50 million fine and to return another $50 million in profits from insider information. Although in 1984, Congress passed the Insider Trading Sanctions Act, which increased fines and criminal penalties for insider trading, even more stringent regulations may be enacted.

COMMON STOCK

Although the technical and legal aspects are important to an understanding of common stock as a source of funds, of more concern are the various decisions that must be made concerning its management. Some

741

CHAPTER 21
INVESTMENT
BANKING AND
COMMON STOCK
FINANCING

must be made at the time the corporation is formed. Other decisions—
listing of stock on an exchange, payment of dividends, stock splits, and
retirement of stock—are generally made at later stages in the corporation's
life.

At the time a corporation is formed, the number of shares of common
stock to be authorized and the par value, if any, must be determined. Let
us consider these in order.

Authorized Shares

State incorporation taxes and annual franchise taxes necessary in order
to do business within certain states are sometimes based upon the number
of shares of capital stock authorized in a corporation's charter. Thus, it
would appear to be an advantage to keep the number of shares authorized
to a bare minimum. When additional shares are needed, the firm can obtain
stockholders' approval to amend the charter to authorize more. However,
in a large corporation this approval may not be given readily, and in any
case it will be expensive to tell the stockholders the reasons for the desired
increase in authorized shares and to obtain their permission. Since a company is likely to need shares in small amounts from time to time, it may be
preferable to estimate the probability of these future needs and to authorize
an adequate number of shares at the time of organization.

For what purposes might a firm need authorized, but unissued, common stock? First, there is always the possibility that it will wish to sell more
common stock to raise funds for expansion. In addition, shares may be
needed to provide stock for conversion of senior convertible issues, for
options (similar to warrants rather than listed options) to officers, and for
dividends in the form of common stock. More important is the possibility
that there will be an opportunity at some future time to acquire another
corporation through an exchange of stock or by the issue of stock for the
assets of the other concern. If the managers must wait to obtain approval
of the stockholders to increase the number of authorized shares, somebody
else could make the acquisition first. Management must weigh the probability of these future needs and the costs of later increasing the authorized
shares against the present cost of paying a somewhat higher tax on incorporation and possibly higher annual franchise taxes.

Par Value

How should one set the par value at the time of incorporation, or
should the firm issue no par stock? There are disadvantages in no par stock.
Some states levy corporation taxes and annual franchise taxes on no par
stock as if it carried a par of $100. If this is true of the state in which the
charter is sought, the company should consider issuance of a low par stock,
say $1 or $5 par value per share.

There are several advantages to this low par stock besides the possible savings in corporation and franchise taxes. Should the par be set at $100, the initial and all future sales of new stock by the corporation must be at $100 or above; otherwise buyers may later be assessed for the difference between the price they paid and the par value. This requirement might seriously hamper any future financing if the market price of the stock should decline in the interim. It would be better to set the par value at $1 per share. The firm might sell the first offering at $100. If the price later declined to $60, it could still sell additional stock. Moreover, the initial sale of common stock at $100 provides a paid-in surplus, against which, in some states, a company may charge losses in its early unprofitable months of operation. Thus the relevant portion of the balance sheet after the initial sale might appear as follows:

Common stock (authorized 20,000 shares)	
Issued, 2,000 shares (par value, $1)	$ 2,000
Paid-in surplus	198,000

The possibility of misleading the investor may be lessened by the use of low par and no par stock. There are still investors who believe that they are getting a "bargain" if they can buy stock with a par value of $100 for only $60. A request that they pay $60 for a par value of $1 hopefully may encourage them to examine the income they are buying, rather than the par value of the stock certificate.

GOING PUBLIC

closely-held companies

A firm whose stock is held by only a few individuals, often related, is termed *closely-held*. Reasons for refusing to sell their common stock to the general public typically center on a desire for privacy and independence. Unless they have more than 500 shareholders and assets of more than $1 million, they do not need to disclose publicly their financial statements.

However, there are strong incentives for eventually going public; that is, for selling common stock (either new shares, shares owned by the family, or both) to the general public. Closely-held concerns find it very difficult to raise additional capital, so that expansion is largely dependent upon retained earnings. Should they wish to expand by acquiring other firms, they are handicapped by not having marketable securities to offer in exchange for those of the company to be acquired. Moreover, owners of a privately-held firm may have estate tax problems, both in terms of raising the funds to pay the taxes and in establishing a fair price for the shares in order to value the estate. These considerations have forced most closely-held firms ultimately to go public.

LISTING

One of the rights of a stockholder is to transfer ownership of her or his shares to another party. The stockholder will probably find a buyer more easily if the stock is listed on a national exchange, such as the New York Stock Exchange, or on a regional exchange, such as the Boston Stock Exchange. A stock that is listed on an exchange may be purchased and sold on the floor of the exchange by its members. Many of these members execute orders to buy or sell which are received from customers located throughout the world.

The problem of whether or not to list securities is faced by the financial managers of relatively few corporations. For example, fewer than 3,000 corporations have their common stock listed on either the New York Stock Exchange or the American Stock Exchange. Probably not more than another 6,000 or so firms would have their common stocks listed or traded on the regional exchanges or in the over-the-counter market. Thus fewer than 10,000 firms would have publicly traded stocks, and only about 3,000 of these firms' stocks are listed on organized exchanges.

Listing may offer advantages, although studies of new listings generally find no statistical evidence that listing *per se* adds significantly to the market value of the firm. An argument sometimes cited for listing is that it provides a channel for future financing. As a counter argument, managers of some companies have pointed out that a growing firm may obtain more "push" in the sale of its securities if it is unlisted. Because brokers handling securities in the over-the-counter market typically obtain a larger margin than if they were dealing in listed stocks, they are often prepared to work harder to sell them.

VOICE IN MANAGEMENT — THE AGENCY PROBLEM

The ultimate authority to determine the management of a business rests with the proprietor, partners, or common stockholders, depending upon the form of business organization. While this authority is exercised directly in proprietorships, partnerships, and many corporations, it is typically exercised only indirectly in a large corporation. Although this indirect control is the only feasible method of operation, it also creates problems in defining the scope of stockholders' rights to certain aspects of management. Moreover, the separation of powers gives rise to situations where management may abuse the prerogatives assigned it by the stockholders.

Right to Elect Directors

Each stockholder has the right to vote for members of the board of directors, his or her voting power being determined by the number of shares of stock that he or she holds. This right may be assigned to others. Thus at one time the Hughes Tool Co. assigned the voting rights of its TWA stock to a board of trustees in order to obtain a large loan. In a few corporations, usually small, there are two classes of common stock: one with voting power and the other without. In all other respects the stock may be identical. Although this is a useful device to maintain control of a corporation, it is frowned upon by the Securities and Exchange Commission. It is also true of many small corporations that the leading common stockholders elect themselves as directors and are appointed as officers. In such cases, stockholders have a direct voice in management.

Once stockholders have elected directors, they have a right to expect them, as their agents, to administer the affairs of the corporation for the stockholders' benefit and not for their own. In case a director does abuse his or her power, even a minority stockholder may sue for the benefit of the corporation to recover any sums lost. For example, if a director caused the corporation to purchase, at an unreasonably high price, property that she or he owned in order to obtain a substantial profit, a stockholder might sue to recover the amount paid above the market price of the property. Any sums recovered by this *derivative suit,* as it is called, would be paid to the corporation too, and not just to the stockholder bringing the suit.[4] To prevent stockholders from making nuisances of themselves, many state laws require that stockholders who bring derivative suits put up "security for expenses" to cover the costs to the corporation of defending against the suit should the charge be found to be without merit.

derivative suit

Right to Inspect Books

Although the right to inspect a corporation's books is given to stockholders under common law, the right is usually satisfied by furnishing the stockholders with audited reports. When a stockholder presses to obtain information that is not provided in the audited statement, he or she may have to prove in court that the information is being requested to appraise management's ability rather than to harm the interests of the other stockholders. Were it not for this protection, competitors might easily buy a few shares of stock to obtain valuable information concerning the concern's operations.

Stockholders also have the right to obtain a list of the names and addresses of their fellow stockholders. Obviously, this information is necessary if an individual stockholder is to enlist the support of others who also seek a change in management. Again, this right may be abused. Therefore, a stockholder seeking this information may have to show in court that he or she has no ulterior motive. Otherwise, the stockholder might obtain the list in order to sell items to the other stockholders or to persuade them to switch to some other security.

---

[4]However, there are also "friendly" derivative suits, whereby a stockholder friendly to the board of directors institutes a suit concerning a questionable practice of the board. If the friendly stockholder loses the suit, the directors cannot be sued again on the same charge.

Methods of Voting

Since it is sometimes difficult to attend the stockholders' meeting in person, a stockholder may vote by means of a *proxy:* that is, a written authorization that delegates to another person her or his rights to vote at the meeting. Proxies are usually mailed out by the group controlling the corporation. If the stockholders are reasonably contented, they sign and return the proxies as a matter of course, thus giving management the power to vote their shares. Those who fail to return their proxies make it easier for management to secure a majority of the votes of those stockholders represented at the meeting. Because of the proxy mechanism, it is usually fairly simple to maintain control of a corporation by owning considerably less than 50 percent of the outstanding stock.

proxy

Ownership of less than a majority of the outstanding stock always leaves one open to a raid by outside interests seeking to seize control. In such cases both the "ins" and the "outs" may hire proxy solicitation firms to seek proxies and to bombard the stockholders with charges and counter-charges. Keep in mind, however, that the "ins" have the use of corporate funds to wage their battle to maintain control. This is one reason why proxy raids are often more spectacular than successful.

The Securities and Exchange Commission requires that proxy material of companies under its jurisdiction be submitted to it for approval. In general the SEC seeks full disclosure of pertinent information and requires that stockholders be allowed to vote for or against key issues that will come before the stockholders' meeting. The problem of eliminating false or misleading information is most acute in the heat of a proxy battle. In addition to the full and truthful disclosure requirements, the regulations also provide that a stockholder, with a proper purpose, can request and receive from management a list of all stockholders in order to be able to communicate with the other stockholders.

Proxy contests are most frequently initiated when firms have shown losses or relatively low rates of return on common equity and low growth in EPS. However, only about one out of three proxy contests have been successful in the past from the point of view of the outsiders. As one might expect, the likelihood of the "outs" being able to overthrow the "ins" seems to increase as the earnings performance of management deteriorates.

Majority Voting. There are two systems of voting in common use. Under the majority-rule system, each stockholder has one vote for each share held. If the stockholder holds 100 shares, she or he may cast that many votes for each director that is preferred. The voting is conducted for each position, one at a time. Thus if there is a group that has 600 out of the 1000 shares outstanding of a corporation, this group will be able to elect every one of the directors that it desires. Unless the majority allows it, there will be no representation of the minority interests on the board of directors.

Cumulative Voting. The alternative system is called cumulative voting. Corporations chartered in some states are permitted to have cumulative voting; in a few states they are required to employ this system. If there were five directors to be elected, a common stockholder with 100 shares would have 500 votes; that is, the number of shares held, multiplied by the number of directors to be elected. Further, he or she could allot all 500 votes to one director. Ballots are cast for all five positions at the same time. A minority group controlling 400 shares out of 1000 would have a total of 2000 votes available in the election of a five-person board of directors. By allocating 1000 votes to each of two directors, they could be assured of placing them on the board and having this degree of representation. The majority with 600 shares and 3000 votes would spread their votes over three directors and be equally certain of electing them.

The two voting methods may be compared as follows:

	Results of Vote			
	Under Majority-Rule Voting		*Under Cumulative Voting*	
Candidates	*Votes*		*Votes*	
Majority A	600	Elected	1000	Elected
Majority B	600	Elected	1000	Elected
Majority C	600	Elected	1000	Elected
Majority D	600	Elected	0	—
Majority E	600	Elected	0	—
Minority V	400	—	1000	Elected
Minority W	400	—	1000	Elected
Minority X	400	—	—	—
Minority Y	400	—	—	—
Minority Z	400	—	—	—

To determine the number of shares needed to control in order to elect a certain number to the board of directors (NE), we can use the formula:

$$\text{NE} = \frac{\text{Total number of shares outstanding} \times \text{Number of directors desired}}{\text{Total number of directors to be elected} + 1} + 1 \qquad (21\text{-}1)$$

If we wish to be sure of electing one director, we would need 167 shares[5]:

$$\text{NE} = \frac{1000 \times 1}{5 + 1} + 1 = 167\frac{2}{3}, \quad \text{or} \quad 167 \text{ (Drop any fractions.)}$$

---

[5]The minority would need 167 shares and would have to cast all votes for one person to elect one director. They would cast 835 votes (5 × 167) for their candidate. If the majority tried to elect the entire board, they would spread their 4165 votes (5 × 833) over 5 candidates. This would give each person 833 votes; the minority representative would win one seat.

The case for or against cumulative voting depends largely on the circumstances. In some cases, the minority representative has been able to bring substantial improvement in the affairs of a corporation through her or his managerial abilities and powers of persuasion. In other cases, the minority representative has been a source of friction who used the position to gather ammunition for future proxy fights. Such activities tend to hamstring effective and aggressive management.

Cumulative voting may be thwarted by several devices. In the previous example, where the minority had 167 shares of common stock, a change in the bylaws to reduce the number of directors from five to four would keep any minority representative off the board. Although 167 shares would be just sufficient to elect one director in five, it would not be adequate to elect one in four. A similar approach is to have only a portion of the directors stand for election each year. If there were nine directors to be elected, 167 shares would be more than enough to elect one. However, if only three were elected each year for three-year terms, the minority group would again be prevented from having representation on the board. The legality of these devices depends in part upon the laws of the state in which the corporation is chartered.

Rights Offering

If an additional issue of common stock were sold to the general public, the share of the corporation's earnings, assets, and rights to management held by existing stockholders might be correspondingly diminished. Under common law they should be offered the chance to maintain their proportionate interest in the company. This right, termed a *pre-emptive* right, is supported by some state laws as well as in the charters of many corporations.

pre-emptive right

When securities are offered first to existing stockholders, it is called a *privileged subscription* or *rights offering.* The procedure is fairly simple. After the issue has been approved, the company sends out notices to stockholders saying that all those who are stockholders as of a certain date may subscribe to additional shares, say one additional share of common stock for each four shares currently held. To keep this orderly, one right is issued for each share of stock that is outstanding at the time the rights offering is made. Thus the number of rights it will take to purchase one additional share of stock depends upon how many new shares will be issued.

privileged subscription

Example

The R Corporation needs $1,250,000 and has decided to issue new shares of common stock to raise the funds. The company currently has 100,000 shares of common stock outstanding, selling for $55 per share. The firm can sell additional shares to existing stockholders at $50 per share. The

747

CHAPTER 21
INVESTMENT
BANKING AND
COMMON STOCK
FINANCING

number of rights that will be required to purchase one additional share can be determined as follows. First, divide the amount of funds to be raised by the price that will be received for each new share. In this example, this is $1,250,000 divided by $50, which gives 25,000 new shares that have to be issued.

Second, division of the existing 100,000 shares by the 25,000 to-be-issued shares indicates that four rights will be required to purchase one new share of common stock. The holder of four shares of common stock will receive one right for each share held. Then if the four rights together with $50 are sent to the company, it will issue an additional share of stock. The stockholder does not have to "exercise the rights" as it is called. Instead, the rights may be sold through a broker. However, the stockholder usually has only 20 days or so to decide before the rights "expire" and become valueless. Stockholders should either exercise or sell their rights; they lose by doing *nothing*.

For a period after the rights offering has been announced, the stock will sell "rights on"; that is, a person buying and holding the stock during this interval will be entitled to receive the rights when they are issued. How can the approximate value of the rights be determined during this period for the R Corporation? It is necessary to take into account the fact that, after the offering, there will be 25 percent more shares outstanding than at present. The owner of four shares of stock with a current market price of $55 is entitled to subscribe to one additional share for $50. If done, the investment in five shares will total $270 ($4 \times \$55 + \$50$), or an average of $54 per share ($270/5$). With this background a formula can be devised to determine P, the theoretical future value of one share of common stock after the offering has expired, using the following notation: M_1 = the present market price of the stock "rights on"; N = the number of rights (or old shares) necessary to purchase one new share of stock; S = the subscription price of the stock. Then,

$$P = \frac{M_1 N + S}{N + 1} \tag{21-2}$$

$$P = \frac{\$55 \times 4 + \$50}{4 + 1} = \frac{\$270}{5} = \$54$$

A schematic picture of the theoretical behavior of the price of the stock and value of a right is shown in Exhibit 21-2 for the R Corporation.

Since the holder of four rights is being asked to pay $50 for stock with an estimated future market value of $54, the total value of the four rights necessary to make this "bargain" purchase must be $4 ($54 − $50). Consequently, the value of each right must be $1. This may also be determined by a formula using the notation above and letting V_1 = the theoretical value of one right when the stock is selling "rights on."

749

CHAPTER 21
INVESTMENT
BANKING AND
COMMON STOCK
FINANCING

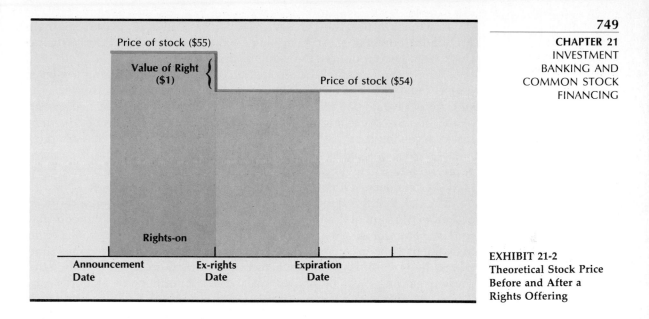

EXHIBIT 21-2
Theoretical Stock Price
Before and After a
Rights Offering

Value of right when stock is selling "rights on":

$$V_1 = \frac{M_1 - S}{N + 1} \qquad (21\text{-}3)$$

$$V_1 = \frac{\$55 - \$50}{4 + 1} = \$1$$

We should observe that the holder of four shares of stock really does not receive anything of value when she or he is issued the rights. Although the rights are worth a total of $4, the holder will lose $1 per share on the market value of the four shares of stock.

At a certain specified date, purchasers of the stock ar no longer entitled to receive the rights, and the stock is said to be selling "ex-rights." When the stock loses the right, we would expect its market price to fall by the value of one right, or from $55 to $54. At this time the rights are traded separately from the stock. A purchaser of four rights could buy one share of stock from the company for $50. How much would be paid for the rights? We would expect that a person might pay no more than $4 for the rights, or $1 each. Together with $50, this would bring the total purchase price of one share of stock to $54, the market price of the stock. In other words, after the stock has gone ex-rights, the new market price of the common stock is M_2, and the theoretical value of the rights, V_2, is as follows:

Value of right when stock is selling "ex-rights":

$$V_2 = \frac{M_2 - S}{N} \qquad (21\text{-}4)$$

$$V_2 = \frac{\$54 - \$50}{4} = \$1$$

stand-by commitment

In actual practice, the rights may sell for more than $1, because of their speculative attractions. An increase of only $4 in the market price of the stock would about double the value of the rights.

If the market price of the stock should fall below $50 during the brief period the rights are outstanding, the rights offering is in trouble. No stockholder would pay $50 for stock that is available at a lower price on one of the organized exchanges. If the firm really needs the money, it may insure receiving it by having the issue underwritten. Under this arrangement, termed a *stand-by commitment*, a syndicate of investment bankers agrees to buy whatever portion of the issue is not purchased by the common stockholders.[6] Of course, there is a charge for this service.

The risk that the rights will not be exercised depends upon a number of factors. (Presumably the greater the risk, the greater the likelihood that the company will wish to underwrite the offering and the greater will be the investment bankers' commission.) Investors know it will be some time before the new funds received will be put to work; therefore, for a while the present earnings will be spread over a larger number of shares. Consequently, if the issue is large in relation to the amount of common stock already outstanding, it is likely to depress the price of the stock on the market. The firm thus runs the risk that the market price will fall below the subscription price. Moreover, the size of the offering in relation to existing shares affects the willingness and ability of stockholders to acquire additional shares. An offering of one additional share for each ten held is likely to move better than an offering of five additional shares for each ten held. It puts a much greater strain on an investor's wealth and loyalty to ask her or him to buy five additional shares than to buy only one additional share.

Of great importance is the spread between the market price and the subscription price in relation to the normal variations in the price of the stock and the general market outlook. If the stock is not extensively traded and fluctuates widely in price, the financial manager would want to set the subscription price well below the current market price. This would reduce the risk that the market price would fall below the subscription price during the period the rights are outstanding. In setting the spread, the general strength of the market should be considered, since any general weakness or uncertainty is likely to be felt by all stocks. Should the spread be too narrow in relation to variations in the firm's own stock and the strength of the general market, we increase the risk that the rights will not be exercised.

---

[6]Underwriters will attempt to hedge their risk by the "layoff technique." When the stock has gone ex-rights, the underwriters will both buy rights on the market and sell the stock "short." By a short sale is meant that the underwriters will sell stock that they have temporarily borrowed from brokers or investors. Then the rights are exercised to obtain stock that is used to make good the borrowed stock. (This is called "covering" the short position.) By this activity the underwriters hope to have as many rights exercised as possible, so that relatively few shares are left for them to buy from the company. Moreover, the shares the underwriters must purchase may have previously been sold by means of the short sales.

Of importance too is the expected rate of earnings from the new capital. The more productive the new funds, the more likely the rights offering will be successful. Finally, the period during which the rights are outstanding should also be considered. The longer the period, the greater the chance of an unfavorable change in market conditions that might force the market price of the stock below its subscription price.

751

CHAPTER 21
INVESTMENT
BANKING AND
COMMON STOCK
FINANCING

SUMMARY

An investment banker performs three main functions: investigating, risk-bearing, and selling. When selling securities on a competitive bid basis, a firm largely eliminates the investigating function. The investment banker usually makes an outright purchase of securities, but not always. When securities are sold on a best efforts basis, the issuer assumes the risk of their not being sold. On a privileged subscription, the issuer undertakes most, or even all, of the selling effort. All three functions may be eliminated in a private placement. For the most part, investment bankers are best able to serve the needs of large corporations. Small companies are rarely able to tap the capital markets for long-term borrowed funds, and few can offer the growth potential necessary to attract external equity capital.

Federal regulation of new issues and the sale of existing securities is designed to provide investors with the information they need to make rational decisions.

MULTIPLE CHOICE QUESTIONS

1. The "gross spread" on a new bond issue is also known as:
   a) The yield to maturity
   b) Bond discount
   c) Bid-ask differential
   d) Underwriting discount

2. A syndicate is:
   a) A secret society
   b) National wire service
   c) Illegal in most states
   d) A group of investment bankers

3. In a "best efforts" security issue:
   a) The issuer participates in the sales effort
   b) Proceeds of the issue are guaranteed in advance

c) Proceeds of the issue are not guaranteed in advance
d) The investment house assigns its best people to the sale

753

CHAPTER 21
INVESTMENT
BANKING AND
COMMON STOCK
FINANCING

4. In an underwriting, the investment banker:

   a) Insures the company
   b) Possesses bonding insurance
   c) Guarantees payment of the corporate debt
   d) Guarantees the proceeds to the company

5. A prospectus:

   a) Is a type of mining claim
   b) Is a financial document filed with the SEC
   c) Is a financial document sent annually to stockholders
   d) Is a good candidate

6. A "red herring" is:

   a) A disclaimer on a prospectus
   b) A security that cannot be sold
   c) A security that cannot be repaid
   d) A delicacy

7. In a direct negotiation, the issuer picks the investment banker. In a competitive bid:

   a) The lowest bidder gets the issue
   b) The highest bidder gets the issue
   c) The investment banker picks the issuer
   d) The company competes with the investment banker

8. In a private placement, the issue:

   a) Cannot be common stock
   b) Has no maturity
   c) Is sold directly to financial institutions
   d) Does not carry a coupon rate

9. A pre-emptive right means that:

   a) The company sells its securities before others do
   b) A new stock issue must first be offered to creditors
   c) A new stock issue must first be offered to existing stockholders
   d) A new stock issue must first be offered to existing minority stockholders

10. Under a rights offering, new stock is:

    a) Not permitted
    b) Sold to existing shareholders
    c) Exchanged for old stock
    d) Convertible into options

11. When a stock is selling "rights on," a purchaser:

    a) Can expect big gains
    b) Is entitled to the rights

c) Is obligated to produce the rights

d) Is not entitled to the rights

12. When a stock goes "ex rights," one would expect:

    a) Law suits

    b) Stockholder protests

    c) Its price to rise

    d) Its price to fall

13. If the stock price of a company falls below the subscription price of a right:

    a) The right will rise in value

    b) The right will be exercised

    c) The right will not be exercised

    d) The stock price is probably being manipulated

14. A major attraction of private placements relative to public issues is that:

    a) Private placements do not require the services of an underwriting syndicate.

    b) Private placements provide for wider distribution to investors

    c) Syndicates are easier to set up with private placements

    d) Interest does not have to be paid on privately placed debt issues

DISCUSSION QUESTIONS

1. Briefly explain the role of the investment banker in helping corporations raise needed long-term debt and equity funds.

2. Identify and describe the investigating function performed by investment bankers.

3. Common stockholders are said to have a major voice in the management of their firms because they have the right to vote for and elect members of the boards of directors. Explain how this is done, including discussion of the two systems of voting currently in use.

4. After operating for a period of time, corporate managements may have to consider going public or having their stocks listed. Explain.

5. What is meant by a "rights offering?" Explain how this distribution method is used in practice by corporations.

6. What is meant by the statement that investment bankers perform a risk-bearing function? How might they minimize the amount of risk that will be assumed?

7. Describe the selling function performed by investment bankers. How are "red herring" and "stabilization" concepts connected with this function?

8. What types of costs are involved when a corporation issues securities through underwriters to the public?

755

CHAPTER 21
INVESTMENT
BANKING AND
COMMON STOCK
FINANCING

9. Describe how flotation costs on new issues are likely to be affected by: (a) size of issue, (b) quality of issue, (c) type of security issued. Also discuss the likely impact of capital market and economic conditions on flotation costs.

10. Investment bankers may be selected by either direct negotiation or competitive bidding methods. Explain. What limitations exist on the likely availability of both methods?

11. Explain the meaning of a "private placement" as a method for distributing securities. Are private placements more likely for stocks or bonds, and what impact does issue size have on the use of the private placement market?

12. Discuss how new bond and stock issues are regulated at the federal and state levels. What instruments or documents are used in the regulatory process?

SOLVED PROBLEMS

SP-1. Western Minerals, Inc. wants to raise $60,000,000 through a rights offering. One right will be issued for each share of common stock held. The market price per share is currently $20, and the subscription price per share will be $16. There are currently 20,000,000 shares outstanding. *rights offering*

    a) How many new shares of common stock will have to be issued?
    b) How many rights will be required to purchase one new share?
    c) Calculate the market price per share of the stock sold "rights off."
    d) Calculate the theoretical value of one right when the underlying stock is sold "rights on."

SP-2. Orafax common stock is selling for $75 per share. The company is considering a rights offering. One right will be issued for each share of common stock held. The new shares will have a subscription price of $65 for each eight rights. *rights offering*

    a) Calculate the theoretical value per share of stock when it sells "rights off."
    b) Calculate the theoretical value of one right when the underlying stock sells "rights on."
    c) Calculate the theoretical value of one right when the underlying stock sells "rights off."
    d) Assume that the stock is selling "rights off" for $81 per share, what is the theoretical value of one right?

SP-3. Vargas Company has one million shares of common stock outstanding. Ten directors are going to be elected, and cumulative voting will be employed. *cumulative voting*

a) How many shares will be needed to ensure the election of one director?
b) If the number of directors is reduced to nine, how many shares will be needed to ensure the election of one director?
c) A minority block controls 200,000 shares. How many directors can they elect if 10 will be elected in all?

PROBLEMS

rights offering

1. The M&M Supply Co. is planning to issue rights to purchase one new share of stock at $20. One right will be issued for each share of common stock held. Four rights will be required for each new share. Current stock price is $25 per share.

a) Assume that you currently hold 100 shares of the company's common stock. What is the total value of your stock holdings (i.e., before the rights offering)?
b) What will be the theoretical value of your stock (ignore rights) holdings when the stock sells "rights off?"
c) What will be the theoretical value of your total *rights* holdings when the underlying stock is selling at the "rights off" price per share calculated in (b)?
d) As a stockholder, how has the rights offering affected your total wealth?
e) Assume that the "rights off" stock price rises above its theoretical value per share and sells for $28.00 per share. What is the theoretical value of your total rights holdings, stock holdings, and total company investment?

cumulative voting

2. A corporation has 600,000 shares of common stock outstanding. Cumulative voting is used. (Show all calculations.)

a) How many shares would you need to control to assure the election of three out of seven directors?
b) If only 500,000 out of the 600,000 shares were voted at the stockholders' meeting, how many shares would you have to control to assure the election of three out of seven directors?

SOLUTIONS TO SOLVED PROBLEMS

SP-1. a) $$\text{No. of new shares} = \frac{\text{Proceeds needed}}{\text{Subscription price}}$$

$$= \frac{60,000,000}{16}$$

No. of new shares = 3,750,000

757

CHAPTER 21
INVESTMENT
BANKING AND
COMMON STOCK
FINANCING

b) $\quad$ No. rights per new share $= \dfrac{\text{No. shares outstanding}}{\text{No. new shares}}$

$$= \frac{20{,}000{,}000}{3{,}750{,}000}$$

$$= 5.33$$

c) $\qquad P = \dfrac{(M_1)(N) + S}{N + 1} = \dfrac{(20)(5.33) + 16}{6.33}$

$$= \$19.375$$

d) $\qquad V_1 = \dfrac{M_1 - S}{N + 1} = \dfrac{20 - 16}{6.33} = \$0.63$

SP-2. a) $\qquad P = \dfrac{M_1 N + S}{N + 1}$

$$= \frac{(75)(8) + 65}{9}$$

$$= \$73.89$$

b) $\qquad V_1 = \dfrac{M_1 - S}{N + 1}$

$$= \frac{75 - 65}{9}$$

$$= \$1.11$$

c) $\qquad V_2 = \dfrac{M_2 - S}{N}$

$$= \frac{73.89 - 65}{8}$$

$$= \$1.11$$

d) $\qquad V_2 = \dfrac{M_2 - S}{N}$

$$= \frac{81 - 65}{8}$$

$$= \$2$$

SP-3. a)   Use equation (21-1) in the text.

$$NE = \frac{\text{Total no. shares outstanding} \times \text{No. directors desired}}{\text{Total Directors} + 1} + 1$$

$$= \frac{(1,000,000)\,(1)}{10 + 1} + 1$$

$$= 90,910$$

b) $NE = \dfrac{(1,000,000)\,(1)}{9 + 1} + 1 = 100,001$

c)   Solve for X.

$$200,000 = \frac{1,000,000(X)^*}{10 + 1}$$

$$X = 2.2; \quad \text{or,} \quad \text{two directors}$$

*Number of directors that can be elected

REFERENCES

Ederington, Louis H. "Negotiated versus Competitive Underwritings of Corporate Bonds." *Journal of Finance,* September 1975, pp. 1129–1133.

Hayes, Samuel L., III. "Investment Banking: Power Structure in Flux." *Harvard Business Review,* March–April, 1971, pp. 136–152.

Johnson, Keith B., T. Gregory Morton, and M. Chapman Findlay, III. "An Empirical Analysis of the Flotation Costs of Corporate Securities 1971–1972." *Journal of Finance,* September 1975, pp. 1129–1153.

Logue, Dennis E., and Robert A. Jarrow. "Negotiation Vs. Competitive Bidding in the Sale of Securities by Public Utilities." *Financial Management,* Autumn 1978, pp. 31–39.

Logue, Dennis E., and John R. Lindvall. "The Behavior of Investment Bankers: An Econometric Investigation." *Journal of Finance,* March 1974, pp. 203–216.

Mandelker, Gershon, and Arthur Raviv. "Investment Banking: An Economic Analysis of Optimal Underwriting Contracts." *Journal of Finance,* June 1977, pp. 683–694.

McDonald, J. G., and A. K. Fisher. "New-Issue Stock Price Behavior." *Journal of Finance,* March 1972, pp. 97–102.

Pettway, Richard H., and Robert C. Radcliffe. "Impacts of New Equity Sales Upon Electric Utility Share Prices." *Financial Management,* Spring 1985, pp. 26–25.

Tallman, Gary D., David F. Rush, and Ronald W. Melicher. "Competitive Versus Negotiated Underwriting Costs for Regulated Industries." *Financial Management*, Summer 1974, pp. 49–55.

Van Horne, James C. "New Listings and Their Price Behavior." *Journal of Finance*, September 1970, pp. 783–794.

759

CHAPTER 21
INVESTMENT
BANKING AND
COMMON STOCK
FINANCING

C H A P T E R

22

LONG TERM DEBT

echnically, all debt with a maturity in excess of one year is long-term debt. However, a distinction is typically made between debt that is repaid within 10 years, known as intermediate-term debt, and debt that matures in more than 10 years. Since the sources and other characteristics of intermediate-term debt differ in significant respects from longer-term debt, each will be discussed separately.

As a company moves from short-term financing to intermediate and long-term financing, it is making a fundamental shift in the sources from which these funds must be repaid. For example, when a company obtains short-term loans, it typically uses this money to finance a seasonal or cyclical increase in inventory and accounts receivable. At the end of the season or during cyclical declines, the company reduces inventories and collects accounts receivable. The conversion of these current assets into cash enables it to repay its short-term loans. Because short-term funds move into and out of current assets or working capital, short-term loans are sometimes referred to as *self-liquidating*, or working capital loans.

In contrast, intermediate- and long-term funds are sought more for investment in plant and equipment and permanent current assets than for financing seasonal changes in current assets. This is consistent with the application of the maturity matching principle discussed in Chapter 9. The source of repayment is the long-run earnings potential of the company rather than the liquidation of the company's assets.

◉ Objectives and Organization of this Chapter

The principal objective of this chapter is to describe the major types and distinctive characteristics of long-term debt arrangements. Included in this category are both intermediate and long-term borrowing. A second objective of the chapter is to demonstrate that, although the interest rate and debt repayment terms are of critical importance in the loan contract, other provisions are also important and should be carefully negotiated by the financial manager. A third objective of this chapter is to illustrate the analysis of a bond refunding decision. Bond refunding usually involves paying off high-cost borrowing with lower-cost borrowing. Since the act of refunding introduces other costs as well, the decision to refund is not obvious. The chapter discusses the steps in a typical analysis.

The first section of the chapter discusses the relationship between the type of debt funds raised and the means of repayment. The second section describes intermediate-term debt. This type of debt, known as "term" debt, is usually repaid in installments during the life of the loan contract. This section demonstrates how the payments are determined and how the cost of such borrowing can be determined.

The third section discusses long-term debt in the form of bonds. It distinguishes between mortgage bonds and debentures. The fourth section describes the loan *indenture*, a document that spells out the duties and rights of the borrower. Overly restrictive provisions in the indenture can add unnecessary expense and unwisely curtail management's freedom of action. However, since such provisions make lenders more secure, carefully structured indentures may reduce the firm's borrowing costs and increase its access to capital markets while not becoming burdensome to the borrower. The fifth section of the chapter examines the rationale and economics of a bond refunding decision.

 ## SOURCES AND REPAYMENT OF LONG TERM DEBT

Because the repayment of funds is closely linked to the use of borrowed funds, let us first discuss how funds are used and then discuss repayment.

Uses of Funds

A basic requirement of intermediate and long-term borrowing is that it be suited to the uses made of the funds. Ordinarily, when a firm borrows funds for long periods, it has two principal uses in mind—purchases of plant and equipment or permanent additions to current assets.

Permanent additions to current assets are necessary to maintain a long-term growth in sales. To illustrate, the dollar investment in inventory is a product of the number of units handled and the price per unit. When sales expand, the number of units grows; during periods of inflation, the price per unit rises. In either case, more dollars become committed to inventory until such time as the trend is reversed.

Repayment of Funds

When borrowed funds are sunk into machinery or permanent additions to current assets, how are they repaid? As will be seen later, funds obtained from intermediate-term debt are typically repaid gradually over the term of the loan. These repayments are ordinarily generated by operating cash flows. In other words, when a company pays back borrowed money, it gradually replaces those borrowings with earnings, with owners' equity.

To sharpen the distinction in the methods of repaying short and intermediate-term borrowings, let us consider the following simple examples. Assume the balance sheet shown in Table 22-1.

If one assumes $5,000 more in short-term debt is needed to finance a seasonal increase in current assets, the balance sheet might appear as shown in Table 22-2.

After the season is over and inventories and accounts receivable have been reduced, the company should be able to repay the $5,000 of current debt from the extra cash accumulated. If profits are paid out as dividends by the owner, the balance sheet will appear just as it did before incurring the debt.[1]

However, the firm may need to increase permanently the level of current assets and to purchase additional equipment. In this case, the balance sheet might appear as shown in Table 22-3.

Usually the company will maintain the plant and equipment at its new level and allow sufficient earnings to accumulate to repay the debt. It is a two-step operation: momentarily, earnings are retained in the form of cash,

---

TABLE 22-1

Before incurring debt			
Cash	$ 1,000	Current liabilities	$ 4,000
Accounts receivable	3,000		
Inventory	4,000	Common stock	11,000
Plant and equipment (net)	7,000		
	$15,000		$15,000

TABLE 22-2

After incurring short-term debt			
Cash	$ 1,500	Current liabilities	$ 9,000
Accounts receivable	5,000		
Inventory	6,500	Common stock	11,000
Plant and equipment (net)	7,000		
	$20,000		$20,000

---

[1]It is assumed that, as equipment depreciates, it is replaced with new equipment of equal cost.

TABLE 22-3

After incurring intermediate-term debt			
Cash	$ 1,000	Current liabilities	$ 4,000
Accounts receivable	4,000	Long-term	
Inventory	5,000	liabilities*	5,000
Plant and equipment (net)	10,000	Common stock	11,000
	$20,000		$20,000

*Accountants classify noncurrent liabilities as "long-term debt." Only the current portions of long-term debt are counted as part of current liabilities.

and then the cash is applied to a reduction of the debt. This is shown in Table 22-4.

In order to trace the source of cash for repayment of the debt, one may refer to a statement of cash receipts and disbursements. It is assumed that revenues are $27,000; cash expenditures, including taxes, are $20,000; and depreciation expense, $2,000. The statement would then appear as shown in Table 22-5.

Observe that, after repayment of long-term debt, the current assets remain at their new, higher level.

TABLE 22-4

After repaying intermediate-term debt				
Cash	$ 1,000	Current liabilities		$ 4,000
Accounts receivable	4,000	Common stock	$11,000	
Inventory	5,000	Add: retained		
Plant and equipment (net)	10,000	earnings	5,000	16,000
	$20,000			$20,000

TABLE 22-5

Statement of cash receipts and disbursements				
Revenues	$27,000	Replacement of		
Expenditures requiring		plant and		
the use of cash	20,000	equipment	$2,000	
		Repayment of		
		intermediate-		
		term debt	5,000	$7,000
Cash generated	$ 7,000	Net addition to cash		0

Lenders engaged in long-term financing are much more concerned with earning power than when they evaluate a firm's financial position for a possible short-term loan. Attention is focused less on the balance sheet, more on the income statement. They attempt to gauge the ability to generate cash over the long run. Earning power thus becomes the main security behind the loan. However, these lenders are still concerned that the company maintains a strong current position, because any failure to pay current obligations is likely to affect the long-term lender adversely as well. There is no diminution in the importance assigned to character and integrity and to the size of the owner's investment in relation to the total debt to be assumed.

TERM LOANS

Term loans are an important source of intermediate-term funds. A distinguishing feature of such loans is that they are usually amortized; that is, regular monthly, quarterly, or yearly payments are made which are applied to pay the interest and to reduce the principal of the loan outstanding. Home mortgages are amortized in the same fashion. Occasionally term loans are made to business that call for an extra-large payment in the last year. Lenders ordinarily do not view these *balloon notes* favorably, since there is no reason to believe a company is suddenly going to have money in the fifth year that it has not been able to generate in the preceding four years.

balloon notes

Example

Let us assume that the Eagle Company asks a commercial bank or other lender for a four-year $100,000 term loan. The loan will carry a 10-percent interest rate and will require annual payments (consisting of principal and interest) to be made at the end of each year, so that the loan will be amortized or paid off in full by the end of the fourth year. What payment amount must be made each year? This question can be answered by using the following basic formula:

$$\text{Annual payment} = \text{Amount borrowed} \div \text{PVIFA} \qquad (22\text{-}1)$$

where PVIFA represents the present value interest factor of an annuity at a stated interest rate and covering a specified time period.[2]

In the Eagle Company example, the PVIFA at 10 percent for four years would be 3.170 (see Appendix A, Table 4) and the annual payment would be calculated as follows:

---

[2]It might be helpful at this time to review the discussion in Chapter 4 dealing with the present value of annuities.

Annual payment = $100,000 ÷ 3.170

= $31,545.74   or $31,546 with rounding

Table 22-6 shows the term loan repayment schedule for the Eagle Company's $100,000, 10 percent, four-year loan.

TABLE 22-6	**Term Loan Repayment Schedule — Eagle Company**			
End of Year	Annual Payment	Interest Payment	Principal or Amortization Repayment	Remaining or Unpaid Loan Balance
0	—	—	—	$100,000
1	$31,546	$10,000	$21,546	78,454
2	31,546	7,845	23,701	54,753
3	31,546	5,475	26,071	28,682
4	31,546	2,868	28,678*	0

*This last repayment of principal is $4 short due to errors caused by rounding all the figures to whole dollars.

Notice that the interest to be paid the first year is $10,000 (i.e., $100,000 × 10 percent). Thus, out of the $31,546 total payment, $21,546 will go towards retirement of the loan principal. This means that the second year's interest will be only $7,845 ($78,454 × 10 percent), and so on until the loan is totally retired. Thus the illustrated term loan requires payment of interest only on the remaining unpaid balance.

term loans

Commercial banks are the major suppliers of term loans. They supply term loans to business concerns for two different purposes. First, they extend term loans for investment in permanent current assets and fixed assets with the expectation that they will be repaid through funds generated from operations. Second, they extend interim credits to "tide the firm over" until it can sell an issue of bonds or stocks. In the latter case, the bank will be repaid by the proceeds from the sales of the securities.[3] This interim financing is most commonly used to finance the initial stages of a plant expansion. Under the usual arrangement the borrower can draw down needed funds as construction progresses. Then, near the end of construction, the loan is repaid from the sale of securities in the capital market or a private placement. Like a seasonal loan, this arrangement economizes on the use of funds, since they are borrowed and paid for only when needed.

---

[3]This type of financing is sometimes known as *bridge* or *construction* financing.

Example	

Assume the Erd Utility Company is going to build a new power plant. The plant will take three years to build and will cost $15 million. First-year construction costs will total $5 million, second-year costs will total $8 million, and third-year costs will total $2 million. If the Erd Company borrows the total $15 million in the first year, much of the proceeds will be invested in low-yielding securities. If the company borrows only the amount needed each year, it will not only incur excessive costs in arranging each loan but will run the very real risk of not being able to get the funds when needed in the event credit market conditions change or the firm's credit standing deteriorates. A third alternative would be for the company to arrange a $15 million loan to be borrowed in three years. With a firm commitment from a lender to lend $15 million in three years, the Erd Company could then go to a bank and request a construction loan totalling $15 million to be used as scheduled and to be repaid in full in three years. With this alternative, the Erd Company will "take down" $5 million in the first year and only pay interest on the amount borrowed. Yet the remaining $10 million would still be available.

Security

Term loans involve the pledge of collateral more frequently than do seasonal, short-term loans. Banks demand security most frequently on loans to small companies. Almost all term loans with maturities in excess of five years that are made to small businesses are secured. This practice is understandable considering the risk inherent in extending credit over this period of time to businesses that are frequently less stable and less protected against competition than larger concerns. Another reason for seeking collateral on term loans to small concerns is the lack of management depth characteristic of many small companies, which are often managed by one person. Bankers are willing to take liens on a variety of assets — showcases, counters, trucks, laundry and dry cleaning equipment, real estate, inventory, and accounts receivable.

Term loans that are to be repaid from earnings may be extended for periods as long as 10 years, although tight money markets often cause bankers to shorten the maximum maturity. Average maturities are probably closer to five years. By their nature, construction term loans mature in two to three years.

INSTALLMENT LOANS

Besides term loans, intermediate-term funds are also available in the form of installment loans. These loans require the payment of interest on the original loan balance even though some payment of principal is being made over the life of the loan. Finance companies make this type of loan to businesses and individuals. Consumer installment loans also are made frequently by commercial banks and other lenders on such items as automobiles and major appliances.

Add On Interest

add-on interest

Interest on installment loan contracts is normally calculated using the *add-on* method. This method usually raises the effective interest cost above the stated rate. This method is also explained in chapter 13.

Example

Assume that the Eagle Company wants to borrow $50,000 from a finance company for three years. The loan will carry an add-on interest rate of 8 percent and will require equal monthly payments so that the loan will be retired at the end of three years. First, calculate the total amount of interest that will be paid. Eagle will be charged $4,000 (i.e., $50,000 × .08) per year and thus $12,000 over the three-year period. This $12,000 plus the original $50,000 principal means that $62,000 in total will be paid. Next by dividing $62,000 by 36 monthly payments, it is apparent that the Eagle Company will have to pay $1,722.22 per month. However, since Eagle is paying back a portion of the loan principal each month but paying interest on the original amount borrowed, the effective cost of borrowing is approximately twice the simple interest rate. This is because the firm has use of approximately one-half of the original amount borrowed during the life of the loan.

APR

The effective interest cost can be approximated with the use of the following formula:

$$i = \frac{2mD}{P(n + 1)} \qquad (22\text{-}2)$$

where i = annual effective interest rate; m = number of installment payments to be made per year; D = total dollar amount of interest to be paid on the loan; P = amount borrowed and available to the borrower; and n = total number of installment payments to be made on the loan.

---

[4]This approximation formula actually overstates the "true" annual percentage rate (APR) as used by the Federal Reserve in terms of Regulation Z.

The effective annual interest rate for the Eagle Company would be:

$$i = 2 \times 12 \times \$12,000 \div \$50,000 \times 37$$

$$= \$288,000 \div \$1,850,000$$

$$= .156$$

Thus this approximation of the effective interest rate is 15.6 percent, or nearly double the 8-percent simple interest rate. The true rate (also known as the annual percentage rate, or, APR) is actually 14.55 percent for this example. Creditors are required to disclose the actual APR on extensions of credit to consumers.

Because the interest charges of finance companies are typically higher than those of commercial banks, a company would be more likely to turn to this source of intermediate-term financing only after finding that its needs could not be satisfactorily fulfilled by a commercial bank. Whether or not a finance company will finance the equipment depends largely on the estimated earning power of the equipment. Even though the company's net worth may be small in relation to the obligations incurred, it may still be able to finance the equipment if the equipment will pay for itself and increase the owners' equity. Because finance companies rely primarily on the earning power of the equipment, they are less concerned with overall financial position and earnings. Consequently, they have less need to control general operations through rather elaborate agreements like those a bank might require.

installment loans

There are two basic methods of financing equipment through a finance company: an installment purchase, or a lease.[5] The installment loan purchase of a piece of equipment, such as a robot, a lathe, or a printing press, is similar to the installment purchase of an automobile by a consumer. Almost any type of equipment may be purchased on installment, although it should have a fairly long economic life and be removable. Should the equipment become a fixed part of the real estate of the installment buyer, it is difficult to repossess. Ordinarily, the borrower must make a downpayment and sign a security agreement that leaves title to the equipment with the holder of the obligation until payment is complete. If the borrower fails to make the required payments, the lender will repossess the equipment.

The buyer/borrower is naturally concerned with the terms of purchase—the downpayment, the maturity, and the interest charge. The downpayment and maturity are interrelated in that the lender tries to adjust them so that the unpaid balance will always be below the resale value of the equipment. For example, if the equipment is highly specialized, its immediate resale value will be low, and the lender is likely to require a high downpayment. If the machine depreciates slowly, the borrower may be able to stretch out the maturity on a note to five or more

---

[5]Lease financing will be discussed in Chapter 23.

years. Or, if the borrower makes a relatively large downpayment, it may be able to stretch out the maturity even though the equipment depreciates fairly rapidly. Downpayments typically range from 10 to 35 percent and maturities from 12 to 42 months, although longer maturities are available.

Most finance companies now provide that payments may be made in accordance with whatever depreciation system is used, or to fit seasonal movements in sales. The philosophy is that payments for the machine are attuned to the rate at which cash is generated.

BONDS

There are two principal types of bonds issued by corporations. Secured bonds, like mortgages, identify specific assets to be used as collateral. Debentures, or unsecured bonds, unlike mortgages, are backed only by the general credit and earning power of the corporation rather than by specific pledged assets.

Secured Bonds

mortgage bond

By pledging specific assets as security, a firm may be able to obtain more funds than it might raise selling unsecured bonds. In some cases a pledge of assets may be necessary to obtain any funds at all. Although bondholders rely primarily on earnings, a lien (mortgage) on assets is valuable to them in that it gives them first claim on the assets secured and also prevents other creditors from obtaining a prior lien on those same assets. Should the firm fail to pay interest and principal when due or otherwise default on the bond, the bondholders are entitled to seize the pledged assets to satisfy their claims. If the amount realized from the foreclosure sale of these assets is not sufficient to satisfy their requirements, the unpaid balance of their debt becomes part of the unsecured creditors' claims on the remaining unpledged assets of the business. If receipts from the sale of the property are more than enough to satisfy the demands of the bondholders, the surplus is applied to the claims of the unsecured creditors.[6]

Almost any asset may be pledged as security. Very commonly, land and buildings may be pledged: that is, the bondholders are given a mortgage on the real estate. This form of security is typical of industries with large amounts of fixed assets, such as the airlines and public utilities. Two typical types of secured bonds are the equipment trust certificates and collateral trust bonds.

equipment trust certificates

Equipment trust certificates. When airplanes, diesel engines or similar equipment serve as collateral, the secured bonds are known as equipment

---

[6]The mechanics of this arrangement are discussed more fully in Chapter 24.

trust certificates. Generally, these certificates are issued by a trustee, who holds title to the equipment. The equipment is then leased to the operator (for example, the airline) in return for annual rental payments sufficient to pay interest on and retire the equipment trust obligations within about 15 years. Equipment trust obligations are usually highly regarded by investors because of the nature of the asset pledged.

Collateral Trust Bonds.   Sometimes a firm's assets include securities of other corporations. Possibly these are kept to maintain control of other concerns, or the securities may not be marketable at a reasonable price. Rather than sell these to obtain funds, a firm may pledge them against bonds that it issues in its own right. These would be termed collateral trust bonds. Inventory may also serve as collateral.

collateral trust bonds

Unsecured Bonds (Debentures)

Bonds that do not have specific assets pledged to secure payment of interest and principal are termed *debentures*. The holders of these securities have a claim on assets prior to that of the owners (common stockholders) but equal to that of the other unsecured creditors. A company can issue debentures if its credit position is so strong that purchasers believe that the claim they share with other creditors on the assets offers about as much protection as would a lien on specific assets. Usually the borrower must promise that assets will not later be pledged to other creditors without giving the debenture holders equal security. As long as the firm can avoid pledging or mortgaging assets, other creditors will be more willing to extend credit. Since bondholders fundamentally look to earnings to satisfy their claims rather than to liquidation of assets,[7] it is entirely possible that, if earnings are clearly adequate, bondholders will forego any claim on assets.

debentures

Subordinated Debentures

In some cases a firm may even be able to persuade bondholders to accept a claim on the general assets subordinate to that of other "senior" creditors. Such securities are called subordinated debentures. These are a particularly useful form of security from the issuer's point of view. In the event of insolvency or bankruptcy, the claims of senior creditors[8] must be settled before any payment is made on the subordinated debentures.

subordinated debentures

---

[7]If bondholders thought they would ultimately have to seize the assets to get repaid, they would not buy the bonds in the first place.
[8]Senior debt is frequently defined as any debt coming due within 12 months; hence, this would include most bank debt. There may also be some long-term debt classed as senior debt.

Example

The effect of the subordination feature in the event of insolvency or bankruptcy may be illustrated very simply. Assume that the liabilities and net worth of a corporation appear as follows:

Liabilities:		
	Senior debt	$ 500
	Subordinated debt	200
	Other liabilities	100
	Total liabilities	$ 800
Net Worth:		
	Common stock and surplus	600
	Total	$1,400

Assume that only $400 is realized from the liquidation of the assets. There are $800 of creditors' claims to satisfy. Without the subordination feature, all of the creditors would receive 50 cents on the dollar, and the common stockholders would have nothing. However, if $200 of the debt is subordinated to the specified senior debt, the senior creditors can enforce both their claim and that of the subordinated debtors until the full amount of the senior claims are satisfied.[9] The claims of other creditors, such as trade creditors, are unaffected by the subordination feature, and the shareholders still receive nothing. The results are summarized in Table 22-7.

TABLE 22-7

	Amount of Claim	Amount Realized without Subordination	Amount Realized with Subordination
Senior debt	$ 500	$250	$350
Subordinated debt	200	100	0
Other liabilities	100	50	50
Common stock & surplus	600	0	0
Totals	$1,400	$400	$400

Calculation of share of senior debt

Without subordination: $\dfrac{\$500}{\$800} \times \$400 = \$250$

With subordination: $\dfrac{\$500 + \$200}{\$800} \times \$400 = \$350$

[9]Chapter 24 contains a more detailed discussion of the distributions in liquidation.

In short, the subordinated debt materially improves borrowing power because it serves as a base upon which to raise additional senior debt. In this respect, it functions as preferred and even common stock, but it has the advantage over preferred stock in that the interest payments are a tax-deductible expense, whereas preferred dividends are not.

Because of their junior position relative to senior debt, subordinated debentures involve greater risk to the bondholders. Therefore, they offer higher yields than senior debentures.

OTHER TYPES OF BONDS

Chapter 5 discussed other types of bonds that have been popular in the 1980s: for example, *zero coupon bonds,* which pay no interest; and so-called *"junk bonds,"* which are viewed as above-average in risk but which provide significantly higher yields. Both types of bonds are designed to appeal to particular investor clienteles and/or to exploit particular features of the tax codes. Since zero coupon bonds and junk bonds are discussed in Chapter 5, the discussion will not be repeated here.

Serial Bonds

A serial bond is a bond that matures in stages. For example, a $20 million, 20-year bond issue may be arranged so that $1 million of the bonds come due each year. Since the maturity date is stated on each bond, an investor may select the maturity that suits her or his needs. Serial bonds are most commonly used when the assets used to secure the bonds are real estate or railroad equipment. In these cases, the annual cash flows generated by the assets are thought to be sufficiently certain that the borrower can assume the risk of meeting the rigid requirements of serial bonds.

serial bonds

Income Bonds

In some instances, firms will sell income bonds. These bonds require the payment of interest only if profits are sufficient to pay it. Typically, any unpaid interest accumulates for only three years, although some income bonds are noncumulative and others are fully cumulative. They often carry long maturities. In a few instances income bonds may be successfully issued to the public. More frequently, they might be offered to preferred shareholders as a substitute for their preferred stock. In such instances, corporations trade nondeductible preferred dividends for a tax deductible interest expense.

income bonds

In earlier years, income bonds were issued only in the case of a reorganization: that is, a basic readjustment of the capital structure because of actual or imminent default on payments on some debt. If the company's position is desperate, existing bondholders may face the alternative of liquidating the company and receiving, say, 20 cents on the dollar or of accepting income bonds in exchange for their present holdings. With the income bonds, the interest charge will still be a claim on income and the principal of the debt a claim on assets prior to that of any stockholder.

Capital Debentures

Other variations are limited only by the imagination of financial managers, investment bankers, and what the market will bear. The 1980's has seen an explosion of innovative and complex debt instruments. For example, additional issues of subordinated debentures may be subordinated to senior debt and other specified issues of subordinated debentures as well. These are sometimes called junior subordinated debentures. The company may even be successful in issuing subordinated income debentures, which are about as close to a preferred stock as one can get and still carry the interest payments as a tax-deductible expense.

Equity Sweeteners

equity sweeteners

Income bonds and subordinated debentures are, in many cases, so risky that they take on many of the characteristics of equity securities. In order to attract lenders to such securities and to avoid high coupon rates, many borrowers offer a mix of coupon interest and capital gain potential. For example, subordinated debentures might allow the bondholder to convert the bond into a specified number of shares of common stock. The bondholder would do so if the stock price rose significantly. However, if the stock price did not rise, the bondholder would still have steady income from the bond. These types of bonds, known as convertible debentures, are described in more detail in Chapter 23.

Other types of equity sweeteners might be in the form of warrants, which are securities giving the holder the right to purchase stock at some specified price. For example, the company might offer a bond/warrant package in exchange for a lower bond coupon rate and other concessions. If the company's stock price rises, the warrants increase in value, adding to the bond investor's total return. Warrants are also discussed in more detail in Chapter 23.

RISK RETURN PROFILE OF THE COMPANY'S SECURITIES

Given the distinctive attributes of a company's securities with respect to risk and yield promised to investors, the securities range from the relatively low risk of secured term notes to the high risk of subordinated debentures with equity characteristics.

THE LOAN INDENTURE

The loan indenture specifies the terms on which funds are lent. These terms include promises ("covenants") by the company to do certain things (*positive covenants*), such as pay interest at stated times or submit financial reports at specified times. The indenture also includes promises by the company not to do certain other things (*negative covenants*), such as not to borrow any more or not to pay dividends.

positive covenants

negative covenants

When a corporation publicly issues bonds with the help of investment bankers, the purchasers or bondholders, located all over the country, are in a poor position to enforce the terms of the contract once the bonds have been issued. To remedy this problem, a *trustee* is appointed to represent the interests of bondholders. The major function of the trustee is to make sure the corporation complies with the provisions of the indenture. A summary of the essential features of the indenture is provided in fine print on the bond itself. Some of the more typical indentures are discussed in this section.

trustee

Event of Default

If the corporation fails to abide by certain specified terms of the indenture, this is considered to be an "event of default." If major lapses are not remedied, the trustee, with the consent of a proportion of the bondholders, must then take action to force the corporation to comply with the indenture or to satisfy the bondholders' demands in some other manner.

Acceleration Clause

In an "event of default," the bondholders have the option of requiring immediate repayment of the debt, even if the liquidation of the company is needed to do so. This covenant is called an acceleration clause because it accelerates the maturity date of the debt. The acceleration clause gives the lender considerable negotiating leverage with the borrower, which enables the lender to act quickly if the company's financial position begins to deteriorate.

Dissipation of Assets

The intent of this provision is to prevent the borrower from taking assets out of the company and thereby reducing the loan collateral or net liquidation value of the company. Some standard loan provisions in this respect include the following:

1. The borrower must maintain a minimum net working capital (current assets minus current liabilities) and possibly a minimum current ratio.

2. The agreement may prevent the owners from taking too much money out of the business by specifically limiting withdrawals or dividends. For example, withdrawals, payments of dividends, or redemption of capital stock may be restricted to earnings realized after the date of the loan was made, or to some percentage of those earnings.

3. The borrower is ordinarily not permitted to sell fixed assets over a certain dollar amount without approval of the lender, nor is he or she allowed to sell the accounts receivable.

4. The lender is likely to require that the borrower obtain its permission before making any investments in fixed assets over a certain dollar amount. Nor will the lender allow the firm to make loans and advances to others or purchase securities other than U.S. government obligations without its approval.

Pledging of Assets To Others

The intent of this provision is to prevent any other lender from getting a lien on the company's assets which would reduce the security value to the existing lender. This may be accomplished in two ways:

1. The indenture will ordinarily contain a negative pledge clause, whereby the borrower promises not to pledge its assets to anybody else.

2. The lender will restrict additional borrowings in some fashion. In part, the requirement that the firm maintain a minimum net working capital restricts its ability to add to current liabilities. Long-term borrowings are usually subject to prior approval from the lender.

Continuation of Management

Since the lender is making a long-run commitment, it is interested in continuation of the borrower's present management and in being regularly informed of developments in the company. Thus, the lender might make the following requirements:

1. The lender may take out, or require the firm to take out, insurance on the lives of key officers.

2. To keep the lender informed of its status, the borrower must provide audited annual reports and often quarterly or semiannual reports.

Limitation on Additional Indebtedness

This provision restricts further borrowing by the corporation in order to protect the current lenders. There are many ways in which this limitation may be specified. For example, there may be an absolute prohibition on further interest-bearing debt without the prior approval of current bondholders (as represented by the trustee). Such a provision is awkward, administratively time-consuming, and expensive, since the borrowing firm needs to check with the lender or trustee every time funds must be borrowed. A more flexible limitation restricts the company's total borrowing to some percentage of assets or long-term capital or net worth or some other measure. For example, there may be a limitation on total interest-bearing debt not to exceed 50 percent of total assets. This allows for the company to increase its borrowing as it increases profits. However, the idea is the same: to keep the borrower from diluting the claims of existing lenders.

After Acquired Property Clause

This clause requires that any property subsequently acquired by the borrower must also be pledged as security for the bonds.

Sinking Fund Requirement

Lenders may seek a *sinking fund* or serial maturities. If a sinking fund is provided in the indenture, the corporation must make a periodic payment of cash to the trustee for the retirement of the bonds or deliver to the trustee a stated principal amount of such bonds. A typical sinking fund provision is illustrated by the following passage taken from a prospectus for a bond issue. The bonds were issued in 1983 and were due in 1995.

sinking fund

> *As a sinking fund for the retirement of the Debentures, the Company will deliver to the Trustee $7,000,000 principal amount of Debentures on or before November 1 in each of the years 1985 to 1994, inclusive, the remaining $6,000,000 maturing on November 1, 1995. In lieu of any part of such delivery the Company may call for redemption at the sinking fund redemption price, on any November 1, a principal amount of Debentures which, together with any Debentures so delivered to the Trustee, will equal the amount required to be delivered on or before such date.*

Notice that the company committed itself to start retiring the debenture issue only two years after the issue was sold (in some instances sinking funds do not begin for five years or more after issuance of the bonds).

The sinking fund may be arranged so as to retire all or only a portion of the bonds before the final maturity date. Frequently, only a portion of the bonds is retired prior to the maturity date, so that the final payment is like a balloon payment on an installment contract. Whatever the method used, it is important to recognize that the sinking fund payments represent a cash drain, and that the amount of debt the firm can assume will depend in part upon the ability to meet the cash payments demanded by the sinking fund. Failure to meet these or any other commitments will constitute an *event of default*, and the trustee may call for the immediate payment of the entire bond issue.

Call Provision

The call provision is of great potential value to the corporation and, simultaneously, represents a risk to the bondholder. In essence, the call provision allows the corporation to pay off the bonds earlier than scheduled. Usually, the corporation will do this because interest rates have dropped significantly and it wants to pay off the expensive borrowing with new, less expensive borrowing. The bondholder, conversely, will have to give up a bond with a high return and reinvest in new bonds with lower yields. In order to protect their investment, bondholders may stipulate that the borrower cannot call the bond within five years or more and that, subsequently, if the bond is called, a penalty or call premium will be paid. The amount of the penalty is usually a year's interest and declines over time.

BOND REFUNDING

Usually refunding is considered when the cost of borrowing has declined, either because of an improvement in the firm's financial position or because of a significant decline in market interest rates. Refunding to remove objectionable provisions in an indenture is also sometimes the motive for retiring an issue. Thus, while this discussion concentrates on the monetary aspects of refunding, these are not the only considerations. Even if the interest rate obtained through a refunding operation is not significantly lower, the company may still decide to refund if it can obtain a more "livable" bond indenture or succeed in postponing the final maturity of the debt to a more suitable time. Nonetheless, the refunding decision should include a consideration of the net cost or savings from the refunding. Consider how this can be done using capital budgeting techniques.

Example

Assume that the Newton Company has an "old issue" of 12-percent bonds outstanding. Other features of the bond are shown below:

Old Issue

- Principal amount outstanding: $30,000,000
- Coupon rate: 12 percent
- Call premium: 8 percent
- Issued: 10 years ago
- Remaining years to maturity: 20 years
- Unamortized underwriting discount: $400,000. The bonds were originally sold at par (100) with the firm receiving 98: that is, the principal amount, or face value of the issue, was $30,000,000, but the corporation

received $29,400,000 (.98 × $30,000,000) from the underwriters. Since the discount of $600,000 was to be amortized over the 30-year life of the bonds on a straight-line basis, it has been reduced by $200,000 during the first one-third of the life of the bonds. That is, $600,000/30 = $20,000 per year and thus $200,000 for 10 years.

● Unamortized issue expense: $80,000. Costs of registration, printing and engraving, legal fees, and so on were $120,000. One-third of this has been amortized. As above, $120,000/30 is $4,000 per year and thus $40,000 for 10 years. Total flotation costs include both underwriting discounts and other issue-related expenses. Thus the total remaining unamortized flotation costs are $480,000 (i.e., $400,000 plus $80,000).

Occasionally a new bond issue is offered in exchange for outstanding bonds. More frequently, the new bonds are sold in the market, and the proceeds are used to call and retire the outstanding issue. Assume that the latter is the case. The following information is available concerning a proposed new issue of 10-percent bonds: (10 percent is the rate investors require today for other securities of similar quality.)

New Issue:

● Principal amount to be outstanding: $30,000,000

● Coupon rate: 10 percent

● Proceeds to issuing corporation: 98. That is, the corporation will receive $30,000,000 less underwriting fees of $600,000, or a new $29,400,000 amount

● Maturity: 20 years

● Legal fees and other issue expense: $110,000. This is not the underwriters' discount or "spread," but various fees and other costs that must be borne by the corporation. Thus the total flotation costs on the new issue would be $710,000.

● Interest overlap period: 25 days. If the 12-percent bonds are refunded, there will be an "overlap" of 25 days of the interest payments on the two bond issues.[10]

With these facts in hand, the net investment required in the refunding operation and the net cash benefits that will result can be calculated. Aside from minor details, the method followed is that used in typical capital budgeting investment decisions.

---

[10]The company could issue the call notice on the old bonds and time the sale of the new bonds so that the cash from the sale would be received just when it was needed to redeem the old bonds. However, should some delay occur in the sale of the new issue, the company would be faced with finding $30 million in a great hurry. Although the probability of such an event might be small, its occurrence would have catastrophic results. Therefore, the company will play it safe and issue a call for the old bonds only after it has sold the new ones. This decision will cost 25 days interest on the old bonds.

The call premium and the unamortized underwriting discount plus other unamortized issue expenses on the old bonds are tax deductible expenses for the year in which the refunding occurs, as shown in Table 22-8.

Observe carefully that some of the expenses are out-of-pocket, or cash, expenditures while others are accounting book entries that affect only the amount of the tax paid. Although the tax savings probably are not realized immediately, it is assumed that they are gained within the year. Consequently, they serve to reduce the net investment required by the tax savings or "tax shield," assuming a 34-percent effective tax rate for the Newton Corporation.

It is also important to note in Table 22-8 that the flotation expenses associated with issuing the new bonds are not immediately deductible for tax purposes but must be written off over the life of the 10-percent bonds (in the same fashion as Newton Corporation was doing on the presently outstanding 12-percent bond issue).

Now let us calculate and show in Table 22-9 the net cash benefits to be realized from the refunding. First, determine the net cash outlays required if the old bonds are kept; then calculate the cash outlays needed for the new bonds. The difference represents the annual net cash benefits to be achieved by the refunding.

TABLE 22-8   Bond Refunding Analysis — Calculation of Net Investment: Newton Corporation

	Accounting Expense On Books	Cash Flow
Retirement of 12% bonds		$30,000,000
Call premium (.08 × $30,000,000)	$2,400,000	2,400,000
Flotation cost of issuing new bonds		710,000
Duplicate interest payments (.12 × $30,000,000) (25/30)	250,000	250,000
Write-off of remaining flotation cost on old bonds	480,000	
Total added expenses	3,130,000	
Total added cash outflow		33,360,000
Less: tax savings (.34 × $3,130,000)	1,064,200	1,064,200
Net expenses after taxes	2,065,800	
Net cash outflow to redeem old issue		32,295,800
Less: gross amount raised by issue of new 10% bonds		30,000,000
Net cash investment in refunding		$2,295,800

TABLE 22-9   Bond Refunding Analysis—Calculation of Annual Cash Benefits: Newton Corporation

	Accounting Expense on Books	Cash Flow
A. Annual cash outlays required on old bonds:		
Interest expense	$3,600,000	$3,600,000
Amortization of flotation costs	24,000	
Total expenses	3,624,000	
Less: taxes saved @ 34%	$1,232,160	1,232,160
Expenses after taxes	$2,391,840	
Net cash outlay		$2,367,840
B. Annual cash outlays required on new bonds:		
Interest expense	$3,000,000	$3,000,000
Amortization of flotation costs ($710,000/20 years)	35,000	
Total expenses	3,035,000	
Less: taxes saved @ 34%	$1,031,900	1,031,900
Expenses after taxes	$2,003,100	
Net cash outlay		$1,968,100
C. Net annual cash benefits from new bond issue:		
Net outlays required on old bonds		$2,367,840
Net outlays required on new bonds		1,968,100
Net cash benefit per year		$ 399,740

In connection with these calculations, it might be noted that the flotation expenses of issuing the new bonds are amortized over the 20-year life of the bonds. Although these adjustments do not represent cash flows, they do affect the payments on income taxes.

It is now possible to evaluate whether to make the bond refunding. This can be done by comparing the present value of the future annual cash benefits of $399,740 (from Table 22-9) against the required investment of $2,295,800 (from Table 22-8). There is little risk associated with the bond refunding decision because the differential cash inflows in the form of interest cost savings are known with virtual certainty. Thus the cash inflows will be discounted at a rate that is lower than the corporate weighted average cost of capital so as to reflect the lower risk associated with the bond refunding decision. This is done by using the cost of new debt. And, since the cash flows are after taxes, the after-tax cost of debt should be used. For the Newton Corporation the bond refunding is evaluated on the basis of a 6.6-percent discount rate (i.e., 10% × .66 = 6.6%). The appropriate calculations are as follows:

$$\text{Present value savings} = \text{Annual cash savings} \times \text{PVIFA}_{(6.6\%, 20 \text{ years})}$$

$$= \$399{,}740 \times 10.932$$

$$= \$4{,}369{,}958$$

$$- \text{Outlay required} = -2{,}295{,}800$$

$$= \text{Net present value} = \$2{,}074{,}158$$

Thus, based on an NPV of more than $2 million, it would be profitable for the Newton Corporation to refund the 12-percent bond issue.

SUMMARY

Long-term debt consists of debt with a maturity in excess of one year. The maturity of the firm's debt should be aligned with the maturity of the assets to be financed, consistent with the maturity matching principle. Term debt is usually repaid in installments during the life of the loan. Interest on installment loan contracts is normally calculated using the "add-on" method, which raises the effective interest cost above the stated rate.

There are two principal types of bonds issued by corporations. Secured bonds, like mortgages, identify specific assets to be used as collateral. Debentures, or unsecured bonds, are backed only by the general credit and earning power of the corporation. The loan indenture specifies the terms on which funds are lent. These terms include covenants by the company to do certain things (positive covenants) and promises by the company not to do certain other things (negative covenants). Bond refunding involves paying off an existing debt with the proceeds from new borrowing. Bond refundings are attractive to corporate borrowers when their costs of borrowing have declined substantially or when new borrowing will permit much less restrictive covenants.

MULTIPLE CHOICE QUESTIONS

1. The role of a trustee in a corporate bond issue is to:
    a) Collect the proceeds from a security issue
    b) Represent the interest of the corporation in a bond sale
    c) Represent the interests of bondholders
    d) Act as the "go-between" in a private placement

2. An indenture is:
    a) A contract specifying bond terms
    b) Technical default by the company on its bond terms
    c) A form of insurance guaranteeing repayment of corporate debt
    d) Illegal in most states

3. A corporation defaults on its bond contract if:

   a) It calls in the bond
   b) The company violates an indenture
   c) The bond is not registered
   d) New stock is sold before the debt is paid off

4. A sinking fund requires:

   a) Periodic cash payments by the borrower to a trustee
   b) Payment of a premium to bondholders
   c) Periodic cash payments by the trustee to the borrower
   d) Periodic dividend payments to bondholders

5. Call premium means that the borrower must:

   a) Pay a penalty to prepay the borrowing
   b) Be ready to repay bonds if called
   c) Permit bonds to be exchanged for the common stock of the company
   d) Call the bonds or pay a penalty

6. An income bond requires:

   a) All net income, if any, is paid to bondholders until the debt is retired
   b) Payment of interest before any other expenses
   c) Payment of interest only if earned
   d) Prepayment of all bond interest

7. Debentures are:

   a) Short-term secured loans
   b) Long-term secured loans
   c) Long-term unsecured loans
   d) Short-term unsecured loans

8. A distinguishing feature of term loans is that:

   a) They have no maturity
   b) They are used for temporary working capital
   c) They can be called by the lender at any time
   d) They are amortized

9. The "add on" method for calculating interest payments results in an effective borrowing rate:

   a) Approximately double the simple interest rate
   b) About double the APR
   c) About equal to the prime rate
   d) Less than the simple interest rate

10. An acceleration clause states that if the borrower fails either to make required payments or to live up to the provisions of the loan agreement:

    a) The interest rate automatically increases
    b) The company has a grace period in order to correct the deficiencies
    c) All future interest is immediately due
    d) The entire loan is immediately due

DISCUSSION QUESTIONS

1. A basic requirement of intermediate and long-term borrowing is that the borrowing should be suited to the uses made of the funds. Explain.

2. What is a term loan? Describe some of the characteristics of a typical term loan.

3. What is the meaning of an installment loan? How does an installment loan usually differ from a term loan?

4. Commercial banks are major suppliers of intermediate-term financing to business firms. Why and how might a commercial bank make use of: (a) a negative pledge clause, and (b) an acceleration clause, when extending intermediate-term loans?

5. Give some examples of kinds of bonds that have specific claims against assets. Also describe an after-acquired property clause.

6. Why do firms sometimes retire debt ahead of schedule? What conditions might lead to a decision on the part of management to refund an existing bond issue?

SOLVED PROBLEMS

SP-1. The Radnor Company is considering an installment loan from the bank. The loan will be for $250,000, payable in equal annual installments over the next five years. The loan will carry an interest rate of 12 percent per annum. *installment loan*

   a) Calculate the annual payment.
   b) Calculate the total interest to be paid on the loan.
   c) Set up a loan repayment schedule like that in table 22-6 of the text.

SP-2. Randolph Enterprises is considering a $100,000 installment loan. The loan will be for three years and will carry a 15-percent simple interest rate. *installment loan*

   a) Calculate the total interest to be paid.
   b) Assume the total interest is to be added to the principal and that both interest and principal payments are to be made in three equal annual installments. Calculate the annual payments.
   c) Estimate the effective annual interest rate under the assumption of yearly installment payments.
   d) Assume the installments are to be made in 36 equal monthly payments. Calculate the monthly payment and the effective interest rate.

SP-3. Spaulding Oil Company is considering a refunding of its existing $10,000,000 debt issue. The existing debt has a coupon rate of 15 percent and 10 years left to maturity. The bond has $75,000 of *bond refunding* unamortized discount and $50,000 of unamortized bond issue expense. If called before maturity, the company will have to pay a premium of 10 percent. A new bond can be sold for $10,000,000 at a coupon rate of 13 percent and a 10-year maturity. Issue costs will amount to $1,000,000. If issued, the company will have to pay overlapping interest on the old and new debt for 60 days. The company is in a 34-percent tax bracket.

a) Calculate the net cash investment required to refund the existing bond issue.
b) What are the annual cash savings that the company can expect by replacing the existing bond issue.
c) Determine whether the refunding would be advantageous. (Round your discount rate to the nearest whole percent.)

PROBLEMS

installment loan

1. The Acme Company is considering an installment loan from the bank. The loan will be for $1,000,000, payable in equal annual installments over the next five years. The loan will carry an interest rate of 10 percent per annum.

a) Calculate the annual payment.
b) Calculate the total interest to be paid on the loan.
c) Set up a loan repayment schedule like that in Table 22-6 of the text.

installment loan

2. Jones, Inc. is considering a $200,000 installment loan. The loan will be for six years and will carry a 12-percent simple interest rate.

a) Calculate the total interest to be paid.
b) Assume the total interest is to be added to the principal and that both interest and principal payments are to be made in six equal annual installments. Calculate the annual payments.
c) Estimate the effective annual interest rate under the assumption of yearly installment payments.
d) Assume the installments are to be made in 72 equal monthly payments. Calculate the monthly payment and the effective interest rate.

bond refunding

3. Break Medical Company is considering a refunding of its existing $2,000,000 debt issue. The existing debt has a coupon rate of 15 percent and 10 years left to maturity. The bond has $15,000 of unamortized discount and $10,000 of unamortized bond issue expense. If called before maturity, the company will have to pay a premium of 15 percent. A new bond can be sold for $2,000,000 at a coupon rate of 10 percent and a 10-year maturity. Issue costs will amount to $200,000. If issued, the company will have to pay overlapping interest on the old and new debt for 60 days. The company is in a 34-percent tax bracket.

a) Calculate the net cash investment required to refund the existing bond issue.

b) What are the annual cash savings that the company can expect by replacing the existing bond issue.

c) Determine whether the refunding would be advantageous. (Round your discount rate to the nearest whole percent.)

4. The Basic Computer Software Company has requested a term loan from the First Bank of Longmont. After several meetings, a bank vice-president in charge of commercial loans offered a $200,000, eight year, 12-percent fully amortized term loan. Basic Computer Software will be required to make annual payments (principal and interest) at the end of each year.

term loan amortization

a) Calculate the annual payment in dollars that will be required each year.

b) Prepare a loan repayment schedule indicating the amount of principal to be repaid each year, as well as the size of the unpaid loan balance at the end of each year.

c) Indicate the size of annual payments if the $200,000 loan had been offered only for five years. Comment on the magnitude of the difference in annual payments between the five-year and eight-year term loans.

5. A local bank has offered a $200,000 installment loan to the Trans-Am Manufacturing Corporation. The loan carries a simple interest rate of 9 percent and is for a five-year period.

installment loan

a) Calculate the total dollar amount of interest that will be paid by Trans-Am over the life of the loan.

b) Determine the size of the installment payments if payments are made at the end of each year. Also indicate the size of payments if quarterly payments were to be made by Trans-Am.

c) Estimate the effective annual interest rate under the assumption of yearly installment payments.

d) How does the effective annual interest rate calculated in Part (c) change if the bank requires quarterly payments over the life of the installment loan?

e) Estimate the effective annual interest rate if Trans-Am Manufacturing is required to make monthly payments to the bank. What would be the size of monthly payments that would be required in order to pay off the loan?

6. The Jones Company is issuing a 20-year, 10-percent, $1,000 par value bond at $900. The bond is callable at the end of 10 years at $1,080. Estimate the bond price at the 10-year call date if the rate of return required in the marketplace for this risk class of bond is 14 percent at that time.

bond value

7. The Voorhew Manufacturing Corp. has been placed in liquidation and $700,000 realized in the sale of its assets. Outstanding claims are shown below. The subordinate debentures are specifically subordinated to the senior debt.

subordinated debt

	Amount of Claim
Senior debt	$ 700,000
Subordinated debt	200,000
Other liabilities	300,000
Common stock and surplus	1,500,000
	$2,700,000

a) How much will each class of claimant realize under the conditions indicated?

b) How much would each class have realized without the subordination feature on one class of debt?

c) How much will each class of claimant realize, given the subordination feature, if $1,000,000 is realized in the sale of assets?

bond refunding

8. The Paper Products Corporation has a 14-percent, $200,000 bond issue that has been outstanding for 10 years and has 10 years remaining until maturity. Unamortized flotation costs are one-half of the $14,000 total flotation costs incurred at time of issue. The existing bond can be called at 8 percent above its par value or face amount issued. Management is contemplating replacement of the existing bond with a new 10-year, 12-percent coupon bond. The new bond will be $200,000 and will require flotation costs amounting to 10 percent of gross proceeds. The appropriate income tax rate is 40 percent, and the firm does not expect to have any overlapping interest payments on the two bond issues.

a) Calculate the net cash investment that will be required in order to replace the existing bond with a new bond.

b) Calculate the annual cash benefits to be derived by refunding the existing bond issue.

c) Would you recommend that the Paper Products Corporation refund the existing bond issue? The firm uses discount rates rounded to the nearest whole percentage rate.

bond refunding

9. The Ball Glass Works Company is considering the possibility of refunding an outstanding issue of 11 percent debentures. The following information is available on the outstanding issue:

- Principal amount: $20,000,000
- Coupon rate: 11 percent
- Call price: 1,070
- Years to maturity: 15
- Unamortized bond discount: $150,000
- Unamortized bond issue expense: $45,000

Conversations with the company's investment banker indicate that the following terms may be obtained on a proposed bond issue:

- Principal amount: $20,000,000
- Coupon rate: 10 percent
- Call price: 1,100
- Years to maturity: 15
- Bond issue expense: $80,000

If the bonds are refunded, the corporation will find it advisable to pay interest on both the old and new bond issues for a period of 60 days. The firm is in the 40-percent tax bracket.

a) Determine the net cash investment that will be required in order to replace the existing bond issue.
b) What are the annual cash benefits or savings that the Ball Glass Works can expect by replacing the existing bond issue?
c) Would you recommend to Ball Glass Works' management that the existing debentures be replaced?

SOLUTIONS TO SOLVED PROBLEMS

SP-1. a) Use Equation (22-1) in the text

$$\text{Annual payment} = \frac{\text{Amount borrowed}}{\text{PVIFA 12\%,5 years}}$$

$$= \frac{\$250,000}{3.605}$$

$$= \$69,348$$

b)

Total payments = (5) (69,348) = $346,741
Less: principal = −250,000
Total interest paid = $ 96,741

c) **Term Loan Repayment Schedule**

End of Year	Annual Payment	Interest Payment	Principal Repayment	Balance
0	—	—	—	250,000
1	69,348	30,000	39,348	210,652
2	69,348	25,278	44,070	166,582
3	69,348	19,990	49,358	117,224
4	69,348	14,067	55,281	61,943
5	69,376*	7,433	61,943	0

*Raised to pay off remaining balance due to rounding differences.

SP-2. a)

$$\text{Annual interest} = (.15)(100{,}000) = 15{,}000$$

$$\times \text{3 years} \qquad \times \quad 3$$

$$\text{Total interest} \qquad \$45{,}000$$

b)

$$\text{Annual installments} = (100{,}000 + 45{,}000)/3$$

$$= \$48{,}333$$

c) Use equation (22-2) in the text

$$i = \frac{2mD}{P(n+1)} = \frac{(2)(1)(45{,}000)}{100{,}000(4)} = 22.5\%$$

d)

$$\text{Monthly payment} = \frac{145{,}000}{36} = 4{,}028$$

$$i = \frac{(2)(12)(45{,}000)}{(100{,}000)(37)} = 29.2\%$$

The faster repayment and fixed total interest result in a much higher effective interest rate.

SP-3. a) Follow the format of Table 22-8 in the text.

Bond Refunding Analysis — Calculation of Net Investment: Spaulding Oil Co.

	Accounting Expense on Books	Cash Flow
Retirement of 15% bonds		10,000,000
Call premium (.09 × 10,000,000)	900,000	900,000
Flotation costs of new bonds		1,000,000
Duplicate interest payments (.15 × $10,000,000)(60/360)	250,000	250,000
Write-off remaining flotation costs on old bonds	125,000	
Total added expense	1,275,000	
Total added cash outflow		12,150,000
Less: tax savings (.34 × 1,275,000)	433,500	433,500
Net expenses after taxes	841,500	
Net cash outflow to redeem old issue		11,716,500
Less: Gross amount raised by issue of new 13% bonds		10,000,000
Net cash investment in refunding		1,716,500

b) Follow the format of Table 22-9 in the text.

Bond Refunding Analysis — Calculation of Annual Cash Benefits

	Accounting Expense on Books	Cash Flow
A. Annual cash outlays required on old bonds:		
Interest expense	1,500,000	1,500,000
Amortization of flotation costs	12,500	
Total expenses	1,487,500	
Less: taxes saved 34%	505,750	505,750
Expenses after taxes	981,750	
Net cash outlay		994,250
B. Annual cash outlays required on new bonds:		
Interest expense	1,300,000	1,300,000
Amortization of new flotation costs (1,000,000/10 years)	100,000	
Total expenses	1,400,000	
Less taxes saved 34%	476,000	476,000
Expenses after taxes	924,000	
Net cash outlay		824,000
C. Net annual cash benefits from new bond issues		
Net outlays required on old bonds		994,250
Net outlays required on new bonds		824,000
Net cash benefit per year		170,250

c)

$$\frac{\text{Annual cash benefit}}{170,250} \times \frac{\text{(PVIFA*, 10 years)}}{6.418} = \text{Present values} = \$1,092,665$$

$$- \text{ Net cash investment in refunding} \qquad\qquad -1,716,500$$

$$= \$-623,836$$

*(13% pretax × .66 = 8.6 = 9% rounded)

The increased investment required exceeds the present value of annual cash benefits. Thus, the refunding is not advisable even with the 2 percent differential.

REFERENCES

Ang, James S. "The Two Faces of Bond Refunding." *Journal of Finance,* June 1975, pp. 869–874.

Bierman, Harold. "The Bond Refunding Decision." *Financial Management,* Summer 1972, pp. 22–29.

Black, Fischer, and John C. Cox. "Valuing Corporate Securities: Some Effects of Bond Indenture Provisions." *Journal of Finance,* May 1976, pp. 351–367.

Johnson, Rodney, and Richard Klein. "Corporate Motives in Repurchases of Discounted Bonds." *Financial Management,* Autumn 1974, pp. 44–49.

White, William L. "Debt Management and the Form of Business Financing." *Journal of Finance,* May 1974, pp. 565–577.

CHAPTER

23

LEASING, "HYBRID" SECURITIES, AND WARRANTS

his chapter reviews several alternative forms of long-term financing that depart from the straightforward debt and equity securities discussed in Chapters 21 and 22. It discusses certain types of leasing arrangements, called financial or capital leases, that have many of the characteristics of debt contracts. The financial manager needs to be able to estimate the implied interest rate on such borrowing arrangements in order to compare leasing alternatives to other forms of borrowing.

The chapter also discusses preferred stock and convertible securities. These securities are known as "hybrid" securities because they possess characteristics of both debt and equity securities. For example, convertible debt securities have characteristics of debt as well as common stock. The hybrid nature of such securities makes them more attractive to investors and can sometimes reduce the company's financing costs because of their unique features.

Last, the chapter considers warrants, a type of security sometimes known as a "derivative" security because its value is driven by the expected value of another security, common stock. Warrants have become popular as a source of corporate financing.

Objectives and Organization of this Chapter

The principal objective of this chapter is to present a look at other important types of long-term financing sources available to corporations. These types of financing arrangements are analytically more complex than the "generic" common stock and long-term debt securities. It is important to understand what they are, how they work, and the features to consider in evaluating them.

The first part of the chapter considers leasing as a source of financing. There are many different types of lease agreements, but the financial manager is only concerned with those that substitute for long-term debt. Thus the focus here is on financial or capital leases. Specifically, leasing arrangements, reasons for leasing, lease versus purchase analysis, and lease versus borrowing analysis, are discussed.

The second part of the chapter discusses preferred stock and convertible debt securities. The third part discusses warrants as a financing source.

CHARACTERISTICS OF LEASE ARRANGEMENTS

lease
lessor
lessee

A *lease* is a contractual agreement whereby the owner of the property (*lessor*) allows another party (*lessee*) to use the services of the property for a specified period of time in return for stipulated cash payments. Title to the property is retained by the lessor. Sometimes the lessee may continue to use the property after the initial period of the lease. In such cases, the lessee may also be given an option to purchase the property.

Leasing involves a fixed contractual obligation and thus must also be viewed as a form of debt financing. In essence, the lessee has borrowed some asset other than cash. The lessee cannot evade periodic rental payments any more than it can ignore interest and sinking fund payments on a bond issue.

Leasing Arrangements

Leases involving two parties, the lessor and lessee, can take the form of either a *direct lease* or a *sale and leaseback* arrangement. At times a third party (a lender) is involved in some lease arrangements that are known as *leveraged leases*.

direct lease

Direct Leases. A direct lease occurs when the lessee leases equipment or other assets not previously owned. This is the most common form of lease arrangement.

sales and leaseback arrangement

Sale and Leasebacks. In this arrangement, the lessee owns assets that are sold to a lessor who, in turn, leases the assets back to the lessee. Firms often use this approach to convert fixed assets such as land, machinery, and buildings into cash in order to improve liquidity positions or to provide funds for other investment purposes.

leveraged leases

Leveraged Leases. A leveraged lease involves a lessor, a lessee, and a lender. The lender lends funds to the lessor in order to purchase the assets that are to be leased to the lessee.

Operating Vs. Financial Leases

There are two basic types of leases available to business firms. These typically differ on the basis of the length of the leasing arrangement and in terms of whether the lease can be cancelled by the lessee.

operating lease

Operating or Service Leases. An operating or service lease is usually rather short term in duration and usually contains a cancellation clause, which permits the lessee the option of an early termination of the lease arrangement. Furthermore, this type of lease generally provides for both financing and maintenance of the leased asset by the lessor. It also is

796

common practice under this type of lease to lease the asset for a period of time that is less than the asset's economic life. Thus, leasing charges associated with a new asset would not be expected to recover fully the original cost, but rather the lessor would expect to be able to sell the asset for an acceptable price when the lease has been terminated.

Assets that are usually leased on an operating or service basis are computers, office copiers, and motor vehicles such as automobiles and trucks.

Financial or Capital Leases. A financial or capital lease is usually a longer-term leasing arrangement and generally does not provide the lessee with a cancellation clause opportunity. Maintenance services are not included under this type of lease, and the leases are usually written so that the lessor recovers the full cost (plus an acceptable return) of the assets from the lease payments received over the life of the lease.

financial lease

Financial or capital leases often are entered into by lessees as a means of acquiring the use of land, buildings, and manufacturing machinery and equipment. Large insurance companies such as Prudential and Aetna, as well as large commercial banks, often are involved as lessors in financial or capital leases. Nearly all sale and leaseback arrangements are handled as financial or capital leases.

Income Tax Implications

Lease payments made by the lessee are deductible for income tax purposes, much like interest expense is, so long as the "lease" is acceptable as a lease by the Internal Revenue Service. The IRS is concerned because the full amount of a lease payment is tax deductible, whereas only the interest portion of the annual payment made on an installment loan is deductible for income tax purposes. The real question becomes one of whether the "lessee" is truly leasing the assets or actually owns the assets (now or through a preferential purchase position at the end of the arrangement) and is, in effect, entering into an installment purchase agreement. If the latter situation is true, then the "lessee" would be receiving maximum tax write-off benefits and still have the ownership benefits when the "lease" terminated. In order to avoid or reduce such situations, the leasing arrangement must meet certain IRS requirements to qualify as a lease for income tax purposes.

Reasons for Leasing

In some cases a firm may have no choice between leasing and purchasing the services of assets. Owners of certain assets may refuse to sell the assets because they wish to reserve for their own benefit any capital gains that may be realized as the property appreciates. For this reason, it may be necessary to lease land to obtain the mineral or oil rights or the privilege of cutting timber. Similarly, the right to use certain patents may be available only through lease rather than purchase.

At other times, a firm will lease property because it seeks only a small portion of the facility or wishes to use it for only a short period of time. Many different reasons are given for choosing lease financing. However, some of them are not correct.

Protection Against Obsolescence.   If a company purchases a machine, such as a computer, it bears the risk of obsolescence. Would it not be better to shift this risk to somebody else and rent the services of the computer until it is superseded by more modern equipment? Consequently, when faced with a lease-or-buy decision on equipment subject to a high rate of obsolescence, leasing should be viewed favorably.

This argument assumes that the lessor is unaware of the rate of innovation in the field. Indeed, since the lessor is a specialist, he or she may be in a better position than the financial manager to judge the rate of obsolescence. Consequently, the lessor will include in the rental fee a charge for obsolescence and for other risks of owning property. It will not be an explicit charge but may be reflected in especially high payments during the early period of the lease so that the lessor recovers the investment as rapidly as possible. If the rate of obsolescence is higher than the lessor had anticipated, the lessee will benefit by having shifted the risk to her or him. Also, if the lessor can spread the risk of obsolescence over many lease contracts, the financial manager may benefit just as he or she does from purchasing fire insurance. The hazard of sudden obsolescence may be a greater individual risk than the financial manager can safely assume.

Flexibility.   A related argument sometimes advanced for leasing is that it provides greater flexibility. For example, if a firm borrows funds to purchase a store that subsequently proves to be poorly located, the company might be bound to that site. If the company leases the property, it can depart when the lease expires.

This argument assumes that the lessor has drawn the lease so that he or she does not recover the investment in the property during the term of the lease. This may be true of leases of equipment, but it is generally not the case on the long-term leases of land and buildings. Thus, by the time a lease expires, the financial manager should expect to have paid, in addition to interest and service charges, most, if not all, of the cost of equipment leased and all of the cost of any real estate leased. The lessee is forced to continue to make rental payments for the full term of the lease unless he or she can sublease the property to someone else. Whether the firm borrows to buy the property or whether it leases it, the company will have paid for it—either directly or over time through the lease payments.

Depreciation of Land. It is sometimes argued that leasing has a cost advantage over owning because it enables the lessee to "depreciate land." A lessee who borrowed to acquire title to land and a building could depreciate only the building for federal income tax purposes. In contrast, should the lessee sell the land and building to an insurance company and then lease them back, the rental payments would include the cost of the land to the insurance company. Through the lease, the lessee is thus able to "depreciate" the cost of the land.

One Hundred Percent Financing. It is sometimes argued that leasing enables the lessee to finance 100 percent of the cost of property, as contrasted with only 50 percent to 75 percent of the cost if the lessee were to raise the funds with a mortgage bond issue. The implication that leasing therefore provides more funds than borrowing is misleading. The conclusion that a lease provides 100-percent financing is based on an erroneous assumption that it has no effect on the company's general borrowing power. This is unlikely. To clarify this, assume that the lessee issues $10 million of debentures on the basis of $100 million of net worth and uses the proceeds to construct a $10-million plant. This could be termed 100-percent financing, but this would also be misleading. Whether the firm borrows or leases, it is "using up" some of its credit. The real question is whether a lease that is equivalent to $10 million of debentures uses up as much of the firm's borrowing power as the issue of debentures. This is a key question. If leasing provides more funds than borrowing in relation to a given amount of equity, it may be desirable even if it is more costly. In 1976, the Financial Accounting Standards Board issued FASB Standard No. 13, "Accounting for Leases." This Standard was formulated to require lessees to provide explicit disclosure of the value of financial or capital lease commitments on their balance sheets. Such lease commitments were to be capitalized by showing the present value of all lease obligations or payments as an asset on the balance sheet. This would be offset by the total dollar amount of lease commitment being reflected as a liability. As one might suspect, the rate at which the lease payment should be discounted in order to calculate the present value of the obligation may be difficult to determine. The FASB provides guidelines to aid the lessee in estimating the appropriate discount rate. Furthermore, the discount rate used to capitalize a financial lease should approximate the cost of financing the appropriate assets if they had been purchased instead of leased. FASB Standard No. 13 does not require the capitalization of operating or service leases. Instead, these types of lease commitments need to be shown only in footnotes to the financial statements.

Since leasing combines attributes of both ownership (i.e., the services of the asset) and borrowing (i.e., contractual payments), it is useful to consider the lease arrangement as an alternative to the borrow-purchase alternative.

Lease vs. Borrow-Purchase

Assume that the Extel Company is considering whether to purchase a piece of equipment financed with a loan, or to lease the equipment. If purchased, the equipment will be depreciated as three-year property with the ACRS 200-percent declining balance method. There will be no salvage value. Annual depreciation charges are shown in Column 3 of Table 23-1. In addition, the company will borrow the full purchase price of $100,000 at an interest rate of 10 percent. Installment payments of $31,546 per year will be required, including principal repayment and interest (Columns 1 and 2, respectively). Installment payments will be due at the end of each year.

Alternatively, Extel can lease the equipment for four years. The lease payment will be $26,000 per year, due at the beginning of each year. Assume that the company's tax rate is 40 percent in order to be able to use the present value tables in the Appendix.

The process of selecting between leasing versus borrow-purchase involves trying to minimize the present values of the cash outflows involved in financing the equipment. Table 23-1 shows the basis for making the financing decision. It first begins with the cash flows associated with the borrow-purchase alternative. The annual loan payment of $31,546 is indicated as a cash outflow. However, part of this payment represents

TABLE 23-1 Cash Outflow Estimates for the Borrow-Purchase and Lease Alternatives: Extel Company

A. Cash Outflows for Borrow-Purchase Alternative

End of Year	Loan Payment (1)	Interest Payment (2)	Depreciation (3)	Tax Shield [(2) + (3)].40 (4)	Cash Outflows (1) − (4) (5)
0	—	—	—	—	—
1	$31,546	$10,000	$33,333	$17,333	14,213
2	31,546	7,845	44,444	20,916	10,630
3	31,546	5,475	14,815	8,116	23,430
4	31,546	2,868	7,408	4,110	27,436

B. Cash Outflows for Lease Alternative

End of Year	Lease Payment (1)	Tax Shield (1) × .40 (2)	Cash Outflows (1) − (2) (3)
0	$26,000	—	$26,000
1	26,000	$10,400	15,600
2	26,000	10,400	15,600
3	26,000	10,400	15,600
4	—	10,400	(10,400)

*The tax shields associated with lease payments are staggered one year because the lease payments are made at the beginning of a year (i.e., the end of the previous year).

tax-deductible interest (Column 2) computed as 10 percent of the remaining balance each year. Depreciation charges are also tax deductible. Both interest payments and depreciation charges are deductible for income tax purposes, and thus they produce a tax shield benefit and reduce cash outflows, as is shown in Column 4. Column 5 indicates the net cash outflows for the loan payment after taking into account tax shield benefits from interest and depreciation expenses.

The bottom portion of Table 23-1 indicates the appropriate cash outflows associated with leasing the equipment. As noted earlier, the Extel Company can lease the equipment under a financial lease arrangement for $26,000 per year, with the first payment being required at the equipment delivery date (end of year zero for these purposes). Lease payments are deductible for income tax purposes and thus create a tax shield much like interest and depreciation charges. The tax shields associated with leasing, however, are staggered by one year to reflect the fact that lease payments are made at the beginning of each period. Consequently no tax shields are shown for year zero, but a tax shield benefit is shown for year four when no lease payment will be made at the end of the year.

In order to compare the leasing arrangement with the borrow-purchase alternative, it is necessary to determine the present value of each set of cash outflows. The alternative with the lower present value will be less expensive and should be accepted. However, considerable controversy exists in the finance literature as to what is the appropriate rate at which such outflows should be discounted. Arguments generally range between the use of the firm's weighted average cost of capital and the firm's after-tax cost of debt.[1] Since the lease is an alternative to debt, and since cash flows have been computed on an after-tax basis, the cash flows will be discounted at the after-tax cost of debt.

Table 23-2 contains the present value calculations. First subtract the annual cash outflows under the leasing alternative from the cash outflows

TABLE 23-2 Selecting Between the Borrow-Purchase and Lease Alternatives: Extel Company

End of Year (1)	Borrow-Purchase Cash Outflows (1)	Lease Cash Outflows (2)	Net Advantage to Leasing (1)−(2) (3)	6 Percent Discount Rate (4)	Present Value of Differential Outflows (5)
0	0	$26,000	($26,000)	1.000	($26,000)
1	$14,213	15,600	(1,387)	.943	(1,308)
2	10,630	15,600	(4,970)	.890	(4,423)
3	23,430	15,600	7,830	.840	6,577
4	27,436	(10,400)	43,036	.792	34,085
			Present Value of Leasing Advantage		8,931

[1]This difference of opinion is largely associated with the degree of risk that is perceived to exist in the lease-versus-purchase decision. The area of most concern is the risk or uncertainty connected with the asset's resale value at some future point in time.

under the borrow-purchase choice. This provides differential cash out-flows that reflect an advantage to leasing. Since the *before-tax* cost of borrowing for the Extel Company is 10 percent, the *after-tax* cost will be 6 percent (this is determined by multiplying the before-tax cost by one minus the 40-percent tax rate). The present value of the differential cash outflows is a positive $8,931, and thus the lease alternative appears to be less expensive.

PREFERRED STOCK

To a considerable extent, preferred stock is a hybrid security — not quite equity, not quite debt.[2] From one point of view it is part of the equity. Because the dividends on preferred stock are regarded as distribution of earnings, they are not a tax-deductible expense. Creditors correctly view preferred stock as part of the equity base that helps support a corporation's debt. If the corporation's charter or the agreement with preferred stock-holders makes no provisions to the contrary, preferred stockholders have almost the same rights as common stockholders. The only exception is the preferred stockholders' claim on cumulative dividends up to a specified amount before payment of earnings to common stockholders.

From the financial manager's point of view, preferred stock is best re-garded as quasi-debt. In the agreement between the company and preferred shareholders, the covenants that are of benefit to the preferred owners are usually detrimental to the common stockholders, and vice versa.

Preferred stock does not have a maturity date. Because preferred stock-holders are regarded as a special class of owners, provisions are sometimes made for compulsory repayment of their investment and are usually made for voluntary repayment.

par value preferred

A company may issue preferred stock that has a *par value* or *no par value.* The par value is the face amount of each share as stated in the corporation's charter. It appears on the front of the stock certificate sent to purchasers of the stock and is usually the amount at which the stock is carried on the corporation's balance sheet. The par value may be $25, $50, $100, or any amount specified.

Dividends on preferred stock are specified either as a percentage of the par value or as an annual dollar amount. Thus, if the company sells a 9-percent preferred stock, the annual dividend per share of stock would be $9 if the par value were $100, but only $1.80 if the par value were $20. Specification of the dividend as a dollar amount is characteristic of no par preferred.

---

[2] It should be noted that sometimes a corporation will have outstanding a "Class A" common stock. Close examination of the terms of the stock may reveal it to be a preferred stock in disguise.

Cumulative Preferred Stock. Dividends on preferred stock are usually cumulative; that is, unpaid dividends are carried forward from year to year. Thus if the dividends are $6 per share and the company has failed to pay dividends for two years, it is said to be $12 in arrears on its preferred stock. Therefore, it must pay $18 per share to the preferred shareholders during the third year before it can make any payments to the common stockholders. Unpaid dividends on noncumulative preferred stock are not carried forward from one year to the next.

cumulative preferred stock

It should be emphasized that preferred stock is unlike debt, in that failure to pay preferred dividends does not give the preferred stockholders the right to take legal action to obtain their unpaid dividends. The only commitment made is that preferred dividends will be paid in the amounts agreed upon before any dividends are paid on common stock. Many corporate directors believe that the terms of their agreement with the preferred stockholders carry a moral commitment to treat the obligation to pay preferred dividends with almost the same respect as they view the interest requirement on a bond issue.

Convertible Preferred Stock. A conversion feature may be added in order to create a *convertible preferred stock.* This is most commonly found on preferred stock issues of industrial concerns and is relatively rare on preferred stock issues of utilities. The conversion feature allows the preferred stockholder to exchange the preferred stock for common stock shares of the company. The conversion would only occur if the common stock price had appreciated over the conversion price. Otherwise, the preferred shareholder would not convert and would continue simply to receive the preferred dividend.

convertible preferred stock

Voice in Management. If no specific provision is made in a corporation's charter, preferred shareholders are also entitled to voting rights. However, the typical practice is to limit the preferred shareholder's voice in management to certain powers over payment of dividends and subsequent issues of prior or equal securities.

In addition, a company will probably have to grant preferred stockholders the right to vote or to elect a specific number of directors if it fails to abide by important features of its agreement with them. Thus the holders of a preferred stock may have no voting power unless six or so quarterly dividends are in default. At that unhappy point, the preferred shareholders, voting as a single class, may be entitled to elect, say, one-third of the board of directors.

CONVERTIBLE DEBT

A convertible bond is one that may be exchanged for a previously determined number of shares of common stock in the issuing corporation. In order to convert such a bond, the bondholder must give up his or her bond and become a common stockholder of the corporation. Since corporations that issue convertible bonds fully expect them to be converted at some time in the future, convertible bonds are an indirect means of selling common stock.

Terms and Characteristics

The conversion privilege associated with a convertible bond may be stated in two ways. On the one hand, the indenture might say that each $1,000 bond is convertible into 20 shares of stock (i.e., the conversion ratio). On the other hand, it might state that the bonds are convertible into common stock at $50; that is, the conversion price of the common stock is $50. By dividing the face value (not the market value) of the bond ($1,000) by the conversion price of the stock ($50), the financial manager can determine that 20 shares of common stock will be received upon conversion. The number of shares that can be received from the conversion of each bond is known as the *conversion ratio*. The common stock price at which conversion takes place is the *conversion price*. Typically the conversion price remains constant or rises over the convertible bond's life.

conversion ratio
conversion price

At any single time, there are two concepts of value associated with a convertible bond. The convertible has a value of a "pure" or nonconvertible bond which the financial manager will call its *straight debt value*. This is the value the bond would trade at in the marketplace if it did not have the convertible option. The second concept of value is the *conversion value*, which reflects the current value of the bond based on the conversion ratio times the current market price for the firm's common stock.

straight debt value

conversion value

Example

Convertible Debt

Let us assume that the Weeks Corporation is planning to raise $10 million through an issue of convertible bonds. Each bond will be convertible into common stock at $50 per share. The convertible bond will carry an 8-percent coupon, have a 20-year life, and will be sold at $1,000.

Instead of a convertible bond, the Weeks Corporation could issue a nonconvertible or "straight-debt" 20-year bond with a 10-percent coupon for $1,000. This is to say that the rate of return being required in the marketplace for nonconvertible bonds in Weeks' risk class is 10 percent. But, because the bond being issued by Weeks is convertible into 20 shares of the firm's common stock, it is carrying only an 8-percent coupon.

The convertible bond's nonconvertible or straight debt value (SDV_0) can be determined as follows (assuming annual interest payments for illustrative purposes):

$$SDV_0 = \sum_{t=1}^{20} \frac{\$80}{(1.10)^t} + \frac{\$1,000}{(1.10)^{20}} \tag{23-1}$$

Using the present value tables in Appendix A for a 10-percent, 20-year annuity results in a present value annuity factor of 8.514. The corresponding present value factor for $1 received at the end of 20 years would be .149. These present value factors multiplied by the appropriate cash flows produce the convertible bond's straight debt value as:

Cash Flow	Amount	Year Received	PVIFA 10%, 20 years	PVIF 10%, 20	Present Value
Interest	$ 80	1-20	8.514		$681
Principal	$1000	20		.149	149

Straight debt value = $830

Exhibit 23-1 illustrates the straight debt value for Weeks' convertible bond. Notice that the initial straight debt value of $830 will ultimately reach $1,000 at the bond's maturity date since, at that time (assuming no

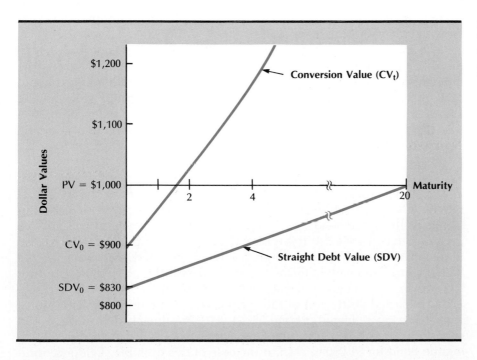

EXHIBIT 23-1
The Straight Debt and
Conversion Values for
a Convertible Bond:
Weeks Corporation

default), Weeks would pay the bondholder the bond's face or par value of $1,000. In actual practice, the straight debt value will fluctuate over time (instead of a smooth gradual rise as depicted in the exhibit) as market interest rates change with changes in investor risk-return expectations. In any event, the straight debt value will reach $1,000 at maturity.

Conversion Value. If the Weeks Corporation is to sell its convertible bond for $1,000, its conversion feature must have a market value of about $170 ($1,000 − $830 SDV) to compensate for the difference in coupon rate of two percentage points. If Weeks' common stock is selling at $45, the issuer might set the conversion price at $50, about 11 percent above the current market price. This is known as the *common stock conversion premium* at time of issue. Usually the issuer would set the conversion price about 10 to 20 percent above the market price of the common stock at the time the convertible bonds are issued.

common stock conversion premium

If the issuer set the conversion price higher, the probabilities of the market price reaching that level within a given period of time are correspondingly diminished. That being the case, the value of the conversion privilege may not reach $170. On the other hand, if the issuer sets the conversion price below $50, the issuer increases the value of the conversion privilege, possibly more than necessary to produce a total package worth $1,000. By observation of market performance of other convertible issues in this risk class, the issuer attempts to "fine tune" the coupon rate and conversion price (as well as other features, such as the call price) in order to hit a market value at time of issue of $1,000.

Assume that the issuer has judged correctly, with the aid of an investment banker, and sells the convertible 8-percent bond at $1,000. At the moment of sale, the straight debt value, or value as a pure bond, is about $830. Since the bond is convertible into 20 shares of common stock having a market value of $45 each, the conversion value of the bond is $900 (20 × $45). That is to say, this is the current market value of the shares of common stock into which it may be converted.

Call Provision. It is important for the issuer of a convertible bond to attach a call provision to the issue. This allows the issuer the option of forcing conversion when the convertible's conversion value reaches a price substantially above the bond's par value of $1,000 and above any call price or premium that might exist. It is typical to place a call price or premium equal to about one year's interest when the bond is issued. For example, the Weeks Corporation might make its convertible callable at $1,080. Only after the conversion value has substantially surpassed the call price, to, say, $1,180 expected at the end of four years, would the firm attempt to force conversion by calling the bond at $1,080. Presumably investors would choose to convert the convertible into stock worth $1,180 instead of returning the bond for $1,080 in cash in the case of this example. Evidence indicates that, when conversion values approach $1,200 and above, they are likely candidates for forced conversion.

Reasons for Issuing Convertible Bonds

One traditional reason cited for issuing convertible bonds is to reduce interest costs. For example, by issuing a convertible bond instead of straight debt, the Weeks Corporation is able to save two percentage points in the coupon rate (i.e., an 8-percent rate instead of 10 percent). A second traditional reason takes the form of delayed equity financing, in that common stock is eventually sold at a higher price than that existing at the time the convertible was issued. It can be argued that Weeks, by selling bonds convertible into common stock at $50, is indirectly selling common stock at five dollars above the current market price (or at an 11-percent premium). Of course, this assumes that conversion eventually takes place. If, instead, the common stock price never rises high enough that voluntary or forced conversion takes place, then the firm is saddled with an "overhanging" convertible, and there is no effective sale of common stock. A third traditional reason for issuing convertible bonds is to enhance the marketability of the issue by offering the possibility of an equity participation in addition to an interest yield.

Dilution Effect of Conversion

Conversion into common stock will lead to an earnings per share dilution. The *dilution effect* on earnings available for common stockholders in the Weeks Corporation is illustrated in Table 23-3. It is assumed that the firm

dilution effect

TABLE 23-3   Dilution Impact of a Convertible Bond Issue on Earnings per Share: Weeks Corporation

Earnings before interest and taxes	$34,000,000
Less: bond interest*	4,000,000
Earnings before taxes	30,000,000
Less: income taxes (40%)	12,000,000
Earnings after taxes	$18,000,000
Actual number of shares of common stock outstanding	1,000,000
Potential number of shares of common stock outstanding	1,200,000
Primary earnings per share	$18.00
Fully diluted earnings per share	$15.44

*Includes $800,000 in interest on the convertible bond during the year.

primary earnings per share

fully diluted earnings per share

issues $10,000,000 of 8-percent bonds that are convertible into common stock at $50 per share.

After the convertible has been issued, earnings before interest and taxes for next year are expected to be $34 million. After subtracting interest (including the interest on the convertible bond) and adjusting for taxes, the earnings available for common stockholders are expected to be $18 million. Since there are actually 1 million shares outstanding, the *primary earnings per share* figure is $18.00. In contrast, if the convertible bond is converted, there will be an additional 200,000 shares outstanding, or a total of 1.2 million shares. The conversion will also reduce bond interest by $800,000 and increase net income by ($800,000) (.66) or, $528,000, resulting in net income of $18,528,000. Dividing the restated in earnings after taxes by the potential 1.2 million shares results in a *fully diluted earnings per share* figure of $1.50. The difference in EPS indicates the dilution impact of full conversion as if it had occurred at the end of the year.

Both the primary and fully diluted EPS figures must be shown, except in the unusual situation where the fully diluted figure is higher, on the firm's income statement. This requirement was established in 1969 by the Accounting Principles Board (APB) in its *Opinion No. 15, Earnings Per Share.* Although beyond the scope of this text, this opinion also required that even a firm's primary EPS must, in certain situations, reflect the potential dilution of "common stock equivalents" because of contractual commitments to issue shares of stock at fixed prices. The APB followed this opinion with *Opinion No. 16, Business Combinations* and *Opinion No. 17, Intangible Assets* in 1970. These were issued to discourage the use of convertible securities to finance acquisitions and mergers — a method used widely during the latter part of the 1960s.

WARRANTS

Besides directly owning shares of common stock, investors can hold indirect positions through warrants issued by corporations.

Warrants to Purchase Common Stock

Warrants entitle the holder to purchase shares of common stock of a given corporation at a specified price over a stated period of time. Usually warrants are detachable when offered in a package with other securities; that is, they may be separated from the bond or preferred stock by the holder and exercised or sold separately in the marketplace.

Warrants are similar to convertible securities in a number of respects. They serve to "sweeten the issue" and thus enhance the marketability of nonconvertible securities by offering the investor an opportunity to share in the firm's future. However, warrants will lead to EPS dilution as do convertible securities. Warrants also are subject to the previously cited Accounting Principle Board's Opinion No. 15, "Earnings Per Share."

Warrants differ from convertible securities in two important respects. First, the issuing corporation usually receives additional cash when the warrants are exercised, whereas this is not usually the case with convertible bonds and preferred stocks. Second, the warrant gives the holder greater flexibility. To exercise the warrant, the holder of a bond-warrant or preferred-warrant package does not sacrifice his or her position as a creditor or preferred stockholder. Also the investor can sell the bond or preferred stock (to which the warrant was initially attached) and hold the warrant, or vice versa. These added options might even make the warrant more valuable than an equivalent convertible bond or preferred stock. Warrants are also offered in packages with common stocks. This has been an approach used by small, relatively unknown companies to improve the marketability of their common stock issues.

Theoretical Value. A warrant has an intrinsic or theoretical value at any point in time prior to its expiration date. This warrant value (WV) can be expressed as follows:

warrant theoretical value

$$WV = (MP - EP)N \qquad (23\text{-}2)$$

where MP is the current market price of the common stock, EP is the exercise price (i.e., the amount that must be paid, usually in cash, for a share of common stock), and N represents the number of shares of common stock that can be bought with each warrant.

Assume that the Weeks Corporation issued an 8-percent, 20-year bond that was convertible into 20 shares of common stock. As an alternative to the convertible bond issue, the firm might have issued a straight or nonconvertible bond with an 8-percent coupon and a 20-year maturity along with warrants to purchase common stock. At the time of issue, nonconvertible bonds in Weeks' risk class were yielding 10 percent. Thus at time of issue the straight debt value of the convertible bond was $830 (see Exhibit 23-1). It follows that a comparable bond with warrants attached (referred to as a bond/warrant unit) would have the same straight debt value.

bond/warrant unit

In order to sell the bond plus warrants package at $1,000 it would be necessary to make the equity participation portion as attractive as the conversion option on the convertible bond. Recall that Weeks placed an 11-percent common stock conversion premium at time of issue on its convertible by setting a conversion price at $50 when the common stock was selling for $45 per share. It is also common practice to set warrant exercise or option prices about 10 to 20 percent above the common stock price at time of issue. The firm might, for example, attach 20 warrants (with each being entitled to purchase one share of common stock) to each bond with an exercise price of $50.[3] Investors would probably value this package at

---

[3]Most warrants are issued with lives of from five to 10 years. Thus the warrant is likely to expire before the bond reaches its maturity date. To this extent, a bond-warrant package is likely to differ from a convertible bond offering.

about the same level as the convertible bond. On the one hand, they would have to put up an additional $50 per warrant exercised (although sometimes issuing corporations allow the use of the attached bond at par value for purposes of exercising the warrants). On the other hand, as the financial manager indicated above, the investor has more flexibility if the warrants are made detachable after a period of time, thus permitting the separate sale of the bond and warrant components.

At time of issue, the theoretical or intrinsic value of each Weeks' warrant would be

$$WV = (\$45 - \$50)1.0 = -\$5$$

This −$5 is analogous to Weeks' conversion value of $900 at time of issue, which was $100 less than the $1,000 being paid for the convertible bond. In a similar fashion, −$5 times 20 warrants also would result in −$100 at time of issue. It is already known from the earlier example that investors were willing to pay $1,000 for a convertible bond with a straight debt value of $830 and thus were willing to value the conversion privilege at about $170 at time of issue. A similar value would be expected for the warrant portion of a bond and warrant package. Obviously the investors are expecting the firm's common stock price to rise above the warrant's exercise price as the firm prospers.

SUMMARY

Leasing is equivalent to borrowing. The firm borrows physical assets instead of cash. Leasing arrangements include direct leases, sale and lease-backs, and leveraged leases. Nearly all sale and leaseback arrangements are of the financial or capital lease type, which are noncancellable and are generally longer-term leases. Operating, or service leases, are generally short-term and cancellable. While qualitative reasons may be used in some instances for deciding to lease, most decisions ultimately come down to choosing on the basis of a numerical lease-versus-borrow-purchase analysis.

Preferred stock is a hybrid security and presents a mixture of features characteristic of both equity and debt. Payment of dividends on preferred stock is typically fixed in amount, much like interest on the firm's bonds. However, unlike debt payments, preferred dividends are not obligatory; the only commitment is that preferred dividends must be paid before dividends are paid on common stock. Also, unlike interest payments on debt, preferred stock dividends are not a tax deductible expense.

As an alternative to straight debt, some corporations issue convertible debentures. The most important reasons for doing so include: (1) to reduce the interest cost of the debt issue, (2) to enhance the salability or market-ability of the issue, (3) to provide a means for selling common stock at a premium, and (4) on the basis of advice and counsel received from investment banking firms. While convertible debentures possess many attractions, they can result in a severe loss of financial flexibility in the event that stock prices do not rise and the firm is saddled with an "overhanging" convertible and associated investor dissatisfaction.

MULTIPLE CHOICE QUESTIONS

1. A "direct lease" applies only to:
   a) Leases made directly to the equipment manufacturer
   b) Assets not previously owned
   c) Operating lease arrangements
   d) Assets previously owned

2. A leveraged lease is one in which:

   a) The lessor borrows against the lease
   b) The lessee has other debt outstanding
   c) Several assets are covered
   d) The lessee borrows against the lease

3. An operating lease is most likely to apply to which of the following:

   a) Buildings
   b) Fixed equipment
   c) Office copier
   d) (a) and (b)

4. A capital lease:

   a) Is made for cash
   b) Is noncancellable by the lessee
   c) Is only made by manufacturers
   d) Involves "sale and leaseback" by lessee

5. According to FASB 13:

   a) Financial leases must be capitalized on the balance sheet
   b) The dilution impact of leases on EPS must be shown on the annual report
   c) Only the interest portion of the lease can be shown as an expense
   d) Lease payments are not tax deductible

6. In choosing between lease and borrowed financing, select the alternative:

   a) With the highest internal rate of return
   b) With the lowest present value
   c) Both (a) and (b)
   d) With the highest present value

7. Preferred stock is more expensive than debt because:

   a) Preferred stock dividends are not assured
   b) Preferred stock dividends are not tax-deductible
   c) In bankruptcy, debtors are paid off before preferred stockholders
   d) All of the above

8. Convertible preferred stock:

   a) Does not receive dividends
   b) Can be exchanged for common stock of the company
   c) Can be sold back to the company
   d) Requires the company to make sinking fund payments

9. A warrant is:

   a) Legal notice that the company has defaulted on its loan indentures
   b) A right to purchase common stock at a specified price
   c) Convertible into common stock
   d) Notice to shareholders of an upcoming election

10. The cumulative feature of preferred stock means that:
    a) Preferred stock dividends are automatically reinvested in the company
    b) Preferred stock dividends not paid in one period must be made up in subsequent periods
    c) New preferred stock is entitled to all dividends previously paid on outstanding preferred stock
    d) No preferred stock dividends can be paid until all outstanding debt is repaid

11. Preferred stock resembles debt in that:
    a) Cash payments by the company are fixed
    b) Failure to make dividend payments can force the company into bankruptcy
    c) Both securities have fixed maturities
    d) Dividends are tax deductible

12. Preferred stock resembles common stock in that:
    a) Cash payments by the company are fixed
    b) Cash payments are tax-deductible
    c) Dividends paid vary with earnings
    d) Failure to pay dividends does not result in bankruptcy

13. A convertible bond:
    a) Is only sold by automobile companies
    b) Can be exchanged for new bonds as they are issued
    c) Can be exchanged for common stock
    d) Pays dividends as well as interest

14. A convertible bond's straight debt value is:
    a) Always higher than its conversion value
    b) Always lower than its conversion value
    c) Always higher than its market value
    d) Is never higher than its market value

15. A convertible bond's conversion value is equal to:
    a) Conversion ratio times common stock price per share
    b) Bond value divided by conversion value
    c) Bond face value divided by common stock price per share
    d) Conversion ratio times bond interest

16. Primary earnings per share usually do not reflect:
    a) Interest paid on convertible debt
    b) Dividends paid on preferred stock
    c) Common stock equivalents of preferred stock
    d) Common stock equivalents of convertible debt

DISCUSSION QUESTIONS

1. What is meant by a convertible bond? Explain the relationship between a convertible bond's conversion ratio and conversion price.

2. Explain the difference between a convertible's straight debt value and its conversion value.

3. Discuss the advantages and disadvantages of convertible bond issues from the standpoint of the corporate issuer.

4. Explain and illustrate the dilution effect of convertible bonds on the firm's earnings per share.

5. What are warrants? In what ways are they similar to convertible securities and in what ways are they different?

6. Define and contrast (a) an operating or service lease and (b) a financial or capital lease.

7. Why are the lease-versus-borrow purchase cash flows discounted at the after-tax cost of debt?

SOLVED PROBLEMS

lease vs. borrow-purchase

SP-1. The Block Company is considering an investment in a machine costing $300,000. The machine, if purchased, would be depreciated according to ACRS as three-year property using the 200-percent declining balance method. The machine has an economic life of four years and will have no salvage value. For ease of computations with the appendix tables, assume that the company's tax rate is 50%. The company is considering the following alternatives:

1. *Borrow-purchase.* With this alternative, the company will borrow the full $300,000 purchase price at an interest rate of 10 percent per year. The loan will be repaid in equal annual installments (including principal and interest) over a four-year term. Payments will be made at the end of each year.

2. *Lease.* The company can lease the equipment from the manufacturer. This alternative will require lease payments of $90,000 per year, payable at the beginning of each year.

   a) Set up a loan repayment schedule for the borrow-purchase alternative. Determine the annual installment payment and the portions allocated to principal and interest.

   b) Determine the annual depreciation charges on the machine, tax shields generated by interest on the debt and depreciation on the machine, and the annual cash outflows for the borrow-purchase alternative.

   c) Determine the annual cash outflows after taxes for the leasing alternative.

   d) Calculate the present value of the leasing advantage.

SP-2. The Starr Company has a 20-year, 8-percent convertible bond outstanding. The bond was issued 10 years ago, is convertible into
50 shares of common stock, and is currently selling at $800 per
bond (par value, $1,000). Assume annual interest payments. *convertible debentures*

    a) Assuming the company's common stock is selling for $15 per
share, calculate (i) the conversion value of the bond; (ii) premium over conversion value.

    b) Assuming the company's nonconvertible debt is selling to yield
15 percent, calculate (i) the straight debt value of the convertible; (ii) premium over straight debt value.

    c) At what common stock price per share will the convertible's
conversion value equal its straight debt value?

SP-3. The Post Company earned $20 million before interest and taxes last
year. Interest expense of $3 million included $1 million for convertible debt. The convertible debt issue has a face value of
$10 million, carries a coupon rate of 10 percent and is convertible
into 80 shares of common stock per $1,000 par value bond. The
company currently has 10 million common stock shares outstanding
and is in a 34-percent tax bracket. Calculate primary and fully
diluted earnings per share for the company. *EPS dilution*

PROBLEMS

1. The Groton Company is considering an investment in a machine costing $1,000,000. The machine, if purchased, would be depreciated
according to ACRS as three-year property, using the 200-percent declining balance method. The machine has an economic life of four years
and will have no salvage value. For ease of computations with the
Appendix Tables, assume that the Company's tax rate is 50 percent.
The Company is considering the following alternatives: *lease vs. borrow-
purchase*

    1. *Borrow-purchase.* With this alternative, the company will borrow
the full $1,000,000 purchase price at an interest rate of 12 percent
per year. The loan will be repaid in equal annual installments (including principal and interest) over a four-year term. Payments will
be made at the end of each year.

    2. *Lease.* The company can lease the equipment from the manufac-
turer. This alternative will require lease payments of $200,000 per
year, payable at the beginning of each year.

        a) Set up a loan repayment schedule for the borrow-purchase al-
ternative. Determine the annual installment payment and the
portions allocated to principal and interest.

        b) Determine the annual depreciation charges on the machine, tax
shields generated by interest on the debt and depreciation on

the machine, and the annual cash outflows for the borrow-purchase alternative.

c) Determine the annual cash outflows, after-taxes, for the leasing alternative.

d) Calculate the present value of the leasing advantage.

convertible debenture

2. The Art Company has a 10-year, 6-percent convertible bond outstanding. The bond was issued two years ago, is convertible into 25 shares of common stock, and is currently selling at $900 per bond (par value, $1,000). Assume annual interest payments.

   a) Assuming that the company's common stock is selling for $30 per share, calculate (i) the conversion value of the bond and (ii) premium over conversion value.

   b) Assume that the company's nonconvertible debt is selling to yield 12 percent, calculate (i) the straight debt value of the convertible and (ii) premium over straight debt value.

   c) At what common stock price per share will the convertible's conversion value equal its straight debt value?

EPS dilution

3. The Quartz Company earned $8 million before interest and taxes last year. Interest expense of $1.2 million included $400 thousand for convertible debt. The convertible debt issue has a face value of $4 million, carries a coupon rate of 10 percent and is convertible into 100 shares of common stock per $1,000 par value bond. The company currently has 5 million common stock shares outstanding and is in a 34-percent tax bracket. Calculate primary and fully diluted earnings per share for the company.

convertible debenture

4. A convertible bond issued by the Downer Office Supplies Corporation carries a $9\frac{1}{2}$-percent coupon, pays interest annually, and has a 10-year life. The bond is convertible into common stock at $40 per share. Comparable straight debt bonds are yielding 12 percent, and the common stock is currently trading at $31 per share. Management anticipates that the conversion value will be about $1,300 at the end of six years.

   a) Calculate the straight debt value for the convertible bond. Also indicate the straight debt value if the interest is paid semiannually.

   b) Calculate the convertible's conversion value. What is the common stock conversion premium?

   c) At what rate will the common stock price have to appreciate or grow to reach a conversion value of $1,300 at the end of six years?

5. The Ash Chemical Company is calling its outstanding issue of convertible debentures which was sold at par ($1,000 each) seven years ago. The bond carries an 11-percent coupon, has 15 years to go before maturity, and is callable at 107 or $1,070. Comparable quality and maturity straight debt is currently yielding 10 percent. The bond is convertible into 15 shares of Ash Chemical's common stock, which was selling for $80 per share just prior to being called.

a) Calculate the bond's straight debt value just prior to being called. Assume annual interest payments.
b) Calculate the conversion value of the debentures just prior to the call.
c) Compare the straight debt value, the call value, and the conversion value for the Ash Chemical Company's convertible bond. As an investor, what action would you take when you receive the call notice?

SOLUTIONS TO SOLVED PROBLEMS

SP-1. a) Annual loan payment = $300,000/(PVIFA, 10%, 4 years)
= $300,000/3.170 = $94,637

Year	(1) Beginning Loan Principal	(2) Installment	(3) Interest	(4) Principal	(5) = (1) − (2) Ending Principal
1	$300,000	$94,637	$30,000	$64,637	$235,363
2	235,363	94,637	23,536	71,101	164,262
3	164,262	94,637	16,426	78,211	86,051
4	86,051	94,656*	8,605	86,051	−0−

*Increased to show payoff of balance

b) Depreciation.

Year	Machine cost	ACRS %	$ Depreciation
1	300,000	.333	$ 99,900
2		.444	133,200
3		.148	44,400
4		.075	22,500
		1.000	$300,000

Year	(1) Loan Payment	(2) Interest	(3) Depreciation	(4) Tax Shield*	(5) = (1) − (4) After-Tax Cash Outflow
1	$94,637	$30,000	$ 99,900	$64,950	$29,687
2	94,637	23,536	133,200	78,368	16,269
3	94,637	16,426	44,400	30,413	64,224
4	94,656	8,605	22,500	15,553	79,103

*Tax shield = (Interest + Depreciation)(Tax Rate)

c) Leasing cash outflows.

Year	Lease Payment	Tax Shield*	After-Tax Cash Outflow
0	$90,000		$90,000
1	90,000	$45,000	45,000
2	90,000	45,000	45,000
3	90,000	45,000	45,000
4		45,000	(45,000)

*Tax Shield = (Lease payment)(Tax rate). Deductions are allowed only when revenues are generated.

d) Present value of leasing advantage.

Year	(1) Loan After-Tax Cash Flows	(2) Lease After-Tax Cash Flows	(3) = (1) − (2) Net Advantage To Leasing	(4) 5% Discount Factor	(5) Present Value
0		$90,000	($90,000)	1.000	($90,000)
1	$29,687	45,000	(15,313)	.952	(14,578)
2	16,269	45,000	(28,731)	.907	(26,059)
3	64,224	45,000	19,224	.864	16,610
4	79,103	(45,000)	124,103	.823	102,137
			Present value of leasing advantage		($11,890)

SP-2. a) i. Conversion value per bond:

$$CV = (MP)(CR)$$

$$= (\$15)(50)$$

$$= \$750$$

ii. Premium over conversion value:

$$= BP_O - CV_O$$

$$= \$800 - 750$$

$$= \$50$$

b) i. Discount the interest payments and maturity value at 15 percent.

$$SDV_O = (80)(\text{PVIFA, 15\%, 10 years}) + 1,000(\text{PVIF, 15\%, 10 years})$$

$$= (80)(5.019) + (1,000)(.247)$$

$$= 648.52$$

ii. Premium over straight debt value:

$$800 - SDV_O = 800 - 648.52$$

$$= \$151.48$$

c) The conversion ratio is 50 shares per bond. When the stock price is about $13 . . .

$$CV_O = 648.52 = (MP)(50)$$

$$MP = 12.97$$

. . . per share, the conversion value will equal $650 dollars, or the straight debt value.

SP-3.

	Primary EPS	Fully diluted EPS
EBIT	$20,000,000	$20,000,000
Interest	3,000,000	2,000,000
PBT	17,000,000	18,000,000
Taxes (40%)	6,800,000	7,200,000
Net income	10,200,000	10,800,000
No. of shares	10,000,000	10,800,000
EPS	$1.02	$1.00

REFERENCES

Alexander, Gordon, J., and R. D. Stover. "Pricing in the New Issue Convertible Debt Market." *Financial Management,* Fall 1972, 35–39.

Brealey, R. A., and C. M. Young. "Debt, Taxes, and Leasing — A Note." *Journal of Finance,* December 1980, pp. 1245–1250.

Galai, Dan, and Mier I. Schneller. "The Pricing of Warrants and the Value of the Firm." *Journal of Finance,* December 1978, pp. 1333–1342.

O'Brien, Thomas, J., and Bennie H. Nunnally, Jr. "A 1982 Survey of Corporate Leasing Analysis." *Financial Management,* Summer 1983, pp. 30–36.

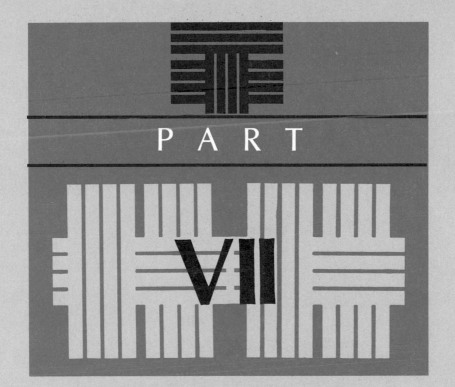

PART

VII

SPECIAL FINANCING SITUATIONS

CHAPTER

24

MERGERS, ACQUISITIONS, AND BANKRUPTCY

his chapter presents topics that may be viewed as polar opposites. At one end of the spectrum, it considers a special type of *expansion* decision: namely the acquisition of an entire company. At the other end of the spectrum, it considers the forced *contraction* through reorganization or liquidation of a company due to financial distress and failure.

Both of these topics are presented in the same chapter because they also have much in common. First, they both contain potential financial consequences of fundamentally larger scope than other financial decisions. For example, the acquisition of a firm may be viewed narrowly as an investment decision. As such, capital budgeting methods would be applied to the analysis. But an acquisition of another company involves more than cash flows: it involves inheriting an ongoing operation with its own policies, corporate culture, markets, and customers. Many of these factors do not fit neatly into standard capital budgeting analysis, and yet they may be of critical importance to the overall success of both the acquired and acquiring companies.

Second, for most firms acquisition and reorganization represent unusual events. They do not constitute the normal operating routine of the financial manager. In other words, they are "episodic," though nonetheless important. Thus, they are treated here as special topics rather than as typical financial decisions.

Third, both of these major events (acquisition or reorganization) have important legal aspects that are beyond the scope of a survey text. Thus, while this chapter indicates the contributions financial analysis can and should make to decisions in these areas, the reader should recognize that nonfinancial considerations may be decisive.

Objectives and Organization of this Chapter

The principal objective of this chapter is to illustrate the role of financial analysis in merger decisions and in financial reorganizations. The discussion of mergers will include the rationale for them, the use of capital budgeting techniques in valuing them, and their financial accounting treatment. In regard to financial reorganizations and liquidations, the chapter examines how the decision is made whether to save the company or liquidate it. Again, the role of financial analysis in making such decisions is considered. Also considered are the alternatives open to the firm when it undergoes reorganization and the distribution process followed when the company is liquidated.

The first section of the chapter describes the various types of business combinations that are possible. The second section examines the rationales given for mergers. The discussion emphasizes the rationales that claim to affect the price of the acquiring firm's stock positively. The third section poses the merger decision as an investment and illustrates how capital budgeting techniques might be applied to determine the economic value of an entire firm. The fourth section of the chapter discusses the calculation and significance of merger terms in relation to financial reporting, earnings per share, and stock price. The fifth section shifts attention to financial distress and business failure. It considers alternatives to liquidation which firms may pursue. Finally, the sixth section discusses some of the more important laws dealing with bankruptcy.

 TYPES OF BUSINESS COMBINATIONS

While the focus of this section is on external expansion through mergers and acquisitions, it is important first to establish a basic understanding of the various forms of business combinations that are available.

holding company

subsidiaries

A *holding company* is a corporation whose sole function is to own a controlling interest in the voting stock of one or more other corporations. The companies that are controlled are referred to as *subsidiaries*. A holding company does not need to own a majority of the voting stock of another corporation to have effective working control. Frequently, ownership of only 10 percent of the stock is sufficient. In all cases, both the holding company and its subsidiaries continue to exist as separate corporations.

A *merger* may be defined as a combination of two businesses in which only one corporation survives. The merged corporation goes out of existence and leaves its assets (and possibly liabilities) to be combined with those of the surviving corporation. It is common practice to refer to the surviving corporation as the acquiring corporation and the corporation that goes out of existence as the acquired corporation. This has led to the interchangeable use of the terms *merger* and *acquisition,* although the term *acquisition* sometimes is preferred when a large corporation acquires a much smaller one.

merger

acquisition

consolidation

Consolidations, in a technical sense, involve the fusion of two or more corporations into a third, entirely new corporation, which absorbs the assets (and usually liabilities) of the old corporations. The old corporations then pass out of existence. As one might expect, it often is difficult to distinguish among the terms merger, acquisition, and consolidation when referring to these forms of combination in practice. As a result, *merger* and *acquisition* are used as general terms throughout the remainder of this section.

825

CHAPTER 24
MERGERS,
ACQUISITIONS, AND
BANKRUPTCY

Holding Company

The first step in a combination is frequently the formation of a holding company. Common stocks of the target company can be purchased without the need for formal approval by either group of stockholders. If purchases are made gradually, there need be no marked rise in the price of the stock, whereas, if it were known that someone was attempting to gain control, a much higher price might result. Once the holding company has acquired control, the companies may live with the situation for a while and test the suitability of a later combination between them. If the companies are incompatible, it is simple gradually to sell the stock that was acquired and disengage from the situation.

Another important reason for the use of the holding company device is that control over extensive amounts of assets may be achieved by a relatively small investment on the part of the residual owners. To illustrate this principle, which is really an improved version of financial leverage, assume that one has working control of corporations by ownership of 20 percent of their common stock. Assume that preferred stock is nonvoting. For illustrative purposes, let us consider the possibilities with an electric utility empire and follow the characteristic capital structure proportions for electric utilities.

Under the foregoing assumptions it is possible to control the holding company with an investment of $1.2 million (20 percent of $6 million). In turn, the holding company holds one-fifth of the common stock of the two subsidiaries A and B. Through the device of a holding company, an investment of $1.2 million controls working assets at the subsidiary level of $212 million. In other words, control is achieved by an investment amounting to about 0.6 percent of the assets at the operating level. The high degree of financial leverage embodied in this structure means that any variation in earnings at the operating level is greatly magnified at the holding company level. This is shown in Table 24-1. The assets of the holding company are comprised of $8 million of Stock A (i.e., 20 percent of A's common stock) and $8 million of Stock B. The holding company thus controls the two firms, A and B. Assuming that one can control the holding company by owning 20 percent of its stock, then an investment of $1.2 million in the holding company (i.e., 20 percent times $6 million) permits control of A and B.

In addition to the attractions of control and leverage, some holding companies are created in response to restrictive state laws. Many state laws favor domestic corporations, i.e., corporations chartered by the state, in relation to "foreign corporations," which are chartered by other states. Taxes may be lower, regulation may be easier, and there are often other differences in treatment. In such cases, it is desirable to maintain the hold-

TABLE 24-1   Holding Company

Assets		Liabilities	
Common stock investments		Long-term debt	$ 8
Company A	$ 8	Preferred stock	2
Company B	8	Common & surplus	6
	$ 16		$ 16
Subsidiary Company A		*Subsidiary Company B*	
Long-term debt	$ 53	Long-term debt	$ 53
Preferred stock	13	Preferred stock	13
Common & surplus	40	Common & surplus	40
Total	$106	Total	$106

ing company structure when operating in a number of states. For example, when personal loan companies expand by purchasing the common stock of firms in other states, they often keep the newly acquired corporations as subsidiaries chartered in the state within which they do business. If they merged the subsidiary into the parent concern, the loan offices would then be offices of a foreign corporation (assuming the parent is chartered in some other state). Still another reason for maintaining the holding company structure is to avoid risks of lawsuits or other contingent liabilities which may be characteristic of the subsidiary's business.

There are important disadvantages to the holding company device. The parent corporation must pay a tax on 20 percent of the dividends received from subsidiaries. This tax would be avoided by a merger or consolidation. There are added costs of maintaining separate organizations and separate corporate relationships. The task of managing and coordinating the activities of two or more distinct corporations is usually difficult. Because directives must pass through the board of directors of the subsidiary, response may be slow and hesitant. If the parent concern does not own 100 percent of the subsidiary's stock, there are minority interests who may harass the board of directors of the subsidiary. It might be preferable to deal with these minority groups once and for all in a merger or consolidation rather than put up with their legal maneuvering over several years. Finally, holding companies are generally viewed with disfavor by the public and by some regulatory bodies, largely because the device has been so abused in the past. When disadvantages outweigh advantages, it may be preferable to merge or consolidate instead of relying on the holding company device.

Merger Types

horizontal merger

vertical merger

There are three basic types of mergers and acquisitions. A *horizontal merger* is a combination of firms in the same line of business, e.g., the merger of two chains of computer stores. A *vertical merger* is a combination of firms involved in different stages of production of the same products or where other forms of buyer-seller relationships are possible, e.g., an automobile manufacturer merging with a steel company.

The third basic type of acquisition is referred to as a *conglomerate merger.* Actually, according to the Federal Trade Commission (FTC), there are three subcategories of conglomerate mergers — *product extension, market extension,* and *other.* Product extension mergers involve combining firms that have functionally related production or distribution systems but do not have directly competing products. An example of this type of conglomerate merger according to the FTC would be the acquisition of a bleach manufacturer by a soap manufacturer. Market extension mergers refer to merging firms that manufacture the same products but operate or sell them in different geographic markets. An example of this type of conglomerate merger is the acquisition of a soft drink bottler operating in Chicago by a Washington-based bottler. The "other," category includes what might be referred to as "pure," conglomerate mergers — mergers between essentially unrelated firms. An example would include the merging or combining of an ice cream manufacturer with a shipbuilding company.

conglomerate merger

product extension merger
market extension mergers

Motives for Mergers

The theoretical objective of a merger is to combine two or more firms so that the market value of the resulting firm is greater than the market values of the firms operating as independent entities. This concept can be depicted as:

$$V(A + B) > V(A) + V(B) \qquad (24\text{-}1)$$

where the post-merger or combined value, $V(A + B)$, is greater than the sum of the pre-merger values for firm A and firm B. In theory, owners of each firm should benefit from such a combination with the relative degree of benefit, depending on the relative bargaining strengths of each firm. This creation of added value through merger and acquisition is the result of *synergy* (i.e., the combined value after merger is greater than the sum of pre-merger parts). The reasons or explanations for synergy most frequently cited by the managements of firms engaging in mergers and acquisitions include economies of scale, management skills, tax factors, lower financing costs, and risk reduction.

synergy

Operating Savings

Certain mergers do offer the opportunities for economies of scale in production or distribution activities. For example, the potential for operating economies would be expected to be high for firms involved in horizontal mergers and acquisitions. Production economies might be achieved when product demand is combined for two firms operating in the same geographic markets. Consolidation of corporate-wide tasks, such as corporate accounting, is also cited as a source of cost savings. Marketing or distribution economies also may be achieved by consolidating these systems for firms joining in horizontal mergers.[1]

Operating economies also are possible in vertical mergers. By integrating and streamlining various stages of production, operating economies may result in a post-merger value that is greater than the sum of the pre-merger firm values. The streamlining of previous buyer-seller relationships could lower inventory carrying costs and possibly eliminate some middle-person markups. Thus a variety of operating economies is at least potentially available in vertical mergers.[2]

Certain types of conglomerate mergers also may involve an opportunity for some degree of operating economies. For example, production economies might be available for firms joining in market extension mergers. Recall that these mergers consist of firms producing the same products and selling the products in different markets prior to merging. Also recall that product extension mergers are comprised of firms that have functionally related production or distribution systems. Thus, while these firms do not handle directly competing products, there may still exist various opportunities for operating economies. Only in so-called pure conglomerate mergers involving the combining of essentially unrelated firms would the possibility of operating economies be highly unlikely.

Managerial Skills

Some mergers and acquisitions may take place for purposes of spreading existing managerial talents or skills over the operation of firms characterized by inefficient performance. For example, an argument made by acquirers during the early 1980s was that they would be able to turn around the relatively poor performance of many of the firms they were acquiring by extending or transferring their superior managerial skills to these firms. However, evidence on the success of these efforts is inconclusive.

Tax Factors

Tax-loss carry-forwards can represent an important reason for merging. For example, a highly profitable firm might seek to acquire a firm having a large tax-loss carry-forward (that otherwise might not be used in order to

---

[1]In addition to possible operating economies, horizontal mergers may offer the opportunity for increased market or monopoly powers by eliminating direct competition. Early antitrust-antimerger legislation directed at monopoly practices included the Sherman Act of 1890 and the Clayton Act of 1914. The Federal Trade Commission Act also was passed in 1914.

[2]Vertical integration through mergers and acquisitions also offers the opportunity for possible increased market or monopoly powers. To restrict vertical and horizontal mergers further, the Celler-Kefauver amendment to the Clayton Act was passed in 1950. Since then the Justice Department and Federal Trade Commission have actively investigated recent merger and acquisition activities.

reduce its taxable income for a period of years). The result could be an improved EPS on a combined basis. Of course, the benefits of such a merger would be short-lived unless the reasons for the tax-loss carry-forward can be corrected — possibly through the transferring of better managerial skills.

Lower Financing Costs

It is sometimes argued that mergers might result in a post-merger lowering of the cost of capital. For example, if one of the combining firms has unused debt capacity, the post-merger combined cost of capital might be lower than the weighted average of the two costs of capital if debt funds are used to consummate the merger.

Some financial economies also might be forthcoming in terms of the costs associated with the obtaining of external debt and equity financing. For example, there are certain flotation or issuing cost economies; i.e., larger security issues have lower flotation cost percentages. Thus, flotation or issuing costs might be reduced after two relatively small firms are combined.

Possibly even more important, financial economies might accrue as a result of improved marketability. Closely held firms find it very difficult and costly to tap external sources of funds. By merging with a firm that is well established in the marketplace, the resulting combined post-merger cost of capital might be lower than the average of the two pre-merger costs of capital. Financial economies also might accrue if, after a merger, the combined firm is large enough to attract institutional investors whereas neither firm was able to do so prior to the merger.

Risk Reduction

As conglomerate mergers became increasingly prevalent during the post-World War II merger movement, an argument was made that, through diversification, a merger reduces the risk of the residual owners. This argument parallels the discussion of portfolio diversification and risk implications in Chapter 6. Proponents contend that risk is reduced by reducing the variability of cash flows and earnings, and this, in turn, causes the value of the merged firm to exceed the values of the companies operating independently.

Of course, unless cash flows are perfectly positively correlated, the merger of two firms will result in a narrower dispersion of expected cash flows. This lower variability implies a lesser likelihood of financial distress and possible bankruptcy. Since investors are risk averse, they view this favorably. However, the argument of reduced risk and thus greater value through merger diversification efforts is countered by the recognition that investors can achieve the same result at less expense by diversifying their own investment portfolios. Hence, they will not pay anything extra to have a firm do this for them through conglomerate mergers and acquisitions.

To summarize, risk reduction through conglomerate mergers is not likely to raise the post-merger combined value. A lowering of risk should be offset by a comparable reduction in expected returns in the market-place when the risk-return trade-off relationship is viewed in an efficient market setting.

However, portfolio diversification may reduce the probabilities of financial distress and bankruptcy and thus be of value to investors as well as managers. Furthermore, reduced cash flow variability may be matched by the willingness of lenders to increase the firm's debt capacity. This can be viewed as a form of financial synergy that could lead to a lower post-merger cost of capital, in that more debt could be added to the post-merger capital structure. Thus, lower bankruptcy costs and the ability to use more debt because of decreased variability in operating cash flows could cause the value of the merged firm to be greater than the sum of the pre-merger parts.

DETERMINING A VALUE FOR AN ACQUISITION

Capital budgeting principles similar to those discussed in Chapters 14 and 15 can be applied to determine the maximum dollar price that can be justified for a potential acquisition. This valuation process can be illustrated with the following example.

Example

Assume that the Chaulk Manufacturing Company is considering the acquisition of the Vortex Machines Corporation. Vortex forecasts sales of $4 million, total assets of $3.5 million, and total liabilities and debt of $1.5 million for this year. The firm also projects annual cash earnings before depreciation and taxes (CEBDT) of $500,000 and annual depreciation of $100,000. It is in the 34-percent tax bracket.

Chaulk's management anticipates that it will be able to achieve certain economies or synergy and thus increase Vortex's annual earnings before depreciation and taxes by $100,000 without altering Vortex's sales, assets, or debt mix. Chaulk's weighted average cost of capital is 10 percent, and the acquisition of Vortex Machines is not expected to cause a change in this required rate of return or discount rate.

The analysis would begin by estimating the future annual cash flows from the pertinent data for Vortex Machines shown in Table 24-2:

TABLE 24-2 Vortex Machines Corp.

	Without Merger	With Merger
Cash earnings before depreciation and taxes (pre-merger)	$500,000	$500,000
Additional savings (synergy related)	—	100,000
Adjusted annual CEBDT	500,000	600,000
Less: depreciation	100,000	100,000
Cash earnings before taxes	400,000	500,000
Less: taxes (34%)	136,000	170,000
Cash earnings after taxes	$264,000	$330,000

Annual after-tax cash flows if the merger takes place are estimated at $430,000 (cash earnings after taxes of $330,000 plus depreciation of $100,000) compared with $364,000 if there is no merger.

If the $430,000 annual cash flow is expected to occur indefinitely into the future, the present value of this stream would be estimated as was done for cash flows associated with perpetual securities in Chapter 5. In this case, Vortex's $430,000 perpetual cash flows would be divided by Chaulk's 10-percent cost of capital as follows:

$$\text{Present Value of Cash Flow Stream} = \frac{\$430,000}{.10} = \$4.3 \text{ million}$$

Thus, Vortex's future cash flow stream is worth a maximum of $4.3 million to Chaulk. However, since Chaulk will be absorbing Vortex's $1.5 million in liabilities and debt, the maximum price that could be justified for the purchase of Vortex Machines' common equity or stock is $2.8 million ($4.3 million − $1.5 million).

It is important to recognize that other developments could alter the price Chaulk would be willing to pay for Vortex. For example, if the acquisition of Vortex would be expected to lower Chaulk's post-merger weighted average cost of capital (e.g., the acquisition could lead to a more optimal capital structure) to, say 9.5 percent, a higher purchase price could be justified. Under this scenario, the present value of cash flows would be:

$$\$430,000 \div .095 = \$4.5 \text{ million}$$

After subtracting the $1.5 in liabilities and debt being absorbed from the present value cash flow stream of $4.5 million, Chaulk could justifiably pay up to $3.0 million to Vortex's common stockholders.

One may also determine the maximum price to be paid for an acquisition by using the common stock dividend discount model described in Chapter 5 as long as there is an active market for the stock of the to-be-acquired firm.

Example

Assume that if the merger were to take place and the expected synergy occurs, Chaulk estimates Vortex's EPS this year to be $3.00 ($330,000 in net income divided by 110,000 shares outstanding). Vortex plans to pay out 40 percent of its earnings in cash dividends, or $1.20 per share. Further assume that Chaulk Manufacturing has forecasted Vortex's earnings and cash dividends to grow at a long-run 6-percent annual compound rate.

In addition, to determine the value of Vortex to Chaulk, one would discount Vortex's future cash dividends at the rate of return required by Chaulk. If Vortex is comparable in risk to Chaulk and is not expected to alter Chaulk's capital structure significantly, the cash dividend stream would be discounted at Chaulk's 10-percent cost of capital.

To illustrate this process of valuation, first recall that the intrinsic value formula can be stated as:

$$P_o = \frac{D_1}{k - g} \tag{24-2}$$

where P_o is the intrinsic value of the company per share; D_1 is the cash dividend expected for next year, k is the required rate of return or discount rate reflecting the appropriate risk class, and g is the long-run compound rate of growth in dividends (and stock prices). Using the data for Vortex gives:

$$P_o = \frac{\$1.20}{.10 - .06} = \frac{\$1.20}{.04} = \$30.00$$

Thus, under the assumptions for this scenario, Chaulk Manufacturing could justify paying a maximum of $30 per share for the stock of the Vortex Machines Corporation. This would amount to a maximum aggregate price of $3 million ($30 times 100,000 shares) for Vortex common equity.

Equity values differ in the above illustrations because of differing assumptions made under each scenario. In some cases, management may choose to use a "most likely" or "expected" maximum value estimate. For example, even though equity value estimates ranged from a low of $2.5 million to a high of about $3.3 million, Chaulk's management may set a maximum purchase price (based on an expected value) of $3.0 million.

MERGER EXCHANGE RATIOS

In most mergers, the common stock of the acquired firm is retired through an exchange of cash or securities by the surviving or acquiring firm.

While many firms are acquired for cash and/or nonvoting securities (debt or preferred stock), many mergers are consummated through the exchange of common stocks. By exchanging securities of "like kind" (shares of voting common stock), the acquired firm stockholders do not declare taxable gains or losses on their holdings until they sell the shares received from the acquiring firm. In mergers where acquired-firm stockholders receive cash or securities viewed as the equivalent of cash, gains or losses are taxable in the year that the merger takes place. Thus selling stockholders may prefer exchange terms that allow them to defer tax liabilities. In addition, the choice of exchange terms influences the accounting methods that may be used for recording mergers and acquisitions, as will be seen shortly.

Let us now return to the Chaulk Manufacturing and Vortex Machines merger example to illustrate the process of determining common stock exchange ratios. Table 24-3 contains some selected pre-merger financial and accounting data for the two firms for the most recent fiscal year:

TABLE 24-3		
	Chaulk Manufacturing	Vortex Machines
Net sales	$12,000,000	$3,700,000
Net income	1,000,000	264,000
Total assets	10,000,000	3,300,000
Common equity	5,500,000	1,900,000
Shares outstanding	300,000	110,000
Earnings per share	3.33	2.40
Price/earnings multiple	12	10
Market price	$40	$24

A starting point for determining a common stock *exchange ratio* is the use of the pre-merger stock or market prices for each firm. Vortex's common stock is currently selling for $24 per share while Chaulk's stock is $40 per share. Thus Chaulk might offer to exchange .60 shares ($24/$40) of its common stock for each share of Vortex's common stock. This means that a Vortex stockholder would be giving up a share of stock worth $24 for six-tenths of a share of stock trading at $40 which is also worth $24 (.60 × $40). An exchange based on current market prices thus is nothing more than swapping of securities of equal value.

exchange ratio

merger premium

In most instances, however, it is unlikely that stockholders in firms that are acquisition candidates will be willing to give up their shares for shares in another firm of equal value. An exception might occur if the future growth prospects are much greater for the acquiring firm than for the to-be-acquired firm. Otherwise, the stockholders in acquisition candidate firms will expect compensation value that is greater than the current pre-merger value of their stock holdings. The payment of cash and/or securities with a value above the acquisition candidate's market value results in the payment of a premium that is usually stated on a percentage basis. For example, if Chaulk exchanged shares with Vortex on a one-for-one basis, Vortex's stockholders would be receiving $40 in Chaulk's stock for each share of their own stock worth $24. Thus a Vortex stockholder would be receiving $16 ($40 − $24) premium per share or a *merger premium percentage* of 66.7 percent [($16/24) × 100].

Recall that, under efficient capital market conditions, existing stock prices should reflect the "real" or intrinsic value of firms based on the then available information. Consequently, merger premiums should not be paid unless the acquiring firm can justify an acquisition price or intrinsic value for the acquisition candidate higher than the candidate's current market price. Higher values may be justified on the basis of operating or financial economies, tax considerations, and even the ability to acquire needed managerial skills. For example, earlier Vortex's intrinsic stock value was estimated to be $30 per share to Chaulk on the basis that Chaulk's management believed operating economies resulting from the two firms merging would raise Vortex's value. This $30-per-share value sets the upper limit or maximum purchase price that Chaulk can justify paying for Vortex. This would amount to a maximum $6 ($30 − $24) premium per share, or a merger premium percentage of 25 percent [($6/$24) × 100].

It is now possible to set a range of plausible values for exchange purposes. The lower limit is set by the acquisition candidate's current stock price of $24 and would involve the payment of a zero premium.[3] The upper limit is the previously determined $30 value per share, or a 25-percent merger premium. One may also examine the range of exchange possibilities in terms of common stock exchange ratios. Recall that a $24 exchange value, if offered by Chaulk, would result in an exchange ratio of .60 shares of Chaulk's common stock for each share of Vortex's stock. If a $30 exchange value were used instead, Chaulk would offer .75 shares ($30/$40) of its stock per share of Vortex's stock. This range of plausible exchange values, merger premiums, and exchange ratios can be summarized as shown in Table 24-4:

---

[3]It is unlikely that most acquisition candidate stockholders would be willing to accept securities with a value less than the price of their own common stock. An exception might occur if a to-be-acquired firm is in financial distress while the performance outlook for the acquirer is very bright.

TABLE 24-4

	Market Value Basis	Intrinsic Value Basis
Exchange value (Vortex's stock)	$24	$30
Merger premium percentage	0%	25%
Exchange ratio (Chaulk's stock for Vortex's stock)	.60:1	.75:1

The final common stock exchange ratio or terms will be determined through the process of merger negotiation. Each merger party would be expected to focus on its strengths while playing down any weaknesses. Expected returns relative to risk should be important to the negotiation process. Obviously stockholder returns are provided through dividend yield and/or capital appreciation over time and long-run realized returns should be commensurate with the riskiness of the investment. When differences exist between merging firms in terms of operating and financial risk, the management of the financially stronger firm will bargain for better relative terms. For example, if the acquiring firm is less risky than the acquisition candidate, then the acquirer's management will bargain for an exchange ratio that is toward the lower limit (market value). A financially stronger acquisition candidate (e.g., in terms of liquidity and capital structure positions) would negotiate for a more beneficial exchange ratio in the form of higher returns as compensation for accepting stock in a riskier firm.

On the return side, there also may be room for substantial negotiation opportunities. While some negotiation may take place concerning possible differences in the dollar amount of cash dividend payments between merging firms because of the clientele effect of stockholders, the more important bargaining issue focuses on growth rates. A merging firm that has relatively greater growth opportunities in dividends, earnings, and stock prices should exercise a stronger bargaining position. Recall that an important determinant of the relative size of P/E ratios as of a point in time is expected growth in earnings. Thus, other things being equal, more rapidly growing firms would be expected to have relatively higher P/E ratios and should be in stronger merger negotiation position. An acquiring firm with a relatively stronger growth position should be able to bargain for the payment of a lower merger premium, whereas, if the acquisition candidate has greater relative growth opportunities, its management would argue for a higher merger premium.

In the case of possible merger synergy benefits, the question of how these benefits should accrue to stockholders of the acquiring firm versus those of the to-be-acquired firm is a complex one. For example, Chaulk Manufacturing expects that operating economies of $100,000 before taxes will occur if it acquires Vortex Machines. If Chaulk wishes to retain all of these benefits for its stockholders, it would exchange common stocks with Vortex only on the basis of stock prices or market values. Of course, the unlikelihood that Vortex's stockholders would accept an exchange ratio of .60:1 has already been acknowledged. The other extreme would be for Chaulk to pass on all merger synergy benefits and argue for, say, an exchange ratio of .70 shares of Chaulk for each share of Vortex. Only through actual merger bargaining will a final exchange ratio be determined.

FINANCIAL REPORTING FOR MERGERS

When two firms merge, the acquiring firm's balance sheet must be adjusted to reflect the acquisition of the acquired firm's balance-sheet accounts as well as the compensation paid by the acquirer. There are two accounting methods for handling a merger. The *pooling of interests method* pools the two firms' assets and liabilities and requires the adjustment of stockholders' equity according to the specified merger terms. In contrast the *purchase method* requires the revaluation of the acquired firm's assets; and, in the event that a purchase price exceeds the revised asset values, the difference is reported on the acquiring firm's balance sheet as *good will.*

pooling of interests method

purchase method

good will

The accounting profession establishes the guidelines for determining which accounting method can be used for a specific merger. In general, the pooling of interests method can be used if the acquiring firm exchanges its voting common stock for at least 90 percent of the acquired firm's outstanding voting stock. Otherwise the purchase method is likely to be required.

Table 24-5 illustrates the difference between the two accounting methods for the acquisition of Vortex Machines by Chaulk Manufacturing.

Assume that Chaulk agrees to acquire Vortex's common stock for $2,800,000 (70,000 shares valued at $40 per share) based on an exchange ratio of .70:1.

Pooling of Interests

Under the pooling of interests method, Vortex's assets would be added to Chaulk's assets to reflect post-merger figures. The same process would be followed for determining the post-merger combined liabilities. In terms of the common equity section, the common stock account would reflect 370,000 Chaulk shares outstanding (300,000 previously outstanding plus the 70,000 additional shares issued for Vortex's shares) times the $5 par value. And, since the sum of the common stock and capital surplus accounts must still equal $4,000,000 (Chaulk's $3,000,000 plus Vortex's $1,000,000 pre-merger figures), the post-merger capital surplus figure must be adjusted upward to $2,150,000 ($4,000,000 − $1,850,000). Notice that, had the exchange ratio been greater than one-to-one in the example, the combined capital surplus would have been adjusted downward. The final

	Pre-merger		Post-merger	
	Chaulk Manufacturing	Vortex Machines	Purchase Method	Pooling of Interests Method
Assets				
Current assets	$ 5,000,000	$1,600,000	$ 6,600,000	$ 6,600,000
Fixed assets, net	5,000,000	1,700,000	7,000,000**	6,700,000
Good will			600,000	
Total assets	$10,000,000	$3,300,000	$14,200,000	$13,300,000
Liabilities and Equity				
Current liabilities	$ 2,000,000	$ 600,000	$ 2,600,000	$ 2,600,000
Long-term debt	2,500,000	800,000	3,300,000	3,300,000
Common stock ($5 par)				
Chaulk shares—300,000	1,500,000			
Vortex shares—110,000		500,000		
Post-merger shares—370,000*			1,850,000	1,850,000
Capital surplus	1,500,000	500,000	3,950,000	2,150,000
Retained earnings	2,500,000	900,000	2,500,000	3,400,000
Total liabilities & equity	$10,000,000	$3,300,000	$14,200,000	$13,300,000

Note: Necessary post-merger changes in the capital surplus and retained earnings accounts are discussed in the accompanying text materials.
*Based on the assumption that Chaulk acquires Vortex's common stock for $2,800,000 (70,000 shares valued at $40 per share) which is an exchange ratio of .70:1.
**Under the purchase method Vortex's fixed assets are revalued upwards by $300,000. Good will is the result of $2,800,000 purchase price less net fixed asset value of $2,200,000 (i.e., Vortex's revalued assets of $3,600,000 less total liabilities of $1,400,000).

step is to sum the retained earnings accounts under the pooling of interests method.

Purchase

If, instead, the merger had been treated as a purchase, Chaulk first would have revalued Vortex's assets to reflect their current "fair" values. For example, assume that Vortex's fixed assets were revalued upward by $300,000 to $2,000,000 but that current assets remained at $1,600,000. This gives a total asset value for Vortex of $3,600,000 and total liabilities of $1,400,000. The amount of good will that will have to be recorded now can be determined, as shown in Table 24-6. Thus total assets will be higher by $900,000 under the purchase method ($300,000 upward valuation of fixed assets plus $600,000 in good will).

The liabilities of the two firms can be combined directly as was done under the pooling of interests method. However, under the purchase

TABLE 24-6

Market value of Vortex's common stock		$2,800,000
Vortex's revised asset value	$3,600,000	
Less: Vortex's total liabilities	1,400,000	
Net value of Vortex's assets		2,200,000
Good will to be recorded by Chaulk		$600,000

method, all of Vortex's common equity is eliminated. Thus the only post-merger retained earnings will be Chaulk's pre-merger $2,500,000 amount. The common stock account will be $1,850,000 ($370,000 shares times the $5 par value). The remainder, $3,950,000 will be allocated to the capital surplus account.

METHODS OF AVOIDING ACQUISITION

Mergers are not always a result of mutual consent. If it is rebuffed by management in its attempt to acquire another company, an acquisition-minded concern may appeal directly to the shareholders of the desired company by a public offer to purchase their shares. Stockholders may be asked to tender (i.e., offer to sell) their shares for cash or in exchange for securities. The use of *tender offers* is preferred to a proxy contest because it is relatively less costly and produces a quick resolution of the battle for control.

tender offer

There are many methods available to fight off a hostile takeover. A common tactic is quickly to find an alternate partner, or "white knight" (the term currently in vogue). For example, when GreatAmerica Corp. sought control of Glidden Co. by asking for tenders on its common stock at $30 per share, Glidden's management quickly arranged a merger with SCM Corporation. The exchange of common stock of SCM for Glidden was valued at $35 per share. Similarly, Commercial Credit Co. successfully fended off seizure by Loew's Theatres, Inc., by merging with the Control Data Corporation. Loew's had to be content with a profit of over $20 million on the shares it had previously acquired.

Another means of avoiding a takeover is to acquire a firm that would make a merger with the raider questionable from a legal point of view. Thus, when B. F. Goodrich was attempting to fend off a tender offer from Northwest Industries, a holding company that included a railroad among its subsidiaries, Goodrich acquired Motor Freight Corp., a trucking concern. The Interstate Commerce Commission could be counted on to view a merger of a railroad and trucking company as objectionable. Similarly, a company might acquire a firm in the same line of business as that of the raider. Then it could complain to the Justice Department that a merger with the corporate raider should be blocked as a violation of antitrust laws.

Still another tactic is to amend articles of incorporation to require approval of a merger by a greater proportion (a supermajority) of the shareholders. Corporations have changed the procedure for electing directors so that only one-third are to be elected each year, thereby substantially delaying any takeover. For example, Goodrich introduced staggered terms for its directors so that Northwest could not possibly win a majority of the board for two years. The raider's voting control may also be diluted by issuing additional common stock in exchange for securities of other companies.

Finally, management of the raided company typically engages in a vigorous campaign of letters and advertisements to its stockholders (at their expense) decrying the offer. Lawsuits against the raider are frequently instituted.

FINANCIAL DISTRESS AND BUSINESS FAILURE

There were more than 40,000 business failures in 1984 in the United States. Even though economic conditions have a major impact on the likelihood of bankruptcy, the single most important factor continues to be mismanagement due to a lack of basic managerial skills.

This section deals with voluntary and involuntary adjustments that may be used during periods of financial distress. However, because of the very complex legal issues involved with bankruptcy, reorganization, and liquidation topics, the discussion must be very limited.

VOLUNTARY ADJUSTMENTS

Depending on the degree of financial distress, management may still be able to make certain voluntary adjustments in an effort to avoid failure. These types of voluntary adjustments are discussed here. They will be followed by a discussion of possible involuntary, or forced, adjustments.

Reduction of Expenditures

At the first sign of impending difficulty in meeting obligations to creditors, the financial manager should take steps to adjust cash flows to fulfill commitments. On the one hand, a firm may attempt to increase cash inflow by selling accounts receivable to a factor or by reducing inventories through special sales. It may be possible to sell all or a portion of the plant and then lease the necessary facilities. In recent years some of the conglomerates that have faced difficulties in meeting payments on their debts have been forced to sell entire divisions to raise needed cash, such as CBS, when it sold its publishing divisions.

On the other hand, it may also be possible to reduce cash outflows by cutting salaries and eliminating dividends to preferred and residual owners. Expenditures for advertising, remodeling, new equipment, and other activities, should often be postponed. Payments to trade creditors may be slowed, although this inevitably incurs damage to the company's credit reputation. It may be possible to substitute some intermediate or long-term debt for existing short-term debt. This process is called *funding*, in contrast with *re*funding, which involves the replacement of one long-term debt issue with another.

Rescheduling Debt Payments

In many cases, the adjustments of cash flows prove to be insufficient to deal with the financial emergency. It then becomes necessary to request creditors to adjust their claims to come within the limits of the firm's financial abilities. The creditors can refuse, forcing the liquidation or reorganization of the business.

Subordination

subordination

Sometimes a company has borrowed funds from its owners or officers. In order to give other creditors, such as the bank, a senior claim on assets in the event of liquidation, the owners and officers may agree to a *subordination* of their claims. This arrangement may so strengthen the position of the senior creditors that they will agree not to demand prompt settlement of their claims. This type of arrangement is the origin of the subordinated debentures discussed in Chapter 22.

Extension

extension

It may be possible to persuade short- or long-term creditors to agree to an *extension:* that is, to a postponement of the maturity of the debt. Such arrangements are most typically made by a small business with its major trade creditors. In return for their agreement to extend the term of their credit, creditors often ask for concessions and some form of assurance that the debt will be paid under the new and longer terms. For example, trade creditors may demand promissory notes, which bear interest and mature at regular intervals. The firm may also have to agree not to increase officers' salaries or pay dividends. In the infrequent cases of extensions of long-term debt, bondholders have been offered a higher interest rate, mortgage security, conversion privileges, and other inducements.

Composition

A more extreme form of adjustment of obligations to meet financial capabilities is a *composition*. Under this type of arrangement creditors agree to accept a partial payment in final settlement of their claims, say 60 cents on the dollar. A portion of the settlement is frequently in the form of promissory notes. Compositions are most characteristic of small companies because of the difficulty of persuading the more numerous and widely-scattered creditors of large corporations to agree to such arrangements. Creditors will agree to such a plan only if they believe they will collect more than by forcing bankruptcy.

composition

Creditor's Committee

A business may be forced to be operated by a *creditor's committee* until sufficient funds have been generated to repay creditors or until a satisfactory composition can be arranged. The aim of such a committee is to enable the business to recover from some random error in management, and it is seldom able to cure more fundamental managerial ills that may have led to the difficulty.

creditor's committee

In each of these cases, individual creditors are not required to accept the proposed adjustment. Because these arrangements are voluntary, there is no legal means of enforcing the will of the majority upon the minority. Any one creditor is entitled to reject the proposal and, if his or her rightful claims are not met, to force the company into liquidation or reorganization. Rather than face this hazard, creditors agreeing to the adjustment often permit payment in full of small creditors who refuse to join the agreement. Thus there is even some incentive for small creditors to dissent. However, these selfish ends cannot be pushed too far, since the owners may always adopt the alternative of liquidation.

Recapitalization

This form of voluntary adjustment includes the elimination of dividend accumulations on preferred stock, stock splits, and the voluntary exchange of one type of security for another.

INVOLUNTARY ADJUSTMENTS

The treatment of business concerns in financial distress is governed by a Federal law, the Bankruptcy Act of 1978. The objective of the act is relatively simple. Once the company is placed in the hands of the court, the situation is "frozen." That is, the *status quo* is temporarily preserved so that no one creditor or group of creditors can make off with an unfair share of the assets. Time is granted to study the situation to determine whether the company can be preserved as a going concern or whether it should be liquidated. If it is possible to preserve the company as a going concern, an opportunity is provided to reduce the amount and cost of debt to a level the company can manage. In this process of scaling down the claims of owners and creditors, their rights are under the protection of the court, so that the priority of their claims on income and assets are supported insofar as possible.

Arrangement

Chapter 11 of the Bankruptcy Act is designed for use by relatively small corporations and partnerships. The chapter applies only to the settlement of unsecured debts; secured obligations are not affected. After the court has accepted a petition by the debtor for reorganization under Chapter 11, it *receiver* may appoint a *receiver* to manage the firm or leave it in the hands of the existing management. The plan proposed by the debtor for settlement of unsecured debt must be accepted by a majority of creditors in number and amount of claims filed, but then the remaining creditors must accept the plan. Note the contrast with the voluntary settlements discussed earlier. In addition, the court must determine that the proposed arrangement is feasible and "for the best interest of creditors."

Reorganization and Liquidation

When there are publicly held securities and a comprehensive reorganization is needed, adjustment usually takes place under Chapter 10 of the Bankruptcy Act. Railroads are reorganized under Section 77 of the Act.[4]

A debtor may voluntarily petition to be adjudged a bankrupt. Alternatively, creditors may seek to have the proper Federal district court declare the debtor a bankrupt under the following circumstances:

1. The debtor's total debts are $1,000 or more.

2. If there are 12 or more creditors, the petition must be signed by three or more with total claims of $500 or more. (If there are fewer, any one creditor owed $500 or more may file.)

act of bankruptcy
3. The debtor has committed an *act of bankruptcy* within the preceding four months. The most important and common act of bankruptcy is the debtor's admission in writing that he or she cannot pay the debts and is willing to be adjudged a bankrupt. Others involve concealment of assets, preferential transfer of some assets to creditors, and various other actions signifying impending doom.

---

[4]The chief difference is the involvement of the Interstate Commerce Commission rather than the Securities and Exchange Commission. The ICC must approve the trustee(s) and the reorganization plan.

If the court finds that the corporation is indeed insolvent or unable to meet maturing debts, it will appoint a trustee to administer the affairs of the corporation. When the debts are greater than $250,000, the court must appoint a trustee who has no connection with the debtor; in other cases the court may either appoint a disinterested trustee or leave the company in the hands of the current management. The trustee has four main tasks:

1. Prepare a compilation of the assets and liabilities of the corporation and guard the assets for the protection of the creditors and owners.

2. By a comparison of its going-concern value and liquidation value, determine whether or not the firm should be liquidated or reorganized.

3. If it is to be liquidated, convert the assets into cash and distribute the cash to creditors and owners in accordance with the rule of absolute priority.

4. If it is to be reorganized, draw up a plan of reorganization with the advice of creditors and stockholders that is fair and feasible.

Liquidating Value Vs. Going-Concern Value

It will be recalled that, in the case of a proposed business combination, the object was to compare the economic value of the company as an independent, going concern to its value in combination with another company. The latter value was determined by the contribution of the individual company to the earnings of the combination. In cases of financial strain, the first objective is to compare the value of the going concern to its value when liquidated. If the liquidating value exceeds the going concern value, the presumption is in favor of liquidation. At times the answer to this question will not determine the final decision. For example, a trade creditor may not wish to gain a reputation for forcing customers into liquidation. However, the creditor must first answer the question so that the cost of preserving a reputation for dealing reasonably with customers is known.

In considering the value of the company *as a going concern,* a creditor must ask why the company got into financial difficulty. Was it a basic fault of management or some situation that might be remedied given time and understanding creditors? Will it be "throwing good money after bad" to continue with the situation? The *liquidating value* of the company is generally much easier to calculate. Fixed assets can usually be sold only at a considerable discount from their book value, depending upon their specialization and the nature of the market. Inventories and accounts receivable will probably bring still more in relation to their book values.

As an application of this principle, small retail stores are frequently liquidated in times of financial strain. If mismanagement has brought a small hardware store into difficulties, there is probably little hope of improvement. After the remedial action — extension, composition, reorganization — the same owner-manager may still be in control. If this is the prospect, the going-concern value cannot be very high. In contrast, most of the assets can probably be sold without excessive losses. If the store leases its space, the assets are largely in the form of inventories and accounts receivable, which may be liquidated fairly readily. Thus the creditors find that the liquidating value exceeds the going-concern value and may reject remedies that involve sacrifices on their part in order to maintain the company as a going concern. On the other hand, the liquidating value of a steel mill is very low because of the high proportion of specialized, fixed assets. Even though the going-concern value is not very high, it is still not as low as the liquidating value. As a result, steel companies that fall into financial difficulties are usually reorganized rather than liquidated.

Rule of Absolute Priority

absolute priority

In a liquidation or reorganization under Chapter 10 of the Bankruptcy Act, claims of creditors and owners must usually be satisfied in accordance with the *rule of absolute priority*. [5] Under this rule senior claims on assets must be settled in full before anything is granted to junior claimants. Thus all creditors must have their claims settled in full before any payments are made to preferred owners, and preferred owners must receive all to which they are entitled before anything is paid to the residual owners. There may also be senior and junior creditors. If there are subordinated debentures outstanding, claims of all senior creditors must be satisfied before any payments are made to the holders of subordinated debentures. The application of the rule of absolute priority is relatively simple in the case of liquidation, but it involves further problems of valuation in the case of reorganization.

Let us consider first the treatment of creditors and owners in the case of liquidation. The required ordering of claims is as follows:

1. Certain priority claims in the order shown.
   a) Costs incurred by the trustee in preserving and administering the assets.
   b) Wages earned within three months before the commencement of bankruptcy proceedings, not exceeding $600 for each claimant.
   c) Reasonable costs incurred by creditors to block an unjustified arrangement or discharge of the bankrupt.
   d) Federal, state, and local taxes.
   e) Certain debts that have been given special priority, such as unpaid rent within three months prior to bankruptcy.

---

[5] In contrast, under Chapter 11 the plan must be "for the best interest of creditors." Because companies under this chapter are often closely held, it may well be in the best interest of creditors to allow the managers-owners to retain a share of the business. Were the reorganization under Chapter 10, application of the rule of absolute priority would wipe them out. Some large concerns also have sought refuge under Chapter 11 in an attempt to preserve some portion of the common stockholders' interest.

2. Secured creditors. Proceeds from assets in which these creditors have a security interest are applied first to senior liens (e.g., first mortgage holders) and then in order to those with junior liens. To the extent that the proceeds are inadequate to satisfy the secured creditors, they become unsecured creditors.

3. Unsecured and subordinated creditors.[6]

4. Preferred owners.

5. Residual owners.

A simple illustration may clarify the application of the rule. Assume that the following amounts are realized from the liquidation of assets to satisfy the claims shown in Table 24-7:

TABLE 24-7

Net cash realized from sale of assets (after settlement of priority claims):		Mortgage bonds (secured by plant and equipment)	$800,000
		Unsecured debts	400,000
Plant and equipment	$600,000	Common stock & surplus	
Other assets	300,000	(deficit)	($700,000)
Cash available	900,000		

Under the rule of absolute priority, the available cash of $900,000 would be distributed as shown in Table 24-8:

TABLE 24-8

Claim of mortgage bonds	$800,000
Cash from sale of pledged assets	600,000
Unsatisfied claim of mortgage bonds	200,000
Claims of unsecured creditors	400,000
Total unsecured claims	600,000
Settlement of unsecured claims: $\frac{\$300,000}{\$600,000}$, or at rate of 50 percent.	
Allocation of cash:	
Bondholders	$700,000 ($600,000 + 50% × $200,000)
Unsecured creditors	200,000 (50% × $400,000)
Common stockholders	0
Total	$900,000

---

[6]For the treatment of subordinated debenture holders, see Chapter 23.

Now let us turn to the adjustment of claims of creditors and owners in the case of a reorganization. It has been shown that settlement of claims under the rule of absolute priority in the case of liquidation is relatively simple. Once the claims have been verified and substantiated and the assets sold, there are two definite sets of figures — claims and cash. This simplicity is not characteristic of a reorganization. Although the claims are readily determined, the values that will be given in satisfaction of these claims are not. If a firm reorganizes, it will not be giving cash to existing security holders; it will be exchanging a new collection of securities for an old group of securities. It does not give them cash, but claims on assets. Whereas a debenture holder might be entitled to receive $1,000 in cash in liquidation, he or she might receive 10 shares of 5-percent preferred stock in a reorganization. The Bankruptcy Act states that creditors are entitled to *fair and equitable* treatment. $1000 in cash is "fair and equitable," but are 10 shares of preferred stock equally fair and equitable? This is the problem, and there are basically three steps involved in the application of valuation principles in reaching its solution.

First, the rate of earnings that can be expected if the company is to be maintained as a going concern must be determined. This estimate is made at an early stage in the proceedings, because it is necessary to determine whether it is better to liquidate the company or allow it to reorganize and continue in business. This process leads to the comparison of liquidating value and economic or going-concern value discussed earlier in this section.

Second, a capital structure must be formulated for the concern that can be supported by the estimated stream of earnings. In addition to requiring that the reorganization plan be fair and equitable, the Bankruptcy Act also requires that it be feasible. The present capital structure clearly will not do; the existing burden of debt is the cause of financial stress. In the case of a reorganization, emphasis must first be upon avoidance of risk. Fixed charges must be minimized so that the reorganized company can avoid falling back into financial difficulties. To relieve a company of fixed charges, trustees frequently propose the issue of income bonds, preferred stock, and common stock to replace a capital structure that was top-heavy with debt. The more serious the financial difficulty, the more likely are existing debts to be replaced by preferred and common stocks. Also, the planned capital structure must provide maneuverability. Since additional funds will probably be needed to rehabilitate the company, there must be "elbow room" in the financial structure. The equity base must be large enough to support the additional borrowings that will probably be needed. In short, the financial plan must be "feasible." The reorganized company should be able to live and prosper with the proposed capital structure for the foreseeable future.

Third, the value of the new securities must be determined and they must be exchanged for the old securities in accordance with the rule of absolute priority. When a trustee has finally evolved a plan, it must be submitted to the court for a hearing. If liabilities exceed $3 million, the judge must submit the proposal to the SEC for advice; he or she may request an opinion from the SEC in other cases. If the court and the SEC find the plan to be "fair, equitable, and feasible," it is then submitted to the creditors and stockholders for approval. To become effective, the plan must be accepted by two-thirds of the amount of each class of debt and by a majority of each class of stock. If the corporation is actually insolvent, that is, if liabilities exceed assets, the stockholders have no vote. When the plan is approved, minority interests must accept the proposal as well. Again, this coercion represents an important departure from voluntary readjustments, such as extensions and compositions.

SUMMARY

Corporate managers have been increasingly willing to expand or grow in recent years through the process of mergers and acquisitions. Ideally, the post-merger value should be greater than the sum of the two pre-merger market values, i.e., merger synergy should take place. Possible opportunities for synergy include taking advantage of operating economies (production, marketing, or distribution economies), managerial skills, tax implications, financial economies, and possibly even increased debt capacity through portfolio diversification efforts. In any case, growth through mergers, like internal growth, should be based on sound investment decisions that are designed to maximize owners' wealth. This can be accomplished by applying capital budgeting principles to determine the maximum dollar price that can be justified for a potential acquisition. This upper limit, coupled with a lower limit established by the acquisition candidate's pre-merger market value, establishes the range for negotiating actual exchange terms. Negotiation efforts likely would address pre-merger risk and return comparisons, as well as covering post-merger values expected to accrue to the acquired firm's stockholders versus the acquiring firm's stockholders.

Mismanagement due to a lack of basic managerial skills continues to be the primary reason for business failure. The problem of mismanagement becomes particularly acute during economic downturns, when there is less room for managerial error before firms suffer financial distress and possibly even bankruptcy. Relief of financial strain involves, as a first step, the comparison of the value of a firm as a going concern with its liquidating value. If the firm is worth more alive than dead, then steps must be taken to adjust downward the various claims on its assets. If the stress is not great, creditors may merely postpone the enforcement of their claims or voluntarily reduce their claims. However, in cases where creditors demand strict adherence to the terms of their contracts, involuntary or forced adjustments will require sacrifices to be made under court supervision. In Chapter 10 reorganizations, the rule of absolute priority prevails, and the reorganization plan must be "fair, equitable, and feasible." That is, creditors and owners must receive their fair share of a new group of securities that can be supported by projected earnings.

MULTIPLE CHOICE QUESTIONS

849

CHAPTER 24
MERGERS,
ACQUISITIONS, AND
BANKRUPTCY

1. A combination of firms involved in different stages of production of the same product is known as:

    a) Vertical merger
    b) Monopoly
    c) Horizontal merger
    d) Conglomerate merger

2. A conglomerate merger differs from a horizontal merger in that the former is:

    a) Vertically integrated
    b) In closely related lines of business
    c) In unrelated lines of business
    d) Illegal

3. The idea that 2 + 2 = 5 represents:

    a) Ratio analysis
    b) Improper financial accounting
    c) Synergy
    d) Diversification

4. The number of shares of common stock of the acquiring company that are to be exchanged for outstanding shares of the acquired corporation is known as:

    a) The P/E differential
    b) The market ratio
    c) The exchange ratio
    d) Good will

5. An extension permits a debtor:

    a) Additional loans
    b) To refund existing debt
    c) To sell common stock
    d) To postpone maturity of debt

6. Under a composition:

    a) The company is liquidated
    b) Debtors take ownership of the company
    c) The company temporarily ceases operations
    d) Creditors agree to accept partial payment

7. Under the rule of absolute priority:

    a) Senior debt is paid off last
    b) Shareholders get nothing until everybody else has been paid off
    c) Claims are paid off in the order in which they are filed
    d) Shareholders are paid off first

DISCUSSION QUESTIONS

1. Provide a brief description of the various forms of business combinations that may be undertaken. Also identify the three basic types of mergers and acquisitions along with their relative importance in major U.S. merger movements.

2. Several reasons are frequently given for engaging in mergers and acquisitions. Identify these and provide brief explanations.

3. Describe how a firm might determine a maximum price or value that it would be willing to pay for an acquisition.

4. Many mergers and acquisitions continue to be consummated through the exchange of common stocks. What factors would be important in arriving at a negotiated exchange ratio?

5. Identify and briefly describe the two basic accounting methods for handling the merger of two firms.

6. What are some of the voluntary adjustments that might be instituted by managers of firms in financial distress as a means of possibly avoiding failure?

7. In the event of forced adjustments on the part of firms suffering financial distress, which chapters of the Bankruptcy Act are likely to be appropriate? How do they differ? Describe the application of the rule of absolute priority.

SOLVED PROBLEMS

acquisition terms

SP-1. Given the following information for the Ajax Co. and Byrd Co:

	Ajax	Byrd
Net income	10,000,000	2,000,000
No. of shares	5,000,000	500,000
EPS	2.00	4.00
MPPS	30.00	40.00
P/E	15X	10X

a) Assume that Ajax tenders $48 per share in a stock-for-stock exchange.

   i. How many new shares will have to be issued?

   ii. Calculate the new EPS for the combined companies after the merger.

   iii. Assume that Ajax's P/E multiple does not change. Calculate the new price per share after the merger. How do you explain the result?

iv. Compare the situation of Byrd shareholders before and after the merger.
    v. Calculate the exchange ratio.
b) What is the maximum price per share (and P/E) that Ajax can afford to pay Byrd without reducing the market price per share of Ajax stock?
c) Assume that, instead of a stock-for-stock exchange, Ajax decides to offer cash for Byrd stock. If Ajax can borrow the amount needed at 10 percent, what is the maximum share price that could be offered without reducing the price of Ajax stock? Assume Ajax's P/E continues at 15X and that all operating and profit levels continue. Also assume that neither Ajax nor Byrd have any debt and that both are in a 40-percent tax bracket.

PROBLEMS

1. Given the following information for the Black Company and the Blue Company:

acquisition terms

	Black	Blue
Net income	$20,000,000	$5,000,000
No. of shares	5,000,000	500,000
EPS	$4.00	$10.00
MPPS	$80	$100
P/E	20X	10X

a) Assume that Black tenders $110 per share in a stock-for-stock exchange.
    i. How many new shares will have to be issued?
    ii. Calculate the new EPS for the combined companies after the merger.
    iii. Calculate the new price per share, assuming no change in Black's P/E multiple, after the merger. How do you explain the result?
    iv. Compare the situation of Blue shareholders before and after the merger.
    v. Calculate the exchange ratio.
b) What is the maximum price per share (and P/E) that Black can afford to pay Blue without reducing the market price per share of Black stock? (Assume Black's P/E multiple will not change).
c) Assume that, instead of a stock-for-stock exchange, Black decides to offer cash for Blue stock. If Black can borrow the amount needed

at 8 percent, what is the maximum share price that could be offered without reducing the price of Black's stock? Assume that Black's P/E multiple continues at 20 times and that all operating and profit levels continue. Also assume that neither Black nor Blue has any debt and that both companies are in a 34-percent tax bracket.

holding company

2. In the illustration of a holding company shown in the chapter, assume that the interest paid on long-term debt is 8 percent and the dividend rate on the preferred stock is 9 percent. Assume the corporate tax rate to be 50 percent.

   a) If each subsidiary had earnings before interest and taxes of $21 million, and all the earnings available were paid out, what would be the profits before taxes of the holding company?
   b) If EBIT of the subsidiaries fell by 10 percent, by what percentage would the profits before taxes of the parent company decline?

valuing an acquisition

3. The ReProm Corporation is considering the purchase of the CLAD Communications Corporation. The after-tax cash flows for CLAD Communications are estimated to be $2 million per year in the future. This forecast, made by ReProm, includes expected merger synergy benefits. CLAD currently has total assets of $10 million with 30 percent of the total assets being financed with debt funds. ReProm's pre-merger weighted average cost of capital is 14 percent.

   a) Based on ReProm's pre-merger cost of capital, what is the maximum purchase price that ReProm should be willing to pay for all of the CLAD common stock?
   b) Now assume that by acquiring CLAD Communications, ReProm will move toward an optimal capital structure such that its weighted average cost of capital will be 12 percent after the acquisition. Under these conditions, what would be ReProm's maximum purchase price for all of the CLAD common stock?
   c) Assume that cash flows for CLAD are estimated at $2 million for next year, will grow at a 10-percent annual rate for the following four years, and then will be level thereafter. Each dollar increase in cash flows will require a $.70 incremental investment in assets. Reestimate the maximum purchase price for CLAD that ReProm could justify, based on the use of a 12-percent discount or hurdle rate.

valuing an acquisition

4. The Magruder Extruder Corporation is considering the possible acquisition of the Forever Plastics Corporation. Following are the financial statements for the most recent fiscal year for the two corporations. Magruder Extruder currently has a 15 times price/earnings ratio and paid $2.17 in cash dividends per share last year. In contrast, Forever

Plastics' price/earnings ratio is 12 times and the firm paid cash dividends of $2.44 per share last year. Forever has 20,000 common stock shares outstanding and Magruder has 25,000.

Income Statements	Forever Plastics	Magruder Extruder
Net sales	$2,300,000	$2,500,000
Cost of goods sold	1,800,000	1,950,000
Gross profit	$ 500,000	$ 550,000
Gen., admin., & marketing	300,000	300,000
Depreciation	20,000	20,000
Interest	44,500	32,500
Earnings before taxes	$ 135,500	$ 197,500
Income taxes paid	54,200	79,000
Earnings after taxes	$ 81,300	$ 118,500
Preferred stk. dividends	—	10,000
Earnings available to common stockholders	$ 81,300	$ 108,500

Balance Sheets	Forever Plastics	Magruder Extruder
Cash	$ 24,000	$ 20,000
Accounts receivable	231,000	300,000
Inventory	425,000	500,000
Total current assets	$ 680,000	$ 820,000
Fixed assets	220,000	280,000
Total assets	$ 900,000	$1,100,000

	Forever Plastics	Magruder Extruder
Bank loan, 10%	$ 85,000	$ 85,000
Accounts payable	129,000	155,000
Accruals	48,000	65,000
Total current liabilities	$ 262,000	$ 305,000
Long-term debt, 12%	300,000	200,000
Preferred stk, 10%	—	100,000
Common stk, $10 par	200,000	250,000
Capital surplus	58,000	145,000
Retained earnings	80,000	100,000
Total liabilities and equity	$ 900,000	$1,100,000

a) Magruder estimates that merger synergy benefits will allow Forever's cash dividends to grow at an 8-percent rate in the future. If Magruder requires a 12-percent rate of return on its acquisitions of Forever's riskiness, estimate the intrinsic value or worth per share of Forever Plastics to Magruder Extruder.

b) Based on the above information, establish a range of common stock exchange ratios that Magruder could presumably justify in acquiring Forever. Calculate the merger premium percentages that would be offered to Forever's stockholders if the common stock exchange took place at the lower limit, the mid-point, and the upper limit of the calculated range.

c) Now assume that Magruder finally agrees to exchange one share of its common stock for each share of Forever's common stock. Calculate the post-merger combined EPS and indicate the resulting increase or dilution that will occur for each firm's stockholders.

d) Estimate the post-merger market or stock price based on an exchange ratio of 1:1 and without any anticipated synergistic benefits. Also estimate the post-merger stock price if the marketplace were to reflect the merger synergy benefits expected by Magruder. Calculate the post-merger P/E multiple under each assumption and show the corresponding per-share dilution or increase that would result for each firm's stockholders.

e) Based on an exchange ratio of 1:1, show Magruder's post-merger balance sheet under the pooling of interests accounting method. Also treat the merger as a purchase and assume that Forever's fixed assets will be revalued upward by $200,000.

bankruptcy

5. The balance sheet of the Phoenix-Sashes prior to liquidation appears as follows:

Assets		Liabilities and Capital	
Cash	$ 3,500	Common stock	$200,000
Accounts receivable	72,800	Earned surplus (deficit)	(46,500)
Inventory	153,600	Preferred stock	50,000
Plant and equipment	411,600	First mortgage bonds	200,000
		Second mortgage bonds	80,000
		Debentures	100,000
		Accounts payable	38,000
		Notes payable — bank	20,000
	$641,500		$641,500

The amounts realized in liquidation are as follows:

Cash	$ 3,500
Accounts receivable	42,000
Inventory	46,140
Plant and equipment	208,500

Assuming that the mortgage bondholders have a mortgage on the plant and equipment, determine how much each class of creditors and owners would receive upon liquidation.

SOLUTIONS TO SOLVED PROBLEMS

SP-1. a) i.

Number of Ajax shares to be issued:

$$= \frac{\$48 \text{ per Byrd share}}{\$30 \text{ per Ajax share}} \times 500{,}000 \text{ Byrd shares}$$

$$= 800{,}000 \text{ new Ajax shares}$$

ii. New EPS

Combined net income	=	$12,000,000
Total Ajax shares	=	5,800,000
Combined EPS	=	2.07

iii. New price per Ajax share:

Combined EPS	2.07
Times Ajax P/E	× 15
Market price per share	$31.00

The market price of the combination is higher than before the merger. Since the P/E has not changed, the real explanation is that, whenever the P/E of the acquiring company (Ajax) is greater than the P/E of the acquired company (Byrd), the new market price will be higher. This is often referred to as "funny money."

iv.

Pre-merger value per Byrd share	= 40.00
Post-merger, 1 Byrd share	= 1.60 Ajax shares
	= (1.60)(31)
	= $49.60

Due to the post merger rise in Ajax stock, Byrd shareholders get an added gain on the exchange.

v.

$$\text{Exchange Ratio} = \frac{\text{No. Ajax shares received}}{\text{No. Byrd shares exchanged}} = 1.60$$

b) Do this backwards. Start out with a post-merger price for Ajax of 30.

Post merger price =	$30.00
÷ P/E	15
= EPS (post-merger)	$ 2.00
Post-merger net income	12,000,000
÷ EPS (post merger)	2.00
= Post-merger shares, maximum	6,000,000
Less previous Ajax shares	5,000,000
= maximum new shares for Byrd	1,000,000
Total new shares for Byrd	1,000,000
÷ Byrd shares exchanged	500,000
= Exchange ratio	2.00

Value per Byrd share = (Exchange ratio)(Ajax price per share)
= (2.00)($30)

maximum price per Byrd share = $60
maximum P/E per Byrd share = $60/4 = 15 times

c) Do this backwards:
Calculate minimum PBT to preserve target EPS.

Target EPS	=	$2.00
No. shares	=	5,000,000
= Target NI	=	$10,000,000
= Target PBT	=	$10,000,000/.6
	=	$16,666,667

Calculate maximum interest deduction for target PBT.

Actual combined NI	= 12,000,000
Actual combined PBT	= 20,000,000
Less target PBT	= 16,666,667
= maximum interest expense for target PBT	$3,333,333

Calculate maximum face value of new debt

$$\text{Face value of new debt} = \frac{\$3,333,333}{.10} = \$33,333,333$$

Calculate maximum price per Byrd share.

Implied price per Byrd share on maximum cash for stock basis	$= \dfrac{33,333,333}{500,000 \text{ Byrd share}}$
	= $66.67 per share

Ajax can offer Byrd shareholders a maximum of $66.67 cash, given its debt cost of 10 percent. However, Byrd shareholders would have to pay taxes on the cash transaction immediately, while in a stock-for-stock arrangement, taxes will not have to be paid until the former Byrd shareholders sell their new Ajax stock.

REFERENCES

Austin, Douglas V. "The Financial Management of Tender Offer Takeovers." *Financial Management*, Spring 1974, pp. 37–43.

Black, Fischer, and Myron Scholes. "The Effects of Dividend Yield and Dividend Policy on Common Stock Prices and Returns." *Journal of Financial Economics*, May 1974, pp. 1–22.

Edmister, Robert O. "An Empirical Test of Financial Ratio Analysis for Small Business Failure Prediction." *Journal of Financial and Quantitative Analysis*, March 1972, pp. 1477–1493.

Gordon, Myron F. "Towards a Theory of Financial Distress." *Journal of Finance*, May 1971, pp. 347–356.

Haugen, Robert A., and Terence E. Langetieg. "An Empirical Test for Synergism in Merger." *Journal of Finance*, June 1975, pp. 1003–1014.

Mandelker, Gershon. "Risk and Return: The Case of Merging Firms." *Journal of Financial Economics*, December 1974, pp. 303–336.

Melicher, Ronald W., and David F. Rush. "Evidence on the Acquisition–Related Performance of Conglomerate Firms." *Journal of Finance*, March 1974, pp. 141–149.

Scott, James H., Jr., "Bankruptcy, Secured Debt and Optimal Capital Structure." *Journal of Finance*, March 1977, pp. 1–20.

Shad, John S. R. "The Financial Realities of Mergers." *Harvard Business Review*, November–December 1969, pp. 133–146.

CHAPTER

25

INTERNATIONAL
FINANCIAL
MANAGEMENT

Growth of international business, especially in the form of direct investment overseas, has materially complicated the task of corporate financial management. The ever increasing international dimension of finance at multinational corporations places entirely new demands on the financial manager, while offering substantial rewards from newly developed financial expertise.

Objectives and Organization of this Chapter

This chapter provides an overview of international finance and its importance to the financial manager. The first section discusses key aspects of multinational financial management. The second section shows how exchange-rate factors affect borrowing decisions. The third section examines exchange-rate effects on operating decisions. Finally, the chapter examines aspects of international finance as they affect capital budgeting decisions.

MULTINATIONAL FINANCIAL MANAGEMENT

Financial management in a multinational context incorporates the same ideas and techniques as domestic financial management, plus several unique and important features. This section identifies the most important of these. Subsequent sections will illustrate their impacts on financial management.

Multiple Currencies

What most obviously distinguishes multinational financial management is its existence in an environment of multiple currencies. For domestic financial managers "a dollar is a dollar," but to the multinational financial manager "a dollar" may be a U.S. dollar, Canadian dollar, Australian dollar, Singapore dollar, New Zealand dollar, or even a Eurodollar. All of these dollars differ in relative value. For example, a Canadian dollar might be worth only 78 U.S. cents. In addition to dollars, the multinational financial manager must keep track of Japanese Yen, German Marks, Mexican Pesos, Italian Lira, Swiss Francs, and other currencies.

Exchange Rates

When investment, borrowing or operating decisions involve non-U.S. currencies, some form of translating or converting them to an equivalent basis is necessary for correct decision making. This conversion is made according to relative *exchange rates* among currencies.

exchange rates

Two methods of quoting foreign exchange rates are prevalent in the New York foreign exchange market: the direct and indirect methods.

direct method

The *direct method* of quotation gives the price of one unit of foreign currency in terms of the domestic currency. Table 25-1 contains some comparative exchange rates for 1977 and 1987, using the direct method. For example, in 1987 the British pound (£) was quoted in New York directly at $1.6160, indicating it would take $1.616 to buy £1.

indirect method

An alternative method of quoting foregin exchange rates is the *indirect method.* The indirect method gives the number of foreign currency units received for one unit of domestic currency. Indirect quotes are not shown in Table 25-1, but they can be determined easily.

$$\text{Indirect quote} = \frac{1}{\text{direct quote}} \tag{25-1}$$

For example, in 1987 the direct quote for marks (abbreviated as DM, meaning Deutsche marks) in Table 25-1 is $0.5469. The indirect quote would be

TABLE 25-1			
Comparative Exchange Rates, 1977 and 1987 (Quoted in U.S. Currency Per Unit of Foreign Currency)			
	1977	*1987*	*Change 1977-87*
Australian dollar	$1.1082	$0.7219	−35%
British pound	1.7449	1.6160	− 7
Canadian dollar	0.9411	0.7471	−21
French franc	0.2034	0.1637	−20
Indian rupee	0.1141	0.0786	−31
Italian lira	0.0011	0.0008	−27
Japanese yen	0.0037	0.0069	+86
Mexican peso	0.0442	0.0008	−98
Spanish peseta	0.0133	0.0079	−59
Swiss franc	0.4171	0.6579	+58
West German mark	0.4308	0.5469	+27

DM 1.8285 per dollar. Someone with $10,000 would be able to purchase 18,285 Deutsche marks.[1]

$$\text{Indirect quote (DM)} = \frac{1}{\text{direct quote (DM)}}$$

$$= \frac{1}{.5469}$$

$$= 1.8285 \text{ DM}$$

Exchange Rate Risk

If exchange rates were stable, the multicurrency dimension would be less severe. However, since 1973, exchange rates have been free to change in response to supply and demand in the foreign exchange marketplace. Table 25-1 shows comparative exchange rates for some selected currencies as of June 18, 1987 and 1977. Note that the value of the Mexican peso has declined 98 percent over the 10 years, while the value of the Japanese yen has increased by 86 percent.

Exchange-rate fluctuations can have enormous impacts on a multinational firm's profitability and thus introduce *exchange rate risk*, which means that adverse changes in exchange rates can arbitrarily reverse a company's expected profitability.

exchange-rate risk

Example

Exchange Rate Fluctuations and Profitability

Assume that the JHC International Corporation sells equipment to a Japanese firm for 100 million Japanese yen, with payment due in 90 days. At the time of sale, the yen is worth .0069 U.S. dollars. Thus, the sale is worth about $690,000 U.S. Also assume that the equipment costs $600,000 to manufacture in the United States and ship to Japan, producing an anticipated profit of $90,000. If the exchange rate drops to .0059 in 90 days, the JHC corporation will receive 100 million yen, now worth only $590,000, a drop of $100,000 simply as a result of exchange-rate fluctuations. JHC's anticipated profit of $90,000 will turn into a loss of $10,000 due solely to the exchange-rate fluctuation during the 90-day period.

---

[1]Prior to 1978, almost all currencies in New York were quoted by the direct method. The changeover to indirect quotation for continental European currencies allowed for easier communication between the New York market and foreign exchange markets in overseas centers.

	Projected	Actual
Sales (yen)	100,000,000	100,000,000
× Exchange rate	.0069	.0059
= Sales (U.S. $)	$ 690,000	$ 590,000
− Expenses	600,000	600,000
Operating profit	$ 90,000	($ 10,000)

Spot and Forward Rates

The exchange rates shown in Table 25-1 represent spot rates, meaning that they are the exchange rates actually in effect. However, arrangements can be made to exchange currency at some future date at a predetermined future or forward rate. The advantage of this arrangement is that risks of exchange-rate fluctuations, such as that of JHC, can be eliminated. Table 25-2 shows some selected forward rates as of June 19, 1987. Normally, forward contracts with commercial banks are readily available for maturities of one, two, three, six or 12 months in the major currencies.

For example, a contract for British pounds with December delivery is available at a forward rate of $1.6175. A buyer of this contract would be obligated to buy pounds at a price of $1.6175 per pound when the contract expires in December. Alternatively, one could sell the contract and thus be obligated to deliver British pounds at $1.6175 per pound.

The forward exchange rate is normally not equal to the spot rate. For example, the spot rate for marks is $0.5469, but the six-month forward rate (i.e., December) is $0.5550. In other words, marks for forward delivery would be more valuable relative to their current value.

Forward Discounts and Forward Premiums

If the direct forward exchange rate is lower than the spot exchange rate, implying that the currency will become less valuable relative to the U.S. dollar, the foreign currency is said to be trading at a *forward discount*. If the direct forward exchange rate is higher than the spot rate, the foreign cur-

TABLE 25-2   Selected Spot and Six-Month Forward Rates, June 19, 1987

	Spot	December Forward	% Change
British pound	$1.6160	$1.6175	+ .09%
Canadian dollar	0.7471	0.7414	− .76
Japanese yen	0.0069	0.0070	+1.40
Swiss franc	0.6579	0.6663	+1.28
West German mark	0.5469	0.5550	+1.48

rency is trading at a *forward premium*. In the example above, marks are at a
forward premium.

The forward premium, or discount percentage ($\% \Delta_f$), can be expressed as an annualized percentage, as shown in Equation 25-2:

$$\% \Delta_f = \frac{(F - S)}{S} \times \frac{[12]}{N} \times 100 \tag{25-2}$$

Where: F = the forward exchange rate; S = the spot exchange rate; and N = number of months forward.

A positive value resulting from this calculation indicates that the currency is at a forward premium. For marks, there is a forward premium of:

$$\% \Delta_f = \frac{(.5550 - .5469)}{.5469} \times \frac{(12)}{6} \times 100$$

$$= 2.96\%$$

Note that this is double the six-month forward premium shown in Table 25-2.

Interest Rate Parity

The relationship between forward rates and spot rates is related to relative interest rates between the two countries whose currencies are being exchanged. This relationship, known as interest-rate parity, is shown for British and U.S. currencies in Equation 25-3.

$$\text{12-month Forward rate}_\pounds/\text{spot rate}_\pounds = (1 + r_\pounds)/(1 + r_\$) \tag{25-3}$$

where $r_\pounds$ = interest rate on 12-month risk-free British securities and $r_\$ =$ interest rate on 12-month risk-free U.S. securities.

Example

Interest Rate Parity

Assume that British risk-free securites are providing a 12-month yield of 6.20 percent and U.S. 12-month Treasury securities are providing a yield of 6.10 percent. If the current spot rate is $1.6160, the implied forward rate is 1.6175.

$$\text{12-month forward rate}_\pounds/\text{spot rate}_\pounds = (1 + r_\pounds)/(1 + r_\$)$$

$$\text{12-month forward rate}_\pounds/\$1.6160 = (1.062)/(\$1.061)$$

$$\text{12-month forward rate}_\pounds = \$1.6175$$

If the forward rate implied by the interest-rate parity relationship gets too far out of line with the actual forward rate, profit-making opportunities will attract currency arbitrageurs, who will exploit the difference.

International Financial Markets

One of the most astounding developments in international finance has been the explosive growth of new international money and capital markets.

Eurocurrency deposit

Eurocurrency Markets. The primary building blocks of this new global international financial system are the Eurocurrency money markets. A *Eurocurrency deposit* is simply a deposit taken by a bank located in one country but denominated in the currency of another country. For example, banks in the Eurocurrency markets in Europe take demand deposits denominated in the United States dollar. These demand deposits are referred to as *Eurodollar deposits.*

Eurobanks take these deposits for the primary purpose of lending them to customers at a profit. Eurobanks will make commercial loans funded in Eurodollars in the form of lines of credit, term loans, or revolving credits.

Eurocredits

LIBOR

The unique aspect of most Eurodollar lending, or *Eurocredits,* is the pricing mechanism. The key interest rate in the market is the *London Inter-Bank Offer Rate* or *LIBOR,* the rate at which key banks in the London market will sell deposits to other banks. When a corporate customer borrows Eurodollars, the interest paid is initially fixed at the present LIBOR rate plus a *spread.* The spread varies from loan to loan, of course, depending on the credit status of the borrower and the availability of funds in the marketplace. However, at six-month intervals, the bank changes the prices it charges to customers.

Given the volume of foreign currency deposits available to support the Euromarket, large sums of money can be raised relatively quickly. Corporate borrowing usually ranges from $10 million to $100 million. Most large Eurocredits are syndicated, with a lead bank or banks arranging the terms of the financing and forming a syndicate of other banks to provide the actual funding. Much larger Eurocredits have been raised for governmental borrowers, and the Eurocredit market has emerged as a leading vehicle for countries that need to finance balance-of-payment deficits.

Eurobond Market. A second market, the Eurobond market provides a very flexible method for multinational corporations to raise long-term capital on short notice. The bulk of these issues are in bearer form, generally with a maturity of no more than 15 years. Most are denominated in U.S. dollars and can be placed at coupon rates closely paralleling those available with U.S. placement. Other currencies are also used for denomination of Eurobonds.

OTHER FACTORS IN THE INTERNATIONAL ENVIRONMENT

In addition to multiple currencies and multinational financial markets, the financial manager must deal with many political risks as well as multiple taxing authorities.

Political Risk

Political risks are another aspect of international finance, and they can take many forms. For example, a multinational firm must deal with possible *nationalization* of foreign businesses. In such cases, the foreign government simply takes over all the local assets of the multinational firm, possibly with no compensation to the parent firm.

nationalization

Another form of political risk arises when certain countries, particularly those generally classified as developing, tend to limit the ability of holders of their currency to exchange it for other currencies. For example, *exchange control restrictions* may limit the ability to make dividend payments from a local subsidiary to a parent corporation, bring in outside funds for investment, make payments for technology through royalties or licensing fees, or pay for vitally needed imported components. Indeed, few countries in the world allow the totally free transfer of the purchasing power of their currency. Until only recently, Taiwan had stringent controls over currency flows. Taiwanese businesses were prohibited from purchasing foreign currency or investing overseas. Due to the possibility of trade retaliation from the United States, Taiwan agreed to relax its currency controls. According to news reports, Taiwan had accumulated over $7 billion in currency reserves in the first five months of 1987, of which about 90 percent was from trade with the United States.

exchange control restrictions

Tax Factors

Although the tax factor is significant in almost every financial decision, the existence of *multiple taxing authorities* and the practice of almost all countries of taxing the dividends, interest payments, or other means by which multinationals move funds across national boundaries makes the tax factor overwhelmingly important in international finance. Scarcely any finance transaction can occur without a specific evaluation of the tax impact of the operation. United States multinationals are particularly affected. Unlike many other countries, the United States bases its taxation on the worldwide income of U.S. corporations. Although some of the more negative aspects of this approach are eliminated by the provision of a tax credit for taxes paid to foreign governments and by the deferral of tax on the income of subsidiaries until the income is brought back to the parent in the form of the dividend, United States-based multinationals must pay particular and continuous attention to these tax impacts. For this reason, all financial decisions should be made on an after-tax basis.

multiple taxing authorities

EXCHANGE RATES AND FINANCIAL DECISIONS

Exchange rate changes affect all the principal areas of financial decision-making in the multinational firm. Let us examine the impacts on the three major types of decision-making: financing activities, operating activities, and investment activities.

Financing Activities

When a company engages in borrowing in a currency other than the dollar, the dollar value of the principal amount due for repayment (as well as any future interest payments) varies with the exchange rate.

Example

Assume that Jones International, a U.S. corporation, needs to provide its subsidiary in West Germany with DM 200,000 for a one-year period, at a time when the direct exchange rate for DM is $0.50. Suppose Jones can provide the local currency through a local German bank loan for DM 200,000 with an interest rate of 12 percent, or by borrowing $100,000 at 9 percent in the United States, converting it to DM at the present exchange rate, and lending the funds to the subsidiary.

We shall refer to the first financing option as the *local currency loan*, and the second financing option as the *dollar loan*. At the end of the one-year period, the subsidiary will repay DM 224,000 (the local currency loan plus interest) if the local currency option is selected. If the dollar loan option is selected, the subsidiary will repay the parent company the equivalent of $109,000 in marks. The parent would then exchange the DM into dollars and then repay principal and interest ($109,000) to the lender. All interest is paid at the end of one year.[2] It is assumed that the funds borrowed under each alternative will be utilized for the same set of operations, and that the local currency cash flows generated by this subsidiary, as well as inflows in other currencies, will not be altered by how the operations are financed.

dollar borrowing cost

The two alternatives can be compared by converting the transactions to a common, dollar, basis. The *dollar borrowing cost* is the dollar equivalent of what is repaid (for interest and principal) minus the dollar value of what has been borrowed.

It is known that the local currency loan will require payment of DM 224,000 (the borrowed amount of 200,000 marks plus 12 percent interest). If the exchange rate remains at $0.50, the local currency loan would have a higher dollar borrowing cost, since the dollar equivalent repaid would be $112,000 compared to the dollar equivalent borrowed of

---

[2]This example, of course, ignores taxation and a number of other important and interesting factors. For a more comprehensive treatment, see William R. Folks, Jr. "The Analysis of Short-Term Cross-Border Financing Decisions." *Financial Management*, Autumn 1976, pp. 19–27, or Alan B. Shapiro. "Evaluating Financing Cost for Multinational Subsidiaries." *Journal of International Business Studies*, Fall 1975, pp. 25–32.

$100,000. This produces a dollar borrowing cost of $12,000, which is higher than the dollar loan alternative.

Dollar Borrowing Cost: Local Currency Option

Amount repaid in local currency	224,000
× Direct exchange rate	.5000
= Dollar equivalent repaid	$112,000
− Dollar equivalent borrowed	100,000
= Dollar borrowing cost	$ 12,000

However, if the local currency depreciates to $0.40, the local currency loan becomes relatively more attractive. The dollar equivalent repaid of $89,600 compared to the dollar equivalent borrowed of $100,000, produces a *negative* dollar cost. The borrowing was actually a source of $10,400 profit! The foreign exchange gain arising from the reduction in dollar value of the company's debt obligation far exceeds the dollar value of interest paid, and local funding is the better alternative.

Dollar Borrowing Cost: Local Currency Option

Amount repaid in local currency	224,000
× Direct exchange rate	.4000
= Dollar equivalent repaid	$ 89,600
− Dollar equivalent borrowed	100,000
= Dollar borrowing cost	($ 10,400)

On the other hand, local currency funding becomes less attractive if the local currency appreciates against the dollar. If the final value of the local currency is $0.60, the equivalent dollar amount repaid would be 224,000 × .60 = $134,400 producing a net dollar borrowing cost of $34,400, a far more costly alternative than dollar borrowing, with its $9,000 interest cost.

The dollar cost of any foreign currency funding is a function of the exchange rate prevailing at the maturity of the funding.[3] Which currency should Jones borrow? Obviously, the answer to this question depends on what Jones' management believes the exchange rate prevailing at maturity one year hence will be. One method of analyzing the decision is to calcu-

---

[3]Where there are interest payments intervening between the time the debt is issued and the time the debt is liquidated, or where there are multiple-period interest payments and principal repayments, calculations become somewhat more complex, although the basic principles remain the same.

late the exchange rate that would prevail when the borrowing costs of the two alternatives are the same. Letting ER_b represent this breakeven exchange rate, one equates borrowing costs of the two alternatives, or:

$$\$9,000 = 224,000 \; ER_b - \$100,000 \qquad (25\text{-}4)$$

which implies that

$$ER_b = \$109,000/224,000 \; Marks = .4866$$

If Jones' financial manager believes strongly that marks would depreciate below \$0.4866, then borrowing the local currency would be superior, even though it carries a higher nominal interest rate. If management believes that the currency will not depreciate below \$0.4866, the appropriate decision is to fund with dollars.

Covered Borrowing

Jones may be able to avoid any uncertainty about the relative costs of the dollar loan and local currency financing options by using information in forward exchange contracts.[4]

Jones knows that, if the local currency loan option is selected, the subsidiary will have to pay DM 224,000 12 months from now. Assume that a forward exchange contract with an expiration 12 months later is selling at a forward rate of .48. If Jones buys a contract for 224,000 marks, the dollar borrowing cost will be known immediately.

Dollar Borrowing Cost	
Amount repaid in local currency	\$224,000
× Direct exchange rate	.4800
= Dollar equivalent repaid	\$107,520
− Dollar equivalent borrowed	100,000
= Dollar borrowing cost	\$ 7,520

The dollar borrowing cost of the local currency alternative is lower than the dollar loan alternative. Since the borrowing is covered, or predetermined, the savings are certain.

Interest Rate Comparisons

As has been seen, it is not possible to compare borrowing alternatives on a simple interest-rate basis, due to exchange rate changes. Thus, the

---

[4]Ideally, the maturity of the contract would match the maturity of the loan being evaluated (12 months in this case).

12-percent mark loan actually could be less expensive on a covered basis than the 9-percent U.S. loan. However, if the exchange rate fluctuations are incorporated into the quoted interest rates, comparisons can be made among financing alternatives denominated in different currencies. To do so, one needs to compute the forward exchange premium or discount (discussed earlier) as an annual percentage.

Example

Forward Discount Percentage

Assume that the current spot rate for German marks is .50 and the 12-month forward rate is .48. The mark would be selling at a forward discount of .02. In percentage terms, the forward discount would be 4 percent (i.e., .02/.50) relative to the current spot rate.

percentage dollar cost of covered borrowing

An equation can be used for determining the interest rate or percentage dollar cost of the covered borrowing (%DCCB) of local currency.

$$\%DCCB = \%I + \%\Delta_f + (\%I)(\%\Delta_f) \qquad (25\text{-}5)$$

where %DCCB is the effective interest rate in dollars; %I is the stated interest rate on the local currency loan; and, $\%\Delta_f$ is the forward premium or discount percentage.

In the example of Jones' local currency borrowing, assuming the forward currency traded at a 4-percent discount, the percentage dollar cost of the covered local borrowing alternative is:

$$\%DCCB = .12 + (-0.04) + (.12)(-.04) = .0752, \quad \text{or} \quad 7.52\%$$

This effective cost of local borrowing on a covered basis is less than the 9-percent cost of borrowing dollars, and thus local currency funding should be selected.[5]

Operating Activities

Changes in exchange rates can affect both the earnings and cash flow performance of the multinational. This was seen earlier in regard to JHC's sales to Japan. While the cash flow exposure of the transaction is clear and relatively simple to understand, the accounting earning implications to the company are complex.

---

[5]Similar calculations can be made on financial investments with a known yield. The dollar investment yield on a covered basis can be assured, providing that all proceeds of the investment, including interest, are sold in the forward exchange market at the maturity date. The covered yield can be calculated directly from a formula identical to the equation above.

Assume that EJC Imports purchases some goods from Spain on August 1. The goods are received on September 1, and payment for the goods is made on November 1.

The impact of exchange-rate changes between August 1, when contract for the purchase of the goods is signed, and September 1, when title passes, is reflected by an increase or decrease in value of the goods as inventory. When the goods are finally sold, this dollar cost of inventory will be used to determine cost of goods sold, which will be higher or lower, depending on how the rate moves between August 1 and September 1. This variability in inventory valuation will either decrease or increase the operating earnings of the company when the goods are finally sold. As the goods may not be sold for several accounting periods, this change in earnings for the subsequent accounting period clearly does not coincide with the exchange rate change that caused it. Nor does this change appear on the income statement as a foreign exchange gain or loss. Rather, it appears as an increase or decrease in the net operating income of the company.

The impact of exchange-rate changes between September 1, when an account payable is entered on the books of the company, and November 1, when the account payable is liquidated by payment, is reflected in the dollar valuation of the account payable. Any changes between September 1 and November 1 in the dollar valuation of the payable are considered as a foreign exchange gain or loss, depending on whether the company paid out less or more in dollars than the dollar value of the payable on September 1. Under present accounting procedures, such foreign exchange gains or losses are included in income in the period in which they occur.

There are two key points to extract from this simple example. First, the results of exchange-rate changes may affect both the timing and amount of the company's cash flows and the timing and amount of the company's reported earnings. Second, the cash flow impact and the earnings impact are not synchronized in effect. Thus, one of the principal responsibilities of corporate financial management is to ascertain the relative importance of managing the earnings impact versus the cash inflow impact of anticipated exchange rate changes.

Liquidity Management

On an almost daily basis, multinational financial executives are faced with the problem of moving funds from one unit in the multinational system that generates excess funds to another unit in need of additional funds.

Multinational corporations, with the assistance and advice of several large multinational banks, have developed sophisticated systems for minimizing the amount of cash necessary for operations. Once again, the essence of the managerial task is to mobilize liquidity reserves in a position within the network of multinational subsidiaries where it can be directed to the unit in need of liquidity.

Pooling Liquidity. One central concept that has emerged is the idea of pooling liquidity. The essence of the pooling technique is to combine the liquidity requirements of a number of subsidiaries and manage that requirement as if it were one. Because every unit in the pooling system will probably not require emergency access to funds at the same time, a lower overall volume of funds is required to support operations than if each subsidiary had to provide funds separately for its own liquidity needs. Technically, pooling is quite difficult when there are substantial barriers to funds movement. As a consequence, only certain subsidiaries of multinationals can pool their liquidity needs.

Netting of Payments. Another technique that has been effective in funds management has been the netting of payments across national boundaries. Whenever a payment between subsidiaries enters into the foreign exchange market, the company as a whole loses, as the banking system profits on all funds transfers through the foreign exchange market. Consequently it becomes advantageous for a multinational to reduce the volume of funds that needs to enter the foreign exchange market. Netting is generally applicable when an integrated multinational network exhibits a large volume of payments between subsidiaries, flowing in both directions.

Example

Assume that subsidiary A owes subsidiary B $600,000, and subsidiary B owes subsidiary A $1 million. If both subsidiaries make payment, a total of $1.6 million flows through the foreign exchange markets. If subsidiary A and subsidiary B net their payments, with subsidiary B sending A only the $400,000 difference between the amount owed to A and the amount owed by A to B, only $400,000 flows through the foreign exchange market, a reduction of 75 percent.

The concept can be extended to a group of subsidiaries involved in such payments; it may be possible to reduce materially the total amount of payment by the process of *multilateral netting*. Each subsidiary totals up the amount to be paid out to other subsidiaries and the amount due from other subsidiaries. At the end of the process, subsidiaries are either in a deficit or surplus position, and those subsidiaries with deficits can transfer funds to subsidiaries in the system with surpluses. Netting requires the close cooperation of local customs and exchange authorities and is really feasible only where payments can be made relatively freely.

multilateral netting

The process of allocating funds to capital investment projects by a multinational corporation is conceptually complicated. One of the primary issues is the determination of the appropriate cash flow stream to be generated by the project, for the investment of capital in a new venture leads to the generation of two different, but interrelated, cash flow streams that require analysis. The first set of cash flows is those generated by the project itself. For example, an investment in a new plant in Brazil for both domestic production and export markets leads to both a cruzeiro cash flow from local sales and a dollar or possibly third currency cash flow from export sales. Given an explicit set of assumptions about exchange rates, the cash flows generated by the project can be developed.

However, because of exchange controls and taxation on international funds transfers, the cash flows generated by the project are not necessarily the cash flows received by the parent. Thus, it is also necessary to develop a schedule of cash flows, measured in the parent's currency, that will be returned to the parent itself.

One controversial issue is whether it is appropriate to analyze the project's total cash flows, or the cash flow stream as it is returned to the parent. One comprehensive survey indicated that 42 percent of the multinational companies questioned analyzed only the project cash flows, that 21 percent analyzed parent cash flows, and 37 percent analyzed both. The method of analysis applied to these cash flow streams also varied, with payback (76 percent), internal rate of return (69 percent), and return on investment (63 percent) the most popular. For those techniques requiring a discount rate, 43 percent of the companies reported choosing a global weighted average cost of capital, 27 percent utilized overseas financial cost, and 30 percent picked a subjective discount rate. Only 25 percent of the companies used a uniform discount rate for all projects, while 53 percent varied the discount rate by the type of project (cost saving investment in existing subsidiaries versus new investment in new markets).[6]

One approach to the international capital budgeting process requires the net present value or internal rate of return (IRR) analysis of both sets of cash flows. Both project and parent cash flows must have a positive net present value (or acceptable IRR). The rationale for subjecting the project cash flows to an internal-rate-of-return or net-present-value test lies in the interpretation of the local currency cost of capital as an indicator of the economic viability of the project to the particular nation where it is located. However, projects that earn an adequate return locally may not be acceptable to the parent corporation if funds cannot be repatriated from the country in a timely fashion or if the profits are taxed away in transfer taxation.

---

[6]Vinod B. Bavishi. "Capital Budgeting Study Among U.S. MNCs Indicates Current Practice Trends." *Business International Money Reports*, June 8, 1979, pp. 194–195.

Repatriation

Repatriation refers to the return of capital from the foreign subsidiary to the parent. Often the foreign country will carefully control the form, timing, and amounts of such repatriation. As a result, multinationals employ a variety of methods for withdrawing overseas investment.

Many channels for funds movement between units are determined by the legal structure of the multinational. Funds may be moved as equity capital from the legal owner of the subsidiary (the ultimate parent or an intermediate subsidiary), and dividend flows move back from the subsidiary to the parent. Normally, new subsidiaries require substantial parent equity investment, although many companies prefer to provide their initial contribution in the form of a package of parent loans and equity. After some initial years of absorbing cash from the parent, the subsidiary (with luck) begins to generate sufficient cash to meet its own funding needs and (perhaps) begins to supply funds to other units in the system. The original capital structure of the subsidiary is often designed to facilitate the withdrawal of funds as necessary.

Loan Vs. Equity Investment. Subsidiaries may receive substantial parent company loans, as loans can be repaid at times when dividends or payouts through parent equity withdrawal may not be politically or financially attractive alternatives. Interest payments and principal repayment sometimes have significant tax advantages over repatriation of capital and dividend payments. Local subsidiaries therefore may be thinly capitalized with parent equity but carry substantial layers of parent-supplied debt to provide the financial muscle needed for local operations.

Intrasubsidiary Transfers. A subsidiary may also receive a loan from a sister subsidiary, either in the form of a direct intrasubsidiary loan or in the form of trade credit. If a multinational has integrated worldwide operations with substantial flows of real goods between subsidiaries, the opportunity for using trade credit as a creative mechanism for transferring funds is seldom overlooked. If it is desired to remove funds from a particular subsidiary, sister subsidiaries and the parent can request more rapid payment for items shipped into the unit. Or they can delay payment for goods shipped out of the unit. On the other hand, if funds must be placed in a particular subsidiary, subsidiaries shipping goods into that unit can extend longer credit terms, and subsidiaries receiving goods from the unit can pay more promptly. The technique of accelerating or decelerating payments to move funds into or out of a country has been a long time standby for moving funds from one currency to another.

Transfer Pricing. Another method of utilizing intrasubsidiary trade flows for intra-unit funds movement (and for the allocation of profit among various taxing units) is *transfer pricing*. Suppose, for example, it is desired to move funds into a particular unit. Other subsidiaries in the multinational system would charge a lower-than-normal transfer price to this unit, thereby reducing the flow of funds out of the unit. If it is desired to move funds out of a particular subsidiary, a higher-than-normal transfer price can be charged to the unit.

Changing the transfer price also changes the earnings of the involved subsidiaries for tax purposes. High transfer prices in and low transfer prices out, a tactic designed to reduce the funds available to a particular unit, also reduces the taxable profits generated in that subsidiary, and consequently the tax bill of the subsidiary. Of course, taxes are increased for supplying and receiving subsidiaries, and it requires a very close calculation as to the desirability of capturing profits in various taxing jurisdictions. A subsidiary that receives low transfer prices in and charges high transfer prices out is being provided with additional funds, but it is also generating an additional tax liability in that particular country and reducing tax liabilities elsewhere.

Technology Payments.   The parent corporation or other units may sometimes provide subsidiaries with management services, technology, and trademarks. Management fees, licensing fees, and royalties thus flow from the receiving subsidiary back to the parent. As there is some flexibility in the original level set for such payments, these payments can be used as a mechanism of funds transfer.

Transfer pricing and technology payments have come under increasing scrutiny from local governments, who recognize the tax avoidance and funds movement capability of the transfer mechanism. Nonetheless, companies can move some funds and allocate profits at the margin using these sophisticated techniques.

Back-to-Back Loans.   Funds transfer between parent and subsidiary or between subsidiaries may also take place indirectly. Rather than lend money directly to the subsidiary, a company may prefer to use the banking system to intermediate the loan, under the hypothesis that local governments would be more reluctant to restrict repayment of loans to financial institutions than they would to restrict repayment of intracorporate loans.

Such *back-to-back* loans involve (1) the parent depositing or lending funds to a multinational bank, (2) the multinational bank's local branch lending local currency funds to the local subsidiary, (3) the local subsidiary repaying the local branch of the multinational bank, (4) and finally, the international bank repaying the parent.

Parallel Loan.   An alternate form, usually arranged by a multinational bank, is the *parallel loan*, whereby company A lends company B funds at the parent level, and company B's subsidiary lends local currency to company A's subsidiary in return. Interest rates are adjusted to take into account exchange rate changes.

Loan Swaps.   Upon occasion, foreign central banks will borrow money from the parent corporation and simultaneously lend local funds to subsidiaries. Such funding arrangements, called *swaps*, usually guarantee a favorable exchange rate for local funds repayment and thus reduce substantially or eliminate the exchange risk to the parent. Swaps provide the central bank of the local currency with foreign currency for a limited period of time.

A knowledge of the nuances and subtleties of intrasubsidiary funds flows and parent-subsidiary funds movement is a vital part of the tool kit of the international financial manager. Although the variety is seemingly infinite, fundamental principles of analysis follow closely those developed in earlier sections on the impact of exchange-rate changes on funding alternatives.

It is particularly important, however, that all analysis be done on an after-tax basis, as particular tax situations may reverse profitable movements. For example, companies with excess foreign tax credit (companies that have paid more in foreign taxes than their U.S. tax liability on foreign source income) have an effective tax rate of zero percent on foreign source income. Such companies might borrow in the United States and re-lend to a subsidiary at a higher rate of interest, replacing higher-cost local currency debt. The interest that the subsidiary would pay to the parent would represent foreign-source income (not taxed), but the interest expense in the United States would be tax deductible. This particular situation might make dollar borrowing more favorable than borrowing overseas at a lower-dollar borrowing cost.

SUMMARY

Multinational financial officers must be capable of making a number of international-level financial decisions in addition to their domestic financial management responsibilities. Since these financial officers are continuously involved with moving funds within the firm from subsidiaries with excess funds to those in need of funds, they need to understand the types and subtleties of intrasubsidiary funds flows and parent-subsidiary funds movements. These financial officers also must be able to manage liquidity within the multinational firm through such techniques as pooling liquidity and the process of multilateral netting of funds. Capital budgeting is conceptually complicated, since financial officers must consider not only the project's cash flows being provided to the foreign subsidiary but also the cash flows that will ultimately be returned to the parent company. Finally, it is imperative for the multinational financial manager to develop an understanding of, and make use of, the rapidly growing and developing international money and capital markets.

MULTIPLE CHOICE QUESTIONS

1. Prices at which currencies trade in terms of each other are known as:
   a) Floating rates
   b) Fixed rates
   c) Interest rates
   d) Exchange rates

2. Rates existing at a particular point in time for immediate exchange of currencies are known as:
   a) Forward exchange rates
   b) Parity rates
   c) Spot exchange rates
   d) Exchange rate premiums

3. Which of the following reflects the direct method of exchange rate quotation?

    b) $1.85 U.S./£ Sterling
    c) 3.45 DM/$U.S.
    d) (a) and (c)

4. Which of the following reflects the indirect method of exchange rate quotation?

    b) $1.85 U.S./£ Sterling
    c) 3.45 DM/$U.S.
    d) (a) and (c)

5. A forward exchange purchase contract obligates the transactor to:

    b) Provide refunds
    c) Buy foreign currency
    d) Provide substitute currencies on demand

6. A currency is trading at a forward discount if:

a) The direct forward exchange rate is lower than the spot rate
    b) The direct forward exchange rate is higher than the spot rate
    c) The spot exchange rate is lower than the direct forward rate
    d) The spot exchange rate is equal to the direct forward rate

DISCUSSION QUESTIONS

1. What is meant by foreign exchange? Briefly describe the two styles of quoting foreign exchange rates.

2. Direct forward exchange rates may trade at forward discounts or premiums. Explain and illustrate.

3. What are some of the implications of exchange rate changes on financial decisions?

4. Explain how financial executives are often involved in the movement of funds between units in a multinational system or corporation.

5. What is meant by the management of international liquidity? What actions can be taken by financial executives in order to maintain liquidity?

6. What factors and considerations are important to multinational firms in the process of deciding how to allocate funds to capital investment projects?

7. Rapid growth in international money and capital markets has led to the use of such terms as *Eurocurrency deposits, Eurodollar deposits,* and *Euro-*

credits. Define each of these terms and indicate their roles in international financial markets.

8. What is exchange rate risk? How can it affect a multinational firm's profitability?

9. Define interest-rate parity. What effect, if any, does it have on forward rates.

SOLVED PROBLEMS

exchange rates

SP-1. Convert the following direct quotes into their indirect equivalents.

French franc $0.1637

Indian rupee $0.0786

Japanese yen $0.0069

Mexican peso $0.0008

Swiss franc $0.6579

exchange rates

SP-2. Assume that the Union Corporation sold equipment to a Mexican import firm for 1 billion Mexican pesos. The equipment cost $700,000 to manufacture and ship. Calculate the operating profit to Union at the following direct exchange rates.

a) $0.0008

b) $0.0010

c) $0.0006

interest rate parity

SP-3. Assume that the 12-month risk-free rates in Switzerland and the U.S. are 5 percent and 6 percent, respectively. If the spot rate, quoted directly, is $0.6579, determine the implied 12-month forward rate according to the interest rate parity relationship.

covered borrowing

SP-4. Assume that the GOA Corporation needs to provide its subsidiary in India with 1 million rupees for a one-year period, at a time when the direct exchange rate for rupees is $0.0800. The alternatives are:

a) A local bank loan in Delhi with an interest rate of 12 percent.

b) A loan from a New York bank at 9 percent.

Determine the percentage dollar cost of covered borrowing (%DCCB) assuming that the forward exchange rate is:

i) $0.0700

ii) $0.0900.

PROBLEMS

exchange rates

1. Convert the following direct quotes into their indirect equivalents.

French franc $0.1842

Indian rupee $0.0541

Japanese yen $0.0035

Mexican peso $0.0040

Swiss franc $0.6666

2. Assume that the VARIC Corporation sold equipment to an Indian *exchange rates* import firm for 1 billion rupees. The equipment cost $55 million to manufacture and ship. Calculate the operating profit to Union at the following direct exchange rates.

   a) $0.0600
   b) $0.0410
   c) $0.0800

3. Assume that the 12-month risk-free rates in France and the U.S. are *interest rate parity* 6 percent and 8 percent, respectively. If the spot rate, quoted directly, is $0.1842, determine the implied 12-month forward rate according to the interest-rate parity relationship.

4. Assume that the MSA Corporation needs to provide its subsidiary in *covered borrowing* Mexico with 100 million pesos for a one-year period at a time when the direct exchange rate for pesos is $0.0008. The alternatives are:

   a) A local bank loan in Chihuahua with an interest rate of 12 percent.
   b) A loan from a New York bank at 9 percent.

   Determine the percentage dollar cost of covered borrowing (%*DCCB*) assuming that the forward exchange rate is:

   i) $0.0010
   ii) $0.0005.

SOLUTIONS TO SOLVED PROBLEMS

SP-1. Use the formula:

$$\text{Indirect quote} = 1/\text{direct quote}$$

	Direct Quote	Indirect Quote
French franc	$0.1637	6.1087
Indian rupee	$0.0786	12.7227
Japanese yen	$0.0069	144.9275
Mexican peso	$0.0008	1,250.0000
Swiss franc	$0.6579	1.5200

SP-2. The answers are shown in the following table:

	(a)	(b)	(c)
Sales (pesos)	1 billion	1 billion	1 billion
× Exchange rate	.0008	.0010	.0006
= Sales (U.S. dollars)	$800,000	$1,000,000	$600,000
− Expenses	700,000	700,000	700,000
Operating profit	$100,000	$ 300,000	($100,000)

SP-3. Use Equation 25-3:

$$\frac{\text{12-month Forward rate}_{fr}}{\text{spot rate}_{fr}} = (1 + r_{fr})/(1 + r_\$)$$

$$\frac{\text{12-month forward rate}_{fr}}{\$0.6579} = (1.050)/(\$1.060)$$

$$\text{12-month forward rate}_{fr} = \$0.6517$$

SP-4. *Step 1:* In order to use Equation 25-5, it is necessary to determine the forward discount or premium percentage for each possible forward rate.

  i) At a forward rate of $0.0700, the forward discount percentage is ($0.0700 − 0.0800)/0.0800 = −12.5%

  ii) At a forward rate of $0.0900 the forward premium percentage is ($0.0900 − 0.0800)/0.0800 = 12.5%

Step 2: Use Equation 25-5 to determine the %*DCCB*:

	%*DCCB*	=	%*I*	+	%Δ*f*	+	(%*I*) (%Δ*f*)
i)	− 2.0		12		−12.5		−1.5
ii)	26.0		12		12.5		1.5

Bavishi, Vinod B. "Capital Budgeting Study Among U.S. MNCs Indicates Current Practices/Trends." *Business International Money Reports,* June 8, 1979, pp. 194–195.

Folks, William R., Jr. "The Analysis of Short-Term Cross-Border Financing Decisions." *Financial Management,* Autumn 1976, pp. 19–27.

Lessard, Donald R., ed. *International Financial Management: Theory and Application.* Boston: Warren, Gorham and Lamont, 1979.

Ricks, David A. International Dimensions of Corporate Finance. Englewood Cliffs, NJ: Prentice-Hall Inc., 1978.

Rodriguez, Rita M. and E. Eugene Carter. International Financial Management, 2nd. ed. Englewood Cliffs, NJ: Prentice-Hall Inc., 1979.

Shapiro, Alan B. "Capital Budgeting for the Multinational Corporation." *Financial Management,* Spring 1978, pp. 7–16.

Shapiro, Alan B. "Nominal Contracting in a World of Uncertainty." *Journal of Banking and Finance* 7, March 1983, pp. 69–82.

POSTSCRIPT: BLACK MONDAY

On October 19, 1987, a day that has come to be known as Black Monday, the stock prices of publicly traded corporations dropped an average of almost 25 percent. This was the biggest one-day drop in history and was more than twice the single-day percentage drop in the Great Crash of 1929. On Black Monday alone, corporations overall lost over $500 billion in value. The financial markets came "within an eyelash," as one authority put it, of a complete collapse. Investigations of the causes and effects of Black Monday are ongoing. Since we take a managerial viewpoint in this text, we will review how the corporate financial manager must deal with the effects of the market crash on corporations.

Share Price Maximization. Throughout this text we assume that one of the objectives of financial management is to maximize the firm's stock price over the long run. The market crash demonstrated vividly that the financial manager cannot control all the factors that determine the firm's share price. For example, many corporations saw their stock prices drop by 30 percent or more in the space of a few hours. Of course the objective of share price maximization is not inconsistent with such widespread market movements. Better managed firms will still be worth more than poorly managed firms, even in depressed stock markets.

Supply and Cost of Capital. An immediate effect of the crash was to frighten investors. Since the average investor lost almost 25 percent of stock wealth in one day, it is understandable that many decided to get out of the financial markets altogether or at least to reduce the level of investments in stocks and bonds. The crash itself thus increased the perceived riskiness of the market. Even prior to the crash, however, the volatility of the stock market increased as a result of enormous trading volumes by financial institutions in pension and mutual funds; computerized trading programs; and arbitrage (in which large volumes of securities may be bought and sold simultaneously) associated with mergers and financial futures contracts.

The reluctance of investors to purchase stocks and bonds had two direct effects on corporations. First, the supply of capital was greatly reduced. Firms were unable to raise money by selling new securities. Second, the costs of capital were increased, reducing the profitability of both existing and planned business investments.

Market Efficiency.   An underlying assumption of much financial theory is that investors value securities rationally, using all available information. In such markets, prices of stocks change to reflect new information. For example, if a company wins or loses a big, profitable contract with the government, its stock price should go up or down accordingly. Yet, on October 19, there was no dramatic negative information justifying a 25 percent decline of stock prices across the board. Does this imply that securities markets such as the New York Stock Exchange are not perfectly efficient all the time? If so, financial managers may find it profitable to exploit such inefficiencies in their dividend, debt, and investment policies.

The effects of the market crash on financial markets or corporate financial management may not be clear for some time. Insofar as the Great Crash of 1929 provides a guide, however, we may expect more regulations to be imposed on all financial markets and large financial institutions using sophisticated computerized trading programs. In addition, we may see industrial corporations reduce their dependence on capital markets for their financing needs. This change will require improved financial management of existing operations.

APPENDIXES

TABLE 1. Future Value Interest Factor (FVIF) of $1

Year	1%	2%	3%	4%	5%	6%	7%	8%	9%	10%
1	1.010	1.020	1.030	1.040	1.050	1.060	1.070	1.080	1.090	1.100
2	1.020	1.040	1.061	1.082	1.102	1.124	1.145	1.166	1.188	1.210
3	1.030	1.061	1.093	1.125	1.158	1.191	1.225	1.260	1.295	1.331
4	1.041	1.082	1.126	1.170	1.216	1.262	1.311	1.360	1.412	1.464
5	1.051	1.104	1.159	1.217	1.276	1.338	1.403	1.469	1.539	1.611
6	1.062	1.126	1.194	1.265	1.340	1.419	1.501	1.587	1.677	1.772
7	1.072	1.149	1.230	1.316	1.407	1.504	1.606	1.714	1.828	1.949
8	1.083	1.172	1.267	1.369	1.477	1.594	1.718	1.851	1.993	2.144
9	1.094	1.195	1.305	1.423	1.551	1.689	1.838	1.999	2.172	2.358
10	1.105	1.219	1.344	1.480	1.629	1.791	1.967	2.159	2.367	2.594
11	1.116	1.243	1.384	1.539	1.710	1.898	2.105	2.332	2.580	2.853
12	1.127	1.268	1.426	1.601	1.796	2.012	2.252	2.518	2.813	3.138
13	1.138	1.294	1.469	1.665	1.886	2.133	2.410	2.720	3.066	3.452
14	1.149	1.319	1.513	1.732	1.980	2.261	2.579	2.937	3.342	3.797
15	1.161	1.346	1.558	1.801	2.079	2.397	2.759	3.172	3.642	4.177
16	1.173	1.373	1.605	1.873	2.183	2.540	2.952	3.426	3.970	4.595
17	1.184	1.400	1.653	1.948	2.292	2.693	3.159	3.700	4.328	5.054
18	1.196	1.428	1.702	2.026	2.407	2.854	3.380	3.996	4.717	5.560
19	1.208	1.457	1.753	2.107	2.527	3.026	3.616	4.316	5.142	6.116
20	1.220	1.486	1.806	2.191	2.653	3.207	3.870	4.661	5.604	6.727
21	1.232	1.516	1.860	2.279	2.786	3.399	4.140	5.034	6.109	7.400
22	1.245	1.546	1.916	2.370	2.925	3.603	4.430	5.436	6.658	8.140
23	1.257	1.577	1.974	2.465	3.071	3.820	4.740	5.871	7.258	8.954
24	1.270	1.608	2.033	2.563	3.225	4.049	5.072	6.341	7.911	9.850
25	1.282	1.641	2.094	2.666	3.386	4.292	5.427	6.848	8.623	10.834
30	1.348	1.811	2.427	3.243	4.322	5.743	7.612	10.062	13.267	17.449
40	1.489	2.208	3.262	4.801	7.040	10.285	14.974	21.724	31.408	45.258
50	1.645	2.691	4.384	7.106	11.467	18.419	29.456	46.900	74.354	117.386

TABLE 1. (Continued)

Year	11%	12%	13%	14%	15%	16%	17%	18%	19%	20%
1	1.110	1.120	1.130	1.140	1.150	1.160	1.170	1.180	1.190	1.200
2	1.232	1.254	1.277	1.300	1.322	1.346	1.369	1.392	1.416	1.440
3	1.368	1.405	1.443	1.482	1.521	1.561	1.602	1.643	1.685	1.728
4	1.518	1.574	1.630	1.689	1.749	1.811	1.874	1.939	2.005	2.074
5	1.685	1.762	1.842	1.925	2.011	2.100	2.192	2.288	2.386	2.488
6	1.870	1.974	2.082	2.195	2.313	2.436	2.565	2.700	2.840	2.986
7	2.076	2.211	2.353	2.502	2.660	2.826	3.001	3.185	3.379	3.583
8	2.305	2.476	2.658	2.853	3.059	3.278	3.511	3.759	4.021	4.300
9	2.558	2.773	3.004	3.252	3.518	3.803	4.108	4.435	4.785	5.160
10	2.839	3.106	3.395	3.707	4.046	4.411	4.807	5.234	5.695	6.192
11	3.152	3.479	3.836	4.226	4.652	5.117	5.624	6.176	6.777	7.430
12	3.498	3.896	4.334	4.818	5.350	5.936	6.580	7.288	8.064	8.916
13	3.883	4.363	4.898	5.492	6.153	6.886	7.699	8.599	9.596	10.699
14	4.310	4.887	5.535	6.261	7.076	7.987	9.007	10.147	11.420	12.839
15	4.785	5.474	6.254	7.138	8.137	9.265	10.539	11.974	13.589	15.407
16	5.311	6.130	7.067	8.137	9.358	10.748	12.330	14.129	16.171	18.488
17	5.895	6.866	7.986	9.276	10.761	12.468	14.426	16.672	19.244	22.186
18	6.545	7.690	9.024	10.575	12.375	14.462	16.879	19.673	22.900	26.623
19	7.263	8.613	10.197	12.055	14.232	16.776	19.748	23.214	27.251	31.948
20	8.062	9.646	11.523	13.743	16.366	19.461	23.105	27.393	32.429	38.337
21	8.949	10.804	13.021	15.667	18.821	22.574	27.033	32.323	38.591	46.005
22	9.933	12.100	14.713	17.861	21.644	26.186	31.629	38.141	45.923	55.205
23	11.026	13.552	16.626	20.361	24.891	30.376	37.005	45.007	54.648	66.247
24	12.239	15.178	18.788	23.212	28.625	35.236	43.296	53.108	65.031	79.496
25	13.585	17.000	21.230	26.461	32.918	40.874	50.656	62.667	77.387	95.395
30	22.892	29.960	39.115	50.949	66.210	85.849	111.061	143.367	184.672	237.373
40	64.999	93.049	132.776	188.876	267.856	378.715	533.846	750.353	1051.642	1469.740
50	184.559	288.996	450.711	700.197	1083.619	1670.669	2566.080	3927.189	5988.730	9100.191

TABLE 1. (Continued)

Year	22%	24%	26%	28%	30%	32%	34%	36%	38%	40%
1	1.220	1.240	1.260	1.280	1.300	1.320	1.340	1.360	1.380	1.400
2	1.488	1.538	1.588	1.638	1.690	1.742	1.796	1.850	1.904	1.960
3	1.816	1.907	2.000	2.097	2.197	2.300	2.406	2.515	2.628	2.744
4	2.215	2.364	2.520	2.684	2.856	3.036	3.224	3.421	3.627	3.842
5	2.703	2.932	3.176	3.436	3.713	4.007	4.320	4.653	5.005	5.378
6	3.297	3.635	4.001	4.398	4.827	5.290	5.789	6.328	6.907	7.530
7	4.023	4.508	5.042	5.629	6.275	6.983	7.758	8.605	9.531	10.541
8	4.908	5.589	6.353	7.206	8.157	9.217	10.395	11.703	13.153	14.758
9	5.987	6.931	8.004	9.223	10.604	12.166	13.390	15.917	18.151	20.661
10	7.305	8.594	10.086	11.806	13.786	16.060	18.666	21.646	25.049	28.925
11	8.912	10.657	12.708	15.112	17.921	21.199	25.012	29.0439	34.567	40.495
12	10.872	13.215	16.012	19.343	23.298	27.982	33.516	40.037	47.703	56.694
13	13.264	16.386	20.175	24.759	30.287	36.937	44.912	54.451	65.830	79.371
14	16.182	20.319	25.420	31.691	39.373	48.756	60.181	74.053	90.845	111.119
15	19.742	25.195	32.030	40.565	51.185	64.358	80.643	100.712	125.366	155.567
16	24.085	31.242	40.357	51.923	66.541	84.953	108.061	136.968	173.005	217.793
17	29.384	38.740	50.850	66.461	86.503	112.138	144.802	186.277	238.747	304.911
18	35.848	48.038	64.071	85.070	112.454	148.022	194.035	253.337	329.471	426.875
19	43.735	59.567	80.730	108.890	146.190	195.389	260.006	344.537	454.669	597.625
20	53.357	73.863	101.720	139.379	190.047	257.913	348.408	468.571	627.443	836.674
21	65.095	91.591	128.167	178.405	247.061	340.446	466.867	637.256	865.871	1171.343
22	79.416	113.572	161.490	228.358	321.178	449.388	625.601	866.668	1194.900	1639.878
23	96.887	140.829	203.477	292.298	417.531	593.192	838.305	1178.668	1648.961	2295.829
24	118.203	174.628	256.381	374.141	542.791	783.013	1123.328	1602.988	2275.564	3214.158
25	144.207	216.539	323.040	478.901	705.627	1033.577	1505.258	2180.063	3140.275	4499.816
30	389.748	634.810	1025.904	1645.488	2619.936	4142.008	6503.285	10142.914	15716.703	24201.043
40	2846.941	5455.797	10346.879	19426.418	36117.754	66519.313	*	*	*	*

* Value is greater than 99,999.

TABLE 2. Present Value Interest Factor (PVIF) of $1

Year	1%	2%	3%	4%	5%	6%	7%	8%	9%	10%
1	.990	.980	.971	.962	.952	.943	.935	.926	.917	.909
2	.980	.961	.943	.925	.907	.890	.873	.857	.842	.826
3	.971	.942	.915	.889	.864	.840	.816	.794	.772	.751
4	.961	.924	.888	.855	.823	.792	.763	.735	.708	.683
5	.951	.906	.863	.822	.784	.747	.713	.681	.650	.621
6	.942	.888	.837	.790	.746	.705	.666	.630	.596	.564
7	.933	.871	.813	.760	.711	.665	.623	.583	.547	.513
8	.923	.853	.789	.731	.677	.627	.582	.540	.502	.467
9	.914	.837	.766	.703	.645	.592	.544	.500	.460	.424
10	.905	.820	.744	.676	.614	.558	.508	.463	.422	.386
11	.896	.804	.722	.650	.585	.527	.475	.429	.388	.350
12	.887	.789	.701	.625	.557	.497	.444	.397	.356	.319
13	.879	.773	.681	.601	.530	.469	.415	.368	.326	.290
14	.870	.758	.661	.577	.505	.442	.388	.340	.299	.263
15	.861	.743	.642	.555	.481	.417	.362	.315	.275	.239
16	.853	.728	.623	.534	.458	.394	.339	.292	.252	.218
17	.844	.714	.605	.513	.436	.371	.317	.270	.231	.198
18	.836	.700	.587	.494	.416	.350	.296	.250	.212	.180
19	.828	.686	.570	.475	.396	.331	.277	.232	.194	.164
20	.820	.673	.554	.456	.377	.312	.258	.215	.178	.149
21	.811	.660	.538	.439	.359	.294	.242	.199	.164	.135
22	.803	.647	.522	.422	.342	.278	.226	.184	.150	.123
23	.795	.634	.507	.406	.326	.262	.211	.170	.138	.112
24	.788	.622	.492	.390	.310	.247	.197	.158	.126	.102
25	.780	.610	.478	.375	.295	.233	.184	.146	.116	.092
30	.742	.552	.412	.308	.231	.174	.131	.099	.075	.057
40	.672	.453	.307	.208	.142	.097	.067	.046	.032	.022
50	.608	.372	.228	.141	.087	.054	.034	.021	.013	.009

Table 2. (Continued)

Year	11%	12%	13%	14%	15%	16%	17%	18%	19%	20%
1	.901	.893	.885	.877	.870	.862	.855	.847	.840	.833
2	.812	.797	.783	.769	.756	.743	.731	.718	.706	.694
3	.731	.712	.693	.675	.658	.641	.624	.609	.593	.579
4	.659	.636	.613	.592	.572	.552	.534	.516	.499	.482
5	.593	.567	.543	.519	.497	.476	.456	.437	.419	.402
6	.535	.507	.480	.456	.432	.410	.390	.370	.352	.335
7	.482	.452	.425	.400	.376	.354	.333	.314	.296	.279
8	.434	.404	.376	.351	.327	.305	.285	.266	.249	.233
9	.391	.361	.333	.308	.284	.263	.243	.225	.209	.194
10	.352	.322	.295	.270	.247	.227	.208	.191	.176	.162
11	.317	.287	.261	.237	.215	.195	.178	.162	.148	.135
12	.286	.257	.231	.208	.187	.168	.152	.137	.124	.112
13	.258	.229	.204	.182	.163	.145	.130	.116	.104	.093
14	.232	.205	.181	.160	.141	.125	.111	.099	.088	.078
15	.209	.183	.160	.140	.123	.108	.095	.084	.074	.065
16	.188	.163	.141	.123	.107	.093	.081	.071	.062	.054
17	.170	.146	.125	.108	.093	.080	.069	.060	.052	.045
18	.153	.130	.111	.095	.081	.069	.059	.051	.044	.038
19	.138	.116	.098	.083	.070	.060	.051	.043	.037	.031
20	.124	.104	.087	.073	.061	.051	.043	.037	.031	.026
21	.112	.093	.077	.064	.053	.044	.037	.031	.026	.022
22	.101	.083	.068	.056	.046	.038	.032	.026	.022	.018
23	.091	.074	.060	.049	.040	.033	.027	.022	.018	.015
24	.082	.066	.053	.043	.035	.028	.023	.019	.015	.013
25	.074	.059	.047	.038	.030	.024	.020	.016	.013	.010
30	.044	.033	.026	.020	.015	.012	.009	.007	.005	.004
40	.015	.011	.008	.005	.004	.003	.002	.001	.001	.001
50	.005	.003	.002	.001	.001	.001	.000	.000	.000	.000

TABLE 2. (Continued)

Year	22%	24%	26%	28%	30%	32%	34%	36%	38%	40%
1	.820	.806	.794	.781	.769	.758	.746	.735	.725	.714
2	.672	.650	.630	.610	.592	.574	.557	.541	.525	.510
3	.551	.524	.500	.477	.455	.435	.416	.398	.381	.364
4	.451	.423	.397	.373	.350	.329	.310	.292	.276	.260
5	.370	.341	.315	.291	.269	.250	.231	.215	.200	.186
6	.303	.275	.250	.227	.207	.189	.173	.158	.145	.133
7	.249	.222	.198	.178	.159	.143	.129	.116	.105	.095
8	.204	.179	.157	.139	.123	.108	.096	.085	.076	.068
9	.167	.144	.125	.108	.094	.082	.072	.063	.055	.048
10	.137	.116	.099	.085	.073	.062	.054	.046	.040	.035
11	.112	.094	.079	.066	.056	.047	.040	.034	.029	.025
12	.092	.076	.062	.052	.043	.036	.030	.025	.021	.018
13	.075	.061	.050	.040	.033	.027	.022	.018	.015	.013
14	.062	.049	.039	.032	.025	.021	.017	.014	.011	.009
15	.051	.040	.031	.025	.020	.016	.012	.010	.008	.006
16	.042	.032	.025	.019	.015	.012	.009	.007	.006	.005
17	.034	.026	.020	.015	.012	.009	.007	.005	.004	.003
18	.028	.021	.016	.012	.009	.007	.005	.004	.003	.002
19	.023	.017	.012	.009	.007	.005	.004	.003	.002	.002
20	.019	.014	.010	.007	.005	.004	.003	.002	.002	.001
21	.015	.011	.008	.006	.004	.003	.002	.002	.001	.001
22	.013	.009	.006	.004	.003	.002	.002	.001	.001	.001
23	.010	.007	.005	.003	.002	.002	.001	.001	.001	.000
24	.008	.006	.004	.003	.002	.001	.001	.001	.000	.000
25	.007	.005	.003	.002	.001	.001	.001	.000	.000	.000
30	.003	.002	.001	.001	.000	.000	.000	.000	.000	.000
40	.000	.000	.000	.000	.000	.000	.000	.000	.000	.000

TABLE 3. Future Value Interest Factor of an Annuity (FVIFA) of $1

Year	1%	2%	3%	4%	5%	6%	7%	8%	9%	10%
1	1.000	1.000	1.000	1.000	1.000	1.000	1.000	1.000	1.000	1.000
2	2.010	2.020	2.030	2.040	2.050	2.060	2.070	2.080	2.090	2.100
3	3.030	3.060	3.091	3.122	3.152	3.184	3.215	3.246	3.278	3.310
4	4.060	4.122	4.184	4.246	4.310	4.375	4.440	4.506	4.573	4.641
5	5.101	5.204	5.309	5.416	5.526	5.637	5.751	5.867	5.985	6.105
6	6.152	6.308	6.468	6.633	6.802	6.975	7.153	7.336	7.523	7.716
7	7.214	7.434	7.662	7.898	8.142	8.394	8.654	8.923	9.200	9.487
8	8.286	8.583	8.892	9.214	9.549	9.897	10.260	10.637	11.028	11.436
9	9.368	9.755	10.159	10.583	11.027	11.491	11.978	12.488	13.021	13.579
10	1.0462	10.950	11.464	12.006	12.578	13.181	13.816	14.487	15.193	15.937
11	11.567	12.169	12.808	13.486	14.207	14.972	15.784	16.645	17.560	18.531
12	12.682	13.412	14.192	15.026	15.917	16.870	17.888	18.977	20.141	21.384
13	13.809	14.680	15.618	16.627	17.713	18.882	20.141	21.495	22.953	24.523
14	14.947	15.974	17.086	18.292	19.598	21.015	22.550	24.215	26.019	27.975
15	16.097	17.293	18.599	20.023	21.578	23.276	25.129	27.152	29.361	31.772
16	17.258	18.639	20.157	21.824	23.657	25.672	27.888	30.324	33.003	35.949
17	18.430	20.012	21.761	23.697	25.840	28.213	30.840	33.750	36.973	40.544
18	19.614	21.412	23.414	25.645	28.132	30.905	33.999	37.450	41.301	45.599
19	20.811	22.840	25.117	27.671	30.539	33.760	37.379	41.446	46.018	51.158
20	22.019	24.297	26.870	29.778	33.066	36.785	40.995	45.762	51.159	57.274
21	23.239	25.783	28.676	31.969	35.719	39.992	44.865	50.422	56.764	64.002
22	24.471	27.299	30.536	34.248	38.505	43.392	49.005	55.456	62.872	71.402
23	25.716	28.845	32.452	36.618	41.430	46.995	53.435	60.893	69.531	79.542
24	26.973	30.421	34.426	39.082	44.501	50.815	58.176	66.764	76.789	88.496
25	28.243	32.030	36.459	41.645	47.726	54.864	63.248	73.105	84.699	98.346
30	34.784	40.567	47.575	56.084	66.438	79.057	94.459	113.282	136.305	164.491
40	48.885	60.401	75.400	95.024	120.797	154.758	199.630	259.052	337.872	442.580
50	64.461	84.577	112.794	152.664	209.341	290.325	406.516	573.756	315.051	1163.865

TABLE 3. (Continued)

Year	11%	12%	13%	14%	15%	16%	17%	18%	19%	20%
1	1.000	1.000	1.000	1.000	1.000	1.000	1.000	1.000	1.000	1.000
2	2.110	2.120	2.130	2.140	2.150	2.160	2.170	2.180	2.190	2.220
3	3.342	3.374	3.407	3.440	3.472	3.506	3.539	3.572	3.606	3.640
4	4.710	4.770	4.850	4.921	4.993	5.066	5.141	5.215	5.291	5.368
5	6.228	6.353	6.480	6.610	6.742	6.877	7.014	7.154	7.297	7.442
6	7.913	8.115	8.323	8.535	8.754	8.977	9.207	9.442	9.683	9.930
7	9.783	10.089	10.405	10.730	11.067	11.414	11.772	12.141	12.523	12.916
8	11.859	12.300	12.757	13.233	13.727	14.420	14.773	15.327	15.902	16.499
9	14.164	14.776	15.416	16.085	16.786	17.518	18.285	19.086	19.923	20.799
10	16.722	17.549	18.420	19.337	20.304	21.321	22.393	23.521	24.709	25.959
11	19.561	20.655	21.814	23.044	24.349	25.733	27.200	28.755	30.403	32.150
12	22.713	24.133	25.650	27.271	29.001	30.850	32.824	34.931	37.180	39.580
13	26.211	28.029	29.984	32.088	34.352	36.786	39.404	42.218	45.244	48.496
14	30.095	32.392	34.882	37.581	40.504	43.672	47.102	50.818	54.841	59.196
15	34.405	37.280	40.417	43.842	47.580	51.659	56.109	60.965	66.260	72.035
16	39.190	42.753	46.671	50.980	55.717	60.925	66.648	72.938	79.850	87.442
17	44.500	48.883	53.738	59.117	65.075	71.673	78.978	87.067	96.021	105.930
18	50.396	55.749	61.724	68.393	75.836	84.140	93.404	103.739	115.265	128.116
19	56.939	63.439	70.748	78.968	88.211	98.603	110.283	123.412	138.165	154.739
20	64.202	72.052	80.946	91.024	102.443	115.379	130.031	146.626	165.417	186.687
21	72.264	81.698	92.468	104.767	118.809	134.840	153.136	174.019	197.846	225.024
22	81.213	92.502	105.489	120.434	137.630	157.414	180.169	206.342	236.436	271.028
23	91.147	104.602	120.203	138.295	159.274	183.600	211.798	244.483	282.359	326.234
24	102.173	118.154	136.829	158.656	184.166	213.976	248.803	289.490	337.007	392.480
25	114.412	133.333	155.616	181.867	212.790	249.212	292.099	342.598	402.038	471.976
30	199.018	241.330	293.192	356.778	434.738	530.306	647.423	790.932	966.698	1181.865
40	581.812	767.080	1013.667	1341.979	1779.048	2360.724	3134.412	4163.094	5529.711	7343.715
50	1668.723	2399.975	3459.344	4994.301	7217.488	10435.449	15088.805	21812.273	31514.492	45496.094

TABLE 3. (Continued)

Year	22%	24%	25%	28%	30%	32%	34%	36%	38%	40%
1	1.000	1.000	1.000	1.000	1.000	1.000	1.000	1.000	1.000	1.000
2	2.220	2.240	2.260	2.280	2.300	2.320	2.340	2.360	2.380	2.400
3	3.708	3.778	3.848	3.918	3.990	4.062	4.136	4.210	4.284	4.360
4	5.524	5.684	5.848	6.016	6.187	6.362	6.542	6.725	6.912	7.104
5	7.740	8.048	8.368	8.700	9.043	9.398	9.766	10.146	10.539	10.946
6	10.442	10.980	11.544	12.136	12.756	13.406	14.086	14.799	15.544	16.324
7	13.740	14.615	15.546	16.534	17.583	18.696	19.876	21.126	22.451	23.853
8	17.762	19.123	20.588	22.163	23.858	25.678	27.633	29.732	31.982	34.395
9	22.670	24.712	26.940	29.369	32.015	34.895	38.028	41.435	45.135	49.152
10	28.657	31.643	34.945	38.592	42.619	47.062	51.958	57.351	63.287	69.813
11	35.962	40.238	45.030	50.398	56.405	63.121	70.624	78.998	88.335	98.739
12	44.873	50.895	57.738	65.510	74.326	84.320	95.636	108.437	122.903	139.234
13	55.745	64.109	73.750	84.853	97.624	112.302	129.152	148.474	170.606	195.928
14	69.009	80.496	93.925	109.611	127.912	149.239	174.063	202.925	236.435	275.299
15	85.191	100.815	119.346	141.302	167.285	197.996	234.245	276.978	327.281	386.418
16	104.933	126.010	151.375	181.867	218.470	262.354	314.888	377.690	452.647	541.985
17	129.019	157.252	191.733	233.790	285.011	347.307	422.949	514.658	625.652	759.778
18	158.403	195.993	242.583	300.250	371.514	459.445	567.751	700.935	864.399	1064.689
19	194.251	244.031	306.654	385.321	483.968	607.467	761.786	954.271	1193.870	1491.563
20	237.986	303.598	387.384	494.210	630.157	802.856	1021.792	1298.809	1648.539	2089.188
21	291.343	377.461	489.104	633.589	820.204	1060.769	1370.201	1767.380	2275.982	2925.862
22	356.438	469.052	617.270	811.993	1067.265	1401.215	1837.068	2404.636	3141.852	4097.203
23	435.854	582.624	778.760	1040.351	1388.443	1850.603	2462.669	3271.304	4336.750	5737.078
24	532.741	723.453	982.237	1332.649	1805.975	2443.795	3300.974	4449.969	5985.711	8032.906
25	650.944	898.082	1238.617	1706.790	2348.765	3226.808	4424.301	6052.957	8261.273	11247.062
30	1767.044	2640.881	3941.953	5873.172	8729.805	12940.672	19124.434	28172.016	41357.227	60500.207
40	12936.141	22728.367	39791.957	69376.562	*	*	*	*	*	*

* Value is greater than 99,999.

TABLE 4. Present Value Interest Factor of An Annuity (PVIFA) of $1

Year	1%	2%	3%	4%	5%	6%	7%	8%	9%	10%
1	.990	.980	.971	.962	.952	.943	.935	.926	.917	.909
2	1.970	1.942	1.913	1.886	1.859	1.833	1.808	1.783	1.759	1.736
3	2.941	2.884	2.829	2.775	2.723	2.673	2.624	2.577	2.531	2.487
4	3.902	3.808	3.717	3.630	3.546	3.465	3.387	3.312	3.240	3.170
5	4.853	4.713	4.580	4.452	4.329	4.212	4.100	3.993	3.890	3.791
6	5.795	5.601	5.417	5.242	5.076	4.917	4.767	4.623	4.486	4.355
7	6.728	6.472	6.230	6.002	5.786	5.582	5.389	5.206	5.033	4.868
8	7.652	7.326	7.020	6.733	6.463	6.210	5.971	5.747	5.535	5.335
9	8.566	8.162	7.786	7.435	7.108	6.802	6.515	6.247	5.995	5.759
10	9.471	8.983	8.530	8.111	7.722	7.360	7.024	6.710	6.418	6.145
11	10.368	9.787	9.253	8.760	8.306	7.887	7.499	7.139	6.805	6.495
12	11.255	10.575	9.954	9.385	8.863	8.384	7.943	7.536	7.161	6.814
13	12.134	11.348	10.635	9.986	9.394	8.853	8.358	7.904	7.487	7.103
14	13.004	12.106	11.296	10.563	9.899	9.295	8.746	8.244	7.786	7.367
15	13.865	12.849	11.938	11.118	10.380	9.712	9.108	8.560	8.061	7.606
16	14.718	13.578	12.561	11.652	10.838	10.106	9.447	8.851	8.313	7.824
17	15.562	14.292	13.166	12.166	11.274	10.477	9.763	9.122	8.544	8.022
18	16.398	14.992	13.754	12.659	11.690	10.828	10.059	9.372	8.756	8.201
19	17.226	15.679	14.324	13.134	12.085	11.158	10.336	9.604	8.950	8.365
20	18.046	16.352	14.878	13.590	12.462	11.470	10.594	9.818	9.129	8.514
21	18.857	17.011	15.415	14.029	12.821	11.764	10.836	10.017	9.292	8.649
22	19.661	17.658	15.937	14.451	13.163	12.042	11.061	10.201	9.442	8.772
23	20.456	18.292	16.444	14.857	13.489	12.303	11.272	10.371	9.580	8.883
24	21.244	18.914	16.936	15.247	13.799	12.550	11.469	10.529	9.707	8.985
25	22.023	19.524	17.413	15.622	14.094	12.783	11.654	10.675	9.823	9.077
30	25.808	22.397	19.601	17.292	15.373	13.765	12.409	11.258	10.274	9.427
40	32.835	27.356	23.115	19.793	17.159	15.046	13.332	11.925	10.757	9.779
50	39.197	31.424	25.730	21.482	18.256	15.762	13.801	12.234	10.962	9.915

TABLE 4. (Continued)

Year	11%	12%	13%	14%	15%	16%	17%	18%	19%	20%
1	.901	.893	.885	.887	.870	.862	.855	.847	.840	.833
2	1.713	1.690	1.668	1.647	1.626	1.605	1.585	1.566	1.547	1.528
3	2.444	2.402	2.361	2.322	2.283	2.246	2.210	2.174	2.140	2.106
4	3.102	3.037	2.974	2.914	2.855	2.798	2.743	2.690	2.639	2.589
5	3.696	3.605	3.517	3.433	3.352	3.274	3.199	3.127	3.058	2.991
6	4.231	4.111	3.998	3.889	3.784	3.685	3.589	3.498	3.410	3.326
7	4.712	4.564	4.423	4.288	4.160	4.039	3.922	3.812	3.706	3.605
8	5.146	4.968	4.799	4.639	4.487	4.344	4.207	4.078	3.954	3.837
9	5.537	5.328	5.132	4.946	4.772	4.607	4.451	4.303	4.163	4.031
10	5.889	5.650	5.426	5.216	5.019	4.833	4.659	4.494	4.339	4.192
11	6.207	5.938	5.687	5.453	5.234	5.029	4.836	4.656	4.487	4.327
12	6.492	6.194	5.918	5.660	5.421	5.197	4.988	4.793	4.611	4.439
13	6.750	6.424	6.122	5.842	5.583	5.342	5.118	4.910	4.715	4.533
14	6.982	6.628	6.303	6.002	5.724	5.468	5.229	5.008	4.802	4.611
15	7.191	6.811	6.462	6.142	5.847	5.575	5.324	5.092	4.876	4.675
16	7.379	6.974	6.604	6.265	5.954	5.669	5.405	5.162	4.938	4.730
17	7.549	7.120	6.729	6.373	6.047	5.749	5.475	5.222	4.990	4.775
18	7.702	7.250	6.840	6.467	6.128	5.818	5.534	5.273	5.033	4.812
19	7.839	7.336	6.938	6.550	6.198	5.877	5.585	5.316	5.070	4.843
20	7.963	7.469	7.025	6.623	6.259	5.929	5.628	5.353	5.101	4.870
21	8.075	7.562	7.102	6.687	6.312	5.973	5.665	5.384	5.127	4.891
22	8.176	7.645	7.170	6.743	6.359	6.011	5.696	5.410	5.149	4.909
23	8.266	7.718	7.230	6.792	6.399	6.044	5.723	5.432	5.167	4.925
24	8.348	7.784	7.283	6.835	6.434	6.073	5.747	5.451	5.182	4.937
25	8.422	7.843	7.330	6.873	6.464	6.097	5.766	5.467	5.195	4.948
30	8.694	8.055	7.496	7.003	6.566	6.177	5.829	5.517	5.235	4.979
40	8.951	8.244	7.634	7.105	6.642	6.233	5.871	5.548	5.258	4.997
50	9.042	8.305	7.675	7.133	6.661	6.246	5.880	5.554	5.262	4.999

TABLE 4. (Continued)

Year	22%	24%	26%	28%	30%	32%	34%	36%	38%	40%
1	.820	.806	.794	.781	.769	.758	.746	.735	.725	.714
2	1.492	1.457	1.424	1.392	1.361	1.331	1.303	1.276	1.250	1.224
3	2.042	1.981	1.923	1.868	1.816	1.766	1.719	1.673	1.630	1.589
4	2.494	2.404	2.320	2.241	2.166	2.096	2.029	1.966	1.906	1.849
5	2.864	2.745	2.635	2.532	2.436	2.345	2.260	2.181	2.106	2.035
6	3.167	3.020	2.885	2.759	2.643	2.534	2.433	2.339	2.251	2.168
7	3.416	3.242	3.083	2.937	2.802	2.677	2.562	2.455	2.355	2.263
8	3.619	3.421	3.241	3.076	2.925	2.786	2.658	2.540	2.432	2.331
9	3.786	3.566	3.366	3.184	3.019	2.868	2.730	2.603	2.487	2.379
10	3.923	3.682	3.465	3.269	3.092	2.930	2.784	2.649	2.527	2.414
11	4.035	3.776	3.544	3.335	3.147	2.978	2.824	2.683	2.555	2.438
12	4.127	3.851	3.606	3.387	3.190	3.013	2.853	2.708	2.576	2.456
13	4.203	3.912	3.656	3.427	3.223	3.040	2.876	2.727	2.592	2.469
14	4.265	3.962	3.695	3.459	3.249	3.061	2.892	2.740	2.603	2.477
15	4.315	4.001	3.726	3.483	3.268	3.076	2.905	2.750	2.611	2.484
16	4.357	4.033	3.751	3.503	3.283	3.088	2.914	2.757	2.616	2.489
17	4.391	4.059	3.771	3.518	3.295	3.097	2.921	2.763	2.621	2.492
18	4.419	4.080	3.786	3.529	3.304	3.104	2.926	2.767	2.624	2.494
19	4.442	4.097	3.799	3.539	3.311	3.109	2.930	2.770	2.626	2.496
20	4.460	4.110	3.808	3.546	3.316	3.113	2.933	2.772	2.627	2.497
21	4.476	4.121	3.816	3.551	3.320	3.116	2.935	2.773	2.629	2.498
22	4.488	4.130	3.822	3.556	3.323	3.118	2.936	2.775	2.629	2.498
23	4.499	4.137	3.827	3.559	3.325	3.120	2.938	2.775	2.630	2.499
24	4.507	4.143	3.831	3.562	3.327	3.121	2.939	2.776	2.630	2.499
25	4.514	4.147	3.834	3.564	3.329	3.122	2.939	2.776	2.631	2.499
30	4.534	4.160	3.842	3.569	3.332	3.124	2.941	2.777	2.631	2.500
40	4.544	4.166	3.846	3.571	3.333	3.125	2.941	2.778	2.632	2.500

SELECTED EQUATIONS

(2-2) Assets = Liabilities + shareholders' equity (p. 28)

(2-3) Effective tax rate = Total taxes paid/taxable income (p. 30)

(2-4) Straight-line depreciation for tax purposes:

$$S - L = C/n$$ (p. 37)

(2-5) Double-declining-balance depreciation for tax purposes:

$$DDB = 2(B/n)$$ (p. 38)

(15-4) Straight-line depreciation (financial accounting):

$$\text{Straight-line depreciation} = \frac{(\text{Original cost} - \text{Salvage value})}{\text{Economic life}}$$ (p. 540)

(4-1) Basic time value equation:

$$FV_n = PV_0(1 + i)^n$$ (p. 86)

(4-2) Future value of annuity (FVIFA table):

$$FVA_n = A(FVIFA_{i,n})$$ (p. 89)

(4-6) Intra-year compounding:

$$FV_n = PV_0[1 + (i/m)]^{mn}$$ (p. 96)

(4-7) Continuous compounding:

$$FV_n = PV_0 e^{in}$$ (p. 97)

(4-3) Present value of future cash flow (formula):

$$PV_0 = FV_n/(1 + i)^n$$ (p. 90)

(4-3b) Present value of future cash flow (PVIF table):

$$PV_0 = FV_n(PVIF_{i,n})$$ (p. 91)

(4-5) Present value of annuity (PVIFA table):

$$PVA = A(PVIFA_{i,n})$$ (p. 94)

Intra-year discounting:

$$PV_0 = FV_n/[1 + (i/m)]^{mn}$$ (p. 96)

(4-8) Continuous discounting:

$$PV_0 = FV_n[1/e^{in}]$$ (p. 97)

(5-1) Fundamental valuation equation:

$$P_0 = \sum_{t=1}^{n} CF_t/(1 + k)^t$$ (p. 124)

(5-4) Bond value (annual interest payments):

$$P_0 \sum_{t=1}^{n} I_t/(1 + k)^t + F_n/(1 + k)^n$$ (p. 128)

(13-1)   Effective cost of missing discounts:

$$\frac{\text{Discount \%}}{100\% - \text{Discount \%}} \times \frac{360}{\text{Net period} - \text{Discount period}}$$ (p. 457)

(13-4)   Approximate effective interest rate on installment loans:

$$i = 2mD/P(n + 1)$$ (p. 461)

(13-8)   Effective interest rate on loans with compensating balances

(cb%) and working balances (WB):

$$\text{Effective interest rate} = (1 - \text{WB/N})\frac{[r]}{(1 - \text{cb\%})}$$ (p. 463)

(13-9)   Effective interest rate (discount loans):

$$\text{Effective interest rate} = \frac{\text{Discount (\$)}}{\text{Face Value} - \text{discount (\$)}}$$ (p. 464)

(14-1)   Average Rate of Return (ARR):

$$\text{ARR} = \text{Average net income}/(\text{Investment}/2)$$ (p. 498)

(14-2)   Net Present Value:

$$\text{NPV} = \text{Present value of cash inflows} - \text{net investment outflows}$$ (p. 499)

(14-3)   Present Value of Cash Inflows:

$$\text{PVCI} = \sum_{t=1}^{n} \text{CF}_t/(1 + k)^t$$ (p. 499)

(14-4)   Profitability Index (PI):

$$\text{PI} = \text{Present value of cash inflows}/\text{Investment outflows}$$ (p. 500)

(14-5)   Internal Rate of Return (r):

$$\text{Net investment (I)} = \text{PVCI} = \sum_{t=1}^{n} \text{CF}_t/(1 + r)^t$$ (p. 501)

(15-2) $$\text{CFAT} = (\text{S} - \text{CGS} - \text{OE})(1 - t) + \text{Dt}$$ (p. 538)

(15-3)   Incremental cash flow after taxes (ΔCFAT):

$$\Delta\text{CFAT} = (\Delta\text{S} - \Delta\text{CGS} - \Delta\text{OE})(1 - t) + \Delta\text{Dt}$$ (p. 539)

(16-2)   Standard deviation, σ:

$$\sigma = \sqrt{\sum_{i=1}^{n} (X_i - X)^2 P_i}$$ (p. 585)

(16-3)   Coefficient of variation (CB):

$$\text{CV} = \sigma/X$$ (p. 585)

Required rate of return on a project, k_{proj}:

$$k_{proj} = R_f + (R_m - R_f)\beta_{proj}$$ (p. 595)

(17-1)   After-tax cost of debt $= k_d \times (1 - T)$ (p. 619)

(17-2)   Weighted average cost of capital, k_a:

$$k_a = w_d k_d(1 - T) + w_p k_p + w_e k_e$$ (p. 620)

(17-3)   Cost of debt, k_d, (bonds):

$$P_b = \sum_{t=1}^{n} \frac{T_t}{(1 + k_d)^2} + \frac{P_n}{(1 + k_d)^n}$$

(p. 621)

(17-4b)   Cost of preferred stock, k_p:

$$k_p = D_p/P_p$$

(p. 622)

(17-5C)   Cost of equity, k_e, (Gordon model):

$$k_e = (D_1/P_s) + g$$

(p. 623)

(17-6)   Cost of equity, k_e, (Capital Asset Pricing Model):

$$k_e = R_f + (R_m - R_f)\beta$$

(p. 624)

(17-7a)   Beta (levered), B_1

$$B_1 = B_u[1 + (D/E)(1 - T)]$$

(p. 632)

(17-7b)   Beta (unlevered), B_u:

$$B_u = B_1/[1 + (D/E)(1 - T)]$$

(p. 632)

(18-1)   Breakeven point (units):

$$BE_u = F_t/(p - v)$$

(p. 651)

(18-2)   Breakeven point (dollars):

$$BE_s = F_t/cm\%$$

(p. 651)

(18-4)   Degree of Operating Leverage (units):

$$DOL_x = \frac{x(p - v)}{x(p - v) - F_o}$$

(p. 652)

(18-5)   Degree of Operating Leverage (dollars):

$$DOL = \frac{Sales - Variable\ costs}{Sales - Variable\ costs - Fixed\ operating\ costs}$$

(p. 653)

(18-7)   Degree of Financial Leverage (units):

$$DFL_x = [x(p - v) - F_o]/[x(p - v) - F_o - F_f]$$

(p. 653)

(18-7a)   Degree of Financial Leverage (dollars):

$$DFL_x = EBIT/PBT$$

(p. 654)

(18-8)   Degree of Combined Leverage (units):

$$DCL_x = x(p - v)/[x(p - v) - F_t]$$

(p. 655)

(18-10)   Degree of Combined Leverage:

$$DCL = DOL \times DFL$$

(p. 655)

(18-11)   Degree of Combined Leverage (dollars):

$$DCL_s = (Sales - Variable\ Costs)/Profit\ before\ taxes$$

(p. 655)

(18-13a)   Degree of Combined Leverage (at any point, X):

$$DCL_x = X/[X - X_{breakeven}]$$

(p. 656)

EBIT/EPS indifference point, financing option #1 vs #2:

$$(EBIT^* - I_{\#1})(1 - T)/N_{\#1} = (EBIT^* - I_{\#2})(1 - T)/N_{\#2}$$

(p. 658)

(19-4)   Total value of levered firm (corporate taxes):

$$V_{tl} = V_{tu} + Dt$$

(p. 686)

(19-7)   Incremental tax shield (corporate and personal taxes):

$$I[(1 - t_j) - (1 - t_c)(1 - t_e)]$$

(p. 688)

(20-3a)   Investment alpha and stock value:

$$P = \frac{(1 - b)EPS_1}{[(1 - b)k_e - b\alpha]}$$

(p. 704)

(21-1)   Number of shares needed to elect N directors (cumulative voting):

$$NE = \left[\frac{\text{Total \# of shares outstanding} \times \text{\# directors desired}}{\text{Total \# of directors to be elected} + 1} \right] + 1$$

(p. 744)

(21-2)   Value of a share of stock selling "rights on":

$$P = [M_1N + S]/[N + 1]$$

(p. 746)

(21-3)   Value of right when stock sells "rights on":

$$V_1 = [M_1 - S]/[N + 1]$$

(p. 747)

(21-4)   Value of right when stock sells "ex rights":

$$V_2 = [M_2 - S]/S$$

(p. 747)

(23-2)   Theoretical value of a warrant:

$$WV = (MP - EP)N$$

(p. 807)

(25-1)   Foreign exchange translation:

Indirect quote = 1/direct quote

(p. 860)

(25-2)   Forward exchange premium or discount:

$$\%\Delta_f = \frac{(F - S)}{S} \times \frac{[12]}{N} \times 100$$

(p. 863)

(25-3)   Interest rate parity between two currencies (pounds and dollars):

$$\text{12-month Forward rate}_\pounds/\text{spot rate}_\pounds = (1 + r_\pounds)/(1 + r_\$)$$

(p. 863)

(25-5)   Percentage dollar cost of covered borrowing:

$$\%DCCB = \%1 + \%\Delta_f + (\%I)(\%\Delta_f)$$

(p. 869)

ANSWERS

Chapter 1 1. b; 2. d; 3. c; 4. b; 5. d; 6. d; 7. d; 8. b. **Chapter 2** 1. b; 2. c; 3. c; 4. b; 5. c; 6. a; 7. c; 8. b; 9. d; 10. a; 11. c. **Chapter 3** 1. d; 2. b; 3. c; 4. c; 5. c; 6. c; 7. a; 8. c; 9. c; 10. c. **Chapter 4** 1. b; 2. d; 3. d; 4. b; 5. d; 6. b; 7. c; 8. d; 9. d; 10. c. **Chapter 5** 1. c; 2. d; 3. d; 4. a; 5. b; 6. d; 7. a; 8. a; 9. b; 10. a. **Chapter 6** 1. c; 2. b; 3. d; 4. c; 5. c; 6. a; 7. c; 8. a; 9. b; 10. c. **Chapter 7** 1. b; 2. c; 3. d; 4. d; 5. c; 6. b; 7. c; 8. b; 9. a; 10. a. **Chapter 8** 1. d; 2. d; 3. d; 4. b; 5. d; 6. b. **Chapter 9** 1. d; 2. a; 3. c; 4. a; 5. d; 6. c; 7. b; 8. c; 9. a; 10. b; 11. b; 12. d. **Chapter 10** 1. a; 2. c; 3. a; 4. c; 5. d; 6. b; 7. d; 8. a. **Chapter 11** 1. d; 2. d; 3. b; 4. b; 5. d; 6. b; 7. d. **Chapter 12** 1. b; 2. a; 3. b; 4. d; 5. c; 6. d; 7. b; 8. b. **Chapter 13** 1. c; 2. c; 3. b; 4. c; 5. c; 6. c; 7. b; 8. d; 9. b. **Chapter 14** 1. a; 2. d; 3. a; 4. d; 5. a; 6. c; 7. d; 8. a; 9. b; 10. d; 11. a; 12. a; 13. a; 14. b; 15. d. **Chapter 15** 1. a; 2. c; 3. b; 4. a. **Chapter 16** 1. c; 2. c; 3. b; 4. d; 5. a; 6. b; 7. c. **Chapter 17** 1. c; 2. c; 3. b; 4. c; 5. a; 6. a; 7. d. **Chapter 18** 1. c; 2. b; 3. c; 4. b; 5. a. **Chapter 19** 1. b; 2. b; 3. d; 4. d; 5. a; 6. a. **Chapter 20** 1. d; 2. d; 3. a; 4. c. **Chapter 21** 1. d; 2. d; 3. c; 4. d; 5. b; 6. a; 7. b; 8. c; 9. c; 10. b; 11. b; 12. d; 13. c; 14. a. **Chapter 22** 1. c; 2. a; 3. b; 4. a; 5. a; 6. c; 7. c; 8. d; 9. a; 10. d. **Chapter 23** 1. b; 2. a; 3. c; 4. b; 5. a; 6. b; 7. b; 8. b; 9. b; 10. b; 11. a; 12. d; 13. c; 14. d; 15. a; 16. d. **Chapter 24** 1. a; 2. c; 3. c; 4. c; 5. d; 6. d; 7. b. **Chapter 25** 1. d; 2. c; 3. d; 4. b; 5. c; 6. a.

INDEX

KEY SYMBOLS USED IN TEXT

A/R = accounts receivable
A/P = accounts payable
CV = coefficient of variation
I = investment outlays
WACC = weighted average cost of capital
SML = security market line
CAPM = capital asset pricing model
P/E = price to earnings ratio
YTC = yield to call on a bond
YTM = yield to maturity on a bond
NWC = net working capital
b = profit retention ratio
FVIF = future value interest factor
FVIFA = future value interest factor for an annuity
PVIF = present value interest factor
PVIFA = present value interest factor for an annuity
FV_n = future value of cash flow to be received in period n
FVA_n = future value of annuity for n periods
PV_0 = present value of future cash flow
PVA = present value of annuity
I = interest payment
k = required rate of return
R = rate of return
p_i = probability of outcome i
Beta = sensitivity of investment to market risk
σ = sigma, standard deviation
σ^2 = sigma squared, variance
R_i = risk-free rate
G = sustainable growth rate in sales
ACP = average collection period
APP = average payment period
CR = current ratio
ROA = return on assets
ROE = return on equity
Q = quantity in units
i = interest rate
D = debt
r = stated interest rate
ARR = average rate of return
NPV = net present value
Σ = sum
CF = cash flow